PACIFIC
ELDORADO

THOMAS J. OSBORNE

PACIFIC ELDORADO

A HISTORY OF GREATER CALIFORNIA

A John Wiley & Sons, Ltd., Publication

Library of Congress Cataloging-in-Publication Data
Osborne, Thomas J., 1942–
    Pacific Eldorado : a history of greater California / Thomas J. Osborne.
        pages cm
    Includes bibliographical references and index.
    ISBN 978-1-4051-9454-9 (hardback) – ISBN 978-1-4051-9453-2 (paperback)   1. California–History.   2. California–History, Naval.   3. California–Commerce–Pacific Area.   4. Pacific Area–Commerce–California.   5. California–Relations–Pacific Area.   6. Pacific Area–Relations–California.   I. Title.
    F861.O63 2013
    979.4–dc23
                                                                        2012031787

A catalogue record for this book is available from the British Library.

Cover image: The Big Sur coastline and Point Sur Lighthouse, California, USA. Photo © Don Smith / Getty Images.
Cover design by Simon Levy

Set in 10/13pt Minion by Toppan Best-set Premedia Limited
Printed in Singapore by C.O.S. Printers Pte Ltd

5   2017

For Ginger, Brooks, Todd, and my students at Santa Ana College – all Californians whose lives have been shaped and enriched by living in this veritable Pacific Eldorado

Contents

3 A Globally Connected Mexican Province   53

4 War and Gold: America's West Coast Eldorado   78

11 America's Pacific Bulwark: World War II and Its Aftermath   267

12 Liberalism at High Tide   295

Illustrations

Foreword

Janet Fireman
(Editor, *California History*)

California was America's dearest object of desire in the mid-nineteenth century, when Manifest Destiny fueled the nation's expansionism. In the 1840s the United States engaged in a desperate quest to acquire California from Mexico, without knowing how very fabulous, how rich, how beautiful, and how loaded with potential the object of its desire actually was. That unknown capacity exceeded all expectations as time passed; that greatest gift of the nineteenth century, as some have said, is a gift that keeps on giving. California is full of surprises, and is famous for imagination and reinvention. One of those surprises is a new system of construing California's history, as the following pages illuminate. *Pacific Eldorado: A History of Greater California* tracks the customary chronology, probing the depths and heights of economic, political, and cultural events; but it also introduces a crystal clear yet completely new lens through which to view the region's past.

Ironically, the inspiration for *Pacific Eldorado* is as old as the sea. In fact, it is this grand body of water, the Pacific Ocean, the largest and deepest on earth, which once extended over surface that is now California land. The chapters herein describe how the state's location came to be where and what it is: Even California, and 47 percent of Californians, started somewhere else and traveled to their current spot on the earth's surface. That creation story of geological migration and accretion established a place over time and became a space like no other, favored by nature and supplied with plentiful resources that people hunted, extracted, nurtured, harvested, pumped, processed, sold, bought, and consumed. The fruit of these natural advantages – most famously gold – defined the state with a come-hither allure, offering prospects grasped, snatched, or secured by Californians from pre-statehood times onward. Capitalizing on the sea, its natural border, and crossing the Pacific and making it a part of their reality, Native Californians, Spaniards, Californios, and Mexicans, as well as peoples from across the Pacific in several directions, had already set the Pacific Eldorado project in motion by the time the United States took over in 1848.

A liaison of location and history furnishes the framework. From its geological assembly millions of years ago to its initial peopling by the first immigrants perhaps 20,000 years ago, through explorations and colonization by Spain, Mexico, and the United States in the past nearly 500 years to the present, California's promise has been broader, deeper, and grander than its borders. Beginning with nature, topography, and natural resources and ending with facts and figures expressing California's economic, political, financial, and cultural power and impact in the Pacific world and beyond, *Pacific Eldorado* draws a through-line from that distant beginning to our time. All this comes with risks and contests: these pages summarize our present concerns and forecast the future demographic and environmental challenges to the state for retaining its remarkable status. We and those coming up – the population is estimated to reach 50 million by 2025 – must be mindful of our drinking water, air quality, climate change, the marine ecosystem, and clean energy.

What does *Pacific Eldorado* deliver to the reader that is unavailable elsewhere? The answer lies in California itself: recognized world-round as special, appealing for its scenic variety, entertainment and recreational attractions, climate and resources, and bountiful possibilities. All this we take for granted. That California faces the Pacific Ocean is appreciated, but even though the long coastline is lionized, the essential truths of relationships between California's location and what Californians have made of that have been ignored. Thomas Osborne brings a new contribution to current discourse about California and its past to reveal a grand tapestry of connections and a multi-hemispheric pattern of interaction with the Pacific world. From the original position California occupied in the American ideal – a foothold on the distant shore – he proffers a parade of Pacific ventures available to the nation because of California's location, its profusion of natural resources, and the cornucopia of human capital, innovation, and imagination that the diversity of Californians have put into operation.

Reading *Pacific Eldorado* stimulates an understanding of the logical pairing of globalization with California. Our minds also focus on the inescapable: the wide Pacific and our entire world are narrowing through digital communication. Even so, the opportunities in our information age are simultaneously expanding the world. Analysis of the Pacific Eldorado concept is yet to be undertaken in the historical literature, but this new reckoning surely will spark broadened consideration of California's links to the Pacific world. Those powerful trans-oceanic links, as this cutting-edge text shows, may best explain why the Golden State was so coveted in the mid-nineteenth century and remains even more so today.

Preface

"The flashing and golden pageant of California,
The sudden and gorgeous drama, the sunny and ample lands, . . .
Ships coming in from the whole round world, and going out to the whole world,
To India and China and Australia and the thousand island paradises of the Pacific . . ."
                                    Walt Whitman, "Song of the Redwood-Tree" (1874)

Whitman's enchanting "Song of the Redwood-Tree" has had a strong basis in the historical record. While this poem omits the gritty details of how "crimps" (owners of boardinghouses for sailors) strong-armed prospective crewmen into sea duty in San Francisco waterfront saloons, it still captures the alluring relationship California has had with the Pacific world for the past 500 years and more. Providing a comprehensive account of that past, *Pacific Eldorado* simultaneously illuminates the historical stepping stones to the state's twenty-first century prominence in the Pacific Basin and globally. In doing so, it aspires to be among those on the cutting edge of internationalizing state and local history and giving the state's long-time Pacific connections their due.

In other words, *Pacific Eldorado* narrates the story of a "greater California," a place whose history in numerous instances extends well beyond the geographical boundaries of the state. These "beyond the borders" connections challenge the prevalent notion of an isolated early California and suggest the need for a history that weaves the local, the national, and the international into a coherent narrative. For example, if Navy Lieutenant Charles Wilkes's epic maritime expedition (1838–42), which brought him to the San Francisco Bay area, is even mentioned in current California history textbooks, they offer virtually no coverage of how that exploration connected California to America's "manifest destiny" of conquering North America and expanding transpacific commerce. In short, the relationship between California and the Pacific world that Walt Whitman expressed in verse, and which the historical record supports, seems to have gone little noticed in current chronicles of the state.

This textbook aims to help students better understand the state's fascinating and complex history by placing it squarely within the context of Pacific geological processes resulting in land formation, prehistoric Pacific voyaging leading to early settlement, international trans-pacific commerce, Pacific immigration, Pacific imaginings that have infused the "California Dream" of a better life for all, and America's expansion beyond its western shoreline and into the world's largest ocean basin. This means a spatial re-framing of California's past. Anticipating this fresh approach to California history, Kevin Starr wrote in *Clio on the Coast* (2010): "Even further down the road, into the twenty-first century, lay the challenge of integrating the Pacific Coast and the nation behind it into a comparative history of the Asia/Pacific Basin of which it was a part. China, Hong Kong, Japan, the Philippines, Hawaii, Chile, Australia, and New Zealand, after all, and the other Asia/Pacific places as well, had long since been important components of the California story." Started two years before and independently of this call for a Pacific-centered California history, this is the first textbook to take up Starr's challenge to historians of the Golden State.

The major theme of this volume could be described as follows: From its beginning, California's history has been shaped increasingly by its Pacific Basin connections – connections that have derived largely from the state's resources, which is why "Eldorado" appears in the title. Throughout California's past, such resources have included sea otter pelts, lumber, whale oil, hides and animal fat (tallow) used for candle-making, gold, borax cleanser, petroleum, farm products, films and media works, Silicon Valley computer technologies, and more.

The book's five related supporting themes include:

- *Greater California*: The Golden State's history has been so international, national, and regional from its outset that it must be understood within a broader or "greater" context than its geographical boundaries would suggest.
- *A Connected California*: The widely accepted notion of an isolated California before 1850 is misleading and overlooks facts to the contrary.
- *A Pacific Population*: Historically, the peopling of California reflects its close ties to the Pacific Basin.
- *A Pacific-infused "California Dream"*: The "California Dream" of seeking limitless wealth and opportunities, that is, the American Dream writ large, contains elements of the area's Pacific connections and imaginings.
- *America and the Pacific World*: California's development markedly illustrates the importance of the Pacific Basin in U.S. history.

Organizationally, the textbook's 14 chapters move chronologically from the geologic formation and earliest peopling of California into the second governorship of Jerry Brown in the years 2011–12. All chapters open with an overview of the topic at hand, followed by a Timeline. Each chapter includes a brief Pacific Profile essay, featuring a person whose life and/or contributions exemplify the role of the Pacific in shaping California history. In some instances such persons have been well known (railroad magnate and former governor, Leland Stanford) and in other instances they have not (restaurateur Norman Asing). Some called California home (former governor, Hiram Johnson); others just visited (mariner and explorer Alejandro Malaspina). The intent has been to humanize the state's past, helping readers see California's Pacific maritime and other connections through the lives of real people. Each chapter ends with a brief Summary, Review Questions, and a Further Readings section that offers an annotated list of written sources for those who wish to explore the "flashing and golden pageant" of Pacific California in more depth and detail.

T.J.O.
Laguna Beach and San Francisco

Acknowledgments

As solitary as researching and writing are, looking back I had a lot of help from many wonderful, thoughtful people in doing this project. A short list of those who were instrumental in providing this help would include:

Ginger T. Osborne, my wife, for patiently listening to me read countless passages from the manuscript to get her recommendations regarding clarity, logic, and brevity, and for supporting this project in numerous other ways.

Janet Fireman, editor of the *California History* journal for more than a decade and adjunct professor of history at USC/Scholar in Residence at Loyola Marymount University, for offering indispensable guidance in making my case for the dominant role played by California's Pacific connections in shaping the state's history.

Peter Coveney, executive editor at Wiley-Blackwell Publishing, for his wise counsel on helping me shape the length of the manuscript and number of chapters, and especially for recognizing the promise of this project when I was still conceptualizing it.

Deirdre Ilkson, development editor (par excellence) at Wiley-Blackwell Publishing, for her attention to the manuscript's organization of content, its clarity of expression, and the numerous sensible suggestions she made regarding chapter revisions.

Isobel Bainton, project editor at Wiley-Blackwell Publishing, for patiently and expertly guiding me through the lengthy process of obtaining permissions for the use of visuals.

Janet Moth, project manager at Wiley-Blackwell, whose obsession with stylistic detail exceeds even my own, and who has ferreted out a number of my errors.

David Igler, associate professor of history at UC Irvine, for incisive comments and constructive suggestions on many chapters of this textbook.

Ted Miles, reference librarian, J. Porter Shaw Library, San Francisco Maritime Historical National Historic Park, for running numerous photocopies of journal articles and his valuable consultation regarding the library's rich collections.

Tom MonPere, dear friend and aficionado of California history, for accompanying me on a history tour of Benicia and Martinez, as well as escorting me on a road trip through the Delta's levees and old Chinatowns, reading many chapters and making helpful suggestions, and whetting my appetite for Wallace Stegner's writings.

Nell Yang, Santa Ana College librarian, for furnishing me with copies of scholarly articles needed for my research on Chinese Americans and transpacific trade in California's past, as well as cheering me on at every stage of this project.

Thomas Lucas, professor of art and architecture at the University of San Francisco, for a private tour of his brilliant "Galleons and Globalization" exhibit and tutoring me on the artworks carried from China to California's missions.

Christina Gold, professor of history at El Camino College, for helping me see some of the teaching benefits of my Pacific-centric/international approach that I did not fully appreciate at the outset of this project.

William Courter, professor of geography at Santa Ana College, for the clearest explanation I've received from anyone on plate tectonics' role in forming California and its landscape.

Patricia Martz, professor of anthropology emerita, California State University at Los Angeles, for fact-checking my coverage on California Indians during the pre-contact period.

Phillip Sanfield, director of media relations for the Port of Los Angeles, who graciously provided me with photocopies of annual reports on exports and imports during the decades of the 1950s, 1960s, and 1970s.

Todd T. Osborne, for helping me with downloading computer graphics and answering my numerous computer-related questions during many late-night telephone calls.

Brooks T. Osborne, for his reading of Chapter 14 with an attorney's eye for argument and organization of material.

Glenna Matthews, independent historian, for reading the entire manuscript and informing me about various aspects of Silicon Valley history pertinent to this study.

Sarah E. Monpere, for help with photographs.

Kristine Ferry, Acting Head of Access Services, UC Irvine Library, for seeing to it that a non-UC Irvine scholar could have full use the Langson Library.

1

Beginnings: From Fire and Ice to Indian Homeland

Fire and ice forged the physical setting of California's storied past. No matter how extensively humans have altered that setting with mining activities, transportation systems, aqueducts, and various other built structures, nature always has been integral to the state's history. Before there was a human record there was pre-history, or a time of beginnings, by far the longest period in California's timeline. During this genesis California literally rose from the Pacific, at times spewing flames and volcanic ash. Violent thrusts from below the Earth's surface formed mountains and valleys that later would be carved by huge rivers of ice. Before these glaciers began melting, some 15,000 years ago, America's first human inhabitants began making their way by foot and watercraft from Asia to North America. On reaching the New World, these mammoth-hunting migrants trekked southward and eastward, some settling in what would become California. Their seagoing Asian counterparts navigated North America's coastline southward to the Channel Islands and mainland. These trekking and sailing Paleolithic, or Old Stone Age, peoples were the first human occupants of this remarkable land. Some scholars speculate that Polynesian and Chinese Pacific voyagers visited Indian California centuries before Europeans arrived in the province.

Pacific Eldorado: A History of Greater California, First Edition. Thomas J. Osborne.
© 2013 Thomas J. Osborne. Published 2013 by Blackwell Publishing Ltd.

Timeline

30 million years ago	California's land mass was formed by Pacific geological processes, especially through plate tectonic subductions and lateral movements
13,000 years ago	Following the "Kelp Highway," Asian Pacific voyagers arrive in the Channel Islands, perhaps becoming the first Californians, according to archeologist Jon M. Erlandson and others
10,000 to 15,000 years ago	As climate warming set in and Beringia melted into the Bering Strait, the descendants of Paleo-Indian migratory hunters continue on their way eastward and southward throughout the New World in pursuit of game
11,000 years ago	The skeletal remains of the so-called Arlington Woman are found at a site on Santa Rosa Island along California's coast
4,600 years ago	A bristlecone pine (*Pinus longaeva*), located in California's White Mountains and dating back more than four millennia, is thought to be the oldest living thing on Earth
2,000 years ago	Some of today's California redwood trees, the world's largest living things, date to the time of Jesus of Nazareth and the Roman Empire
1000 CE	Chumash Indians build a seafaring culture in and around today's Santa Barbara and on a few of the Channel Islands
400–800	Early Polynesians may have reached California in watercraft, according to a small group of anthropologists and linguists
1500s	Specialists estimate that 15,000 Chumash lived in California at the time of European contact
Late 1700s	Between 300,000 and 1,000,000 indigenous people inhabited California most of them living in villages of 100 to 500 dwellers

Landforms

Not only was California born of the Pacific, also it is situated on the Ring of Fire, an intercontinental perimeter of volcanoes and earthquake faults that line the Pacific Rim in a sweeping arc from Japan to Chile. Like many other areas along the Ring of Fire, the state's varied landmass was assembled over time from geologic fragments of rocks and sediments, called "terranes," lying on the crust or floor of the Pacific long after the Earth was formed some 4.6 billion years ago. Before these fragments began uplifting from the ocean, North America's western shoreline extended to about where the Rocky Mountains are situated today. West of that ancient coastline loomed the vast, heaving Pacific.

According to widely accepted plate tectonics theory, formulated by geologists in the mid-1960s, California's landmass has evolved over hundreds of millions of years. The process has been global and ongoing. Eons ago 20 huge subterranean masses of material, called plates, comprised the Earth's crust and upper mantle. These plates meandered due to heat and pressure from deep within the planet, creating continents. The largest of these subterranean masses, the Pacific Plate, lies beneath roughly two-thirds of the ocean by that name. The eastward-moving Pacific Plate collided with the western edge of the North American Plate in a zone somewhat west of the Rockies. At the point of collision the Pacific Plate subducted, that is, pushed beneath the North American Plate, thereby generating enormous heat. The heat, in turn, melted subterranean basalt rock that combined with deeply buried sediments to produce ores – including gold that in the mid-1800s sparked a worldwide rush to California – while pushing up the Earth's crust and forming granite outcroppings. In this way western mountains and their basins came into existence. The initial collision was followed by subsequent ones, called "dockings" or "accretions," that assembled California's topography, which included off-shore volcanic islands. "Wherever you stand in this state," says geologist Keith Heyer Meldahl, "if your feet are on bedrock, the odds are that you're standing on an immigrant [piece of ground], reeled in by subduction from the far reaches of the Pacific in the process of assembling California." About 30 million years ago, when the area for the most part assumed its present geographical configuration, these west-to-east collisions stopped and a lateral south-to-north movement of the Pacific Plate began that continues to this day.

This lateral movement has had major consequences for the region, especially in terms of earthquakes. The Pacific Plate has been moving northwestward at about 2 inches a year. Consequently, part of Baja California was carried over millions of years to the coastline and interior reaches of southern California and up to San Francisco. This movement has been characterized by gnashing and grinding along the Pacific–North American plates' subduction zone. Stresses from the lateral movements of the two plates force an unlocking of surface-area terrain on both sides of the fissure known as the San Andreas Fault. The forced unlocking of these blocks results in powerful earthquakes along this fault system that extends from Point Reyes Peninsula just above San Francisco southeastward for 350 miles to the mountains of southern California. Earthquakes along that fault line have devastated cities, leaving many dead and striking fear into survivors. Such was the case in 1906 when much of San Francisco was flattened and burned (due to ruptured gas lines and water mains in the city) by a severe earthquake along the San Andreas Fault. Since 1769, when the Spanish began colonizing the province, there have been 117 measured or recorded earthquakes along this fault. Geology and geography augur more to come on this and other faults in the state.

Volcanoes, plate tectonics, earthquakes, winds, and waves have formed California's coast-line, offshore islands, mountains, and basins or valleys. That coastline, with its many pic-turesque coves and tree-crested cliffs, is one of the most photographed and tourist-visited in the world, extending 1,264 miles in length. Monster waves, or tsunamis, generated by distant earthquakes, have on occasion reportedly reached 195 feet in height before bombarding northern California's shores. Such a wave struck just north of Humboldt Bay in 1913. Less noteworthy yet still powerful currents of wind and sea have been sculpting coastal California for eons.

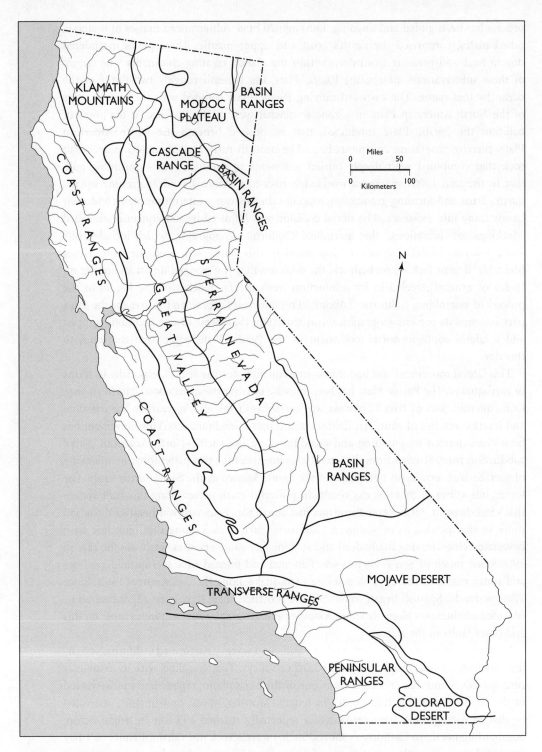

Figure 1.1 California topography. The variation in the state's topography is unmatched nationwide. Based on Mary Hill, *California Landscape: Origin and Evolution*, revised edition (Berkeley: University of California Press 1985), p. 24. Reprinted by permission of University of California Press.

Inland from the coast, mountain ranges and plateaus of dramatically varying elevations dominate most of the state's nearly 100 million acres of surface area. America's third-largest state, after Alaska and Texas, California features at least half a dozen ramparts.

Two mountain chains and a high plateau occupy much of the far northern reach of the state's boundaries. The Klamath range is located in the northwest corner of the state. Two major rivers, the Klamath and Trinity, flow through the mountains' gorges, emptying into the Pacific. To the east the volcanic-created Cascades, which lie on a north–south axis from Washington to northern California, feature such peaks as Mt. Shasta (14,162 feet) and Mt. Lassen (10,457 feet), both of which resulted from thunderous, fiery eruptions along the Pacific Ring of Fire. Mt. Shasta's volcanic origin goes back about 50 million years ago, while Mt. Lassen is around 200,000 years old. The Modoc Plateau, covered with rugged lava flows and site of an 1873 war between whites and Indians, is tucked in the northeastern corner of the state.

Slightly south of the Cascades, California's highest range – the Sierra Nevada – begins its more than 400-mile span along part of the state's eastern boundary. This relatively young rampart, the world's longest and some 50 million years old (according to a team of Stanford scientists), is still rising, unlike the Appalachians in the eastern United States. The twin jewels of the Sierra, some say, are the glacial-carved Yosemite and Hetch-Hetchy valleys. The former is world-renowned for its granite cliffs and majestic waterfalls; the latter was transformed into a reservoir for San Francisco in the early twentieth century. A major obstacle to early overland migrants and the major construction challenge to builders of the nation's first transcontinental railroad, the Sierra boasts the highest peak in the contiguous 48 states – Mt. Whitney (14,495 feet). Fifty other Sierra peaks measure above 13,000 feet. The eastern slopes of the Sierra Nevada, which rise abruptly out of a largely treeless basin, are especially steep as those who have hiked in that region will attest.

Beyond impressive recreational opportunities and perhaps unparalleled aesthetic endowments, the Sierra Nevada range has been a storehouse of riches in pelts, ores, timber, and water. For, example, Chinese miners in the 1850s referred to the Sierra as *Gam Saan*, Gold Mountain. Other valuable ores, like tungsten (used in weapon-making), were mined in the twentieth century. Rivers flowing from the Sierra, like the Feather and Tuolumne, have furnished hydroelectric power and water to farmers and thirsty Californians. Sapphire-blue Lake Tahoe, the state's largest body of fresh water, is but one of the many lakes carved by Sierra glaciers.

The Great Basin – comprising parts of Utah, Arizona, and California – lies just east of the Sierra. Its historical importance has much to do with the early twentieth-century diversion of the Owens River into an aqueduct built to provide the inhabitants of Los Angeles with water. The resulting conflict between Owens Valley farmers and the City of Los Angeles became a major event in California's more recent past. East of Owens Valley the White Mountains extend across the state border into Nevada.

Close to and paralleling the Pacific seaboard, the Coastal Ranges run much of the length of the state from Cape Mendocino down to Point Conception. The ranges were formed by the same subduction process, described above, which produced the state's larger landmass. Younger than the Sierra Nevada, the Coastal Ranges – with some exceptions – generally ascend to between 3,000 and 4,000 feet. In addition to shale and sandstone, a good deal of serpentine, the state rock, can be found in these mountains.

Situated between the Coastal Ranges and the Sierra, the 450-mile-long and 50-mile-wide Central Valley was once immersed in sea water. The retreating ocean left in its wake what would evolve into one of the most fertile and productive farmlands in America, watered by the southward-flowing Sacramento River and the northward-flowing San Joaquin River. Together these two rivers formed a delta region in the state's interior that remains linked to the Pacific by San Francisco Bay's tributaries. The Bay's narrow entrance and 400 square miles of inlets, which render Stockton and Sacramento Pacific ports, make it one of the world's finest natural harbors.

Two more ramparts complete the mountainous profile of California. The southern end of the Great Valley gives way to the Transverse Ranges, so called because they extend for about 250 miles along an east–west axis that stretches to the offshore Santa Barbara Channel Islands. Still farther south, the Peninsular Ranges form the northernmost extremity of mountains that run the length of Baja California.

The state's final landform comprises the adjoining Mojave and Colorado deserts, occupying California's southeast corner. Death Valley, located in the Mojave, has the distinction of being the lowest point (282 feet below sea level) in North America. South of Death Valley, the Colorado Desert stretches to the Mexican border.

Climates

Just as California's land mass was Pacific-born much the same is true for its climates, which are as diverse as its topographic features. Rainfall, temperature, and sunlight vary so significantly throughout the state that meteorologists speak of its micro-climates. Even *within* distinct geographical areas climates, especially temperatures, can fluctuate dramatically on a seasonal basis. Since the beginning of European settlement in California, climate has become increasingly important in shaping the state's economy.

As elsewhere, California's climates are influenced by many variables including wind patterns, ocean currents, and high-elevation mountains. The dominant weather pattern is for the westerly winds (precipitation-bearing onshore winds from the Pacific) to blow during the winter months, depositing rain – and in some places snow – from the northern to the southern end of the state. These somewhat warm winds have a swirling effect that draws colder ocean water to the surface, creating coastal fogs from the resulting air–moisture mix and condensation. Inland from the fog-shrouded coast, high-elevation mountains intercept the moisture carried by the prevailing westerlies while blocking their flow eastward. Hence the much drier and often arid weather east of the Coastal, Sierra Nevada, San Gabriel, and San Bernardino mountains.

The flow pattern of the westerlies is largely inoperative in the spring, summer, and early fall months when hot, dry winds blow from interior deserts toward the ocean. In southern California, for example, the Santa Ana winds often produce drought conditions, which, in turn, have resulted in hazardous fires. The Witch (Creek) fire in October 2007, for example, destroyed more than a thousand homes north and east of San Diego. Drought and Santa Ana wind gusts of up to 100 miles per hour forced the closure of many schools; the entire town of Julian was evacuated. Such wildfires have become more frequent and severe in recent decades.

Drought and wildfires occur throughout California despite the plentiful rainfall in the northern as compared to the southern part of the state. Temperatures rarely rise above 70 degrees Fahrenheit (F) in the northwestern corner of the state, where average annual rainfall exceeds 100 inches. The Mojave Desert in the southeastern part of the state represents the other end of the climate continuum. There temperatures can swing from below freezing in winter to summer highs above 120 degrees F. The average annual precipitation is 1.5 inches. In Furnace Creek, Death Valley, located in the Mojave, the American heat record was set on July 10, 1913, when the thermometer reached a hellish 136.4 degrees F! In what is billed as "the world's toughest foot race," athletes compete annually in the Badwater ultra-marathon, a grueling 135-mile run from Badwater, Death Valley to Mt. Whitney – from the lowest to the highest elevations in the 48 contiguous states. The race is held in mid-summer when Badwater temperatures reach a blistering 130 degrees F.

The most problematic and consequential aspect of California's rainfall pattern is that three-fourths of the state's water supply originates in the mountain snow packs in the northern third of the state while more than three-fourths of the demand comes from agriculture and the teeming population in the southern two-thirds. As a result, the state has constructed one of the world's most extensive systems of aqueducts and dams to redistribute water to the otherwise parched farmlands in the Central and Imperial valleys as well as to Southland residents.

From this survey it is clear that there is no single California climate. Still, to the extent that there is a public image of such a climate, that image is based on the so-called Mediterranean weather conditions that prevail along the coastline from Santa Barbara to San Diego. The weather in this region is the most moderate in the state; summers are warm and dry and winters rarely get down to freezing while rainfall seldom exceeds 12 inches. This rare climate is found only in three parts of the world other than California and the Mediterranean Basin: central Chile, the Cape of South Africa, and southern and western Australia.

Such an ideal climate is marred principally by firestorms (already discussed) and smog. Smog (a term concocted from the words "smoke" and "fog") is an unhealthy gray haze created when nitrous oxide, an air pollutant, reacts with sunlight to produce ozone. In the Los Angeles Basin the ozone is trapped by a combination of mountains, westerly winds, and temperature inversions. Instead of the ozone escaping into the atmosphere, which would happen under normal conditions, it is blocked by warmer air above it and sealed in the Basin by nearby mountains. Consequently, the ozone stagnates near ground level causing respiratory and other ailments among humans, and in the lower-elevation forests it slows tree growth, particularly that of the ponderosa pine. Smog has been a serious problem in southern California at least since the mid-twentieth century.

While air quality has suffered because of smog, the otherwise ideal Mediterranean climate in the Southland has spurred the regional economy. The movie and aircraft industries located in the region largely because of the weather. As a beach culture emerged in the twentieth century, bathing suits and other ocean-oriented apparel gave rise to a very profitable sportswear enterprise.

Plants and Animals

California's diversity of climates is matched by that of its plants and animals. From prehistoric times – when mammoths, mastodons, camels, and saber-toothed tigers roamed much of the area – to today, the environment has proved conducive to life in its many forms.

Redwood trees rank among the state's most prominent plants. These stately giants grow almost exclusively along the coast from Big Sur to Humboldt County and in Yosemite and Sequoia national parks. Only a small number grow outside California – in Oregon and China. Those growing in coastal California, *Sequoia sempervirens*, are the tallest living things in the world, ascending to heights of 370 feet or more. Sierra redwoods, *Sequoia-dendron giganteum*, have the largest mass of any life form on Earth. The General Sherman tree in Sequoia, for example, is 273 feet high and 36.5 feet thick at its base. Its lower branches alone have more bulk than any single tree growing east of the Mississippi River. Redwood trees are both insect- and fire-resistant, yet require the heat from blazes in order to reproduce. Such heat causes the cones, which remain on the trees about 20 years, to burst and drop their seeds on the scorched ground where competing vegetation no longer remains. Rain and sunlight will then bring about germination. The life cycle that will follow is a long one: scientists have dated many living California redwood trees at more than 2,000 years old, to the time of Jesus of Nazareth and the Roman Empire. Experts consider such specimens as "old growth;" unfortunately, only 5 percent of the original two million acres still exist. Because of their sheer majesty and other distinctive qualities, the California legislature has designated both the coastal and Sierra redwoods as the official state trees.

In addition to redwoods, other notable California trees exist. The bristlecone pine, *Pinus longaeva*, is among them. These are the oldest extant forms of life in the world; some having lived 4,600 years. Bristlecone pines are native to the White Mountains. Numerous varieties of other pines grow throughout the non-desert parts of the state. The sugar pine is the largest and tallest of these in the world. One living specimen located on the western slope of the Sierra in Tuolumne County is 216 feet high and 10 feet in diameter. The Australian eucalyptus offers a good example of a non-native tree found in parts of coastal and central California. More importantly, the Australian tree should be thought of as being part of a transpacific exchange of goods, people, and diseases that have influenced much of California's history. Australian miners and sea captains brought eucalyptus seeds and seedlings to California aboard vessels crossing the Pacific during the gold rush years. In fact, many Australian ships sailing into San Francisco Bay were constructed of eucalyptus. By the 1860s and 1870s farmers used the trees for windbreaks and firewood, and developers for beautification of areas undergoing urbanization. Oil from the tree was thought to relieve pain and cure insomnia, malaria, dysentery, venereal disease, and much else. Nearly all of the above trees and others as well, like firs and oaks, have contributed to the profits of logging companies in the state. Three-fourths of the original acreage of conifer forests that existed 150 years ago has been cut down. Environmental organizations have mounted strong campaigns to save what is left of these old-growth stands of trees, especially the redwoods.

Palm trees, a southern California icon, were imported in the real-estate boom of the 1880s to give the area an exotic, biblical look. Only one species of palm – the fan palm – is native to the state and its habitat is found in the desert.

Since settlement by Europeans, California's environment has provided habitats for a variety of animals. The largest and most legendary of these has been the now extinct California grizzly bear (*Ursus californicus*), a representation of which graces the state flag and seal. Sitting atop the food chain, these powerful beasts coexisted with the California Indians. An estimated 10,000 roamed the coastal valleys, mountains, and even seashores when Spaniards began settling in the province. The giant bears ate mainly salmon, beached whales, and acorns. The last known grizzly in the state was killed in 1922 by a Fresno County rancher.

California, including its 15 islands (seven in the Farallon archipelago and eight Channel Islands) and coastal waters, has been home to many other animals as well. Among the terrestrial creatures are mountain lions, black bears, deer, elk, mountain sheep, badgers, bobcats, rattlesnakes, and more. Beavers, which are semi-aquatic, live in streams and lakes. They were hunted for their fur by California mountain men in the early decades of the nineteenth century. Trout and other freshwater fish have long populated the state's lakes and rivers, affording anglers an opportunity to test their skills. Salmon, which are fished commercially, spawn in many rivers flowing to the Pacific. Among marine mammals, the California sea otter, whose fur was prized in faraway Canton, China, was hunted to near-extinction in the first half of the nineteenth century. Migrating California gray whales provided a valuable resource for the San Francisco-based Pacific whaling industry in the latter half of that century. Located on the Pacific Flyway, a West Coast flight corridor for birds that extends from Alaska into South America, California is regularly visited by migratory waterfowl. Residentially based airborne animals include more than 500 species of birds. Of these the California condor, a vulture with a wing span of up to 9 feet, is the largest. Nearly extinct in the twentieth century, the state's condor population is beginning to rebound. More than half of the state's resident and migratory seabird nests are located on the Farallon Islands, situated about 30 miles west of San Francisco.

First Peoples and Their New Homeland

Who were the first Californians? When was the area settled? What is known about how the earliest aborigines lived? How did countless generations of their descendants interact with the natural environment? These are important questions for which there are few simple, definitive answers. This is the case for several reasons. Because there were few written records before the arrival of Europeans in the 1500s (the pre-contact period), historians are dependent on the often conflicting and tentative findings of scientists, especially anthropologists and archeologists. Also, what passes for the prehistory of California must correlate with what geologists, physicists, and ecologists have learned about landforms, the dating of human and animal bones, and sustainable habitats for game, plants, and people. Such correlations, likewise, can be problematic. For example, anthropologists and archeologists sometimes dispute the results of radiocarbon tests used to date the arrival of the first humans in the area.

With these cautions in mind, historians are in general agreement that perhaps as early as 50,000 years ago humans had followed big game – such as mammoths, mastodons, and bison – eastward across the Beringia ice bridge that once connected Asia to Alaska. Ten to fifteen thousand years ago, as climate warming set in and Beringia melted into the Bering Strait, the descendants of these Paleo-Indian migratory hunters continued on their way eastward and southward throughout the New World in pursuit of game. They traveled through ice-free corridors, "Paleo-Indian superhighways" according to UC Santa Barbara anthropologist Brian Fagan, into lands that would become California and the remaining bulk of the Americas. From the California mainland, various groups built watercraft that carried them to the Channel Islands of the Santa Barbara Channel, contend some anthropologists. The skeletal remains of the so-called Arlington Woman at a site on Santa Rosa Island have been radiocarbon dated to as early as 11,000 years ago.

Until recent years, this ice-free corridor explanation was clearly the dominant one regarding the earliest human inhabitants of North America's western coastline. Today, however, anthropologist Jon M. Erlandson of the University of Oregon and other researchers have found that prehistoric Asian seafarers most likely voyaged along the northernmost coastal waters of the Pacific Rim, reaching California's Channel Islands at least 13,000 years ago, and possibly even millennia earlier. This so-called coastal migration theory refers to the ancient offshore route as the "Kelp Highway," in reference to the clusters of edible marine life inhabiting these lush kelp beds, as well as accessible birds and nearby terrestrial game.

Archeological evidence, including fish hooks and other gear, have been excavated on the Channel Islands and carbon-dated to 13,000 years ago. Moreover, Erlandson claims that geologic evidence suggests that the ice-free corridor may not have been passable until 14,000 years ago, if then, and archeological remains found in 14,300-year-old caves on Oregon's coastline seemingly predate the ice-free corridor migration. In short, a growing body of scientific evidence holds that California's first human inhabitants were probably northeast Asian Pacific Rim voyagers. Whether or not they predated the Beringia land-crossers (the archeological debate continues), ancient Pacific seafarers were clearly among the first human settlers of what became California.

As the Arlington site suggests, Indians have been living in California for between 12,000 and 15,000 years or longer. For thousands of years afterward the growing aboriginal population spread into all regions of the land, adapting to the diverse, ever-changing environmental conditions they encountered.

Long before Europeans arrived, California natives had lived in considerable harmony and balance with their natural surroundings. Food, prepared by the women, was usually plentiful and its sources were diverse. Indians ate ocean and freshwater fish, mollusks, sea otter, deer, elk, birds, reptiles, insects, acorns, piñon seeds, mushrooms, squash, corn, and more. Nutritionally, their diets were superior to those of the Europeans who would later claim the land. Men hunted and fished; women gathered, stored, and processed acorns and other foods. Acorns were a high-fat dietary staple that required leaching out the tannic acid

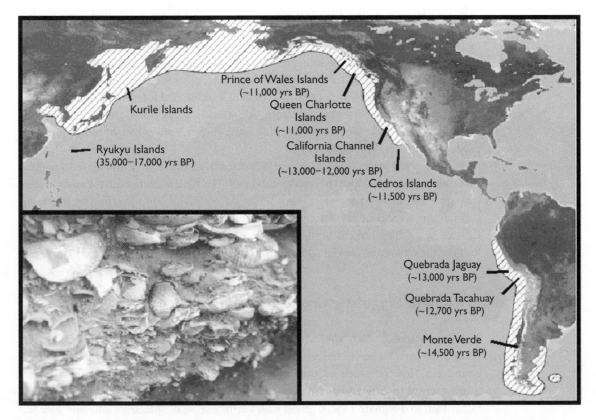

Kurile Islands

Ryukyu Islands
(35,000–17,000 yrs BP)

Prince of Wales Islands
(~11,000 yrs BP)

Queen Charlotte
Islands
(~11,000 yrs BP)

California Channel
Islands
(~13,000–12,000 yrs BP)

Cedros Islands
(~11,500 yrs BP)

Quebrada Jaguay
(~13,000 yrs BP)

Quebrada Tacahuay
(~12,700 yrs BP)

Monte Verde
(~14,500 yrs BP)

Figure 1.2 The Kelp Highway. Drawn by Michael H. Graham. Source: Jon M. Erlandson, Michael H. Graham, Bruce J. Bourque, et al., "The Kelp Highway Hypothesis: Marine Ecology, the Coastal Migration Theory, and the Peopling of the Americas," *The Journal of Island and Coastal Archaeology*, 2/2 (2007). Reprinted by permission of Taylor & Francis Ltd and Michael H. Graham.

by rinsing and using mortars and pestles for grinding the meal into flour for cooking. While these activities entailed work they seldom required excessive labor since many carried out these tasks. If ever there were a Pacific Arcadia, a terrestrial paradise of rustic beauty and relatively simple living, California came as close as anywhere else to realizing that ideal.

During the millennia before European contact, California's Indians built an extraordinary knowledge base about how elevation and climate related to food resources, about edible and medicinal plants, and forestry management. Tribal territories sometimes spanned different elevation levels, each level featuring its own edible vegetation and animal resources as well as climatic characteristics. For example, Indians crowded into the foothill woodland areas because of the widespread availability of acorns. The Indians in the Colorado Desert used creosote bushes to treat nausea and other intestinal problems as well as respiratory ailments.

By the standards of their time and today, the California Indians of the distant pre-contact period excelled in forestry management and plant cultivation. Their major management tool was the controlled burning of trees and the dense underbrush that otherwise choked more valuable vegetation. The frequent fires they set in forests and oak woodlands favored the growth of such flame-tolerant trees as black oak, giant sequoia, and ponderosa pine. Certain native grasses also benefited. As a result of less cluttered forests native hunters could better see game and dangerous predators, like grizzlies, black bears, and mountain lions. By pruning trees and plants, and relocating some species, natives sought to maximize the productivity of their environment.

As forestry managers, California's early Indians lived sustainably and close to nature's rhythms and balance, which they understood well. Their interactions with the environment were governed by two precepts: do not waste; do not hoard. Hunting, fishing, gathering, and farming were conducted accordingly, ensuring ample food resources for the future. Favored by an environment of plenty, the natives' stewardship of resources and the land fostered the ecology of aboriginal California.

Tribal and Linguistic Groupings

The word "tribes," when applied to California's Indians, requires a brief explanation. Usually the term suggests Indian groupings tied to specified or recognizable territorial boundaries. However, when anthropologists and linguists refer to California tribes the term is often meant to differentiate between language families traceable to general living areas rather than to designate a social group with a strong sense of shared identity and a leadership structure.

When Indians had California to themselves their numbers expanded and their distinct groupings enjoyed a large measure of self-determination. On the eve of colonization in the late 1700s, between 300,000 and 1,000,000 indigenous people inhabited California. Most of them lived in villages of 100 to 500 dwellers. The village residents constituted an autonomous social group that anthropologists call a "tribelet." Generally, the dwellers in these village communities, or tribelets, recognized only the authority of their local chieftain or headman, who resided in a central village. These leaders were responsible for managing the tribelet's food and other resources and settling disputes. Except among the relatively more militant Mojaves and Yumas in the southeastern region, political organization and a broad sense of group identity were lacking, which eased the work of Spanish missionaries.

The absence of a broader Indian identity was due in part to the fact that natives tended to live within the territorial boundaries of their respective tribelets. This resulted in what anthropologist Robert Heizer characterized as a "deep-seated provincialism and attachment to the place of their birth." For example, Mattole mothers impressed on the children of their northwest coastal tribelet that wandering beyond their group's boundaries was perilous. Still, such boundaries were somewhat permeable; neighboring tribelets at times negotiated agreements allowing border-crossings for hunting, gathering, and trade. Also, Indians at times traveled beyond California's borders to exchange goods.

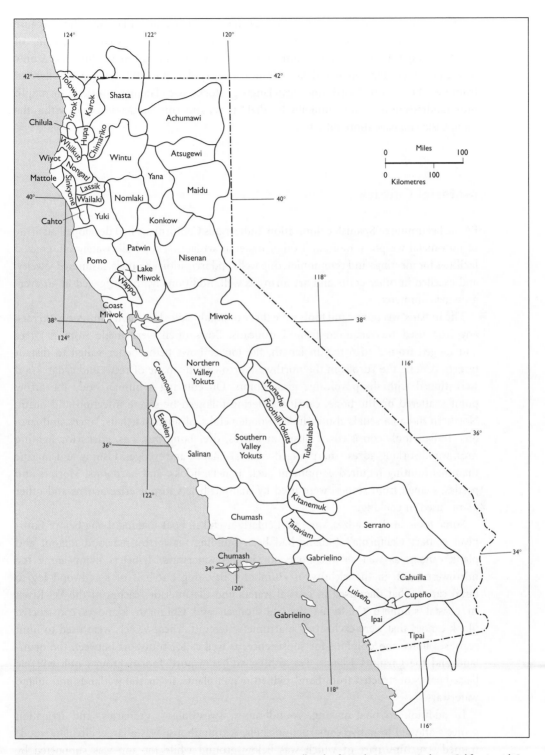

Figure 1.3 Indian living areas. Based on Robert F. Heizer, *Handbook of North American Indians: California*, vol. 8 (Washington, D.C.: Smithsonian Institution, 1978), p. ix. Used by permission of the Smithsonian Institution.

The provincialism and boundary-consciousness of native Californians were both a cause and a result of the numerous languages they spoke. These Indians constituted one of the most linguistically diverse populations in the world, surpassed in this regard only by the peoples of the Sudan and New Guinea. They spoke up to 80 languages that derived from five of the Native North American language stocks. Each language stock, in turn, split into hundreds of mutually unintelligible dialects, making communication even within the same basic language more difficult.

Material Culture

By the beginning of Spanish colonization, indigenous Californians had developed an array of non-metal weapons, tools, and other material artifacts. They built watercraft, erected facilities for meetings and ceremonies, dug wells and irrigation channels, fashioned jewelry, and excelled in other crafts and art forms as well. Additionally, they engaged in an ever-growing commerce.

The Indians' weaponry and tools were those of highly skilled Stone Age hunter-gatherers; any iron used was acquired from Europeans. Bows often were made from fir trees and ranged from 3 to 6 feet in length, the longer bows being better suited to distant targets. Among the Yuroks in the northwest, arrow shafts made of reeds and cedar wood were tipped with sharp volcanic glass points. On entering a human body the arrow point shattered on the bone, causing festering followed by severe infection and death. Northern Indian arsenals also included wooden clubs, obsidian hatchets, lances, and javelins. Indian tools consisted of obsidian knives, deer-bone punches, sticks for lighting fires, woodworking adzes (sharp-edged cutters), mauls, and wedges. Fishing and marine mammal hunting required equipment such as nets, hooks, and harpoons. Mortars and pestles, shaped from stones, were used by many tribelets to pulverize acorns and other plants used in cooking.

Some tools, such as adzes, were particularly useful in boat-making. Long before European contact California's Indians had been building seaworthy redwood dugout and plank canoes, as well as tule boats for inland waterways. Tribelets living along the northwest coast, in the vicinity of Humboldt Bay, dug out half of a redwood log to build canoes that they used in coastal waters and the interior reaches of the Eel River. In coastal southern California the Shoshonean and Chumash islanders constructed plank canoes that were exclusively maritime watercraft. These vessels were used to hunt seals, sea lions, and dolphins for subsistence, as well as for transport between the mainland and the Channel Islands. For fishing and transport, Indian groups utilized Tule balsa boats, constructed from hand-twined marsh plants, in coastal wetlands and inland waterways.

In addition to boat-making, roundhouses, sweathouses, granaries, and irrigation projects attested to native construction skills. A roundhouse was a large, circular, wood-framed structure, part of which was below ground while the top was supported by rafters and covered with earth. It was used for rituals. Sweathouses served as ceremonial centers and men's saunas. The sweathouse consisted of a sealed room heated by an open fire. When sufficiently hot, males exited and bolted to nearby ponds of cool water and submerged themselves. These rituals were intended to cleanse the body of scents that could alert game to a hunter's presence as well as to appeal to spirits in nature. Women in the central region customarily built thatched granaries for food storage, some of which reached 15 feet in height. The Owens Valley Paiutes used communal labor to dig irrigation ditches and dam streams to enhance the productivity of edible wild plants.

In basketry California's Indians were virtually unsurpassed worldwide. Women dominated the craft and art form; Pomo males were the only ones of their gender to make baskets. These portable containers had multiple uses: gathering, storage, and cooking of food; the carrying of infants; headwear; ritual observances; and commerce. They often featured geometric and animal designs. Some were so tightly woven that they could carry water, even without tar caulking, and be used for cooking. Pomo baskets were particularly ornate, exhibiting intricate designs coupled with decorative feathers and inlaid mother-of-pearl.

Clothing was fashioned from sea otter, rabbit, and deer skins, as well as plant materials; the latter also were used by men and women for body painting. In summer men often wore nothing, while women dressed in skirts made of plant fibers. Both sexes covered themselves in furs during colder periods of the year. Special rituals called for more elaborate apparel: feathered headdresses and capes, shell necklaces, and jewel and shell earrings. Footwear for most northern tribelets consisted mainly of moccasins; southern groups preferred sandals. Body tattoos, sported by men and women, were common in Indian California. Yurok girls, for example, received facial tattoos beginning at age 5. Black stripes were etched into the skin from the corners of their mouths to below their chins. Every five years another line was added, making clear their age. Imagine what age-concealing women in the Western world would have thought about that practice!

Indian art was gendered. Just as women excelled in basketry and costume design, men dominated wood and bone carving, storytelling, music, and rock-carving (petroglyphs) and rock painting (pictographs). Most of these art forms were practiced widely, though the petroglyphs and pictographs were limited to the interior parts of southern California. The Chumash were particularly adept at executing these artworks. Boulders and the walls of caves were used to carve and paint representations of humans, animals, and assorted abstract shapes – all of which usually derived from religious beliefs.

Some of the Indians' material artifacts became articles of exchange in a steadily growing commerce. By the time of European colonization, native Californians had been carrying on a brisk trade with both neighboring and distant aboriginal groups. Surplus food, redwood dugout canoes, abalone shells, whalebone, baskets, and many of the weapons and tools mentioned above were both bartered and sold (often using shell currencies). Commercially, Indians exchanged their goods in a "greater California." Trails crisscrossed and extended beyond California's current borders into Arizona, Nevada, Oregon, and the Baja peninsula of Mexico, thereby facilitating long-distance trade.

The near-absence of metal in aboriginal trade was an important factor in earlier assessments of the California Indians' material culture. Coupled with the lack of a written language, unfamiliarity with the wheel, and relative non-use of animals as beasts of burden, the absence of metal instruments led some earlier whites to disparage the California Indians. Nineteenth-century fur trappers and, later, some writers viewed the natives as culturally and racially inferior to Euro-Americans and other North American indigenes. They often used the term "Digger" when referring to Native Californians, some of whose women used pointed sticks to unearth roots and wild vegetables, presumably for food. Only primitives, many whites believed, would subsist on such a crude diet. The term "Digger" was a racist misnomer since the plant material that California Indians dug up was used mainly for basketry, though they ate some roots and bulbs. More importantly, white Americans' use of the term showed little understanding of the wide array of Indian foods and the natives' sophisticated grasp of plant ecology. Dehumanizing California's aborigines in this fashion made it easier to divest them of land and other resources. In recent decades scholars have repudiated this older view and recognized the modern environmental stewardship at the heart of the natives' material culture.

Religion and Social Practices

The natives' religious beliefs shaped their social practices. Considerable variation existed in both matters, rendering generalization difficult. Still, some commonalities can be identified as long as important qualifications and exceptions are noted.

Most California Indians believed in the existence of a hierarchical universe comprised of three interrelated worlds, or in a variation of this view. An upper world was inhabited by quasi-human and animal-like beings in the form of the Sun, Moon, and constellations. A second or middle world contained humans, their environment, and non-mortal beings. A third or underworld was home to reptilian and amphibious spirits harmful to people. In short, to natives, spirits were everywhere, punishing or rewarding humans depending on how faithfully they followed their religion.

The religions of the California Indians were ecologically based. A core principle ran through virtually all of their spiritual beliefs: The earth and all life on it comprised a sacred, interdependent whole of which humans were but one part among all the other coequal parts. Instead of being separate from the environment and above other species, humans – in order to survive – must reverence their connection to the Earth and care for it. This is not to say that California's Indians always practiced environmental stewardship, for in fact they at times over-hunted and over-fished. The important point is that they learned from their mistakes, as survival was a grim teacher.

Caring for the Earth would assuredly address the needs of generations to come, but Indian seers also believed that in the distant future the universe would be depleted of life-sustaining energy and that nature's bounty would eventually give out. Such a religion-inspired cosmology is consistent with the modern notion of entropy, of considerable interest to physicists who foresee a similar ending of the Cosmos.

Other beliefs also reflected the importance of the natural world in Native Californian religions. Indians, for example, differed on whether there was one god or many. Most groups believed in the existence of many deities or spirits that were to be found in animals, places, streams, trees, natural processes, and landforms. The spirits would punish wasting and hoarding, that is, behaviors that upset the ecological balance and threatened life. Being on good terms with the spirit world, then, was required for the maintenance of a stable, predictable environment.

Rituals aimed at conciliating the spirits followed from these and related beliefs. Ceremonies marked the year's first salmon catches and acorn harvests. Though tribelets differed in the ways they conducted ceremonies, indigenous rites in and beyond Indian California focused largely on the major stages of the human life span: birth, puberty, marriage, sex, childbearing, sickness, and death.

Coming-of-age or puberty ceremonies were held for both sexes, though such rites were generally more involved for girls than for boys. For girls on the cusp of womanhood a lengthy dance was usually performed. Many northern California native groups believed that a female's potential for evil greatly intensified when going through puberty. Accordingly, elders gave pubescent girls detailed rules for gathering firewood and performing other chores as well as for comporting themselves with modesty. In the southern parts of California tribelets applied direct means to counter the supposed consequences of the physiological changes associated with blossoming womanhood. Warmth was thought essential in this process. Adolescent females were not allowed to drink cold water and bathing had to occur only in heated water. Among the Gabrielino and Luiseño peoples girls being initiated were placed in a warm pit simulating roasting in an earthen oven. In this instance the elders saw themselves as providing for the girls' future health rather than combating any presumed evil tendencies.

Initiation rites for males often included the infliction of pain and suffering, such as being whipped by a bow string and fasting. Such were the ways of the Achomawi and Shasta natives in the northeastern corner of California. Additionally, the Achomawi pierced young men's ears. Completion of these rites gained males (and in some locales females) membership into California's two major religious cults, the Kuksu and the toloache. The former cult impersonated spirits by using distinctive disguises in their rituals. The latter cult used jimsonweed (*Datura stramonium*), a narcotic, to induce sacred trances.

For young initiated natives – indeed for virtually all North American Indians – shamanism, the belief that priests have powers drawn from the spirit world that among other things cause and cure diseases, was a central component of religion. Sickness was thought to result from foreign objects that had lodged in one's body. Shamanistic cures, therefore, involved the removal of any such objects, usually by sucking, accompanied among the Colorado River tribes by blowing tobacco smoke on the injured body area. Throughout California singing and dancing were often integral to the curing process as well. A shaman's presumed power to *produce* diseases at times led to inter-tribal war, especially in cases where rival groups attributed a disease to a shamanistic curse imposed by their foes. As can be seen from the fact that priests in the northwestern areas usually were women, shamanistic customs varied throughout Indian California.

As mentioned, Indian social practices derived largely from religion. This was partially true with respect to war. Connections between religion and social practices are also evident in matters of class and wealth distribution, gender roles, and marriage.

Regarding war, California natives engaged in occasional violent conflicts but overall were comparatively peaceful, except for the Mojave and Yuma groups, as noted. In addition to charges of being victimized by the casting of shamanistic curses, other causes of war included poaching game, boundary intrusions, and the capturing of women. The Chumash are reported to have gone to war over insults directed at their chiefs. Though gruesome, hostilities usually did not last long. The weapons of choice included bows and arrows, war clubs, stones, and slings. The Yuma, Mojave, and Diegueño were the only tribes to use shields – usually constructed of unornamented animal hides. Generally, prisoners were not taken. Men seized in battle were summarily killed and decapitated; women and children were slaughtered, though females sometimes were taken as captives. With the exception of warring northwestern Shasta, and Wintun groups, victorious tribes commonly took scalps.

A consideration of Indian wealth, its importance, and its distribution illustrates the importance of looking beyond California's physical borders when attempting to understand its past. Significantly, the Indians of northern California were culturally linked to the aboriginals of Alaska and the Pacific Northwest (Oregon and Washington), who attached great importance to wealth and the social status it represented. Northern Indians with the most property controlled rituals. For them, religion and socio-economic status were closely linked. In northwestern California, Indians enslaved one another for unpaid debts. Servitude existed nowhere else in the province during the pre-contact period. Throughout much the rest of California, Indians showed relatively little interest in property acquisition and class distinctions.

Gender roles throughout California, on the other hand, tended to be more clearly defined than class distinctions and, again, had a religious dimension. Females raised the children, assisted with births, and made family clothing. As mentioned, they gathered, processed, and cooked foods, and constructed granaries. Mothers transmitted knowledge, both practical and folkloric, to their children. They weaved baskets, danced, and sang. Among the Chumash, with their highly advanced hunter-gatherer culture, matrons often ruled villages; in more northern areas, as shown, females served as priests. Men hunted, fished, fought, gambled, controlled most of the property, and wielded the bulk of political and religious authority.

California natives viewed the family as society's most important institution, and marriage lay at the heart of it. Bride-purchase was practiced widely, except for groups east of the Sierra and along the Colorado River. Sometimes marriages involved religious rites; in other instances tribelets recognized a couple as being married if the two had lived together for a length of time. Divorce was rare but possible. Husbands often had more than one wife; this was particularly true for chiefs and shamans, who valued the multiple political ties afforded by polygamy. Among some tribelets, if a wife was unfaithful the husband could claim the wife of his wife's lover. Prostitution was practically unknown.

Usually the lineage (a large, extended family of blood relatives and in-laws) was traced through the man's ancestry. Lineages, far more than tribal affiliations, marked a person's identity and exerted authority over individuals.

Pacific Profile: Anthropologist Alfred L. Kroeber

When the last survivor of the Yani tribe emerged starving and near-naked in the northern California town of Oroville in 1911, the so-called "savage" ended up in jail. California's leading anthropologist, Alfred L. Kroeber, on hearing about the capture, telegraphed the arresting sheriff in clipped language: "Hold Indian till arrival professor State University who will take charge and be responsible for him. Matter important account aboriginal history." Given custody of reportedly the last Stone Age Indian in America, Kroeber named his new ward "Ishi" – meaning "man" in the Yahi subgroup dialect of the virtually extinct Yani tribe. Subsequently, the anthropologist and the Indian formed a short-term working relationship that made possible the recovery of the language and culture of an indigenous people who otherwise would have vanished through the cracks of California history. Lacking immunity to whites' diseases, Ishi lived for a little less than five years after being brought to the University of California at Berkeley for study. Saddened and depressed by Ishi's death in 1916, Kroeber sought psychoanalysis for a while before returning to his research in cultural anthropology. Theodora Kroeber, the anthropologist's second wife (his first having died of tuberculosis in 1913), told the Indian's story and described her husband's relationship with him in *Ishi in Two Worlds: A Biography of the Last Wild Indian in North America* (1961).

Alfred Louis Kroeber (1876–1960) was born in Hoboken, New Jersey, and grew up in New York City. As a Columbia University graduate student he studied Eskimo languages and the cultures of several Californian tribes – the Yurok, Yokut, and Mojave. While finishing his studies, Kroeber secured a job as curator of the anthropological collections at the small California Academy of Sciences in San Francisco. Shortly after receiving in 1901 the first doctorate in anthropology awarded by Columbia, the young scholar accepted a teaching position in the University of California at Berkeley's newly established anthropology department.

In addition to teaching dozens of graduate students, some of whom became leading anthropologists, Kroeber poured himself into travel research and publications on indigenous cultures in California, Mexico, and Peru. His massive *Handbook of the Indians of California* (1925), an anthology of writings, secured his reputation as the preeminent authority on the subject matter. During World War II the U.S. government commissioned him to teach an Army Specialized Training Program at Berkeley in Chinese, Japanese, Thai, and Vietnamese languages to select military personnel who would accompany American invasion forces in Asia. A heart attack forced Kroeber to carry out this task only in an advisory capacity.

Toward the end of his lengthy career, Kroeber became a venerated generalist, devoting himself to studying the diffusion of culture based on his findings regarding California's aborigines. One major product of this shift was his 1923 publication of the first textbook in his field, titled *Anthropology*. The work, updated in 1948, is noted for its position that there is no objective evidence indicating the inferiority of any racial group. This view stood in opposition to earlier and popular Euro-American pronouncements about the supposed inferiority of the California Indians. He died in 1960, revered for his work on the indigenous peoples of the Golden State and parts of the Pacific Rim.

The Chumash: Pacific Coast Mariners and Traders

According to anthropologists, no group of California Indians was more skilled and involved in seafaring than the Chumash. Their trade goods, currency, and wealth derived largely from maritime resources.

Around 1000 CE (Common Era, equivalent to AD) they began settling villages in central California, along the coast from San Luis Obispo to Malibu, and on a few of the Channel

Islands. Some Chumash goods, however, circulated far beyond this settlement area and even beyond California's borders. For example, their shell beads produced in Santa Barbara and the Channel Islands have been found in Oregon, the Southwest, and the Great Basin.

The Chumash maritime region was rich in resources that provided for a flourishing economy. Coastal waters and those surrounding the Channel Islands abounded with kelp forests (kelp wraps were used to cure leg swelling), fish, sea otters as well as other marine mammals, and valuable shells (used in fashioning money, and in making fish hooks and ornaments). Islanders exported to the mainland shell beads, fish, otter skins, and steatite ollas (soapstone cooking pots from Santa Catalina Island). In return, mainlanders exported to the islands acorns, seeds, bows and arrows, furs, roots, and baskets. Villages in and around today's Santa Barbara served as exchange centers in commerce that brought together natives from the interior, the mainland coast, and the Channel Islands.

The same waters that abounded in resources also abounded in seagoing hazards. Watercraft sometimes capsized in high seas and drownings were common. Fernando Librado, a Chumash boat-builder and expert on tribal lore, told an anthropologist in the early twentieth century: "Canoe faring is dangerous, and drownings are frequent. There would be no coming home, for a wind or wave might capsize a *tomol* [boat]. . . ." When the Santa Ana winds blew, Chumash canoes remained on the beach due to high waves. The natives rarely made passages during the night; when they did they navigated by the stars.

Chumash sailors usually built the ocean-going vessels they rowed. These seamen comprised a select group known as the Brotherhood-of-the-Canoe. In order to protect their monopoly on inter-island and island to mainland shipping, they guarded closely their knowledge about plank-boat construction, seamanship, and currents. Canoe owners, usually chiefs, paid Brotherhood members to conduct the voyages and load and unload cargoes. As this payment and the commerce with which it was connected suggests, the Chumash maritime economy constituted an early form of capitalism.

Modern researchers estimate that about 15,000 Chumash lived in California at the time of European contact in the 1500s; by the late nineteenth century few remained. Visiting the Santa Barbara Channel coastline in 1602, Spanish navigator Sebastian Vizcaíno wrote in his journal that the Indians were "well formed and of good body, although not very corpulent [fat]." Though the Chumash enjoyed a bountiful environment, they experienced their share of self-imposed suffering that was only compounded by the arrival of the Spanish. Physical evidence indicates that during times of stress, for example food shortages, the Chumash turned on one another in occasional outbursts of violence that led to deaths. Polluted water on the Channel Islands, coupled with possible venereal disease throughout the tribal area, also led to population declines.

For all of these difficulties, on the eve of European contact the Chumash and their fellow California Indians had registered impressive achievements. Their knowledge of plants and animals as well as their sustainable ecology especially stand out. They excelled in basketry and rock art. With the possible exception of indigenous Alaskans, the Chumash may have been unsurpassed in all of native North America in seafaring. Despite all these accomplishments, in the early 1500s California's Indians were about to see their homeland visited and later invaded by a light-skinned people who had traveled from afar.

Figure 1.4   A replica of a Chumash plank canoe (*tomol/tomol'o*), ashore on San Miguel Island, located off Santa Barbara's coast. Watercraft like this may hold clues regarding the possibility of pre-Columbian Polynesian voyagers visiting California's coast. Courtesy of the Santa Barbara Museum of Natural History.

Other Possible Early Voyagers to California

Before the arrival of light-skinned people, or Europeans, had other non-Indian Pacific voyagers reached California in ancient times? Scholarly speculation centers around two possibilities: Polynesian and Chinese Pacific-crossers.

A small group of anthropologists and linguists is currently investigating whether early Polynesians reached California in watercraft sometime between 400 and 800 CE. UC Berkeley linguist Kathryn Klar and Cal Poly San Louis Obispo anthropologist Terry Jones published an article in the July 2008 issue of *American Antiquity*, claiming linguistic and archeological evidence for ancient Polynesian voyaging to southern California. They noted, for example, that the Chumash Indians, who inhabited the area around present-day Santa Barbara, continue to use the word *tomol* or the variant *tomolo'o* for "boat." Moreover, *tomol* or *tomolo'o* did not refer to simply any kind of boat; instead it described an ocean-going, hand-sewn, redwood plank canoe. Polynesians are known to have used such canoes, built from redwood logs carried along Pacific currents to distant islands across that ocean. Klar and Jones note that the term *tomolo'o*, which appears in no other North American Indian language, is rooted in a Polynesian word. From this fragmentary evidence, the two scholars and others reason that the Chumash may have learned their extraordinary skills as Pacific mariners from ancient Polynesians who likely visited southern California's shores centuries before the arrival of Europeans. Research into this matter is robust and ongoing.

A second possibility, based on scantier evidence than the first, is that in 458 CE an Afghan Chinese Buddhist monk, Hwui Shan, sailed across the Pacific with several other Chinese monks, exploring much of North America's western coastline from Alaska southward to the tip of Baja California. According to Chinese records dating to the late fifth century CE, such a round-trip voyage was undertaken and Hwui Shan noted his sighting of tall trees of red wood and topographical features resembling the diverse land masses found from the Northwest Coast to that of Baja. While such a voyage was possible, physical evidence remains lacking and present-day scholars in the United States are hesitant to affirm or deny a Chinese discovery of America nearly a millennium before Columbus.

SUMMARY

California's land mass, climates, and other physical features were shaped largely by Pacific forces, and these features profoundly influenced the state's subsequent human history. The earliest human inhabitants migrated from Asia's Pacific Rim in watercraft and afoot, and lived mainly in coastal areas, adapting their cultures – especially their foods, dress, and tool-making – to a hospitable marine environment. This was less true, naturally, for tribelets living in the interior regions, though trade between coastal and hinterland Indians remained brisk throughout most of the pre-European contact period. California's tribelets were severely provincial, as evidenced by the scores of languages and hundreds of dialects they spoke, making communication between these linguistic groups extremely difficult. Anthropologists give the physically healthy California Indians high marks not only for living in an ecologically sustainable manner, but also for their artistry, especially seen in their basketry and petroglyphs. Alfred L. Kroeber, an early researcher of California's native peoples, attained a national reputation and helped shape the field of his expertise throughout most of the twentieth century.

Among all of California's Indian groups, the Chumash developed the most advanced maritime culture, based on a trade network that extended in many directions beyond the present boundaries of the state. In short, their economy embraced a Greater California. Aside from Paleo-Indian seafarers, California may have been visited by Polynesian and Chinese Pacific-crossers centuries before the arrival of Europeans in the province. Much more evidence, however, will be needed to substantiate the likelihood of Polynesian and Chinese transpacific visits to California before the arrival of Europeans in the 1500s.

REVIEW QUESTIONS

- In what ways were California's landmass and climates shaped by Pacific forces?
- How and when did California's first human inhabitants arrive in the area that much later became the Golden State? What was the so-called "Kelp Highway," as explained by anthropologist Jon M. Erlandson, and why was it significant?
- What evidence do scholars offer to support their claim that the lifestyles of California's Indians were sustainable before the arrival of Europeans?
- Who was Ishi and why was he significant in California history? What was anthropologist Alfred Kroeber's connection to Ishi?
- How did the Pacific maritime economy of the Chumash impact the interior reaches of California, Oregon, the Southwest, and the Great Basin?

FURTHER READINGS

Lowell J. Bean, "Indians of California: Diverse and Complex Peoples," *California History*, 71 (Fall 1992), 302–23. The author offers a readable and well-illustrated overview of the California Indians from pre-contact times to the late twentieth century.

Warren A. Beck and Ynez. D. Haase, *Historical Atlas of California* (Norman, OK: University of Oklahoma Press, 1974). Though dated, this is still a useful source especially for geography, climate, and other natural features of the state.

Thomas C. Blackburn, ed., *December's Child: A Book of Chumash Oral Narratives* (Berkeley: University of California Press, 1975). The study affords a description of anthropologist John P. Harrington's huge collection of unpublished notes and writings on the Chumash plus tribal oral narratives drawn from those materials.

Thomas C. Blackburn and M. Kat Anderson, eds., *Before the Wilderness: Environmental Management by Native Californians* (Menlo Park, CA: Ballena Press, 1993). This book covers Indian adaptations to California's diverse landforms and biological zones.

Joseph L. Chartkoff and Kerry Kona Chartkoff, *The Archaeology of California* (Stanford, CA: Stanford University Press, 1984). Readers are treated to a highly detailed and well-illustrated account of California's earliest Paleo-Indian settlers and how they lived.

J.M. Erlandson, M.L. Moss, and M. Des Lauriers, "Life on the Edge: Early Maritime Cultures of the Pacific Coast of North America," *Quaternary Science Reviews*, 27 (2008), 2232–45. This is a cutting-edge source

for the maritime explanation of California's earliest settlements.

Brian M. Fagan, *Ancient North America: The Archaeology of a Continent* (New York: Thames & Hudson, 2005). A comprehensive college-level anthropology textbook, this volume pays particular attention to ancient peoples living along North America's Pacific coastline.

Brian M. Fagan, *Before California: An Archaeologist Looks at Our Earliest Inhabitants* (Walnut Creek, CA: AltaMira Press, 2004). An anthropological-archaeological tour through Indian-occupied California, this study contains testimonies drawn from travelers, scholars, and natives.

Philip L. Fradkin, *The Seven States of California: A Natural and Human History* (Berkeley: University of California Press, 1995). This work provides a traveling journalist's view of the state's major geographical regions and their respective histories.

Lynn H. Gamble, *The Chumash World at European Contact: Power, Trade, and Feasting Among Complex Hunter-Gatherers* (Berkeley: University of California Press, 2008). This specialized work offers a distillation of the most recent scholarly findings regarding the Chumash.

Ramon A. Gutierrez and Richard J. Orsi, eds., *Contested Eden: California Before the Gold Rush*, a special issue of *California History*, 76/2 and 3 (Summer and Fall 1997). See especially the articles by M. Kat Anderson, Michael G. Barbour, and Valerie Whitworth, "A World of Balance and Plenty: Land, Plants, Animals, and Humans in a Pre-European California" (pp. 12–47), and William S.

Simmons, "Indian Peoples of California" (pp. 48–77). These writings cover both the early and later history of the California Indians, particularly their ecologically informed lifestyles.

Derek Hayes, *Historical Atlas of California* (Berkeley: University of California Press, 2007). This book contains original maps and commentaries plus excerpts from historical documents related to the historical geography of California.

R.F. Heizer and M.A. Whipple, *The California Indians: A Source Book* (Berkeley: University of California Press, 1971). This is a classic compendium of information on California's Indians from prehistoric times to the late twentieth century.

David Hornbeck, *California Patterns: A Geographical and Historical Atlas* (Palo Alto, CA: Mayfield Publishing, 1983). This dated but otherwise excellent collection of maps and charts elucidates California history from the pre-contact period to the 1980s.

Douglas J. Kennett, *The Island Chumash: Behavioral Ecology of a Maritime Society* (Berkeley: University of California Press, 2005). This account offers a synthesis of the cultural and environmental history of the Northern Channel Islands and their Chumash inhabitants who arrived 13,500 years ago.

Theodora Kroeber, *Ishi in Two Worlds: A Biography of the Last Wild Indian in North America* (Berkeley: University of California Press, 2004). The author reveals the human and tragic consequences of a lone Indian's brief experience of living in a white world.

Leif C.W. Landberg, *The Chumash Indians of Southern California* (Los Angeles: Southwest Museum, 1965). This is a brief, scholarly yet readable introduction to the basic aspects of Chumash culture, including tools, foods, seasonality, and ecology.

Kent G. Lightfoot and Otis Parrish, *California Indians and Their Environment* (Berkeley: University of California Press, 2009). The author provides a recent synthesis of the latest scholarship on the complex and environmentally sophisticated cultures of California's Indians.

John McPhee, *Assembling California* (New York: Farrar, Straus & Giroux, 1993). This book is the starting point for understanding the role of plate tectonics in the geological formation of California.

Mains'l Haul: A Journal of Pacific Maritime History, 47/1 and 2 (Winter/Spring 2011). The theme of the issue is "Prehistory: Pacific Seafarers and Maritime Cultures." The articles make a strong case for Asian Pacific seafarers being the first peoples to inhabit the western coastline of the Americas.

Malcolm Margolin, *The Ohlone Way: Indian Life in the San Francisco-Monterey Bay Area* (Berkeley: Heyday Books, 1978). This work focuses on the pre-contact history of these northern California aborigines.

Keith Heyer Meldahl, *Rough-Hewn Land: A Geologic Journey from California to the Rocky Mountains* (Berkeley: University of California Press, 2011). The connection between California gold and the primordial floor of the Pacific Ocean is explained in this readable account of plate tectonics and the ever-changing Far Western landscape.

James J. Rawls, *Indians of California: The Changing Image* (Norman, OK: University of Oklahoma Press, 1984). With effect, the author argues that nineteenth-century white American images of Native Californians reveal more about the observers than those being observed.

John W. Robinson, *Gateways to Southern California: Indian Footpaths, Horse Trails, Wagon Roads, and Highways* (Arcadia, CA: Big Santa Anita Historical Society, 2005). This book connects early Indian trails with later Euro-American overland routes into southern California.

Allan A. Schoenherr, *A Natural History of California* (Berkeley: University of California Press, 1992). This is an encyclopedic work detailing the diverse landforms and flora and fauna of the state.

2

Spain's Greater California Coast

A dream was born and the modern age of global trade opened in the 1500s. The dream was that of a Spanish novelist who envisioned a land of riches called "California." Distant from Atlantic world slave-trading and colonizing ventures, California during that century was drawn into the beginnings of global commerce and an Anglo-Spanish rivalry for Pacific supremacy. Between 1542 and 1821 Spain consolidated and then lost its hold on California, which had become active in a transpacific fur, manufactures, and grain trade while encountering foreign intrusions.

Timeline

1510   Spanish fiction writer Garcí Ordóñez de Montalvo depicts California as an island near "the terrestrial paradise"

1521   Spanish conquistador Hernán Cortés seizes Mexico from the Aztecs

1535   Cortés claims Baja California for Spain

1539   Francisco de Ulloa discovers that Baja is a peninsula, not an island

1542   Mariner Juan Rodríguez Cabrillo, sailing for Spain, leads an expedition resulting in the first documented Europeans setting foot on Alta California and Spain's claim to most of North America's western coastline

1565   The Manila galleon trade, linking California to Spain's Pacific empire, begins

(Continued)

Pacific Eldorado: A History of Greater California, First Edition. Thomas J. Osborne.
© 2013 Thomas J. Osborne. Published 2013 by Blackwell Publishing Ltd.

1579   After pillaging Spanish churches on South America's Pacific Coast, Drake sails the *Golden Hind* to an anchorage at the Point Reyes Peninsula; after a sojourn there, he claims Nova Albion, which amounted to much of North America's western coastline, for England

1595   Portuguese merchant-adventurer Sebastián Rodríguez Cermeño, sailing for Spain, voyages from the Philippines to California's coast, stopping at Point Reyes Peninsula where he is shipwrecked while exchanging gifts with Coast Miwok Indians

1602   Spaniard Sebastián Vizcaíno launches a maritime expedition that explores Alta California's coast possibly north of Cape Mendocino, making landfalls and renaming sites along the way

1769   Two maritime and two land expeditions, famously including Franciscan monk Father Junípero Serra as a leader, depart New Spain to occupy and settle Alta California; Serra establishes Alta California's first mission, San Diego de Alcalá

1774   Spanish Captain Juan Bautista de Anza launches an overland expedition from Tubac presidio in Arizona to Monterey, Alta California, establishing a land route to the new province

1775   Anza embarks on a second overland expedition from New Spain to Alta California that results in selecting sites for a mission and presidio in San Francisco; Lieutenant Juan Manuel de Ayala sails into San Francisco Bay, exploring and mapping the huge inlet

1776   Father Francisco Palóu dedicates Mission San Francisco de Asís

1777   San José de Guadalupe is established as Alta California's first civil pueblo

1781   Yuma Indians conduct the bloodiest and most successful Indian rebellion in California history, killing more than 30 Spanish soldiers plus four missionaries; Spaniards establish the Pueblo de Nuestra Señora la Reina de Los Angeles, the second civilian settlement in Alta California

1784   Father Serra's death occurs at Mission San Carlos Borromeo

1785   Toypurina, an Indian medicine woman, leads male warriors from at least six villages in an attack on Mission San Gabriel

1786   French mariner Comte de La Pérouse spends ten days in Monterey before completing his circumnavigation of the globe

1791   Alejandro Malaspina, an Italian commander exploring the Pacific for the Spanish Crown, surveys the Alta California coast and sojourns in Monterey

1792   British Captain George Vancouver explores America's Pacific Northwest Coast and that of California, returning to the Spanish province twice the following year

1796   *The Otter*, captained by Ebenezer Dorr and engaged in the Pacific maritime fur trade, is the first American vessel to visit California, anchoring in Monterey Bay

1806   Russian Count Nikolai Petrovich Rezanov sails from Sitka, Alaska, into San Francisco Bay seeking supplies

1812   To supply Alaska with food and hunt for sea otters, the Russian American Company establishes Fort Ross along the northern California coast above San Francisco

1818   Hippolyte de Bouchard, a French-born pirate claiming to sail for Argentina, raids California missions, including that at San Juan Capistrano, supposedly to overthrow Spanish rule in the Latin American wars of independence

A Name, a Dream, a Land

Europeans named California before exploring and settling it. In 1510 Spanish novelist Garcí Odóñez de Montalvo published a popular story, *Las Sergas de Esplandián* (The Exploits of Esplandian). The novel describes the adventures of a medieval knight, Esplandián, who goes on a crusade to Constantinople. He heroically defends this Christian city against a pagan army of black Amazonian women led by a ferocious Queen Calafia. She and her all-female army hail from a distant island "on the right hand of the indies" and "very near to the terrestrial paradise." California, the fictional realm of these female warriors, is depicted as a land of riches. Gold, used to fashion weapons, is the only metal on the island and pearls abound there.

The gold-seeking soldiers led by Hernán Cortés, whose army seized central Mexico from the Aztecs in 1521, were familiar with Montalvo's tale. The Spanish conqueror affirmed as much in a 1524 letter he sent to his king, telling of the gold Cortés expected to find when he reached Calafia's land after a prospective northwestward voyage of several days. On making that voyage in 1535, Cortés claimed Baja, California, thought to be the mythical Amazon queen's island of riches, for Spain. Spanish voyager Francisco de Ulloa discovered by 1539 that Calafia's supposed island was instead a peninsula that his countrymen had named California. Still, some European maps erroneously portrayed California as an island as late as the 1750s.

The island myth persisted, in part, because Spaniards wanted to believe that an inland water passageway at the supposed northern end of an insular California would prove to be the long-sought Strait of Anián. The legendary strait, also called the Northwest Passage, was thought to course its way from North America's Atlantic shoreline westward across the continent to the Pacific. Such a strait, Europe's rulers believed, would provide the safest and shortest water route to the fabled riches of Asia. Consequently, navigators and their sponsoring governments eagerly (and futilely) searched for the Pacific terminus of such a waterway into the late 1700s and beyond.

In the 1500s, the Spanish had seen to it that a name and a dream were connected to a land. However, given the rudimentary state of geographical knowledge at that time the location and boundaries of that land, California, remained vague and unfixed. What can be said for certain is that mapmakers in general and Spaniards in particular conceived of what today might be designated a "greater California." That is, they understood the province as extending from the southern tip of Baja northward to the undiscovered Strait of Anián. On some maps that strait was located just above the Gulf of California; on other maps it was situated much nearer the icy inlets of the far northern Pacific (today's Alaska). Even in the late 1700s, according to historian David J. Weber, Spain thought of "the unoccupied Pacific coast of North America" as constituting what it termed "California." After all, maritime expeditions headed by Juan Perez and Juan Francisco Bodega y Quadra, in 1774 and 1775 respectively, resulted in Spanish land claims along Alaska's shoreline. Both of these expeditions made stops along the California coast. Thus, more than 200 years ago the Spanish conceived of a far greater California, spatially, than is portrayed on today's maps.

Beginning in the 1500s European mariners made the claims that resulted in California's vague and shifting boundaries that appeared on maps. Juan Rodríguez Cabrillo was the first of these sea explorers to chart North America's western coastline from Baja northward into Oregon's waters and claim the land for Spain.

Cabrillo's Coastal Reconnaissance

Most likely a Spaniard, though some earlier authorities assumed he was Portuguese, Cabrillo ranks among the founders of Spanish California, which was part of New Spain, a colonial viceroyalty or imperial province that included today's Central America, Mexico, and the American Southwest. In 1542, New Spain's highest official, Viceroy Antonio de Mendoza, directed Cabrillo to lead a northern voyage comprised of three ships in search of the Strait of Anián. At about the same time, Mendoza commissioned a second voyage, led by Ruy López de Villalobos, to sail to the Philippines. The aim of both of these maritime expeditions was to enhance trade prospects with Asia's Spice Islands. At the time, virtually all of the maritime powers of Europe had this same goal.

Departing Navidad, a port on Mexico's mainland just above Acapulco, on June 27, Cabrillo began a reconnaissance that would gather important information regarding California's islands, coastline, Indians, and natural resources. Rounding the tip of Baja, his party at first enjoyed easy sailing, stopping occasionally to chart islands and land along the peninsula to make claims of possession for Spain. Some Indians came on board to trade goods; they used sign language to indicate that they had recently learned of men looking like Spaniards who had been exploring in the interior region to the east. The tribesmen may have been referring to Ulloa's expeditionary force of three years earlier.

On September 28 Cabrillo's party dropped anchor in San Miguel Bay, renamed San Diego early in the next century. That same day, he and his men became the first Europeans known to set foot on present-day California. The Kumeyaay Indians they encountered proved wary. Cabrillo soon learned that the natives, some of whom had attacked his men with bows and arrows, were agitated by news of Spanish atrocities committed on tribesmen to the east. When Cabrillo gave gifts to the Kumeyaay tensions relaxed and the Spaniards were able to take on needed supplies for the voyage northward.

From San Diego Cabrillo's expedition sighted and visited offshore islands, where members encountered large Indian populations. Reaching Santa Catalina, the expedition's journal noted: "They went ashore with the boat to see if there were people; and when the boat came near, a great number of Indians emerged from the bushes and grass, shouting, dancing and making signs that they should land." The women fled in fear, continued the account, and the Spanish responded by giving assurances that they came in peace. Accepting these assurances, the Indians "laid their bows and arrows on the ground and launched in the water a good canoe which held eight or ten Indians, and came to the ships." Gifts were then exchanged on the ships followed by the Spaniards going ashore. "All felt secure," concluded the journal entry.

Afterward the expedition sailed for the mainland. The voyagers sighted the bay at San Pedro and then visited a nearby Indian fishing village named Town of Canoes, where a

Figure 2.1   An artistic depiction of Cabrillo's vessel *San Salvador* under full sail. Courtesy of the artist, Richard DeRosset.

customary possession ceremony in the name of the king was held. Such ceremonies involved praying, singing the Catholic Latin hymn Te Deum (Thee, O God, we praise), and claiming the land and its inhabitants for the Spanish Crown. After the possession ceremony, the Spaniards plied the waters of the Santa Barbara Channel off Point Conception. They encountered the prosperous Chumash settlements that greatly impressed the white men, who marveled at the Indians' nautical skills and seaworthy canoes. Strong northwest headwinds convinced Cabrillo to sail back to San Miguel Island, where he fell and apparently broke an arm. This mishap did not stop the expedition from resuming its explorations and mapping of coastal waters. Without landing, he viewed what later was named Monterey Bay. More bad weather set in, along with gangrene in Cabrillo's arm, resulting in a return to San Miguel Island; on January 3, 1543, Cabrillo died there. His crew buried him on the windswept island.

Bartolomé Ferrer, second in command, then assumed leadership of the expedition. Confronting gales and high waves, the explorers reached a northern point somewhere between Monterey Bay and the present Oregon–California border (42 degrees latitude). Overtaken by exhaustion, a shortage of supplies, scurvy (a life-threatening disease caused by lack of ascorbic acid in one's diet), and heavy seas, Ferrer and his party reversed course and sailed back to Navidad.

Aside from being the first documented Europeans to set foot on Alta (upper) California, that is, what would later constitute the Spanish claim above the Baja Peninsula, the record of the Cabrillo–Ferrer expedition is mixed. The search for the Strait of Anián remained as elusive as ever. No gold or other precious metals were found. The charts of the rugged coastline lacked sufficient detail. Eldorado, or the land of riches that Spaniards imagined California to be, now seemed a wilderness filled with dangers to ships and crewmen alike. Still, the expedition registered at least one major accomplishment: it established Spain's claim to California, meaning most of North America's western coastline.

Globalization Begins: The Manila Galleon Trade

Viceroy Mendoza's efforts to locate transpacific trade routes between Southeast Asia and New Spain eventually led to Spain's colonizing of Manila, in the Philippines, in 1571. By then the so-called Manila galleon (a large square-rigged sailing vessel) trade had been going on for six years and would last for a total of 250 years.

This trade was significant because it generated tremendous wealth for the Spanish Crown and the foreign pirates who preyed on the participating treasure vessels. Before the Manila trade developed nearly all of the inhabited continents were linked together commercially with one major exception: the Americas had not established trade relations with Asia. By providing this last link, the Manila trade ushered in the modern age of economic globalization. Spanish California, whose port at Monterey was occasionally visited by the galleons, played a role in this historic occurrence. Raymond Ashley, director of the San Diego Maritime Museum, captured the significance of the Manila trade for California when he noted in 2002: "In the case of San Diego and other West coast cities, the foundation of our Pacific Rim economy was laid when the galleons established . . . a pattern of regular trade across the Pacific."

The story of how this regular trade began reveals how Spanish California was affected by and connected to developments in New Spain, Europe, and Southeast Asia in the 1500s and afterward. While Spanish interest in Alta California lapsed in the several decades following Cabrillo's reconnaissance, silver discoveries took place in Zacatecas and elsewhere in Mexico. Meanwhile, China needed and wanted to purchase silver coin as legal tender. Spain could not ship silver to China via the Cape Horn route around Africa as Portugal exercised the exclusive right to that seaway by a Vatican-brokered agreement. That meant that Spain needed to locate a sea route from Mexico and Peru to the Philippines, from where a lucrative trade with nearby China and the Spice Islands of Southeast Asia could be conducted.

In 1564 Spanish Commander Miguel López de Legazpi established the westward route to the Philippines, seizing the port of Manila. Next, he needed to locate the eastward return

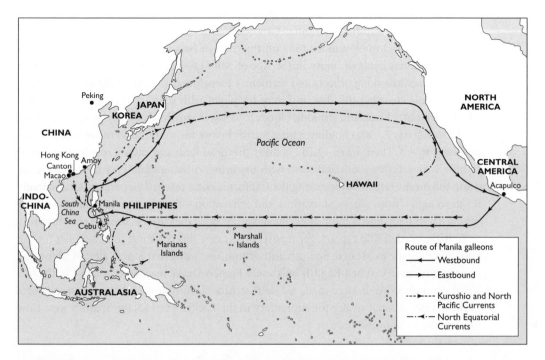

Figure 2.2   The sailing routes of Manila galleons. From Thomas W. Chin, ed., *A History of the Chinese in California: A Syllabus* (San Francisco: Chinese Historical Society of America, 1969), p. 5. Compiled by H.M. Lai. Illustrated by James B. Wong. Courtesy of the Chinese Historical Society of America (CHSA).

route from the islands back to Mexico. Fray Andrés Urdaneta, who had accompanied Legazpi, was to test the theory that a vessel could sail northeasterly until it picked up the Japanese current and westerlies and then follow the California coastline southward to Acapulco. In 1565 he commanded a vessel that completed the exhausting return voyage in 129 days. This signal event marked the opening of the Manila galleon trade, which peripherally would link California to Spain's Pacific empire.

In order to maintain tight control over the export of New World coins and bullion (gold or silver bars), in 1593 the Spanish king decreed that with few exceptions only one galleon would sail the Pacific circuit yearly. Cargoes were not to exceed 250,000 pesos in value and profits were supposedly limited to 140 percent. However, documents reveal cargoes valued at far greater sums and profits. For example, the galleon *Santa Ana* departed Manila for Acapulco with gold in the amount of 600,000 pesos and 1,500,000 pesos' worth of silks, musk (a perfume-like substance), and pearls. Profits sometimes ran as high as 400 percent. Customarily, these returning treasure vessels carried silks, spices, porcelains, wax, camphor chests, samurai swords, ivory carvings, and more. The Spanish silver coin known as a "piece of eight," used to purchase these wares in Manila, became the first global currency in history.

The historic Manila trade was replete with dangers, particularly shipwrecks along the rugged California coast, piracy, and scurvy. Strong currents, storms, and jagged rocks from

Mendocino southward claimed a fair share of the returning galleons. One of the most notorious pirates, Englishman Thomas Cavendish, attacked the Acapulco-bound *Santa Ana* (mentioned above) in November 1587 off the coast of Baja California, and made off with one of the largest hauls of booty in the Age of Sail (1400s to mid-1800s). Scurvy caused numerous deaths among officers and seamen. A Frenchman aboard a galleon sailing along the California coast left this description of his plight with scurvy: "It rotted all my gums, which gave out a black and stinking blood. . . . I [used] my knife on my gums. . . . I went on deck each day . . . and holding a little mirror before me in my hand to see where it was necessary to cut. Then, when I had cut away this dead flesh and caused much black blood to flow, I rinsed my mouth and teeth with my urine, rubbing them very hard." Often the death toll on the return voyage along the California coast reached 50 percent. Occasionally it was so high – from scurvy, starvation, and exhaustion – that no one survived aboard the vessels. These unmanned "ghost ships" floated eerily along the currents back toward Acapulco.

To make needed ship repairs, get reports on pirates, and replenish food supplies for the remaining voyage to Mexico, Spanish authorities concluded that a port along California's coast was necessary. When English buccaneer Francis Drake reached that coast in the late 1500s, Spanish officials were made aware that Alta California was at the crossroads of a growing international rivalry for supremacy in the Pacific. Even so, the Spanish were slow to establish a California port.

Drake, Nova Albion, and Cermeño

The slowness of the Spanish to fortify their claim to Alta California invited a brief, emergency visit from Francis Drake. Afterward, a Portuguese navigator sailing for Spain, Sebastián Rodríguez Cermeño, sought a port of refuge for the Manila galleon along the California coast.

Sailing under orders from Queen Elizabeth I, in late 1577 Drake crossed the Atlantic and passed through the stormy Strait of Magellan, at the southern tip of South America. Entering the Pacific and sailing up the coasts of Chile and Peru he pillaged Catholic churches of their gold altarpieces and other ornamentation. Also, he raided Spanish vessels he encountered, including a treasure galleon. After this seizure in 1579, Drake's vessel, the *Golden Hind*, was so overloaded with literally tons of booty that it was scarcely seaworthy; still, he outran a Spanish patrol ship and made his way up to the northern California coast where on June 17 he anchored for repairs and a sojourn that was to last five weeks.

The English corsair's California visit resulted in friendly encounters between the whites and local Miwok Indians. Francis Fletcher, the ship's chaplain and chronicler of the voyage, noted what modern scholars would call the culture shock that ensued on both sides of the racial divide. At first the hundreds of Indian warriors visiting Drake's encampment assumed a warlike attitude toward the English sailors. After signs of friendship from the seamen, the threat of armed conflict diminished. Next, gifts were exchanged followed by the Indian women engaging in a mourning ceremony. They began "crying and shrieking piteously, tearing their flesh with their nailes from their cheeks in a monstrous manner, the blood streaming downe along their brests. . . ." Seemingly horrified by this, Drake and his men sang Christian hymns and prayed, "lifting up our eyes and hands to heaven . . . beseeching God . . . to open by some means their blinded eyes." This seemed to soothe the Miwoks, who on later occasions asked the English to sing.

As they continued to make cultural comparisons, the English took the physical measure of the natives. Fletcher observed that the Indians were "commonly so strong, that that which 2 or 3 of our men could hardly beare, one of them would take upon his back, and without grudging carrie it easily away up hill and downe hill an English mile." Moreover, the Indians were described as "exceedingly swift in running, and of long continuance." Judging by European encounters with other indigenous peoples throughout the Pacific Basin, the seamen most likely had sex with the Indians.

The Miwoks' placing of a feathered crown on Drake's head led the party of Englishmen to assume wrongly that this symbolized the transfer of the Indians' ancestral land, called Nova Albion (Latin for New England) by the Britons, to Queen Elizabeth's island kingdom. Before departing Nova Albion, Drake fashioned a brass plate claiming possession of the land for England. The plate was nailed to a post at his encampment, which a good many historians (but not all) locate at today's Drake's Bay on the Point Reyes Peninsula.

Drake's voyage was more significant as a feat of navigation and catalyst of international rivalry for supremacy in the Pacific than as a factor in shaping California history. In completing his journey in 1580, he became the second person in history to circumnavigate the globe. His vessel was the first English ship to sail around the world, and his voyage marked the first time this was accomplished under a single commander. Afterward, Spain's domination of the Pacific could no longer be taken for granted. Though displeased by the English sojourn in California, the Spanish took no immediate steps to secure their own claim to the province. Instead, they focused on extracting silver and gold from their mines in Mexico and Peru.

Still, the Manila galleons, which carried precious output from these mines, remained in jeopardy. The Spanish needed to establish a safe harbor on the California coast that could resupply vessels returning to New Spain from the Philippines and furnish naval escorts to fend off pirates. To that end, Spanish officials directed the Portuguese *adelantado*, or merchant-adventurer, Sebastián Rodríguez Cermeño, to sail from the Philippines in 1595 to the California coast, where he was to locate a port of call.

Crossing the Pacific, Cermeño's treasure-laden galleon, the *Agustín*, reached the north coast of present-day Eureka, from which he headed southward. Stormy coastal waters forced him to seek refuge in Drake's Bay. A month-long sojourn there included gift exchanges with the Coast Miwoks and a customary Spanish possession ceremony. The voyage's chronicler, Pedro de Lugo, detailed what the Indians ate, how they dressed, and their reaction to the Spaniards. Accordingly, Lugo noted that the natives were well built and wore nothing, going about their activities "with their private parts exposed." Peaceful relations were ensured by Spanish gift-giving.

Meanwhile, storm waves battered and wrecked the *Agustín* as it lay anchored in the bay. Twelve crewmen died and the ship's cargo and provisions were lost. Cermeño and a party of his men scavenged the countryside for acorns, wild nuts, and whatever else might be edible and stored on the small boat – the *San Buenaventura* – that they would use to limp back to Acapulco. Despite all of these hardships coupled with the near-starvation of his surviving 80 crewmen, on the remaining leg of the journey to Mexico Cermeño managed to chart part of California's coastline and some of the offshore islands.

Barely avoiding punishment after returning to Acapulco without having found a safe California port for Manila galleons, Cermeño had nevertheless accomplished something. His maps and surveys were the most accurate of their time. Also, he had managed to bring his men home safely. Until further notice, however, Manila galleons were prohibited from exploring California's hazardous coast.

The Spanish Pacific, Vizcaíno, and Monterey

Disappointment with Cermeño's voyage did not prevent the Spanish authorities from commissioning another sailing expedition to discover a safe haven for Manila galleons along California's treacherous coast. This search, however, is best understood in the context of a growing European rivalry for maritime supremacy in the Pacific and Indian oceans.

Envious of Spain's maritime wealth, as evidenced in the prosperous Manila galleon trade, Holland and England pushed for a share of the Asian market. At the end of the 1500s Dutch ships had passed through the Strait of Magellan, entering the Pacific, followed in 1600 by Dutch pirate Oliver van Noort, whose presence would imperil the Manila galleons. The voyages of Drake and Cavendish as well as the formation of the British and Dutch East India companies, in 1600 and 1602 respectively, further attested to a growing international rivalry for Pacific supremacy. California entered this scenario as Spain's hoped-for site of a harbor that could offer safety and provisions for galleons returning from the Philippines to Mexico.

Within this Pacific Basin context, Spanish officials made repeated attempts to locate a port of refuge on California's coast. Accordingly, on orders from the Crown, the viceroy of New Spain, Gaspar de Zúñiga y Acevedo, count of Monterrey, organized a reconnaissance voyage under the command of Sebastián Vizcaíno, a seasoned explorer. More than a year was invested in planning and outfitting the maritime expedition. With three ships and more than 130 men, including cartographers, the voyages commenced from Acapulco on May 5, 1602. Father Antonio de la Ascensión, a chaplain, recorded parts of the journey. The expedition was to survey and map bays, coastal islands, and landmarks from San Diego northward to Cape Mendocino.

Encountering gales, the vessels tacked (zigzagged) northward, making stops for water and food. Many of the stopover sites were densely inhabited by Indians. A 10-day sojourn in San Diego furnished an opportunity to trade European goods with natives for their animal skins. As with earlier Spanish voyages, the Indians spoke of other white men trekking in the interior regions, which Vizcaíno thought were part of Juan de Oñate's campaign to reconquer New Mexico several years earlier. Going ashore at Santa Catalina Island the Spaniards interacted with Gabrielinos, who seemed familiar with the foreign visitors. The islanders' seaworthy plank canoes, their harpooning skills, and their coastal trade network impressed Ascensión. He also noted the Indians' talent for thieving Spanish goods, beating even "the gypsies in cunning and dexterity." Nearer land, friendly Chumash seamen paddled boats out to the expedition's ships to welcome and trade with the Spaniards.

Trade and friendly exchanges with Indians, however, could not fully compensate for the storms, starvation, and scurvy that ravaged the expedition's sailors by the time they passed Point Conception. On December 16, 1602, Vizcaíno's ships anchored in what he called Monterey Bay, which he tactfully named after his superior, New Spain's viceroy. Vizcaíno's fanciful description of the site probably accounts for Monterey becoming the first capital of Spanish California. It was "the best port that could be desired, for besides being sheltered from all the winds, it has many pines for masts and yards, and live oaks and white oaks, and water in great quantity, all near the shore." More to the point, he continued, Monterey was at the right latitude to offer "protection and security for the ships coming from the Philippines." The local Costanoan Indians were not nearly as numerous as Vizcaíno had claimed. Most likely, he exaggerated the bounties of Monterey because the pension and other rewards offered by his superiors depended on the establishment of a port there.

Departing Monterey with two ships (the third had been sent back to Mexico with the sick and disabled), the expedition proceeded northward to what Vizcaíno thought was Cape Mendocino and beyond, perhaps into the coastal waters of southern Oregon. By then heavy fogs, towering waves, sickness, injuries, and scant provisions forced a turnaround and a hurried course for Mexico. On March 21, 1603, Vizcaíno's vessel reached Acapulco. The other two ships had already arrived. More than 40 men, about a third of the entire exploration party, had died in the venture.

What had been accomplished and what resulted from the arduous undertaking? Vizcaíno's logs and charts proved useful to mapmakers for more than a century afterward. Monterey, though not nearly as ideal as Vizcaíno described it, thereafter provided Spanish California with a capital and needed port of call that would itself become commercially prosperous. Against official orders, Vizcaíno renamed many of the sites at which he landed, and the new names have largely remained to this day. For example, he rechristened San Miguel as San Diego. Despite the fact that Viceroy Zúñiga praised Vizcaíno, the next viceroy, the marqué de Montesclaros, saw the entire enterprise of establishing a port on the California coast as wasteful of limited resources. Monterey was located so close to Acapulco, he reasoned, as to make it an unnecessary and costly stop for the returning Manila galleons.

Colonizing California: Missions, Indians, and the Sea

Spain's colonization of Alta California occurred within an international maritime context. King Carlos III's efforts to inject Enlightenment rationality and efficiency into his nation's overseas imperial policy while defending his American frontier provinces against foreign intrusion led to Spanish settlement of Alta California. In the initial planning stage, directed by *visitador-general* José de Gálvez in Mexico City (whose authority at times may have exceeded that of the viceroy), missions, that is, religious compounds, and Indians were not essential to this colonizing venture. Both quickly became central to it. To Gálvez a military outpost at Monterey would enable the pacification of the Indians of the coastal province, and ensure the collection of tribute taxes from them that would bolster the

Spanish treasury. Gálvez had developed his colonizing plans for California before receiving premature news of an imminent Russian advancement by sea into the province. Still, the wily Spanish official exploited this presumed foreign threat – which did not materialize until later – to get the full backing for his colonizing venture from the viceroy in New Spain, marquis de Croix.

In Spanish America, as in some rival colonial projects elsewhere, religion and empire-building went hand in hand. Under Gálvez, the extension of Spain's imperial frontier into Alta California beginning in the late 1700s exemplifies this. By establishing a string of missions from the southernmost part of the province to the San Francisco Bay area between 1769 and 1817, Spain's Catholic padres dominated a large part of North America's Pacific Coast, which they transformed into a Spanish cultural zone. These padres came from the Franciscan Order, which in 1768 replaced the Jesuits, or churchmen from the Society of Jesus, in Baja California because Spanish officials grew uneasy about the latter's independence and power in the New World. With the Jesuits removed from their 18 Baja missions and others they had established in Sonora, Mexico, and southern Arizona, Spain's evangelization of Alta California became entirely a Franciscan enterprise. Today's restored Franciscan mission adobes, vanquished Indians, and Spanish place names afford only a glimpse of this formidable period in California's not-so-distant past.

In what Gálvez collectively termed "the Sacred Expedition," he launched in 1769 two maritime and two land migrations to occupy Alta California. All four parties were to reach San Diego Bay about the same time. The overall undertaking was exhausting, costly, and consequential.

In January and February, the vessels *San Antonio* and *San Carlos* respectively set sail from La Paz to San Diego with seamen and supplies. Sailing northward into the prevailing winds and currents, this was always a difficult voyage; rough seas, scurvy, and dysentery took their usually high toll. Of the 90 seamen on the two ships only 16 were healthy when the vessels anchored at San Diego.

The two land expeditions encountered hardships of their own. In late March, Captain Fernando Rivera y Moncada led the first trek from Baja northward. The slow-moving party covered 250 miles in 52 days, suffering heat exhaustion, hunger, and thirst most of the way. Captain Gaspar de Portolá and Franciscan monk Junípero Serra jointly led the second overland party of soldiers and Baja mission Indians from the arid peninsula overland into San Diego. At times barely able to walk due to a painful varicose, ulcerated leg condition that the self-flagellating friar refused to treat, Serra's journey was, in effect if not intent, a pilgrimage into history and possible sainthood.

By July 1 all four migrant groups had arrived at their destination, with a little less than half of their original 300 or so men still alive. In the face of desertions, sickness, and hunger, only the timely arrival of additional supplies by sea from San Blas kept the settlement project viable.

In mid-July the starving, ailing pioneer remnant founded the mission of San Diego de Alcalá – the first of nine such religious stations established under Serra's able leadership. By 1823 his successors had raised the number of California missions to 21, spanning the 500 miles from San Diego to Sonoma. Each of these was located on or near the coast roughly one day's journey apart.

In addition to converting and pacifying local Indian populations, the Catholic padres sought to Hispanicize the natives, that is, to train them to speak Spanish, farm, and serve as craftsmen and cowboys in the missions and at the nearby ranchos. In this way, reasoned the Franciscan fathers, the missions could become self-sustaining agrarian communities while providing the neophytes, or converted Indians, with the skills to support themselves as autonomous individuals after the missions would be downsized into ordinary churches and the land returned to the native peoples. This so-called "secularization" process was to begin 10 years after the founding of each mission.

California's second mission – San Carlos Borromeo – was founded, again by Serra in concert with Portolá, on June 3, 1770, at Monterey. Serra had arrived by sea a few days earlier. Portolá, who had led a party that trekked as far north as San Francisco Bay in late 1769, commanded an overland expedition of 12 soldiers who set out from San Diego and reached Monterey in time to join with Serra for the mission's founding. His route became the track for the El Camino Real (The King's Highway), which corresponds roughly with Highway 101 today. In 1771 Serra relocated Mission San Carlos Borromeo to the Carmel Valley, on the other side of the Monterey Peninsula. The relocated mission thereafter became his California headquarters and site of his death in 1784. Weary of overland marches and eager to rid himself of California's settlement challenges, Portolá installed Pedro Fages as governor of the province and returned by sea to Mexico. With the establishment of the first two missions in San Diego and near Monterey the work of the Sacred Expedition was brought to a successful conclusion.

Contemporaries and historians have been assessing the impact of the California mission system on the Indians ever since the 1780s, when foreigners began visiting these religious compounds. The oral and written commentaries of observers, scholars, and the Indians and their descendants form a considerable body of evidence and opinion about what has been a highly controversial subject. A number of matters have been at issue. These include but are not limited to: the padres' assumptions about the maturational level and capacity of the Indians; the padres' treatment of neophytes; and the sickness and mortality rate of mission Indians.

The way the Franciscan fathers viewed the unconverted Indians must be seen in the context of the padres' fearful reaction to the eighteenth-century Enlightenment and Age of Revolution. At roughly the same time that California's missions were being established, Anglo-Americans along the continent's eastern seaboard were heralding the rights of individuals in such documents as the Declaration of Independence and the Constitution. The French enshrined individual liberty in the Declaration of the Rights of Man and Citizen. This new, secular thinking clashed with the Franciscan ideal of self-denial and building spiritual communities in the California wilderness. The missions, then, became enclaves where friars and Indians could restore the simpler piety of the early Church. Thick adobe mission walls and resolute clergy, however, were not enough to withstand the onslaught of the heresies and vices of the changing times.

These heresies and vices were close at hand; missionaries saw them at work among the so-called *gente de razón* (the people of reason). *Gente de razón* included the padres, their Spanish kinsmen, and those of mixed Iberian, Mexican, and Indian descent – called Californios – who spoke Spanish and often lived near the missions. The people of reason

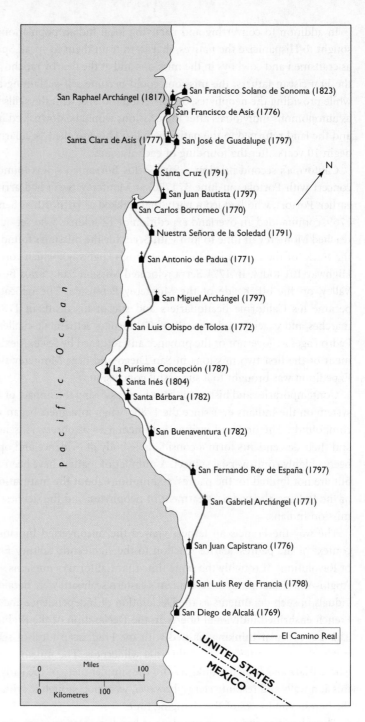

Figure 2.3 The 21 Upper California missions. Most of these missions were located on or near the Pacific Coast, which facilitated their being supplied by ships from Mexico.

constituted Spanish California's upper class that supposedly embodied the superior racial and cultural endowments of Western civilization. Catholicism, land ownership, and political and clerical offices were their entitlements. For the most part, only the first of these, Catholicism, was within reach of the Indians. They occupied the lowest order of what was essentially a two-tiered caste system that lacked a middle class of lawyers, shopkeepers, and skilled craftspersons.

California's padres viewed unconverted Indians as "heathens" whose behavior ranged from "gentle and friendly" to "barbarian." Many friars described their Indian wards, even when adults, as "children" in terms of their simple hunter-gatherer lifestyles and mental development. Yet there is evidence that at least some of the priests believed neophytes could and should be shepherded to adulthood. Despite the good intentions of the padres, that shepherding was not happening according to some foreign visitors. French mariner the comte de La Pérouse, who in 1786 spent 10 days in Monterey before completing his circumnavigation of the globe, observed that the neophyte was "too much a child, too much a slave, too little a man." On the other hand, five years later Alejandro Malaspina, an Italian commander exploring the Pacific for the Spanish Crown, reached Monterey and found the mission Indians peaceful, healthy, and pious thanks to the padres. So from the outset the missionary project had its critics and supporters.

Mission Indians at times became targets of discrimination and abuse. The so-called "gentiles," that is, non-mission Indians who remained in the wilds living with their tribelets, were beyond the authority of the padres. Ordinarily, this was the case unless such Indians were captured and forcefully brought into a mission to be punished for an alleged crime and then released, which occasionally happened. As a rule, gentile Indians were not forced into the mission system and made to convert to Catholicism, which would have violated Franciscan principles. Neophytes, on the other hand, could not leave the missions without permission. Franciscans held that once an Indian converted he or she remained a Catholic for life. A convert, then, could not renounce Christianity and return to an Indian village. Those who tried were captured and punished.

Regarding neophyte punishments, overseers whipped, shackled, pilloried, jailed, cut food rations, and increased workloads for violating rules. Of these methods, scholars have often focused on whippings or floggings. Looking back, Native Californian Lorenzo Asisara testified in 1877 to the cruelty of a certain Padre Ramon Olbés. "He was never satisfied to prescribe less than 50 lashes; even to the little children of 8–10 years he would order 25 lashes given at the hand of a strong man, either on the buttocks, or on the stomach. . . ." Asisara said that "the women as well as the men" fell under the lashes of rawhide whips that drew blood. Instances like this abound; even Father Serra acknowledged that some of the whippings were excessive. Foreign visitors, as well, noted the frequency and severity of the whippings. More recently, Franciscan monk and scholar Frances F. Guest advanced two points in defense of the padres. First, they said repeatedly that they loved the Indians and defended neophytes as much as possible from mistreatment by soldiers. If the Indians were whipped excessively it was due to the fact that floggings were an integral part of eighteenth-century Spanish culture. So by Spanish standards the Indians did not suffer cruel or unusual punishment. Second, the floggings that Indians received were no worse than the self-flagellation of the Catholic friars. They avowedly whipped themselves three times a week (while wearing coarse robes under which tight belts with iron spikes pierced their skin) and for longer periods of time than they whipped the Indians in order to experience the suffering of Christ. This latter point raises the question of human agency. Assuredly, the padres were influenced by the Spanish Catholic culture in which they found themselves. At the same time, they acknowledged some measure of choice or free will. Indians, for example, supposedly could choose or reject conversion. By the same logic, padres must have possessed some measure of agency or choice when it came to inflicting neophyte beatings.

While beatings were bad enough, even worse was the appallingly high death rate of mission Indians, due mainly to Euro-Asian diseases to which the neophytes had no immunity. The poor diets of the Indians who were crowded into foul-smelling, insanitary, flea-infested mission quarters virtually ensured the weakening of the Native Californians' bodies. Investigating the high death rate of mission Indians in 1797, Governor Diego de Borica identified insanitary conditions as the major threat. He could barely inspect the Indian quarters at one unnamed mission due to the filth and odor of raw human sewage. In such conditions Indians suffered epidemics of smallpox, and, after the 1820s, measles, dysentery, influenza, and venereal disease – spread largely by Spanish soldiers who raped or had consensual sex with Indian women. Indian women suffered the most from all of these diseases and died in the greatest numbers. Babies born to syphilis-infected mothers were delivered dead, or inherited the disabling disease. The Franciscans acknowledged that many more neophytes died each year than were born. Mission records indicate that between 1769 and 1834, 62,600 Indians died and only 29,100 were born. Fewer than half of the Indian children born in missions lived to the age of 5. Rarely did a mission-born Indian live beyond 20 or 25 years of age, according to anthropologist Kent G. Lightfoot. Recent studies indicate that the crude death rate, an overall calculation rather than one pinpointing a particular cause of death, of pre-contact California Indians was 50 deaths per 1,000 persons. By 1800 the number had risen to 85 per 1,000. One of the major unintended consequences of missionizing the Indians was the decimation of their population. Throughout the province, the overall Indian population dropped from an estimated minimal 300,000 in 1769 to 100,000 by 1846. This population decline was most evident in the regions where missions were located.

Both neophytes and gentiles put up considerable resistance to the missions, including but not limited to fleeing, hunger strikes, stealing livestock and other property, abortion, and launching rebellions. Authority Sherburne Cook estimated that on average 10 percent of the mission Indians fled each year. By the early 1800s neophytes had gained access to the horses recently introduced by Spaniards, and had become skilled riders. They began stealing their mounts, using them to escape into the interior regions, and selling horses to other Indians, some as far away as New Mexico. Punitive Spanish expeditions to capture neophyte horse thieves at times erupted into open Indian rebellion. The first Indian revolt against the Franciscan missionaries occurred in San Diego on August 15, 1769, shortly after the mission's founding. Six years later the Indians there attacked a second time, killing Father Luís Jayme.

In 1781 the Yumas carried out the bloodiest and most successful Indian rebellion in California history. The conditions leading to the revolt existed elsewhere throughout the province but few other Indian groups matched the ferocity and independence of the Yumas. In June of that year Captain Fernando Rivera y Moncada had led an expedition of settlers whose accompanying cattle had destroyed part of the Indians' crop of mesquite beans. On July 17, the Yumas attacked two Spanish settlements on the California side of the Colorado River. The following day the Indians assaulted Rivera and his soldiers, killing more than 30 of them plus four missionaries. Women and children were unhurt.

For a month in 1824 Chumash neophytes took over and occupied the mission at La Purísima Concepción. As usual, Spanish arms, including muskets acquired secretly and illegally from Russians at Fort Ross, prevailed. Despite such defeats, a strong neophyte resistance movement continued throughout California in the years ahead.

While combating Indian resistance during the Spanish period the missions struggled to attain some measure of self-sufficiency. Still, without supplies from Mexico and Peru reaching California by sea the missions might not have survived. Realizing that Alta California would have to be supplied by sea, Gálvez established a naval post at San Blas, along the coast of Mexico some 60 miles above Puerto Vallarta, in 1767. Voyaging northward from San Blas, Spanish supply ships carried needed foodstuffs and other items to the California missions. For example, in 1771 one such ship set sail for Monterey carrying biscuits, ham, sugar, corn, flour, rice, beans, wheat, wine, and brandy, as well as chickens and pigs. Manufactures, including agricultural tools and cooking implements, were also on board. Moreover, from that port Spanish vessels could explore and name sites along North America's Pacific Coast up into southernmost Alaska.

Often these San Blas supply ships were piloted by Juan Pérez, probably the most important maritime figure in the history of Spanish California. A seaman in the Manila galleon trade, he had lived in the Philippines and China before plying the California coast during the early mission period. His reconnaissance of the western seaboard up into Alaskan waters, resulting in Spain's claim to the Pacific Northwest up to 54 degrees 40 seconds latitude, as well as his timely provisioning of the San Diego and Monterey settlements by sea in the 1770s, attest to his role in shaping the province's history.

By the late 1780s California's missions were at the center of the province's maritime economy. For a short while, they produced an agricultural surplus. In addition to corn, wheat, beans, and barley, the Franciscans sold bulls, cows, oxen, hogs, and sheep to Spanish soldiers. The missions also cultivated hemp, used for rope in mining and shipping, and directed Indians to hunt sea otters, some of whose skins the padres sold illegally to foreign smugglers who in turn marketed the furs for profit in China. Both the hemp and the legal share of the otter pelts were sent by sea to San Blas. This profitable Pacific trade (about which more will be said below) ended by 1810, when Mexico joined with its Latin American sister colonies in a war for independence that lasted until 1821. During that time, the missions were unable to produce enough food to sustain the Pacific province and only one official supply ship from San Blas arrived in California. However, at least 20 Spanish merchant vessels, mainly from Peru, supplied the province, buoying its economy during that period. Also, the Franciscans engaged in an illicit seagoing trade with Russian, British, American, and French merchants for necessities, all of which underscores the importance of Pacific transport and the numerous maritime connections to California's Spanish missions.

Ranchos, Presidios, and Pueblos

Though missions served as Spain's primary colonizing institutions, ranchos, presidios, and pueblos also played roles in that regard. A cluster of colonizing institutions, then, dotted Spain's coastal frontier in California.

Ranchos consisted of land grants issued by viceroys in New Spain. The earliest such grants were made by Viceroy Antonio de Bucareli in 1773. Tracts varied considerably in size from a small plot measured in Spanish yards to more than 150,000 acres. Laws prescribed that ranchos must not intrude on mission holdings and that grantees (rancheros) had to build a house and situate at least 2,000 head of cattle on the land. Rancho lands served as grazing commons, that is, they were not for the exclusive use of cattle belonging to the grantee. If the land remained unused it reverted to the government. Though they spread from the San Francisco Bay Area to San Diego, half of the ranchos were located near Los Angeles.

Presidios served as forts that housed Spanish and Mexican soldiers, whose responsibilities included protecting the missions, controlling both neophyte and gentile Indians, and defending California from imperial rivals. Strategically located at San Diego, Monterey, San Francisco, and later Santa Barbara, presidios consisted of stockades, firearms, and artillery. Food grown at the missions fed the soldiers.

The Spanish established presidios and missions almost simultaneously. Serra's Sacred Expedition founded the first presidio at San Diego in 1769. At Monterey the following year Portolá erected a presidio at the same time that the San Carlos Mission was established. As will be shown, the same held true for the presidio and mission at San Francisco in the mid-1770s.

With a sea route from San Blas to the Alta California presidios and missions firmly established, as well as peninsula trails reaching northward into the province, it remained for the viceroy in New Spain to establish a dependable supply and settler route from Sonora, Mexico, to Monterey and the Bay Area, as it is called today. Bucareli and Serra were only too happy to support a proposal from Captain Juan Bautista de Anza to open such a northern overland route in order to advance Spain's California frontier to the Bay of San Francisco.

Anza launched the first of his two expeditions from the Tubac presidio, in southern Arizona, in January 1774. Yumas furnished their tule boats to ferry the party across the Colorado River. After getting lost amid the sand dunes of the Colorado Desert, Anza and his men slowly made their way to Mission San Gabriel, founded three years earlier. From there the expedition trekked to Monterey, returning by the same route to Tubac in May 1774. Pleased that an overland route had been established, Bucareli promoted Anza to the rank of lieutenant colonel and ordered a follow-up expedition for 1775. That was the same year in which Anglo-American colonists on the continent's eastern seaboard fired the opening shots of the American Revolution at Lexington and Concord.

Leaving from Horcasitas, Mexico, Anza's second expedition swelled to 240 persons upon reaching Tubac. The party included three missionaries, three officers, and 20 soldiers, along with wives and children and hundreds of horses, cattle, and mules. Gifts to the Yuma

Indians assured their assistance with crossing the Colorado River. After resting briefly at Mission San Gabriel and punishing rebellious Indians at San Diego, the expedition pushed northward in two groups, reuniting at Monterey in early 1776. Its next destination would be San Francisco, whose enormous bay had been entered by sea, explored, and mapped the preceding year by Lieutenant Juan Manuel de Ayala. At San Francisco Anza chose sites for a presidio and the Mission de Asís (or Dolores), the latter of which Father Francisco Palóu dedicated in June. Anza also explored the east bay to Carquinez Strait, which a century later would lead to the establishment of Pacific/river ports at Sacramento and Stockton.

With Bucareli's strong support, Anza's two overland expeditions had helped secure Spain's outposts of empire as far north as the Bay Area. San Francisco Bay itself, the largest natural harbor on the Pacific Coast, could now be defended by Spanish forces at the new presidio – for the time being.

Shortly after Anza's exploits, Minister of the Indies José de Gálvez ordered a reorganization of Spain's northern frontier provinces. In 1776 these provinces were detached from the viceroyalty in Mexico City and placed under a commandant general of the "Interior Provinces" who governed from Sonora. Felipe de Neve, the newly appointed governor of the now single province of Alta and Baja California, was headquartered at Monterey. On orders, he established pueblos, or frontier towns, largely for the purpose of increasing the food supply. Missions, alone, could not provide sufficient rations for the presidios and the voyages of supply ships from San Blas had proven costly, dangerous, and prone to delays.

Founded in 1777, San José de Guadalupe became California's first pueblo. Its original 15 settlers and their families derived largely from the presidios of San Francisco and Monterey. The administrative machinery for subsequent pueblos began to take shape. An *alcalde* would run the pueblo government, ensuring that settlers grew crops on their assigned lands and that irrigation and granary projects were completed.

Next, Neve turned his attention southward, overseeing the founding of California's second pueblo, Nuestra Señora La Reina de Los Angeles del Río Porciúncula (the Town of Our Lady the Queen of the Angels by the River of Porciúncula) on September 4, 1781. Characteristically, the 46 Los Angeles *pobladores*, or colonists, came from the ranks of impoverished Mexicans from Sinaloa. Ethnically, except for two who claimed to be Spaniards, they were of mixed mestizo and mulatto background with a predominance of partial African heritage. Mestizos were the offspring of Spanish–Indian sexual unions, and mulattos were born of such unions between whites and blacks. All of the mestizos and mulattos were unschooled, and missionaries viewed the males as idlers, gamblers, and seducers of Indian women. Such was the modest beginning of a pueblo that within two centuries would become a world-class city.

Villa de Branciforte, the third and last pueblo founded during the Spanish era, was sited at Santa Cruz, at the far northern end of Monterey Bay. This settlement had many of the trappings of a penal colony. In 1797 Governor Diego de Borica sought "poor but honest colonists" to inhabit an agricultural town near Mission Santa Cruz. He ended up with a nucleus of lawless men and unskilled workers, nine of whom had been convicts. This group was joined by eight others and four retired soldiers who owned several hundred head of horses and cattle. The following year six more convicts arrived from Monterey. Adobe homes and tools, which Monterey officials had offered as inducements to settlers, never materialized. Short of resources and populated largely by poor colonists, the villa pueblo left only a trace of its existence after two decades.

Gender and Sexuality in a Frontier Society

Gender roles and sexual conduct, within and between the various kinds of frontier settlements just discussed, were major determinants of social life in the Spanish period. Patriarchy, Catholicism, and social status influenced greatly the interactions between all males and females in provincial California.

As throughout the early modern world, gender roles for virtually everyone in Spanish California were prescribed by patriarchy, that is, male dominance, which included a societal double standard in sexual behavior. Church officials and the ruling class of Californios reinforced these social standards or norms. Male rule, however, did not go unchallenged by females.

With respect to gender roles, the exemplary woman of all classes and backgrounds was chaste if single, faithful if married, subservient to male authority, timid, and homebound. Her honor and her family's social standing were linked to her virginity at marriage. A man's honor, on the other hand, centered on conquest and protecting female family members, whom he dominated. A female's domination of males was unacceptable. The case of Toypurina, an Indian medicine woman, illustrates this point. On October 25, 1785 she led male warriors of at least six villages in an attack on Mission San Gabriel. The attack failed and Toypurina was arrested along with three of her leading male companions. Public whippings and mission imprisonment followed. During sentencing, Governor Pedro Fages scorned her three male accomplices for allowing themselves "to be dominated by the aforesaid woman." In matrimony, *gente de razón* males nearly always wed females of their own social class, and the new brides were expected to remain submissive to their husbands.

Moreover, all married couples were expected to bear children; this was the gender role and duty of all husbands and wives. Childless married neophytes suffered more indignities at the hands of authorities than did their *gente de razón* counterparts at the higher end of the social scale. At the Mission Santa Cruz, for example, Father Olbés demanded of an infertile Indian couple that they perform sexual intercourse in his presence. They refused. So the padre next inspected the husband's penis to learn "whether or not it was in good order." When the priest tried to examine the woman's genitalia she struck and bit him, for which Olbés ordered her hands to be tied while 50 lashes were administered, followed by her being shackled and locked up in a women's dormitory. Missionaries demonized Indian women who resisted this type of treatment as witches.

Gender roles were more easily governed by the Church and society than was sexual conduct. As noted, among *gente de razón* a double standard prevailed: males commonly engaged in extramarital sexual relationships, fathering illegitimate offspring. For example, General Mariano Guadalupe Vallejo fathered 16 illegitimate children. Such children were neither entitled to their father's surname nor to equal shares of his wealth. If male, they could not hold public office, a privilege conferred only on their gender. Females who engaged in fornication, adultery, or other sexual misbehaviors were punished more severely than males. Forty-year-old Josefa Bernal, one such sexual transgressor, was subject to her son's supervision and that of other family males. She barely escaped being beaten by him when he found her in an adulterous relationship with Marcelo Pinto.

Neophytes, occupying the lower rung of the social ladder, suffered the worst consequences of the sexual double standard. Females served the *gente de razón* males, especially the soldiers, as concubines and prostitutes; they were the primary victims of rape by soldiers and of venereal disease. In mission confessionals, priests remained especially alert to any hint of female sexual impropriety and were quick to impose Church discipline in such cases.

Still, neophyte women rebelled against sexual mistreatment in a number of ways. These included abortion, infanticide, and harming or killing unfaithful husbands or lovers. Sometimes mission women poisoned the priests' food, and worshipped their own gods. Aborting a fetus or killing a baby brought severe punishment at the hands of the padres. Floggings, the wearing of iron shackles around the ankles for three months, head shaving, and public ridicule awaited female neophytes found guilty of these crimes.

Gentile Indians, on the other hand, lived in a different world regarding gender and sexuality. Females among some groups, like the Chumash, served as chiefs and healers. Non-mission Indians generally accepted premarital sex, polygamy, polyandry, homosexuality, same-sex marriages, cross-dressing, and ritual erotic dancing. Men and women celebrated sexuality. Under certain circumstances these Indians condoned and practiced abortion and infanticide. Divorce was easily obtained.

Such were the gendered social ways of Spanish California. In this frontier society, they remained firmly in place as vestiges of Hispanic Catholic culture long after Spain's rule ended in the early 1800s.

Pacific Profile: Alejandro Malaspina, Mariner-Explorer

As an able young commander, Italian-born Alejandro Malaspina (1754–1810) rose quickly through the ranks of the Spanish navy during the latter half of the eighteenth-century Enlightenment. For Spain, the voyage on which Captain Malaspina embarked in 1789 had two major objectives: the gathering of scientific information about the physical features of the Crown's Pacific claim as well as ethnographic data on indigenous peoples; and gauging the extent to which Russia and other rivals had established a presence along North America's Pacific Coast. While the two vessels of the expedition, *Descubierta* (Discovery) and *Atrevida* (Daring), crossed the Atlantic and plied the Pacific coasts of Chile, Peru, North America, and China, the scientist-mariners also visited numerous islands in Polynesia and Micronesia. During the course of this epic maritime reconnaissance from 1789 to 1793, Malaspina's party surveyed much of the greater California coast, which at this time of indistinct boundaries extended as far north as Alaska. Also, it located major sites along the shoreline in terms of latitude and longitude, and produced artistic renderings of the peoples and landscapes of the province.

For 15 days in 1791, Malaspina sojourned in Monterey. He described the bay as much to his liking: "In a serene and unlimited sea view toward the northwest and the north a thousand kinds of aquatic birds appeared to the spectator . . . The monstrous whale, the sea lion and the sea otter occasionally applauding the smiling

(Continued)

aspect of the atmosphere, and at other times the complete tranquility that they were enjoying, did not [prevent them from amusing] themselves almost on the same beach. . . ."

The indigenous peoples did not fare as well in the opinion of the visiting Spaniards. One expedition observer grumbled: "The Indians of the Mission of Monterrey are the stupidest, as well as the ugliest and filthiest that can be found. In their Rancherias [villages] they make their meals of seafood that the sea spreads upon the beach in unspeakable abundance, thus saving them the work of fishing and of preparing the equipment necessary for it. . . . they lack the stimulus of private property and the advantage that the most active and hardworking would achieve, and thus only engage in the tasks which they are obliged to perform."

In contrast to the local Indians, Malaspina and his men greatly admired Father President Fermín Francisco de Lasuén, who directed neophytes to gather plant specimens and Indian artifacts for the expedition. Malaspina had only praise for the Spanish mission system, though he was silent about the methods padres used to control neophytes. Since expedition scientists interviewed two Monterey Indians who spoke fluent Spanish, the interviewers believed that their process of gathering information was sound in terms of accurate communication. Historian Donald Cutter concluded that if this was true, the captain conducted the first "detached study of California Indians." The Spanish visitors noted that five Indian groups near Monterey's San Carlos Mission engaged in continual warfare with each other. Contradicting the views of French navigator La Pérouse

and other foreign visitors, Malaspina trumpeted the achievements of the Franciscans in converting the Indians, noting that "without the slightest shedding of blood," the padres had ended "a thousand local wars that were destroying them," and gave the Indians "social beginnings, a pure and holy religion, [and] safer and healthy foods."

Regarding biological inquiry, expedition botanist Thaddeus (Tadeo) Haenke gathered approximately 250 specimens of California plants in and around Monterey. Included among these specimens was a redwood tree, which he reputedly introduced to Spain and which remains standing near the Alhambra of Grenada.

Returning to Spain by retracing the route that had brought his expedition into the Pacific, Malaspina expressed liberal ideas that had blossomed during this lengthy voyage – ideas greatly at odds with those of the absolutist Crown. The commander urged independence for Spain's New World colonies. He argued that transoceanic voyages should be franchised, which would have reduced royal control, and that Spain should establish a duty-free port for foreign trade. Falling out of favor with King Carlos IV, Malaspina was arrested, imprisoned, stripped of his new rank (bestowed immediately on his return) as a naval admiral, and eventually banished from Spain. He died of yellow fever in a remote Italian village on April 9, 1810. Not until well into the twentieth century did his maritime exploits gain the international recognition they deserved. Malaspina's California visit and the information he gathered added to the growing importance of the province as a venue for mariners and traders in the Pacific world.

The Transpacific Fur Trade

In addition to the voyages of Malaspina and other mariners, sea otter and fur seal hunting, beginning in the late 1700s, were responsible for bringing California into the sweep of Pacific and international history. For at least four decades, the hunting and marketing of these skins connected the province to Latin America, Polynesia, Asia, and Europe.

As a result of British Captain James Cook's Pacific voyaging in the late 1770s the word spread about the lucrative market in Canton, China for the skins of sea otters and fur seals. John Ledyard, an American aboard one of Cook's vessels, published an account in 1783 of

the profits to be made in this commerce. Ledyard urged that New Englanders ship manufactures to the Northwest Coast, where they could be traded for pelts that would be
exchanged in Canton for products saleable in America. Otter pelts at one point fetched
$120 each in Canton. Along the U.S. northeastern Atlantic seaboard a growing demand
developed for Chinese teas, porcelains, silks, nankeens (inexpensive cottons), furniture, and
art. California and Northwest Coast sea mammal furs constituted the pivotal article in this
transoceanic commerce. Spanish officials were primarily interested in exchanging pelts for
Chinese mercury, which was needed in Mexico's mines to extract silver from ore. Britain
remained interested in the transpacific fur trade despite the remarkable understatement of
Captain George Vancouver, who during his 1792–3 reconnaissance of the California coast
(which he referred to as New Albion) reported to his government: "though the sea otter
skins obtained in these parts are certainly inferior to those procured further to the north,
they could not fail of becoming a profitable article of traffic."

Arriving in Monterey in 1796, the *Otter*, captained by Ebenezer Dorr, was the first
American merchant vessel to anchor in California. In the ensuing decade numerous
other "Boston ships" frequented California waters in search of otter and seal skins to barter
in the China trade. Missionaries, Indians, and soldiers swapped pelts for American manufactures. The entire traffic was illegal, for Spanish colonial policy forbade all foreign
commerce with the Crown's dependencies. Occasionally, foreign traders – including
Americans – would be caught and punished by Spanish officials, yet the illicit trafficking
in goods only grew. Some of the Yankees, as Americans were often called, relocated in
California, marrying into Spanish families and facilitating the eventual U.S. takeover of
the province.

Yankee merchants brokered an agreement with agents of the Russian American Company
(RAC), which in 1804 had established its North American headquarters in Sitka, Alaska.
Accordingly, RAC officials used native Alaskans to procure sea otter pelts that would
be carried in Yankee ships to Canton. The Russians would pay the freightage and share
half the profits with the American merchants. As the otter supply declined in Alaskan
waters, the RAC extended its hunting operations southward to coastal California. With
Sitka hit by starvation and scurvy during the winter of 1805–6, Russian Count Nikolai
Petrovich Rezanov voyaged to San Francisco, aboard the *Juno*, seeking food supplies
and scouting otter-hunting prospects. In violation of Spanish regulations, Governor José
Joaquín de Arrillaga granted Rezanov's request to buy provisions for Sitka. Logic would
suggest that the governor's decision was to some extent influenced by the Russian visitor's
one-month whirlwind courtship of and engagement to the San Francisco presidio
commander's beautiful 15-year-old daughter, Concepción Argüello. The couple's romance
entered the annals of California history after Rezanov brought the foodstuffs back to Sitka
and afterward died on a return trip to Russia reputedly undertaken to seek the czar's
approval for marriage. The senorita awaited her lover's return, learning of his death 35
years later, by which time the unmarried woman had become a nun.

The Russian venture in California did not end with Rezanov's departure, as in 1812 the
RAC established several settlements in the vicinity of Bodega Bay. Collectively they were
known as Fort Rus (later Americanized as "Ross"). Overlooking the Pacific, the redwood
stockade employed an international and multicultural workforce that included Russians,

Creoles (persons of mixed Russian and aboriginal blood), Native Alaskans, and local Pomo and Miwok Indians. The fact that the San Francisco presidio lacked the military clout to stop Russian expansion in California speaks to the tenuous hold that Spain had on its coastal flank. For all practical purposes, Fort Ross could be said to have been located in Russian California, which indicates just how internationally contested and connected the Pacific province was.

California was at the same time connected via the Pacific otter trade to Hawai'i and Canton in a triangular pattern of exchange. In its earliest and simplest phase, otter and sometimes fur seal skins acquired along Spain's greater California coast from Baja to Alaska were shipped to Honolulu, Hawai'i, and then transported to Canton. Return cargoes included the usual Chinese goods already noted. While ships from various nations partici-pated, after 1800 Yankee vessels came to dominate the trade. For example, the *Lelia Bird*, commanded by William Shaler, crisscrossed the Pacific several times from 1803 to 1805, both eluding and defying Spanish officials in Chile, Guatemala, and California. Meanwhile his illicit cargoes of otter pelts gathered in San Francisco, Santa Barbara, San Pedro, and San Diego were shipped to Honolulu and then on to Canton. A return voyage would restart the pattern, or a variation of it.

By the end of the Spanish period in California, foreigners – mainly Russians, Britons, and Americans – had greatly depleted the sea otter and fur seal stocks. Other resources in the region, however, would quickly surpass the profitability of pelts and strengthen Cali-fornia's ties to the Pacific world.

Hippolyte de Bouchard's Pirate Raids

Few events underscore early California's connection to the Pacific and Latin America's wars of independence (1810–24) like Hippolyte de Bouchard's pirate raids along the California coast in 1818. These raids, coupled with the already mentioned supply ships from Peru that helped sustain the province, attest to the fact that California was not nearly as cut off and isolated from the wider world as many historians have suggested.

Reacting against centuries of Spanish imperialism and inspired by the American Revolu-tion, in 1810 Latin Americans launched their own fight for independence. The timing for this struggle was dictated by French Emperor Napoleon Bonaparte's toppling of Spanish King Ferdinand VII in 1807. The ripple effects of that dethronement reached all the way to California's shores in that nearly all of Spain's New World colonies, beginning with Mexico, took advantage of the ensuing turmoil in the mother country by waging wars of independence.

Into these politically stormy seas sailed Bouchard's pirate ships. Born in France, where he joined the navy at age 9, Bouchard eventually relocated to Argentina, from where his two ships – the *Argentina* and the *Chacabuco* – embarked on their voyages of piracy in the Pacific. His well-armed international crew of 200 men included Hawaiians, Yankees, Span-iards, Portuguese, Creoles, blacks, Filipinos, Malays, and Englishmen. After pillaging vessels in the Philippines and Hawai'i, Bouchard's vessels sailed to California in late 1818, suppos-edly to further the cause of independence – which the province did not support.

His first anchorage was in Monterey Bay. After encountering initial resistance from the forces of Governor Pablo Vicente de Solá, the presidial troops retreated to present-day Salinas. Bouchard's men then took over the presidio, raised the Argentinian flag, and proceeded to burn virtually all public buildings. According to Peter Corney, who captained the *Chacabuco*, "all the sailors were employed in searching the houses for money, and breaking and ruining every thing." Gardens, orchards, and livestock were destroyed and the settlement lay in smoking ruins when Bouchard's ships departed and headed south for more plundering in and around Santa Barbara.

The pirate's last California raid took place on December 14, while his ships anchored off San Juan Capistrano. After easily occupying the mission, followed by a leisurely breakfast, the crewmen sacked the town and other buildings. According to Corney: "We found the town well stocked with everything but money and destroyed much wine and spirits and

Figure 2.4   A painting of the San Juan Capistrano Mission at time of Bouchard's pirate raid. Artist unknown. Courtesy of the Maritime Museum of San Diego, *Mains'l Haul – A Journal of Pacific Maritime History*, 36/4 (Fall 2000), p. 30.

all the public property; [and] set fire to the king's stores, [and] barracks . . ." On the way back to their waiting ships, many of the buccaneers were so inebriated that "we had to lash them on the field-pieces and drag them to the beach . . ." Before setting sail, 20 of the men were flogged for drunkenness.

So ended California's stormy encounter with the revolution that had swept across most of Latin America. Three years later, in 1821, a Mexican vessel arrived in Monterey carrying news of independence. The Spanish flag that had flown over the Pacific province's capital was lowered and replaced by Mexico's eagle-and-snake banner.

SUMMARY

Spanish officials and mapmakers envisioned a California extending from the southern tip of Baja northward to a mythical Strait of Anián near Alaska, that is, a much greater California than that depicted on today's maps. A legendary warrior queen, Calafia, supposedly reigned over her namesake land, a seaside Eldorado brimming with pearls and gold. Beginning in 1542, the maritime explorations of Cabrillo and his successors resulted in the establishment of a safe haven, eventually at Monterey, for the famed Manila treasure galleons that for centuries visited that port en route from Asia to Acapulco, Mexico. Through the Manila trade, in the late 1500s the province became tangentially connected to the beginnings of globalization. By the late 1700s Spanish California emerged as a Pacific Eldorado for the hunting of sea otters and fur seals, whose pelts attracted high prices in Canton, China. Alejandro Malaspina's 1791 voyage of scientific reconnaissance demonstrated Spain's concern about Russian and other foreign sea otter hunters in California waters.

Missions, presidios, and civil pueblos located on or near the coastline anchored the province to Spain, which became increasingly wary of British and Russian intrusions. From the Spanish standpoint, Indians basically fell into two groups: those brought into the missions, and those outside that system. Patriarchy, Catholicism, and social status shaped gender roles and sexual behavior in California long after Spain's rule ended. Hippolyte de Bouchard's pirate raids along California's coast in 1818 show that the Spanish province was not isolated during the Latin American wars of independence.

REVIEW QUESTIONS

- What was the geographical reach of the Spanish claim to California from the mid-1500s to the late 1700s?
- How was California connected to Spain's Manila galleon trade?
- What roles did missions, presidios, and pueblos play in Spain's conquest of California?
- What were the rights and roles of females in Spanish California?
- How was California connected to the transpacific fur trade?

FURTHER READINGS

Robert Archibald, *The Economic Aspects of the California Missions* (Washington, D.C.: Academy of American Franciscan History, 1978). Much of the information found in this volume is hard to find in any other single work.

John Francis Bannon, "The Mission as a Frontier Institution: Sixty Years of Interest and Research," *Western Historical Quarterly*, 10 (July 1979), 302–22. This article offers a state-of-the-field assessment of scholarship on the mission system.

William J. Barger, "Furs, Hides, and a Little Larceny: Smuggling and Its Role in Early California's Economy," *Southern California Quarterly*, 85/4 (Winter 2003), 381–412. More than "a little larceny" occurred in early California, as this article shows.

Rose Marie Beebe and Robert M. Senkewicz, eds., *Lands of Promise and Despair: Chronicles of Early California, 1535–1846* (Berkeley: Santa Clara University and Heyday Books, 2001). Filled with maps and other useful visuals, this volume offers numerous primary source documents addressing life in California before the American takeover.

Donald C. Cutter, *Malaspina in California* (San Francisco: J. Howell, 1960). This volume is the only book-length treatment of the subject.

William Deverell and David Igler, eds., *A Companion to California History* (Malden, MA: Wiley-Blackwell, 2008). This anthology offers the most recent interpretations of the major developments in California history.

Iris H.W. Engstrand, "Seekers of the 'Northern Mystery:' European Exploration of California and the Pacific," in Ramon A. Gutierrez and Richard J. Orsi, eds., *Contested Eden: California before the Gold Rush* (Berkeley: University of California Press, 1997), 78–110. The author's research into the early European voyages along California's coast is grounded in primary sources.

Felipe Fernández-Armesto, *Pathfinders: A Global History of Exploration* (New York: W.W. Norton, 2006). Spain's exploration of the Pacific is examined within a global context.

Dennis O. Flynn and Arturo Giraldez, "Globalization began in 1571," in Barry K. Gills and William R. Thompson, eds., *Globalization and Global History* (New York: Routledge, 2006). The authors' case for globalization beginning with the Manila galleon trade is formidable.

Steven W. Hackel, ed., *Alta California: Peoples in Motion, Identities in Formation, 1769–1850* (Berkeley: University of California Press, 2010). Drawing on the Huntington Library's Early California Population Project online database, contributors to this anthology provide insights into the changing identities of missionaries, Indians, soldiers, and settlers in California before the American conquest.

Steven W. Hackel, *Children of Coyote, Missionaries of Saint Francis: Indian–Spanish Relations in Colonial California, 1769–1850* (Chapel Hill, N.C.: University of North Carolina Press, 2005). The unintended consequences of Spain's mission policy, which severely depleted California's Indian population, are treated in this major foray into social/religious history.

Steven W. Hackel, "Land, Labor, and Production: The Colonial Economy of Spanish and Mexican California," in Ramon A. Gutierrez and Richard Orsi, eds., *Contested Eden: California before the Gold Rush* (Berkeley: University of California Press, 1997), 111–46. This piece focuses largely on the economic functioning of the missions.

Kent G. Lightfoot, *Indians, Missionaries, and Merchants: The Legacy of Colonial Encounters on the California Frontiers* (Berkeley: University of California Press, 2005). Currently, this is the only study comparing the Russian and Spanish impacts on California's Indians.

Mains'l Haul: A Journal of Pacific Maritime History, 35/4 (Fall 1999). This entire issue is focused on the theme "Baja California and the Sea." See also 41/4 and 42/1 (Fall 2005/Winter 2006). The issue's theme is "Spain's Legacy in the Pacific." For Hippolyte Bouchard's pirate raids, see 36/4 (Fall 2000), 22–33. Cabrillo's expedition is the theme of 45/1 and 45/2 (Winter/Spring 2009).

W. Michael Mathes, *Vizcaíno and Spanish Expansion in the Pacific Ocean, 1580–1630* (San Francisco: California Historical Society, 1968). This highly detailed study, replete with drawings and other visuals, shows how Vizcaino's exploration of the California coast contributed to Spain's expansion in the Pacific.

James D. Nauman, ed., *An Account of the Voyage of Juan Rodriguez Cabrillo* (San Diego, CA: Cabrillo National Monument Foundation, 1999). Containing translated excerpts from primary source documents, this booklet offers a good introduction to Cabrillo's expedition.

James A. Sandos, *Converting California: Indians and Franciscans in the Missions* (New Haven, CT: Yale University Press, 2004). This volume is particularly strong in its extensive coverage of disease in the California missions.

Freeman M. Tovell, Robin Inglis, and Iris H.W. Engstrand, eds., *Voyage to the Northwest Coast of America, 1792: Juan Francisco de la Bodega y Quadra and the Nootka Sound Controversy* (Norman, OK: The Arthur H. Clark Company, 2012). Three historians specializing in the history of the Pacific Coast present a late eighteenth-century account of a major Spanish voyage that sheds light on the natural resources of California and the interactions between Spaniards and Indians in and around Monterey.

David J. Weber, *The Spanish Frontier in North America* (New Haven, CT: Yale University Press, 1992). This study is arguably the most reliable and comprehensive to date on Spain's North American frontier.

3

A Globally Connected Mexican Province

With Mexico's winning of independence from Spain in 1821, California's interactions with the wider world increased substantially. This was due to several key factors: Mexico's liberalized trade laws, her weak hold over the province, the area's need for imported manufactures, the steady arrival of foreign newcomers, and, most importantly, the United States growing presence in the Pacific Basin.

Timeline

1821	California passes from Spanish to Mexican control
1822	Britons Hugh McCulloch and William E.P. Hartnell immigrate to California, purchasing hides, horns, furs, and wines for the English firm of John Begg and Company
1823	A twenty-first mission, San Francisco Solano de Sonoma, is established
1826	Hudson's Bay Company fur trappers enter northern California
	Fur trapper Jedediah Smith makes the first known American entry into California
	William G. Dana, a relative of the more famous Richard Henry Dana, sails from Boston, resettling in Santa Barbara
1827	French Captain Auguste Duhaut-Cilly buys horses at Fort Ross that he sells at a profit in Honolulu, where he takes on a cargo of sandalwood before proceeding to Canton, China
	Trapper James Ohio Pattie leads a group of mountain men overland into California
1829	Estanislao, of the Lakisamni Yokuts in the San Joaquin Valley, leads nearly a thousand warriors in battle against the forces of Lieutenant Mariano Vallejo
	An army revolt at the Monterey presidio, launched by unpaid soldiers, is suppressed but leads to Governor José María Echeandía's resignation
	New Englander Abel Stearns voyages to California, where he becomes a prominent Pacific trader and cattleman

(Continued)

Pacific Eldorado: A History of Greater California, First Edition. Thomas J. Osborne.
© 2013 Thomas J. Osborne. Published 2013 by Blackwell Publishing Ltd.

1830s	Between 20 and 30 vessels regularly trade at California ports; illicit foreign maritime commerce flourishes, especially in offshore islands like Catalina
1830	Hawaiian King Kamehameha III imports California vaqueros to herd cattle and teach ranching skills
1831	A southern California rebellion, led by Californios, results in bloodshed and the removal from office of California Governor Manuel Victoria, who is sent by ship back to Mexico
1831–6	Eleven governorships come and go in the province
1832	Thomas O. Larkin, of Massachusetts, a Pacific trader and later the first U.S. consul in California, voyages to Monterey, where he resettles
1833–4	The Joseph Reddeford Walker brigade constitutes the first Americans to make the east-to-west crossing of the Sierra and the first whites to see the Yosemite Valley and giant sequoia trees
1834	Some 200 Padrés–Híjar colonists voyage from San Blas, Mexico, and arrive in Alta California
	Governor José Figueroa issues an order to begin the secularization of the province's missions
1836	American Isaac Graham assembles about 30 riflemen to help Juan Bautista Alvarado and José Castro successfully unseat California's Mexican-appointed governor
1839	Swiss businessperson John A. Sutter arrives by sea in San Francisco, shortly afterward establishing the fort, colony, and port of New Helvetia, near the confluence of the American and Sacramento rivers
1840	Richard Henry Dana's classic *Two Years before the Mast* is published, narrating his experience as a seaman voyaging across the Pacific and along California's coast
early 1840s	The English-owned Hudson's Bay Company extends its North American fur empire by establishing a trading post in Yerba Buena (San Francisco)
1841	Lieutenant Charles Wilkes's epic naval-scientific expedition into the Pacific arrives in San Francisco Bay, beginning a six-week reconnaissance and sojourn
	The (John) Bidwell–(John) Bartleson settler group arrives in California
1843	Lansford W. Hastings, a lawyer and promoter of westward migration, heads a party migrating from Oregon to California
1845	Lansford W. Hastings's *The Emigrants' Guide to Oregon and California* appears, providing dangerously misleading information on overland trails
1846	Seafaring Santa Barbara hide trader Alfred Robinson publishes his book, *Life in California*, providing a description of the Mexican province during the hide-and-tallow era
	The Donner party, consisting of 87 overland pioneers, attempts an early winter crossing of the Sierra, resulting in 40 deaths and a resort to cannibalism

Mexico's Misrule of California

Governmental misrule took many forms in Mexican California, whose northern and southern borders were basically the same then as today. That misrule is seen in the lack of enforcement of policies devised in Mexico, political instability due to coups and counter-coups, and spasms of lawlessness and anarchy intermingled with military despotism. Such turmoil was not peculiar to California; it existed throughout much of Latin America in the aftermath of the wars of independence.

The severely hierarchical nature of Spanish governance carried over into independent Mexico. In 1821 Agustín de Iturbide intimidated the Mexican Congress into naming him the constitutional emperor of Mexico, a title thereafter hereditary. This may not have been so bad had he and his retinue not focused so much on royal protocol, including the appropriate titles for his family members, the months of silly debate over whether the motto on Iturbide's bust on the coinage should be in Latin or Spanish, and on making Iturbide's coronation a lavish three-day spectacle. All of these monarchical trappings were indicative of the kind of leader he would prove to be: a *caudillo*, a military despot on horseback. Less than one year after his coronation, he was forced to resign, and liberal criollos (Mexican-born Spaniards) and mestizos took power. Still, after the coup the legislature, or *Cortes*, remained subservient to the succession of presidents whose powers went largely unchecked. The struggles of the criollos and mestizos against the Catholic Church and wealthy landed conservatives kept the newly proclaimed republic in turmoil, leaving few resources and little serious thought to be directed toward governing Alta (also called Nuevo, or new, or simply) California.

Under the authority of a succession of military despots in Mexico City, California's governors from 1821 to 1846 were rarely men of talent; their short terms in office contributed to the chronic instability of the province. During that time they often relied on unpaid presidio soldiers to enforce official policy. Mexico's rule might have been harsher if it had had sufficient soldiers to police the population and keep foreign intruders out. As in the preceding Spanish era, civilian rule or self-government was never robust in Mexican California. During those two-and-a-half decades California was administered first as a territory, and then in the 1830s as a "department" of Mexico. It never attained the higher status of a state, which suggests how marginal the province was to officials in Mexico City.

Mexico's constitution of 1824, a liberal document reflecting principles found in the U.S. Constitution and guaranteeing political and racial equality, was seldom enforced in California. This was due largely to the *pobladores'* (town settlers') lack of acquaintance with the principles of individual rights derived from basic charters of governance. Moreover, there were few lawyers in the province to wage legal battles on behalf of the common people. Governors were the appointees of officials in Mexico City. Instead of having a legislative branch of government, a *diputación* served as an advisory body to the governor. The body's members were to be elected by the *ayuntamientos* (town councils) and army officers. In actuality, the governor exercised the lawmaking, judicial, and military powers, rendering California a frontier garrison polity – as it had been under Spain.

Military rule, unfortunately, did not provide political stability. For example, during the five years from 1831 to 1836, 11 governorships came and went in the province. Three additional governors were appointed in Mexico City but Californians refused to seat them. Between 1832 and 1846 rival parties for the governorship mustered troops and engaged in five armed clashes. Continuity in policymaking was virtually impossible given such disorder, which was compounded by Mexico transferring settlers to California who lacked experience with the demands and processes of self-governance.

An example of this disorder is seen in the attempt of American Isaac Graham, a former fur trapper turned liquor producer, who in 1836 assembled about 30 riflemen to help Juan Bautista Alvarado and José Castro successfully unseat California's Mexican-appointed governor. Four years later Graham and about five dozen Americans and Britons were arrested for treason by officials and sent to Mexico for trial. The resulting "Graham Affair" ended with his release and that of his men, secured by British intervention.

Against this backdrop of developments, the province wrestled with some key political issues. The most pressing of these was secularizing the missions.

Secularization of the Missions

The eventual secularization of the missions, that is, divesting them of their extensive lands, establishing parish churches on their property, and discharging the neophytes, had been the aim of Spanish colonial policy since the arrival of the Franciscans in California in 1769. Mission lands were to be transferred to adjoining pueblos, each of which would receive 4 square leagues of property, with the remaining parcels going to the neophytes. Parishes were known as secular houses of worship and distinct from mission churches, which were operated by monastic orders.

Secularization took a much longer time arriving than either the clergy or government officials had anticipated. The padres sensed that their Indian wards required more training, occupational as well as religious, before being turned loose to function on their own in an often turbulent frontier province. That secularization took place when it did (in the mid-1830s and early 1840s) was due mainly to three factors: a residual anti-clericalism that carried over from the Latin American wars of independence; pressure on the governments in Mexico and California from ranchers, known as rancheros, eager to acquire more grazing lands for their growing cattle herds; and mounting Indian resistance to the missions.

Of these three factors, Indian resistance was probably the one felt most acutely by officials. The 1824 Indian uprising at Mission La Purísima Concepción has been mentioned (Chapter 2). That same year, however, witnessed additional brief Indian takeovers at the missions of Santa Barbara and Santa Inés. Some lives were lost and much property destroyed before soldiers suppressed the Indians, killing a good many of them. In 1829 Estanislao, of the Lakisamni Yokuts, inflamed the San Joaquin Valley by leading nearly a thousand warriors – both neophytes and gentiles – in battle against the forces of Lieutenant Mariano Vallejo. In a message warning Padre Narcíso Durán, Estanislao declared that the Indians "have no fear of the soldiers because they, the soldiers, are few in number, are very young, and do not shoot well." Though Vallejo's troops prevailed after a three-day battle, Valley Yokuts continued to raid coastal settlements and steal horses that were traded to New Mexico rustlers. In short, the missions were no longer effective at pacifying the Indians. Prospective settlers from Mexico, as a result, were not inclined to relocate in California.

This bothered officials in Mexico City because they viewed such emigration as necessary to defend California from foreign intruders, particularly Russians and Americans.

As Estanislao's rebellion suggests, by virtue of occurring away from the coast in the Central Valley, the Indians of California's interior regions – such as the Shastans, San Joaquin Valley Yokut, the Plains and Sierra Miwok, and Mohaves – were not internationally connected through Pacific trade like the coastal tribelets. Instead, the Indians in California's interior parts had their own exchange networks linking them to indigenous peoples in the Great Basin and elsewhere in the West. Moreover, these and other interior Indian groups who remained largely beyond the jurisdiction of Catholic missions generally fared better in terms of diet and other living conditions than neophytes.

Though a twenty-first mission, San Francisco Solano de Sonoma, was established in 1823, by the early 1830s most secular authorities in Mexico and California were convinced that the missions had outlived their usefulness. Nevertheless, José María Echeandía, the first governor of California or *jefe político superior* and *comandante general militar* under Mexico's republican constitution, approached secularization cautiously. Arriving by ship at San Diego, he made that port his home and the unofficial capital of the province, whose designated headquarters remained Monterey. In San Diego, as throughout the area, the missions still supplied the presidios and the cow hides and tallow (animal fat used for candle-making) that were exchanged for foreign imports – imports that brought needed customs revenues into the governor's province. An 1829 army revolt at the Monterey presidio, launched by unpaid soldiers, was suppressed but led to Echeandía's resignation.

A new pro-Church government that came to power in Mexico in 1830 appointed Lieutenant Colonel Manuel Victoria as governor of California. He adamantly opposed secularization and embodied *caudillo*-style military rule. Shortly before he took office, the previous administration in Mexico had appointed liberal firebrand José María Padrés as California's governor. Before Padrés was installed, however, a coup in Mexico resulted in Victoria's appointment and seating in Monterey, California's capital.

This power shift and the accompanying instability in California temporarily stalled secularization. Padrés had persuaded Echeandía, just before the latter left office, to issue a general secularization order. On taking office, Victoria nullified that order, imposed several repressive measures, and banished some of the opponents of his regime – including Padrés. Led by Californios, these harsh actions resulted in a southern California rebellion. Uncharacteristic of the province's political conflicts, the insurrection brought bloodshed in a battle north of Cahuenga Pass on December 4, 1831. Seriously wounded in the skirmish by a rebel lance-thrust, the governor drew his sword and killed the assailant. The governor's role in this violent outbreak led to his recall and departure by ship to Mexico. For the better part of the following year no progress was made on secularization as the province divided into two rival political camps: Echeandía ruled in the south, and Agustín Zamorano in the north. Worried about the chaos in California and determined to make headway on secularization, officials in Mexico City appointed a new provincial governor, Brevet Brigadier General José Figueroa.

A mestizo and the most able of Mexican California's governors, Figueroa's brief term (1833–5) ended with his death but marked the effective launching of a secularization policy; later Mexican governors would carry it to completion. A vague secularization law passed by the Mexican Congress in August 1833 provided a legal basis for Figueroa's implementation of the policy. Some 18,000 mission Indians were affected. On August 9, 1834, Figueroa issued an order to begin secularization. Neophytes were to receive half the mission lands but they were not authorized to dispose of the holdings; secular administrators were to oversee the policy. The governor visited some of the missions and instructed the neophytes on the benefits they would enjoy as a result of secularization, namely the opportunity to farm or ranch their own land. Six missions were secularized in 1834; 11 years later the policy was completed.

Native Californian reactions were mixed while non-Indian observers had little good to say about the results of secularization. Some Indians rejoiced at the prospect of gaining their freedom and owning land. Others cast off Catholicism and the trappings of Hispanic civilization to rejoin gentile groups in the wilds. Some lived in poverty on the outskirts of pueblos; these ex-neophytes took jobs as vaqueros (cowboys), servants, and outdoor laborers, usually receiving food and clothing rather than wages. Visiting Monterey in the late 1820s, British sea captain Frederick W. Beechey found that "many [former neophytes] having gambled away their clothes, implements and even their land, were compelled to beg or plunder, in order to support life."

Figure 3.1 Neophyte Indians gambling at Mission San Francisco de Asís, drawn by Louis Choris in 1816. Choris accompanied Otto von Kotzebue, commander of the Russian ship *Rurik*, on a round-the-world voyage, 1815–18, during which the California coast was explored. Courtesy of the Bancroft Library, UC Berkeley.

Numerous Indians had no idea that a portion of mission land was to revert to them. Father President Narcisco Durán lamented that Indians living in the Los Angeles pueblo suffered more deprivation and punishment at the hands of their new employers than had been the case in the missions.

Californios, on the other hand, anticipated and enjoyed great benefits from the closing of the missions. They covetously eyed the real-estate opportunities awaiting them when secularization unfolded. Officials in Mexico saw in the availability of mission land a chance to attract their countrymen to California, where settlements could be established north of San Francisco to arrest Russian expansion from Fort Ross. This prospect helped advance secularization policy. José María Padrés partnered with his associate José María Híjar to link that policy to the land hunger of colonists by authoring a plan to resettle Mexicans sailing from San Blas and arriving in California, where the newcomers would live on what had been mission lands. By promising vacant mission land, the two partners recruited roughly 200 settlers in Mexico, bringing them to the province in 1834. On learning that they had rivals for the Church's lands, Californios were furious. Before the colonists arrived a new government in Mexico cancelled the Padrés–Híjar project. On reaching California, the colonists ignored the cancellation order and Governor Figuero's demand that they return to Mexico immediately. Instead, they settled as far north as the Sonoma Valley, thereby helping to secure Mexico's always tenuous hold on the province.

Because of the 1836 independence movement launched by Americans in Texas, who had been recruited as colonizers by the Mexican government, that authority no longer encouraged foreign immigration to California. Nevertheless, to the anguish of officials in Mexico and California the mere chance of obtaining mission land provided all the encouragement needed to attract foreigners.

By the time of Governor Figueroa's death, little mission land remained in the hands of the Indians despite the prohibition against the selling of their individual shares to rancheros. The secular administrators were to see that as few cattle as possible were slaughtered so that the ex-neophytes would receive their promised share of livestock. Instead, missionaries killed numerous cattle in order to sell the hides and thereby feed the Pius Fund, an endowment that the Church used to support missions in Baja and Alta California. Whatever good intentions served as a basis for secularization, the inability of the ex-neophytes to protect their interests, coupled with the land-lust of Californios and others, paved the way for ranchos to replace the missions as the leading institutions of the province in the 1830s.

Hides, Tallow, and Rancho Society

With the advent of secularization, California's pastoral economy and society revolved around cattle-raising, which made the province dependent on transpacific exports and imports. The 20 or so ranchos that had existed during the Spanish period ballooned up to roughly 800, comprising about 10 million acres, in the Mexican era. They were nearly all located along the coast so that their products, hides and tallow, could be loaded aboard oceangoing vessels. Just as sea otter pelts had rendered California a Pacific Eldorado in the Spanish era, hides and tallow largely performed that function in the Mexican period. From the 1820s onward, the province's international Pacific Basin connections strengthened and multiplied dramatically. Meanwhile, a ranchero oligarchy, led by wealthy patriarchs, ran the province.

California's hide production and trade were driven mainly by the needs of New England shoe- and boot-makers. Locally, hide leather was used to fashion bridle reins, *riatas* or lassos, chair bottoms, and floor mats. Some of the tallow was used as cooking oil. Most of the substance, however, was enclosed in large rawhide bags (*botas*) weighing as much as 1,000 pounds, that were shipped to Peru. There the tallow was processed into candles and soap, which were sold to silver miners. Though the quantity of California hides and tallow traded in Mexican California is unknown, historian Douglas Monroy puts the figure at nearly 1.25 million hides and 60 million pounds of tallow in the years 1826 to 1848.

The cattle needed to satisfy these international market demands were raised on California ranchos that were run in ways traceable to medieval Spain. Land grants, bestowed in the name of the Crown and revocable, conveyed the right to *use* rather than own the land. Consequently, since the missions did not own these properties, thorny legal questions arose during the Mexican and later periods as to whether the neophytes actually possessed the plots distributed to them that they sold or bartered away to rancheros. The tracts varied in size between 10,000 and 20,000 acres. A few families, though, like the Yorbas and Castros, managed to acquire grants of several hundred thousand acres. California's climate and natural grass provided abundant fodder on these enormous spreads. An open-range policy allowed cattle to roam and forage across indistinct tract boundaries. Because this resulted in herds mixing, annual roundups or rodeos were held so that rancheros could find and brand their stock. Besides the work involved, these were festive occasions highlighted by feats of horsemanship.

A mix of workers was involved in the hide-and-tallow industry. Indians, both ex-neophytes and gentiles, and poorer Mexicans performed rancho labor. They herded, slaughtered, and skinned cattle, and salted hides to preserve them for shipping. Additionally, they rendered tallow from the carcasses. The hides, stacked compactly, were transported to waiting ships by American and kanaka (Hawaiian) sailors.

The province's commerce was closely connected to Hawai'i, which served as the international commercial crossroads of the Pacific, meaning that due to its fairly central location ships plying that ocean stopped there more than anywhere else to make repairs, load and unload cargoes, and rest crewmen. Horses, cattle, and ranching were introduced to those Polynesian islands from California. For example, in 1827 French Captain Auguste Duhaut-Cilly bought a deckload of horses at Fort Ross that he sold at a profit in Honolulu, where he took on a cargo of sandalwood before proceeding to Canton, China. In 1830 Hawaiian King Kamehameha III imported vaqueros from California to herd cattle and teach ranching skills.

The hide-and-tallow trade operated largely on a barter basis. Scarce money and ample hides in Mexican California helped ensure that the skins would be treated as currency, informally called "California bank notes." Foreign ships served as floating department stores, bringing needed manufactures to California. Britons Hugh McCulloch and William E.P. Hartnell took up residence in California in 1822, purchasing hides, horns, furs, and wines for the English firm of John Begg and Company, which secured a three-year monopoly on the province's surplus hides and tallow.

Later that same year New England merchants entered and soon dominated the trade. The first of these, William Gale, represented the Boston shipping firm of Bryant and Sturgis. As supercargo (the officer conducting business) on the vessel *Sachem*, Gale enjoyed some success in transacting business with padres willing to evade the contract with John Begg and Company. When that agreement expired the English lost out to American traders. Richard Henry Dana, Jr., a Harvard student in the early 1830s, took a leave of absence due to illness and joined the crew of the Bryant and Sturgis-owned *Pilgrim*, one of many clipper supply ships sailing from New England to California and other West Coast destinations. Dana wrote about his seafaring and onshore hide-loading days along California's coast in his classic account, *Two Years Before the Mast* (1840). Nearly a third of all foreign vessels departing California ports in this period, like the *Pilgrim*, carried cargoes of hides and tallow. From California, the majority of these vessels voyaged to the Pacific Northwest Coast, Alaska, and/or Hawai'i to acquire or sell trade goods before returning to their home ports along the United States Atlantic seaboard or in Europe. Already by the 1830s, however, Yankee and English hide traders were resettling in California port towns in order to participate more fully in the growing Pacific commerce.

Alfred Robinson of Massachusetts furnishes an example of a seafaring Yankee hide trader who took up residence in Santa Barbara. There he married into the prominent de la Guerra family, whose patriarch, José de la Guerra, amassed great wealth as a merchant and middleman in transpacific trading with Mexico, Peru, and the Philippines. Robinson's book, *Life in California* (1846), provides a description of the Mexican province during the hide-and-tallow era. The oceangoing commerce, in which Robinson and other Americans engaged, paved the way for the later U.S. takeover of California. American ambitions for the province were expressed succinctly by Dana in his popular narrative: "In the hands of an enterprising people what a country this might be!"

In the early 1840s, the English-owned Hudson's Bay Company (HBC) extended its North American fur empire by establishing a trading post in Yerba Buena (San Francisco). Until 1846, when it left California, HBC exchanged its wares for hides and tallow, which it sold elsewhere.

Because so little was manufactured in California, Pacific traders supplied virtually all such goods in exchange for hides and tallow. Typical import cargoes included: dry goods, liquors, cigars, raisins, sugar, spices, silks, hardware, cutlery, guns, powder, caps, combs, toothbrushes, shoes, furniture, an occasional piano, even Chinese fireworks. Censored books, that is, those that Catholic clerics saw as too liberal, were smuggled into California, mainly by New England merchant shippers. For example, in 1831 Mariano Guadalupe Vallejo exchanged 400 cowhides and 10 kegs of tallow for an unknown quantity of smuggled books, which he shared with two friends. All three were excommunicated by a Church official, though later they were reinstated and allowed to keep the books. Apart from

Figure 3.2   A replica of the brig *Pilgrim* at sea, off the coast of California. Courtesy of the Ocean Institute, Dana Point, CA.

smuggled goods, Mexican customs officials collected port duties ranging from 5,000 to 15,000 pesos at Monterey. Between 20 and 30 vessels regularly traded at California ports, San Diego being the busiest of those from which hides were shipped. The fact that annual revenues from port duties seldom exceeded $75,000 suggests that illicit foreign commerce with California thrived, especially in the offshore islands, such as Catalina. Despite such evasions, duties from Pacific trade constituted the sole financial means for paying the costs of governing Mexican California, underscoring the dependency of the province on transoceanic commerce. Yet the duties worked no hardship on Yankee traders. Even after payment of legitimate fees and sometimes bribes, Dana claimed that American profits from these voyages often reached 300 percent.

Though less consequential than California's maritime commerce, overland trade also contributed to the province's economy. Beginning in the late 1820s a caravan trade developed along the Old Spanish Trail that ran from Santa Fe, New Mexico, to Los Angeles. Westward-bound pack trains brought silver, blankets, and other items. Eastward-bound return cargoes included such Californian and Asian products as hides, tallow, and Chinese silks. American and New Mexican horse thieves augmented this trade by seizing mounts from ranchos located between San Jose and Los Angeles and transporting them out of California to other Mexican frontier provinces.

Like Yankee and non-Anglo-Pacific traders, rancheros also amassed wealth in Mexican California. Such wealth kept these Californio land barons and their families atop a three-tiered social pyramid. American and other foreign immigrants occupied the larger middle tier of society. Many of them intermarried with *gente de razón*, with whom they identified, and, as indicated, prospered as merchants and landowners. This group included Abel Stearns, Alfred Robinson, Thomas O. Larkin, John Marsh, William Wolfskill, John Temple, and John Sutter. Numerous *cholos* (Mexican workers) and Indians constituted the base of the social pyramid. Often landless, exploited, unruly, and sometimes violent, they performed the province's manual labor.

Though rancheros had the most property, they lacked an attribute common among the aristocracies in the American states along the Atlantic seaboard: education. Because mission-associated schooling did not go beyond memorization of religious catechisms, there were, in effect, no educational institutions in either Spanish or Mexican California. Consequently, the level of literacy in the province, even among the upper class, was low. There were no post offices, newspapers, magazines, libraries, museums, theaters, or art galleries. Many of the wealthiest rancheros could not sign their own names; instead, they drew a sign of the cross on documents requiring a signature. Some scholars estimate that probably no more than 100 Californians were literate in 1845. Evidently, more important to Californians than learning was the enjoyment they experienced at fiestas, rodeos, bull and grizzly-bear fights, cockfights, and other gatherings where social classes mingled and celebrated the occasion of the moment.

Family life among the Californios was governed largely by patriarchy. Ranchero fathers at times locked up their daughters to safeguard their virginity. Family patriarchs arranged marriages, afterward often controlling the lives of their wedded children. Wives could expect to give birth to numerous children. Among the wealthy de la Guerras, Ortegas, and Vallejos some parents had 13 to 19 children. A double standard favoring males prevailed regarding punishment for sexual offenses. A man, unlike a woman, would not forfeit his honor by engaging in promiscuity. In Mexican California a woman who gave birth out of wedlock thereby reduced her chances of success in the marriage market. Californio Mariano Guadalupe Vallejo, for example, sired several children by women below his social rank. Two of these women were sisters. When asked by a padre in 1827 what his intentions were, Vallejo responded he "could marry neither" of them. Punishments for fornication and adultery were more severe for women than men.

Some women found their own ways to resist patriarchal control over their lives. Apolinaria Lorenzano, who taught in a girls orphanage, rejected marriage though an offer had been made to her. "I refused his offer . . . because I was not particularly inclined toward that state [of matrimony] even though I knew the merits of that sacred institution." Other women, both single and married, challenged male control by engaging in illicit sex.

Despite patriarchy and its controls, women could and did own land, that is, those who were members of the socially elite *gente de razón,* and enjoyed some legal safeguards while girls' gender roles were flexible. Women owned roughly 60 ranchos, comprising 335,000 acres. For example, Juana Briones de Miranda held a land grant of 4,439 acres near

San Jose. Also, under Mexican law wives retained ownership of any property belonging to them at marriage and received community property rights after they wed. Moreover, laws protected wives from abusive husbands. Girls as well as boys of all social classes were taught horsemanship and grew into what some foreign observers described as the best riders in the world.

While Californians adjusted to secularization and enjoyed what pleasures a pastoral economy and lifestyle had to offer, Americans in greater numbers – beginning with fur trappers – entered the province. Mexico's hold on California would weaken further.

Fur Trappers

The coming of American beaver trappers to California in the 1820s had two major consequences. First, it further internationalized the province by strengthening its ties to the United States. Second, it linked a westward-moving United States to a globalizing Pacific commerce.

Jedediah Smith and his party of 15 mountain men were the first Americans to enter California via an overland route. His two related goals were to gain access to an abundance of beavers, whose pelts brought $5 each at Rocky Mountain trade rendezvous (raucous trading fairs), and traffic in furs and other items in California. Led by two Indian guides, they arrived at the San Gabriel Mission in November 1826, "nearly naked" and exhausted from having crossed the Rocky Mountains and coursed their way southwestward through the Great Salt Lake area and the parched Mojave Desert. Lacking documents permitting him to trade, Mexican officials at the mission awaited instructions from Governor José María Echeandía in San Diego. Captain William H. Cunningham, a Boston-based hide and tallow trader whose ship *Courier* had just arrived at San Diego, learned of Smith's plight and left his vessel to accompany him on the journey to meet the governor. After receiving the governor's permission to trade, Smith joined Cunningham aboard the *Courier*, by which time the trapper had been introduced to several other Yankee Pacific traders who had been voyaging between California, Hawai'i, and Mexico.

In 1827 Smith had another brush with Governor Echeandía, and again was helped by New England and British Pacific traders. After leaving California to attend a trappers' July rendezvous at Bear Lake, Utah, Smith returned to the province, and Spanish officials imprisoned him first at San Jose and then at Monterey. With a Russian fort and settlements in and around Bodega Bay and increasing numbers of foreign ships along California's coast, Echeandía feared international designs on the province. With English trader William Hartnell serving as translator, Bostonian sea captain John Rogers Cooper, a resident of Monterey, secured Smith's release from that customs port. From Monterey, Smith sailed to San Francisco where he rejoined his mountain men, who had recently sold their supply of beaver skins and otter pelts. A farewell dinner for Smith was held aboard the U.S. warship *Blossom*, with her captain and four Yankee captains, some of whom were Pacific whalers. As historian Nancy J. Taniguchi notes, this gathering symbolized the first coming together of interior trappers and Pacific sea captains whose cargoes, crisscrossing that ocean, included whale oil, Hawaiian sandalwood, Chinese silks and porcelains, and California hides and sea otter pelts. In 1828 Smith trekked northward to the HBC's headquarters at Fort Vancouver, becoming the first American to reach the Oregon Country overland from California. Comanche killed the thoughtful, highly literate trailblazer three years later on the Santa Fe Trail.

Trapper James Ohio Pattie, a hot-tempered and profit-driven young man, led the next group of mountain men into California in 1827. With his father Sylvester and a group of American trappers from New Mexico, Pattie hunted beavers in Arizona's Gila Valley. From there the party moved down the Gila River to the Colorado, where Yuma Indians attacked and stole the expedition's horses. The thirsty trappers resorted to drinking their own urine before stumbling into the care of Dominican missionaries in Baja California. After providing aid, the padres sent the hunting party under guard to Governor Echeandía in San Diego, who was still bothered about Jedediah Smith's intrusions.

Oddly, James Ohio Pattie's life may have been saved by a smallpox epidemic in northern California. Both father and son were imprisoned in San Diego, where Sylvester Pattie languished and died from the exhaustion of the trek and the squalid conditions of his cell. James Ohio Pattie later wrote that his release from prison was due to the fact that he had brought with him a vaccine for smallpox and Echeandía needed him to administer it to Californians. As "Surgeon Extraordinary to his Excellency, the Governor of California," Pattie inoculated some 22,000 inhabitants from San Diego to Bodega Bay. The Russians at Fort Ross paid "Dr." Pattie $100 for these services.

Pattie's audacity seems to have been limitless. When Echeandía refused to pay the trapper's bill for medical services, Pattie appealed to President Anastacio Bustamante of Mexico, who, likewise, did not authorize payment in money. However, the president did offer a land grant on the California coast and a thousand head of cattle if the American would become "a Catholic and a subject of the government." Pattie indignantly refused and returned to his home state of Tennessee, bringing a close to his brief but memorable exploits in California. His legacy consists in having opened the Gila route into the province.

Other well-known mountain men entering California in the 1830s included Americans Ewing Young and Joseph Reddeford Walker. Young formed a partnership with David Jackson that combined trapping with conveying California horses and mules to New Mexico. Young and his men hunted beavers along the Gila and Colorado rivers before going after sea otters on the California coast in 1832. Jackson's group was beset by Mohave attacks, with the result that more than half of the horses and mules he acquired were taken by Indians. Young found that supplying California horses and cattle to Oregon buyers brought more profit than trapping, even though he temporarily joined forces with HBC fur hunters in the San Joaquin Valley. He perfected the routes from New Mexico to California and from California to Oregon.

Captain Benjamin Bonneville, on leaving the army, arranged for trapper Joseph Reddeford Walker to blaze a central pathway across the Sierra for California-bound travelers. With 60 men under his supervision, in 1833 Walker and his party started westward from the vicinity of Great Salt Lake. They passed by the Nevada river and lake named after him and crossed the Sierra over a pass that afterward also bore his name. The Walker brigade constituted the first Americans to make the east-to-west crossing of that rampart, and probably the first whites to see the magnificent Yosemite Valley and giant sequoia trees. From there the party proceeded to San Francisco Bay, where half a dozen of his men decided to stay. The brigade then went to Mission San Juan Bautista and Monterey. In the spring of 1834 Walker and his men headed eastward across the San Joaquin Valley, traversed the Sierra, and explored Owen's Valley before exiting the province. Walker, like other mountain men, discovered the routes into California that would be taken by overland emigrants who would settle the area, and publicized the bounties of the land sufficiently to ensure an ever-increasing flow of newcomers.

Early Settlers and Overland Emigrants

Not all newcomers to California came with the intention to settle, yet many remained to carve out bright futures for their families in what publicists billed as the land of plenty. The research of late nineteenth-century historian Hubert Howe Bancroft and other early scholars reveals much about those foreigners who relocated in the Pacific province.

Two accidental settlers included John Gilroy and Joseph Chapman. Gilroy, a Scottish seaman, arrived sick and never left. He married into a prominent landowning Californio family, on whose holdings the town of Gilroy, today's "Garlic Capital of the World," was established. Chapman voyaged aboard one of Hippolyte de Bouchard's pirate ships, reaching California in 1818. Spanish officials held him captive, with other buccaneers, in Monterey. He insisted that Bouchard had "shanghaied" him, that is, physically coerced him into sea duty, in Honolulu and forced him into committing acts of piracy. After his release from jail, he became a boat builder, thereby adding to the province's pool of skilled labor.

New England provided California with most of the leading merchants of the period. Usually, they came by sea and their businesses were dependent on Pacific Basin trade routes and exchanges.

William G. Dana, a relative of the more famous Richard Henry Dana, exemplifies the Yankee businessman who adapted to the culture of Mexican California. Sailing from Boston, he arrived in Santa Barbara in 1826. In accordance with the province's naturalization law he converted to Catholicism and became a Mexican citizen, entitling him to acquire land. Next, he married the socially prominent 16-year-old Josefa Carrillo of that town, by whom he sired 21 children. His principal income came from ranching and trade. Dana had a license to hunt sea otters, and served as captain of the port, *alcalde* (the chief local official), and in various other governmental positions.

Abel Stearns, also from Massachusetts, sailed as a 12-year-old orphan to China, the East Indies, and Latin America. As a young man he voyaged to Mexico – where he obtained citizenship – and then entered California in 1829. Stearns prospered as a trader, especially in smuggled goods from Latin America and Hawai'i, and in ranching. A knife wound on his face inflicted by an irate store customer left him disfigured. Nevertheless, he married a beautiful Californio woman, Maria Francisca Paula Arcadia Bandini, and enjoyed all of the economic advantages that her wealthy family could confer on the new son-in-law. Before long he became the largest landowner and richest cattleman in southern California.

Henry D. Fitch, another New Englander and occasional trading partner of Stearns, plied Pacific waters from Peru and Chile, to Hawai'i, Mexico, and along California's coast, acquiring goods to be sold in his San Diego merchandise store. His store was also supplied by shippers from the United States and these other countries, whose vessels anchored in San Diego. Yankee merchantmen furnished ploughs, kegs of powder, axes, hammers, screwdrivers, hatchets, paint, textiles, pans, copper pots, knives, and other assorted items. Mexican ships unloaded serapes, ponchos, rebozos (rectangular women's garments), hats, and ornamental shell combs. Hawaiian vessels brought Chinese tea and other Asian goods, plus coffee, sugar, and other American products. Fitch paid hunters to bring him sea otter pelts and sea lion oil. He voyaged to Chile with Joséfa Carrillo of San Diego and a cargo of hides to be traded; they married in Valparaíso in 1829 before returning.

Thomas O. Larkin, of Massachusetts, was arguably the most influential American in Mexican California. In search of merchandising profits, he voyaged around Cape Horn en route to the Pacific province, arriving in Monterey in 1832. Aboard ship he had met Mrs. Rachel Hobson Holmes, who planned to meet her seafaring husband in Hawai'i. Apparently, a shipboard romance had developed between Larkin and Holmes, for when Rachel learned, on reaching those islands, of her husband's recent death she wrote to Larkin in California, who then proposed by mail. A civil wedding ceremony took place on a vessel off the coast of Santa Barbara; thereafter, the new bride became the first American woman to reside in California. With the addition of his wife's assets to the sizable earnings from his Santa Barbara store, and his profits from trading in Hawai'i, China, and Mexico, Larkin became rich and powerful. In 1844 he was appointed U.S. consul at Monterey. Probably reflecting his own successes and positive feelings about the province, he told readers of the *New York Herald*: "Solomon, in all his glory, was not more happy than a Californian."

"Dr." John Marsh, also from Massachusetts, voyaged to southern California in 1836, settling in Los Angeles. A graduate of Harvard College, he apprenticed with an army surgeon in Minnesota without completing his medical training due to the surgeon's death. Marsh nevertheless proclaimed himself a physician and offered his services for payment in cowhides. Soon he sold his accumulated hides for $500 and converted to Catholicism in order to fulfill naturalization requirements. Marsh bought a large rancho on the eastern slope of Mount Diablo, located in the San Francisco Bay area. He accepted cattle in payment for his medical services, and paid his Indian ranch hands in food and shelter rather than money. From his new quarters he wrote numerous letters to acquaintances in the Midwest and the East, describing the promise and beauty of California. Consequently, he drew more settlers to the province.

One particularly influential newcomer to Mexican California came by land and sea. John A. Sutter was born in Baden (now in Germany) of Swiss German parents. There he married, fathered five children, and ran up debts before abandoning his family and sailing for New York in 1834. From New York he moved briefly to Missouri, and then traded unsuccessfully in Santa Fe. The lure of profits drew him toward the Pacific as he joined with HBC trappers

Figure 3.3   An 1849 portrait, painted by Joseph Knapp, of Rachel Hobson Holmes Larkin, wife of American Consul Thomas O. Larkin. © 2012, California State Parks, Larkin House Collection, City of Monterey, CA.

and then with Protestant missionaries in a trek to Fort Vancouver. By then, if not before, he had decided to head for California but was warned about the hazards of traveling over-land, where Indians or nature's elements might claim his life. So he boarded a company ship that took the circuitous route of sailing to Hawai'i, and then recrossing the north Pacific to Sitka, Alaska, and finally voyaging to San Francisco in 1839. Soon after arriving, Sutter, armed with letters of introduction he had cajoled from officials in Honolulu and Sitka, met with Governor Juan B. Alvarado in Monterey. The governor, seeking a barrier to Russian expansion from Fort Ross, granted Sutter permission to start a colony, Nueva Helvetia (New Switzerland), on the American River near the junction with the Sacramento River.

Sutter's fort was a highly internationalized and multicultural facility; it combined the functions of a manufacturing, farming, ranching, and fur trade center, while serving as a Pacific port and sanctuary for pioneers crossing the Sierra en route to California. Hawaiian workers built the first structures within the compound: thatched roof huts. Indians, former neophytes and gentiles, constructed the thick adobe walls. French Canadian trappers, a Nova Scotia carpenter, an Irish blacksmith and about 1,000 Nisenan and Miwok Indians were all part of New Helvetia's diverse workforce. Sutter bought livestock, artillery, and other equipment from the Russians at Fort Ross for $30,000. The master of this international colony, Sutter spoke four languages, and claimed U.S., Mexican, and Swiss citizenship. Yet his national loyalty always remained fluid, opportunistic, and highly questionable. His significance during the Mexican period lies in the fact that he embodied and brokered many of California's international and Pacific connections, dominated the economy of the Sacramento Valley, and facilitated the flow of settlers coming to central California via overland routes.

In the 1840s organized groups of overland parties began to trickle into the province. The first of these was the Bidwell–Bartleson group of 1841. Based on John Marsh's upbeat reports about California's climate and resources, the Western Emigration Society was formed in Missouri in 1841. Some 500 members joined and planned to migrate overland to the Pacific province. However, on learning of the arrest and imprisonment of Tennessean Isaac Graham and 38 other foreigners, mostly Yankees, on suspicion of launching an American takeover of California, the society's roster dwindled down to a former teacher, John Bidwell. Sixty-eight others joined his party. John Bartleson was elected to command the journey. They started in May 1841, following the Oregon Trail and then leaving it to cross the Great Salt Lake Basin. Half of the party wisely remained on the course to Oregon; the others were subjected to Bartleson's temporary desertion and the perils of crossing the Sierra. By then Bidwell had assumed the leadership. On November 4, 1841, the group reached Marsh's ranch, where members of the party were overcharged for needed supplies. Several weeks later they arrived at Sutter's Fort and were treated hospitably.

Another emigrant party of the time included that led by William Workman, John Rowland, and Benjamin D. Wilson, which consisted of 25 Americans and New Mexican traders who traveled from Santa Fe to Los Angeles in the fall of 1841. They followed the Old Spanish Trail through the deserts of the southwest to southern California. The ease with which the party received passports from local officials reflects the breakdown of centralized Mexican authority. Despite the fact that after the Texas independence movement of 1836 that authority became less yielding regarding passports, local Mexican officials at times accepted bribes, thereby undermining their government's restrictive policy and facilitating American migration into the southwest.

In 1843 Lansford W. Hastings, a lawyer and promoter of westward migration, headed a party migrating from Oregon to California. The party's unprovoked killing of several Indians in the upper Sacramento Valley ensured problems for future emigrants following in the wake of Hastings's group.

During the next two years two more parties came overland into the province. In 1844 the Stephens–Townsend–Murphy company departed Missouri for California. This company constituted the first group of settlers to travel in covered wagons over the Sierra via what would later be designated Donner Pass. A year later Hastings's *The Emigrants' Guide to Oregon and California* appeared, trumpeting the wonders and opportunities awaiting newcomers to these far western lands while providing dangerously misleading information on overland trails. That same year at least 250 people followed various trails into California. For example, the Grigsby–Ide party of more than 100 emigrants traversed the Sierra via the Truckee River route near Lake Tahoe.

The perils and horrors of an ill-timed Sierra crossing were made evident in the 1846 Donner party tragedy. Starting from Independence, Missouri, in May, the group, later led by George Donner, followed the California Trail from Fort Bridger, Wyoming, westward to the "Hastings Cutoff," where they veered south of the Great Salt Lake to take the short cut urged by the route's namesake. Whatever distance they might have saved was far overshadowed by the parched terrain, dying stock, depletion of essential supplies, and the extended time required to reach the eastern foot of the Sierra. An early Sierra winter mired the bulk of the party in 10 feet of snow near Donner Lake. Exposure to the cold, exhaustion, and starvation put everyone's life at risk. Some resorted to cannibalism, eating the flesh of those who had died. Party members killed and ate two Indian guides whom Sutter had earlier sent to the forlorn expedition. In desperation, James Reed and several companions left the group and somehow made their way to Sutter's Fort, which resulted in four rescue parties being sent to aid those who were still alive. Reed's children, meanwhile, had been cared for by the family of Patrick and Margaret Breen, showing that among the surviving emigrants the bonds of humanity could still be found. Of the 87 Donner party pioneers who had set out on the trek, 40 died. Thus ended the greatest catastrophe in the history of the California Trail.

While sea routes to California remained perilous, due mainly to storms, no maritime tragedy of comparable scope to that of the Donner party has been recorded in the Mexican period. During that era, a good many of the exhausted travelers and traders arriving by sea hailed from New England, as suggested above. They relocated along California's coast, perhaps to replicate the marine environment of the northeast Atlantic seaboard.

Pacific Profile: Alpheus B. Thompson, China Trader

As was shown in Chapter 2, California's connection to the China market can be traced back to the Manila galleon trade begun in 1565. That connection was strengthened in the late 1700s and early 1800s when Yankee sea otter traders began arriving in increasing numbers along California's coast. Soon after, they established refitting stations on Oahu, in the Hawaiian Islands, which became the center of Pacific commerce. New Englander Alpheus Basil Thompson (1797–1869), who engaged in this commerce, settled in Santa Barbara in the early 1830s, when hides and tallow surpassed sea otter pelts as a major item of exchange. He, like other prosperous Yankee shippers from Monterey to San Diego, trafficked in the California–Hawai'i–China trade during the middle decades of the nineteenth century.

Before settling in California, Thompson acquired a close familiarity with transpacific mercantile pursuits. He lived in Canton, China from 1821 to 1825, serving as a merchant-representative of his uncle's Boston firm, Wildes and Marshall. In the latter year, he relocated to Oahu, where again he oversaw commercial affairs for the family business. His responsibilities included serving as supercargo of several vessels engaged in the Hawai'i–California trade.

Like many other New Englanders settling in California during the Mexican period, Thompson married into a prominent Californio family. In 1834 he exchanged wedding vows in Santa Barbara with 19-year-old Francisca Carrillo, described by Richard Henry Dana as "a delicate, dark complexioned young woman, of one of the respectable families of California." As a son-in-law of Don Carlos Antonio Carrillo, Thompson added large land holdings to his considerable wealth from Pacific commerce. Many of his trade dealings were with Abel Stearns and other leading Santa Barbara merchants.

The extent to which these Yankee-bred California merchants maintained ties considerably beyond the province's borders is seen in their correspondence. For example, on November 26, 1837 Thompson, in Hawai'i, wrote to his sister Mary in Maine that he had just arrived in Oahu "with a Cargo of Salted Hides and Furs" and would return in about two weeks with "a Cargo of Merchandise suitable for the California Market." The letter, he said, would reach her "by way of Panama." From Hawai'i, such California-bound cargoes usually contained Chinese porcelains and other Asian commodities plus New England manufactures.

The Pacific hide-and-tallow trade dwindled in the 1840s, eclipsed by the international race for Chinese tea and other Asian items carried in swift Yankee clipper ships. Thompson's correspondence indicates that he paid attention to the arrival of these vessels in California ports, especially as his relatives sometimes voyaged to China aboard the sleek craft. Throughout the Mexican period, he and his fellow merchant-traders as well as whalers strengthened California's and America's commercial ties to the Pacific Basin.

"Thar She Blows:" New England Whalers

California whaling surged with the large-scale entrance of New England hunters into the Pacific Basin in 1819, beginning a bonanza that lasted to the 1860s. During the course of three- to five-year voyages around Cape Horn and eventually into California waters, they sought sperm, right, and humpback whales. The sperm whale was larger and more esteemed than the right. It measured from 30 to 70 feet in length and weighed between 35 and 65 tons. Humpbacks, like sperm whales, were huge, sometimes 50 feet in length, and weighed between 34 and 45 tons. On sighting a spouting behemoth, a ship's lookout would yell: "Thar she blows," alerting his crew to prepare immediately for the chase and harpooning.

In the pre-petroleum era of Mexican California, and of the world as well, whale carcasses served a variety of purposes. For example, from a sperm whale of the size just mentioned crewmen might obtain 2,000 gallons of high-quality oil to be used as a fuel for lighting and as a machine lubricant. The large teeth could be exchanged as ivory for the products of Pacific islanders, including wood, food, and water. Ambergris, a secretion from the giant mammal's intestine, was used in perfumes, spices, and as an aphrodisiac, that is, an enhancer of sexuality. One whale captain claimed to have received $10,000 for 800 pounds of the substance. In addition to being valued for their oil, right whales were prized for their baleen, that is, for the elongated comb-like strainer in the mouth of the creature that when processed sold for $3 a pound. Baleen was used in chair springs, buggy whips, and corsets.

By 1840 American whalemen had found that their prey migrated throughout the Pacific Basin. Accordingly, Yankee hunters began traveling a seasonal circuit. To avoid the worst weather at Cape Horn, they rounded the tip of South America during the southern hemisphere's summers, hunting in the coastal, "onshore" fisheries of Chile, Peru, and Ecuador.

Then they sailed west to the Society, Samoan, and Fiji islands. Next, they crossed the equator, arriving in the Hawaiian ports of Honolulu, Lahaina, and Hilo for repairs, storage of oil, reprovisioning, and rest. By then the northern hemisphere's milder weather had set in, and voyages continued to Japan's whaling grounds. From there, whale ships proceeded north to Siberia's coastal fisheries, and then on to the Arctic's whale habitats. Whalemen then sailed southward along the Northwest Coast to California for a hunt, and back to Hawai'i for the usual repairs, storage, and reprovisioning. On the arrival of summer in the southern hemisphere, whale fleets sailed for the waters of the Philippines, Australia, and New Zealand before backtracking to the fisheries off Antarctica. Yankees, who dominated the Pacific whaling circuit, established small supply stations at most of these sites.

California's role in this transpacific whaling circuit, as noted, increased after 1819. For one thing, the achievement of Mexican independence in 1821 resulted in an opening of California's harbors to foreign commerce. Of 20 vessels known to have been along the province's coast in 1822, at least six were whalers that had anchored in San Francisco for refitting and supplies. The enormous bay there did not provide a hunting ground due to its narrow opening at the Golden Gate; instead, its shoreline was dotted with whaling supply and repair stations. Doubtless, few sea captains foresaw the not too distant time when San Francisco would become the world's leading whaling port. Regardless, in 1825 at least 17 whalers had been counted along the province's coast. An early Californian reported to a newspaper during the Mexican period that he had seen "as many as forty sail of whaling craft in the harbor of Monterey in one season. . . ." French whalers often hunted along the coast near that port. In a letter published in the *New York Journal of Commerce* in the early 1840s, Consul Thomas O. Larkin wrote: "There now [are] 500 to 1000 American whalers with 20,000 seamen in the Pacific. Half of them will be within twenty days' sail of San Francisco." In short, whaling, like many of California's other maritime activities, contributed to the internationalization and especially the strong Pacific connections of the province by the mid-1840s. Officials in Washington, D.C., were not content for the United States simply to remain one among the several nations competing for whales and the other bounties of North America's Pacific coastline.

The Charles Wilkes Pacific Expedition

California's connection to the Pacific Basin and U.S. interest in the province were both demonstrated in the U.S. Exploring (or Wilkes) Expedition, of 1838–42. Since the epic Pacific voyages of Englishman James Cook in the late 1760s and the 1770s, Europe's leading powers had conducted similar explorations of that ocean, which increasingly became a contested maritime frontier. With an ever-growing commercial stake in Asian and Pacific commerce, the U.S. government commissioned naval Lieutenant Charles Wilkes to lead an expedition of six ships into the Pacific for the purpose of gathering commercial and scientific information. Specifically, Wilkes was to map that ocean basin, locating uncharted islands and anchorages, to help Yankee whalers. Also, he was to gather information about the geology, zoology, botany, and other natural features of the Pacific waterscape as well as report on the various human cultures encountered.

During the course of the globe-circling expedition, Wilkes's squadron rounded Cape Horn and surveyed various Polynesian archipelagos before reaching Oahu, whose coastline and possible harbors were charted. From there, the flotilla sailed to the western coast of North America, mapping potential anchorages. At Vancouver (in today's Washington), the expedition split in two: Lieutenant George F. Emmons led an overland reconnaissance, which included Canadian and other HBC trappers, to California; Wilkes and others sailed to Yerba Buena, entering the Golden Gate on August 14, 1841, and beginning a six-week stay in the province. Emmons and his men encountered rugged terrain, grizzly attacks, and some unfriendly Indians before reaching Sutter's Fort, from where they received aid before rejoining Wilkes in San Francisco Bay.

The expedition's activities in the area varied. From his ship, the *Vincennes*, Wilkes sent a land party out to explore and map the interior region between San Francisco Bay and the Sacramento River. The men saw lynx, herds of elk, and foxes whose pelts were said to fetch $20 each in China. When they camped at night wolves and grizzlies remained a constant menace. They returned to the *Vincennes* exhausted, and some suffered from poison oak. The commander personally visited the nearby mission of Santa Clara and pueblo of San Jose. Most important, the huge bay was surveyed, along with the adjoining San Pablo Bay, and part of the San Joaquin River. All was not work, however; the expedition's officers and crew socialized on board the *Vincennes* with Yerba Buena's Mexican officials and other notables in the area. Sutter was among them, as was the Russian head of the settlement at Bodega, and several padres.

On October 31 the expedition's ships weighed anchor to depart California. Just outside the entrance to the Golden Gate, where the flotilla had assembled in the darkness of the next morning, a sandbar posed a risk. An incoming tide was accompanied by towering 30 foot breakers that for five hours crashed over the decks of the vessels causing them, in Wilkes's words, "to tremble throughout." A watchman aboard one of the ships was killed by a blow to his abdomen from a piece of equipment loosened by the giant waves. Limping away from San Francisco Bay, the squadron recrossed the Pacific, making stops in Hawai'i, Manila, Singapore, and Cape Town, surveying and mapping along the route. Entering the Atlantic, the expedition returned to New York in June 1842.

What was significant about this maritime expedition? The crew surveyed 280 islands and prepared 180 charts, one of which was the first to trace global whaling grounds. By mapping 1,600 miles of Antarctica's coastline, the voyage determined that the huge frozen landmass was a continent. The expedition brought back thousands of species of plants and seeds, which were turned over to the U.S. Botanic Garden in Washington, D.C. So extensive was the new knowledge gained that it took 30 years to publish all the atlases, charts, and reports that followed in its wake. One of the written works resulting from this venture was Wilkes's own five-volume account, *The Narrative of the United States Exploring Expedition* (1845).

Wilkes recorded in his journal the impressions he had of California under Mexican rule and the maritime value that the province had should it be acquired by the United States. The presidio at Yerba Buena had "fallen into decay, [and] the guns were dismounted." No one seemed to be in charge. Moreover, at that same pueblo, "there was a similar absence

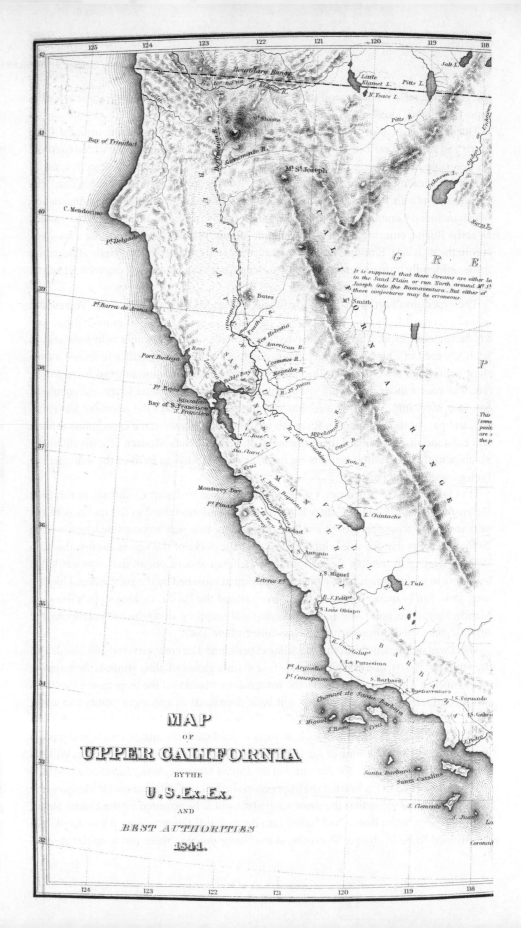

MAP

OF

UPPER CALIFORNIA

BY THE

U.S. Ex. Ex.

AND

BEST AUTHORITIES

1841.

Figure 3.4   A photographic image of a map of Upper California's coast prepared by a scientist participating in the U.S. Exploring (or Wilkes) Expedition, 1838–42. Courtesy of the Smithsonian Institution Libraries, Washington, D.C.

◄───

of authority" and "anarchy and confusion" reigned. In other words, California was ripe for the taking. What did the province offer the United States? Plenty. "It is very probable that this country [California]," he wrote, "will become united with Oregon, with which it will perhaps form a state that is destined to control the destinies of the Pacific. . . . [The straits of Juan de Fuca and San Francisco] have . . . within themselves every thing to make them increase, and keep up an intercourse with the whole of Polynesia, as well as the countries of South America on the one side, and China, the Philippines, New Holland, and New Zealand, on the other."

Wilkes's comments on California and North America's western coastline fueled a growing interest in Washington, D.C., about the future of Mexico's province and the U.S. presence in the Pacific Basin. Great changes loomed for the Far West and beyond.

SUMMARY

Under unstable Mexican rule from 1821 to 1846, California became more globally connected and Pacific-oriented. The secularization of the missions had the unintended consequence of linking the province to the Pacific Basin and America's Atlantic seaboard through the hide-and-tallow trade, which grew rapidly as former Church lands were acquired by rancheros, who dominated a patriarchal society.

Throughout the Mexican period, Americans began arriving in California by sea and via overland trails blazed by fur trappers and followed by immigrant parties. Miscalculations in timing a Sierra crossing could have horrific results, as seen in the Donner party tragedy that included incidents of cannibalism.

As more Americans arrived, California's Pacific Basin ties increased. Yankee coastal shippers, mainly headquartered in San Diego and Santa Barbara, carried hides and tallow that they exchanged for trade goods at ports along the Oregon coast and across the Pacific in Peru and Chile. From Latin America their vessels often sailed to Honolulu, where sandalwood and other products were acquired for trade in porcelains, silks, and teas in Canton, China. The heavily laden ships then completed the Pacific circuit, returning to California ports. Among others, Santa Barbara China trader Alpheus B. Thompson prospered greatly from this commerce. Meanwhile New England merchant shippers carried manufactures aboard cargo vessels – virtual floating department stores – around Cape Horn for sale in California and Oregon. As the hide-and-tallow trade declined in the 1840s, San Francisco began its ascent into the leading whaling port in the Pacific and later in the world.

The famed Charles Wilkes maritime expedition of 1838–42 demonstrated the growing interest of the U.S. government in California and the Pacific Basin. An American takeover of the province was in the making.

REVIEW QUESTIONS

- How would you characterize Mexican governance in California from 1821 to 1846?
- In what ways was California connected to the Pacific Basin in the Mexican period? Who was Alpheus B. Thompson?
- Why were the missions secularized, and what were the results of the policy for the neophytes? How did secularization impact the province's economy?
- What was California's role in the Pacific whaling enterprise?
- What was the Charles Wilkes Pacific Expedition and what was its significance for California and the United States?

FURTHER READINGS

Rose Marie Beebe and Robert M. Senkewicz, eds., *Testimonios: Early California through the Eyes of Women, 1815–1848* (Berkeley: Heyday Books, 2006). Women in early California speak for themselves in this work, that is based on interviews conducted in the late nineteenth century by historian Hubert Howe Bancroft.

D. Mackenzie Brown, ed., *China Trade Days in California: Selected Letters from the Thompson Papers, 1832–1863* (Berkeley: University of California Press, 1947). The 25 letters to and from Alpheus B. Thompson presented in this volume provide rich details about California's mid-nineteenth-century China trade.

Miroslava Chávez-Garcia, *Negotiating Conquest: Gender and Power in California, 1770s to 1880s* (Tucson, AZ: University of Arizona Press, 2004). The author examines the ways in which Indian and Mexican women maneuvered within the bounds of a patriarchal society to maximize their agency, at times challenging male control from the 1770s to the 1880s.

Robert Glass Cleland, *The Cattle on a Thousand Hills: Southern California, 1850–80* (San Marino, CA: Huntington Library, 1990). Focusing heavily on the gold rush period, the economic and social development of southern California is traced in this volume.

Richard Henry Dana, Jr., *Two Years Before the Mast & Other Voyages* (New York: Library of America, 2005). This remains the unsurpassed first-hand account of Mexican California's Pacific-oriented hide-and-tallow trade and the society revolving around that commerce.

Auguste Duhaut-Cilly, translated by August Frugé and Neal Harlow, *A Voyage to California, the Sandwich Islands, & Around the World in the Years 1826–1829* (Berkeley: University of California Press, 1999). California's Pacific and international connections during the Mexican period are highlighted in the record left by this French sea captain.

Arrell Morgan Gibson and John S. Whitehead, *Yankees in Paradise: The Pacific Basin Frontier* (Albuquerque, NM: University of New Mexico Press, 1993). The authors treat America's growing Pacific presence after the Revolution of 1776 as an extension of the frontier movement across the Republic's interior landmass.

Lloyd C.M. Hare, *Salted Tories: The Story of the Whaling Fleets of San Francisco* (Mystic, CT: Marine Historical Association, 1960). Though dated and short on documentation, this is one of the few studies of San Francisco's rise to the top of global whaling ports in the last half of the nineteenth century.

Albert L. Hurtado, *John Sutter: A Life on the North American Frontier* (Norman, OK: University of Oklahoma Press, 2006). The volume provides a detailed and fully internationalized treatment of Sutter and the California of his times.

David Igler, *The Great Ocean: The Transformation of the Eastern Pacific, 1770s–1840s* (New York: Oxford University Press, 2013). This is a major study connecting pre-statehood California with China, Hawai'i, Peru, Mexico, and the Northwest Coast up to Alaska.

Robert Kirsch and William S. Murphy, eds., *West of the West: The Story of California from the Conquistadores to the Great Earthquake, as Described by the Men and Women Who Were There* (New York: E.P. Dutton, 1967). This is one of the few anthologies of eyewitness writings that situate California within the larger spatial context of international and Pacific Basin happenings.

W. Michael Mathes, *The Russian–Mexican Frontier: Mexican Documents Regarding the Russian Establishments in California, 1808–1842* (Jenner, CA: Fort Ross Interpretive Association, 2008). The complex and important story of Russian–Mexican relations in California in the first half of the nineteenth century is told in the annotated documents appearing in this volume.

Doyce B. Nunis, Jr., ed., *The Journal of a Sea Captain's Wife, 1841–1845: During a Passage and Sojourn in Hawaii, and of a Trading Voyage to Oregon and California* (Spokane, WA: Arthur H. Clark, 2004). Lydia Rider Nye's journal provides a rare glimpse at how an observant, articulate New England woman, sailing the Pacific with her hide-trading husband, viewed the people and circumstances she encountered in Hawai'i, Oregon, and California.

Nathaniel Philbrick, *Sea of Glory: America's Voyage of Discovery, The U.S. Exploring Expedition, 1838–1842* (New York: Viking Penguin, 2003). The human drama of the Wilkes expedition is brought to light in this poignant, fair-minded, and detailed account.

Louise Pubols, *The Father of All: The de la Guerra Family, Power, and Patriarchy in Mexican California* (Berkeley: University of California Press, 2009). In addition to tracing the social connections and political influence of a prominent Santa Barbara family, the author highlights José de la Guerra's lucrative Pacific trade ties to Mexico, Peru, and the Philippines.

Alfred Robinson, *Life in California during a Residence of Several Years in that Territory*, with an introduction by Andrew Rolle (Santa Barbara, CA: Peregrine, 1970). First published in 1846, Robinson's account details his trafficking in the lucrative transpacific hide trade, while sketching the lifestyles of prominent Californio families.

Nancy J. Taniguchi, "Jed Smith, U.S. Trade, and Global Connections," *Southern California Quarterly*, 88 (Winter 2006–7), 389–407. This article appropriately and effectively views the full international reach of Jedediah Smith's activities in California.

David B. Tyler, *The Wilkes Expedition: The First United States Exploring Expedition (1838–1841)* (Philadelphia: American Philosophical Society, 1968). The author provides a fully documented, comprehensive history of arguably the most important maritime exploring expedition in America's past, with attention paid to California.

David J. Weber, *The Mexican Frontier, 1821–1846: The American Southwest Under Mexico* (Albuquerque, NM: University of New Mexico Press, 1982). The Mexican frontiers of Texas, New Mexico, and California are described and analyzed in this major study.

John Whitehead, "Hawai'i: The First and Last West?," *The Western Historical Quarterly*, 23 (May 1992), 153–77. The author argues for including Hawai'i as part of America's frontier movement into the Far West.

4

War and Gold: America's West Coast Eldorado

Events that were international in scope and of lasting effect spotlighted California during the 1840s. War between the United States and Mexico swept the Pacific province into America's hands. Shortly after hostilities ended, miners from all over the world rushed into California, dramatically expanding and diversifying the population and shaping the future of what came to be known as the Golden State.

Timeline

1820	The single U.S. warship *Constellation*, according to Secretary of the Navy Smith Thompson, is "cruising the Pacific Ocean for the protection of our trade and whale fisheries"
1840	Mexican officials imprison a group of Americans and Britons for trying to set up an independent government in Monterey; the U.S. warship *St. Louis* arrives at that port and U.S. Secretary of the Navy Abel P. Upshur intervenes and secures the release of the captives
early 1840s	The U.S. Pacific Squadron of six warships and a supply vessel intensifies its focus on Hawai'i and California as areas critical to American trade expansion in that ocean
1842	Thomas ap Catesby Jones, commander of the U.S. Pacific Squadron, sails from Peru to Monterey, where he raises the American flag, declaring California under American rule; discovering that his seizure of the province was based on false information, the following day Jones orders the flag lowered and the province returned to Mexico
	Captain William D. Phelps, of the American merchant vessel *Alert*, captures the presidio at San Diego; he holds the fort for three days before learning that war has not erupted between the United States and Mexico and that Jones has relinquished Monterey; Phelps, like Jones before him, withdraws
1845	President James K. Polk sends John Slidell to Mexico to negotiate the transfer of Upper California and New Mexico to the United States for up to $40 million; the Mexican government refuses to receive Slidell

Pacific Eldorado: A History of Greater California, First Edition. Thomas J. Osborne.
© 2013 Thomas J. Osborne. Published 2013 by Blackwell Publishing Ltd.

1846	The United States declares war on Mexico
	Americans in Sonoma arrest Mexican General Mariano Guadalupe Vallejo and proclaim the independent Republic of California, which lasts less than a month
	John D. Sloat, commander of the U.S. Pacific Squadron, raises the American flag over California's capital at Monterey, proclaiming that "henceforth California will be a portion of the United States"
	Andrés Pico leads Mexicans in a victory over U.S. General Stephen Kearny at the Battle of San Pasqual
1847	Yerba Buena is renamed San Francisco by U.S. Navy Lieutenant Washington Bartlett
	Mexican California surrenders to American forces in the so-called Cahuenga Capitulation
	President James K. Polk declares that the harbors on the California coast "would afford shelter for our navy, for our numerous whale ships, and other merchant vessels employed in the Pacific ocean, [and] would in a short period become the marts of an extensive and profitable commerce with China, and the other countries of the East"
1848	James Marshall, an employee of John Sutter, discovers gold on the South Fork of the American River
	The Treaty of Guadalupe–Hidalgo ends the war with Mexico, transferring most of the Southwest, including California, to the United States
	Mormon elder Sam Brannan waves a bottle of gold dust and shouts in San Francisco: "Gold! Gold! Gold! from the American River," touching off the California gold rush
	Outside of California, the earliest news of the gold discovery travels by sea and is first publicized in the Honolulu *Polynesian* newspaper on June 24
	The Pacific Mail Steamship Company is founded in New York with an office, wharf, and other facilities in and around San Francisco Bay; the shipping company provides the world's first transpacific service linking the United States to Asia
1849	The California gold rush is in full force as multitudes of so-called "forty-niners" pour into the Mother Lode country
1850	According to the June 6 edition of the *Alta* (San Francisco) newspaper, 509 ships – mostly carrying gold miners – are in port
	According to the 1850 federal census females comprise less than one-tenth of California's population
1851	The California clipper ship *Flying Cloud* voyages from New York to San Francisco in 89 days and 21 hours, setting a sailing record that held until 1989
1852	California's Chinese number 25,000, constituting a tenth of the non-Indian population
1855	American international shipping magnate William H. Aspinwall completes the construction of a 65-mile transcontinental railroad across the Panamanian Isthmus, reducing the time of an isthmus crossing for gold-seekers from four or five days to three or four hours
1867	The Pacific Mail Steamship Company has 47 vessels, and has become America's largest and most profitable maritime carrier

California and the Pacific Squadron

U.S. interest in California, much like Spain's earlier claim to the province, derived largely from Pacific trade prospects, to which Americans added whaling. In the late 1700s, Yankee China traders and whalers began plying the Pacific. As Spain's Latin American colonies were fighting for independence in the early 1800s the U.S. government lost no time in securing an ever-growing naval presence along the western coast of the Americas and in Polynesia.

Operating from the ports of Callao, Peru, and Valparaíso, Chile, the U.S. Navy established a small Pacific Squadron to protect America's interests in that vast ocean. In 1820 the single warship *Constellation*, according to Secretary of the Navy Smith Thompson, was "cruising the Pacific Ocean for the protection of our trade and whale fisheries." Yankee warships also assisted with repairs of merchant vessels and served as depositories for specie (gold or silver coin) belonging to American traders, often carrying specie back to the United States for them. By 1826 Secretary of the Navy Samuel L. Southard regularly referred to the Pacific Squadron, then comprising three ships, as being among four such groups stationed throughout the world's oceans. In addition to policing the western coast of South America, the Pacific Squadron was expected to operate in California waters as well as in Hawai'i and elsewhere throughout Polynesia.

As America's Pacific trade grew throughout the 1830s and 1840s so, too, did the squadron's presence along the coasts of California and Mexico. By 1839 the ranking officer of the Pacific Squadron, Commodore Alexander Claxton, received orders from the Navy Department stating: "The increasing commerce of the U. States, within the Gulf [of California] and along the coast, of California, as far as the Bay of San Francisco, together with the weakness of the local authorities and their irresponsibility to the distant Government of Mexico, renders it proper . . . that occasional . . . protection should be afforded to American enterprise in that quarter." Claxton was to send one or two vessels to the California coast "as occasion may require."

The enforcement of this directive reveals a bizarre development: English–American cooperation in policing California's coast at the very moment that Britain and the United States were rivals in that far western frontier. For example, when Mexican officials in Monterey imprisoned a group of English and American citizens for allegedly trying to set up an independent government, the U.S. warship *St. Louis* arrived at that port in June 1840. U.S. Secretary of the Navy Abel P. Upshur scolded the Mexican authorities for beating, imprisoning, and destroying the property of the captured men "without even the forms of a trial." As a result of the U.S. Navy's intervention the men were quickly released. Upshur exulted that "the rights not only of American citizens, but of British subjects in California" had been upheld. Why the Pacific Squadron would defend Englishmen in California is not entirely clear given the antagonism between Britain and the United States. Examples of this antagonism included ongoing clashes between the United States and Britain over the Maine–New Brunswick boundary, a dispute over the border between British Columbia and the Oregon Territory, and Britain's disapproval of American slavery. Despite this antagonism, however, both the United States and Britain aimed to increase their respective trade throughout the Pacific Basin and some measure of cooperation in California could be mutually beneficial.

By the early 1840s the Pacific Squadron's patrol boundaries were stretched to the limits that would prevail until the twentieth century. They included all of America's West Coast and westward from the meridian of Cape Horn to the 180th degree of longitude, and southward between those meridians to the South Pole. Northward, the squadron's boundary reached to the Arctic. By then the U.S. government, with a Pacific Squadron of six warships and a supply vessel, had intensified its focus on Hawai'i and California as areas critical to American trade expansion in that ocean. To foster that expansion and protect the ensuing transoceanic commerce, in 1841 the Navy Department appointed Thomas ap Catesby Jones as commander of the Pacific Squadron.

Jumping the Gun at Monterey

Commodore (naval squadron commander) Jones had the reputation for being an able officer fully committed to expanding American influence in California and throughout the Pacific Basin. In 1826 he commanded the warship *Peacock* on a voyage to the Marquesas, Society, Tahitian, and Hawaiian Islands. In Honolulu Jones negotiated a treaty with native leaders ensuring the safety of shipwrecked American sailors and providing for terms of trade equivalent to the most favorable treatment Hawai'i extended to any other nation. Though the pact failed to gain U.S. Senate approval, largely because it had been executed by a naval officer rather than a Department of State official, it exemplified Jones's initiative in advancing America's commercial interests in the Pacific.

Jones, who believed that California was less important than strategically located Hawai'i, assumed his squadron's command when he arrived in Callao in May 1842. This was at a time when naval officers stationed at distant ports were accorded decision-making power they would not have been given had communications been more timely. Jones and others in his position, then, exercised considerable discretion in handling their responsibilities. Yet they remained vulnerable to recall and disciplinary action if their decisions turned out badly in the judgment of federal officials.

In the absence of timely, reliable information and orders, unverifiable rumors at times became the basis for naval actions; such was the case when Jones faced a difficult decision regarding California. On arriving at Callao, he learned that two months earlier a French squadron had departed Valparaíso for an undisclosed destination. British sources and Jones believed that the French warships had sailed for California with colonization in mind. Then on September 5 a steamer reached Callao from Panama carrying news that the United States and Mexico were at war. That same day several British warships had departed Callao under secret orders. Jones promptly met with J.C. Pickett, an American diplomat in Lima, Peru, to discuss possible courses of action. As they met dispatches arrived, including excerpts from American newspapers, convincing the two that Britain had purchased, or was about to purchase, both Upper and Lower California from Mexico for $7 million.

Ignorant of the facts that the true destination of the British ships had been the Mosquito Islands off the Caribbean coast of Nicaragua and that the French vessels had sailed for the

Marquesas Islands in the South Pacific, Jones assumed mistakenly that the naval craft of both of those nations were en route to California. Fearing that his country was about to be out-maneuvered by these rival powers, Jones readied the vessels *United States* and *Cyane* for a quick departure to Monterey.

Within a day's sailing from Callao, he arranged a conference on board the *United States* with the commanders of the two vessels plus the lead officer of a third ship, the *Dale*, which would thereafter sail to Panama. The officers concluded that the rumors of war between the United States and Mexico were probably true, which provided sufficient justification for the Pacific Squadron to sail from Peru to California. Furthermore, if war had in fact erupted "it would be our bounden duty to possess ourselves of every point and port in California that we could take and defend." Finally, they decided that any acquisition of California by a European power would constitute a violation of the Monroe Doctrine of 1823, in which President James Monroe warned European powers not to interfere in the political affairs of western hemisphere nations.

A few hours outside of Monterey, Jones delivered a stirring speech to the sailors aboard the *United States* and *Cyane*. He declared it their duty, once on shore, to lower the Mexican flag and replace it with the Stars and Stripes. They must seize California and "keep it afterward, at all hazards." Jones insisted on not harming any peaceful civilians. America's forces must be the "protectors of all, and not the oppressor of any."

Seldom in U.S. history has such an aggressive and unwarranted military action been carried out with so little resistance and no bloodshed. On the morning of October 19 one of Jones's two warships fired a warning shot at a lone Mexican vessel near the southern tip of Monterey Bay. At 2:45 in the afternoon the *United States* dropped anchor near the Spanish fort at Monterey. Jones was now within striking distance of the supposed "enemy." A few hours later a boat flying the Mexican flag approached. Jones questioned its officers, who said they "knew nothing of war." A sailor on a merchant ship, *Fame*, told Jones that a recently received report stated that the British were to acquire Upper California and guarantee Mexico's continued possession of Lower California. That information coincided with what Jones had heard in Callao. The moment for action had arrived.

At 4 that afternoon Jones sent one of his officers ashore to demand the surrender of Monterey. Acting governor Juan Bautista Alvarado was given 18 hours to capitulate or suffer an American attack. Alvarado turned the matter over to his commander of the fort, Don Mariano Silva, who concluded that his 29 presidio soldiers and 11 artillery pieces were insufficient to defend the town. At 7:30 on the morning of October 20 two Mexican officials, accompanied by American merchant and translator Thomas O. Larkin, boarded the *United States* to sign surrender papers that provided for an American landing party to go ashore, collect all weapons, take over the presidio barracks, and seize the fort. Larkin informed Jones that recent newspapers on shore made no mention of war between the United States and Mexico. Suspecting Larkin's motives, Jones dismissed the reference to such writings. The bloodless American takeover seemed complete.

That same day a landing party of 150 American seamen went ashore. They accomplished their mission without firing a shot. The townspeople put up no resistance. The Mexican flag at the presidio was lowered and Old Glory was raised in its place, followed by a 26-gun salute. Jones concluded that the takeover had been "conducted in a most orderly manner."

Figure 4.1 *Harbor and City of Monterey, California 1842.* Painting commissioned by Thomas O. Larkin. City of Monterey, Colton Hall Museum, Monterey, California. Monterey was a thriving port town and Pacific maritime trade center in the 1840s. Courtesy of the Colton Hall and Presidio Museums, City of Monterey Art Collection.

The next day, October 21, brought surprises. Jones went ashore in the morning to inspect the secured town and fort. His secretary then handed him the newspapers that Larkin had mentioned the previous day. The papers contained nothing about a war between the United States and Mexico, or transference of California to Britain. Jones realized then that he had been wrong on both counts. After consulting with several of his officers, Jones ordered the lowering of the American flag at 4 that afternoon. The Mexican flag was flown again. Property that had been seized was returned, the American troops were recalled to their ships, and normal relations restored.

Unfortunately, there were unintended consequences. Apparently encouraged by Jones's aggressive actions, Captain William D. Phelps, of the American merchant vessel *Alert*, captured the presidio at San Diego. He held the fort for three days before learning that war had not erupted between the United States and Mexico and that Jones had relinquished Monterey. Phelps, like Jones, retreated. These "jumping the gun" incidents derailed what had been the United States ongoing negotiations with Mexico for the purchase of California. The Mexican government expressed outrage at the violation of its sovereignty by the Americans. Both Mexican officials and their press condemned the barbarities of Thomas "ape" Catesby Jones. Meanwhile, the U.S. minister to Mexico assured that government that Jones had acted without orders. Secretary of the Navy Upshur recalled Jones, stripped him of his command of the Pacific Squadron, and reassigned him to less important duties.

There were other outcomes as well for the United States. Californians seemed to hold no grudge against Americans. Jones's seizure of Monterey cooled French and British interest in taking California by putting the leaders of those powers on notice that if war with Mexico occurred the United States would probably seize the province. Lastly, Jones exposed Mexico's inability to defend California, signaling to American policymakers the ease with which the United States could take the Pacific province.

Polk, the Pacific, and the Outbreak of War

America's acquisition of California was based on maritime considerations linking the province to Oregon and U.S. trade across the Pacific. Since the presidency of Thomas Jefferson (1801–9) federal officials, naval officers, and American traders spoke and wrote of Oregon and Alta California mainly within the context of transpacific commerce. Similarly, one of the main causes of war between the United States and Mexico in 1846 was the latter's rejection of President James K. Polk's bid to buy California. Should purchase fail, Polk put into operation another plan calling for an independence movement among Californians encouraged and co-opted by military adventurer John C. Frémont.

Even more than his immediate predecessors in the White House, President Polk's administration (1845–9) was determined to acquire a huge portion of the western coast of North America for the United States. His aim was to expand American commerce throughout the Pacific Basin. Consequently, he focused on Pacific ports: Puget Sound, San Francisco, Monterey, and San Diego. Of these the president attached the greatest importance to San Francisco. In Polk's message of December 1847 he declared that the harbors on the California coast "would afford shelter for our navy, for our numerous whale ships, and other merchant vessels employed in the Pacific ocean, [and] would in a short period become the marts of an extensive and profitable commerce with China, and the other countries of the East." In other addresses that same year the president had made the same points, as did a number of congresspersons and other U.S. officials. The governments of Britain and France were equally keen on California's maritime advantages pertaining to the China trade. With commercial ambitions of their own in the Pacific Basin, those nations did not want to see the province, especially San Francisco Bay, acquired by the United States.

An additional international influence that may have affected Polk's thinking about California were reports he received about an Irish priest, Eugene McNamara, who had been given permission by Governor Pío Pico in July 1846 to settle 10,000 Irish colonists in the San Joaquin Valley. McNamara viewed his project as a bulwark to protect Catholics in the province from becoming "the prey of the Methodist wolves." Such a reference doubtlessly referred to North Americans, among whom the Methodist faith had been spreading. The possibility of such a settlement scheme could not have pleased the American president.

Having listed annexation of California as a major goal in the election of 1844, Polk sent John Slidell to Mexico the following year to negotiate the transfer of Upper California and New Mexico to the United States for up to $40 million. The Mexican government refused to receive Slidell; the sale of California, especially to the United States, would have invited more political turmoil for the already shaky regime of President José Joaquín Herrera, which was about to be toppled.

At the same time that Polk angled to buy California, his administration embarked on a second strategy to take over the province: it sent instructions to Consul Larkin in Monterey to cultivate support among Californios for peacefully severing ties with Mexico and ceding their territory to the United States. Mariano Vallejo and General José Castro assured Larkin of their help. This strategy was abandoned shortly after events in the Southwest brought Mexican–American relations to the breaking point.

While the Larkin intrigue was under way, the Polk administration contended with an explosive U.S.–Mexico boundary clash over territory claimed by both Texas and Mexico lying between the Nueces and Rio Grande rivers. Texas was admitted into the Union as a slaveholding state in 1845, after annexationists overcame years of opposition from anti-slavery members of the Whig Party in Congress, led by John Quincy Adams and other northerners. At the time of its admission, Texas claimed that its southern border extended to the Rio Grande River, thereby embracing the disputed territory. Mexico, on the other hand, insisted that Texas's southern boundary ended farther north at the Nueces River, putting the contested land under Mexican sovereignty.

This boundary dispute provided the proximate cause of the Mexican War that erupted in 1846 and ended two years later. Upper California provided the major prize at stake. Combat started in the contested southwestern territory between the Nueces and Rio Grande rivers shortly before war was declared. In late April 1846, troops of both nations battled each other in that area. Nearly a dozen American soldiers were killed, prompting Polk to deliver a war message to a joint session of the House and Senate on May 11. In addition to denouncing Mexico's shedding of "American blood on American soil," the president listed other grievances. These included that nation's refusal to negotiate with Slidell on the sale of Upper California to the United States. Two days later, while Britain was in the process of agreeing that Puget Sound's harbors belonged to the United States, Congress declared war on Mexico. America's permanent acquisition of California, and especially its coveted seaports, was now in sight.

Amid opening hostilities, in the summer of 1846 an additional development in California propelled the United States takeover of the Pacific province: the Bear Flag Revolt. John C. Frémont was a highly visible figure in this episode. An American who eloped with Jesse Benton, the talented and ambitious daughter of powerful U.S. Senator Thomas Hart Benton of Missouri, Frémont had journeyed overland to California in 1843–4. On that occasion, as a lieutenant in the army's Corps of Topographical Engineers, Frémont led a scientific expedition to the province. His influential father-in-law, who championed America's westward expansion and domination of Pacific commerce, had lobbied in Washington, D.C., for the expedition. Frémont and his wife jointly wrote a report of the journey that enthralled the nation and guided later emigrants to California. His familiarity with the province and its unstable governance (the Spanish-speaking populace rebelled at least 12 times during the Mexican period) set the stage for Frémont's shadowy role in the Bear Flag uprising.

Determined to bring California into the Union, Frémont, encouraged by Senator Benton and Secretary of the Navy George Bancroft, returned to the province with 60 armed men in December 1845. In February 1846 he appeared in Monterey, claiming that his intention was to survey a route to the Pacific. Colonel José Castro ordered Frémont and his soldiers to leave California. Defiant to the point of recklessness, the American officer and his men journeyed to Hawk's Peak in the Gabilán Mountains located near the Salinas Valley, where they hoisted the American flag. While Castro raised a force of 200 men, Larkin mediated Frémont's retreat northward to Oregon "slowly and growlingly."

Near Klamath Lake in southern Oregon, Frémont was overtaken by U.S. Marine Lieutenant Archibald Gillespie, who had been commissioned by President Polk to deliver important messages to several Americans in California – particularly Larkin and Frémont. The contents of these messages remain debated by historians; about all that can be said with certainty is that they communicated that war with Mexico was imminent. One vaguely worded message, from Senator Benton to Frémont, was interpreted by the son-in-law as saying: "the men who understood the future of the country . . . regarded the California coast as the boundary fixed by nature to round off our national domain."

Whatever else may have been communicated, Frémont reversed his direction and led his 60-man force back to California. No longer the surveyor and explorer, he saw his new duty as that of an American army officer. Much later, he recalled that this new duty meant preventing England (which had a battleship situated off the coast of Monterey) from interfering, and carrying the expected war against Mexico into California, which the United States could claim by conquest when hostilities ended.

With this secret mission in mind, later in May Frémont and his men camped near present-day Marysville, a short distance from Sutter's Fort. Americans in the vicinity came to the camp, warning that Mexican General José Castro was preparing to oust Yankees from the province. Covertly, Frémont encouraged the Americans to provoke the Californians into attacking them, which would draw him and his soldiers into the conflict. Such an incident could furnish a pretext for Polk sending sufficient U.S. troops into California to claim the province in a war with Mexico. On the other hand, as happened in Texas in 1836, a settler revolt could lead to California independence and eventual American annexation without a U.S. war against Mexico. Frémont gauged his activities to meet either of these scenarios. (It must be stressed that not until August 17, 1846, when official U.S. dispatches arrived by sea at San Pedro, did people in California know for certain that America was at war with Mexico. Until then Frémont had to exercise caution in order to safeguard the Polk administration from possible charges of trying to seize California through a U.S.-sponsored Yankee revolt in the province.)

Emboldened by Frémont's encampment, American settlers in the Sacramento and Napa valleys launched an uprising on June 10, at which time revolutionary Ezekiel Merritt captured horses intended for Castro's forces. The animals were taken to Frémont's camp. This theft was simply an early step in the rebels' larger plan of overthrowing Mexican rule.

On June 14 more than 30 of Merritt's comrades-in-arms seized control of the village of Sonoma, home to General Mariano Guadalupe Vallejo, California's wealthiest and most prominent citizen. The grimy marauders included horse thieves, trappers, and runaway sailors, "about as rough a looking set of men as one could well imagine," according to one witness. They immediately surrounded Vallejo's residence. The general invited their leaders – the raw-boned and illiterate Merritt, Robert Semple, John Grigsby, and William Knight – into his home, where Vallejo treated them to large quantities of brandy. When William B. Ide joined these "well lubricated" men a little later, the terms of capitulation were finalized. The insurgents then seized whatever horses and arms could be found on the property.

Despite the fact that the hospitable Vallejo was known to favor American annexation of California, he was imprisoned at Sutter's Fort for two months. During that time Frémont scolded Sutter, who by then had opportunistically resigned his commission in the Mexican military and declared his support for the American settlers, for trying to make the general's confinement less harsh. Rosalía, Vallejo's daughter, bristled with "a large dose of hatred" against the Americans. Her anger over her father's humiliation was shared by other Californios, whose fears of Yankee domination seemed justified.

Soon after capturing Vallejo, Ide emerged as the visionary leader of the American guerrilla force calling itself the Bears. Their goal was to establish an independent Republic of California. In Sonoma on June 14, 1846, they raised a roughly made banner, the handiwork of William Todd (a nephew of Abraham Lincoln), and then issued a high-sounding proclamation. The homemade Bear Flag featured a red star in the upper left corner (reminiscent of the 1836 Texas revolt). To the right of it appeared the crude rendering of a grizzly bear. Below these emblems large black letters spelled out: "California Republic." A broad red stripe of flannel ran horizontally across the bottom of the banner, which by an act of the state legislature in 1911 has since become the official state flag. The following day, Ide read a long, windy statement he had just written. It decried Mexican "despotism," applauded the "rectitude" and "bravery" of the insurrectionists, and declared the founding of a republic.

Figure 4.2 The Bear Flag of 1846. Used by permission of the Society of California Pioneers.

Under their new flag the Bears brought closure to their coup by waging a skirmish, the "Battle of Olompali." Two Americans and five or six Mexicans died. In the aftermath, Frémont took charge of the Bears, merging his group with theirs. On July 1 he marched his force into the undefended San Francisco presidio, an exploit far more symbolic than substantive. All of these activities, Frémont acknowledged in 1848, were "without expressed authority from the United States, and revolutionary in . . . character." Four days later he organized the California Battalion that he would soon command under the auspices of the U.S. government, which commenced military operations in California on July 7. No longer was there any reason for the existence of the Bear Flag Republic.

The new republic and its flag have been fantastically romanticized. Historian Neal Harlow has rightly dubbed the supposed polity a "paper nation," for its straw government lasted less than a month, only until July 9, when U.S. naval forces arrived and claimed all ruling authority. The significance of the short-lived Bear Flag movement is that it antagonized Californios, fueling their determination to fight against the American military forces that had begun arriving in increasing numbers. Given the arrival of these forces, a development independent of Frémont's filibustering, it is difficult to see how the outcome of the struggle for California would have turned out much differently had there been no Bear Flag Revolt. Undoubtedly, though, the incident assured Frémont a highly visible role in the California theater of the Mexican War and propelled his subsequent political career.

California and the Mexican War

While the major armed clashes of the war took place in Mexico, California was the scene of considerable conflict as Polk made sure that U.S. forces would be positioned there. That way when Mexico surrendered the United States could claim the province as an indemnity for the costs incurred. Overall, the earliest and least amount of fighting occurred in the northern half of California. The later, more ferocious and determinative battles occurred in the southern parts of the province. A critical challenge facing the Californios was recruiting sufficient soldiers from a population whose loyalties were often divided. The American forces, superior in numbers and weaponry, were challenged mainly by the difficulties of maintaining a united front amid the sometimes conflicting views of Commodore Robert F. Stockton, General Stephen Watts Kearny, and Frémont. Regarding American military operations in California, the U.S. Navy played the central role.

When John D. Sloat, commander of the Pacific Squadron, received definite but unofficial news that war had erupted between the United States and Mexico, he sailed from Mazatlán to Monterey, arriving on July 2, 1846. Fearful of repeating the Thomas ap Catesby Jones incident of four years earlier, Sloat waited five days at Monterey before taking action. Unwilling to chance British naval intervention and mindful of the uprising at Sonoma, Sloat raised the American flag over Monterey on July 7, proclaiming that "henceforth California will be a portion of the United States." Similar flag raisings were held two days later at Yerba Buena, Sonoma, and Sutter's Fort. A response was not long in coming. On July 16 Governor Pío Pico issued a call for all Californians to repel the Yankee invaders.

At this juncture the aged and ailing Sloat was replaced by the younger and far more aggressive Commodore Robert F. Stockton, who assumed command of the Pacific Squadron and all American forces – including those of Frémont – in California. With no Californian resistance in the northern half of the province, the focus shifted southward. Governor Pico, who had been headquartered in Los Angeles, fled to Mexico before Stockton arrived by sea at San Pedro, from where he traveled overland to the "city of the angels," arriving on August 13. At the same time Frémont, promoted by Stockton to the rank of major, and his seasick mountain men sailed from Monterey to San Diego, reaching that port on July 29. Within a few days San Diego was secured, for the time being, and flying the American flag.

As in the north, Stockton's forces encountered no resistance in Los Angeles. On August 17 he issued a proclamation: "The Flag of the United States is now flying from every commanding position in the Territory, and California is now entirely free from Mexican dominion." While that was true, it was not welcome news to all Spanish-speaking residents. It was also true that the war in southern California was just beginning, due in part to subsequent mistakes made by Stockton and his excitable aide, Archibald Gillespie.

Stockton's imposition of martial law in Los Angeles, including a prohibition on carrying arms and a 10 o'clock evening curfew, struck the population as unduly harsh. When the commodore departed for San Francisco, leaving Gillespie in charge, the situation in Los Angeles deteriorated rapidly due to the latter's mishandling of some of the troublesome local residents. Gillespie treated violators of the martial law edict as rebels. If rebellion had not yet fired their imaginations and resolve, it soon would.

On September 24 Gillespie found himself confronted by Captain José María Flores and his band of rebels, who proceeded to unleash a resistance movement that rapidly engulfed the southern regions of the province. A group of American riflemen surrendered to Californians at a Chino rancho, thereby heartening the rebels who next pinned Gillespie down at Fort Hill, located just behind the Los Angeles plaza. A messenger rode some 500 miles to alert Stockton at San Francisco to the urgent need for help. Meanwhile, the terms of his surrender allowed him to march his men to San Pedro for departure.

At that port Gillespie's force was met by a just-arriving contingent of marines and sailors voyaging from San Francisco. The combined forces marched back to Los Angeles, all the horses in the area having been taken by the rebels.

Before the American forces reached Los Angeles they were attacked by José Antonio Carrillo and his men near the Domínguez Rancho on October 8. His secret weapon was an old cannon that had been hidden in the garden of Señora Inocencia Reyes. Recovered and lighted with a cigarette, the artillery piece inflicted enough punishment on Gillespie's troops to ensure a decisive Californio victory in the Battle of the Old Woman's Gun. Consequently, Los Angeles would remain under rebel control for several more months.

Meanwhile, in June 1846 General Stephen Watts Kearny, stationed at Fort Leavenworth (Kansas), received orders from the secretary of war instructing him to seize New Mexico and then proceed overland to California where he was to establish civilian and military rule. Polk wanted Kearny's army in California during hostilities to make it that much easier for the United States to claim the territory at war's end. Starting out with an army of 300 soldiers, Kearny was met by scout Kit Carson, sent eastward to Washington, D.C., by Stockton to notify officials that the United States had conquered California. Kearny acted on this premature news, sending most of his force back to Santa Fe, where it was not needed, to serve garrison duty. The roughly 2,000-mile trek was completed in early December when he and his worn-out 100-man contingent arrived at John Warner's ranch, located at the eastern edge of today's San Diego County.

With insufficient recovery time, Kearny's force attacked the rebels, led by the governor's brother, Andrés Pico, at the Indian village of San Pasqual on the fog-shrouded morning of December 6. Located about 35 miles northeast of San Diego, San Pasqual was the scene of fierce combat on that memorable day. Pico's mounted lancers were more than a match for the fatigued Yankees, 22 of whom were killed and an equal number wounded, including Kearny. There were no enemy casualties. A relief force was sent to Kearny; with this aid the general and his hungry, wounded, and weary troops slowly made their way to San Diego on December 12. Strangely, Kearny reported an American victory at San Pasqual to his superiors, an assessment at odds with the facts and shared by few historians.

While skirmishes were fought between Californios and Americans up and down the coast of the province, in early 1847 both sides began concentrating their strength in and around Los Angeles, a population center where Yankee control was contested. Just southeast of the pueblo the Battle of San Gabriel was waged on January 8 by the combined forces of Stockton and Kearny against the army of José María Flores. The San Gabriel River separated the opposing camps. Poor-quality powder compromised Flores' artillery fire, enabling the Americans to cross the river and proceed toward Los Angeles. The next day Stockton's and Kearny's troops encamped just outside Los Angeles, fighting sporadically with few casualties on either side. On January 10 the pueblo yielded to the entering American troops, and Flores fled to Mexico after leaving Andrés Pico with authority over the Californians. Fearful of the terms that Stockton might exact, Pico rode to San Fernando in order to surrender to Frémont. On January 13 the two men struck an agreement pardoning the rebels, the so-called Cahuenga Capitulation, which ended seven months of war in California.

The struggle over authority among Kearny, Stockton, and Frémont, however, remained to be resolved. Before sailing away to Mexico's west coast, Stockton had appointed Frémont as governor of the conquered territory. Kearny refused to recognize Stockton's power to make that appointment, claiming that a naval commander did not have such authority over a brigadier general – especially one, like himself, who had specific orders to organize a civil government in California. Dispatches from Washington, D.C., confirmed Kearny's view. Despite support from his influential father-in-law, Kearny arrested Frémont and sent him to the nation's capital where in late 1847 and early 1848 he was tried and convicted of mutiny, disobedience, and conduct detrimental to good order and military discipline. President Polk intervened, striking the mutiny conviction, granting clemency, and ordering the defendant back to duty. Still, the court martial had taken its toll on Frémont, who resigned from the army. For whatever reason, the ordeal enhanced his popularity, bolstering his political future.

The Treaty of Guadalupe–Hidalgo, signed on February 2 and ratified by the U.S. Senate on March 11, 1848, ended the Mexican War. By its terms California was acquired by the

United States. The effort at purchase had failed, as had the hope of a peaceful American takeover from within the province. For Polk, that left only war, and war worked. In California, as shown, the war was mainly a naval affair. Warships cruising the provincial coast transported the marines and sailors (and even Frémont's army at times) who secured control over the ports and hinterlands. Supplies for the American forces often came by sea. California, whose harbors were thought essential to building a commercial empire on the Pacific, was America's most important conquest in that fateful, uneven clash between neighboring powers. During the course of hostilities, on January 31, 1847, Yerba Buena had been renamed San Francisco by U.S. Navy Lieutenant Washington A. Bartlett, thereby linking the name of that town to the bay that had been so coveted by the Polk administration. Within two years, San Francisco would become known worldwide as the Pacific port of entry for multitudes of California-bound gold miners.

Gold, Ships, and Wagon Trains

One of the signal events in world history, the gold rush (c.1848–60) further enhanced California's image as a Pacific Eldorado. Long after the yield of glittery ore tapered off, the story has been told and retold of men leaving families behind and embarking on heroic journeys to discover treasure. Like the ancient Greek myth of Jason and his crew aboard the *Argo* in search of the Golden Fleece, the tale of California's Argonauts – who proudly took their name from this legend – is one of epic proportions. It involved fortune-seekers, ports, ships, wagons, merchants, shovels, pans, guns, greed, murder, luck, and more. And like Jason's famed quest, the gold rush was mainly a maritime venture.

On January 24, 1848, more than a month before the U.S. Senate approved the peace treaty with Mexico, James Marshall, an employee of Sutter, inspected a ditch soon to be used to channel the flow of the South Fork of the American River to power a new saw mill. Thirty miles from New Helvetia, the mill was located in Coloma, named after the nearby Maidu village of Cullumah. A glittery substance lodged in gravel caught Marshall's eye. Thinking it was gold, he brought a sample to Sutter, who consulted his *American Encyclopedia* and concluded that Marshall was right. The two men and Sutter's other employees at the site agreed to keep the discovery a secret.

Still, a secret involving untold riches was not likely to be kept for long. Sutter himself told friends John Bidwell and Mariano Vallejo. Though a small amount of gold had been found in 1842 at Placerita Canyon, just north of Mission San Fernando, many of those who heard of Marshall's discovery remained skeptical. Even when the San Francisco *Californian* printed news of the finding on March 15, and the *California Star*, the town's and province's only other newspaper, 10 days later carried an account, there was no stampede to the gold fields. Instead, prospectors merely trickled into the surrounding area.

The rush of 1848 got under way on May 12. On that day Mormon elder Sam Brannan, who previously had organized a party of 200 emigrants sailing from New York to California, waved a bottle of gold dust and shouted in San Francisco: "Gold! Gold! Gold! from the American River." "The whole country, from San Francisco to Los Angeles, and from sea shore to the base of the Sierra Nevadas, resounds with the sordid cry of gold, GOLD,

GOLD! while the field is left half-planted, the house half-built, and everything neglected by the manufacture of shovels and pickaxes," reported the *Californian*. Publication of both newspapers was suspended because their employees had gone prospecting. They were joined by a good number of Indians; some worked for whites; others labored for themselves, exchanging their findings for goods.

After 1848, as more white gold-seekers poured into the state, increasing the competition for riches, Indian–Caucasian relations broke down as Anglos set out to exterminate Native Californians. According to some historians, in one example in about March 1849, a group of Oregon men likely raped some Maidu women along the American River. When Maidu men attempted to protect the women, white miners shot and killed the Indian males. A short while later, the incident escalated into mutual retaliatory killings that resulted in whites murdering at least seven Indian "prisoners" at Coloma, all of whom had been shot down after having been told to run. A witness to much of this violence, Theodore Johnson, wrote: "The late emigrants across the mountains, and especially from Oregon, had commenced a war of extermination upon them [Indians], shooting them down like wolves, men, women and children, wherever they could find them." By the early 1850s the once numerous Indians in the gold fields had largely been driven out by white miners.

Beyond California, news of the discovery at Sutter's mill was spread mainly by ships reaching ports throughout the Pacific Basin and Europe, and horse travel to Washington, D.C. As a consequence of the strong California–Hawai'i maritime trade connection, news of the gold discovery was first publicized in the Honolulu *Polynesian* newspaper, on June 24, 1848. This was before even neighboring Oregon had received this information. In fact, news of the California gold rush had been carried throughout the Pacific Basin by whalers and seagoing traders before reaching people in the Middle West, the East, the South, and Europe. Navy Lieutenant Edward F. Beale brought news and a sample of gold to Washington, D.C. in September 1848. Virtually all doubt about the California bonanza was swept away with President Polk's confirming words to Congress on December 5: "The accounts of the abundance of gold in that territory are of such an extraordinary character as would scarcely command belief were they not corroborated by the authentic reports of officers in the public service." The following year a cascade of Argonauts descended on El Dorado; they became the well-known forty-niners.

American gold-seekers traveled to California by ships, wagon trains, and sometimes a combination of land and water transport. From the United States, the gold fields could be reached by three basic routes (each of which had some variations): Panama, Cape Horn, and overland. The winter snows of 1847–8 meant that the first emigrants would come by sea, since ocean routes were open year round. Between April 1849 and April 1850 alone roughly 62,000 Argonauts arrived in San Francisco by ship. According to the June 6, 1850, edition of the *Alta* newspaper, 509 ships were in port; many would be abandoned and turned into wharves, and waterfront factories and hotels. Throughout the gold rush era supplies reached California mainly by sea, and mail to and from El Dorado was transported almost exclusively by oceangoing vessels.

California-bound residents living along the Atlantic seaboard and the Gulf Coast generally came by ship. The greatest number of these passengers opted for the Panama route, which initially took six to eight weeks. Charges ranged between $350 and $1,000, depending on accommodations, mode of voyaging (passage was cheaper on sailing than on steam-powered vessels), and fare prices in the ticket speculation market. Accordingly, speculators bought large blocks of tickets and then resold them so as to exact the highest prices during times of peak demand, which was usually in winter when miners often returned home. The Argonauts' journey to California involved sailing or steaming southward from their home port, and into the Caribbean, stopping at Chagres, Panama, or on Nicaragua's Caribbean coast. From there gold-seekers boarded dugout canoes, rode mules, and walked – led by local guides – to Panama City on the Pacific side of the isthmus, where they awaited a steamer or sailing vessel bound for San Francisco. Bandits, tropical diseases, snakes, alligators, heat exhaustion, and death threatened the isthmus-crossers. These problems were eased in 1855 when American international shipping magnate William H. Aspinwall (see Pacific Profile below) completed the construction of a 65-mile transcontinental railroad across the Panamanian Isthmus. The isthmus crossing, which formerly took four or five days, could afterward be made in three to four hours, reducing even more the transit time from America's Atlantic ports to San Francisco.

Clearly, the Panama route to and from the gold fields was best. From 1848 to 1851 at least 36,097 people followed it to El Dorado. Not only fastest and safest for passengers, particularly after the isthmian railroad was operating, California's gold, its most important export, was transported via that ship and train pathway. Between 1849 and 1869 at least $710,753,857.62 in specie was shipped from San Francisco by way of the Panama route. Whether they came to California by sea or land, nearly all gold-seekers returned home on ships via Panama, and in fewer instances Nicaragua. In 1851 return tickets on sailing vessels sold for as little as $50 to $85. Steerage accommodations aboard a steamer went for $125. The meat aboard the Panama-bound steamer *Oregon*, complained passenger Isaac Lord in 1851, was so infested with worms that had it been thrown overboard it would "have proved a vomit for sharks."

The Cape Horn route around the southern tip of South America had been the traditional sea path to California for whalers, China traders, and hide-and-tallow shippers. Not surprisingly, it became a major artery for the transport of passengers, mining equipment, and other goods during the gold rush. The voyage from New York to San Francisco covered more than 13,000 miles and often involved encounters with icy winds and high waves whether passing by the Cape or through the narrow Straits of Magellan. Motion sickness, naturally, was rampant. Generally, passengers spent five to eight months at sea before reaching San Francisco. Ticket costs varied from $500 to $1,000. At least 1,400 vessels sailed to California via Cape Horn in 1849 and 1850.

After 1852 passenger traffic shifted increasingly to the Panama route and Cape Horn vessels carried mostly machinery and other bulky cargoes. The famed California clippers, first built in the 1840s for the China trade, greatly reduced the time required to voyage from the Atlantic to the Pacific Coast via Cape Horn. They were so called for their sleek hulls, large sail area, and speed. *Flying Cloud*, for example, departed New York on June 2, 1851, and arrived 89 days and 21 hours later in San Francisco on August 21, setting a sailing record that held until 1989! The early 1850s marked the heyday of clippers.

American gold-seekers from many walks of life voyaged to El Dorado. Passengers included lawyers, merchants, farmers, mechanics, preachers, gamblers, prostitutes, and

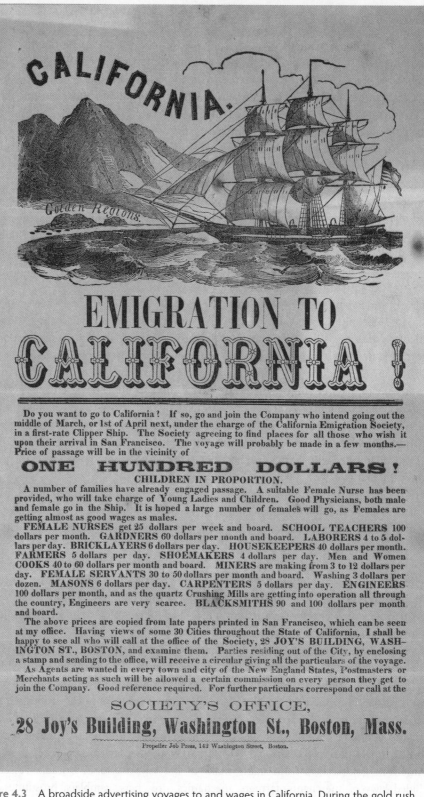

Figure 4.3   A broadside advertising voyages to and wages in California. During the gold rush broadsides like this one promoted visions of California as the Pacific Eldorado. Reproduced by permission of the Huntington Library, San Marino, California.

more. The monotony of the lengthy transit was relieved by watching spectacular sunsets, spotting dolphins and whales, catching sharks, singing, dancing, reading, journaling, listening to lectures and sermons, staging theatricals, playing high-stakes poker, fighting, sexual promiscuity, and engaging in practical jokes. Passengers were especially grateful for shore leave in such ports as Rio de Janeiro, Valparaíso, Callao, and Acapulco.

Historians differ on whether more Argonauts came to California by land or sea. They agree, however, that emigrants from the Middle West, the Southwest, and Mexico were mainly overlanders.

In the 1850s some 200,000 people traveled overland in wagon trains, usually organized into companies. As with seafarers, not all overlanders remained. American gold-seekers journeyed to El Dorado mainly along the Oregon Trail and its spur, the California Trail. This 2,000-mile route opened up in the 1830s (see Chapter 3) and under the best conditions took 100 days. Council Bluffs, Iowa, and St. Joseph and Independence, Missouri, served as major starting points. From there prairie crossers followed the Platte River to South Pass in the central Rockies, which took them across the Continental Divide to Fort Bridger. Two forks presented themselves at that point: a northern trail to Soda Springs and Fort Hall that met the Humboldt River in Nevada; and a southern path to Salt Lake City that extended to Hastings Cut-off en route to the Humboldt. From the intersection of these two forks at the Humboldt, emigrants either proceeded toward one of the passes through the Sierra or they pursued a northern course around that range to the gold fields. Alternate routes to the south, where trekkers did not have to contend with winter snows, included the Old Spanish Trail from Santa Fe to Los Angeles, and the Santa Fe Trail from that town, along parts of the Gila River, to San Diego. Regarding the overland routes, transportation and equipment costs ranged from $750 to $1,000 in the early years of the rush.

Pacific Profile: William H. Aspinwall, President of the Pacific Mail Steamship Company

William Henry Aspinwall (1807–75) was born and died in New York City. Like other Yankees whose roots were on the Atlantic seaboard, Aspinwall played an important role in connecting California to the Pacific Basin and the East Coast of the United States. He did this through his transoceanic shipping business and the railroad he operated across the Isthmus of Panama.

Aspinwall's early maritime transport experience was gained in the 1830s as a merchant whose sail-driven ships traded with Europe, South America, and China. The China market, in particular, excited his imagination, triggering a grand vision of Pacific commerce with his mid-1800s fleet of clippers and steamboats plying the waters of that ocean. The firm of Howland and Aspinwall, in which he was the key partner, built the famous clipper *Sea Witch*, which set a record in 1849 of sailing from New York to China in 79 days.

A consummate businessman, Aspinwall saw in the California gold rush a rare opportunity to transport people, supplies, and mail from Panama northward to California and Oregon. In the process he would continue trading with Hong Kong and reach out to other Asian and Pacific ports as well, including Honolulu. With the American military in control of California in late 1847, the federal government entered a contract with Aspinwall to deliver U.S. mail between Panama and Oregon. To provide the mail service, Aspinwall and Howland established the Pacific Mail Steamship

(Continued)

Company in April of the following year. By 1867 the Pacific Mail fleet had grown to 47 vessels, and the company had become America's largest and most profitable maritime carrier. Such growth was a sure sign of California's and the West Coast's rapidly increasing ties to the Pacific Basin.

The cargoes of Pacific Mail vessels departing San Francisco for the Far East included California flour, gold and silver bars, and Mexican and U.S. dollars, the latter coined at the U.S. Mint in that port city. Incoming goods from Asia included rice, tea, silk, and other assorted Chinese wares.

In addition to its transport services, at Aspinwall's direction in 1850 Pacific Mail built a repair and mainte-nance facility at Benicia, located on the north shore of Carquinez Strait in the San Francisco Bay Area. A coaling station, provisioning warehouse, repair depot, and eventually an iron foundry, comprised the facility, which constituted California's first industrial establishment.

In a fitting tribute to Aspinwall, a *New York Times* obituary, dated January 19, 1875, stated that as a result of his shipping and rail lines: "The Way was opened to direct communication between Asia and America and Oceanica and Australasia, besides an immense coast line extending from Panama to Behring's Straits [Alaska]." California, whose gold rush spurred the growth of Pacific Mail, was the hub of Aspinwall's Pacific enterprise.

The World Rushed In

During the gold rush era California became the most internationalized and culturally diverse place on Earth, and San Francisco the world's most cosmopolitan city. Foreign emigrants outnumbered American newcomers in California in 1848. Even when that situation reversed itself a few years later, foreigners continued coming to El Dorado seeking their fortune. In November 1851, of the 452 vessels in San Francisco harbor, 242 were American-registered, 36 came from Britain, 11 from France, 10 from Germany, 5 from Chile, 3 from Sweden, 3 from Austria, 2 from Holland, and 1 from Italy. Miners from these and additional countries joined an already ethnically diverse California population in the quest for riches.

Polynesians, Americans, and Europeans living in Hawai'i were the first emigrants to come. Native Hawaiians, called "kanakas" by American Californians, sailed in scores aboard ships carrying needed foodstuffs and merchandise for miners and others. Unaccustomed to the chill of a Sierra snowfall, kanakas often sailed home to their islands in the winter months, returning to the mining camps when spring arrived.

Thousands of Latin Americans were next in the sequence of arrivals. These included Mexicans coming mainly overland from Sonora, though some voyaged from the Sea of Cortez, and seagoing Chileans and Peruvians. Of these, Mexicans were the most numerous, numbering 15,000 in 1850. Passage of a foreign miners' license tax of $20 a month in that year led to the exodus of 10,000 of these miners to Mexico. (Protests from foreign miners and their governments helped secure the California legislature's repeal of the tax in March 1851.) Estimates of the numbers of Chilean gold-seekers vary between 3,000 and 5,000. Information on Peruvian emigrants is not available. The Pacific Mail vessel *California* transported a large number of both South American groups to San Francisco.

Argonauts from Britain's Pacific dependencies were also part of the world that rushed into California. New Zealanders learned of the California gold strike in November 1848 when an American whaler arrived carrying copies of the Honolulu *Polynesian*. Copies of that newspaper reached Australia a month later, resulting in thousands of its citizens boarding vessels to California. A gold strike in Australia in 1851 resulted in a reverse migration of its Argonauts from California to their homeland. Despite the return migration, Australia continued exporting needed goods to California, including jerked beef, bacon, butter, cheese, beer, medicines, woolen blankets, nails, axes, window glass, cooking utensils, and prefabricated wooden houses. By land and sea, British Columbians made their way south to El Dorado as well, working mainly the mines in the Trinity–Klamath–Shasta region.

The Chinese were the largest group of transpacific emigrants to gold rush California. Numbering 25,000 in 1852, they constituted a tenth of the non-Indian population. Eight years later nearly 35,000 Chinese lived in the Golden State. In some of the mining areas they comprised nearly a third of the population. In many of these rural areas, as in cities like San Francisco and Sacramento, they established sections called Chinatowns. These neighborhoods featured grocery stores, gambling casinos, laundries, brothels, opium dens, sleeping quarters, and eateries.

French-speaking gold-seekers arrived, mainly by sea, in increasing numbers in the early 1850s. From France they came via the Cape Horn route and from Tahiti, a French colony in Polynesia, they crossed the Pacific. Others journeyed to California from Quebec, Canada, and Louisiana, presumably by a combination of land and sea routes. By 1853 French-speaking miners in California numbered between 25,000 and 30,000.

To this international multitude must be added California's own diverse *residential* ethnic groups consisting of Indians, Californios, and Anglos, plus African Americans entering the state as both free persons and slaves. The story of how these groups fared in the social ferment of a new state is taken up in Chapter 5.

Life in the Diggings

Life in the mining camps, or diggings as they were called, was influenced by numerous factors. The most important of these were the technologies used to extract gold, the absence of duly constituted authority to resolve disputes over claims, the scarcity of women, and the presumption of many white Americans that they were entitled to the lion's share of California's and the West's resources, especially in view of the United States' victory in the Mexican War.

Most of the gold extraction technologies, from the simplest to the more involved, used water to separate the metal from clumps of ore, gravel, and dirt. Panning was the earliest and most elementary method of rendering precious particles and nuggets. Miners simply sloshed river sediment in a water-filled, hand-held pan, gathering the heavier gold particles that gravitated to the bottom. Among teams of miners, sluices or wooden cradles were popular. Also called "Long Toms," a sluice was an elongated, shallow wooden structure of varying lengths, open at one end. Water would be channeled via inclined conveyances, called flumes, into the sluice as gravel and bits of ore were fed into the device. Cleats or raised surfaces in the sluice would catch the gold particles, preventing them from being washed away in the man-made current. Miners also built and used rockers, or sluices that rolled from side to side during the water flow, in order to separate gold from river sediment. These relatively inexpensive techniques were in widespread use during the first three or four years of the rush, when surface gold was plentiful. During that time, 1848–52, some $200 million in gold was obtained in California. On average, according to one estimate, gold-seekers using these methods gathered $20-worth of the metal a day in 1848 and $2-worth in 1853. Multiply these figures by 20 to gauge their equivalent value today.

In the mid-1850s, as the surface deposits of gold became scarcer, other extraction technologies came into use. Hydraulic mining utilized canvass-constructed high-pressure water hoses, sometimes called water cannons, carrying sufficient force to blast away entire hillsides to get at ore deposits. The resulting debris was then channeled into sluices for the rendering of gold. Because of the required capital investment in equipment, only mining companies could afford this method. In 1870 some 22 percent of the gold extracted in California was garnered by this technique. Hydraulic mining was environmentally destructive, and one can see the devastation today in such places as Malakoff Diggins State Park, where a portion of the damaged landscape has been preserved. The water cannons toppled trees, denuded hillsides, and silted waterways feeding the Sacramento River. When heavy rains descended in winter 1861–2, the bed of the river running through Sacramento had risen to such a level from this silting that the city was flooded. Scientist William Brewer, who visited the surrounding area, wrote in his journal in January 1862: "The Central Valley of the state is under water."

Similarly, companies employing work crews engaged in hard-rock mining, especially in the so-called Mother Lode area, which extended for roughly 120 miles along today's Highway 49 from Eldorado County southeast to Mariposa County. This zone, 4 miles wide at some points, was thought to possess the richest veins of gold in California. Using winches, pulleys, and drills, crews entered mine shafts and bored into the surrounding walls, unearthing quartz and other gold-bearing substances. The ore was then crushed in "stamp mills" and gold was extracted from the amalgamation by the application of mercury, much of which was mined at New Almaden. In addition to its use in the gold country, California mercury was shipped throughout the West and overseas. By the late 1860s one-half of the gold mined in the state was from quartz. The mercury-laced tailings polluted some of California's waterways, endangering fish and other aquatic life.

With tens of thousands of miners of diverse ethnic and national origins, laboring often in close proximity to one another, problems of law and order were bound to arise given the absence of lawmen and courts. Add large quantities of liquor, firearms, greed, and xenophobia to the mix and combustible situations were guaranteed. The mere names of some of the mining towns are suggestive of trouble: Hell's Delight, Gouge Eye, Devil's Retreat, and Murderers' Bar. In the early 1850s murder and theft pervaded nearly all mining camps and lynch law, that is, the imposition of the death penalty without due process, was common. For example, in Dry Diggings (later renamed Hangtown and finally Placerville)

Figure 4.4   Hydraulic mining at Malakoff Diggins, now a California State Park. Courtesy of the California History Room, California State Library, Sacramento, California.

in January 1849 a Chilean and two Frenchmen stood accused of robbery and attempted murder. The accused were tried by an armed and drunken crowd. When Edward G. Buffum protested on behalf of the defendants, the mob threatened to hang him, until he backed off. All three of the accused men, none of whom spoke or understood English, were then lynched. This was not a rare occurrence.

Women, on the other hand, were rare. According to the 1850 census females comprised less than one-tenth of California's population. In the state's mining counties they constituted only 3 percent of the inhabitants. So whatever restraining force they might have provided in the diggings was largely absent. Among the few living in the gold fields, some mined, others washed clothes and cooked for males, and a contingent engaged in prostitution.

Like the men, women in the diggings struggled with success and failure. Lucy Stoddard Wakefield wrote from Placerville to friends on September 18, 1851: "I love California and probably now shall make my home and final resting place here," adding, "I have been toiling hard for the last two and a half years and am still doing an almost incredible amount of work." To avoid sexual harassment, some female Argonauts dressed in male garb. A popular Frenchwoman, who had left Paris for California's mines, reported that she "cut off her hair, donned men's clothes, took the name of Marie Pantalon, and went prospecting in the gold country."

Writer Louise Clappe, better known by her pen name of Dame Shirley, narrated the stories of some female gold-seekers, one of whom lost her husband to cholera on the overland trail and had to provide for her nine children by washing and cooking for male miners. "She used to wash shirts, and iron them on a chair – in the open air, of course; and you can fancy with what success. But the gentlemen were too generous to be critical, and as they paid her three or four times as much as she asked, she accumulated quite a handsome sum in a few days. . . ."

Most of the prostitutes in the gold fields were women of color: Mexican, Chinese, Chilean, and Indian. They lived and plied their trade mostly in the southern mines, that is, those located south of the Mokelumne River, separating Amador and Calaveras counties. The northern mines, situated above that line, were largely the province of single white males. They occasionally traveled southward to engage the services of female sex workers. There, for example, they would have found Chilean Rosario Améstica, who had sailed to California with a group of male miners from her country. Still, the scarcity of white females in the northern mines at times led to attacks on non-white women, often regarded as little more than prostitutes. The consequences of the imbalance in the ratio of white men to white women for the sexual behavior of Anglo miners is a subject deserving of more study.

Probably the most determinative factor of life in the diggings was the Anglo presumption of entitlement to all of California's and the West's riches – precious metals, land, forests, fisheries, everything. In accordance with the spirit of Manifest Destiny in the 1840s, dominant in Washington, D.C., and especially among settlers of the West, God gave the North American continent to the United States. Some Protestant ministers preached that God had hidden California's gold from the Catholic Spaniards and Mexicans, revealing Eldorado's wealth only when the sway of the Vatican over the province diminished.

California's white miners may have been the most presumptuous of all. They flooded into Nevada during the Comstock Lode era from 1859 to 1881. Nearly $300 million, mostly in silver but some in gold, was extracted from the area, where some of the world's most advanced technology was used to move workers and equipment thousands of feet into hard-rock hillsides. Mining companies capitalized by San Francisco banks and stockholders further illustrate the economic reach of California in western extractive enterprises. George Hearst and James Flood were among the many San Francisco millionaires profiting from the Comstock mines. For them life in the diggings was something they read about rather than experienced.

The Gold Rush's International Economic Impacts

Historian Gerald D. Nash put it best: "The California Gold Rush precipitated a veritable economic revolution in the state, the nation, and the world. Production of precious metals affected price levels, labor, wages, capital investment, the expansion of business, finance, agriculture, service industries, and transportation." Other gold strikes and rushes, with somewhat similar but shorter-lived results, occurred in other parts of the world throughout the 1800s.

California most assuredly felt the effects of this economic revolution. San Francisco replaced Honolulu as the commercial hub of the Pacific. The state became a major exporter of flour and beef to regional, Pacific Rim, and world markets. Hoses, stamp mills, steam engines, and nozzles were manufactured and exported. Levi Strauss established a jean-manufacturing business in San Francisco to outfit miners with durable pants. The gold rush led to the start of banking in California, Wells Fargo & Company being among the most prominent firms. Collis P. Huntington, Mark Hopkins, Leland Stanford, and Charles Crocker – known as the Big Four – profited from supplying miners with equipment and other merchandise; they parlayed their earnings into the founding of the Central Pacific Railroad in 1861. California mining was doubtlessly helped when British stock companies invested roughly $10 million in that extractive enterprise.

Regarding the impact on the United States, California gold exports helped create a favorable trade balance for the nation. This was possible because the state produced 59 percent of the country's gold output from 1850 to 1900. During the rush, some $1.4 billion (or $25 billion in 1990 dollars) was unearthed from California. American shippers, like Pacific Mail and Cornelius Vanderbilt's Accessory Transit Company, prospered from transporting Argonauts across the Central American isthmus en route to and from San Francisco.

The international reach of California's gold rush is seen in its impact on specific countries. Hawai'i redirected its trade away from America's Atlantic ports to San Francisco. In 1850, 469 ships from those islands entered the Golden Gate, carrying goods valued at $380,000. The rush created a labor shortage in Hawai'i that was remedied by the importation, beginning in 1852, of Chinese cane field workers. Goods from China and Japan were shipped to El Dorado, including Chinese clothing and prefabricated houses. Australian wheat, beef, coal, and dray horses were sold in California. New Zealand profited from lumber sales to the Golden State. Chile, Peru, and Brazil benefited from Cape Horn voyagers, whose California-bound vessels stopped at their ports for supplies. In December 1850, for example, 12 American ships visited Brazil's Saint Catherine's Island. By 1856 British exports to California exceeded $2 million annually. That nation's economy profited greatly as wages rose faster than prices. French immigrant companies invested in California real estate, agriculture, and mining. German gold-seekers came in such numbers as to create a labor shortage in their homeland. New capital flowed into the Italian states, providing for the building of railroads and telegraph lines. In all of these nations and others as well commodity prices rose in the 1850s, in part due to California's and Australia's gold production. A gold strike in Peru in 1849–50, and full-scale rushes in South Africa in 1885 and the Yukon–Klondike region of Canada in 1897 were of shorter duration than the California phenomenon but, similarly, bolstered prices and fueled international economic growth.

In the gold rush era, then, California solidified its Pacific Eldorado stature and advanced as an important player in the global economy. Though prosperity was assured, whether

California could meet the challenges of statehood and the national crisis that lay ahead remained uncertain.

SUMMARY

The Mexican War and the gold rush following on its heels solidified California's status as America's West Coast Eldorado. As the Latin American wars for independence wound down in the early 1820s, the U.S. Navy beefed up its Pacific Squadron and included the California coast within its patrols. By the early 1840s the United States was poised to take California, as Thomas ap Catesby Jones's premature seizure of the province in 1842 showed. When President James K. Polk found that Mexico refused to sell California, he maneuvered America's neighbor to the south into a war that would bring the Pacific province into the Union. The resulting Mexican War was fought mostly outside of California but the region was the great prize for the victorious Americans, who formalized the cession of the province in the Treaty of Guadalupe–Hidalgo of 1848.

While that treaty was being negotiated an epic gold rush was about to begin near Sacramento. California's gold rush was basically a maritime phenomenon since so many miners and their equipment arrived by sea, and most of the gold transported elsewhere was carried in ships. Miners from throughout the Pacific Basin and much of the world made their way by sea and overland to the storied gold fields of the Sierra Nevada Mountains. William H. Aspinwall, co-founder and president of the Pacific Mail Steamship Company in 1848, which transported miners and gold, built that firm into America's largest maritime shipper, dominating the carrying trade of the Pacific world. Reflective of the violence in the mining camps, white gold-seekers raped and killed Indian prospectors, who within a few years left the diggings. The gold rush transformed San Francisco into a leading cosmopolitan city while inflating currencies and launching businesses throughout the Pacific Basin and the world. Though similar rushes occurred in Australia, Peru, South Africa, and Canada in the 1800s, none of these had impacts as lasting as California's.

REVIEW QUESTIONS

- Why did the U.S. Pacific Squadron begin patrolling California's coastline in the 1820s and increasingly thereafter?
- Why was President James K. Polk so intent on annexing California in the mid-1840s?
- What role(s) did the Pacific Mail Steamship Company play in shaping California history during the gold rush era?
- How numerically unbalanced were the genders in gold rush California? What were the results of this imbalance?
- What were the major international impacts of California's gold rush?

FURTHER READINGS

Charles Bateson, *Gold Fleet for California: Forty-Niners from Australia and New Zealand* (East Lansing, MI: Michigan State University Press, 1963). The strength of this work is that it combines maritime, economic, and social history into a compact narrative.

Peter J. Blodgett, *Land of Golden Dreams: California in the Gold Rush Decade, 1848–1858* (San Marino, CA: Henry E. Huntington Library and Art Gallery, 1999). This is a richly illustrated, wide-ranging, introductory account.

Robert J. Chandler and Stephen J. Potash, *Gold, Silk, Pioneers & Mail: The Story of the Pacific Mail Steamship Company* (San Francisco: Friends of the San Francisco Maritime Museum Library, 2007). The authors provide a useful introduction to the history of this important shipping firm.

James P. Delgado, *Gold Rush Port: The Maritime Archeology of San Francisco's Waterfront* (Berkeley: University of California Press, 2009). Based on the archeological study of shipwrecks and wharves, the author crafts an account of San Francisco's global connections during the gold rush era.

James P. Delgado, *To California by Sea: A Maritime History of the California Gold Rush* (Columbia, SC: University of South Carolina Press, 1990). This is a highly detailed, comprehensive study of voyaging to gold rush California.

Norman A. Graebner, *Empire on the Pacific: A Study in American Continental Expansion* (New York: Ronald Press, 1955). The author argues that President James K. Polk's expansionist policy derived from his determination to make America dominant in the trade of the Pacific.

Neal Harlow, *California Conquered: War and Peace on the Pacific, 1846–1850* (Berkeley: University of California Press, 1982). This is a highly detailed account of the California theater of the Mexican War.

John A. Hawgood, ed., *First and Last Consul: Thomas Oliver Larkin and the Americanization of California, A Selection of Letters* (Palo Alto, CA: Pacific Books, 1970). Larkin's correspondence offers a glimpse into the growing American interest in California just prior to statehood.

Albert L. Hurtado, *Indian Survival on the California Frontier* (New Haven, CT: Yale University Press, 1990). An authority examines how Indians survived the white invasion of their homelands in the 1800s, keeping much of their culture intact.

David Igler, "Alta California, the Pacific, and International Commerce before the Gold Rush," in William Deverell and David Igler, eds., *A Companion to California History* (Malden, MA: Wiley-Blackwell, 2008), 116–26. California's growing importance in Pacific commerce on the eve of the American takeover is treated in this essay.

Oakah L. Jones, Jr., "The Pacific Squadron and the Conquest of California, 1846–1847," *Journal of the West* (April 1966), 187–202. This article is one of very few scholarly treatments of the subject.

John H. Kemble, *The Panama Route, 1848–1869* (New York: Da Capo Press, 1972). This is a reprint of Kemble's earlier classic study on an important maritime dimension of the California gold rush.

Thomas M. Leonard, *James K. Polk: A Clear and Unquestionable Destiny* (Wilmington, DE: Scholarly Resources, 2001). President James K. Polk's skillful blending of aggressiveness, tact, and vision in directing foreign policy is highlighted in this concise political biography.

Joann Levy, *They Saw the Elephant: Women in the California Gold Rush* (Norman, OK: University of Oklahoma Press, 1992). Using diaries and other primary writings, the author tells the stories of gold rush women with wit and verve.

Oscar Lewis, *Sea Routes to the Gold Fields: The Migration by Water to California in 1849–1852* (New York: Alfred A. Knopf, 1949). While dated and short on bibliographic citations, this book is especially strong on narrating the experiences of passengers taking the Cape Horn route to San Francisco.

Aims McGuinness, *Path of Empire: Panama and the California Gold Rush* (Ithaca, NY: Cornell University Press, 2008). The author situates Panama's role in the gold rush in a transnational context, emphasizing U.S. and Latin American nation-building.

James J. Rawls and Richard J. Orsi, eds., *A Golden State: Mining and Economic Development in Gold Rush California* (Berkeley: University of California Press, 1999). This is an indispensable anthology of writings treating the technological and economic aspects of the gold rush in an international context.

Malcolm J. Rohrbough, *Days of Gold: The California Gold Rush and the American Nation* (Berkeley: University of California Press, 1997). A social history of the gold rush, this volume draws heavily from diaries and letters.

Ralph J. Roske, "The World Impact of the California Gold Rush, 1849–1857," *Arizona and the West*, 55/3 (Autumn 1963), 187–232. This is one of the few comprehensive, published monographs on the gold rush in global perspective.

John H. Schroeder, *Shaping a Maritime Empire: The Commercial and Diplomatic Role of the American Navy, 1829–1861* (Westport, CT: Greenwood Press, 1985). The role of the U.S. Navy as a protector of maritime trade is stressed in this work.

Kevin Starr and Richard J. Orsi, eds., *Rooted in a Barbarous Soil: People, Culture, and Community in Gold Rush California* (Berkeley: University of California Press, 2000). This anthology focuses on the migratory, ethnic, demographic, and cultural dimensions of the gold rush.

5

National Crisis, Statehood, and Social Change

From the rush of 1849 to the end of the Civil War in 1865 and its immediate after-math, America faced the crisis of disunion and the challenge of social change. The crisis was aggravated by the prospect of slavery spreading westward to the continent's Pacific shores. Though geographically far removed from the states and territories usually associated with the North–South divide, California, nonetheless, could not escape the strife-ridden prelude of the sectional showdown. During the ensuing Civil War, the Golden State's role was mainly maritime in nature and scope. The forces of national disunion, coupled with major demographic shifts in California, especially large-scale Chinese immigration, set the context within which the new state would struggle to build a viable civil government and ordered society. Aside from absorbing large numbers of Chinese, racial relations involving other ethnic groups as well compounded the challenges facing the state. In the 1850s and 1860s California's population, adventurers in foreign lands, and commercial interests reflected a strong and growing orientation toward the Pacific Basin.

Pacific Eldorado: A History of Greater California, First Edition. Thomas J. Osborne.
© 2013 Thomas J. Osborne. Published 2013 by Blackwell Publishing Ltd.

Timeline

1849	48 delegates attend California's constitutional convention held in Colton Hall, Monterey; the constitution requires that "all laws, decrees, regulations, and provisions" be published in both English and Spanish, thereby mandating an early bilingualism in governance; the constitution is approved later that year by voters in a referendum; state officers are elected
	The first legislature convenes in San José; two members of the U.S. Senate are elected
	Captain Henry Halleck's report on Mexican land claims in California concludes that most of the claims had not been supported by documentation, and that many were fraudulent
1850	Attorney William Carey Jones's report, authorized by the U.S. secretary of the interior, holds that most of the Mexican claims constituted "perfect titles," meaning they are complete regarding documentation
	With Congressional passage of the Omnibus Bill, California is admitted to the Union as a free state, meaning slavery is disallowed
	About 15,000 Californios inhabit the state, among a total population of 92,597 people
	The California legislature approves the Act for the Government and Protection of Indians, according to which unemployed adult Indians are subject to prosecution for vagrancy, in which case the courts can hire them out; Indian boys until 18 and girls until 15 can be apprenticed to employers under conditions similar to enslavement, beginning with the bidding at auction for the services of these youths
1851	Congress passes the (William M.) Gwin Land Act authorizing the president to appoint a three-member commission to investigate and decide Mexican land grant claims, with a provision for appealing decisions through the federal courts
	Amid rising crime and gang violence, San Francisco establishes its First Committee of Vigilance
	San Francisco's Sam Brannan leads filibustering expedition to Hawai'i for the purpose of seizing the islands
1852	The California legislature enacts a fugitive slave law
1852–3	Hysteria grips the public concerning what is believed to be Joaquín Murieta's robberies and murders of Chinese and others in and around Calaveras County
1853	California Superintendent of Indian Affairs Edward F. Beale conceives a plan for reservations that is applied in the West
1854	In *People v. Hall*, the California supreme court holds that Chinese, being similar to Indians in that they are of Asian origin, cannot witness in legal proceedings against a white
1855	California filibusterer William Walker organizes American mercenaries for an armed takeover of the government of Nicaragua
1856	In response to several publicized killings, a second vigilance committee is organized in San Francisco
	Onetime U.S. Senator for California John C. Frémont becomes the Republican Party's first presidential candidate
1858	The California supreme court rules against granting freedom to black man Archie Lee despite the fact that slavery has been outlawed in the state
1859	California supreme court Chief Justice David S. Terry kills David C. Broderick in a duel, inflaming state Democratic politics for years afterward

1860	In an unprovoked attack, whites kill 60 Indians, mostly women and children, living on an island in Humboldt Bay
	California filibusterer William Walker is captured by the British and turned over to Hondurans, who execute him before a firing squad
1862	Congress passes and President Abraham Lincoln signs the Pacific Railroad Act, providing for the construction of America's first transcontinental railroad and accompanying telegraph system; these measures are aimed at linking California's economic well-being to the northern, pro-Union states
	A Union fort is built next to the town of El Monte to guard southern California against a possible Confederate-led insurrection
1863	A secessionist conspiracy to send arms to the Confederacy aboard the schooner *J.M. Chapman* is thwarted in San Francisco Bay by U.S. Navy officials from the U.S.S. *Cyane*
1864	The Modocs are relocated from their northern California homeland to southern Oregon, where they are forced to share a reservation with their enemies, the Klamaths
1865	The Confederate raider Shenandoah attacks Pacific whalers and merchantmen sailing to and from California's coast
1872–3	The Modoc War marks the last Indian armed conflict against whites in the state

A Constitution, a Legislature, a State

Extreme turmoil best describes California in 1849. Overrun with gold-seekers and faced with mounting violence in the mining camps and nearby towns, some Americans in San José, Monterey, and Sacramento urged military governor Bennett Riley to organize a government. Generally, Congress had overseen the process whereby the federal government acquired territories that, after meeting certain requirements, were admitted to statehood. Caught in the crossfire of sectional politics and stymied by the thorny issue of slavery's status in the Mexican land cession of 1848, Congress failed to provide a governing structure for California in 1849. For good reason, Riley exceeded his authority and called for the election of delegates to attend a constitutional convention to accomplish that task. Next, a legislature was established, followed by statehood.

Monterey, a principal Pacific port and the capital of early California, served as the site of the six-week convention that wrote the constitution of 1849. In Colton Hall, beginning September 1, 48 delegates assembled: 37 represented northern districts, 11 came from southern districts; 14 were lawyers, 11 were farmers, none were miners; 8 were Californios, 6 were European-born immigrants. The Californios included Pablo de la Guerra, José Carrillo, and Mariano Vallejo. Pre-Mexican War Anglo settler delegates included Thomas O. Larkin, Abel Stearns, and convention president Robert B. Semple. Apropos of the times, there were no women, Native Americans, African Americans, or Asians among the constitution-writers. English was spoken, with translators for the delegates who only spoke Spanish. Moreover, the resulting constitution required that "all laws, decrees, regulations, and provisions" be published in both English and Spanish, thereby mandating an early bilingualism in governance.

Attendees looked to the constitutions of Iowa and New York for guidance, and generally divided on the key issues along north–south lines. Their major concerns included whether California would be a state or a territory, how to handle slavery, who should receive citizenship, where the eastern boundary should be drawn, and the property rights of married women. Delegates from southern California favored territorial status because they correctly feared that the landowners in and around Los Angeles would carry a disproportionate tax burden under statehood. By majority vote statehood won. Led by William E. Shannon, delegates from both the northern and southern reaches of California decided to disallow slavery. While moral considerations were not entirely absent, the determining factor was that attendees did not want non-slaveholding gold miners to have to compete with gangs of chattel workers. Such competition was thought to be unfair and would "degrade [white] labor." As in the United States as a whole, citizenship was extended to whites only. Californios fell within that category. With citizenship went voting rights. Accordingly, the constitution affirmed that the suffrage could be exercised by "every white, male citizen of Mexico who shall have elected to become a citizen of the United States." Indians, but not African Americans, could be given voting rights in the future if both houses of the state legislature passed, by a two-thirds vote, a measure to that effect. Besides women and non-whites, voting was also denied to "idiots," "insane persons," and those convicted of "any infamous crime."

The eastern boundary issue aroused considerable debate at the convention. Some delegates wished to include parts of today's Nevada, Arizona, and Utah, as all of these areas fell within the Mexican cession contained in the 1848 Treaty of Guadalupe–Hidalgo. Delegate Charles T. Botts responded sarcastically: "Why not indirectly settle it [the eastern boundary controversy] by extending your limits to the Mississippi [River]? Why not include the island of Cuba?" The sense of the majority was that land east of the Sierra Nevada was mainly desert and of little value. Consequently, the constitution-writers settled on the present eastern boundary, which basically follows the length of the Sierra Nevada range. (See Chapter 1 for a detailed explanation.)

Delegates deliberated on the property of married women. Spanish and Mexican law recognized the separate property of women both before and during marriage. Under English common law, which prevailed throughout much of the United States, upon marriage a woman's property was transferred to her husband. According to Botts, "the God of nature made women frail, lovely and dependent . . . the only despotism on earth that I would advocate is the despotism of the husband." Botts was answered by Henry Wager Halleck, who argued pragmatically that by protecting the property rights of female spouses the delegates could not "offer a greater inducement for women of fortune to come to California." Halleck's call for adopting the Spanish–Mexican legal precedent in this matter carried. California, thereby, became the first state to safeguard constitutionally the separate property rights of married women.

Besides these specific issues, the framers included in their document a more philosophical statement regarding individual rights. Among these was the right of "pursuing and obtaining safety and happiness." This was truly novel, particularly the *achievement* and not merely the pursuit of happiness. No other state constitution contained such a promise. Some authorities, for good reason, view this feature of the charter as characteristically Californian.

Reminiscent of the outsized vision of citizen happiness, the delegates not only accepted federal land grants for support of public schools, a standard procedure for new states, but went a step beyond and anticipated the founding of a university. Such an institution was thought necessary "for the promotion of literature, the arts and sciences."

Before adjourning, conventioneers adopted a state seal. The Great Seal of the State of California brims with lofty aims and hopes. In the foreground it features Minerva, the Roman goddess of wisdom and the arts, who sprang fully formed from Jupiter's head – a reference to California's bid to bypass territorial status in favor of immediate statehood. A grizzly bear crouches at her feet, while nearby a prospector wields a pick, and ships and isles dot San Francisco Bay. Hillsides and snow-sprinkled Sierra peaks form the background. Inscribed above this idyllic scene is the Greek motto "Eureka," meaning "I have found it." An arc of 31 stars, indicating California's position in the order of statehood, graces the upper reaches of the design.

The constitution was approved by voters in a referendum on November 13, 1849: 12,061 in favor, 811 opposed. Argentina's leaders were so impressed with the document that it became the model for their nation's constitution of 1853. With a charter in hand, California's lawmakers set about completing a governmental framework for America's first Pacific state.

On the same day as the referendum, elections were held for the state's first officeholders. Peter H. Burnett won the governorship; John McDougal became lieutenant governor. The

Figure 5.1 The great seal of the state of California. Photo Atlaspix / Shutterstock.com.

first legislature convened in San José, on December 15. The two houses of the legislature, the senate and assembly, elected John C. Frémont and William M. Gwin to the U.S. Senate. Audaciously, Californians established the apparatus of a state government without statehood. In short, lacking Congressional approval, decisions made in San José meant little if anything.

Undaunted, the first legislature went about its business. Locating a permanent capital proved elusive, as rival towns put in their bids. From 1849 to 1854 the capital shifted six times, mainly around San Francisco Bay among San José, Vallejo, Benicia, and finally the river and Pacific port city of Sacramento, which became the permanent seat of state government, due mainly to its central location, influential advocates, and access to the sea. Legislators gained greater traction on such policy issues as organizing local and county governments, establishing law enforcement agencies, and collecting revenues. Despite such achievements, many of the delegates remained fixated on their narrowest political interests, and repaired to a local saloon often enough to be dubbed "The Legislature of a Thousand Drinks."

Congress's decision on statehood was entangled in sectional and partisan disputes ultimately tied to the slavery question. As that question became increasingly divisive, states were admitted to the Union in pairs so as to ensure an equal balance between those allowing and those prohibiting slavery. Importantly, this method prevented either the North or South from gaining a numerical advantage in the Senate. California's admission would tip the nation's sectional balance in favor of the non-slaveholding northern tier of states. Southerners in Congress would not allow that, unless in so doing they could receive compensatory concessions.

Thanks to the wits of Kentucky Senator Henry Clay and others, the impasse was broken by a political bargain between leading Whigs and Democrats: the Compromise of 1850. Incorporated into the so-called Omnibus Bill, the compromise provided for: (1) California's admission into the Union as a free state; (2) the organization of Utah and New Mexico as territories that could decide locally whether to allow slavery when they applied for statehood; (3) the termination of the sale of slaves (but not the ending of slavery itself) in Washington, D.C., and a stronger federal fugitive slave law. On September 9, 1850, the Omnibus Bill became law, granting California statehood.

Land Disputes and Independence Movements

California's politics, always fractious, were extremely so in the 1850s. Litigation and uncertainty over land titles led to prolonged strife. Controversy also arose from southern Californians' bona fide objections to paying a disproportionate share of taxes, compared to northern residents, while being underrepresented in the state legislature. Then, too, the growing North–South divide in national politics fueled sentiment among some Californians to dodge the crisis of the Union by somehow transforming the new state into an independent Pacific republic.

No issue in the new state was more complex and contentious than that of dealing with land claims in the aftermath of the American takeover of California. Most of the contested land lay in coastal valleys located as far north as the Russian River. Large tracts also existed in the Sacramento and San Joaquin valleys. The Treaty of Guadalupe–Hidalgo promised that Mexican "property of every kind" in the ceded territory would be "inviolably respected" by U.S. laws and officials. Such property, the bulk of which was in the form of huge land grants, was claimed by a relatively small number of Californios. American settlers rejected the idea that some 13 million acres of undeveloped grazing land should be held by several hundred rancheros, the majority of whom had received their tracts within the five years prior to the U.S. takeover. For example, the Pico family claimed 532,000 acres of land. Moreover, purported Mexican deeds often referenced vague boundaries, as indicated in the frequently used expression *poco más o menos* ("a little more or less"). Maps, when they existed, offered little help as they lacked the precision of a survey. Mexican record-keeping, by American standards, was slipshod, and there were no archives housing documents that could prove the legitimacy of Hispanic deeds. For all of these reasons, Mexican claimants faced major hurdles in securing land titles.

Mindful of the uncertainties involved, Governor Richard B. Mason commissioned Captain Henry Halleck to investigate the Mexican land claims in order to determine their legitimacy. His report, submitted in 1849, concluded that most of the claims had not been supported by documentation, and that many were fraudulent. News of these findings emboldened American settlers who had been occupying some of the contested lands. These so-called "squatters" rioted in Sacramento in 1850, insisting on their right to acquire parcels from unproven Mexican claims. Manifest Destiny, that is, the belief that God had given North America's landmass to the United States' white citizens, pervaded the thinking of Anglo settlers.

Armed with Heaven's sanction, it is little wonder that American squatters did not back a second land inquiry, this one authorized by the secretary of the interior and conducted by attorney William Carey Jones. Jones's report, issued in March 1850, held that most of the Mexican claims constituted "perfect titles," meaning they were complete regarding documentation.

Ultimately, U.S. settlement of the resulting disputes rested on a law introduced in Congress by California Senator William M. Gwin. As passed, the Gwin Act provided for the president's appointment of a board consisting of three commissioners. They would determine the validity of all land claims proffered by the Mexican grantees. Rejected claims would become the property of the federal government. Both grantees and the United States had the right to appeal a decision to the federal district court, and even to the U.S. Supreme Court.

The board deliberated in San Francisco and Los Angeles from January 1852 to March 1856. Of the approximately 800 cases it reviewed, 604 claims (involving some 9 million acres) were upheld, while 209 claims (involving nearly 4 million acres) were denied. On average, cases took 17 years to resolve. The 4 square leagues pueblo grant on which the City of San Francisco was situated was not confirmed until 1866. Land claim proceedings left nearly all parties, except the attorneys, poorer than they had expected to be. One historian estimates that lawyers extracted fees amounting to between 25 and 40 percent of the value of the land. Many of the grantees whose claims were upheld found that after such a lengthy litigation period squatters had settled on the disputed tracts and had to be removed by private police. Grantees who lost their cases often became embittered if not impoverished. Ranchera Apolinaria Lorenzano, a dispossessed one-time owner of three tracts, lamented: "I find myself in the greatest poverty, living by the favor of God and from handouts."

Successful land claimants faced a new system of state taxation and representation not to their liking. Under this regimen, the revenue burden fell more heavily on the so-called cow counties in the Southland than on the mining counties to the north. This was because a state law exempted from taxation mines located on federal property, leaving cattle ranchers in the south with large tax liabilities based on their extensive holdings of land and livestock. Yet, the same under-taxed mining counties had more legislators in the state capital than did the high-taxed cow counties.

This unfair situation sparked movements in southern California for separation. In 1859 the state legislature approved a measure supported by a majority of voters in the southern counties calling for the division of California into two sections, the southern part incorporating the counties from San Luis Obispo south and eastward into the Territory of Colorado. The measure reflected the wishes of Hispanic rancheros to shape their own society without undue influence from northern California Anglos. Preoccupied with the growing threat of civil war, Congress took no action on the separation measure, which some of its members wrongly saw as an attempt to extend slavery.

Others in the new state wanted to take matters even further. The idea of forming an independent Pacific republic can be traced at least as far back as the Bear Flag Revolt. Throughout the 1850s, whenever Californians felt a strong need for better mail service, protection from Indians, and more ports of entry, some voices called for creating a separate nation. California Governor John Weller, for example, supported the creation of "a mighty republic" on the Pacific, "which may in the end prove the greatest of all" as a way to escape choosing between the Northern and the Southern states in the growing national divide. California's commercial ties with the northern tier of states, however, helped ensure that the state remained intact and pro-Union.

Vigilance Committees and Untamed Politicians

California's first decade of statehood was stormy. Besides land disputes and independence movements, the new state contended with vigilance groups, political violence, and military adventurers, called "filibusterers," interfering in Latin American and Pacific island affairs.

As in the mining camps, California's cities in the mid-nineteenth century had yet to develop a credible system for administering justice through law enforcement. Again, as in the camps, citizens took matters into their own hands. These "vigilantes" (from a Spanish word meaning "guards"), often led by city merchants, arrested, tried, and summarily punished those they convicted of crimes. Punishments ranged from whippings to ear-cropping, branding, and even hanging. Convictions could not be appealed, nor could clemency be granted.

While California's first vigilante committee was formed in Los Angeles in 1836, San Francisco, with its own violent crime problem, soon took center stage in that regard.

San Francisco's lawlessness was largely the handiwork of a disbanded New York regiment, variously called the Regulators or Hounds, led by Lieutenant Sam Roberts. Originally formed to capture runaway seamen, the Hounds became thugs who ran a protection racket, shaking down city storeowners. They portrayed themselves as guardians of public order, in the course of which they hounded Latinos and other foreigners out of California. A notorious instance of this occurred on the evening of July 15, 1849, when they attacked a Chileno encampment in San Francisco, robbing and beating their victims, and murdering a mother and raping her daughter. San Franciscans were furious. Sam Brannan led some 230 militiamen who arrested 20 of the perpetrators, tried them, and meted out punishments of fines, prison, and deportation. Still, problems persisted. The Sydney Ducks, a gang of Australian ex-convicts, sometimes joined the Hounds, who continued to brutalize foreigners and others. In the wake of a beating of a prominent downtown merchant in February 1851 and several fires that smacked of arson, William Tell Coleman and Brannan organized San Francisco's first Committee of Vigilance in the latter's office on June 9.

The following day it took custody of John Jenkins, who had been caught stealing a small safe. Jenkins threatened his captors with reprisal from his friends, which doubtlessly steeled the resolve of the committee to punish him quickly. A crowd that had gathered in the plaza that same day witnessed with approval the trial and moonlight hanging of Jenkins. Thus the first person apprehended by the committee was executed within hours of committing a relatively minor crime. In July the committee caught Australian James Stuart, who had escaped the Marysville jail, where he had been incarcerated for the murder of a sheriff. The committee hanged Stuart after securing a confession from him, and in August lynched two more Sydney Ducks, whom Stuart's testimony had implicated in robberies.

In September the committee, having learned that hundreds of known criminals had left California and others had gone into hiding, ceased its operations. The final tally of its activities included: nearly 90 arrests, 4 hangings, 1 whipping, 28 deportation sentences, 15 turned over to authorities, and 41 released. Five years later, before a legal infrastructure of courts, attorneys, and regard for "rule of law" became sufficiently robust in San Francisco, the citizenry would once again take the law into its own hands.

Meanwhile, San Francisco's example of vigilante activity influenced other communities throughout American California. In the mining town of Downieville a Mexican woman, Josepha Segovia (called Juanita), became the focus and victim of a clash between cultures and sexes. Beginning on the evening of July 4, 1851, and continuing into the early morning hours of the next day the town's citizenry partied in the aftermath of Independence Day speeches and festivities. Sometime the next morning Josepha killed one of the revelers, Joseph Cannon, who had forcefully entered her adobe hut the night before. Cannon's friends testified that he had returned only to apologize for having broken down her door in his drunkenness the preceding night. A witness for Josepha, on the other hand, stated that Cannon, on his return, had called her a "whore." Juanita claimed that Cannon wanted "to sleep with me." Fearing rape, she pulled out a knife and stabbed Cannon to death. News quickly reached Downieville and a mob soon assembled, chanting "Hang the greaser devils!" Despite her explanation, which may not have been understood by the angry crowd of onlookers, that the killing was in self-defense, she died on the scaffold on July 5. Justice, if that is what it could be called, was swift but assuredly not color-blind.

Wilder and smaller than San Francisco, Los Angeles, too, was the scene of vigilante activity in the early years of statehood. The mayor and city council organized a vigilance committee in 1851. Among those it hanged were three men convicted of murdering Major General J.H. Bean. The innocence of one of the three was proved later.

San Francisco's vigilance committee of 1856 was larger and better organized than its predecessor of 1851. By 1856 a powerful urban merchant class, generally distrustful of the city's Irish Catholic-led Democratic officialdom, recoiled at the shooting deaths of General William Richardson and of the editor of the *Daily Evening Bulletin* newspaper, James King of William (so named to distinguish him from others named James King in Washington, D.C., his birth city).

Richardson's murder resulted from a confrontation on the occasion of the opening of the American Theater in November 1855. The general's wife complained about being seated in close proximity to gambler Charles Cora and his mistress, the madam of a notorious brothel. Two nights later, Richardson exchanged heated words with Cora at the Blue Wing saloon. Cora, later claiming that Richardson had reached for a gun, drew his own pistol and fired, killing the general. The gambler was immediately arrested by police.

While Cora sat in jail awaiting trial, King editorially attacked James Casey, who had recently won election to the San Francisco county board of supervisors. Casey was known to be part of the state's reputedly corrupt Democratic regime, headed by David Broderick. When King revealed in the *Bulletin* that Casey had been imprisoned in New York's Sing Sing prison, the latter shot and killed the editor in the street.

On the day of the shooting, William Tell Coleman, a San Francisco merchant whose fleet of clipper ships amassed him a fortune in maritime trading, organized the Committee of Vigilantes of 1856. The group included many of the city's leading businesspersons. The fact that some equally prominent citizens formed the Law and Order Party, to counter the vigilantes, shows that the rule of law had by then secured a strong foothold in the developing city. Nevertheless, four days after the shooting of King 2,500 armed vigilantes stormed the county jail, apprehending Cora and Casey. On the day of King's funeral, the committee publicly hanged both men.

Nicknaming their headquarters Fort Gunnybags, the committee held together for three months, virtually displacing the city's law enforcement officials. Appeals from Law and Order advocates, so called because they insisted on courtroom trials and due process, resulted in Governor J. Neely Johnson proclaiming San Francisco to be in insurrection. After a few violent altercations between vigilantes and Law and Order men, led by state Supreme Court Justice David S. Terry, the committee disbanded in August 1856. In its three months of operations, it had hung four accused murderers, including Cora and Casey, and issued deportation orders to 30 others, warning that execution awaited any returnees. Most historians agree that California's vigilantism must be understood within the context of the violent times: one observer noted that more than half of the members of the first state legislature in 1850 appeared for their duties "with revolvers and bowie knives fastened to their belts." Most also agree that vigilantes shortchanged due process.

A number of politicians, like vigilantes and gangs, remained untamed in the 1850s. The most publicized instance of this was the Gwin–Broderick feud. Both were Democrats who had come to California in 1849 to get elected to the U.S. Senate. So end their similarities.

David C. Broderick was 29 when he arrived in California, after doing his political apprenticeship in New York City's corrupt Tammany Hall machine. Fifteen years younger than his rival, William M. Gwin, Broderick had little formal education, spoke against slavery, and was impulsive by temperament. He became San Francisco's first major political boss, and led the Free Soil wing of the Democratic Party statewide. That faction opposed the extension of slavery into the western territories. In 1850 Broderick won a state senate seat, thereby positioning himself for a U.S. Senate bid in the near future. Gwin, on the other hand, had been a Congressperson from Mississippi, and was a well-educated lawyer with proslavery views, though he voted to ban servitude in California at the 1849 constitutional convention. He led the Chivalry or "Shiv" faction of the state's Democratic Party.

The intraparty feud erupted in 1854 when Broderick began jockeying to replace Gwin as U.S. Senator. Gwin's term would expire the following year and he sought reelection. One year before the 1855 election the two rivals became so deadlocked in their respective bids for the Democratic nomination that neither prevailed, nor could anyone else run. Consequently, one of California's two Senate seats remained vacant for two years.

The feud so paralyzed the Democrats that the Know-Nothings briefly gained control of the state's government. They constituted a national party, and were so called because when people inquired about their agenda, party members replied that they knew nothing. The aim of the Know-Nothings was to stop the flow of immigrants, especially the Chinese, into the United States. A strain of anti-Catholicism, usually played down, was also in evidence among party members.

In 1857 both of California's U.S. Senate seats were open, and members of that chamber were selected by state legislatures. One of those two seats, however, came with only a four-year term, instead of the prescribed six years. This was because two years earlier, as noted, one California seat went unfilled. Broderick used all of his tricks and leverage in the party to bully Gwin into agreeing to run for the four-year seat, leaving the six-year seat available for himself. For instance, Gwin was made to promise that he would not seek any federal appointments for his supporters; otherwise, Broderick would use his influence to prevent Gwin from even receiving the four-year Senate term. When President James Buchanan learned of Broderick's schemes, he gave prized government positions to Gwin's supporters, rejecting Broderick's recommendations for office and thereby incensing him. In a Senate speech, Broderick lashed out at both Buchanan and Gwin, attacking the president for supporting a proslavery government in the Kansas Territory. The extent to which Broderick's criticisms were based on principle, as opposed to his own shameless ambition, remains uncertain.

The clash between the two Senate aspirants entered its final stage in the California elections of 1859, though the political fallout would continue for years afterward. Those in the Broderick camp referred to themselves as Douglas Democrats (Democrat Stephen Douglas authored an 1854 measure giving Kansans and Nebraskans the opportunity to block the spread of slavery within their jurisdictions when they applied for statehood). Still, the Gwin faction won most of the state offices. Shortly after the election, former California Supreme Court Chief Justice David S. Terry challenged Broderick to a duel for having denounced him publicly during the recent election, in which Terry lost his campaign to remain on the court after the imminent expiration of his old term. On September 13, 1859, the two met in a San Mateo County ravine to settle matters with their pistols. Broderick's bullet missed its mark, while Terry's lodged in Broderick's chest, killing him and any chances of reconciliation between the opposing sides in California's Democratic Party. The pro-southern views of the Gwin faction were not shared by the majority of the state's electorate before the duel; this was even more the case after Broderick's "martyrdom" to the antislavery cause.

Pacific Filibusterers

In the 1850s, Californians' disregard for domestic law, as seen in vigilantism, was mirrored in breaches of international law as well. Such breaches were evidenced in the many unauthorized, illegal, and aggressive expeditions on the part of the state's filibustering citizens in foreign countries throughout the Pacific Basin. Filibustering was not uniquely a Californian phenomenon; adventurers from other states as well were involved. Yet the Golden State assuredly had more than its share of intruders on foreign soil. Nearly all of the state's filibustering exploits were launched from San Francisco and were of a maritime nature, occurring in areas accessed by Pacific waters. These areas included Sonora, Baja California, Hawai'i, Central America, and Ecuador. Though not necessarily intending to extend the state's influence across borders and into these areas, filibusterers nevertheless had the effect of doing just that – in a sense, fashioning a greater California.

Joseph C. Morehead was California's first filibusterer. As a former military supply officer, he had access to surplus goods, including the ship *Josephine*. In the spring of 1851 he sailed southward with some 200 men to La Paz, expecting to seize Mexican land for the United States. After engaging in some trading there, his force dispersed. A second attachment of Morehead's men traveled overland through Los Angeles toward the Sonora frontier. It, too, disbanded. Morehead, himself, led a third, seaborne, contingent headed for Mazatlán that narrowly escaped arrest in San Diego. Mexican officials awaited him, though on arrival they found no weapons or munitions aboard Morehead's vessel. Nothing came of the ill-fated venture.

In November 1851, San Francisco filibusterers again targeted Sonora. This time 88 Frenchmen from that city sailed for the Mexican harbor at Guaymas, on the Sea of Cortés. The anchorage was a gateway to the Sonora frontier. On arriving they established a mining and agricultural colony, which aimed also at pacifying the Apache, who soon ran off with the colony's livestock. The settlement dissolved, only to be succeeded by another venture involving San Franciscan Frenchmen. Still looking for a colony to buffer Apache attacks and invest in a French mining enterprise, some Mexican officials in Sonora again invited French filibusterers in San Francisco to establish a settlement in their frontier province. The Mexican population of the province was not pleased about this seeming foreign invasion. In 1852, 240 or so filibusterers disembarked at Guaymas, and marched headlong into strong resistance from Sonorans. Count Gaston de Raousset-Boulbon, the French group's reckless leader, thereafter shuttled between Guaymas, San Francisco, and Mexico City, preparing for yet another incursion. This time he sailed southward to Mexico with 400 men aboard an overloaded schooner. Their defeat in the Battle of Guaymas on July 13, 1854, dealt the final blow to French filibustering from California.

In November 1851 Sam Brannan of San Francisco led a filibustering expedition of some 25 Californians, who sailed aboard the clipper *Game Cock* to Hawai'i. They believed false rumors that King Kamehameha III wanted to abdicate and sell his kingdom. News of their plans leaked out. At the request of the Hawaiian cabinet, the warship U.S.S. *Vandalia* was kept at Honolulu to defend the island kingdom against the California filibusterers. The intruders found that the king would not see them, native Hawaiians would not help them, and American whalers in the islands opposed their plans. The undertaking ended in a fiasco. During the next three years a number of Californians immigrated to Hawai'i. Officials in the islands viewed these arrivals as restless, ambitious men with revolution in mind. Their presence probably contributed to the ongoing rumors buzzing about Hawai'i of new filibustering expeditions being outfitted in California.

While the credibility of such rumors remains doubtful, what is certain is that in the early 1850s some Golden State members of Congress urged the American annexation of Hawai'i to defend the West Coast and, especially, advance the California–Pacific–China trade. California Representative J.W. McCorkle, for example, stated in a House speech on November 22, 1852: "It is essential to our Pacific interests that we should have the possession of the Sandwich Islands [as they were often called then], and upon this point the people of California will speak with one voice." By the 1850s, in short, filibustering was merely one link in an ever-growing California–Hawai'i connection.

Perhaps the most publicized of California's filibustering expeditions were those of William Walker in Central America. The so-called "grey-eyed man of destiny," Walker practiced both medicine and law in the South before relocating to San Francisco, from where he launched a number of forays into lands south of the border. Though he intruded in Baja California and Sonora, his name is most closely linked with Nicaragua, where from 1855 to 1857 he attempted to establish himself as a dictator. His original force of 56 armed men eventually grew to over 2,000 American mercenaries who heeded his promise of pay and land bonuses. Transportation magnate Cornelius Vanderbilt employed Walker's army briefly in hopes of stabilizing Nicaragua's politics sufficiently for Vanderbilt and his business partners to rake in profits from their shipping and rail transit service across the Central American nation. When Walker proved conniving and unreliable, Vanderbilt aided disaffected Nicaraguans in overthrowing him in the so-called revolution of 1857. Undaunted, the filibusterer made two attempts to retake the country. Both failed, followed by his capture off the coast of Honduras by a British sea captain who turned him over to the Hondurans. On September 12, 1860, they summarily shot and killed him.

A few years earlier, farther southward along Latin America's Pacific Coast, a band of Californians intervened in Ecuador's politics. A former president of that nation, Juan José Flores, had been overthrown, and in 1852 he attempted to regain his office. Forty or so Californians voyaged to that troubled land to reinstate Flores. An explosion aboard their vessel took the lives of half of the force, and the venture thereafter petered out.

So ended some but by no means all of the inglorious escapades of Californians in foreign parts of the Pacific region. In the mid-nineteenth century few, if any, other states had populations as restless at home and as meddlesome abroad as California. Meanwhile, a great clash of arms was about to erupt on America's eastern seaboard. Though distant from where the battles would be waged, California's role in the impending hostilities would be consequential.

California, the Pacific, and the Civil War

Rarely do historians' accounts of the Civil War give much coverage to California's role, or to that of Pacific developments, in that epic conflict. The fact that no major battles were fought on the West Coast perhaps makes this understandable. Moreover, some writers of California history claim that there was little, if any, chance that the state would join the Confederacy. They may be right; however, as in the first instance, hindsight has obscured the immediacy of the historical moment as felt and attested to by contemporaries. To state residents and Union and Confederate officials in their respective capitals, California and the Pacific Coast figured importantly in both the approach to war and military operations after hostilities commenced in 1861. Similarly, the state's loyalty to the Union seemed less assured to contemporaries than it does to some historians in our own time. The state's politics during the 1860s shifted with the onset, course, and outcome of the war.

Though the federal government did not extend the draft to California, about 16,000 men in the state volunteered and served the Union in what some historians have termed "The Army of the Pacific." Some did garrison duty along western routes to the Northeast, but most remained in the state. These garrison forces relieved army regulars, who were then ordered eastward to augment Union forces. The "California Hundred" and the "California Battalion" were absorbed into the Second Massachusetts Cavalry. A "California Column" had been ordered to secure the New Mexico frontier from an expected Confederate attack that was repelled before the coastal contingent arrived.

San Francisco Unitarian minister Thomas Starr King singlehandedly raised $1,233,831.31 for the Sanitary Commission (forerunner of the Red Cross), more than a quarter of the total amount received by that agency. Arriving in San Francisco by an oceanic steamer from New York, King's eloquent speeches and writings on behalf of the Union went far toward sustaining morale among the state's supporters of the North. He portrayed California as integral to God's plan of uniting the Atlantic and Pacific coasts, and all of the land between (including the South), into a continent-wide nation. To King, California's role in the Civil War took on mystical, cosmic dimensions.

The Golden State's Civil War involvements are especially evident in maritime matters. Cheering crowds gathered at dockside San Francisco to see the California Hundred sail through the Golden Gate en route to Boston to aid Union forces. The U.S. Navy was sufficiently concerned about California secessionists gaining a foothold on the Baja peninsula to order three of the Pacific Squadron's six warships to police the coasts of Mexico and the Golden State. The Lincoln administration's greatest Pacific maritime concern, however, was safeguarding the waterborne shipments of gold from California to Panama. California's gold, according to Howard R. Lamar's *The New Encyclopedia of the American West*, was "indispensable in bolstering the North financially." During the war more than $173 million in California gold and Nevada silver reportedly passed through San Francisco's Golden

Figure 5.2 Painting by an unknown artist of the U.S.S. *Cyane*, a Pacific Squadron vessel policing the Pacific Coast. MacMullen Collection D11.22000. Courtesy of the San Francisco Maritime Historical Park, J. Porter Shaw Library.

Gate en route to Panama by sea, and from there to Washington, D.C. These precious metals were carried aboard the Pacific Mail's treasure steamers.

Two maritime developments involving California attest to the Confederacy's efforts to prosecute the war along the Golden State's Pacific Coast. The first of these concerned a secessionist conspiracy to equip the schooner *J.M. Chapman*, anchored in San Francisco Bay, with war matériel in order to prey on Pacific Mail treasure steamers. Local authorities had been keeping a close watch on the vessel and its provisioning. Moments after it had left its dock on the morning of March 15, 1863, the Pacific Squadron's U.S.S. *Cyane* overtook the privateer, and U.S. naval officials boarded her. They arrested the armed crew and confiscated incriminating documents outlining plans for a Confederate seizure of San Francisco's forts and Alcatraz Island. Instead of seizing Alcatraz, some of the crewmen – after being tried and convicted of treason – were imprisoned there.

A second development involved attacks of the Confederate raider *Shenandoah* on Pacific whalers and merchantmen. While voyaging toward San Francisco, the Rebel ship had sunk a number of vessels sailing from that harbor in the spring of 1865. News of these sinkings, and exaggerated fears of others to come, spread alarm from San Diego to Puget Sound, prompting surveillances and the erection of coastal fortifications. While still in North Pacific waters, the *Shenandoah*'s commander, James Waddell, received news from a British ship departing San Francisco that the South had surrendered, which caused him to drop plans to attack that port and complete a circumnavigation of the globe. Maritime developments like those just described help explain why seaboard Californians felt that the Civil War involved them.

Despite the pro-Union stance of Civil War governors John Downey and Leland Stanford, and the majority of Californians, strong pockets of pro-Confederacy sentiment existed in the state, mainly in the Central Valley and southern counties. The towns of Visalia, Los Angeles, El Monte, and San Bernardino harbored such pro-South secret societies as the Knights of the Golden Circle, the Knights of the Columbian Star, and the Committee of Thirty. The *Los Angeles Star* newspaper openly supported the Confederacy. At the port of San Pedro, Union officers intercepted a cache of arms sent by El Monte to aid Rebel forces in the South. In 1862 a Union fort was built next to the town of El Monte to guard against insurrection. Judge David S. Terry and General Albert Sidney Johnston were among those Californians who went to the South and assumed command positions in the Confederate Army. In part to keep California in the Union, says historian Bruce Cumings, "Abraham Lincoln signed the bill for a transcontinental railroad in 1862," a measure that would link the Golden State to markets in the northern states.

On the home front, California politics in the 1860s shifted and realigned in accordance with national and statewide considerations. Democrats dominated in Washington, D.C., and – as has been shown – Sacramento in the 1850s. During the course of the Civil War, Republicans came to power in both of the capitals, as outside of the South Democrats were widely viewed as a threat to the preservation of the Union. Yet when the conflict ended in 1865 Republicans continued their control of the national government while California reverted to its 1850s partisan preferences and elected a Democrat, Henry Haight, to the governorship in 1867.

Ocean Crossings: The Chinese on Sea and Land

During the last few months of the Civil War, Congress passed a law authorizing "the Establishment of Ocean Mail-Steamship Service between the United States and China." Passage of the measure reflected the United States rapidly growing interest in the Orient. In the 1850s and 1860s American ships out of San Francisco voyaged to Asian ports, mainly in China, returning with laborers and cargoes of porcelains, silks, and mail. "Celestials," as Americans often referred to the Chinese passengers aboard these vessels, swelled their numbers in the Golden State and spread into surrounding parts of the Far West during these decades. The new transpacific emigrants played a lasting role in shaping California's economy and society.

China, throughout her lengthy history, has not been known for spawning epic overseas migrations. Only the combined disasters of the mid-nineteenth century could have eventuated in the diaspora of that period, during which tens of thousands of Chinese shipped as laborers to Hawai'i, Cuba, Peru, California, and elsewhere abroad. China's crises included the Opium Wars (1839–42, 1856–60) against Britain, the Taiping Rebellion (1850–64) that took millions of lives, famine, and a plummeting economy. Desperation, then, pushed Chinese peasants to seek jobs overseas. Also, visions of opportunity, even riches in California's gold diggings and fertile soil, drew these sojourners across the Pacific. While planning to return to their homeland upon making their fortune in California, only about 40 percent left the Golden State.

Transporting people, parcels, and trade items, Pacific Mail quickly grew into the world's third-largest oceanic shipping line. With an office and wharf in San Francisco and repair facilities in nearby Benicia as well as lobbying clout in Sacramento and Washington, D.C., the company's steamers averaged 33 days traversing the roughly 5,000 miles from that Golden Gate port to Hong Kong via Yokohama. The company's nearly 400 foot wooden vessels featured coal-powered side-wheels and, at times, screw propellers, the latter greatly upping efficiency and speed.

Most Chinese emigrants to San Francisco came from the ports of Canton and Hong Kong; few could afford to pay their passage without a loan. By the late 1850s they used the credit-ticket system. Accordingly, a Hong Kong broker advanced the passage fare, about $40, to an emigrant, who agreed to repay the loan from future earnings on arrival at his destination.

Mirroring the race and class differences on land, Caucasian officers and Chinese crewmen manned the seagoing transports. These ocean giants carried an average of 1,000 steerage passengers on each trip to San Francisco. Steerage constituted the lowest deck, and was the cheapest, least ventilated, and most crowded and squalid quarters on the Pacific side-wheelers. Federal laws placed limits on the number of passengers aboard, but captains frequently exceeded those limits, sometimes by more than 400 in excess of the maximum allowed. Sickness and shipwreck took the lives of numerous Chinese aboard these so-called "coolie" ships.

The vast majority of America's Chinese emigrants from the 1850s to the 1870s arrived in San Francisco. They called San Francisco "Dabu," that is, "First City." This title meant that that urban center was of first importance in their lives. Sacramento was named "Second City," and Stockton "Third City." From 1848 to 1876, according to historian Yong Chen, 233,136 Chinese arrived by sea in San Francisco; 93,273 left America by that city's port, which had become a major gateway of their transpacific travels. According to the 1860 federal census virtually all of the Chinese in the United States lived in California. While the vast majority remained in the Golden State, 10 years later thousands of them had migrated throughout the West to Nevada, Washington, Montana, Idaho, and Oregon.

On arrival in San Francisco, the Chinese gained employment as miners, farmhands, merchants, fishermen, tailors, laundrymen, makers of footwear, restaurateurs, and railroad-builders. The story of Chinese in the mines and laundries has been told in Chapter 4, while their role in railroad construction is examined in Chapter 6. Thus, some mention of their other employments is in order here.

Those employments varied. Beginning in the 1860s, as farm laborers Chinese predominated in the harvesting of wheat, hops (used for making beer), strawberries, and any other crops requiring bending and squatting. They also worked in the sugar beet fields, and earned $1 a day laboring in California's vineyards and orchards. As import-export

Figure 5.3 An illustration of Chinese arriving at the San Francisco Customs House, from *Harper's Weekly* cover, February 3, 1877. Teeming with human cargoes of Chinese immigrant workers, the San Francisco Customs House was the major point of arrival for Asian Pacific-crossers during the Civil War era in California history. Courtesy of the Bancroft Library, UC Berkeley.

merchants and grocers, Chinese businessmen sold Asian foods to emigrant miners that included rice, yams, noodles, dried vegetables, bamboo shoots, tea, salted fish, dried bean curd, and fresh fruits from nearby orchards. Non-food sales items included rice paper, Chinese ink and brushes, firecrackers, joss sticks (for burning incense), pans, and opium. Chinese fishermen plied the waters between Oregon and Baja California, and along the Sacramento River delta, catching salmon, sturgeon, and shrimp. About tailors and seamstresses, Reverend A.W. Loomis wrote in 1869: "Pantaloons, vests, shirts, drawers, and overalls are made extensively by Chinamen." Regarding the manufacture of footwear, by 1870, 11 of San Francisco's 12 slipper factories were Chinese-owned, and one-fifth of the city's boot- and shoe-workers were Chinese. That city's numerous Chinese restaurants drew a good number of whites, including public officials.

On the darker side, courts afforded the Chinese little protection, a new foreign miners' tax fell most heavily on Chinese, and a criminal element arose in their neighborhoods. In *People v. Hall* (1854), the California supreme court held that Chinese, being similar to

Indians in Asian origin, could not witness in legal proceedings against a white. The court claimed to be protecting whites from the "corrupting influence" of testimony of "degraded and demoralized blacks from Africa, Indians from Patagonia, South Sea Islanders, Hawaiians, Chinese and other peoples of color." In effect, both whites and non-whites were denied legal redress as crime victims if the only witnesses were Chinese, blacks, or Indians. In 1855 the state legislature exempted from the foreign miners' tax all sojourners declaring their intention for citizenship. The Chinese were the only foreigners unable to receive the exemption because California's constitution stated that only whites could be state citizens. Compounding these difficulties, prosperity and disorder gave rise to the "highbinders," or Chinese gangsters, in the 1860s. Besides extorting protection money from Chinese merchants, they dealt in gambling, prostitution, opium dens, and labor racketeering. Gangsters organized themselves into groups called "tongs," which at times fought wars for control over assorted illegal activities and markets. Besides injuring tong members, sometimes innocent bystanders suffered from being caught in the crossfire of these feuds.

To meet the challenges of surviving and maintaining their culture in the face of discrimination, during the 1850s the new arrivals established the Chinese Consolidated Benevolent Association, a coalition of six self-help societies also known as the "Six Companies." The Six Companies featured elected officers and a paid staff, who saw to it that San Francisco's Chinese had sufficient water, fuel, candles, and oil, while providing medical and funeral services. The vast majority of the city's Chinese were members of the Six Companies. Given its numbers and organization it is little wonder that San Francisco was home to the first, most visible, wealthiest, and largest Chinatown in the United States.

Pacific Profile: Norman Asing, Chinese American Restaurateur

"We are not the degraded race you would make us," wrote Norman Asing, a leader of San Francisco's Chinese community in 1852 in a letter to California Governor John Bigler. The governor had previously called for limiting Chinese immigration into the state. "When your nation [the U.S.] was a wilderness, and the nation from which you sprung [England] *barbarous*, we exercised most of the arts and virtues of civilized life . . . we are possessed of a language and a literature, and . . . men skilled in science and the arts are numerous among us," continued the writer.

Norman Asing, born Sang Yuen in southeast China's Pearl River delta, wrote the letter. His birth and death dates are unknown; what is known is that he developed a remarkable command of English and demonstrated impressive leadership in San Francisco's Chinatown. Around 1820 he voyaged from Macao, China, to Europe

and America, changing his name in transit. After a period of residency in New York City he became a merchant and relocated briefly to Charleston, South Carolina. In his response to Governor Bigler, Asing also said that he had become a Christian and a naturalized U.S. citizen. Although a 1790 federal law restricted naturalization to "free white persons," some eastern courts agreed to naturalize Chinese. So Asing's claim to American citizenship may have been valid, though confirming evidence is lacking.

In 1849 Asing turned up in gold rush California. That year he opened America's first Chinese eatery of record in San Francisco, quickly becoming a community spokesperson. His Macao and Woosung Restaurant was located at the corner of Kearney and Commercial streets, about one block from today's Portsmouth Square in the heart of Chinatown. The city's politicians

(Continued)

and police regularly banqueted at the establishment, ensuring the owner's prosperity. That same year Asing's fellow immigrants elected him leader of the Chew Yick Kung Shaw (Luminous Unity Public Office), America's first Chinese mutual aid society. In 1854 he was listed as a "foreign consul" in the city directory, indicating his prominence and role as a representative of San Francisco's Chinese as well as some connection with the land of his birth.

Norman Asing's story, however, may not be as simple and straightforward as this suggests. In addition to being a champion of his people, he may have also opportunistically positioned himself to take advantage of the plight of those he supposedly defended. Along with John Lipscomb, a labor importer, Asing urged the vigilance committee of 1851 to deport an attractive brothel owner, Madam Atoy, because of her "free and

easy style of living." Her business defied venerable Confucian values, lending community support for her deportation. Asing, reportedly, wanted to acquire either the brothel itself or the property on which it was housed. Selim Woodworth, an influential merchant and developer, suspected Asing's motives and warned the committee accordingly. While much about the episode remains unclear, the charge against Asing remains just plausible enough, especially in the 1850s "race for riches" in San Francisco, to deserve mention. Doing so brings to light the powerful acquisitive urge of that time and place; in no way does it diminish the importance of Asing's otherwise courageous efforts on behalf of China's Pacific-crossers to the Golden State. California and American history are replete, after all, with examples of those who not only did good, but also did well.

Californios and Other Spanish-Speakers

During the first two decades after statehood, Anglos forced large numbers of Spanish-speaking Californians (along with Mexicans from Sonora and other Latin Americans) out of the gold fields and off lands for which a court-recognized title was lacking. For Californios and others Hispanics these setbacks were followed by political decline, discrimination against Latinos/as, and acculturation.

In mid-nineteenth-century California, demographics augured a grim destiny for Spanish-speakers. About 15,000 Californios inhabited the state in 1850, among a total population of 92,597 people. A good many of the Californios possessed wealth, mainly in land holdings that would soon be greatly reduced in number and size.

While their material circumstances deteriorated, Californios were beset by social tensions within the wider Hispanic population of the state and racial discrimination from newly arrived Anglos. In effect, Californios were positioned between these two groups and, like metal particles in a magnetic field, they were pulled simultaneously between two opposite poles. In the 1850s, and increasingly in the subsequent decades, lower-class Mexican immigrants – cholos – outnumbered the well-to-do Californios. This class difference, important to long-time resident Spanish-speakers, was ignored by the incoming Anglos, who lumped all Latin Americans together as lawless, lazy "greasers." In the late 1850s the San Francisco *Herald* complained: "Californios are a degraded race; a part of them are so black that one needs much work to distinguish them from Indians; there is little difference between them and the Negro race." In 1857 Manuel Dominguez, a landowner and signer of the California constitution of 1849, was barred from the witness stand in a court trial because a gringo lawyer charged that Dominguez had Indian blood, which by law disqualified him on racial grounds from testifying. Socially prominent Californios, not surprisingly, recoiled at such sweeping public insults and humiliations.

At the same time, Californios, as a social class, accommodated the Anglos, at times forming business partnerships with them, even intermarrying on occasion. The Californio presence was strongest in the Southland, among the influential de la Guerra, Pico, Bandini, and similar landed families living along the coast from Santa Barbara to San Diego. The intellectually gifted Francisco Ramirez, who at 14 was fluent in three languages, served as a cultural mediator. At 18 he edited *El Clamor Público*, a Spanish-language weekly newspaper in Los Angeles, and was often a spokesperson for the Californios, as was Mariano Vallejo in the north. On an occasion in which he wrote in English, Ramirez told readers "we are Native California Americans born on the soil. . . ." However, the land and its people were now part of the United States "and there is every probability that we shall remain so for all time to come. . . . [Therefore] let us divest ourselves of all bygone traditions, and become Americanized all over – in language, in manners, customs and habits." At the same time, he reminded whites that: "A dark skin may harbor beneath it a noble heart as well as a profound intellect." His was the voice of pragmatic acculturation, and a fair number of his compatriots heeded it. Chivalry Democrats, on the other hand, steeped in Southern racism, joked about "free niggers and frijoles."

Some of the Spanish-speakers who did not heed Ramirez's call to Americanize, mainly *cholos* but also a few members of leading Californio families, turned to banditry. Joaquín Murieta was California's most celebrated outlaw, his exploits having become legendary. Actually, there were five Joaquíns, all bandits with different surnames, in the 1850s, of which Murieta was one. In the winter of 1852–3, hysteria gripped the public resulting from what was believed to be Joaquín Murieta's robberies and murders of Chinese and others in and around Calaveras County. Mexicans, for some reason, despised the Chinese nearly as much as the gringos did. With public pressure mounting for bringing the elusive Joaquín to justice, Governor Bigler offered a $1,000 reward for his capture and authorized army captain Harry S. Love and a posse of 20 to run down the bandit.

After coming upon an encampment of Mexican suspects at Panoche Pass in the Coast Range, Love and his men fought a gun battle with the supposed outlaws. The posse captured their leader, a man thought to be Murieta, and beheaded him while cutting off the hand of another, assumed to be Joaquín's sidekick, "Three-fingered Jack [Manuel Garcia]." These grisly "trophies" were pickled in a bottle of alcohol as proof of the posse's success. Though no positive identification had been made and Joaquín-like bandit attacks continued for several more years, the state legislature appropriated $5,000 as a bonus to Love and his men. Similarly, San Francisco's grateful Chinese community awarded Love and his band $1,000. Half-Indian author John Rollin Ridge wrote a book titled *The Life and Adventures of Joaquín Murieta, Celebrated California Bandit*, published in 1854. In this work Murieta emerged as a Robin Hood figure, avenging gringo mistreatment of Mexicans, especially in the mines. Isabel Allende's novel, *Daughter of Fortune* (1999), recounts the legend of Joaquín Murieta for modern readers, noting that Chileans in California viewed the heroic figure as one of their own countrymen. In addition to Hispanics, Native Americans looked to their own leaders of Joaquín-like repute for protection from land-hungry whites.

Indians: A People under Siege

During the first few decades of statehood no ethnic group received worse treatment at the hands of whites than Native Americans. Rejecting victimhood, California's Indian bands did what they could, at times waging war, to retain some of their lands and simply survive.

The decimation of the Indian population during the first few decades of the American takeover indicates how fatal the confrontation with the Anglo settlers was for the state's First People. In 1845, on the eve of the U.S. conquest, about 150,000 Indians inhabited the province. By 1870 their number had dropped to approximately 30,000. That figure had nearly halved by 1900. Most deaths were due to disease; starvation and physical attacks by whites accounted for the remainder of the casualties.

The first state legislature passed a law contributing to the tragic plight of Native Californians. In 1850 that body approved the Act for the Government and Protection of Indians. Accordingly, unemployed adult Indians were subject to prosecution for vagrancy, in which case the courts could hire them out. Indian boys until 18 and girls until 15 could be apprenticed to employers under conditions similar to enslavement, beginning with the bidding at auction for the services of these youths. A worker for the U.S. Mail Department in northern California affirmed: "Indians seven or eight years old are worth $100." Ten years later that law was amended to extend the time period during which employers could have custody and control over the earnings of Indian apprentices. Usually, those entrusted with their custody used the children to perform household chores such as washing, cleaning, and child care. In some documented instances, Anglos kidnapped and sold Indian girls into sexual slavery. In December 1861 the *Marysville Appeal* newspaper reported that young females served both the "purposes of labor and lust." At times the kidnappers murdered both of the parents before stealing the children. California's indigenous peoples retaliated by killing whites, some of whom had not been involved in this horrific commerce. Anthropologist Sherburne F. Cook and other authorities estimate that as many as 4,000 Indians, and possibly more, were victims of these legal measures and the practices that ensued.

Worse for the Indians, whites acquired most of the aboriginals' land. In 1851 and 1852 federal agents negotiated 18 treaties with 139 California Indian bands, providing 11,700 square miles of reservation space for the natives. The treaties were rejected by the U.S. Senate in the latter year, largely because whites wanted much of the allotted real estate. Congress approved an alternative policy in 1853, the handiwork of the superintendent of Indian affairs for California, Edward F. Beale. His plan put Indians on smaller reservations that would also function as army posts. The first and largest of these settlements was established in the Tehachapi foothills at Tejon. There conditions grew so bad that in 1858 the Indians revolted. Soldiers suppressed the uprising and its leaders were punished with severe whippings. The reservation system, begun in California, soon spread throughout the West, where it was administered by incompetent, corrupt officials for decades afterward. In California as in the western region, famine and starvation often followed in the wake of Indians losing their land. Desperate, the displaced natives sometimes stole cattle and other stock simply to survive, which resulted in army and white paramilitary attacks on Indian settlements. Overall, whites killed 100 Indians for every Anglo death resulting from these interracial clashes. William H. Brewer, a participant in the Geological Survey of California, wrote in 1862: "as yet I have not heard a single intelligent white man express any opinion but that the whites were vastly more to blame than the Indians."

One of the most lethal white attacks in the state's history occurred on Indian Island in Humboldt Bay and at nearby villages on February 26, 1860. On that fateful morning a gang of whites armed with axes, hatchets, and knives butchered and hacked to death 60 Indians, nearly all women and children. This massacre was unprovoked, for the victims constituted "a band of friendly Indians," according to Major G.J. Raines, commander of Fort Humboldt at the time. Viewing the carnage in the aftermath, writer Bret Harte observed: "Here was a mother fatally wounded hugging the mutilated carcass of her dying infant to her bosom; there a child of two years old, with its ear and scalp torn from the side of its little head." Two more massacres in the immediate area that same day brought the total Indian deaths to 188. This was merely one among many other unprovoked and brutal white assaults, which included scalpings, on California's First Peoples.

Amid such massacres and land losses, the Modocs in northeastern California fought the last Indian war against whites in the state in 1872–3. Expulsion from the Modocs' ancestral lands along the Lost River was at the root of their problem with white officials. In accordance with the federal reservation policy, in 1864 the Modocs were relocated from their California homeland to southern Oregon, where they were forced to share a reservation with their enemies, the Klamaths. In Oregon the Modocs split into two groups, one of which – led by Kintpuash (often called Captain Jack) – returned to the Lost River area. As negotiations for a reservation there bogged down, Kintpuash and a clique within his band thought that their bargaining power would be increased if they made a show of physical force by killing the whites with whom they were conferring. The American officials knew of the danger yet attended the meeting of April 11, 1873 unarmed. General Edward Canby and a Methodist missionary were killed, while an Indian agent was severely injured by Modoc warriors, who then fled to the nearby lava beds and outcroppings. Disagreements split these Modocs into two groups, one of which was captured by U.S. Army troops. In return for the promise that they would not be tried, the prisoner group helped the American forces pin down and defeat the remaining contingent of Modocs. A trial was held and four of the Indian leaders, including Kintpuash, were hanged; two other defendants were sentenced to prison.

While the Modocs survived the war, other Indian groups – such as the Yahi – were pushed by whites into extinction after the 1870s. Living in the Mill Creek area south of Mount Lassen, the Yahi people were hunted like game by gold-seekers. In 1911 the last known survivor of his tribe wandered into Oroville hungry and emaciated. The survivor's story is briefly recounted in Chapter 1's Pacific Profile.

African Americans: Up from Bondage

While California entered the Union as a free state, white racism was sufficiently strong to make life very difficult for its small African American population, numbering about 1,000 in 1850. During the next three decades their numbers grew slowly, still constituting only 1 percent of the total people in residence.

In the 1850s the state legislature passed a series of laws that threatened some presumptively free blacks with a return to bondage, and prohibited African Americans from voting, testifying in state courts, serving on juries, and marrying whites. Besides facilitating re-enslavement, these measures prevented blacks from being able to defend their property holdings and other assets in a court of law. Additionally, racially based legal obstacles made it nearly impossible for their children to attend white public schools.

State lawmakers enacted a fugitive slave statute in 1852, reminiscent of the measure that was part of the federal Omnibus Bill that brought California into the Union two years earlier. The 1852 state law was not so much aimed at returning fugitive slaves, for there were practically none in California, given its distance from Dixie. Instead, that law became a weapon of Southern masters who had brought slaves into the state to mine gold and afterward intended to return to the South with their human "property." Ordinarily, slaves brought to California, where they resided, would thereby gain their freedom since the state had outlawed servitude. To get around this, masters claimed that in accordance with California's fugitive slave law they had the legal right to round up their "fugitive slaves" and take them back to the South.

Slave masters also were helped by California's judiciary. In an 1858 case involving African American slave Archie Lee, the state supreme court ruled that despite the fact that Lee would ordinarily have been freed by residing in California, he should remain in bondage because his master was ill and needed help. Fortunately for Lee, a U.S. commissioner intervened and secured his freedom.

Bridget "Biddy" Mason's rise from bondage exemplified just how successful some African Americans became in the latter half of the nineteenth century. Arriving in southern California in 1851 as a slave, she gained her freedom five years later. Afterward, Mason worked as a nurse in Los Angeles for $2.50 a day. She saved enough money to buy several pieces of real estate, which she eventually parlayed into a fortune. As a wealthy landowner, Mason turned to philanthropy, founding a nursery school and a rest home for poor blacks. Her success, and that of a few others, was the exception for African Americans. Still, it exemplified what was possible in a society permeated with white racism and undergoing rapid socio-economic change on the eve of the railroad-building era.

SUMMARY

Because of the chaos of the gold rush in 1849, Californians hastily framed a state government before attaining statehood itself the following year. They drafted a constitution requiring that all laws be published in English and Spanish, outlawing slavery, extending citizenship to whites only (including Californios), setting the eastern boundary, and recognizing the property rights of married women. California's constitution is unique in that it is the only state charter that guarantees the rights of "pursuing and obtaining safety and happiness."

Figure 5.4 Bridget "Biddy" Mason. Courtesy of Golden State Mutual Life Insurance Co. Records, Department of Special Collections, Charles E. Young Research Library, UCLA.

Legal battles and lawlessness pervaded the times. Californio rancheros struggled to retain their huge land tracts but lost much of their holdings through lengthy and costly court proceedings. Amid the chaos in the diggings and the violence that spilled over into San Francisco, powerful vigilante movements in 1851 and 1856 attempted to provide law and order in the Far West's largest, wealthiest port city. California politics, particularly the Broderick–Gwin feud, both reflected and fueled the state's untamed political landscape. Meanwhile, San Francisco-spawned filibustering ventures in Hawai'i, Mexico, and parts of Central and South America, demonstrated California's aggressive reach in the Pacific Basin.

California's Pacific maritime importance was underscored by huge Civil War-time gold shipments by sea to the Union government, and the ocean crossings of Chinese immigrants to the Golden State. During the Civil War and its immediate aftermath, the San Francisco-based Pacific Mail Steamship Company transported tens of thousands of these immigrants, who became a major force in agriculture, fishing, mining, and railroad-building. Some, like Norman Asing, became leading merchants in San Francisco, home to America's oldest and largest Chinatown.

The Chinese, like other non-Anglos, suffered discrimination in housing, jobs, and the administration of justice, as these ethnic minorities could not bear witness against a white person in a court of law. All of these minorities fought back, often by forming self-help associations, taking advantage of the few opportunities open to them, or turning to crime. Indians fared the worst as their population declined substantially due to disease and treatment at the hands of whites that approached genocide.

REVIEW QUESTIONS

*   In what sense was bilingualism established as a principle in the California constitution of 1849?
*   What forms did public disorder and violence take in the 1850s? To what extent was Anglo racism a factor leading to these social problems?
*   Where throughout the Pacific Basin were California filibusterers active?
*   What evidence supports the view that California's involvement in the Civil War was mainly maritime in nature?
*   How well did Californios and other Spanish-speakers fare in California during the first decade of statehood? Who were their leaders and how did they deal with the American takeover of the former Mexican province?

FURTHER READINGS

Robert R. Alvarez, Jr., *Familia: Migration and Adaptation in Baja and Alta California, 1800–1975* (Berkeley: University of California Press, 1987). The author treats the Baja peninsula and California to the north as one region based on strong historical and familial links.

John F. Burns and Richard J. Orsi, eds., *Taming the Elephant: Politics, Government, and Law in Pioneer California* (Berkeley: University of California Press, 2003). This work is strong on the details of establishing a governmental framework for the new state.

Tom Chaffin, *Sea of Gray: The Around-the-World Odyssey of the Confederate Raider Shenandoah* (New York: Hill & Wang, 2006). The Pacific exploits of this much-feared Confederate war vessel are treated in this engaging account.

Yong Chen, *Chinese San Francisco, 1850–1943* (Stanford, CA: Stanford University Press, 2000). The author provides a detailed social and cultural history of America's oldest and largest Chinatown.

Thomas W. Chinn, ed., *A History of the Chinese in California: A Syllabus* (San Francisco: Chinese Historical Society of America, 1969). This thin volume offers invaluable, documented information on California's Chinese.

Bruce Cumings, *Dominion from Sea to Sea: Pacific Ascendancy and American Power* (New Haven, CT: Yale University Press, 2009). This book is part of a new genre of scholarly works addressing the role of the Pacific world in shaping American history.

William Deverell, *Whitewashed Adobe: The Rise of Los Angeles and the Remaking of Its Mexican Past* (Berkeley: University of California Press, 2004). The author shows how Los Angeles, ever America's "city of the future," came of age by appropriating and at times obliterating its Mexican past.

Richard A. Garcia, ed., "Turning Points: Mexican Americans in California History," *California History*, 74 (Fall 1995), 226–339. The entire issue is devoted to Mexican Americans in the state.

Benjamin F. Gilbert, "California and the Civil War, a Bibliographic Essay," *California Historical Society Quarterly*, 40 (December 1961), 289–307. Though dated, this article introduces investigators to the earlier literature on the subject matter.

Lisbeth Haas, *Conquests and Historical Identities in California, 1769–1936* (Berkeley: University of California Press, 1995). The complex process of identity-formation among Indians and Californios, especially in the southern part of the state, is treated with sophistication in this work.

Sam W. Haynes and Christopher Morris, eds., *Manifest Destiny and Empire: American Antebellum Expansionism* (College Station, TX: Texas A & M University Press, 1997). In multiple essays, each of which is devoted to a separate theme, six authors address the political, diplomatic, military, artistic, and other aspects of the Manifest Destiny movement that brought California into the Union.

Robert F. Heizer and Alan J. Almquist, *The Other Californians: Prejudice and Discrimination under Spain, Mexico, and the United States to 1920* (Berkeley: University of California Press, 1971). This early study of racism in California is distinctive for its presentation of minority voices, reflective of the more than 50 pages of pertinent documents at the end of the book.

Corinne K. Hoexter, *From Canton to California: The Epic Chinese Immigration* (New York: Four Winds Press, 1976). This sympathetic account of Chinese immigration to California chronicles the racism and other hardships they encountered along with their contributions and spread into communities from San Francisco to New York City.

Aurora Hunt, *The Army of the Pacific, 1860–1866* (Mechanicsburg, PA: Stackpole Books, 2004). This study focuses largely on California's military role in the Civil War.

Rudolph M. Lapp, *Afro-Americans in California* (San Francisco: Boyd & Fraser, 1987). Like the author's other works, only broader in scope, this book provides a reliable guide to the experiences of African Americans in the Golden State.

Glenna Matthews, *The Golden State in the Civil War: Thomas Starr King, the Republican Party, and the Birth of Modern California* (New York: Cambridge University Press, 2012). This is the most comprehensive and up-to-date study on Civil War California in print.

Shirley Ann Wilson Moore, ed., "African Americans in California," *California History*, 75 (Fall 1996), 194–283. An indispensable resource, this issue provides a "state-of-the-field" assessment of the African American experience in California.

Leonard Pitt, *The Decline of the Californios: A Social History of the Spanish-Speaking Californians, 1846–1890* (Berkeley: University of California Press, 1966). The pioneering work on the subject, it treats the factions within Californio ranks and their expedient partnerships with American merchants, while analyzing the fall of this elite Spanish-speaking cohort from power.

Leonard L. Richards, *The California Gold Rush and the Coming of the Civil War* (New York: Vintage Books, 2007). This study traces the impact of antebellum America's growing sectional divide on the politics of gold rush California, while touching on the state's military role in the Civil War.

Andrew F. Rolle, "California Filibustering and the Hawaiian Kingdom," *Pacific Historical Review*, 19 (1950), 251–64. This article focuses on an often marginalized episode in the history of California filibustering.

Robert J. Schwendinger, *Ocean of Bitter Dreams: Maritime Relations between China and the United States, 1850–1915* (Tucson, AZ: Westernlore Press, 1988). The hardships suffered by Chinese laborers aboard California-bound American ships are detailed in this authoritative book.

6

Pacific-Bound Rails, Hard Times, and Chinese Exclusion

California's economic growth and influence throughout the Far West increased dramatically with the gold rush and the building of the nation's first transcontinental railroad in the 1860s. Like the mining bonanza era, the railroad-building period was closely linked to the Golden State's lucrative Pacific maritime involvements extending all the way to Asia. The good times ended with the onset of the nationwide economic depression of the 1870s. Unemployed laborers and their political spokespersons looked for scapegoats. In California and elsewhere in America the Chinese received a large share of the blame for the troubles of workingmen, whose leaders helped write a new state constitution in 1879. Largely at California's behest, three years later Congress framed and implemented a new policy of excluding most Chinese from entry into the United States.

Pacific Eldorado: A History of Greater California, First Edition. Thomas J. Osborne.
© 2013 Thomas J. Osborne. Published 2013 by Blackwell Publishing Ltd.

Timeline

1861 The Central Pacific Railroad is chartered in Sacramento

1862 In part to facilitate Asian Pacific trade, the Pacific Railroad Act is passed and signed, providing for the construction of America's first transcontinental railroad and accompanying telegraph system

1865 The Southern Pacific Railroad is incorporated in California; the Big Four buy it, still unbuilt, three years later

50 Chinese, the first contingent of thousands who would cross the Pacific to build the first transcontinental, are employed by the Central Pacific Railroad

1867 The Central Pacific rejects its Chinese laborers' requests for $40 a month and a 10-hour workday (8 hours in the tunnels), with the result that some 2,000 Chinese go on strike; the railroad withholds food and other supplies, breaking the strike one week after it began

1869 Secretary of State William H. Seward dubs San Francisco, envisioned as the western terminus of a transcontinental railroad and telegraph network, "the Constantinople [a world-renowned Mediterranean port] of American empire"

The Central Pacific and Union Pacific railroads meet at Promontory Point, Utah, completing the first transcontinental rail network

1871 Led by Anglos and some Hispanics, the state's bloodiest anti-Chinese massacre occurs in Los Angeles, resulting in the deaths of between 19 and 21 Chinese

1873 Regarding the building of the first transcontinental railroad, New York journalist Charles Nordhoff rightly declares: "Not a foot of iron was laid on the road on all the eight hundred miles to Ogden [Utah], not a spike was driven, not a dirt-car was moved, nor a powder-blast set off, that was not first brought [by vessel] around Cape Horn"

1874 The Big Four create the California-based Occidental and Oriental Steamship Company, capitalized at $10 million in stock, to compete with the Pacific Mail Steamship Company

Charles Nordhoff publishes *Northern California, Oregon, and the Sandwich Islands*, whose chapters situate the Golden State in the Pacific world

1876–7 A report issued by the San Francisco Board of Supervisors states that the Chinese are viewed as "a social, moral and political curse to the community"

1877 Denis Kearney, in San Francisco, organizes the Workingmen's Party, whose demands include: the eight-hour workday, direct election of U.S. Senators, compulsory education, state regulation of banks and railroads, a fairer tax system, and a ban on all Chinese immigration into the state

1878 1,500 unemployed workers in San Francisco demonstrate for "work, bread, or a place in the county jail;" another group of men threatens to destroy the wharves and vessels of the Pacific Mail Steamship Company and bomb Chinatown; the U.S. Navy sends a warship to the Bay Area to defend federal mail docks

A Sacramento constitutional convention is attended by 152 delegates

1879 California's second constitution, aimed at regulating the Southern Pacific Railroad and limiting Chinese employment opportunities, is approved by voters

(Continued)

1882	Under pressure from California interests, Congress passes the Chinese Exclusion Act, suspending the immigration of Chinese workers, skilled and unskilled, to the United States for 10 years and prohibiting the naturalization of Chinese in America; teachers, students, merchants, and travelers are exempted from the immigration ban
1883	A second transcontinental railway, the famed "sunset route" connecting San Francisco and New Orleans, gives the Big Four access to the carrying trade of the Gulf of Mexico
1885	A competitor of the Southern Pacific, the Atchison, Topeka & Santa Fe Railroad, reaches San Diego
1898	The Southern Pacific launches *Sunset* magazine, a San Francisco monthly promoting tourism and settlement in California
1900	Headquartered in San Francisco, the Southern Pacific has branch offices in major cities throughout the United States and Europe, and boasts the world's largest transit network; Southern Pacific's federally granted California land holdings range between 3 and 5 million acres

A Transcontinental Railroad, California, and Pacific Commerce

The railroad era in California history marked a significant departure from the prior mule caravans, stage lines, and pony express modes of overland travel and communication. In 1857 Congress passed the Overland California Mail Act, resulting in a federal contract let to the Butterfield Overland Express Company to transport mail some 2,800 miles between St. Louis and San Francisco. The 24-day trip was shortened time-wise by the pony express, which was made obsolete by completion of the first transcontinental telegraph line in 1861. The Pacific Mail Steamship carrying service, on the other hand, was supplemented rather than supplanted by the coming of rails to California.

For two decades before construction on America's first transcontinental railroad began in the 1860s, businesspeople and federal officials conceived, refined, and publicized the bold idea of such a project – tying it to America's, particularly California's, role in capturing maritime trade with Asia. The leading spokespersons for the idea included Asa Whitney, Thomas Hart Benton, and William Henry Seward.

China merchant Asa Whitney may have been the first to develop and articulate the idea of a coast-to-coast rail network and to link that notion to expanding America's presence in the Orient. As a maritime trader Whitney made a fortune from his transactions in China in 1842–4, in the aftermath of the first Opium War that resulted in the opening of five Chinese ports to American shippers. On his return he conceived of the possibility of a transcontinental railroad connecting America's Atlantic coast, via Chicago, with northern California. When completed, such a transportation project would provide an "iron path" to the nation's far western markets and capture the China trade. "The vast commerce of all India, of all Asia, which has been the source and foundation of all commerce from the earliest ages," would be wrested from England and transferred peacefully to the United States. Whitney converted the nationally prominent politician John C. Frémont, who eloquently stated: "The golden vein [of commerce] which runs through the history of the world will follow the track to San Francisco, and the Asiatic trade will finally fall into its last and permanent road." In 1845 Whitney moved beyond conceptualizing and, at his expense, conducted a survey expedition that explored a possible transcontinental route from the Missouri River to the Pacific Coast. He would build the railroad himself, he said, if the federal government would give him a land grant 60 miles wide along his proposed route. Sections of the grant could be sold to cover construction costs. Whitney's northern route aroused the fears of Southerners in Congress, who saw the project as benefiting the industrial North, and they rejected it for that reason.

Unlike Whitney, Senator Thomas Hart Benton had not traveled to Asia. Still, Benton took a large, Pacific worldview of a prospective transcontinental railroad and was influential in the nation's capital. In a Senate speech on January 16, 1855, he called for federal sponsorship of a rail line from Missouri to California. Such would be "the true and good route for the road which is to unite the Atlantic and the Pacific, and to give a new channel to the commerce of Asia." Europe, too, figured in Benton's grand scheme. Goods exported from Europe would be shipped across the Atlantic and reach "Asia through America" via rails and sails.

Among the advocates of a transcontinental railroad, William Henry Seward, secretary of state under President Abraham Lincoln, developed the most profound geopolitical understanding of the enterprise in all of its Pacific world implications for U.S. foreign policy. More than any policymaker of his time, he conceived a blueprint for America's acquisition of a Pacific empire in the late nineteenth century. A transcontinental railroad was integral to his view of world history and his plan for the United States to emerge as the dominant global power. He stated in 1850 that "the commercial, social, [and] political movements of the world" were "in the direction of California, which bounds at once the [American] empire and the Continent." Several years later he affirmed that a transcontinental railroad would become the major carrier of the world's goods from Europe to the Far East. The prospective line would constitute "the shortest route for merchandise from England and the [European] continent to China, India, Australia and South America by way of New York and San Francisco." To him the trade of the Pacific would be the most contested prize in international affairs in the coming decades. California and its ports would provide the necessary launch sites for acquiring Hawai'i and Alaska, and eventually building a canal across Central America – all for the purpose of controlling the northern Pacific sea lanes to the markets of Asia. In 1869 Seward dubbed San Francisco, envisioned as the western terminus of a transcontinental railroad and telegraph network, "the Constantinople of American empire."

Such ambitious thinking picked up considerable support in the Northern states in the 1850s. In the South, however, it ran into strong planter opposition to large-scale, federally subsidized internal improvements projects – especially ones that seemed to offer few benefits to the slow-to-industrialize slave states. The fact that the proposed routes had been decidedly northern ones further antagonized the South's ruling class. Not until Southern states began seceding from the Union in 1861 could supporters of a Pacific railroad begin to muster the votes necessary in Congress to advance their grand ideas.

Theodore Judah, the Big Four, and the Pacific Railroad Act of 1862

Conceiving the grand idea of a transcontinental railway was an indispensable first step toward achieving the related goals of strengthening America's Pacific presence and trade with Asia; founding a railroad, formulating a plan to build such a line, and securing government funding for the project constituted equally important next steps. The upshot of this colossal undertaking was that a "greater" California and its transportation giant, the Central Pacific Railroad, would exert considerable economic influence throughout the Far West and beyond. Moreover, as radical economist Henry George had predicted, San Francisco – the Central Pacific's headquarters – would emerge, if it had not done so already, as western America's preeminent city.

Theodore Judah spearheaded the process of converting the dream of a transcontinental trunk line, that is, a long-distance rail pathway with connector tracks or spurs, into a reality. A 28-year-old construction engineer and surveyor, he voyaged from the Atlantic Coast to California in 1854. In the ensuing six years, he solved the critical problems of where and how to lay rails through the Sierra and recruited initial investors.

Judah's greatest contribution to the transcontinental railroad project was in discovering and surveying what became the route through the towering Sierra. Figuring out how to span this rugged rampart with track and tunnels was clearly the thorniest engineering challenge of the entire transcontinental enterprise. Until a workable plan was devised, investment capital could not be raised. Understanding this, Judah went into the Sierra in 1860 with druggist friend Daniel W. Strong and a few assistants, and located a sloping ridge above Dutch Flat that extended between the Yuba and Bear River gorges and the American River toward Donner Pass. The gradual grade of 105 feet per mile convinced Judah that here was the route that could take eastward-bound trains up and over the 7,000-foot-high Donner Pass summit. Now he could form a railroad company, the Central Pacific of California, and bring in business partners.

Four Sacramento dry-goods merchants met with Judah in November 1860 on the second floor of a hardware store on K Street owned by two of them. The prospective investors, who came to be known as the "Big Four" or the "Associates," were Charles Crocker, Mark Hopkins, Collis P. Huntington, and Leland Stanford. All four of them had come to gold rush California to seek their fortune either through mining or supplying prospectors with shovels and other needed equipment. Judah convinced them to invest in his project. Their joint undertaking resulted in strengthening the Central Pacific, largely because of the business savvy of the Big Four. In April 1861, the Central Pacific was reorganized to admit new stockholders and elect officers: Stanford became president, Huntington vice president, Hopkins treasurer, and Crocker oversaw construction financing and labor. Judah served as chief engineer. All four investors plus Judah served as directors of the company.

Their financial partnership was essential to the launching of the railroad venture, which soon enriched the Big Four. California's incorporation law required stock purchases of $1,000 per mile of track to be laid. That meant $115,000 would be needed to authorize rail construction across the 115 miles between Sacramento and the state's eastern boundary.

The Associates barely amassed the requisite 10 percent down payment on the $115,000; doing so allowed their project to proceed. From total combined assets of about $100,000 at the incorporation of the Central Pacific Railroad of California on June 27, 1861, the Associates later acquired an aggregate personal fortune of about $200 million.

Since these businessmen became titans of industry in California and nationwide, biographical profiles of them are in order. Charles Crocker was born in Troy, New York, and raised in Indiana, where from an early age he sold newspapers, split rails, and managed a small iron forge. Large, brawny, and independent, he left home in his teens and traveled overland to California intent on making a fortune mining gold. Mining, however, made for sore muscles and uncertain income; before long the once strapping youth ballooned into a 250-pound, back-slapping, wheeler-dealer Sacramento shopkeeper and politician.

Mark Hopkins, another native New Yorker, sailed to California via Cape Horn, arriving in Sacramento in such desperate straits that he and several companions were reduced to eating the bone marrow of a dead ox along the road to the state capital. He met with some success as a grocer before opening a hardware store with Collis Huntington.

Huntington was born in Connecticut to an impoverished family with nine children. Looking back on his growing up, he declared: "I could whip any boy in school, old or young, I excelled in geography." He also handled numbers well. In 1849 he voyaged from New York to San Francisco, picking up $3,000 en route by buying and selling supplies to gold-seekers crossing the Panamanian isthmus. Nearly monopolizing the California shovel trade, Huntington loved the combat of the marketplace and the political arena.

Born near Troy, New York, Leland Stanford sailed to California in 1852 via the Nicaragua route. He was far more a politician than a businessperson. Though Stanford was "not distinguished by intellect or political deftness," according to historian William Deverell, he had sufficient aptitude and the good luck of entering California's fledgling Republican Party at a time when advancement through the organization's hierarchy was open to men of his ilk. Elected governor of California in 1861, he was well placed politically when the Central Pacific sought government funding at the national and state levels.

The New York connection among Crocker, Hopkins, and Stanford was emblematic of that state's role in securing financing for transcontinental railroads throughout the last four decades of the nineteenth century. According to historian Richard White, author of *Railroaded: The Transcontinentals and the Making of Modern America* (2011), New York and Massachusetts were homes to the family and social networks, enriched by the transoceanic China trade, which built most of the transcontinentals during that period.

Federal funding for the first transcontinental railroad came with Lincoln's signing on July 1 of the historic Pacific Railroad Act of 1862. By then the 11 secessionist Southern states had no representation in Congress; no longer could their voting delegates block a federal government-sponsored transcontinental railroad project following a northern route. By then the case for building a Pacific railroad and telegraph network had grown only stronger. Acutely aware of this, Huntington and Judah voyaged to Washington, D.C., to help write the landmark law along with collaboration from Congressperson Aaron A. Sargent and Senator James A. McDougall, both of California.

The Pacific Railroad Act of 1862, authorizing the building of a telegraph line to complement the rail system, had several major objectives. These included providing for the defense of America's Pacific Coast and growing maritime trade, integrating the nation's economy by linking markets and resources, pacifying western Indians when necessary, transporting mail, and unifying the country through improved transportation and communication.

Toward these ends, the measure: (1) authorized the Central Pacific Railroad to construct tracks from San Francisco Bay to the eastern state line, and the Union Pacific Railroad to complete the connection from the Missouri River; (2) provided 200-foot rights of way on both sides of the track to the two railroads; (3) granted 10-square-mile (increased to 20-square-mile in 1864) tracts of public land on alternating sides of the roadbed, including timber and stone (but not mineral) rights on these lands; and (4) extended 30-year bond loans yielding 6 percent interest to the two railroads, issued at the rate of $16,000 in bonds per mile of construction for the easy grades, $32,000 for the high plains, and $48,000 for mountainous sections. The bounteous terms of the federal Act and the unprecedented scope of the project reflected the national influence of California businesspersons and politicians.

Bounteous federal aid was still not enough to satisfy the Associates, who created their own contract and finance company to build their eastbound leg of the first transcontinental. This construction company, according to historian White, charged the Central Pacific "roughly twice the actual cost of construction per mile." Thus, the stockholders in that railroad were being price-gouged and exploited by the men who simultaneously ran the Central Pacific and its construction company. Years later, Collis Huntington admitted that the contract and finance company was "as rotten a corporation as ever lived."

Shortly after the passage of the Pacific Railroad Act, if not before, a rift between Judah and the Big Four emerged. As chief engineer for the Central Pacific, Judah insisted on overseeing all aspects of construction. His partners, for whom business profits were everything, responded by denying Judah any voice in Central Pacific matters. The rift widened when the Big Four sought to receive the $48,000 per mile federal bond award for construction in foothills some 20 miles distant from the Sierra and Judah refused to certify the deception. Disgusted with his partners, Judah sailed for New York in October 1863 hoping to persuade railroad barons there to help him buy back the Central Pacific from the Associates. Unfortunately, this hero of the first transcontinental railroad contracted yellow fever in Panama and died in his wife's arms, at the age of 37, on November 2 in New York. His former partners did not so much as name a railroad crossing after him.

That same year the Central Pacific induced the state legislature and counties to help finance its project by providing subsidies in addition to those granted by the federal government. Specifically, the cash-strapped Big Four succeeded in getting the state legislature and several counties, such as Placer and Sacramento, to buy $1.5 million-worth of Central Pacific stock. Moreover, these jurisdictions pledged to assume the interest payments on a like amount of bonds. This timely assistance from the state and county governments enabled the Central Pacific to collect the much-needed first installment of federal aid. Amid this search for more funds, construction began.

Groundbreaking in Sacramento took place with much fanfare at noon on January 8, 1863. The Sacramento Union Brass Band serenaded a gathering crowd beneath a clear sky. Following a prayer invoking God's blessing, Crocker stepped forward and bellowed: "The

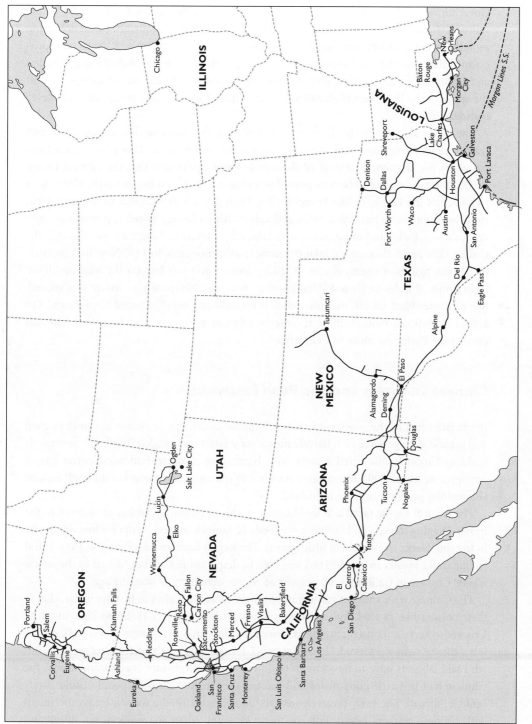

Figure 6.1 Route of the Central Pacific Railroad and the later extension of its rail lines by its successor, the Southern Pacific Railroad Company. Based on map appearing in Richard J. Orsi, *Sunset Limited: The Southern Pacific Railroad and the Development of the American West, 1850–1930* (2005), pp. 42–3. Used by permission of University of California Press.

Governor of the State of California will now shovel the first earth for the great Pacific railroad." California senators and assemblymen looked on admiringly, afterward delivering remarks to the audience. One speaker, echoing Asa Whitney's dream of Pacific trade, proclaimed that over the road about to be built "the skills of India, the rich tribute of China and Japan, the gold, the wine, and the wool of Australia, the treasures of California, and the spices of the [Far] East shall roll in a mighty tide of wealth such as mankind has never realized before."

The above statements clearly suggest that the Pacific maritime dimension of the first transcontinental railroad project was of paramount importance. This point was underscored by the fact that nearly all of the supplies and equipment that the Central Pacific needed for its work had to be transported from the war-torn East by sea via the Cape Horn route across the Pacific to San Francisco Bay. Such shipments included all iron products, from locomotives to handcars, rails, and spikes. Also, blasting powder, percussion caps, nails, shovels, picks, and more were carried aboard steamers making their way through the Golden Gate and following the inland waterway to Sacramento. In 1873 New York journalist Charles Nordhoff rightly declared: "Not a foot of iron was laid on the road on all the eight hundred miles to Ogden [Utah], not a spike was driven, not a dirt-car was moved, nor a powder-blast set off, that was not first brought [by vessel] around Cape Horn." On arrival at their destination, these shipments supplied a Chinese workforce that had also crossed the Pacific en route to California.

Chinese Laborers and the Push Eastward

In the latter half of the nineteenth century railroad-building was mainly the work of men and muscle. A large force of relatively inexpensive labor was needed. While the westward-building Union Pacific hired mainly Irish hands, the eastward-building Central Pacific employed nearly 12,000 Chinese laborers, most of whom were recruited in the southeastern Guangdong province of their homeland.

The Central Pacific faced a labor-shortage problem. Generally, whites were lured to the mines. Digging tunnels and building roadbeds 12 hours a day, especially for low wages and in freezing Sierra weather, held little appeal. The largest number of toilers that the Central Pacific could muster in spring 1865 was 800. In desperation, Crocker turned to the nearly 50,000 Chinese in California, 90 percent of whom were men of working age.

The Chinese were small in stature and thought by some whites to be effeminate, clad in their pajama-like clothes and sporting pigtails. Irishman James H. Strobridge, hired by Crocker to serve as construction boss, feared that the Anglo crewmen would walk off the job if these Asians were hired. "I will not boss Chinese," he grumbled. Crocker replied: "But who said laborers have to be white to build railroads?" Strobridge was reminded that the Chinese had invented gunpowder and erected the Great Wall; such people could surely build a railroad. The surly boss relented and in February 1865 a month-long experiment with Chinese workers began. Fifty of them were put under his supervision, filling and driving dump carts and excavating with picks. They received $26 in gold for their labors and performed superbly, Strobridge grudgingly admitted.

Surprised and impressed by what he had seen, the construction boss scoured California's towns in search of more Chinese. When the state's population of Chinese had been exhausted, the railroad turned to Asia. Crocker contracted with the San Francisco firm of Sisson and Wallace to import workers directly from China. Stanford, who had previously denounced Chinese as "the dregs of Asia" and "that degraded race," reversed his view and now urged increasing their immigration to California by at least half a million more. Eventually, 80 percent of the Central Pacific's laborers were Chinese. To address the challenge of communication Crocker hired Sam Thayer, who was fluent in several Chinese dialects, to serve as both a translator and a teacher of English to selected immigrants.

Working conditions for the Chinese crewmen remained hard and dangerous. Toiling from sunrise to sunset, six days a week, they worked in gangs of 12 to 20. Laborers were paid $35 per month, out of which expenses for food and clothing were deducted, leaving each man about $20 to $30 in net monthly salary. Each gang elected a "head man" to buy provisions and collect and distribute pay, and a cook. Earning this pay was at times perilous. In one especially difficult stretch of the trans-Sierra route aptly known as "Cape Horn Passage," a nearly perpendicular rock wall, Chinese workers were lowered from atop a cliff in wicker baskets. Thus dangling nearly 1,400 feet above the American River, the basket men drilled holes in the granite for the insertion of gunpowder. Next, the workers scrambled up the lines to escape the explosion that followed. In this fashion, said historian Thomas W. Chinn, "inch by inch, a road bed was gouged from the granite." Snow avalanches presented a hazard, at times causing deaths in the winter months. The Dutch Flat *Enquirer* reported on December 25, 1866, that "a gang of Chinamen employed by the railroad was covered up by a snow slide and 4 or 5 died before they could be exhumed. . . . Then snow fell to such a depth that one whole camp of Chinamen was covered up during the night and parties were digging them out when our informant left."

Such conditions and perils may have been slightly ameliorated by aspects of Chinese culture that made camp life more tolerable. At the end of the workday, for example, men regularly heated water in large containers and enjoyed sponge baths and a change of clothes before eating their dinners. Workers' diets included familiar Chinese foods, some of which were imported from their homeland: dried oysters, dried fish, sweet rice, dried bamboo, salted cabbage, dried fruits and vegetables, noodles, dried seaweed, dried abalone, dried mushrooms, peanut oil, tea, pork, and poultry. This was a more varied and balanced diet than that of white workers, who consumed salted beef, beans, bread, butter (sometimes rancid), and potatoes. The Chinese also drank large quantities of warm tea, whereas whites quenched their thirst with cold water, coffee, and strong whiskey. Unfortunately, that unheated water at times was contaminated, causing illness. Some railroad officials commented that Chinese workers were physically healthier than their Anglo counterparts.

At least three other aspects of Chinese culture could be found in the railroad work environment: religious shrines, opium, and gambling. At various points along the right of way, workers erected religious structures such as "joss houses," or temples of worship for Buddhists, Taoists, and Confucians. Statuary and incense sticks were common furnishings in these constructions. In addition to their religious practices, opium-smoking in the evenings tended to bring a measure of calmness and relaxation into the lives of harried Chinese workers. The drug, along with foodstuffs and other items, was imported from

China. Strobridge and Crocker hated the narcotic, but since workers' productivity seemingly remained unimpaired by the substance, no effort was made to prohibit its use. The alcohol guzzled by white workers, on the other hand, led to fights, hangovers, and slowdowns. Gambling, railroad officers observed, was a deeply ingrained cultural habit among Chinese. Generally, head men regulated the activity to counter indebtedness, bankruptcy, and the discord that could follow.

Though the Chinese were industrious, reliable, low-wage workers who posed few problems for their employer, on one major occasion they registered their discontent with labor conditions. When the Central Pacific rejected their requests for $40 a month and a 10-hour workday (eight hours in the tunnels), some 2,000 Chinese went on strike in June 1867. A spokesperson for them put it bluntly: "Eight hours a day [in the tunnels] good for white men, all the same good for Chinamen." With no support from other workers and Crocker cutting off food and other supplies for the Chinese, the strike collapsed after only a week, and work resumed.

Having built across the Sierra by mid-1868, the Central Pacific's crew found it much easier to construct roadbeds and lay track in the flat terrain of Nevada. Pushing eastward at the rate of nearly a mile per day, the Central Pacific reached the Great Salt Lake Basin in January 1869. Farther east the Union Pacific was descending from the Rockies. Public and worker excitement mounted as the two railroads approached each other.

In late April the two railways were 14 miles apart, and the Central Pacific took up the challenge of beating the track-laying record just set by the Union Pacific. As newspaper reporters watched, the Chinese and European immigrant workforce of the Central Pacific laid 10 miles and 56 feet of track in slightly less than 12 hours, surpassing the Union Pacific record by more than 2 miles. Acknowledging the importance of the Central Pacific's Chinese workforce, Edwin B. Crocker, an attorney for the railroad and brother of Charles Crocker, observed: "The early completion of this railroad we have built has been in large measure due to that poor, despised class of laborers called the Chinese, to the fidelity and industry they have shown."

On May 10, 1869, a jubilant crowd assembled at Promontory Point, Utah, designated by Congress as the meeting point, to celebrate the completion of the transcontinental line. The hundreds of onlookers included political dignitaries, railroad executives, crewmen, and reporters. A photograph that became famous was taken; it did not include a single one of the 10,000 Chinese workers present. Prayers and speeches were followed by Leland Stanford's driving of a golden spike, symbolically anchoring the last rail. Telegraph wires sent word of the achievement to a waiting world. The streets of Chicago were clogged with a 4-mile procession of people rejoicing at the news; in Philadelphia the Liberty Bell peeled an acknowledgment of the triumph.

In a sense, Columbus's quest for a western route to Asia had been brought to a successful end, but the benefits for American railroads turned out to be much less than promoters had anticipated. The fabled Northwest Passage waterway or Strait of Anián, sought by Cabrillo and other mariners since Columbus's time, in effect, turned out to be a manmade overland conduit spanning the North American continent. Ironically, in mid-November 1869 the Suez Canal was completed, providing an all-water route to the Orient from the Mediterranean. Consequently, much of Europe's Far Eastern trade flowed through the new

Figure 6.2   Dignitaries and laborers at the Golden Spike ceremony. Andrew J. Russell, 227 East and West, shaking hands at "Laying Last Rail," May 10, 1869. Collection of the Oakland Museum of California, City of Oakland. Museum Purchase.

canal, reducing the importance of America's Pacific railroad as a carrier of transatlantic goods to West Coast ports and on to Asia.

The Southern Pacific Railroad and the American West

To some extent the growth of California's economy in the 1870s and 1880s, and that of western America as well, was tied to the expansion of the Southern Pacific Railroad. Literally and figuratively the emergent railroad giant was an engine powering the development of a greater California. Headquartered in San Francisco, the Southern Pacific's sprawling network of tracks constituted the first nationwide and international transportation system.

By 1900 it had branch offices in major cities throughout the United States and Europe, and boasted the world's largest transit network. The Southern Pacific achieved its domination of western railroading by absorbing the Central Pacific and taking over smaller carriers, establishing numerous routes within California and between states in the western and southwestern regions, selling subdivided land grant parcels to settlers, providing refrigerated rail cars for eastward-bound produce and agricultural information to growers, and developing an effective advertising program to lure farmers and others to the Golden State.

Chartered in California in 1865, the still unbuilt Southern Pacific Railroad was bought by the Big Four three years later. The Associates then folded the Central Pacific into their growing corporation, continuing to acquire other lines as opportunities presented themselves. Anxious to eliminate the possibility of a competing transcontinental line into southern California, the Big Four hastily built a Southern Pacific line south from the Central Pacific junction at Lathrop through the San Joaquin Valley to Los Angeles and then the Colorado River. Three thousand Chinese workers laid the roadbed, bridging that river and making Yuma, Arizona railroad-accessible by autumn 1877. During the 1870s the Southern Pacific began construction on a second north–south route from San Jose to Los Angeles. In 1876, amid great fanfare and after paying the Big Four a $600,000 subsidy plus ceding the rail line to San Pedro, Los Angeles was linked to the state's northern transcontinental route. This so-called "coastal route" was opened in sections and finished in 1901.

In addition to these main lines, the Southern Pacific bought or built numerous branch lines throughout the state during the last three decades of the nineteenth century. Railroad historian Richard Orsi notes that by the late 1870s the Southern Pacific had established a monopoly on rail traffic in California. The company was capitalized at $225 million, and owned 2,340 miles of track and 85 percent of the railroads in the state, including all the important lines in the San Francisco Bay Area, Los Angeles, and the Sacramento and San Joaquin valleys.

During the 1880s the Southern Pacific registered even more spectacular growth, causing some organizational restructuring. The completion in 1883 of a second transcontinental railway, the famed "sunset route" connecting San Francisco and New Orleans, gave the Big Four access to the carrying trade of the Gulf of Mexico. Simultaneously, the Associates extended tracks from the Sacramento Valley into the Pacific Northwest, reaching harbors at Portland and Coos Bay as well as the fertile Willamette Valley.

The rapid growth of the Big Four's railroad enterprise necessitated corporate reorganization. Because some states did not allow out-of-state railroads to operate within their jurisdictions, separate Southern Pacific Railroad companies had to be established in different states, which added to the costs and burdens of management. Moreover, the railroad's mergers and acquisitions increased its size and complexity. To address these challenges posed by growth, the Big Four established a large holding company – the Southern Pacific Company – in 1884 to manage their far-flung transportation empire. Holding companies bought controlling shares of stock in businesses operating within the same industry, thereby reducing competition. Though incorporated in Kentucky, because of California's business-friendly laws the California-created rail giant remained headquartered in San Francisco. Leland Stanford served as president. Due to Stanford's time-consuming work as a U.S. Senator, however, Huntington, resentfully at times, handled financial matters in both Washington, D.C., and New York.

The following year, by which time the new holding company operated some 5,000 miles of track and owned dozens of railroad companies in addition to extensive interstate and international maritime shipping enterprises (discussed later), the Southern Pacific Company bundled management into two huge systems. Operating rail lines west of El Paso, Texas, Alban N. Towne oversaw the Pacific System from his San Francisco office. Working out of New Orleans, A.C. Hutchinson supervised the Atlantic System, which included rail business east of El Paso. In order to make informed decisions, the Big Four instituted coherent and comparable accounting procedures among the Southern Pacific's affiliates. These efficiency measures came just in time, for in November 1885 a transcontinental competitor arrived in California – the Atchison, Topeka & Santa Fe Railroad had reached San Diego.

The Southern Pacific's land dealings, criticized by contemporaries and many historians, added to the company's profits from 1865 to the end of the century. According to the railroad's documents the sale of subdivided government land grants was aimed at providing "limited quantities [of acreage] to those who will cultivate the soil, and who will own the land they cultivate." Numerous small farms would foster regional prosperity and build an expanding customer base for traffic as growers would need rail access to markets. To feed this traffic, the railroad operated an international land sales office in London, resulting in the settlement of immigrant European farmers in California. Regarding these arrivals, the *Reno Gazette* grumbled in an 1876 issue that "this afternoon the westbound emigrant train disgorged the shabbiest lot of mortals it has been our misfortune to see for some time. The bell rang, all got aboard and went off. Reno . . . [was] relieved, but we could not help feeling for California."

Such social commentaries aside, historian Richard Orsi places the Southern Pacific's federally granted California land holdings in the range between 3 million and 5 million acres by 1900. However, the railroad owned an aggregate of some 18 million acres in such grants in California, Oregon, Nevada, and Utah. Still, the bulk of the Southern Pacific's profits came from its transport operations, which were greatly enhanced by the carrier's founding of farm towns in the San Francisco Bay and Los Angeles areas, the San Joaquin Valley, Oregon, Nevada, Arizona, and Texas.

The Southern Pacific's provision of refrigerated rail cars made possible the nationwide marketing of California's fruits and vegetables, while the railroad's dissemination of agricultural information among growers promoted an important new sector of the state's economy. Moreover, the company contributed financially to the growth of agricultural colleges in California, Arizona, Nevada, Oregon, and Texas. The resulting boost given to scientific agriculture ensured a steadily increasing flow of produce that would be carried by the railroad. A clearer example of the Southern Pacific acting on the basis of enlightened self-interest would be hard to imagine.

Because more settlers meant a larger customer base for its carrying services, the Big Four developed an effective promotional campaign to lure people, especially farmers, to the Golden State and other parts of the West. Both company and outside writers were employed. For example, nationally prominent journalist Charles Nordhoff, a freelancer hired by Collis P. Huntington, published *California: For Health, Pleasure, and Residence* (1873). Nordhoff assured readers that California's violent frontier conditions were in the past; good farmland was plentiful and just waiting to be tilled. From the 1870s through the 1890s, the railroad used the world fairs, held in Europe and the United States, to display lavishly the fruits and other products of the state, including woods, wines, cereals, minerals, and a host of manufactures. The fact that California won 42 prizes for its fruit displays at the World's Industrial and Cotton Exposition, held in New Orleans in 1884–5, was due largely to the efforts of the Southern Pacific. The railroad's 1898 launching of *Sunset* magazine, a San Francisco monthly, did much to boost the fortunes of the Southern Pacific and the state. By 1904 the publication boasted 58,000 subscribers nationwide, and the railroad constituted the largest corporation in the West.

Pacific Profile: Seafaring Journalist Charles Nordhoff

Charles Nordhoff (1830–1901), was born in Erwitte, Prussia, and immigrated to the United States in 1845. He received some education in Cincinnati but mostly was schooled informally during a boyhood printing apprenticeship and especially his nine years at sea in the U.S. Navy, serving on a whaler, and in the merchant marine. Most of his sea wanderings and journalistic writings centered on Pacific venues: California, the West Coast, and Hawai'i. *Nine Years a Sailor* (1857) and *Stories of the Island World* (1857) chronicled his early years afloat.

In the early 1870s, Nordhoff moved into political and travel journalism, writing and editing for the New York *Evening Post* and reporting for the *New York Herald*. During these years he voyaged to San Francisco, Honolulu, and the Columbia River. Either by ship or stagecoach (the record is not clear), he made his way down to San Diego as well.

It was the Southern Pacific Railroad that commissioned him to write the book on these ventures referred to just above, *California: For Health, Pleasure, and Residence*. His promotional volume covered numerous subjects, including climate, scenery, the Central Pacific Railroad, the Chinese, and more. In it he wrote, "California has certainly the finest climate in the world." He made this statement with reference to the coastal areas of Santa Barbara and San Diego, whose sea breezes and mild temperatures he loved and equated with health. California's landscapes and seascapes enthralled Nordhoff. The several books he read about Yosemite did not prepare him for the grandeur he witnessed: "No man

can so describe the Yosemite Valley as to give to one who has not seen it even a faint idea of its wonderful, strange, and magnificent scenery." Beyond Yosemite's giant redwoods and granite peaks, he urged readers to voyage along California's coast, which "has a great deal of fine scenery." Concerning other topics the book addressed, Nordhoff was full of praise for his literary patron, the Central Pacific Railroad and its founders. The Big Four were credited for their vision, honesty, and establishment of one of the "most thoroughly built and equipped and best-managed [railroads] in the United States." Being on their payroll, what else was he to say?

The Chinese, employed by that railroad and as agricultural field hands and abalone-hunters, also fared well in the book. "They learn very quickly, are accurate, painstaking, and trustworthy, and especially as gardeners and for all hand-labor they are excellent." Nordhoff urged that the U.S. government allow more Chinese women to immigrate to America's shores to reduce the number of brothels in the state's Chinatowns. Education and conversion to Christianity would, he thought, enable the Chinese to discontinue opium-smoking. Nordhoff traced the lives of Chinese American abalone-hunters in arid Baja California. Supplied with food and water by a San Diego sea captain, these border-crossing hunters sent back with the schooner master cargoes of cut, cured, and packed abalone meat that would then be shipped up the coast to San Francisco. There the cargoes would be loaded onto China-bound merchant vessels. Here is another illustration of California's growing ties to the Pacific Basin. Nordhoff's own ties to a greater, Pacific California solidified when he purchased a ranch near Ensenada, and settled during the later years of his adventurous life in Coronado, near San Diego.

Northern California, Oregon, and the Sandwich Islands (1874) constituted a second book of his, connecting the Golden State to the Pacific world. It also evidenced the anti-imperialist views that informed his New York *Herald* writings against America's possible annexation of Hawai'i in 1893–4.

Nordhoff died in San Francisco, a city whose population was "more uniformly civil, obliging, honest, and intelligent than they are anywhere in this country, or . . . in Europe." Highly respected and influential in his day among politicians and journalists, curiously he has no biographer. Far more famous is his Polynesia-sojourning grandson, Charles Bernard Nordhoff, co-author of the acclaimed *Mutiny on the Bounty* trilogy that was adapted for the award-winning film by that title in 1935.

Transpacific Steamers

The Southern Pacific grew into such a leviathan because in addition to operating its extensive rail lines it became a major maritime shipper. Beginning in the 1870s, the railroad and steamship businesses were integrated into a huge transport network that connected the eastern United States with the West Coast and transpacific trade. San Francisco, the West Coast's busiest port for international trade, was the network's major hub through which goods and people flowed. Consequently, the state's Asian Pacific orientation became increasingly pronounced.

Unwilling to let the Pacific Mail Steamship Company (see Chapter 5) dominate the maritime West Coast and transoceanic trade, in 1874 the Big Four founded a competing line – the California-based Occidental and Oriental Steamship Company. Capitalized at $10 million in stock, the company was jointly controlled by the Central Pacific and Union Pacific railroads, which is indicative of how important the prospect of Pacific trade was to these transcontinental railway giants. Leland Stanford served as president of the company during most of its first two decades of operation. The wharves of the Central Pacific were placed at the disposal of the new steamship line free of charge, and steamers were to make runs to and from Asia monthly.

While the two steamship companies were supposedly competitors, a large measure of cooperation obtained in order to ensure predictable, stable profits. For example, each company agreed to offer a monthly transpacific voyage, undertaken at 15-day intervals. Earnings on tea and other through cargoes (those routed from Asia, across the Pacific, and onto trains destined for markets between California and the eastern seaboard) were divided between the railroads and Pacific Mail. Further, the railroads guaranteed to Pacific Mail the profits from at least 600 tons of freight monthly. Lastly, Pacific Mail agreed that its San Francisco wharf could be used by both shipping firms.

The firms used an ever-widening range of routes and ports. In the early years of service, the Occidental and Oriental steamers sailed from San Francisco at the middle of each month (Pacific Mail vessels sailed on the first) en route to Yokohama, and then to Hong Kong. In the 1880s voyages were launched from San Francisco every 10 days. By the early 1890s Honolulu had become a stopover port; not long afterward Manila was added to the transpacific route of both shipping lines. In 1896 the two lines entered the Far East's coastal trade. This resulted in their vessels carrying goods and passengers from Yokohama to Kobe, Nagasaki, and Shanghai before anchoring in Hong Kong. These same ports were revisited on the return voyage to San Francisco.

Regarding crossing times and crews, the Occidental and Oriental ships traversed the Pacific faster than those of Pacific Mail. Steaming from Yokohama to San Francisco usually took 15 or 16 days. Both companies employed Chinese crews, recruited in Hong Kong. They received wages below what would have been paid to whites.

Passengers ranged from those few, usually Anglo-European, in first-class cabins, to the many, most of whom were Chinese, in steerage. Asians carried to the United States sometimes numbered more than 1,000 on a single vessel.

Cargo-carrying was far more profitable than the passenger business. Income from the eastbound Asian trade was more than three times that of the westbound cargo departing from San Francisco. In order of their revenue-generating prospects, the major eastbound commodities included tea, silk, merchandise, rice, burlap sacks, sugar, and opium. In 1899, for example, the *Doric* dropped anchor in San Francisco with 2,346 bales of raw silk aboard, valued at approximately $2,500,000. Among westbound cargoes, flour was the most lucrative product, followed by silver, Mexican dollars, ginseng (a medicinal herb), and jewelry. In the period 1878–1900 the Occidental and Oriental provided its stockholders an average of a 60 percent return on their investments. So at the same time that the company facilitated through sea and rail traffic between Asia and America's eastern seaboard, via San Francisco, the shipping line turned a nice profit. California, whose role was pivotal in this maritime–overland interchange, became increasingly Pacific-involved.

Depression and the Anti-Chinese Movement

At the heart of California's economic development, railroads were also at the center of America's hard times during the depression of the 1870s. Over-speculation in railroad stocks coupled with the collapse of a major Philadelphia bank that financed the Northern Pacific Railroad triggered the nationwide business downturn. A great railway strike in 1877 unleashed waves of violence in New York and Chicago that swept across the country to California. As has often been the case in hard times, some segments of the public sought scapegoats, especially among immigrant laborers.

In the fields, mines, and urban workplaces jobs were scarce. Widespread unemployment among white farm- and ranch-hands, aggravated by drought in the winter of 1876, resulted in rural workers occupying abandoned barns for shelter. Comprising half the workforce in the state's mines in 1870, many Chinese left the diggings for railroad construction jobs, or moved into towns and cities, gaining employment in restaurants and laundries. Often they lived in ethnic enclaves called Chinatowns, scattered from Chico to San Diego. The scarcity of jobs alone would have led to blaming the Chinese for white unemployment; the arrival in 1876 of 22,000 Chinese laborers in San Francisco compounded the job shortage and fed existing anti-Asian prejudice. By then, such workers constituted about one-fourth of the state's toilers available for hire. Numerous and easily identified, for many Anglos Chinese became what historian Alexander Saxton termed "the indispensable enemy."

S.S. Doric

Figure 6.3   The Occidental and Oriental steamer, *Doric*. This steel-hulled vessel regularly sailed between San Francisco and Hong Kong. According to the July 6, 1902, edition of the *New York Times*, this steamer had arrived the day before in San Francisco carrying the largest ever shipment of opium (33,210 pounds) and 129,492 chests of tea. © Mystic Seaport, Photography Collection, #1999.175.615.

On October 24, 1871, Los Angeles was the scene of the bloodiest anti-Chinese massacre in the state's history. Resistance to a police raid and an assault by 500 mainly Anglos and some Hispanics, deputized as members of a posse, sparked the ensuing race riot, resulting in the killing of between 19 and 21 Chinese. Most of the victims were lynched. Competition for jobs was a factor but probably not the most important one causing this outburst of violence.

A combination of statewide anti-Chinese prejudice and the death of a white man in a local feud precipitated the carnage in Los Angeles. Since the early 1850s the Chinese had been depicted as unclean and diseased; their women were commonly viewed as prostitutes. Tongs were characterized as un-American crime syndicates; Chinese religion was treated as paganism; and the foods of these people were often seen as disgusting. To this combustible mix of prejudice and hard times was added the sporadic feuds that set the residents of Los Angeles' Chinatown against each other. In the resulting crossfire, occasioned by a dispute between two Chinese companies, that is, community organizations, over a woman, a white man – Robert Thompson – was accidently killed and two officers injured. Within hours police and a posse went on a rampage, murdering Chinese indiscriminately, burning their buildings, and looting their stores.

Indicative of the public's blaming of the city's Chinese residents for the violence, the justice system failed to imprison even those few who were convicted of wrongdoing. The Los Angeles district attorney's indictment was so sloppy that it neglected to charge any of the defendants with murder. Eight rioters, who had been sentenced to the state prison at San Quentin, regained their freedom shortly after incarceration when the California supreme court overturned their convictions by lower tribunals. The time had not yet arrived when the state's Chinese could defend themselves in court against the wrath of lynch mobs and the partiality of local police departments.

As economic conditions worsened nationwide, anti-Chinese violence erupted in Chico, San Francisco, and elsewhere throughout the state and the West in 1877. When a Chico businessman, employing Chinese in his soap factory, leased a slaughterhouse to some Chinese people, the facility was burned and a note sent to the property owner, John Bidwell: "Sir, you are given notice to discharge your Mongolian help within ten days or suffer the consequences." More incidents like that followed. On March 14 the anti-Chinese rage reached a crescendo. At a ranch just outside of town, five armed men shot four Chinese hired to clear land, and then set their homes ablaze. One of the gunshot victims died. The *Chico Enterprise* newspaper revealed on March 30, 1877, that members of the Laborers' Union – connected to a white supremacist group called the Order of Caucasians – were responsible for the terror. Court trials and convictions followed but all those imprisoned were paroled long before their sentences had been served.

San Francisco's outburst of anti-Chinese violence, while not as deadly as that in Los Angeles, was deeply rooted in racial bigotry. The bigotry was fed by the large flow of Cantonese immigrants arriving at San Francisco, the hub of Chinese transpacific voyaging. Between 1848 and 1876, 233,136 Chinese arrived in that city, while 93,273 departed for China from that port. In 1876 alone about 20,000 came. Some Anglos saw the growing numbers of these immigrants as dangerous to public health and morals. In a report issued in 1876–7 the San Francisco Board of Supervisors stated that the Chinese were viewed as "a social, moral and political curse to the community." Brothels, opium smoking, gambling, and communicable diseases (especially syphilis and leprosy) were attributed to these foreigners, who, additionally, were thought to be inassimilable. Chinatown, according to that report, was "a laboratory of infection," inhabited by "lying and treacherous" aliens. Jobless, working-class whites resented these newcomers, who offered their services for paltry wages. As employment competition intensified during the depression-ridden mid-1870s, previously simmering anti-Chinese prejudice boiled over. Steamships arriving in San Francisco from China were met by angry, club-wielding mobs that attacked the disembarking Asians. Bloody riots ensued.

To restore order, William T. Coleman, famed vigilante leader, formed a Committee of Safety. With a force of more than 1,000 men, armed with pick handles, the more stable, merchant-class of the city stood ready to exercise a measure of restraint on outraged laborers. Still, some rioting occurred with loss of life; however, conditions remained more volatile in the East, particularly Philadelphia.

San Francisco's anti-Chinese movement then returned to the political arena, where it had been effective earlier. For example, in 1870 the city had passed a Sidewalk Ordinance outlawing the use of a bamboo pole placed across one's shoulders, from which loads were

Figure 6.4 A *Wasp* magazine cartoon showing arrival of Chinese in San Francisco. White laborers blamed the Pacific Mail Steamship Company and its Canadian affiliate for transporting Chinese workers to San Francisco, where the new arrivals established businesses that threatened local white merchants who could not compete with the cheap Asian labor. Courtesy of the Bancroft Library, UC Berkeley.

suspended. This method of conveyance had been customary for the Chinese peasantry. In San Francisco white boys were known to upend the loads for amusement, causing spillage onto the street.

The need for a movement leader was met with the arrival in the city, by clipper ship, of a fiery Irish seaman, later turned wagon master, Denis Kearney. A gifted orator and polemicist, Kearney established the Workingmen's Party. Organized in early October 1877, the party's demands included: the eight-hour workday, direct election of U.S. Senators, compulsory education, state regulation of banks and railroads, and a fairer tax system. Capitalists and monopolists were denounced. Uppermost, however, was the demand for ridding California of the Chinese. Kearney's inflammatory speeches, often delivered to huge outdoor audiences gathered at a sandlot across from the city hall, ended with such phrases as "The Chinese must go" and "Every workingman should get a musket." "Are you ready to march down to the wharf and stop the leprous Chinamen from landing?" Kearney roared to one throng. Five days after haranguing a crowd of 2,000 near Charles Crocker's Nob Hill mansion, Kearney and five of his accomplices were arrested and jailed for two weeks. After being released, the mantle of the martyr added even more effect to his resumed anti-Chinese rhetoric. He was repeatedly arrested for inciting riots, and each freeing brought him more popularity. On the occasion of one of his prison releases, 7,000 workingmen celebrated by parading through the city.

Tension mounted in January 1878 as 1,500 unemployed workers demonstrated for "work, bread, or a place in the county jail." At another such gathering men threatened to destroy the wharves and vessels of the Pacific Mail Steamship Company, and bomb Chinatown. Coleman again called out his law and order forces, and the U.S. Navy sent a warship to defend federal mail docks.

Amid this backdrop of unease and terrorist threats, the Workingmen's Party held its first convention on January 28, 1878. Speakers scorned "capitalists and their willing instruments" in government. With its base energized, the party's political clout grew. The following year it elected a mayor of San Francisco, several state supreme court justices, 11 senators, and 16 assemblymen. Despite these results, the party collapsed nearly as rapidly as it had formed. Its demise was due to internal strife and suspicion that Kearney had taken bribes from the railroad. Though withering and suffering from dissension within its ranks, the Workingmen's Party had drawn considerable attention to the need for reform and managed to seat 51 delegates, a sizable minority, at the upcoming state constitutional convention.

The Constitution of 1879

In the nearly three decades since statehood, new economic and social issues arose that galvanized into political action groups within California's dramatically increasing population. One such issue was an inequitable tax system that placed undue burdens on farmers. Another was the seemingly limitless power of the Southern Pacific Railroad and abuses by other corporations, including banks. A third concerned a white backlash to the influx of Chinese immigrants. Many politically active Californians decided that these and other matters could not be addressed effectively by mere legislation. In state elections in September 1877, voters approved the call for a new constitutional convention.

Beginning in September 1878 and ending six months later, a Sacramento constitutional convention was attended by 152 delegates, three times the number assembled in Monterey in 1849. Fifty-seven were lawyers, 39 were farmers, and the rest came from diverse occupations. All were white males. They wrote one of the longest, most detailed charters in the world, much lengthier than its U.S. counterpart. That happened as provisions were included relating to nut trees and wrestling.

In addition to rejecting a proposal for women's suffrage and eliminating the 1849 requirement that all laws be published in Spanish and English, the delegates addressed the issues primarily responsible for the convention. Regarding tax relief for growers, the results were disappointing. Still, in principle, some headway was made with the establishment of a state board of equalization, whose mission was to oversee tax collection fairly and efficiently. Also, the document contained a provision making mortgage holders liable for taxes on the equity they held in farm lands. While a rate- and fine-setting railroad commission of three members was established, it came to be seen as a pawn of the Southern Pacific. Real railroad regulation was several decades away. Regarding the Chinese, the constitution authorized the state to protect itself from "aliens, who are, or may become . . . dangerous or detrimental." Corporations and the state were prohibited from employing Chinese, except "in punishment for crime." Cities were permitted to restrict Chinese to prescribed districts, as well as to disallow their residence entirely. "Asiatic coolieism" was equated with "human slavery."

The finished document satisfied few. Conservatives warned that it was communistic; liberal reformers complained that it failed to protect the rights of workingmen. Politics being "the art of the possible," it probably represented the best blending and balancing of voting factions and their interests attainable at that time. With little enthusiasm, the electorate approved the document on May 7, 1879, by a numerical majority. More than 80 percent of the electorate cast ballots. Northern California's larger cities, where the Workingmen's Party had clout, opposed ratification. Southern California's rural counties, dependent on rail transport for crops, voted for approval. The charter has been amended more than 350 times and has undergone other substantial revisions. It remains the fundamental law of California.

Halting Chinese Immigration

California's Caucasian-led anti-Chinese movement, strongly represented at the Sacramento constitutional convention, garnered national support at the end of the 1870s. New York City's Chinatown, emerging at that time, was home to about 2,000 residents in the 1880s. By then, the same anti-Chinese rhetoric and racist cartoon caricatures found in San Francisco newspapers appeared in those of New York.

The late nineteenth-century campaign to halt the flow of Chinese into America, assuredly, was nationwide; however, California launched the inglorious movement. A first step in stemming the influx of Chinese required modifying the (Anson) Burlingame Treaty of 1868, which had provided for their unlimited entry into the United States. The treaty was amended in 1880, giving the United States the right to "regulate, limit, or suspend such coming or residence, but may not absolutely prohibit it." This amendment became the basis for the drafting of the law that would virtually halt Chinese immigration into America.

In early 1882, California Republican Senator John F. Miller introduced a bill in Congress establishing a 20-year embargo on Chinese laborers entering the United States. Having bipartisan support, the measure passed both houses but President Chester A. Arthur vetoed it. Shortly afterward, effigies of Arthur were hanged or burned in the settlements of Merced, Napa, Williams, and Tomales. The Miller bill thereafter underwent change. A 10-year embargo replaced the longer one. So revised, the Chinese Exclusion Act again passed both houses, and this time President Arthur signed it into law on May 6.

The new law contained basically two provisions: first, it suspended the immigration of Chinese laborers, skilled and unskilled, for 10 years; second, it prohibited the naturalization of Chinese in America. Teachers, students, merchants, and travelers were exempted from the immigration ban. The statute was extended twice for successive 10-year periods in 1892 and 1902.

The enactment of the Chinese exclusion law was significant in American and California history. Passage of the measure marked the first time the U.S. government had restricted the immigration of a group based on ethnicity. Also, support for exclusion by many Republicans indicated that by the early 1880s that party's abandonment of African Americans' civil rights had broad implications for other non-white minorities as well. California's tradition of anti-Asian discrimination was markedly reinforced by the Act. Even after its passage, the prejudice did not abate. An 1885 report issued by San Francisco's Special Committee declared that the alleged filth and immorality of Chinatown were "inseparable from the very nature of the race." While deportations were not part of the exclusion measure, the state's Chinese population declined sharply from a highpoint of 136,000 in 1883 to fewer than 46,000 by 1900. In 1943, at which time China was a World War II ally of the United States, President Franklin D. Roosevelt lifted the ban.

Even with the consequent shortage of Chinese labor in the wake of exclusion, the state's economy rebounded and grew by leaps and bounds in the last decades of the 1800s. The dramatic recovery infused the dream of Eldorado with fresh possibilities and gave rise to a cultural flowering that commanded national attention.

SUMMARY

The federal government subsidized the building of the transcontinental railroads in the latter half of the nineteenth century mainly to develop West Coast markets and transpacific trade with Asia. California, as home to the Central Pacific Railroad, played a major role in this epic undertaking, as members of the Big Four – or the "Associates" – and several of the state's politicians helped write the federal Pacific Railroad Act of 1862. That measure launched the transcontinental railroad-building era. The San Francisco-based Pacific Mail Steamship Company transported thousands of Chinese contract laborers to the Golden State, where they served as the backbone of the Central Pacific's workforce. Meanwhile the Associates bought the Southern Pacific Railroad, which subsumed the Central Pacific. The merger enabled the Southern Pacific to monopolize railroad traffic in California and throughout the entire western United States, with tracks extending also to the Gulf Coast. In 1874 the Southern Pacific founded its own profitable Pacific shipping line, the California-based Occidental and Oriental Steamship Company. By then California shippers dominated the passenger and cargo trade of the Pacific Basin. Preeminent seafaring journalist Charles Nordhoff, on the Southern Pacific's payroll, wrote books and magazine articles luring Americans to the Golden State, Hawai'i, and the Pacific Northwest. In 1900 the Southern Pacific constituted the largest transit network in the world. The commercial reach of Greater California had become ever greater.

At the same time that California's economic clout had grown, so too did its vulnerability to downturns in the nation's business cycle. Such was the case in the nationwide depression of the 1870s. The hard times led to widespread unemployment in the Golden State, and out-of-work whites blamed low-wage Chinese workers for the downsized labor market. In 1871 Anglos and some Hispanics in Los Angeles rampaged through Chinatown, sparking the violence that resulted in the looting of Chinese-owned stores, the burning of buildings, and the deaths of residents. At the insistence of labor leaders, Californians wrote and passed a new constitution in 1879 that contained provisions aimed at regulating railroads, providing for a fair apportionment of taxes, and restricting the rights and employment opportunities of Chinese. At that time, Irish American Denis Kearney was leading angry, unemployed whites in San Francisco in a sometimes violent crusade to stop Chinese immigration into the United States. As a result of this unrest, California played a major role in Congress's passage in 1882 of the Chinese Exclusion Act, which prohibited nearly all Chinese from entering the United States for 10 years. With extensions the measure remained in force until 1943.

REVIEW QUESTIONS

- What were the connections between the federal transcontinental railway project of the 1860s, the Pacific Rim, and California? How did the Big Four's founding of the Occidental and Oriental Steamship Company fit into those connections?
- In what ways did journalist Charles Nordhoff exemplify California's Pacific Basin orientation?
- What were the effects of the nationwide economic depression of the 1870s on California?
- What were the major features of the California constitution of 1879?
- What was California's role in the framing of Congress's policy of Chinese exclusion in 1882?

FURTHER READINGS

David Haward Bain, *Empire Express: Building the First Transcontinental Railroad* (New York: Viking Penguin, 1999). This is a comprehensive, even-handed, and highly detailed account of one of the signal events in California and American history.

Dee Brown, *Hear that Lonesome Whistle Blow: The Epic Story of the Transcontinental Railroads* (New York: Henry Holt, 1977). The building of all of the late nineteenth-century U.S. transcontinental railroads is covered in this brief volume, which is distinctive in its presentation of foreign opinion of these long-distance carriers.

California History, 57/1 (Spring 1978). The entire issue is devoted to "The Chinese in California."

Sucheng Chan, *Asian Californians* (San Francisco: Boyd & Fraser, 1991). Though the volume's thematic organization sometimes seems to scramble chronology, the work brims with information and insights unlikely to be found in any other single book.

Yong Chen, *Chinese San Francisco, 1850–1943* (Stanford, CA: Stanford University Press, 2000). In addition to chronicling the history of America's oldest and largest Chinatown in the period covered, this study is greatly enriched by the author's focus on transpacific connections between Guangdong Province and San Francisco as well as the use of Chinese-language sources.

Thomas W. Chinn, ed., *A History of the Chinese in California: A Syllabus* (San Francisco: Chinese Historical Society of America, 1969). This syllabus, compact and filled with vital information, is a starting point and indispensable resource for any inquiry into Chinese California's past.

Bruce Cumings, *Dominion from Sea to Sea: Pacific Ascendancy and American Power* (New Haven, CT: Yale University Press, 2009). The work is one of the first to call out the importance of the Pacific world and California's maritime role in shaping American history.

William Deverell, *Railroad Crossing: Californians and the Railroad, 1850–1910* (Berkeley: University of California Press, 1994). The public's changing reactions to the Southern Pacific Railroad, from unrealistic hopes to a sense of betrayal, are traced with care in this well-researched book.

Victor Jew, "The Anti-Chinese Massacre of 1871 and Its Strange Career," in William Deverell and Greg Hise, eds., *A Companion to Los Angeles* (Malden, MA: Wiley-Blackwell, 2010), 110–28. This chapter treats anew the 1871 Los Angeles massacre as "the starting point of the city's modernization."

John Haskell Kemble, "The Big Four at Sea: The History of the Occidental and Oriental Steamship Company," *The Huntington Library Quarterly*, 3/3 (April 1940), 339–57. This is still the most detailed, authoritative account of the topic, written by a master of California maritime history.

David S. Lavender, *The Great Persuader: The Biography of Collis P. Huntington* (Boulder, CO: University of Colorado Press, 1999). The author shows how Huntington, ruthlessly at times, operated outside of the law but within the morality of Gilded Age America to promote the building of the rail complex that transformed California, the West, and the nation.

Susie Ling, ed., *Bridging the Centuries: History of Chinese Americans in Southern California* (Los Angeles: Chinese Historical Society of Southern California, 2001). An array of topics is covered in this anthology, seasoned by numerous first-hand accounts by persons identified with the Southland's many Chinese communities.

Charles Nordhoff, *California: For Health, Pleasure, and Residence. A Book for Travelers and Settlers* (Berkeley: Ten Speed Press, 1974). This reprint of Nordhoff's 1873 book offers detailed written sketches of the state's topography, climate, farming, manufactures, cultures, and much else.

Paul M. Ong, "The Central Pacific and Exploitation of Chinese Labor," *Journal of Ethnic Studies*, 13 (Summer 1985), 119–24. Using social science theory and methods the author shows that Chinese railroad workers were exploited more than previous studies had shown.

Richard J. Orsi, ed., "Railroads in California and the Far West," *California History*, 70 (Spring 1991). The entire issue is devoted to railroads in the history of California and the western states.

Richard J. Orsi, *Sunset Limited: The Southern Pacific Railroad and the Development of the American West, 1850–1930* (Berkeley: University of California Press, 2005). This is a comprehensive and sympathetic study of the operations and impacts of the Southern Pacific Railroad throughout the West.

Ernest N. Paolino, *The Foundations of the American Empire: William Henry Seward and U.S. Foreign Policy* (Ithaca, NY: Cornell University Press, 1973). Immersed in Seward's writings, the author lays out the secretary of state's vision for a San Francisco-based American Pacific empire, of which the transcontinental railroad is an integral feature.

Jean Pfaelzer, *Driven Out: The Forgotten War against Chinese Americans* (New York: Random House, 2007). Using an array of first-hand and secondary sources, the author details white California's often violent efforts to rid the state of Chinese, while showing how this ethnic minority fought back through the courts, boycotts, and arming themselves.

Robert Chao Romero, "Transnational Commercial Orbits," in William Deverell and David Igler, eds., *A Companion to California History* (Malden, MA: Wiley-Blackwell, 2008), 230–45. The author traces the increased flow of Chinese immigrants to Baja California and other parts of Mexico and Latin America as a result of being shut out of the United States in 1882.

Alexander Saxton, *The Indispensable Enemy: Labor and the Anti-Chinese Movement in California* (Berkeley: University of California Press, 1971). The author argues that California settlers carried into the state nationwide prejudices against blacks, that these prejudices were then applied to the Chinese, and that the resulting massacres helped unify the state's otherwise heterogeneous Caucasian community.

Norman E. Tutorow, *The Governor: The Life & Legacy of Leland Stanford*, 2 vols. (Norman, OK: Arthur H. Clark, 2004). Extensively researched and written by an authority, this is possibly the only comprehensive biography of this major figure in California and American history.

Richard White, *Railroaded: The Transcontinentals and the Making of Modern America* (New York: W.W. Norton, 2011). The author details the greed, graft, corporate arrogance, and exaggerated claims of the transcontinental railroads as the harbingers of American progress, thereby reassessing the government–railroad partnership in late nineteenth-century America.

John Hoyt Williams, *A Great and Shining Road: The Epic Story of the Transcontinental Railroad* (Lincoln: University of Nebraska Press, 1996). A lively and highly readable narrative, the work is distinctive in its coverage of how Asian trade, via California, figured prominently into plans for building the first transcontinental railroad.

7
Eldorado's Economic and Cultural Growth

California's vital economic and cultural development from the 1870s to the early twentieth century strengthened both its Pacific Basin connections and its ties to the North American West. In the economic arena, that development is seen most vividly in the harnessing of water resources, the rise of commercial agriculture, the emergence of the petroleum and boride enterprises, the electrification of municipal railways, the land and population boom in southern California, and the growth of maritime trade and naval facilities. As the Golden State broadened its economic base, it acquired sufficient cultural polish to draw national, and in some instances international, attention to its writers, artists, photographers, newspapers, and institutions of higher learning. In short, California's reputation as a Pacific Eldorado where riches abounded and dreams came true took on fresh meaning and credibility.

Timeline

1852	What later becomes Mills College for Women is founded in the Bay Area town of Benicia
1855	Jesuits establish Santa Clara College
1863	The San Francisco *Examiner* is founded
1865	California's first oil well is drilled in Petrolia, Humboldt County
	The San Francisco *Dramatic Chronicle*, forerunner of the *Morning Chronicle*, begins publishing
1868	The California legislature charters the University of California; the campus is situated initially in Oakland and shortly thereafter moves to Berkeley
1870	California is ranked first in the quantity of wine produced in the United States, accounting for more than half of the nation's output
1873	Andrew S. Hallidie of San Francisco invents the world's first electrically powered cable car system
1874	The state adopts compulsory elementary education
1879	Political economist Henry George publishes *Progress and Poverty*, espousing his single-tax theory
	The University of Southern California is founded in Los Angeles

Pacific Eldorado: A History of Greater California, First Edition. Thomas J. Osborne.
© 2013 Thomas J. Osborne. Published 2013 by Blackwell Publishing Ltd.

1880s	Southern California's real-estate boom extends into Mexico
	San Francisco is the world's leading whaling port
1881	Helen Hunt Jackson publishes *A Century of Dishonor*, detailing the mistreatment of the California Indians
	The *Los Angeles Times* is founded
1884	George Chaffey founds the Los Angeles Electric Company, resulting in the City of Angels becoming America's first electrically lit municipality
1885	California's wheat flour exports to Hong Kong reach nearly 450,000 barrels
1886	In *Lux v. Haggin*, the state supreme court holds that the downriver riparian rights of Miller & Lux trump the prior appropriation claim of Haggin's firm (and by implication any similar future claims based on the old Hispanic doctrine)
1887	The Wright Irrigation Act is passed by the state legislature, recognizing the public's right to establish irrigation districts, exercise eminent domain, and raise revenue to finance irrigation projects
	Pomona and Occidental colleges are founded in Claremont and the Eagle Rock neighborhood of Los Angeles, respectively
1888	Built largely by Chinese immigrants and sited at the edge of the Pacific, the palatial Hotel del Coronado opens in San Diego
1890	The Union Oil Company of California is founded, with headquarters in Santa Paula
	The Pacific Coast Borax Company is founded by Francis Marion "Borax" Smith
	Hawaiian King David Kalakaua visits, and dies in, California
	Yosemite National Park is established
1891	Leland Stanford Junior University is founded in Palo Alto
1892	The Sierra Club is created and headquartered in San Francisco by UC Berkeley and Stanford professors; John Muir is elected president of the organization, which today is nationwide
1893–4	The midwinter International Exposition is held in San Francisco, marking the first world's fair held on America's Pacific slope
1898	In the Spanish–American–Cuban–Filipino War, 80,000 men from Washington, Montana, Iowa, Wyoming, Kansas, Tennessee, and Utah ship out across the Pacific from San Francisco harbor to the Philippines
1901	Robert Dollar enters the San Francisco shipping industry, developing a steamship line that becomes a major carrier in the growing China trade
	Frank Norris publishes *The Octopus, a Story of California*, a novel depicting the Southern Pacific as a heartless exploiter of San Joaquin Valley wheat growers
1903	The transpacific submarine cable is completed, connecting San Francisco to Manila via Hawai'i, Midway, and Guam
	Francis Marion "Borax" Smith establishes the East Bay Key System of rapid transit from Piedmont and Berkeley to San Francisco, using rail and ferries
	Bay Area author Jack London publishes his most popular book, *The Call of the Wild*, a novel about a San Francisco dog that adapts to the Alaskan wilderness

Water, Land, and Rural Development

From the 1850s to the 1910s water, land, and development were critical issues facing California. Each was thorny in itself. To compound the challenge presented by each, they were all linked closely together. Water resources had to be released from monopolistic control and then managed so as to avoid flooding and yet provide irrigation for farmland. Moreover, in order to be fully harnessed, those resources had to be transported long distances to facilitate the development of rural areas.

California's water, like the state's landform itself (see Chapter 1), has come from the Pacific, making possible the creation of an agrarian Eldorado. For millennia westerly winds have blown moisture-bearing clouds from the Gulf of Alaska and the vicinity of the Hawaiian Islands over the West Coast's landmass, supplying rainfall for the loam-rich Santa Clara and Central valleys. Aquifers, too, were filled by seepage from this precipitation. Pacific tides coursing inland from San Francisco Bay daily raised and lowered Sacramento River flows in the delta by as much as 2 to 3 feet.

Miners, farmers, developers, shippers, and settlers squabbled over control of the region's precious water resources during the latter half of the nineteenth century and beyond. River water rights, particularly in the upper reaches of the Central Valley, were especially contested. Until the American takeover of California, the Spanish system of "prior appropriation" governed the use of river water. Accordingly, regardless of where one's property was located, an owner could claim exclusive right to the use of a watercourse, and the sale of that claim, if he were the first party to divert and use a given stream or river. After statehood in 1850, American settlers largely rejected prior appropriation, insisting instead on the old English common law doctrine of "riparian rights." This meant that only those parties whose property bordered a stream or river could claim use of that water source. The rivalry between prior appropriation and riparian claimants was muddled and intensified greatly in the 1850s when the state legislature recognized the legitimacy of both approaches. One result of the ensuing confusion was that by 1870 only 60,000 acres of the state's farmland was being irrigated. This was but a fraction of the available irrigable soil.

A major court case arose out of the struggle for control of water flowing down the Kern River into the fertile, semi-arid San Joaquin Valley. Two titans in the business world, Miller & Lux Land and Cattle Company and the Kern County Land Company, vied for water rights to the Kern. Miller & Lux invoked riparian doctrine based on its ownership of a 50-mile-long parcel hugging the Kern. Its rival, led by James B. Haggin and Lloyd Tevis, asserted prior appropriation to justify its diversion of water upriver to land far from the Kern. In the landmark case of *Lux v. Haggin* (1886), the state supreme court held that the downriver riparian rights of Miller & Lux trumped the prior appropriation claim of Haggin's firm (and by implication any similar future claims based on the old Hispanic doctrine). Irrigation of farmland distant from a watercourse suffered a major setback.

Farmers not possessing riparian lands, however, won a major victory with the California legislature's passage of the Wright Irrigation Act in 1887. This path-breaking measure provided the public's right to establish irrigation districts, exercise eminent domain (usurp private water rights and seize publicly useful irrigation works), and impose taxes and sell bonds to finance irrigation projects. Fifty such districts had been established by 1911. The growth of California agriculture was no longer restricted by monopolizing business interests bent on controlling the state's valuable water resources.

Beyond irrigation, farmers and towns faced the challenge of floods. The flooding issue, especially in the soil-rich Sacramento Valley, derived from the gold rush period. Hydraulic mining (see Chapter 4), in which workers used high-pressure hoses to loosen ore from rock walls and hillsides, silted northern California rivers, rendering some impossible to navigate in parts. Worse, the muddy gravel washed into the Sacramento River from its tributaries – the Feather, the Bear, and especially the Yuba – at times caused horrific floods in Sacramento and throughout the Sacramento–San Joaquin delta. Humans and livestock both were victims of the liquid torrents that buried entire houses and other buildings while submerging valuable farmland and destroying crops. According to an 1891 Congressional report authored by scientists and engineers, 39,000 acres of California farmland had recently been buried in flood-carried mine tailings, resulting in nearly $3 million in losses. The longer that hydraulic mining continued, the greater the threat of deluge became because hillside debris settled along river bottoms, raising beds ever closer to their embankments.

Valley farmers erected levees (elevated embankments) and tried repeatedly to make hydraulic mining illegal. The "each man for himself" ethos of the times resulted in a patchwork of insufficiently high levees aimed at protecting one farmer's acreage while redirecting floodwaters toward another farmer's fields across the raging Sacramento. At times growers hired armed guards to defend their levees against sabotage by cross-river farmers whose lands would be swamped by the redirected river flows caused by the levees. Often, the imperiled cross-river farmers succeeded in overpowering such guards and destroying the problematic earthen bulwarks. The notion that growers on both sides of the Sacramento had a shared interest in a systemic, community-wide solution would take decades more to evolve. Not until the twentieth century did Central Valley growers benefit from the use of modern water storage facilities, aqueducts, and flood channels.

Southward, in the Los Angeles Basin (extending from Ventura County in the north to Riverside and Orange counties in the south) and California's Colorado Desert, the water issue also loomed of critical importance. Without water availability, economic growth could not take place.

George Chaffey, a self-taught engineer and entrepreneurial genius from Canada, was instrumental in building a water and electrical infrastructure in southern California. Because of his projects deserts would bloom and cities would be lit. His business involvements exemplified California's transpacific connections with Australia in irrigation-related matters.

Leaving Canada, Chaffey came to Riverside, where he and his brother opened a land-development business. The brothers bought 2,500 acres in Cucamonga, which they subdivided and brought water to via cement pipes. Buyers of each of the 10-acre parcels became shareholders in the brothers' Etiwanda Water Company. Within months fellow Canadians bought lots from the Chaffeys, establishing the colony of Etiwanda, the most innovative agricultural settlement west of the Rockies. Etiwanda was forward-looking not only because of irrigation and its cooperative stock feature, but also because it received electricity. George

Chaffey hit on the idea of harnessing the water power of streams descending from the San Gabriel Mountains to Cucamonga. Installing a hydroelectric generator near his irrigation works, he directed the resulting current by wire to his Etiwanda home. The result was electricity to light the house and power an arc light atop its roof. His home, thus, became the first in the Far West to be illuminated by electricity. Soon afterward, Chaffey installed a telephone line linking Etiwanda to San Bernardino. The brothers next duplicated their Etiwanda infrastructure in the nearby town of Ontario. Other towns close by, including Pomona, Pasadena, and Redlands, adopted various features of the Ontario model.

As these innovations suggest, George Chaffey developed infrastructures to improve living conditions in rural and urban areas. His signal contribution to urban life was his founding in 1884 of the Los Angeles Electric Company, which succeeded in making Los Angeles the first electrically lit city in the United States. By then Chaffey's achievements were drawing international attention.

A delegation of Australian officials visited Ontario, California, and concluded that the town's irrigation, electrification, schools, library, and churches offered a model to be replicated in the rural, arid parts of their colony. Intent on investigating how well his Ontario model might work in Australia, George Chaffey sailed across the Pacific from San Francisco to Sydney in 1886. By design or chance, he spent the next 11 years there, establishing irrigation settlements in Mildura and Renmark. Returning to California in 1897, Chaffey had learned from his Australian venture that whites could survive in extremely hot and arid climates (a notion that ran contrary to public thinking at that time) and government participation in irrigation and town-development projects could prove beneficial.

Equipped with this knowledge, Chaffey next undertook the challenging tasks of water engineering and town-building in California's Colorado Desert, a pocket of 600,000 acres of immensely fertile land located in the southeast corner of the state. Under his guidance, the Alamo Canal was built, which served as an overflow channel carrying Colorado River water from a point slightly below the Mexican border northward into the United States. In 1901, via this canal, the Colorado Desert (renamed by Chaffey as the Imperial Valley) underwent development. Within eight months, 2,000 settlers moved into the newly irrigated region, with more coming afterward. There, as elsewhere in the state, engineering genius tapped nature's bounty to spark economic growth.

Commercial Agriculture

Just as in the nation at large, California's farming sector in the last three decades of the nineteenth century moved increasingly from subsistence to commercial tilling. What distinguished the state's agricultural output in this era was the preeminence attained with respect to the cultivation of wheat, citrus and deciduous fruits, raisins, nuts, viticulture (grape growing), and sugar beets.

Nature, technology, and the built environment coalesced to foster California's wheat production, which, according to the 1870 census, surpassed gold as the state's most valuable commodity. In the ensuing decade wheat farming overtook ranching as the dominant form of California agriculture. The Sacramento and San Joaquin valleys were home to the sufficient rainfall, fertile soil, and heavy machinery that produced a wheat bonanza in the late 1800s. California's lead in inventing and utilizing steam-powered tractors and combines assuredly benefited the state's wheat growers. The building of rail lines connecting the Central Valley to San Francisco's waterfront enabled farmers to get their crops from distant fields onto waiting ships that would transport the grain to markets across the Pacific and elsewhere.

Though not representative of most growers, a few "wheat barons" and finance-shipping moguls conducted business on a vast scale. Hugh Glenn, for example, owned 66,000 acres of Sacramento Valley farmland on which he employed a thousand workers. Investing $300,000 in machinery, Glenn produced a million bushels of wheat a year by 1880. Isaac Friedlander facilitated the credit arrangements and sale of bulk grain cargoes by working with burlap sack companies, banks, warehouses, and shippers, ensuring that harvested wheat would reach the intended overseas markets.

While the bonanza lasted, both the quality and quantity of the state's wheat were impressive. Grower John Bidwell's wheat won the gold medal at the 1878 Paris International Exposition, meaning that his grain was judged the finest in the world. In 1889 California, with some 3 million acres of wheat fields, was the nation's second-largest producer of the staple crop. Such intensive and extensive cultivation, however, exhausted the soil. Simultaneously, competition arose from growers in the Mississippi Valley, Argentina, Russia, and Australia – many of whom imported techniques and machinery developed in California. Prices dropped and wheat cultivation gave way to a citrus fruit bonanza.

Spanish missionaries had introduced citrus orchards into Alta California to combat scurvy among crewmen aboard vessels plying coastal waters. Citrus crops included oranges, lemons, grapefruit, tangerines, and limes. Like so many other commodities connecting California to the Pacific world, the Far East – especially China – had been home to oranges and lemons. These fruits had been part of a much larger and ongoing Pacific exchange between Asia and the Americas dating back to the beginnings of the Manila galleon trade in the latter 1500s (see Chapter 2). While the yield from orange trees reduced the incidence of seagoing scurvy, the missions' Valencia variety did not meet the taste test for many. Still, gold rush miners opted for scurvy prevention over flavor. They thereby ensured a market for the seedy and often tart Valencias harvested from the orchards of growers like William Wolfskill, Los Angeles' mid-nineteenth-century pioneer citrus planter. In the late 1800s California planters imported eucalyptus trees from Australia, another article in the ongoing Pacific exchange, to serve as windbreaks for the proliferating orange groves in the Southland.

More than any other citrus crop, oranges captured statewide acreage and national markets. Sometimes referred to as "fruit of golden hue" by advertisers, the orange emerged as California's signature crop. America's nineteenth-century Orange Empire, says scholar Douglas Sackman, was centered in the Los Angeles Basin. Within this 50-mile north–south swath, orange production increased dramatically from about 1870 to the early twentieth century and beyond. In 1870 only 30,000 orange trees were growing in the state, mainly in this region. Twenty years later that figure had jumped to 1.1 million trees. In 1893 more than 70 million California oranges were sold nationwide, bringing in receipts totaling $32

Figure 7.1   A Pomona-like goddess holding
California oranges looks toward a ship in port.
Reproduced by permission of the Huntington
Library, San Marino, California.

million. By the early 1900s, southern California grew two-thirds of America's oranges and
at least 90 percent of its lemons.

A number of factors made this remarkable growth possible. The introduction of sweet,
seedless navel oranges, facilitated by the replanting of cuttings from Bahia, Brazil, in Riverside, California, in 1873, resulted in a year-round harvesting cycle. Valencias ripened in
summer, and Brazilian (renamed Washington) navels did so in winter. Refrigerated railroad
cars, in use by the 1880s, reduced spoilage of these perishable cargoes en route to national
and global markets. The creation of the California Fruit Growers' Exchange in 1905, later
rebranded as "Sunkist," removed middlemen from the business and provided growers with
cost-sharing technologies, packing, advertising, and marketing operations. Similar agricul-

tural cooperatives were formed by producers of seasonal fruits (peaches, apricots, and plums), nuts, raisins, poultry, and dairy products. Criticized as communistic by independent contractors who recoiled at the idea of nonprofit cooperatives, the fruit exchange was replicated by growers across the Pacific in Australia and elsewhere.

Little of the wealth enjoyed by the genteel growers living on Pasadena's "millionaire's row," later called Orange Grove Avenue, fell into the pockets of the fruit pickers. Generally, orchard workers were ethnically non-white males and came from throughout the Pacific Basin – China, Japan, Mexico, and the Philippines. They stood atop tall ladders, often harvesting oranges in sizzling temperatures and receiving a small wage calculated on the quantity of fruit a man picked. At most, pickers made a few dollars a day. From the 1870s to the 1890s, the Chinese predominated in the fields largely because orchard owners learned that rough treatment of oranges caused spoilage. The Chinese were thought to be the most skillful fruit handlers, and growers saw them as particularly suited by nature to withstand the harsh conditions and low pay. According to one planter, "the short-legged, short-backed Asiatic performs all of the stoop-over-work, the squat work. He stands any temperature." In the packing houses, where the washed and labeled fruit was wrapped in paper and placed in wooden crates for shipment, women performed the labor. Because they were paid by the box, or piece-rate, their hands flew practically without interruption. A 1914 report prepared by UC Berkeley economics Professor Carlton Parker, on conditions in the packing houses, noted: "By closing time the girls are pale and worn looking, almost wilting before one's eyes as the days drag along, leaning forward on their boxes for an occasional rest."

Prune plums, a deciduous fruit, were grown in abundance by Pacific-crossing Chinese and then Japanese workers in the Santa Clara Valley beginning in the late 1800s. In 1891 the valley's output reached 22 million pounds. By the early decades of the twentieth century, Santa Clara County produced half of the world's supply of prunes. With the opening of the Panama Canal in 1915, millions of cases of canned prunes and other California fruits were shipped across the Pacific and through the new waterway to markets along the Atlantic seaboard and elsewhere overseas.

California viticulture, like other agricultural enterprises, can be traced to the Franciscan padres. Their unremarkable sacramental libation was greatly surpassed in quality when a French commercial winemaker, Luis Vignes, closed his distillery business in Hawai'i and immigrated to California in 1831, settling in Los Angeles. A master vintner, he brought vine cuttings from France that he replanted on his southern California property. Twenty years later Hungarian immigrant Agoston Haraszthy grew Zinfandel grapes at his Sonoma vineyard. Within a decade French vintners Étienne Thée and Charles Lefranc were plying their trade in Los Gatos, and Charles Krug was operating a Napa Valley winery. Meanwhile, in what came to be known as Anaheim, a group of Germans established a wine-producing colony sustained by their planting of 400,000 grapevines. In later decades vineyards proliferated from Sonoma County in the north to Cucamonga in the south. By 1870 California ranked first among America's wine-producing states, responsible for more than half of the nation's output.

While not as stately as a wheat stalk, or as picturesque as a golden orange, or as sensuous as a wine grape, the lowly sugar beet nevertheless played an important role in late nineteenth-century California agriculture. Moreover, beet sugar magnates Claus Spreckels and the

Oxnard brothers (Robert and Henry) became influential businessmen in the state and the western region. After having liquidated his extensive Hawaiian cane sugar holdings, German-born Spreckels immigrated to California in 1888, underscoring the close relationship between Hawai'i and the Golden State. In San Francisco he entered the recently established beet sugar business. Sometimes called the "Sugar Emperor," he dominated the market for the sweet substance west of the Missouri River before partnering with the Oxnard brothers in the 1890s. Spreckels's Watsonville factory in Santa Cruz County was the largest of its kind in the United States before 1900, by which time California led the nation in the profitable beet sugar enterprise.

Despite Spreckels's and the Oxnards' dominance of the western sugar market, the Hawaiian-based maritime shipping firm of Castle & Cooke sent cargoes of island-grown cane sugar to their California and Hawaiian Sugar Refining Company factory in Crockett, California. The C and H brand, as it is familiarly known, has been a staple on grocers' shelves in California and beyond since the company's founding in 1905. Both the shipping firm and the sugar-refining company illustrate California's business ties to the Pacific Basin.

Black and White Gold

Just as California was a Pacific Eldorado agriculturally, that is, figuratively an extremely fertile seaboard land, similarly it possessed a wealth of other resources, especially petroleum and sodium borate (commonly known as borax). At times writers have referred to these two resources as black gold and white gold, respectively.

Though California's oil bonanza did not occur until the 1890s, drilling for the viscous substance started back in the 1860s. George S. Gilbert, previously a whale oil vendor, set up a small petroleum refinery on his ranch near Ventura in 1861. He sold the kerosene yield, which buyers used for home lighting. In that same decade Phineas Banning explored for petroleum near Wilmington, while up north in Humboldt County San Francisco investors drilled the state's first well at Petrolia in 1865. News of Gilbert's venture reached Thomas A. Scott of the Pennsylvania Railroad, who sent Yale University geologist Benjamin Silliman to California in 1864 to assess the state's petroleum prospects. The geologist's report, based largely on Gilbert's optimism, led Scott to purchase more than 250,000 acres, mostly in and around Ojai. Scott then sent his nephew, Thomas R. Bard, to drill on the purchased land. While little came of Bard's petroleum probes, he managed to make a fortune off the sale of lands belonging to his uncle and himself.

While Bard temporarily withdrew from oil ventures, a host of smaller operators, mainly in southern California, tried their luck in the 1870s and 1880s. Lyman Stewart and Wallace L. Hardison, Pennsylvania oilmen, drilled at Newhall, in northeastern Los Angeles County, in 1883. They met with enough success to buy land for further exploration while turning to the added pursuits of refining and marketing. Three years later and short of investment capital, Stewart and Hardison persuaded the cash-equipped Bard to join them in forming the Sespe Oil Company. By the end of the company's first year of operation it had produced 50,000 barrels of oil, which constituted about 15 percent of California's total output. When in 1890 the triumvirate founded Union Oil Company of California, headquartered in Santa

Paula, the state was poised for a petroleum future. Within the next decade, Union established refineries at San Pedro and at a location on the Carquinez Strait, built tankers and pipelines, and operated numerous wells in several Southland counties. In 1900 the firm ranked as a leader in the nation's oil industry.

Union was not the only successful petroleum corporation in California during this time. In the Bay Area, the Pacific Coast Oil Company was active. Southward, in Los Angeles Edward L. Doheny and Charles Canfield partnered in 1892 in developing the city's first oil field. The site was located near the La Brea Tar Pits, where the skeletal remains of entrapped prehistoric animals have since been found. In the resulting oil boom, 2,300 wells were dug during the next five years. Thereafter, Doheny became a major supplier of fuel oil for the Southern California Railway, a subsidiary of the Santa Fe Railroad. During that time, as railroads turned from coal to petroleum fuel, he opened drilling fields in Fullerton, Brea Canyon, and outside Bakersfield. In 1902 he sold his Petroleum Development Company to the Santa Fe Railroad. By then Doheny was probably the best-known oil promoter in the state. Also by then, he had founded the Mexican Petroleum Company, the first business of its kind to secure an oil contract from the nation south of the border. His spinoff asphalt company paved a good many of the streets in Mexico's major cities. For most of the early twentieth century Doheny's oil operations in California, Mexico, and, later, Peru linked him closely to the Pacific Rim as well as to Washington, D.C., where he lobbied on behalf of his extensive interests. By the 1920s, this Los Angeles-based tycoon was one of the richest men in the United States.

Standard Oil was also a major factor in the rise of California's oil industry. From the 1870s to the 1890s it transported by rail large quantities of its eastern oil products to the Golden State. These products, which the state's other petroleum firms also marketed, included oil for fuel, street paving, lighting, and machine lubrication. Standard bought the above-mentioned Pacific Coast Oil Company in 1900, six years later renaming it the Standard Oil Company (of California). By then the black gold of "Oildorado" had become a coveted prize in the nationwide competition among the petroleum giants of the day.

From the 1890s through the early 1920s and beyond, Union Oil and other California petroleum companies shipped much of the state's oil to West Coast markets aboard tankers docked and loaded at the Port of Los Angeles. The opening of the Panama Canal resulted in huge quantities of California oil being transported across the Pacific and through that passageway to destinations in the Atlantic Basin.

Though small compared to the oil-extraction industry, borax mining constituted a further broadening of California's economic base in the late nineteenth century. In 1881 Aaron and Rosie Winters, a couple living in the Ash Meadows region of Death Valley, learned of the search by Nevada prospectors for borax, a mineral used in laundry detergents and other products. California orange growers used it to kill blue mold on their golden globes. Borax is found in salt beds, and when refined could be sold profitably. Gathering a sample of the crystalline substance, Aaron conducted the prescribed flame test. When the flame burned green, indicating the authenticity of the substance, he is supposed to have exclaimed to his wife: "She burns green, Rosie. We're rich, by God!"

The Winters sold their Death Valley claim for $20,000 to William T. Coleman, a San Francisco businessman and former vigilante leader. Coleman started the Harmony Borax

Works near present-day Furnace Creek, located in Death Valley. He hired Chinese workers to scrape the "white gold" ore from the parched lake beds. They labored in temperatures that sometimes reached 130 degrees Fahrenheit, earning about $1.50 per day. Large wagons pulled by so-called "twenty-mule teams" carried the ore to a rail station in Mojave. The cargo was then transported to a refinery at Alameda in the Bay Area. After processing and packaging, the borax was marketed.

At the end of the nineteenth century California's infant borax business began its climb to international stature. In 1890 Francis Marion "Borax" Smith, an Oakland businessman, bought Coleman's properties for $550,000. He then combined his Nevada borax holdings with those he purchased from Coleman, forming the Pacific Coast Borax Company. Next, the newly consolidated firm adopted the "Twenty-Mule Team Borax" trademark that would become famous throughout the West and beyond. Smith invested his earnings in Bay Area real estate, amassing a fortune. Today's U.S. Borax Incorporated, headquartered in California, traces its roots back to the days of the Death Valley mule train. It is global, with offices throughout the Americas, Europe, and Asia, and is one of the major transoceanic shippers operating out of the Port of Los Angeles. Again, maritime commerce played a key role in California's development as a Pacific Eldorado.

Interurban Railways and Southern California's Rise

Municipal electric railways helped transform the state's two leading cities, San Francisco and Los Angeles, into modern metropolises in the decades preceding and following 1900. Though San Francisco served as the Pacific West's financial powerhouse and leading city, Los Angeles made great strides as an urban center, driving much of the Southland's robust growth.

The home of the world's first cable car system, late nineteenth-century San Francisco blazed the path toward modernization for cities in the Far West. Andrew S. Hallidie, a rope wire maker in San Francisco, invented the electricity-powered light rail system in 1873. Cable cars were so called because they were pulled up and down steel rails by underground wire cables. The first such rail line ran on Clay Street. The system was adopted throughout much of the developed world at that time until the invention of the overhead trolley in Richmond, Virginia, in 1888. Thereafter, San Francisco installed its own trolley system while retaining a scaled-down version of its old cable car network that is still in operation to the delight of its citizenry and tourists alike.

Francis Marion "Borax" Smith provided the entrepreneurial drive and capital, from his mining enterprise, to build interurban street rail lines for the East Bay area. The so-called Key System resulted. Thought by some to resemble a skeleton key shape, the mass transit system founded in 1903 was originally designated the San Francisco, Oakland & San Jose Railway. Smith's primary aim was to sell East Bay real estate, and the best way to do that was to provide convenient rail access into San Francisco from outlying communities, including Berkeley and Piedmont, which formed the loops of the key. Ferry ships constituted the "teeth" of the key; these bay-crossing vessels transported passengers from a 17,000-foot-long pier in Oakland to San Francisco.

Southern California was equally blessed with the entrepreneurial prowess necessary to develop a light rail transit system – one of several components (the others including the already discussed citrus industry and oil drilling) essential to the region's economic growth. Henry E. Huntington, nephew of Collis P. Huntington, had such talent.

Having no son of his own, Collis groomed Henry for leadership of the Southern Pacific's railroad empire. Though serving as vice president of the corporation, Henry's presidential prospects were dashed when in 1900 Edward H. Harriman, then president of the Union Pacific, gained control of the Southern Pacific as well. The resulting blocked promotion benefited southern California, for thereafter Henry invested his fortune and abilities in developing a trolley system that would eventually serve much of the Los Angeles Basin. Like "Borax" Smith, Huntington was keenly interested in selling suburban real estate and to do so he had to provide accessible transit into and out of central Los Angeles. Consequently, Huntington founded the Pacific Electric Railway Company (PE). The Los Angeles-based PE interurban rail system, featuring the signature "Red Cars," embraced 42 surrounding cities.

In addition to rails and real estate, Henry Huntington spurred Southland economic growth through his venture into electric power generation and distribution. On his uncle Collis's advice, in 1902 Huntington and a group of investors incorporated the Pacific Light and Power Company (PL&P). The company was formed to supply electricity to the trolley system and provide power to segments of Los Angeles County. PL&P's major project was the building of a hydroelectric power station on the Kern River in the Sierra Nevada range. Construction was slowed by legal wrangling between PL&P and two competing water firms, Miller & Lux and the Kern River Land Company. A costly settlement cleared the path for completion of a power-generation station and a concrete canal conveying river water to the hydroelectric plant. In 1905 PL&P began supplying parts of Los Angeles with electricity.

With a booming economy for most of the two decades following 1868, southern California's population grew rapidly, largely through the arrival of newcomers. In addition to those looking for affordable land and other economic opportunities, many came for the climate. *Sunset* magazine acknowledged that southern California had no gold but "eastern prospectors discovered an inexhaustible supply of twenty-two carat climate." The climate was especially valuable, said the many advertisers and publicists, because of its supposed health benefits. Uprooting herself from New England, Charlotte Perkins Gilman, an internationally known feminist and health-seeker, settled in Pasadena, where she enjoyed "heavenly" days that she contrasted with the East Coast's "sickly winters." Journalist Charles Nordhoff (see Chapter 6, Pacific Profile) wrote that Santa Barbara, San Diego, and San Bernardino had especially healthful climates. "In each of these places I have met men and women who have been restored to health and strength by residence there. . . ." By 1900 medical practitioners had disputed many of the sweeping claims that had brought thousands of health-seekers into southern California. Still, the health myth – symbolized by depictions of oranges on the doors of rail cars – had taken on a life of its own that would extend well into the twentieth century.

In addition to climate and health, some boosters stressed the richness of the region's Hispanic culture. Charles Fletcher Lummis, for example, was variously an influential *Los*

Angeles Times reporter, poet, Indian advocate, amateur anthropologist, and flamboyant magazine editor, who frequently dressed in southwestern garb. He enticed many out-of-state readers with his tales of the Franciscan missions and the glories of Spain's legacy in the Southland. A Harvard dropout in his senior year, Lummis walked from Ohio to California, via a route that took him 3,500 miles, arriving in Los Angeles in 1885. A love of the Southwest and all things Spanish and Indian resulted from his trek. Lummis himself built his stone-walled, hybrid mission-Indian pueblo-styled home, named El Alisal (now the headquarters of the Historical Society of Southern California) on the west bank of the Arroyo Seco in Highland Park. Some historians credit him for launching the Spanish mission revival/preservationist movement in Los Angeles and spreading it to Santa Barbara in the early 1900s. Lummis claimed that the Ramona myth alone, drawn from Helen Hunt Jackson's novel *Ramona* (1884) and romanticizing an unhurried Hispanic lifestyle in southern California in the 1850s, netted the region $50 million from tourism.

Their imaginations aroused, Americans took advantage of the rate war between the Southern Pacific and Santa Fe railroads and took the train to southern California. For a brief period in 1885, the price of a ticket from Kansas City to Los Angeles dropped to $1. Such a bargain provided an additional incentive, if any were needed, to get on board.

Available land, advertising, and low railroad fares touched off real-estate booms in southern parts of the state. Land sales there had shown an appreciable increase going back to the 1860s, when ranching declined due largely to prolonged drought. The downturn in ranching resulted in huge tracts of former grazing areas being put on the market for eventual subdivision into town sites, farms, and home lots. The combination of modest-priced land parcels, effective promotion, and affordable rail tickets sparked the real-estate boom of the 1880s, which marked the highpoint of Southland economic development in the latter half of the nineteenth century.

Most of the region's development occurred in Los Angeles and San Diego. Los Angeles' growth peaked in 1887, a year when tens of thousands of mostly white tourists and immigrants arrived. The city's population was estimated to have increased from 11,000 in 1880 to 80,000 by 1887 (though official records put the latter figure in the 50,000s). The 1887 boom attained its height during the months of June, July, and August, when some $38 million in real-estate transactions occurred. In San Diego the boom began with the arrival of the transcontinental railroad in 1885. Electric lighting was installed the following year, and the first electric streetcar line began operations in 1887. The city's population leapt from 2,637 in 1880 to 30,000 in 1887, thereafter trailing off and not surpassing the latter figure until 1910. John D. Spreckels, sugar refiner and steamship magnate as well as a son of Claus Spreckels, developed much of the city, including high-end Coronado properties. Built largely by Chinese immigrants and sited at the edge of the Pacific, the palatial Hotel del Coronado opened in 1888. The resort attests to the robust economy and rising stature of both San Diego and southern California in the late nineteenth century.

San Diego's real-estate boom extended south of the border into Mexico in the 1880s. A flurry of construction, including road building, took place in Tijuana, whose hot springs were touted as being among the best anywhere. Farther south down the Baja peninsula an 18,000,000 acre tract of land owned by the International Company of Mexico was subdivided into parcels for homes and farms. Los Angeles and San Diego newspapers advertised the opportunities awaiting the "man of small means." In the Mexican state of Sinaloa a cooperative colony known as Crédit Foncier attracted a number of Southlanders. The southern California boom mentality even reached to Mexico City, where land subdivisions began taking place. Greater California's influence in Mexico and especially Baja, through real-estate transactions and tourism, has increased fairly steadily ever since the late 1800s.

California's Maritime Economy

California's economy in the late nineteenth and early twentieth centuries was closely tied to the sea. The state's Pacific ports, so integral to prosperity, included San Francisco Bay and its up-channel delta waterfronts at Sacramento and Stockton, Los Angeles, and San Diego.

California's extensive maritime activity spread northward into Alaskan and Siberian waters, down the coast to Baja, up the Sea of Cortéz and into the Colorado River, across the Pacific to China and neighboring countries, to various Pacific archipelagos, to the western coast of Latin America, and around Cape Horn – until the Panama Canal was completed – to ports on both sides of the Atlantic. Seaborne shipments of some foods and oil have been mentioned briefly above. More extensive illustrations of the geographical reach and scale of the state's maritime economy can be seen in the shipping of wheat and wheat flour, quicksilver, and lumber, and in the shipbuilding, whaling, and fishing industries. In maritime matters, as has been implied in real-estate dealings, it makes sense to speak of a Pacific-oriented, "Greater California" whose reciprocal influences extended far beyond the state's borders.

California wheat and wheat flour were dry enough to withstand spoilage on long voyages to distant markets in Europe and Asia. Largely as a result of Isaac Friedlander's efficient organizing of the wheat and wheat flour trade in the 1860s and 1870s, San Francisco's grain exports increased significantly. In 1868, 193 ships carrying wheat and flour departed from that port; the corresponding figure for 1882 was 559 vessels. In addition to a strong overseas demand, the trade increased because transportation costs decreased due to the improvement in ship design. In 1868 the British introduced iron-hulled clippers, which marked an advancement over earlier vessels in carrying capacity and durability in storms. By the 1880s shipping rates between San Francisco and Liverpool, England, were less than half what they had been in the 1860s.

Given the high demand and reduced shipping costs, California wheat exports to Europe increased from 4,732,787 centals (1 cental equaled a hundredweight or 100 pounds) in 1869–70 to 12,786,534 centals in 1889–90. This threefold increase spurred the development of San Francisco's flour-milling industry. The plant of the state's leading flour miller, Abraham Dubois Starr, reached a daily capacity of 2,200 barrels in 1885. Ships departing San Francisco laden with flour milled by Starr and others at times sold some of their cargo in East Coast cities before crossing the Atlantic en route to Liverpool.

As early as 1854 Friedlander sent a trial shipment of wheat flour to China. The venture paid handsomely. He became more drawn to China than Europe for three reasons. First,

Figure 7.2   Grain ships near Martinez, c.1880. Courtesy of the Contra Costa County Historical Society, ID 1144. These grain vessels are sailing westward from the inland ports of Stockton and Sacramento through the Carquinez Strait toward the Pacific. Reproduced by permission of Contra Costa County Historical Society.

"down easters" (fast ships constructed in Maine) could sail from San Francisco to Hong Kong, the usual Chinese terminus for the flour trade, in roughly one month, compared to 100 days for those vessels to reach England. Second, the China voyage did not entail rounding the treacherous Cape Horn. Third, there was as yet no competition in the Hong Kong grain market, which as early as 1863 received 40,000 barrels of California wheat flour. During the next two decades, wheat became a dietary staple of the Chinese, second only to rice consumption. The Chinese used the wheat flour, prized for its purity and high gluten content, to make noodles and cakes.

In the 1880s the Golden State's wheat trade peaked before declining in the following decade. By 1885 California wheat flour exports to Hong Kong had reached nearly 450,000 barrels a year. California millers, with offices there, often reshipped some of their flour as far south as Singapore and as far north as the Russian port of Vladivostok. By 1900 Chinese farmers and factory operatives had learned enough about the growing and milling of wheat to supply their own market, and, consequently, California grain exports to the Celestial

Kingdom slumped, never to regain their once vaunted position. Still, those exports had provided a transpacific commercial bridge to China, opening that country in the early twentieth century to a brisk trade in other California-produced commodities, including lumber and kerosene.

Meanwhile, California led the nation in another article exported throughout the Pacific Rim in the latter half of the nineteenth century – quicksilver, or mercury. Until the 1890s, quicksilver ranked second only to gold in the value of the state's mineral output. The substance had a number of uses. In addition to producing the prized orange-red pigment/dye vermilion, quicksilver served to manufacture explosives, plate mirrors, fabricate scientific instruments, and make medicines. Its main use, however, was to recover gold and silver from ore. The recovery was done by crushing, wetting, and adding salt, copper, and quicksilver to make an amalgam that was spread onto a large flat surface called a patio. The amalgam was heated, thereby vaporizing the mercury (some of which was recaptured for future use), leaving the precious metals separated from the mix. From 1850 to 1900, California's mines, the most productive of which was New Almaden, supplied half the world's quicksilver. Drawn from Pacific-bordering nations, the workforce at that mine was composed largely of immigrant Mexicans, Chileans, and Chinese. About 57 percent of California's output, in the years 1852–90, was exported, mainly to the Pacific Rim nations of Mexico, Peru, and China (which used the substance for vermilion production). The remainder was sold to mining interests in the state and throughout the Far West, and to vermilion producers in New York.

California's logging industry, centered in the northern counties, shipped large quantities of lumber up and down the coast, inland to Sacramento, and across the Pacific. In some instances it was closely connected to timber and shipping enterprises whose operations extended from San Diego northward into Oregon and Washington. For example, lumber leviathan Pope & Talbot, Incorporated started as a San Francisco-based barge transport service in 1849. Several years later it entered the lumber trade. Headquarters were established in Oregon's Puget Sound area, yet the company had marketing offices in San Francisco, the hub of a vast Pacific Rim business zone. Co-founder Andrew J. Pope ran the San Francisco operations, which provided lumber shipments to Chile, Hawai'i, Australia, Japan, Hong Kong, and the West Coast of the United States. The firm's California branches expanded significantly in 1887 when it opened the San Francisco Lumber Company. During the next 20 years Pope & Talbot chartered lumber companies and distribution yards in Los Angeles and San Diego. In 1895 lumber magnate Robert Dollar, who similarly owned huge stands of timber from British Columbia to northern California, entered the San Francisco shipping industry. His Dollar Shipping Company initially transported lumber from the Sonoma coast to San Francisco. In 1901 Dollar expanded his operations by developing a steamship line that became a major carrier in the growing China trade. Known as the Grand Old Man of the Pacific, he eventually took over the Pacific Mail Steamship Company, established the American Presidents Line of vessels, made the cover of *Time* magazine, and amassed a maritime shipping fortune of $40 million.

Reflective of California's rising Pacific maritime profile, shipbuilding, concentrated around Humboldt and San Francisco bays, was a major business during the latter half of the nineteenth century. In both of these areas the transport of lumber was an important

Figure 7.3   African American whaling captain William T. Shorey and family. When the whaling industry moved from New England to California in the 1870s, African Americans comprised a large percentage of the crews. Courtesy of San Francisco Maritime National Historical Park, Victoria V. Francis Collection, photo number POO.21578X.

factor in establishing shipbuilding yards. On Humboldt Bay, Hans Bendixon's yard supplied at least 113 vessels to the trade, one of which was the lumber schooner *C.A. Thayer*, currently on display at San Francisco's Maritime National Historical Park. In the 1880s, as steam schooners began to displace wind-powered vessels, the San Francisco Bay area emerged as a prominent West Coast shipbuilding center. Benicia, a port on the bay since the 1850s, served as such a center for Matthew Turner, his brother Horatio, and John L. Eckley, beginning in 1882. Their firm, Turner and Eckley, specialized in constructing some of the fastest sailing vessels in the cargo trade between San Francisco, Hawai'i, and Tahiti.

Like shipping, whaling contributed greatly to American California's economy. In the mid-nineteenth century, New England ports, especially New Bedford, and the port of Lahaina on the island of Maui in Hawai'i, were the world's centers of deep-sea whaling. By the 1880s, however, San Francisco emerged as the unrivaled leader of the multi-million-dollar international whaling industry. From the Gulf of Alaska to Mexico's Sea of Cortés, San Francisco hunters preyed on the California gray whale, whose oil was used as a lighting fuel and lubricant, and whose bone matter strengthened women's corsets. Humpbacks and blue whales were also hunted. Crews came from diverse ethnic and national backgrounds, including Portuguese, Anglos, African Americans, Caribbean islanders, Hawaiians, and more. San Franciscan William T. Shorey gained fame and some fortune as the only African American whale boat captain of record on the Pacific Coast.

Fishing, too, brought wealth to the Golden State. Salmon and cod catches enriched the owners of the California-based Alaska Commercial Company, whose vessels traversed waters as far north as the coast of Siberia. In southern California Latinos and Asians fished the abundant offshore stocks of sardines, tuna, halibut, mackerel, sharks, barracudas, mussels, clams, and abalone. As early as the 1850s more than 500 Chinese fishermen worked the deep waters off Monterey. Women, mainly Asians and Hispanics, staffed the canneries in Monterey, San Pedro, and San Diego in the early 1900s. Chinese shrimpers, following the lead of Italians, set up dozens of camps around San Francisco Bay to catch and dry the small creatures, a sizable share of which were exported profitably across the Pacific to China. From the 1860s through the 1880s, Chinese abalone hunters, operating out of San Diego, regularly voyaged southward down to Baja's Cabo San Lucas in search of the lucrative mollusks whose iridescent, pearl-colored shells and prized meat brought high prices. Once caught, the abalone were dried and shipped from San Diego to China, where the demand was insatiable. As this maritime trade suggests, California's Pacific Basin economic ties grew ever stronger in the half-century or so after statehood.

The extent to which the Golden State's maritime economy aroused global attention is seen in the 1893–4 Midwinter International Exposition in San Francisco. This marked the first time the world's fair was held on America's Pacific slope. During the fair's five-month run, one and a half million visitors strolled through the 160 acre site at Golden Gate Park, in view of the state's spectacular fruit, wine, and olive displays. California's deserved reputation as an Eldorado on the shores of the Pacific was greatly enhanced by the extravaganza.

While San Francisco was clearly the Pacific Coast's dominant port city throughout the 1800s, Henry Huntington foresaw a time in the near future when the center of maritime trade and influence would shift southward as the United States became increasingly Pacific-oriented. Los Angeles, he said, was "destined to become the most important city in this country, if not the world. It can extend in any direction as far as you like; its front door opens on the Pacific, the ocean of the future. The Atlantic is the ocean of the past. Europe can supply her own wants. We will supply the wants of Asia." As the Pacific world loomed ever more important to the United States, California and its ports served as America's primary gateway to that vast ocean basin.

Pacific Profile: David Laamea Kalakaua, King of Hawai'i and Visitor

David Laamea Kalakaua (1836–91), Hawai'i's monarch from 1874 until his death, was one of several Hawaiian rulers to visit California in the nineteenth century, and because the Golden State was part of the Union after 1850, he became the first monarch to enter the United States. He visited California three times: in 1874, 1881, and 1890. The first visit was of particular importance in that it greatly strengthened the island kingdom's economic ties to both California and the United States,

facilitating eventual annexation of Hawai'i to the Union in 1898.

His 1874 visit to California and Washington, D.C., was for the purpose of supporting passage of a treaty of commercial reciprocity, whereby Hawaiian cane sugar and other products would enter the United States duty free, and American articles would likewise not be subject to tariffs on entering Hawai'i. Kalakaua sailed from his island kingdom aboard the U.S.S.

(Continued)

Benicia, accompanied by an entourage of advisers, including U.S. Minister to Hawaii Henry A. Peirce. Arriving in San Francisco, the royal party was greeted with all possible courtesy and fanfare. On behalf of the U.S. government, Kalakaua was welcomed by General John M. Schoefield, and on behalf of the city the king was greeted by Mayor James Otis. After spending a week in San Francisco the monarch traveled by railroad to Washington, D.C., where he met with President Ulysses S. Grant. The American president pledged his support for the reciprocity treaty, which was ratified by both governments and took effect in June 1875. Hawaiian cane growers thereafter became dependent on the market advantage of shipping their sugar to San Francisco, the West Coast's leading port and refining center. Under the treaty, island planters reaped millions of dollars in profits by underselling their tariff-paying foreign competitors. Kalakaua worked closely with Hawaiian grower and San Francisco refiner Claus Spreckels, and they both enjoyed the benefits of trade reciprocity.

The occasion for Kalakaua's 1881 10-day California stay was his round-the-world trip, undertaken in part to strengthen Hawai'i's standing in international affairs. His first and last stops were in San Francisco. After being entertained by U.S. officials and Spreckels, the king traveled to Sacramento before sailing across the Pacific to Japan. On encircling the globe, he returned to San Francisco for 11 days, visiting the Lick Observatory and spending two days at Spreckels's Aptos ranch, where the king was presented with a pair of bay horses and a thoroughbred colt. From there the monarch returned to Hawai'i.

In 1890 Kalakaua's health was in decline. On his physician's advice, he sailed to California in search of a cooler climate. Arriving in San Francisco on December 4, the king received the usual warm welcome and met with many of his longtime friends. In a private letter he wrote of his reception: "A spontaneous ovation. I have never seen the like before. . . . Not one moments rest. . . . Receptions, Balls, Dinners . . . Sunshine, Rain, Storm . . . Wonder that I am not half dead yet. . . . Good People and all that but awfully damn cold, Whio!" He was banqueted at the city's exclusive Union and Bohemian clubs, and ushered everywhere by high-ranking naval and civilian officials. After a visit of two weeks, the king traveled to San Diego, staying at the posh Hotel del Coronado, and to Mexico. On returning north, his health rapidly deteriorated. In Santa Barbara he suffered a slight stroke. Shortly after reaching San Francisco, his physician diagnosed the king's malady as Bright's Disease, a serious kidney ailment. On January 20, 1891, Kalakaua, staying in the city's Palace Hotel, slipped from unconsciousness to death. By then California's economic bond with Hawai'i was stronger than the island kingdom's connection to any other American state.

California and the Spanish–American–Cuban–Filipino War

California's commanding economic role on the Pacific seaboard was matched by its strategic importance, especially in time of war. In the late nineteenth century San Francisco served as America's primary staging area for all military operations in the Pacific. The importance of such operations in U.S. naval planning cannot be overstated. According to Admiral Alfred Thayer Mahan, the foremost American naval strategist of the time, during "the last quarter of the closing [nineteenth] century, the Pacific Ocean in general and eastern Asia in particular are indicated as the predominant objects of interest, common to all nations, both in the near and in the remote future." California's turn-of-the-century military importance can be understood only when viewed in this larger international maritime context.

The Spanish–American–Cuban–Filipino War (1898–1902), a compound of two closely related conflicts, resulted in the United States becoming an overseas empire and one of the foremost powers in the Pacific Basin. In the first war, lasting little more than three months in 1898, Yankee forces secured Cuba's independence from Spain. Through the peace treaty later that year the United States acquired the Philippines from Spain, but the takeover led immediately to Filipino military resistance. The path to America's victories in both wars ran through California, specifically San Francisco.

Shortly after the outbreak of war with Spain in April 1898, American Commodore George Dewey won a spectacular naval victory on May 1 over Spanish forces at Manila, in the Philippines. (His flagship *Olympia* had been built in San Francisco.) What had begun as a war in the Caribbean suddenly and dramatically now had a Pacific theater. San Francisco's Presidio served as the West Coast's troop-training center and point of embarkation for forces voyaging to Hawai'i (where needed coal would be loaded on steam-powered warships) en route to Manila. The mission of the troops was to reinforce Dewey's position in the event that a new Spanish naval squadron should be sent to recapture the Philippines. As assurance against this remote possibility, some 80,000 men from Washington, Montana, Iowa, Wyoming, Kansas, Tennessee, and Utah shipped out from San Francisco harbor to the Philippines.

Echoing the views of many naval strategists and West Coast maritime shippers, contemporary historian Hubert Howe Bancroft exulted in the aftermath of Dewey's Manila victory: "San Francisco Bay [would become the commercial] open door to all the world. . . . And as the [Pacific] ocean is the largest, its borders more extended and containing more natural wealth, its islands more numerous and opulent than those of any other sea or section, its ultimate destiny and development will be correspondingly great." California's commercial ties to the Pacific Basin became even more numerous and profitable after America staked out and secured its military position in the Philippines.

Securing that foothold near the coveted China market required America's suppression of Filipino resistance. That resistance developed in February 1899, as soon as islanders learned that the United States had annexed their Philippine homeland. In the ensuing three-year imperial war to put down the native "insurrection," troop ships crossing the Pacific departed from and returned to San Francisco. For example, the 9th and 10th U.S. Cavalry units, composed entirely of African American soldiers, voyaged to the Philippine battlefields from the Golden Gate port.

California's role in these turn-of-the-century wars had three lasting results. First, the state's major harbors and naval shipyards, like Mare Island in San Francisco Bay and the base established later at San Diego, kept California in the forefront of West Coast military planning. Second, the wars led to the completion in 1903 of the transpacific submarine cable connecting San Francisco to Manila via Hawai'i, Midway, and Guam. America now had streamlined communication with its new Pacific dependencies. Third, Filipino immigrants began coming to California in increasing numbers, often settling in port cities. In San Diego the first arrivals, beginning in 1903, were students enrolled at the State Normal School (now San Diego State University). Their fellow islanders, coming in the following decades, often worked in the canneries and fields. They were the children of a war they did not fight and part of the Pacific Rim immigrant labor force that helped build the Golden State's twentieth-century economy.

A Cosmopolitan Culture

Despite the hard times of the 1870s and 1890s, California's spectacular economic growth from statehood to the early 1900s nurtured an equally impressive cultural maturation. A wild and often lawless frontier society developed into a more civil, cosmopolitan one. By the turn of the century the state's writers, artists, and educational institutions would attain national and, in some instances, international recognition.

Mark Twain, born Samuel L. Clemens, was a transitory figure in the state's literary coming of age. In 1864 Twain entered California from Nevada, where two years earlier he had begun his writing career as a reporter and then editor for the Virginia City *Territorial Enterprise*. One of the most original and critically acclaimed American authors of his time, he elevated the quality of California writing to a higher tier of satire and irony, exemplified in such works as *The Celebrated Jumping Frog of Calaveras County and Other Sketches* (1867). The late 1860s found him reporting from the Sandwich (Hawaiian) Islands, "the loveliest fleet of islands . . . anchored in any ocean," voyaging to the East Coast to give popular lectures on his Pacific travels and other western topics, returning to California and Nevada briefly, and then leaving the Golden State for good.

Ambrose Bierce, like Twain a member of San Francisco's literati, was the most caustic of the state's writers, gaining him the nickname of "The Wickedest Man" in the city. Embittered by an unhappy childhood, his anger was poured out in venomous attacks on the Southern Pacific Railroad. In *The Devil's Dictionary*, he cynically defined truth as "An ingenious compound of desirability and appearance."

Rejecting cynicism, a number of talented political and environmental activists contributed their writings to the promotion of various causes. Henry George, Frank Norris, Helen Hunt Jackson, Charles Fletcher Lummis, Mary Austin, Jack London, John Muir, and Gertrude Atherton constituted a pantheon of reform-minded author luminaries that could be matched by few other states. All were well recognized far beyond California, and some were known internationally.

One of the most original social thinkers in the country, Henry George attributed the rise of wealth for the few and poverty for the many to the inequitable distribution of land. As populations increase, so do land values. The possessors of huge undeveloped holdings, like the Southern Pacific, unjustly received the unearned increment from rising real-estate prices. If governments would tax this unfair windfall, railroads would be incentivized to sell their unused acreage thereby spreading the wealth. This was the single-tax theory George espoused in his 1879 treatise, *Progress and Poverty*. This was the policy that when adopted would usher in "the Golden Age . . . the culmination of Christianity. . . ." Such were the views of a millennial-minded reformer who, on the other hand, vehemently opposed unions and characterized the Chinese as "utter heathens, treacherous, sensual, cowardly and cruel."

From his four years at the University of California at Berkeley, where he read the gritty, realistic fiction of Emile Zola, Frank Norris developed an interest in dramatizing the plight of the dispossessed in his own fiction writing. While sharing Henry George's contempt for the Chinese, Norris's national reputation derived largely from his publication of the propagandistic novel *The Octopus, a Story of California* (1901). The novel spoke to the public's deep-seated anger toward powerful trusts, in this case the Southern Pacific Railroad, which he portrayed as a heartless exploiter of San Joaquin Valley wheat growers (see Chapter 8). Norris wrote five other novels, among them *McTeague* (1899) and *The Pit* (1903).

Helen Hunt Jackson, Charles Fletcher Lummis, and Mary Austin advocated for Indians, while Maria Amparo Ruiz de Burton sympathized with Californios dispossessed of their lands. Though living in Colorado, Jackson researched the treatment of California's mission Indians and wrote *A Century of Dishonor* (1881), a government-commissioned *Report on the Conditions and Needs of the Mission Indians* (1883) with Abbot Kinney, and *Ramona* (1884), a popular novel romanticizing Indian life in Mexican California. Lummis, as noted, was a Los Angeles resident and similarly studied and defended Native American rights while venerating Spain's legacy in the Southland. As editor of the *Land of Sunshine* magazine, he recruited articles from the gifted Mary Austin. She wrote *The Basket Woman* (1904) and numerous other accounts of California and southwestern Indians. Ruiz de Burton, the state's first published Latina writer, authored *The Squatter and the Don* (1885), a novel depicting the struggles of a cultivated Mexican landowner in dealing with vulgar Anglo squatters as the don's nameless and poorly paid Indian ranch-hands looked on.

Jack London, a one-time oyster pirate on San Francisco Bay and later University of California at Berkeley dropout, became the world's most highly paid and well-known author. The setting for nearly all of his many books was the Pacific Basin. Though an avid socialist and political propagandist, his best-selling works centered on the struggle of men and dogs against such forces of nature as blizzards, scorching heat, and towering waves. *The Call of the Wild* (1903), a novel about a San Francisco dog that adapted to the Alaskan wilderness, was his most popular book. Infatuated by his reading of Herman Melville's South Sea tales, London taught himself sailing and voyaged aboard the schooner *Snark* with his wife Charmian. They stopped in Hawai'i, Bora Bora, Tahiti, the Marquesas Islands, Australia, and other exotic Pacific archipelagos. His near-death encounters and exhilarating experiences became material for his gripping and lyrical travelogue, *The Cruise of the Snark* (1911).

Josiah Royce and Hubert Howe Bancroft advanced historical studies in California. Though a philosopher by profession, graduating from the University of California and then completing a Ph.D. at Johns Hopkins University at age 23, Royce authored the influential *California: A Study of American Character: From the Conquest in 1846 to the Second Vigilance Committee in San Francisco* (1886). In this historical work Royce emphasized California's progression from a lawless mining frontier to a civil society built by pioneer settler families. Far more engaged in history than was Royce, Bancroft, a San Francisco bookseller and amateur scholar, traveled from California to Alaska buying books, manuscripts, and maps dealing with Pacific slope history. He then assembled a team of assistants to compose what became a 39-volume history of the Pacific Coast from California to Alaska. Seven of the tomes focused on California's past. Bancroft then sold his large collection of materials to the University of California, where it formed the nucleus of Berkeley's famed Bancroft Library.

As Half-Dome has towered over Yosemite Valley, so has the visage of John Muir hovered over the mighty Sierra, his beloved "Range of Light." From wood cutting and sheep herding,

Figure 7.4   Jack and Charmian London aboard
Snark. Courtesy of the Department of Geography,
UC Berkeley.

Muir moved on to mountaineering, environmental preservation, fruit farming, and nature
writing. Though he explored glaciers along the Pacific Rim from California to Alaska, and
then toured Australia, New Zealand, and Asia, much of the time he lived in and for the
Sierra, with regular stays at his family home in the Bay Area town of Martinez. Muir campaigned successfully for the establishment of Yosemite National Park in 1890 (it had been
a state park since 1864). Next, in San Francisco he and a cluster of hiking Berkeley and
Stanford professors founded the Sierra Club in 1892. They elected Muir president. The San
Francisco-headquartered organization aimed at conserving the Sierra and other Pacific
Coast wilderness areas. Today it is national in scope.

Gertrude Atherton, a suffragette and author of 34 novels, epitomized the writer as cosmopolitan. San Francisco born and raised, she lived in New York City and London, and
traveled in France and Germany before returning home to the City by the Bay. While in
France, Atherton finished the first of her several novels set in California, *Los Cerritos* (1890).
The Californians (1898), a later novel about man versus woman and restrictive Spanish

mores, won acclaim. The heroines in her works were often independent-minded women who challenged social conventions.

The doings of all these authors and much else were covered by the leading California newspapers of the day. The *San Francisco Examiner* was founded in 1863 and later sold to George Hearst, who in 1887 turned it over to his son William Randolph Hearst, whose nationwide chain of papers would soon become known for journalistic sensationalism. In 1865 brothers Charles and Michael deYoung started the forerunner of what three years later became San Francisco's *Morning Chronicle*. With the help of writers Bret Harte and Mark Twain, the paper soon enjoyed the widest circulation west of the Mississippi. The other leading paper of the period, the *Los Angeles Times*, was founded in 1881. Three years later Harrison Gray Otis bought the publication, building it into a powerful morning daily by the end of the century.

Painters and photographers, working in California, produced high-quality, nationally esteemed art in the late nineteenth and early twentieth centuries. William Wendt's seascapes and landscapes, particularly his oil painting *Old Coast Road* (1916), sited in Laguna Beach, has since become a classic. Similarly, the notable works of Albert Bierstadt, William Keith, and Thomas Ayers exemplify the magnetic pull of California's Yosemite Valley and other natural wonders on artists of the period. Charles Christian Nahl painted rambunctious historical scenes, such as *Joaquin Murieta: The Vaque* (n.d.) and portraits. Photographers Carlton Watkins and Eadweard Muybridge excelled in the new art form. What iconic Yosemite Valley and the Mariposa Grove did for painters, it also did for Watkins, as seen in his photographs *Vernal Fall* (c.1858) and *Section of the Grizzly Giant* (c.1866, sequoia redwood). These and other Sierra photographs brought Watkins fame in Paris. In addition to receiving notoriety by shooting and killing his wife's lover and allegedly poisoning her, Muybridge achieved international recognition for his Yosemite and so-called locomotion photographs, the latter depicting running horses.

Schools and colleges, as much as art, reflect the health and maturity of a culture. In this regard, California made tremendous progress during the half-century after the gold rush. The state adopted compulsory elementary education in 1874. Secondary education lagged, as five years later the state boasted only 16 high schools.

To provide for the anticipated crop of future students, the state established "normal schools." These publicly funded, two-year post-secondary institutions trained teachers for grades one through eight. In 1900 state normal schools were providing teacher education in Chico, Los Angeles, San Diego, San Francisco, San Jose, and Santa Barbara.

While pre-collegiate education for students and teachers was off to a slow start, higher learning registered major gains in a matter of mere decades. With few exceptions, California's leading universities and colleges were located in or near Pacific port cities. The state's Agricultural, Mining, and Mechanical Arts College was renamed and chartered in 1868 as the University of California. It was initially situated in the East Bay Area city of Oakland and later moved to Berkeley, an adjacent community just to the north. The new institution was named after George Berkeley, an Irish philosopher and bishop. Classes opened in 1869, and women were admitted with no numerical quotas the following year. From modest beginnings as a public, land grant college of applied learning the new public university had skyrocketed to international prominence by the early 1900s.

The University of California's first law school, Hastings College of the Law, was established in San Francisco in 1878. When two female applicants were rejected for admission, the new school became embroiled in a major controversy. Despite objections from the college's board of directors that women, because of their gender, were unfit for legal study, Clara Shortridge Foltz and Laura de Force Gordon won admission by triumphing in their 1879 law suit against the board. Foltz, the intellectually formidable mother of five children, thereafter became the first woman to practice law in California and to try cases before the California supreme court. She was also the inventor of the concept and role of the public defender, that is, an attorney employed and paid by the government to defend those too poor to afford private counsel. Both of these Hastings alumnae went on to distinguished careers and leadership roles in the state's women's suffrage movement.

Thirty-six miles away from San Francisco in the South Bay Area, Leland Stanford Junior University, named after the deceased only son of the Southern Pacific Railroad magnate, was established in 1891. Well-endowed with railroad money and ably led by biologist and president, David Starr Jordan, Stanford rose to eminence almost overnight. Women and men were to compete on an equal basis for entrance. However, due to the insistence of Jane Lathrop Stanford that female students never number more than 500, it would take decades before the university removed that gender-based admissions barrier.

A host of other fine private colleges and universities also appeared in the state in the latter half of the 1800s and early 1900s. Again, most were in or near Pacific port cities; nearly all had sectarian connections with Protestant or Catholic churches. Methodists founded the College of the Pacific in 1851 in the port city of Stockton. The following year Mills College for women, initially known as the Young Ladies' Seminary, opened in the port city of Benicia, afterward moving to Oakland. Santa Clara College (later university) was established in the South Bay Area by Jesuit priests and chartered in 1855. In 1879 Methodists founded the University of Southern California in the Pacific port city of Los Angeles. Congregationalists established Pomona (the oldest of the Claremont Colleges) and Presbyterians founded Occidental in 1887 in Eagle Rock, a suburb of Los Angeles. Whittier, a Quaker college, commenced instruction in 1901, while Redlands, a Baptist institution, did so in 1909.

California's amazing economic and cultural growth took place amid mounting public anger targeting the Southern Pacific Railroad, and increasing labor union activity. These matters await examination in the next chapter.

SUMMARY

California's economic and cultural growth from the 1870s to the 1920s catapulted it into the front rank of states in an increasingly Pacific-oriented America. The Golden State grappled with its perennial water-distribution problem sufficiently well to become the dominant farming state in the Far West, whose grain and other agricultural exports were shipped throughout the Pacific Basin and beyond. Similarly, in oil extraction, mining, manufacturing, development of its urban infrastructures, and especially its maritime economy California led the region, augmenting its status as America's Pacific Eldorado. Visits to the state by Hawai'i's King David Kalakaua underscored California's close economic connection to that island nation that the United States annexed in 1898 to increase the China trade and defend America's Pacific Coast. California's role as a training and staging area in the ensuing Spanish–American–Cuban–Filipino War, erupting in that year, was pivotal and determinative. Completion of the transpacific submarine cable in 1903, linking San Francisco to the Far East, was simply the final development needed to render California as America's Pacific fortress.

California's unequaled and diversified economic growth, coupled with its new military importance, was matched by a surge in its cultural achievements. The Golden State had become cosmopolitan. Its writers were regionally, nationally, and in a few instances internationally acclaimed. Newspapers flourished, as did scholarship and the arts. Often located in or near Pacific port cities, the state's institutions of higher education, especially the University of California and Stanford, had gained national prominence by 1900. Smaller institutions, such as Pomona and Occidental colleges, tended to have close Church ties when they were founded.

REVIEW QUESTIONS

- What was the Ontario (California) model of irrigation and electrification developed by George Chaffey? How and when did that model get transplanted across the Pacific in Australia?
- How were California's agricultural and oil enterprises, often centered in the state's interior regions, connected to Pacific maritime commerce?
- How was David Laamea Kalakaua, King of Hawai'i, linked to California's history?
- What was California's role in the Spanish–American–Cuban–Filipino War, 1898–1902?
- What evidence is there of Pacific Basin ties in the life and writings of Jack London?

FURTHER READINGS

J.A. Alexander, *The Life of George Chaffey: A Story of Irrigation Beginnings in California and Australia* (Melbourne: Macmillan, 1928). The author makes a strong case for his view that Chaffey's 11-year sojourn in Australia prepared him for bringing irrigation to California's Colorado Desert.

Barbara Babcock, *Woman Lawyer: The Trials of Clara Foltz* (Stanford, CA: Stanford University Press, 2011). Clara Foltz's brilliant, reform-oriented legal career is detailed in this thoroughly researched and engagingly written study.

John E. Bauer, *Health Seekers of Southern California* (San Marino, CA: The Huntington Library Press, 1959). This is one of the few in-depth studies of a topic vital to the rise of southern California.

California History, 74 (Spring 1995). The entire issue is devoted to "Citriculture and Southern California."

Daniel E. Cletus, *Bitter Harvest: A History of California Farmworkers, 1870–1941* (Berkeley: University of California Press, 1981). The origins of the ongoing marginalization of California field workers are expertly chronicled in this work.

Edwin T. Coman, Jr., and Helen M. Gibbs, *Time, Tide & Timber: Over a Century of Pope & Talbut* (Palo Alto, CA: Stanford University Press, 1949). Though celebrating Pope

& Talbut's first hundred years, this pro-company account offers useful material on California lumbering.

Bruce Cumings, *Dominion from Sea to Sea: Pacific Ascendancy and American Power* (New Haven, CT: Yale University Press, 2009). This may be the first study to place California's development at the center of America's westward thrust across the continent and into the Pacific Basin.

William Deverell, *Whitewashed Adobe: The Rise of Los Angeles and the Remaking of Its Mexican Past* (Berkeley: University of California Press, 2005). The book shows how after statehood an Anglo-dominated Los Angeles at times utilized and obliterated the area's connections to Mexican places and people.

William Deverell and Greg Hise, eds., *A Companion to Los Angeles* (Malden, MA: Wiley-Blackwell, 2010). See chapter 12, by David Vaught, for an up-to-date analysis of rural California's economic and social development.

Glenn S. Dumke, *The Boom of the Eighties in Southern California* (San Marino, CA: Henry E. Huntington Library and Art Gallery, 1944). Though dated, this is still essential reading on the meteoric rise of late nineteenth-century southern California.

William B. Friedricks, *Henry E. Huntington and the Creation of Southern California* (Columbus, OH: Ohio State University Press, 1992). This well-researched volume stresses Huntington's entrepreneurial talents, which were vital in modernizing early twentieth-century Los Angeles.

Norris Hundley, Jr., *The Great Thirst: Californians and Water, A History* (Berkeley: University of California Press, 2001). This is the most thorough, balanced, and insightful work on the critical subject of water in the state's history.

David Igler, *Industrial Cowboys: Miller & Lux and the Transformation of the Far West, 1850–1920* (Berkeley: University of California Press, 2001). Through the operations of one powerful company, the author shows how western land and water rights were consolidated and the environment degraded as industrialization advanced in the Far West.

Robert Kelley, *Battling the Inland Sea: American Political Culture, Public Policy, and the Sacramento Valley, 1850–1986* (Berkeley: University of California Press, 1989). Though not the last word on delta hydraulics and public policy, this book is the starting point for any serious exploration of these matters.

Carey McWilliams, *Southern California: An Island on the Land* (Salt Lake City, UT: Gibbs M. Smith, 1983). In this classic account, the author stresses what he sees as the insularity of southern California up to World War II.

Daniel Meissner, "Bridging the Pacific: California and the China Flour Trade," *California History*, 76 (Winter 1997–8), 82–93. This is one of the first studies to link wheat-growing in the Central Valley to the Asian Pacific market.

Richard J. Orsi, "The Octopus Reconsidered: The Southern Pacific and Agricultural Modernization in California, 1865–1915," *California Historical Quarterly*, 54 (Fall 1975), 196–220. The Southern Pacific's role in fostering California agriculture is persuasively presented in this journal article.

Thomas J. Osborne, "Claus Spreckels and the Oxnard Brothers: Pioneer Developers of California's Beet Sugar Industry, 1890–1900," *Southern California Quarterly*, 54 (Summer 1972), 117–25. The largely ignored role of these sugar magnates in shaping California's agricultural development is highlighted in this study.

Donald J. Pisani, *From the Family Farm to Agribusiness: The Irrigation Crusade in California and the West* (Berkeley: University of California Press, 1984). The work situates California's irrigation challenges and agricultural development within a regional economy.

Paul W. Rodman, "The Wheat Trade between California and the United Kingdom," *Mississippi Valley Historical Review*, 45 (December 1958), 391–412. An authority on western economic development details the profitability and market dynamics of California's wheat trade with Britain.

Douglas C. Sackman, *Orange Empire: California and the Fruits of Eden* (Berkeley: University of California Press, 2005). In addition to covering the economics of California's emergent citrus industry, this work places that industry within a Pacific Basin exchange zone.

David J. St. Clair, "New Almaden and California Quicksilver in the Pacific Rim Economy," *California History*, 73 (Winter 1994–5), 278–95. This article traces the uses of and markets for this California-mined substance.

Robert J. Schwendinger, *International Port of Call: An Illustrated Maritime History of the Golden Gate* (Woodland Hills, CA: Windsor Publications, 1984). Whaling, mining, fishing, shipping, exploring, warring, and more are covered in this volume that clearly shows the global importance of San Francisco's harbor from precolonization times to the 1980s.

Kevin Starr, *Americans and the California Dream, 1850–1915* (New York: Oxford University Press, 1973). The chapters on selected authors of the period offer insights into how the state influenced their works and, conversely, how their writings both shaped and reflected the elusive California dream.

Kevin Starr, *Material Dreams: Southern California through the 1920s* (New York: Oxford University Press, 1990). The built environment takes center stage in this account of how hydroelectric works, oil, automobiles, trains, Hollywood, architecture, and USC shaped a "brassy" and somewhat "noisy" component of the California dream.

E. Mowbray Tate, *Transpacific Steamers* (New York: Cornwall Books, 1986). Replete with photographs, this volume provides a useful overview of West Coast steam shipping throughout the Pacific Basin up to American entry into World War II.

Donald Worster, *Rivers of Empire: Water, Aridity, and the Growth of the American West* (New York: Oxford University Press, 1985). California's quest for water is viewed within the broader sweep of American empire-building in the "hydraulic West."

8
Anti-Railroad Politics, Municipal Graft, and Labor Struggles

California was fully integrated into the national economy and political arena by the late nineteenth century. Industrialization and its technologies, as well as the spread of union organizing and the farm-based People's Party, had seen to that. Consequently, California's anti-monopoly movement was part of a larger American anti-trust crusade beginning in the 1880s and lasting into the 1910s. The Southern Pacific Railroad, the state's dominant corporation, became the prime target for disgruntled farmers and reformers of all kinds. At the same time that state government was under fire for allegedly being a pawn of the railroad, voters in San Francisco, Los Angeles, and other cities charged that their local officials had taken bribes from moneyed interests. Compounding these vexations, California laborers in the depression-ridden 1890s struggled for better treatment amid wage cuts and layoffs that were nationwide. In short, for the Golden State as for America at large the period was one of mounting public anger.

Pacific Eldorado: A History of Greater California, First Edition. Thomas J. Osborne.
© 2013 Thomas J. Osborne. Published 2013 by Blackwell Publishing Ltd.

Timeline

1878–84	San Francisco's Trades' Assembly serves as the umbrella labor organization for Bay Area factory workers
1880	A gunfight at Mussel Slough is fought over land claimed by both the Southern Pacific Railroad and farmers
1883	In the case of *Ellen M. Colton v. Leland Stanford et al.*, Mrs. Colton releases as evidence of her husband's importance in the Southern Pacific's hierarchy several hundred letters that tarnish the railroad's reputation
1885	Burnette G. Haskell founds the Coast Seamen's Union (CSU) in San Francisco
1886	John D. Spreckels's Oceanic Steamship Company organizes the Shipowners' Association, which passes over CSU members and continues to work with crimps in hiring seamen
1888	The Los Angeles Chamber of Commerce is founded
	California's Labor Commissioner estimates that 81 unions operate in San Francisco with more than 19,000 members
1891	The Sailors' Union of the Pacific is organized in San Francisco and led by Andrew Furuseth
	In San Francisco workers' leaders establish the Union Labor Party; this is a rare occurrence in American politics in that it is a labor party, like those in Australia, New Zealand, and Britain
1892	Phineas Banning's three sons buy nearly the entire island of Catalina, developing its resort facilities and infrastructure while providing a steamer service to and from its anchorage at Avalon
	The San Francisco Labor Council forms, embracing 31 unions
1899	With a federal appropriation, construction begins on building a major harbor at San Pedro
1901	Hundreds of San Francisco waitresses go on strike for higher wages, resulting in the shutting down of nearly 200 restaurants
1906	A major earthquake/fire destroys much of San Francisco; recent research puts the death count at above 3,000 people; property damage, in 1906 dollars, was in the range of $500 million
	A major bribery investigation into San Francisco politics begins; the city's Republican boss, Abraham Ruef, is prosecuted for graft, resulting in his later imprisonment in San Quentin Penitentiary
1907	In San Francisco female laundry workers and female employees at the Ghirardelli chocolate factory go on strike for higher pay and better working conditions
1909	The Southern Pacific Railroad's entire bonded debt to the federal government is repaid
1910	In Los Angeles Mexican workers on the street trolleys are joined by laborers in other industries in striking to gain recognition
	As a labor strike grips Los Angeles, an explosion traced to union operatives destroys the *Los Angeles Times* building, killing 20 men and injuring 17 others
1913	The Wheatland riot erupts, resulting from a clash between migrant workers and labor organizers on the one hand, and a ranch owner and law enforcement officers on the other

The Battle of Mussel Slough

Farmers' anger flared into violence in 1880 at Mussel Slough, a flatland crop-growing area along a fork of the Kings River about five miles northwest of Hanford in Tulare County. A gunfight occurred there that would influence public opinion throughout the state and long be remembered as a tragedy. At issue were allegedly broken promises by the Southern Pacific Railroad, the price of more than 60,000 acres of fertile land, and the monopolistic power of the railroad. While the occupants of Southern Pacific-claimed land emerged as heroes and the railroad as villain in this conflict, according to contemporary and later accounts, the complexity of the event calls into question such one-sided verdicts.

The dramatic battle between local land claimants and the railroad was more than a decade in the making. Beginning in the late 1860s an array of forces leading to a conflict was set in motion. From 1867 to 1870 the Southern Pacific squabbled with a group of land speculators over the legitimacy of the railroad's claim to a federal land grant to build through Mussel Slough. These land speculators included a small group of homesteaders and squatters, both of whom were farmers who lived there. Homesteaders gained title to their land in accordance with the 1862 Homestead Act, which enabled settlers to own 160-acre tracts of the public domain if they made some improvements and paid nominal closing fees. Squatters, on the other hand, were occupiers who lacked land deeds to the vacant properties they cultivated and on which they resided. In 1870 both Congress and the California legislature confirmed the legality of the Southern Pacific's Mussel Slough land claim. Nevertheless, squatters remained ignorant of this confirmation, disbelieved it, or regarded it with indifference. For whatever reason or combination of reasons, they moved into the area in growing numbers, and dug an extensive network of irrigation ditches to get needed water to their crops. Many of these people believed John J. Doyle, an admitted squatter arriving in 1871, who assured neighbors that the federal government would void the railroad's land grant in the area because the carrier had not quite completed the contractually required rail link to Mussel Slough. Based on this flimsy advice, squatters staked out 500–600 claims on land the railroad insisted was part of its grant from the federal government.

As a result of the Southern Pacific completing its line through Mussel Slough in 1876, the federal government issued patents, or land deeds, to the carrier. Afterward, local resistance to the railroad mounted as it sought to assert its land claim by selling parcels. In the early months of 1878 500 local squatter claimants organized the Settlers' Grand League to resist Southern Pacific's takeover of Mussel Slough. Under the leadership of Thomas Jefferson McQuiddy, a former Confederate cavalry officer, the resisters formed a secret paramilitary society, donning red robes, masks, and hoods. Paying late-night calls Ku Klux Klan-style, they terrorized settlers willing to buy land parcels from the Southern Pacific. In November, these nightriders evicted a tenant family living on the property of Perry Phillips, who had purchased his land from the railroad. Next, League members torched the family's house. The following year, at the League's invitation, San Francisco anti-monopoly and Workingmen's Party of California leader Denis Kearney delivered an incendiary speech to Mussel Slough settlers. "Murder the red-eyed monsters" (presumably referring to all parties aligned with the railroad), he shouted to the throng.

Opposition to the railroad's land sales was based mainly on the asking price. The League insisted on a price of no more than $2.50 an acre, the customary government price for public land. Citing recent Southern Pacific pamphlets, League squatters called attention to the railroad's offer to sell the land at "various figures from $2.50 upward per acre." In the late 1870s the railroad countered that that price reflected the 1867 market value, not the increased worth of the land at the completion of the roadbed. As a result, most of the parcels were priced at $10 to $20 per acre, while a small number near the railway towns sold for $25 or more per acre.

So went the bickering and League intimidation of the few land purchasers who tried to cultivate their farms. Realizing that prospective buyers were frightened off by this, the railroad began filing lawsuits to evict the masses of squatters occupying company land. A court decision in 1879, *Southern Pacific Railroad Company v. Pierpont Orton*, upheld the legality of the railroad's title to the land. Still, militant Leaguers warned against any attempt at their eviction. Amid growing tensions, in March 1880 Leland Stanford went to Hanford, a small town in the disputed area, and negotiated with Doyle and other squatter leaders. According to them, Stanford promised that the railroad would substantially compensate local farmers for their irrigation ditches, which would lower by $5 the price per acre. Briefly, it seemed the price issue had been resolved. Big Four magnate Charles Crocker, however, refused to go along with Stanford's purported promise, thereby ending any chance of compromise.

The Settler's Grand League then arranged for a Hanford rally to be held on May 11. By then some land buyers had threatened to sue the Southern Pacific if it did not remove trespassers from their parcels. Three such buyers – Mills Hartt, Walter Crow, and Perry Phillips – met with U.S. Marshal Alonzo Poole at a Mussel Slough field site. Before Poole could read an eviction notice, he was interrupted by angry squatter settlers, who would not let him carry out his court-authorized removal orders. Shouting erupted between the three buyers and angry squatters. When an excited horse lunged, knocking Poole to the ground, Hartt and Crow, sitting in nearby wagons, assumed Poole had been attacked and grabbed their guns. Shots were exchanged, after which Hartt toppled over dead. Another hail of bullets fired by several dozen men killed five more people. Crow escaped only to be hunted down, shot, and killed later that same day at a nearby irrigation ditch.

Assessing responsibility for the tragic incident is complex. That a conflict would arise seems certain due to the initial confusion about ownership of the disputed land, the large number of claimants, and the unpopularity of the Southern Pacific. Neither the railroad nor the Leaguers were blameless. True, the Leaguers were given to violence, as was shown by their terrorizing of settlers willing to pay the railroad for land. Yet the militants showed a willingness to accept what they understood as Stanford's agreement to reduce significantly the price of land parcels. In annulling Stanford's supposed offer, Crocker – and by implication the railroad – likely rejected a last, clear chance to reach a peaceful resolution of the conflict.

Despite the complexity of the dispute, the Southern Pacific emerged in the public eye as the sole villain. To author Frank Norris the railroad had grown figuratively into a giant octopus (the title of his 1901 novel), with tentacles reaching into capitals, courts, and boardrooms in California and beyond. The battle of Mussel Slough against this monster may have been lost by California's yeomanry, according to press accounts, but the political war against the railroad had just begun.

An Angry Widow Sues: The Colton Letters

Before his death in October 1878, David D. Colton served as the Southern Pacific's Sacramento lobbyist. Contemporary press accounts referred to him as the fifth member of the "Big Five" or the "Half" of the "Big Four and a Half." His specialty was buying off politicians in the state capital to secure needed votes on measures affecting the Southern Pacific. Colton's counterpart in Washington, D.C., was Collis P. Huntington, the shrewdest of the Associates and the most detested among them by contemporaries.

In the stormy aftermath of Colton's death in his late seventies, his widow received slightly more than half a million dollars from the railroad in settlement of her husband's stock shares. Trouble began brewing when she learned that Mark Hopkins, who had died earlier that same year, had amassed a much more valuable Southern Pacific stock portfolio than her husband even though both men had possessed comparable shares. Evidently, shares of the same stock had been valued differently for Colton and Hopkins. Mrs. Colton's initial curiosity about this disparity quickly turned to outrage at the thought of being defrauded by her late husband's business partners, the Big Four. She retained a lawyer and sued the Associates for $4 million.

A lengthy, publicized lawsuit, *Ellen M. Colton v. Leland Stanford et al.*, followed. To establish her husband's key role in the corporation, as well as his close ties to the Associates, in 1883 she furnished the court with several hundred letters written by Huntington and addressed to her spouse. Many began with the advice "Burn after reading," or words to that effect. In one such letter, Huntington stated that "it costs money to fix things . . . I believe with $200,000 I can pass our bill, but that it is not worth this much to us." As the letters became available, *The Chronicle* in San Francisco and the *New York World* printed them. Soon readers around the country were learning of the Southern Pacific's bribes of Congresspersons, lower court judges, commissioners, and even a U.S. Supreme Court justice. For eight years the trial dragged on before a verdict resulted in denying Mrs. Colton any additional money.

The railroad had won the case but at the further cost of its reputation. Any doubt as to whether the Southern Pacific was a menace to democratic politics was removed by the revelations contained in Huntington's infamous letters. Moreover, to the public, a lone bereaved widow had been exploited by a heartless, greedy, and hopelessly corrupt corporate monster.

Pacific Gateway: Locating a Harbor in Los Angeles

Southern California's economic boom of the 1880s (see Chapter 7) gave rise to Los Angeles' bid in the 1890s for federal aid to build a harbor and breakwater to accommodate the anticipated growth of Pacific maritime trade. Though San Diego had the best natural harbor in southern California, that city did not have the lobbying clout in Sacramento and the nation's capital to compete for funds with such rivals to the north as Santa Monica and San Pedro. Each of these two rival sites in the vicinity of Los Angeles had powerful advocates.

Phineas Banning (see Pacific Profile below), an entrepreneurial-minded resident of the coastal town of Wilmington, took the initiative and began the lengthy process of transforming San Pedro into a world-class port. In the 1850s Banning built a San Pedro wharf atop a rock jetty, foreseeing great profits in facilitating Los Angeles' ocean-going commerce. Between 1870 and 1890 he helped secure federal assistance to improve San Pedro's inner harbor and build its first breakwater to shield the port from Pacific swells. The Los Angeles Chamber of Commerce, founded in 1888, overcame its uneasiness about involving the federal government and invited Washington, D.C., officials on fact-finding junkets to San Pedro. As a result, in 1890 the Corps of Engineers studied several sites for harbor construction, selecting San Pedro and recommending an outlay of $4 million to build a breakwater.

Collis P. Huntington, however, worked mightily to steer Congress away from San Pedro and toward Santa Monica, where the Southern Pacific had bought waterfront property that would give his company a monopoly on rail traffic to and from Los Angeles. Huntington had powerful friends in Congress, especially Senator William P. Frye of Maine, chair of the Committee on Commerce. Frye mocked the San Pedro harbor proposal, criticizing its advocates for "calling on the government to give you what nature refused." Dissatisfied with the results of the earlier Corps of Engineers study, in 1892 Huntington persuaded Congress and the administration to conduct a second study. Again, the Corps recommended San Pedro. Ignoring the finding, Huntington designated the world's longest wharf, constructed by the railroad at Santa Monica, as Port Los Angeles. The secretary of the treasury extended Customs District certification, authorizing Port Los Angeles to participate in international trade. In its first 18 months of operation, Port Los Angeles berthed some 300 ships. San Pedro registered a consequent loss in business.

Alarmed by Huntington's boundless determination to push for a harbor site at Santa Monica, supporters of a San Pedro port were galvanized into action. For example, the Los Angeles Free Harbor League formed. The term "Free," in this instance, meant that the Southern Pacific would not dominate the prospective port, which would be open to virtually all trading and transport enterprises. Los Angeles newspapers, particularly the *Times*, gave editorial support to San Pedro. On the East Coast, the *New York World* asked whether this was "a government for the people, or a government by Mr. Huntington, for Mr. Huntington." The Santa Fe Railroad notified Washington, D.C., officials that its $500 million investment would be lost if the federal government financed improvements to the Southern Pacific's Santa Monica harbor.

In the face of increasing opposition (even his fellow Associate, Stanford, favored San Pedro), Huntington persisted, bringing his clout to bear on Washington, D.C., legislators. As a result, a congressional committee deliberating on the 1896 Rivers and Harbors Bill approved the measure's $2.9 million appropriation for construction of a breakwater at Santa Monica.

But for the doggedness and oratorical brilliance of California Senator Stephen M. White, immortalized in a 1908 bronze statue placed in the heart of the City of Angels, San Pedro might have lost its bid to be Los Angeles' harbor. White effectively debated Frye on harbor location, with the result that another (third) commission, composed of engineers, was tasked with deciding whether the $2.9 million appropriation should be spent at Santa Monica or San Pedro. The commission's choice of San Pedro must have galled Huntington, for he had been instrumental in securing the sum from Congress in the first place.

In April 1899 the first rocks splashed from a barge, settling into San Pedro Bay. Construction of the long-awaited breakwater had begun. Born of a clash between political titans, the Los Angeles–San Pedro harbor, when joined with that of Long Beach, would one day become the largest and busiest port complex in the United States.

Pacific Profile: Phineas Banning, Port of Los Angeles and Santa Catalina Promoter

"A massive frame, dynamic in action, a keen brain, violent passions, and an abundant heart" – these were the words used by a contemporary to describe Phineas Banning (1830–85). Banning played a critical role in southern California's maritime development, including that of Santa Catalina Island. His meteoric rise as an entrepreneur during the latter half of the nineteenth century both promoted and reflected the growth of Los Angeles itself.

Born in Wilmington, Delaware, into a large, struggling family, young Banning made his way to southern California by ship via the Isthmus of Panama route, arriving in San Pedro in 1851. Taking on business partner David Alexander, Banning opened a stagecoach line to Los Angeles, roughly 20 miles distant from San Pedro. Soon the two partners had warehouses, 15 wagons, and 75 mules to facilitate their freight-hauling business. Their wagon service eventually connected San Pedro to such faraway points as Santa Fe, New Mexico, and Salt Lake City, Utah.

Banning's inland ventures were complemented and eclipsed by his Pacific operations. Realizing that Los Angeles' growth was closely tied to maritime trade, he built two San Pedro wharves in the early 1850s, the first having been destroyed by storms. Within a few years he founded the seacoast town of Wilmington (where he lived and which he named after his hometown), had vessels built in San Francisco to carry passengers and baggage from offshore steamships to his new beach resort on Santa Catalina, and inaugurated a shipping service between San Pedro, San Francisco, and San Diego. In 1857, for example, he shipped 21,000 crates of wine grapes to San Francisco. Banning had become so identified with seagoing traffic that throughout Los Angeles he was known as "Port Admiral." All of

Banning's various shipping and transportation ventures just mentioned – plus lumbering and stevedoring – eventually came under the umbrella of his Wilmington Transportation Company.

In the early 1860s the state awarded the Port Admiral a franchise to build a railroad from Wilmington to Los Angeles. State, county, and city funding measures financed the rail line, which was completed in 1869. In the following decade the Southern Pacific bought it and made Banning an officer of the corporation. Meanwhile, he secured federal funding for a lighthouse and improvements for the harbor at Wilmington–San Pedro.

Besides championing a harbor for Los Angeles, Banning's other major maritime project was promoting the development of Santa Catalina, one of California's Channel Islands located 22 miles from San Pedro. Beginning in 1859 he organized visits to Santa Catalina for friends and business associates. Convinced of the island's resort and mining possibilities, he tried to purchase it with a partner in 1883. Before a sale could be completed, Banning suffered severe injury when he stepped off a trolley in San Francisco and was struck by a passing express wagon. He lived only a few years afterward until declining health took him to an early grave. Banning's three sons, who had often vacationed on Santa Catalina while growing up, bought nearly the entire island in 1892, developing its resort facilities and infrastructure while providing a steamer service to and from its anchorage at Avalon.

Eventually a Los Angeles street was named after the Port Admiral, as well as a town in southern California, and a high school in Wilmington. His greatest contribution to the Golden State, however, was his initiation of the San Pedro–Los Angeles Port project.

Figure 8.1   Rocks quarried on Santa Catalina Island and used to construct the Los Angeles–San Pedro breakwater. Photo: T.F. Keaveney. Courtesy of the Los Angeles Harbor Department.

Debt Dodging Denounced

As fierce as the harbor fight had been in the 1890s, the Southern Pacific was even more determined to scale down its huge debt to the federal government. The company's earlier incarnation, the Central Pacific Railroad, had received about $27 million in federal subsidies to cover initial construction of the Far Western link of the first transcontinental railroad. The subsidies took the form of 30-year bonds payable in 1899 at 6 percent interest, which amounted to an additional $50 million. A federal law enacted in 1878 required the railroad to establish a sinking fund drawn from profits in order to repay the loan, but the Central Pacific ignored the measure.

In 1896, with the repayment date approaching, Huntington conceived a plan to reduce vastly the amount owed. Members of Congress doing his bidding crafted a Funding Bill that would have extended the repayment period by 99 years at an interest rate of 0.5 percent. Huntington justified the debt dodging bill by recounting the material benefits that the railroad had brought to the nation, adding that repayment of the original obligation at that time would bankrupt the Southern Pacific.

Given the economic depression of the 1890s and the farmer-based hatred of the railroads, the measure provoked a public outcry. San Francisco Mayor Adolph Sutro, elected on a People's Party ticket in 1894, led his city's opposition. William Randolph Hearst collected 200,000 signatures on petitions denouncing the Funding Bill and his *Examiner* commissioned Ambrose Bierce to write venomous commentaries on Huntington and his proposed measure. Also, Hearst unleashed cartoonist Homer Davenport to skewer the railroad at every opportunity.

The California legislature, in a rare display of defiance against the Southern Pacific, passed a resolution urging the federal government to collect the money owed and, moreover, to assume ownership of the railroad if the debt were not repaid in full. Congress voted down the Funding Bill in January 1897. So thrilled was California's governor, James H. Budd, that he declared January 16 a public holiday in celebration of the vote outcome. To the surprise of few, the Southern Pacific repaid its entire bonded debt to the federal government by 1909 – and did not go out of business in the process.

The Southern Pacific Political Machine

The Southern Pacific Railroad was the most powerful influence shaping California politics from 1870 to 1910. That does not mean that the railroad always got its way, that it was the only force shaping the state's policies, or that its opponents were above reproach in public affairs. During that 40-year period, as throughout the state's past, many happenings were too complex to be reduced to a simple morality play involving unvarnished heroes and villains. That said, the Southern Pacific was a colossus, exercising considerable influence in California's legislature, its courts, and its official regulatory commissions. Newspapers, too, were influenced by the railroad to provide friendly coverage of company operations.

Such influence-peddling was overseen by skilled practitioners of the art. David Colton, the railroad's earlier Sacramento lobbyist, was succeeded by attorney William F. Herrin, who from 1893 to 1910 headed the Southern Pacific's legal and political departments. Herrin saw to it that every California county had a Southern Pacific political boss. He and his protégé in charge of Los Angeles operations, Walter Parker, directly or through county bosses bribed government officials to do the railroad's bidding. Herrin and Parker were basically nonpartisan dispensers of cash, offering money to officials regardless of party affiliation, though most went to Republicans.

If newly elected state legislators were not already recipients of railroad bribes, shortly after installation they often found a cash-stuffed envelope in their mailboxes. A letter would accompany the cash, stating that the Southern Pacific wished to retain their legal services. As the confidentiality of the attorney–client relationship is protected by law, it was nearly impossible to prove in a court that the "retainer" was really a bribe.

Regulating and taxing the railroad proved very difficult since California judges were often appointed by state senators influenced by the Southern Pacific. Once on the bench, judges at times received free rail passes. While the 1879 state constitution prohibited such passes, enforcement of the ban was lax.

Southern Pacific influence also reached to the highest tribunal in the nation. U.S. Supreme Court Justice Stephen J. Field, a friend of the Big Four, received his appointment with railroad support and afterward rendered legal opinions that protected the Southern Pacific and other carriers from taxation and regulation. He argued in *The Sinking Fund Cases* (1879) that Congress could not amend the Pacific Railroad Act in such a way as to ensure that the Central Pacific and Union Pacific railroads repaid their federal government loans that had been extended to build the transcontinental line. Moreover, he championed the doctrine granting personhood to corporations under the terms of the Fourteenth Amendment's Due Process and Equal Protection clauses. The U.S. Supreme Court's adoption of that interpretation helped shelter the Southern Pacific from taxes imposed by the State of California and several of its counties. Such taxes, the court held, deprived corporations – the equivalent of persons – of their property without due process of law.

Though the Southern Pacific sought to influence various state regulatory bodies, it focused most intently on the bank and the railroad commissions. Banks lending money to businesses or persons who publicly denounced the company might be dogged by the commissions and pressured into denying loans to anti-railroad interests. Authorized by the 1879 California constitution, the state Railroad Commission was largely ineffective in its work during the next three decades. The assembly committee on commerce conducted an investigation in 1883, finding that one of the three commissioners had accumulated $20,000 that he could not account for coherently, and a second commissioner – who had close ties to the Southern Pacific – had made more than $100,000 in an ethically questionable transaction.

While larger newspapers, like the *San Francisco Examiner* and the *Los Angeles Times*, had the financial resources to remain independent of the Southern Pacific, smaller publications found it harder to reject railroad subsidies in exchange for favorable coverage. Also, the smaller presses could least afford to risk losing railroad advertising contracts by being openly critical of the Southern Pacific.

The "Queen City of the Pacific:" Boss Ruef's San Francisco

Americans moving westward across the Great Plains and mountains to the Pacific's shores brought with them the Gilded Age political culture of Atlantic seaboard cities. Urban bosses, that is, political power brokers, were a centerpiece of that political culture. New York City's William M. Tweed, commonly known as "Boss Tweed," headed the notoriously corrupt Tammany Hall Democratic political machine. Republicans had their city machines as well. Often uneducated, bosses rarely held high-profile public office; instead, they tended to control those who did through bribes and other unsavory means. Party bosses offered aid to needy, recently arriving European immigrants in exchange for their electoral support of machine candidates for public office.

Late nineteenth-century San Francisco, the Pacific Coast's leading city commercially and in practically every other way, had become a variant of this transplanted model of municipal politics. This is especially important because of San Francisco's regional influence. As Lord James Bryce, the famed British observer and diplomat, noted, San Francisco was "more powerful . . . than is any Eastern city over its neighborhood." The City by the Bay's "neighborhood" extended to the seal fisheries of Alaska, the sugar fields of Hawai'i, and the tea plantations of Asia. San Francisco's money financed a fair amount of Portland, Oregon's development, and its steamers – as has been shown – fed much of Arizona's economy via the Pacific–Gulf of California maritime trade. Called the "Queen City of the Pacific" because of its commercial dominance in that ocean, San Francisco happenings, including politics, had ripple effects far beyond the state's borders.

A peculiarity of San Francisco's Republican political machine was that it was not run by a rough-talking bully schooled in the often violent underworld of city politics but, rather, was headed by a man of education and considerable refinement, Abraham Ruef. A more unlikely person for such a job would be hard to imagine. Born into a wealthy San Francisco family of French and Jewish heritage, young Ruef had been a reform-minded idealist as a college student. Graduating in 1883 with high honors in classical languages from the University of California at Berkeley at the age of 18, three years later he earned a law degree from the University of California's Hastings College of the Law. By birth, education, and temperament, then, he seemed on the path to high-minded public service.

Once outside these citadels of learning, the brilliant young lawyer became slowly immersed in the gritty realities of San Francisco's ward politics. With a scholar's curiosity and eye for detail and patterns, he stepped into Republican backroom strategy meetings, becoming ever more fascinated with how power was wielded. Apprenticed in backroom, ballot fraud politics to Phil Crimmins and Martin Kelly, Ruef was awakened to his own political ambitions, hoping to one day become a U.S. Senator. "I drifted with the machine," he wrote. "Whatever ideals I once had were relegated to the background." Still a young man, his transformation from reformer to opportunist had been complete.

Ruef opened his law office in San Francisco's Latin Quarter, a working-class neighborhood that was home to Italian-, French-, and Spanish-speaking families. They would comprise a component of his following, as he soon emerged as the area's leading Republican organizer. Seeing no future as an underling to Crimmins and Kelly, in 1901 Ruef formed his own faction within the city's Republican Party – the Republican Primary League. The League would draw its membership from the various segments of San Francisco's population: the diverse religious communities, laborers, merchants, professionals, and politicians. This splinter organization failed to displace the Crimmins- and Kelly-led dominant faction. Undeterred, Ruef took advantage of a major San Francisco dock strike that year, in which five wage-earners died, to assume leadership of a labor organization that emerged in the wake of that upheaval.

Disenchanted with the Democratic Party, whose mayor, James D. Phelan, had called in strikebreakers and police to quell the dock melee, workers' leaders founded the Union Labor Party (ULP) of the city and county of San Francisco in September 1901. This was a rare organization in American politics in that it was a labor party, like those in Australia, New Zealand, and Britain. Major American labor unions, like the American Federation of Labor, eschewed party politics in order to work for very limited, well-defined goals such as higher wages, fewer hours, and safer working conditions. European-like labor parties, on the other hand, sought broader, structural reforms encompassing workers' compensation benefits, health care, pensions, and government ownership of public utilities. Similarly, the breadth of the ULP's goals are seen in its platform, which read in part: "We favor the acquisition and public ownership of all public utilities and means of communications, such as public buildings, street railways, gas, electric light, water, telephone and telegraphs. We regard the acquisition of a public water supply and the operation of the municipality of the Geary-street railway as of primary and special importance. In the event of their acquisition we pledge our nominees to a progressive and economical operation thereof."

Having shown little earlier regard for labor interests, Ruef opportunistically plunged into ULP politics, quickly becoming the party's leader. In that capacity, he arranged the party's nomination of his close friend and president of the Musicians Union, Eugene Schmitz, for city mayor in the 1901 election. Schmitz had been reluctant to pursue the nomination, telling Ruef "I have no experience. I don't know anything about municipal affairs. . . . I never made a public address. . . . The whole thing is preposterous." To which Ruef replied, "What you lack can easily be supplied." The boss saw electability in Schmitz's good looks, his German and Irish ancestry that would appeal to voters, and the candidate's Catholicism. All would go well, Ruef assured Schmitz, because of a basic principle of electoral politics: "The psychology of the mass of voters is like that of a crowd of small boys or primitive men. Other things being equal, of two candidates they will almost invariably follow the strong, finely built man." Schmitz won, ushering in a city government that became legendary for corruption. So effective was the Ruef–Schmitz team that the mayor won reelection in 1903 and 1905.

In San Francisco government, opportunities for graft, that is, unfair or unethical gain, abounded throughout the Schmitz era. The ULP picked up only a few of the 18 supervisorial seats in 1901 and 1903. In 1905, however, all 18 seats went to ULP members, as well as the offices of city treasurer, district attorney, city attorney, county clerk, and coroner. Ruef was careful not to hold public office himself so that he could legally serve as an attorney for such public utility corporations as the Pacific State Telephone and Telegraph Company, United Railroads of San Francisco, and the Home Telephone Company. All of these corporations paid him a monthly retainer. He, in turn, saw to it that the Schmitz regime enacted policies congruent with the wishes of his corporate clients.

Moreover, Ruef and his organization exacted tribute from a mix of other legitimate and illegitimate businesses. Outright bribes were not solicited, but payments to him were made by dairies, theaters, saloons, gambling houses, brothels, and other enterprises. The boss forbade his business clients to offer money or gifts directly to supervisors or others on the City payroll. That way, reasoned Ruef, whatever payments he received could be justified as legal fees. He was then free to distribute such "fees," after paying himself, among city officials.

Foiled Reform: The 1906 San Francisco Earthquake and Graft Trials

The epic earthquake, of approximately 8.0 magnitude, that shook parts of San Francisco to the ground beginning at 5:13 a.m. on April 18, 1906, also helped break the political hammerlock that the Ruef–Schmitz regime had on the city. These two happenings, connected in some ways, marked major turning points in the city's history. A municipal reform impulse, which had been building nationwide since the 1890s, had little to show for itself in San Francisco in the immediate aftermath of the earthquake and graft trials of public officials that began in October 1906. Yet the city would not return to business as usual and longer-term changes in governance were soon coming.

With its epicenter located on or near the ocean floor 2 miles west of San Francisco, the 1906 earthquake furnishes a striking natural example of how the Pacific has shaped – in this case dramatically so – California's history. It was felt as far north as Coos Bay, Oregon, southward down to Los Angeles, and westward into central Nevada, underscoring the seismic reach of Greater California. Most of the shaking occurred along a 400-mile rupture of the San Andreas Fault. The destruction zone along that fault line was about 25 miles wide.

One of the great earthquakes in modern world history, the toll in lives and property was staggering. Recent research puts the death count at above 3,000 people. Property damage, in 1906 dollars, was in the range of $500 million. Afterward, much of the city looked like a smoldering, war-decimated refuse pile.

Most of the devastation was caused by the 50 separate fires ignited by the breaking of gas pipes. The earth's violent movement also punctured water mains, making it extremely difficult to get sufficient water pressure to put out the fireball that burned much of the city.

Investigations, photographs, and eyewitness accounts attest to the extent that the calamity was seared into the consciousness of those surviving it. An official report prepared by UC Berkeley geology Professor Andrew C. Lawson in 1908 contained a description of the power of the quake near Point Reyes, about 30 miles north of San Francisco: "At Point Reyes Station at the head of Tomales Bay the 5:15 train for San Francisco was just ready. The conductor had just swung himself on when the train gave a great lurch to the east, followed by another to the west, which threw the whole train on its side." In downtown San Francisco, one survivor, a certain G.A. Raymond, was staying in the city's famous Palace Hotel when on the morning of the disaster he was "thrown out of bed." Grabbing his clothing, he rushed from the hotel. "Outside I witnessed a sight I never want to see again . . . All around me buildings were rocking and flames shooting. As I ran people on all sides were crying, praying and calling for help. I thought the end of the world had come."

Chinatown was leveled and many of its 14,000 inhabitants left homeless. However, for many there was a silver lining in the dark clouds of smoke: the birth records of the city's Chinese perished in the flames, making it exceedingly difficult for immigration authorities to dispute the residents' claims to American citizenship. Like the rest of the City by the Bay, Chinatown rebuilt itself into the nationally prominent enclave that it remains today.

As the city dug itself out of its physical and psychic ruins, it also began the process of digging itself out from the public scandals of the Ruef–Schmitz years. The city would rebuild itself structurally and politically. Fremont Older, editor of the San Francisco Bulletin, led the political housecleaning, laying plans even before the earthquake. The district attorney pledged his help, as did wealthy sugar heir Rudolph Spreckels. Even President Theodore Roosevelt assisted by arranging for federal prosecutor Francis J. Heney and investigator William J. Burns to play lead roles in preparing cases for the anticipated graft trials.

Figure 8.2   Much of the renowned Palace Hotel, like San Francisco itself, was reduced to rubble by the 1906 earthquake. Courtesy of the California History Room, California State Library, Sacramento, California.

Headway was made when the prosecutor trapped a supervisor into taking a staged bribe. In exchange for an offer of immunity, the supervisor divulged the names of his colleagues who had received bribes. Soon the other supervisors confessed, on being offered similar immunity. Going up the prosecutorial food chain, Heney offered protection from charges to Ruef, thereby obtaining a confession that implicated top corporate executives. Grand Jury indictments for bribery were then issued against the president of the United Railroads, Patrick Calhoun; against the chief counsel for that company, Tirey L. Ford; and against executives of various utility firms. Heney's ultimate aim, implicit in this strategy, was to go to the top rung of the corporate influence ladder and indict and convict the Southern Pacific's general counsel, William F. Herrin, and his superior, railroad president Edward H. Harriman.

The prosecutor's aim was highly ambitious, which, under the circumstances, made convictions unlikely. His strategy depended on Ruef testifying in accordance with his confession. Unless the boss testified in court, under oath, that the corporate leaders paid him fees knowing that some of those monies would be disbursed to public officials, the cases against these defendants would fall apart. When the executives of United Railroads stood trial in 1907, Ruef, the prosecution's star witness, refused to provide the testimony for which Heney had bargained. Ultimately, none of the executives were convicted. Exasperated, Heney withdrew Ruef's immunity and prosecuted him in 1908 for trolley bribery. A prospective juror, angry that Heney had exposed him as a former convict, shot Heney in open court. Though surviving the resulting head wound, Heney was replaced by Hiram Johnson, who won a conviction of Ruef that landed the boss in San Quentin prison.

Figure 8.3   Abraham Ruef on steps of the Court House during graft trials. Ruef's personal transformation from idealist to big city "boss" greatly impacted San Francisco's politics. Courtesy of Bancroft Library, UC Berkeley.

In the end, no bribe-givers were convicted. Ruef was the only defendant who served prison time. Schmitz, whose conviction was overturned on a technicality, won election to the Board of Supervisors in 1917! In 1909 San Francisco's business leaders, who had helped to initiate the graft investigation, became less supportive when the prosecution turned its sights in their direction. That year voters installed a new set of city officials who discontinued the trials. While Ruef's career had ended, Johnson's had just begun.

Maritime and Factory Labor

Nationwide, from the 1880s to the 1910s, labor organized to meet the challenges of a corporate-dominated economy and government at all levels that was slow to respond to workers' interests. Organizing, however, was fraught with internal battles at the national level over what the goals should be and who unions should admit to membership. Founded in Philadelphia in 1869, the nationwide Knights of Labor union was fractured by these internal battles as it struggled for the rights of working people. When the press blamed that union for a deadly bombing at an outdoor Chicago labor rally on May 1, 1886, a serious blow was struck to the Knights' radical vision of overthrowing capitalism by uniting all workers into one big organization regardless of trades and skills. Repudiating the goals and organizational structure of the Knights, Samuel Gompers of New York fashioned a new union that same year – the American Federation of Labor (AF of L). Whereas the Knights had been highly political and advocated government ownership of the means of production, the AF of L spurned politics and embraced capitalism. Unlike the Knights, the AF of L pursued three clear, concrete goals: higher wages, shorter hours, and safer working conditions. In California, maritime and factory labor in the 1880s and afterward moved increasingly in concert with Gompers's pragmatic approach.

California, especially its cities of San Francisco and Los Angeles, was a major arena for America's struggles between labor and capital. The Golden State's struggles were distinguished by a Pacific Rim racial factor, namely, that a fair number of its workers were of Asian and Hispanic ethnic backgrounds. To varying degrees, this factor was present in the campaigns of workers.

White seamen toiled under conditions that differed significantly from those of laborers on land. Crimps, or managers of boardinghouses and taverns for sailors, entered into agreements with ships' captains to provide needed crewmen. Generally, seamen could not obtain a job without going through a crimp, and captains could not secure a crew without doing likewise. If workers were in short supply, sometimes captains paid crimps "blood money" to "shanghai" seamen. Shanghaiing usually involved plying sailors with alcohol, beating them into submission or unconsciousness, and turning the hapless victim over to a shipmaster. By the time the sailor regained consciousness, the vessel he was aboard might be on its way to Shanghai, China, or some other distant port. Once in the employ of a captain, seamen, unlike workers on land, could not quit a job that they found unrewarding. Under the U.S. laws of that time, sailors abandoning their jobs were guilty of the crime of desertion, making them subject to arrest and imprisonment. Moreover, unlike most toilers on land, seamen could be legally flogged for "justifiable cause."

Already bad, these conditions worsened in 1885 when shippers reduced monthly pay to $20 and $25 for work done inside and outside ports, respectively. To address these circumstances, Burnette G. Haskell founded the Coast Seamen's Union (CSU) in San Francisco in that year. By August the CSU had 3,000 members out of approximately 3,500 coasting (distinguished from deepwater) sailors. The following year it was strong enough to force an increase in wages on all coasting vessels to $35 and $40 for work inside and outside ports, respectively.

In 1886 San Francisco shippers, including John D. Spreckels's Oceanic Steamship Company, fought back by organizing the Shipowners' Association, which passed over CSU members and continued to work with crimps in hiring seamen. The union picketed the waterfront, blood was spilled, and several men were killed before the CSU ran out of funds and capitulated on September 30. Union membership declined to slightly more than 1,000. Morale was low. Haskell, an avowed socialist whose utopian Kaweah colony in the Sierra would drain union funds, was blamed for the defeat and ousted from leadership.

Distancing itself from socialism and adapting to the change from sail to steam, the union discontinued the office of president, investing the new secretary, Andrew Furuseth, with executive power. These changes paid handsomely, as he – like his friend AF of L President Samuel Gompers – was a pragmatic organizer with financial management skills. Under Furuseth's leadership, in 1891 the CSU combined with the Steamshipmen's Protective Union to form the Sailors' Union of the Pacific (SUP). The SUP was headquartered in San Francisco and led by secretary Furuseth, who saw to it that the union joined the city's powerful Federated Trades Council (see below) an alliance of labor organizations. SUP branch offices would eventually extend to Seattle, Honolulu, and Norfolk, Virginia – exemplifying the sweep of a Greater California labor organization. Furuseth was the driving force behind the passage of the La Follette Seamen's Act of 1915, which ended imprisonment for desertion and mandated better working conditions for sailors.

The white SUP members were not the only sailors on the West Coast. According to historian Robert J. Schwendinger, at least 80,523 Chinese employees served on American commercial vessels during the years 1876–1906. They were not slaves, indentured workers, or contract laborers, but wage earners and free men. Most were Chinese nationals, but toward the end of the century an increasing number of crewmen were Chinese Americans, mostly from California. They were employed by the two dominant San Francisco-based steamship companies: Pacific Mail and Occidental and Oriental. The crews aboard these vessels were largely Chinese with some whites; the officers were invariably Caucasians. Wages for Chinese crewmen ranged from a low of $14 to $18 per month for coal handlers to a high of $45 to $60 per month for cooks.

California labor unions despised and denigrated Chinese maritime workers, who, consequently, were not admitted into membership. Furuseth, who did more than anyone to upgrade the treatment of American seamen of European ancestry, shared the prejudice of white laborers toward Asians, warning at a 1902 Senate Immigration Committee hearing that unless more white men entered maritime work "yellow" men would take over the seagoing labor force. Chinese sailors were cowards, he testified; they allegedly showed a lack of courage in several shipwrecks that he mentioned. Additionally, Furuseth insisted that ship hands be drawn from "native born" workers. This seems especially odd given the fact that he had been born in Norway and came to the United States as an adult immigrant before becoming a Pacific Coast seaman.

Either out of ignorance or oversight, Furuseth did not mention the role of Chinese sailors in the Battle of Manila during the Spanish–American War of 1898. Commodore George Dewey enlisted the aid of 29 Chinese on his flagship *Olympia*. Moreover, his squadron had leased two Chinese support vessels from Hong Kong, carrying munitions and coal. The crews of both vessels were mainly Chinese. Because of the "courage and energy" shown by these crewmen, Dewey petitioned Congress to allow them to immigrate to America. Given the rampant anti-Asian sentiment across the land, and especially in California, the naval hero's request was denied.

The shipping companies employing Chinese crews also expressed positive views about their workers. Owners and officers of these firms attested to the value of their Asian crews and defended successfully the right of their companies to employ Chinese, Japanese, and Filipino seamen. Most likely the comparative advantage of lower labor costs for non-unionized employees was a major factor responsible for these positive assessments. However, the fact remains that these Asian maritime workers were judged to be among the best in the labor pool.

Like maritime workers, California factory employees struggled to improve their lot amid the depression-driven wage cuts and layoffs of the 1870s and 1890s. By the latter decade San Francisco had emerged as the strongest center of trade union activity west of Chicago and remained so until about 1920. In the early twentieth century Los Angeles gave birth to a less powerful though more radical labor movement of its own.

From 1878 to 1884 the San Francisco Trades' Assembly served as the umbrella labor organization for Bay Area factory workers. While it shared the goals of the Workingmen's Party of California, its leaders distrusted Denis Kearney and did not want the Trades' Assembly to become a pawn of Kearney's political party. Led by socialist Frank Roney, Trades' Assembly members were vehemently anti-Chinese. The organization fell victim to factionalism, leading to Roney's resignation and its demise in 1884.

The following year a larger and more effective labor organization emerged in San Francisco, the Federated Trades Council. It was animated by the same virulent anti-Chinese sentiment as its predecessor but differed in that the Federated Trades Council included unions outside the Bay Area, even in other western states. In 1886 the Council led a boycott of Chinese goods and several anti-union newspapers, whose printers had gone on strike. That year Roney took the helm of the Council as strikes and boycotts spread in the Bay Area and throughout other large American cities. In effect, a labor renaissance swept the City by the Bay. Two years later California's Labor Commissioner estimated that 81 unions operated in San Francisco with more than 19,000 members. The Council had been a major generator of this growth. Factionalism, as often was the case with unions, began to plague the Council in the early 1890s, and was compounded by antagonism with the newly formed San Francisco Building Trades Council. After mediation, the two rival organizations combined, forming the San Francisco Labor Council (SFLC) in 1892, which embraced 31 unions. Due largely to the SFLC, San Francisco workers in the early 1900s enjoyed higher pay and better working conditions than their non-union counterparts across the nation.

By the turn of the century San Francisco's women, who in increasing numbers had entered clerical and service occupations, had organized their own labor unions. In 1901 hundreds of city waitresses went on strike for higher wages, resulting in the shutting down of nearly 200 restaurants. Female laundry workers did likewise in 1907, as did female employees at the Ghirardelli chocolate factory, who demanded higher pay and an end to dangerous and insanitary working conditions.

These actions brought positive results that spurred more action. Four years later, a state law limited the workday to eight hours for women (excluding farm labor), and in 1913 California passed a minimum wage law for women. In 1919, 1,300 female telephone operators stopped work and successfully battled for the right to bargain collectively.

Meanwhile, Los Angeles began showing signs of labor activity. With a much smaller population than San Francisco in 1880 (11,000 Angelinos compared to 233,000 San Franciscans), Los Angeles was on the cusp of a real-estate boom (see Chapter 7) that would transform the "cow county" metropolis into a port city with a broadened economic base. Amid this transformation, marked by labor strife, the city would become a national leader of the "open shop" movement. Theoretically, open shop businesses were those that hired irrespective of whether a job-seeker was a union member. Often, however, union membership disqualified an applicant seeking employment. An open shop city or business, in other words, was anti-union.

In the Southland, *Los Angeles Times* publisher and conservative Republican Harrison Gray Otis led the campaign against labor unions, eventually heading the most powerful anti-union business association in America. This is a bit ironic given the fact that as a 15-year-old printer he had quit a job with a newspaper because the proprietor refused to unionize, and later as an employee of the Government Printing Office in Washington, D.C., he had joined the Typographical Union.

In 1890, by which time southern California's economic boom had ended and few labor organizations existed in Los Angeles, Otis announced a 20 percent pay cut and locked his union printers out. When the printers picketed, Otis brought in well-paid strikebreakers from San Diego and elsewhere, all the while keeping up a steady stream of anti-union and anti-reform articles in the *Times*. The strike collapsed, as did the subsequent union-led boycott of the newspaper.

In the early 1900s Los Angeles corporations organized to combat growing union strength. By 1903 the Merchants' and Manufacturers' Association (M&M), founded in the 1890s to promote free enterprise, had become an anti-union juggernaut, smearing boycotters as "un-American, unjust, unwarranted, and illegal." M&M member-businesses refused to work with employers who negotiated with unions. The consortium also arranged with banks for the withholding of loans from such businesses. To broaden the base of anti-union efforts, Otis and Henry Huntington helped launch a so-called Los Angeles Citizens' Alliance, which served as a chapter of a larger national organization with that same goal.

This anti-labor activity generated renewed energy for organizing among the city's toilers, which, in turn, produced a counter-offensive led by the M&M. In 1910 Mexican workers on the street trolleys were joined by laborers in other industries in striking to gain recognition. The city council, pushed by Otis and the M&M, responded by outlawing picketing and striking.

By then labor relations in Los Angeles were a tinderbox. Union funds from San Francisco helped finance a strike of 1,500 Los Angeles metal trades workers on June 1, 1910. It constituted the largest work stoppage so far in the city's history. The *Times* denounced the strike, and major labor unions nationwide denounced the *Times*.

Then, early in the morning on October 1, amid the metal trades strike, a stupendous explosion destroyed the *Times* building, resulting in what the city's anti-union forces called the "crime of the century." Twenty men died and 17 were injured. Labor leaders, including Samuel Gompers, denied any union responsibility. However, a federal investigation, followed by a trial and confessions by three defendants, confirmed that the dynamite bomb had been the work of extremists in the International Association of Bridge and Structural Iron Workers Union. That union was headquartered in Indianapolis, and its three convicted members included Ortie McManigal, John J. McNamara, and his brother James B. McNamara. In the face of compelling evidence, their attorney, Clarence Darrow, convinced the men to plead guilty to save their lives. Tarnished by the violent episode, Los Angeles remained a citadel of the open shop for decades afterward.

Figure 8.4 The ruins of the *Los Angeles Times* building, 1910. The destruction of this building inflamed business–labor relations in the city for decades afterward. Reproduced by permission of the Huntington Library, San Marino, California.

Field Work and the Wheatland Riot

California farming differed from tilling in the Midwest and elsewhere in the United States. For one thing cultivation here took place on huge tracts of land, owing to the state's tradition of Spanish grants that through lawsuits, sales, and coercion wound up mainly in the hands of white American growers. This is somewhat in contrast with the Great Plains region, where more modest family-owned farms prevailed at least into the early 1900s. Also, the state's farms were distinct in their production of seasonal, specialized crops (see Chapter 7). In the Midwest, on the other hand, farms were more likely to produce a greater variety of crops.

As a result of these salient characteristics of California agriculture, the state's farm workers had been employed for shorter periods of time and received lower pay than their counterparts elsewhere in the nation. Agrarian toilers in California had also been more migratory and non-white than field workers in most other states. In succession, Chinese, Japanese, Asian Indians, Mexicans, and Filipinos worked the orchards and fields of the Golden State. Until more recent times, this labor force, drawn mostly from the Pacific Rim, has been non-unionized. The chronic poverty experienced by California's farm hands has occasionally led to violent clashes with their employers and law enforcement agents.

Given the abject conditions of farm labor, from the 1880s most of the jobs went to cash-needy, highly mobile immigrant workers. In that decade the Chinese predominated among the seasonal hands in California's fields. One and two decades earlier they had built many of the levees protecting farmland in the Sacramento Valley. As mechanization costs rose for growers, especially on wheat farms, employers kept wages low in order to offset their increasing equipment expenses. In such circumstances, the Chinese were thought to be ideal laborers because of their stamina, organization, and reliability. Chinese cooks received higher wages than their fellow field workers, and in some instances served as account managers and advisers to employers. During the 1880s, the bumper harvests of the state's wheat fields, sugar beet farms, and orchards were made possible by their highly productive, low-cost labor. According to the *Pacific Rural Press* (July 30, 1881): "It is difficult to see how the present fruit crop, which is bringing such fine prices, or the immense grape crop now ripening could be handled at all without Celestial [Chinese] aid." With the passage of the 1882 exclusion law, opposed by many large growers who panicked at the thought of losing their cheap workforce, the influx of Chinese ended rapidly, and most of those in the rural areas moved into towns and cities.

"Japanese Rapidly Supplanting Chinese," announced the *Sacramento Bee* on May 20, 1891. "They are more Tractable and Find Life Luxurious on a Dollar a Day." The news coverage was half-right – Japanese field workers indeed began replacing their Asian brethren in the 1890s. The Japanese, however, were less tractable than other field hands and initiated work stoppages to obtain higher pay. Growers occasionally brought in white strikebreakers and fired the troubling Japanese crews. The economic depression of the 1890s led to staggering job losses for whites. They directed much of their fury at these Pacific-crossers from Asia, some of whom were beaten and forced from their farm jobs by itinerant, unemployed Anglo-Americans, sometimes referred to as "fruit tramps." Through organizing, aggressive negotiating, and outworking their competition, Japanese farm workers earned an average of $427.18 (without board) in 1912. They had become the highest-paid field hands in the state. With their earnings, Japanese workers pooled their resources to lease or buy their own farms. Caucasian growers responded by joining with urban labor unions to block what the *Sacramento Bee* characterized in 1905 as dozens of "little brown men [Japanese] crowding out white laborers and getting hold of ranches."

Two new groups of alien migrant workers entered California's agricultural labor force in the 1910s. Asian Indians tilled in the Imperial Valley. Below the border, a revolution in Mexico (1910–20) led to many of its peasant families fleeing northward into the American Southwest and California. They were the forebears of Mexican American writer Victor Villaseñor, whose book *Rain of Gold* (1992) recounts the trials and triumphs of these border-crossers as they sought field and other work to support their families. As with the various ethnic work groups that preceded these refugee arrivals, the state's labor unions considered them ineligible for membership.

The fact that California's urban labor unions ignored the plight of farm workers literally left the field open to overtures from radical organizers whose revolutionary doctrines were sure to inflame employers and conservative rural populations. Seeking to unionize the state's desperate, disenfranchised field workers, the Chicago-based Industrial Workers of the World, known variously as the IWW and Wobblies, sent representatives into farming areas. They preached the overthrow of capitalism "through any and all tactics."

The volatile mix of inhumane working conditions and Marxian socialist union organizing was a sure recipe for the explosion of violence that rocked the farmland just outside of the town of Wheatland, located just southeast of Marysville, in early August 1913. Ralph Durst, a major hop (an ingredient in beer) grower in the state and owner of a large ranch near Wheatland, advertised throughout California and beyond the state for pickers. Some 2,800 mostly alien job-seekers arrived; yet Durst needed only half that many. The oversupply of labor lowered wages to 75 cents a day. Ten percent of that paltry amount was held back by Durst to cover workers' purchases of over-priced food and other essentials from the ranch store. Eight filthy outdoor toilets were provided to accommodate the throng of men, women, and children. Durst failed to supply drinking water, and would not allow workers to rent a water wagon. To quench the laborers' thirst in the more than 100-degree Fahrenheit heat, he arranged for one of his relatives to sell watered-down lemonade for 5 cents a glass.

Amid these barbarous conditions, the angry toilers decided to take matters into their own hands. About a hundred of them were IWW members. Their leaders organized a protest meeting, demanding water, sanitary facilities, and higher wages. Durst made a few concessions before ordering several IWW organizers off his property and calling in a sheriff's posse of deputies. A day later, August 3, the tension led to a riot when the assembled workers refused to disperse and a deputy fired his weapon in the air to calm the crowd. About 40 shots ensued, fired by both workers and lawmen. When the bullets stopped flying, four people lay dead – the district attorney of Yuba County, a deputy, and two workers.

In the wake of the melee, two of the IWW organizers were tried for murder, on the theory that their incendiary speeches led to the shooting that caused the deaths. They were convicted of conspiracy to murder the district attorney. Durst, whose exploitative treatment of the workers set the stage for the violent outburst, went unpunished.

The Wheatland tragedy drew public attention to the travails of migrant labor. Progressive Era reformers soon afterward took the first steps to improve conditions for California's field workers.

SUMMARY

California in the late 1800s and early 1900s, as earlier, was closely connected to the rest of the nation. Consequently, the anti-railroad politics, municipal corruption, and labor strife that characterized the nation at large played out in the Golden State as well. The gunfight at Mussel Slough, the scandalous revelations in the Colton letters, the Southern Pacific's attempt to discount its debt to the federal government, and that railroad's efforts to monopolize the maritime trade of southern California ignited and fueled a firestorm of public anger. Much of that anger first erupted in San Francisco, the so-called "Queen City of the Pacific." A socialistic third party, the Union Labor Party, formed there, intent on securing government ownership of the city's utility companies. San Francisco political boss Abraham Ruef seized leadership of the ULP and proceeded to line his pockets and those of city and county officials with money he extorted from local utility companies.

San Francisco's colossal 1906 earthquake devastated much of the municipality while exposing the rampant corruption of its government. Out of the rubble emerged a movement to prosecute the city's corrupt officials and rebuild both the infrastructure and reputation of the Pacific Coast's leading city. Bustling Los Angeles had big plans of its own to become a commercial force in the state. Entrepreneur Phineas Banning helped see to it that a harbor would be built in San Pedro that would one day eclipse San Francisco's maritime supremacy.

In the late 1800s and early 1900s labor and capital battled each other in the state's leading cities and farmlands. Mirroring workers' struggles to organize in Chicago and New York, toilers in San Francisco and Los Angeles campaigned for collective bargaining rights. San Francisco quickly became home to the most powerful labor union movement in the western United States. In 1891 that city's maritime workers founded the Sailors' Union of the Pacific, which, under Andrew Furuseth, unionized dockworkers and seamen along America's entire West Coast and beyond, demonstrating the reach of Greater California. Men and women in the state's factories formed separate unions. Organized labor fought the admission of low-wage Asian immigrant workers into the state. Los Angeles, due to the efforts of Republican leaders Harrison Gray Otis and Henry Huntington as well as the Merchants and Manufacturers Association, was the state's center of anti-union activity. Labor elements were involved in the bombing of the *Los Angeles Times* building in 1910. Agricultural workers suffered the worst conditions of employment, leading to the Wheatland riot of 1913.

REVIEW QUESTIONS

- Why was so much public anger aimed at the Southern Pacific Railroad, which had brought economic growth to California? How did Collis Huntington fit into the rising discontent of Californians?
- Why did a major struggle develop in the 1890s over where a harbor would be located in Los Angeles? What was Senator Stephen M. White's role in that struggle?
- What was Abraham Ruef's role in the political scandals that rocked San Francisco in the early 1900s?
- What working conditions led to the formation of maritime unions in San Francisco? How did Andrew Furuseth go about addressing those conditions, and how did he view Chinese seamen?
- What circumstances led to the Wheatland riot of 1913?

FURTHER READINGS

Walton Bean, *Boss Ruef's San Francisco: The Story of the Union Labor Party, Big Business, and the Graft Prosecution* (Berkeley: University of California Press, 1968). The transformation of an idealistic, scholarly sophisticate into a big city boss and his influence on San Francisco politics is told with skill.

Sucheng Chan, *Asian Californians* (San Francisco: Boyd & Fraser, 1991). The subject matter is treated with attention to the role and treatment of Asian women in the state.

Daniel Cletus, *Bitter Harvest: A History of California Farmworkers, 1870–1941* (Berkeley: University of California Press, 1981). The author traces the state government's response to the Wheatland tragedy, noting how the 1913 Commission on Immigration and Housing took the first halting steps by investigating and documenting farm workers' miserable living conditions.

Daniel Cornford, ed., *Working People of California* (Berkeley: University of California Press, 1995). This anthology of gendered writings focuses on urban and rural labor, skilled and unskilled toilers, and the dynamics of race within the working class.

Ira B. Cross, *A History of the Labor Movement in California* (Berkeley: University of California Press, 1935). This is a dated though still useful survey of the state's labor history.

William Deverell, "The Los Angeles 'Free Harbor Fight,'" *California History*, 70 (Spring 1991), 12–29. Without defending the Southern Pacific Railroad, the author

critiques the widely accepted view that the opponents of a Santa Monica harbor were virtuous paladins of the public interest.

Philip Ethington, *The Public City: The Political Construction of Urban Life in San Francisco, 1850–1900* (Berkeley: University of California Press, 2001). Highly conceptual, this work analyzes how group identities of race, class, ethnicity, and gender shaped San Francisco's "public sphere."

Philip Fradkin, *The Great Earthquake and Firestorms of 1906: How San Francisco Nearly Destroyed Itself* (Berkeley: University of California Press, 2006). With detail and compelling logic, the author argues that unprepared San Franciscans and their municipal government were partially to blame for the extent of the ruins caused by the great temblor of 1906.

Michael Kazin, *Barons of Labor: The San Francisco Building Trades and Union Power in the Progressive Era* (Urbana, IL: University of Illinois Press, 1989). The volume narrates how building trades organizers, working with other union leaders and San Francisco officials, built the strongest labor movement in any American city.

Carey McWilliams, *Factories in the Field: The Story of Migratory Farm Labor in California* (Berkeley: University of California Press, 2000). This is a paperback reprint of a classic work recounting the struggles of various ethnic groups of farm workers to redress the harsh labor conditions imposed by corporate agriculture in the state.

Ernest Marquez and Veronique de Turenne, *Port of Los Angeles: An Illustrated History from 1850–1945* (Santa Monica, CA: Angel City Press, 2007). The photographs, captions, and narratives contained in this volume chronicle the rise of the Port of Los Angeles to world-class stature.

Gerald D. Nash, "The California Railroad Commission, 1876–1911," *Southern California Quarterly*, 54 (December 1962), 287–305. The author attributes the ineffectiveness of the Railroad Commission to the inexperience of its members as much as to the machinations and influence of the Southern Pacific Railroad.

Spencer Olin, *California Politics, 1846–1920: The Emerging Corporate State* (San Francisco: Boyd & Fraser, 1981). In covering the rise of California as a corporate state, the author makes a case for not viewing the Southern Pacific Railroad as the sole embodiment of the money power that shaped politics from statehood through the Progressive Era.

Jean Pfaelzer, *Driven Out: The Forgotten War Against Chinese Americans* (New York: Random House, 2007). Drawing on well-documented cases, this book describes in vivid detail the lawful and unlawful means used by whites, assisted at times by African Americans, to drive the Chinese out of towns, cities, and farmlands in California and the Pacific Northwest.

Alexander Saxton, *The Indispensable Enemy: Labor and the Anti-Chinese Movement in California* (Berkeley: University of California Press, 1971). Focusing on labor's crusade against Asians, the author locates the roots of the state's anti-Chinese movement in Civil War-era Southern white racism against blacks.

Robert J. Schwendinger, *Ocean of Bitter Dreams: Maritime Relations between China and the United States, 1850–1915* (Tucson, AZ: Westernlore Press, 1988). This is a highly authoritative work that integrates maritime, diplomatic, and Chinese American history.

David F. Selvin, *A Place in the Sun: A History of California Labor* (San Francisco: Boyd & Fraser, 1981). This reliable, brief survey offers a point of entry into subject matter that is receiving increasing attention from historians.

Tom Sitton, "The Bannings on the Magic Isle: Santa Catalina Island, 1892–1919," *California History*, 87 (December 2009), 6–23. Santa Catalina's turn-of-the-century development as a "pleasure island" and sport fisherman's paradise, under Banning family ownership, is chronicled in this article.

Tom Sitton, *Grand Ventures: The Banning Family and the Shaping of Southern California* (San Marino, CA: Huntington Library Press, 2010). This work traces the important business activities of Phineas Banning and his sons in spurring the growth of southern California's maritime economy and philanthropic endeavors during the decades before and after 1900.

Errol Wayne Stevens, *Radical L.A.: From Coxey's Army to the Watts Riots, 1894–1965* (Norman, OK: University of Oklahoma Press, 2009). The author argues that much of Los Angeles' history since the depression-ridden 1890s has been shaped by conflict between right-wing business interests and left-wing unionists, socialists, communists, and ethnic minorities.

Grace Heilman Stimson, *Rise of the Labor Movement in Los Angeles* (Berkeley: University of California Press, 1955). A bit dated, this book remains the most comprehensive and in-depth history in print of Southland labor conditions and union organizing.

Richard S. Street, *Beasts of the Field: A Narrative History of California Farmworkers, 1769–1913* (Stanford, CA: Stanford University Press, 2004). As a study of California field labor during the lengthy time span covered, this copiously cited and engagingly written book is unmatched.

Hyman Weintraub, *Andrew Furuseth: Emancipator of the Seamen* (Berkeley: University of California Press, 1959). This well-researched biography acknowledges Furuseth's white racism while crediting him for steadfastly working to improve employment conditions for sailors.

9

Governor Hiram Johnson and Pacific-Oriented Progressivism

The Progressive Era reform movement of the late nineteenth and early twentieth centuries was part of an international response to the excesses and inequities of industrial capitalism. Essentially, it was a campaign for social democracy in the form of the regulatory state, that is, an effort to provide citizens with a measure of economic security and protection against the fluctuations of the business cycle. Such protections, including old-age pensions and government inspection of hospitals and childcare facilities, gained increasing public attention in Europe, New Zealand, and the United States during this time, giving momentum to social democracy in the Western world. In America this reform impulse occurred during an upswing in the business cycle in the Progressive Era, rendering this a period of prosperity nationwide. In California, prosperity was enhanced by maritime trade that stood to grow even further by the opening of the Panama Canal. More importantly, Golden State progressivism bore the imprint of Pacific leanings.

In the United States progressivism operated at the national, state, and local levels. In each of these political arenas, urban reformers addressed the unchecked power of corporations, the corruption of politics by railroads and private-sector utilities companies, the exploitation of women and children in the workforce, the demand of women to vote, the need to supply cities with clean water, and more. During this period government assumed increasing responsibility for the public welfare, particularly of middle-class whites. In California and the rest of America, this new role for government marked a departure from the unregulated capitalism of the late 1800s. Hiram Johnson, the Golden State's progressive governor and later U.S. Senator, attained legendary status for his leadership in cleaning up politics and modernizing governance.

Pacific Eldorado: A History of Greater California, First Edition. Thomas J. Osborne.
© 2013 Thomas J. Osborne. Published 2013 by Blackwell Publishing Ltd.

Timeline

1907   California's Republican reformers create the Lincoln–Roosevelt League to break the grip of the Southern Pacific Railroad on politics

Hawaiian surfing legend George Freeth (who had taught writer Jack London to surf on Oahu) moves to the Golden State, introducing wave-riding in southern California

1907–8   President Theodore Roosevelt negotiates a Gentlemen's Agreement whereby all over-age children of foreign background and those unable to speak English will be sent to segregated schools, and Japan will no longer permit its workers to immigrate to California

1910   Angel Island Immigration Station is established in San Francisco Bay to limit Asian immigration to America's Pacific Coast

Revolution erupts in Mexico, resulting in tens of thousands of Hispanic border-crossers entering California and the American Southwest

An explosion destroys the *Los Angeles Times* building

Hiram Johnson, a progressive Republican, is elected governor

1911   The Stetson–Eshleman railroad regulation bill is passed into law, empowering the Railroad Commission to set railroad passenger and freight rates, subject to judicial review

Constitutional amendments extend the Railroad Commission's authority over utility companies as well

The Public Utilities Act is passed, activating the Commission's new authority to regulate public utilities companies

The State Board of Control is established to conduct audits of government agencies, cut waste, and improve efficiency

A workers' compensation law goes into effect

Constitutional amendments establish the initiative, referendum, and recall processes

Voters can directly elect their U.S. Senators

Male voters ratify a women's suffrage constitutional amendment

1913   A state law establishes a minimum wage for women

A constitutional amendment providing for cross-filing goes into effect

The Alien Land Act prohibits land ownership and leasing acreage for more than three years to persons ineligible for U.S. citizenship

The Raker Act, a federal law, authorizes San Francisco to use the Hetch Hetchy Valley as a reservoir and electric power-generation site

The Owens Valley–Los Angeles Aqueduct is completed

Fullerton Junior College, the first public two-year institution in the state, is founded in Orange County

The California legislature passes the Red Light Abatement Act criminalizing pimping and allowing police to padlock brothels

1914	John Muir, world-renowned environmentalist and mountaineer, dies
1915	The Panama Pacific Exposition, a world fair, is held in San Francisco, showcasing that city's Pacific trade and recovery from the 1906 earthquake
	Made entirely in California, David W. Griffith's pro-Ku Klux Klan film *The Birth of a Nation* is released, sparking protests from blacks
1916	A World War I preparedness parade in San Francisco is marred by a terrorist bombing that kills nine people and injures 40; Warren K. Billings and Thomas J. Mooney are convicted and sent to prison despite evidence that prosecution witnesses committed perjury
1918	Frederick M. Roberts, California's first black assemblyman, is elected in Los Angeles' 74th District
	Evangelist Aimee Semple McPherson settles in Los Angeles, shortly afterward founding the Four Square Gospel Church that eventually becomes international
1919	The southern branch of the University of California (later renamed UCLA) is founded in Los Angeles
	The Criminal Syndicalism Act is passed, making it unlawful to advocate the use of force or violence to bring about political change or changes in industrial ownership or control of businesses

The Beginnings of Reform

While the heyday of California progressivism occurred in the 1910s, signs of a coming reform movement can be traced back to the early 1890s. Such signs included modern ballots, the appearance of Nationalist Clubs, the rise of the People's Party, the Good Government movement in Los Angeles, and the formation of the Lincoln–Roosevelt League in the state.

The Australian secret ballot was a transpacific cultural artifact adopted in California in 1891, and elsewhere throughout the United States in the preceding decade, Massachusetts being the first state to take this step. Australians adopted secret voting in order to prevent bullying and buying of votes at polling places, which had been common in England. Before this reform came into effect in California and elsewhere in America, party organizers provided their loyal followers with ballots listing that party's candidates. Voters' names were called out at polling places and the person identified in this public manner would step forward and be handed a ballot that he would, in the presence of observers, place in a box. The adoption of the Australian ballot marked a departure from this crude, manipulative voting method that limited voters' choices. Thereafter, at official polling places the state provided voters with a ballot listing all the candidates, to be cast in secret. This innovation applied only to general elections and not to party-controlled nominating conventions; still, it constituted a major advancement in democracy supported by California reformers, including labor leaders, prohibitionists, and feminists.

Nationalist Clubs sprang up in the state and across much of the nation in the early 1890s. They grew out of grassroots enthusiasm for the Christian socialist ideas of Edward Bellamy, author of *Looking Backward: 2000–1887* (1887). Such ideas adapted the compassionate teachings of Jesus of Nazareth to public policy, meaning that governments should care for those unable to fend for themselves: orphans, the sick and disabled, widows, the aged.

Bellamy's controversial novel tells of a Bostonian, Julian West, who awakens from a long sleep in the year 2000 and finds an America in which a business-led aristocracy no longer exists and economic resources are evenly distributed among the populace. A moral transformation has taken place: cooperation has replaced competition, and the national government guarantees "the nurture, education, and comfortable maintenance of every citizen from the cradle to the grave." In 1890 California featured 62 Nationalist Clubs, boasting some 3,500 members, most of whom lived in San Francisco and Los Angeles. The purpose of the clubs was to work toward the non-violent achievement of Bellamy's dream of a communal society. By the mid-1890s, amid strikes and a worsening depression, the movement folded.

While Nationalist Clubs were urban-based, the People's or Populist Party garnered support both in cities and farm country. California's Populists, like their fellow party members throughout the West and South, campaigned against the railroads and for direct democracy, championing the initiative (a mechanism allowing voters to put a measure on the ballot), the referendum (offering voters a means to repeal a law), and the recall (providing voters with an opportunity to remove officials). These measures would become centerpieces of California progressivism. Equally important, if not more so, they would have profound future consequences, as when voters recalled Governor Gray Davis and replaced him with Arnold Schwarzenegger in 2003 (see Chapter 14).

Shortly after the turn of the century, a group of middle-class professionals in Los Angeles – including newspaper editor Edward A. Dickson, attorney Meyer Lissner, physician John Randolph Haynes, and others – launched the Good Government League. It aimed at wresting control of the city council from Walter Parker and his band of Southern Pacific Railroad-tied politicians. These mostly Republican reformers orchestrated the 1902 rewriting of the city's charter to include provisions for the initiative, referendum, and recall. Two years later the League saw to it that Los Angeles became the world's first city to employ the recall, which resulted in the removal of a council member who had voted to award the *Los Angeles Times* a printing contract even though a bid $15,000 lower had been received. An infuriated Harrison Gray Otis, the arch-conservative publisher of the *Times*, denounced the Leaguers as "Goo-Goos." He disliked them almost as much as he detested the Southern Pacific Railroad, unions, and socialists. Despite opposition from Otis and others, the League swept 17 reformers into the 23 available political offices in the 1906 municipal elections, though the Southern Pacific's candidate for mayor of Los Angeles, A.C. Harper, prevailed. A scandal the following year involving Harper's purchase of oil and sugar stocks led to his eventual abandonment of office.

Buoyed by the Good Government movement in Los Angeles and the contemporaneous San Francisco graft trials (see Chapter 8), in 1907 California reformers created a statewide organization to revamp politics, the Lincoln–Roosevelt League. Angelinos Dickson, Lissner, and Haynes, were again involved in carrying reform to this next level, as were like-minded public figures in the Central Valley and Bay Area. Dr. Haynes, a Christian socialist whose highly successful medical practice and real-estate investments gave him the means to effect change, was particularly adept at building a Southland coalition that would add momentum to a California-wide drive for reform. Haynes organized a banquet in January 1907, to which he invited Edward A. Dickson, and arranged for prominent journalist Lincoln Steffens to be the featured speaker. Steffens urged reformers to expand their successful work in cities to the entire state. Several weeks later, Dickson, as correspondent for the *Los Angeles Express*, went to Sacramento to cover the January session of the state legislature. There, by chance, he encountered for the first time Chester H. Rowell, editor of the *Fresno Morning Republican*. The two pledged to collaborate on forming a statewide organization to free California from the grasp of the Southern Pacific "Octopus."

Next, two major meetings were held to create the intended organization. The first drew heavily from southern California and was held in Los Angeles on May 21, 1907. "Lincoln Republicans," so named by Dickson, framed an "emancipation proclamation" declaring their goal of freeing the Republican Party from control by the Southern Pacific Railroad's Political Bureau. The initiative, referendum, recall, and direct primaries (whereby voters and not parties chose candidates) were endorsed. Other proposals called for state regulation of railroad and utility rates, forest conservation, workers' compensation, a minimum wage standard for women, and women's suffrage.

The second meeting was held in Oakland on August 1. There, E.H. Harriman, head of the Southern Pacific, was ridiculed along with other "malefactors of great wealth." President Roosevelt's role in pushing for federal railroad regulation was extolled. A compromise between the relatively more progressive Roosevelt followers and the more moderately inclined Lincoln admirers resulted in naming the new statewide reform organization the Lincoln–Roosevelt League. In effect, it constituted a markedly autonomous liberal wing of the Republican Party. All it needed was a titular leader.

The League's search for a gubernatorial candidate took more than a year. Their eventual choice, Hiram Johnson, was at first very reluctant to run. A prosperous attorney with a home in Marin County overlooking San Francisco Bay, he saw little reason to spend his days in hectic Sacramento, squabbling over politics. Only after Rowell, Lissner, Dickson, and others appealed to Mrs. Johnson, who in turn used her powers of persuasion, did her husband agree to run. Having made the decision, Johnson threw his all into the campaign for governor in the 1910 election.

An "Aggressive Advocate" and the 1910 Election

Chester Rowell once described Hiram Johnson, known for being strong-willed and combative, as "an aggressive advocate." The son of Grove Johnson, a conservative lawyer and politician who had served as a railroad spokesman in the California legislature, Hiram grew up in Sacramento. He attended the University of California at Berkeley for three years, before dropping out to marry Minnie McNeal. The young groom then studied law in his father's office until passing the bar examination in 1888. His legal practice included defending labor unions and prosecuting San Francisco's notoriously corrupt political machine under Boss Ruef and Mayor Eugene E. Schmitz (see Chapter 8). Johnson disagreed with his father about railroad influence, unions, and other political matters, but absorbed his toughness, shrewdness, and temper. He would carry these traits with him into his electoral debut in 1910.

As the gubernatorial choice of the Lincoln–Roosevelt League, Johnson still had to gain the Republican Party's nomination in what became the state's first direct primary, as provided by a 1909 law. His running mate as lieutenant governor was southern Californian Albert J. Wallace, president of the Anti-Saloon League, an organization working in many states to outlaw the manufacture, sale, and consumption of alcoholic beverages. Wallace lent geographical balance to the ticket and appealed to the prohibitionists, whose greatest numbers and influence were in the Southland. The two League candidates succeeded in besting their rivals, some of whom had been put up by conservative Republicans with Southern Pacific endorsement. With the League firmly in control of the Republican Party, California headed into one of the most determinative elections in the state's history.

From the start, Johnson managed his own campaign. Seeing Leaguers' mishandling of several news stories convinced him to take charge of his own race for the governorship. "Of all the Damn Fool Leagues that ever existed," fumed the testy candidate, "The LINCOLN–ROOSEVELT LEAGUE not only is the worst, but the worst that could ever be conceived. . . ." He made no apologies for refusing to travel with other League candidates for office. Nevertheless, the League remained supportive of Johnson despite his at times intemperate barbs directed at it. The candidate's rancor toward the League did not let up as he took his campaign on the road.

Up and down the state Johnson went by automobile, covering 20,000 miles and trumpeting repeatedly his one theme: "Kick the Southern Pacific out of politics." Audiences roared their approval. He dismissed advice to include other issues because he sensed that what he was doing worked. It worked particularly well in the Central Valley, where wealthy owners of large farms and ranches had scores to settle with the Southern Pacific for charging high freight rates. Thus, Johnson was not so much the defender of small farmers and ranchers exploited by the powerful railroad as he was the champion of one segment of rich capitalists against another. His shrewdness in enlisting support from wealthy backers in the Central Valley paid off at election time.

Theodore Bell, the Democratic Party's gubernatorial candidate, ran on a similar anti-Southern Pacific platform but addressed a wider range of issues than Johnson. As historian Spencer Olin notes, since Johnson and Bell agreed on the railroad issue, the campaign was decided largely though not entirely on the personalities of the two men. Johnson, who exuded vigor and spirit, was clearly better able to arouse large audiences than his opponent. In addition, his valid charge that Bell received financial backing from Walter Parker, chief political operative for the Southern Pacific in Los Angeles, tarnished the Democratic candidate's reform credentials. There is no evidence that Bell solicited any help from the railroad, yet the help he was given ruined his chances at the polls.

The outcome of the election could scarcely have been better for the Lincoln–Roosevelt reformers. Johnson won the governorship with 177,191 votes to Bell's 154,835. Berkeley's socialist candidate J. Stitt Wilson came in a distant third with 47,819 votes.

Regulating the Economy

Swept into office on an incoming tide of public anger toward the Southern Pacific, Governor Johnson took action beginning in 1911 to attend to that matter and regulate the economy in other areas as well. This meant reining in the power of railroads and utilities

Figure 9.1   Hiram Johnson relaxing at home just before the 1910 election. Courtesy of the Bancroft Library, UC Berkeley.

companies, while closely monitoring governmental expenses, protecting injured and sick workers, and regulating child labor. In many of these endeavors California reformers were inspired by policies across the Pacific in New Zealand, a self-governing British "dominion" in the vanguard of social democracy.

Effective regulation of the Southern Pacific came in the form of the Stetson–Eshleman bill, championed by Johnson and approved on February 9, 1911, and three later constitutional amendments aimed at greatly strengthening the state Railroad Commission. The Stetson–Eshleman law empowered the commission to set transportation and passenger rates, subject to judicial review, for all railroads and other transport businesses. By the end of June 1912, the commission had saved shippers and passengers an estimated $2 million in railroad fares. The three constitutional amendments, adopted in October, 1911, authorized the legislature to further broaden the commission's power by, for example, extending its regulatory control over public utilities. Such utilities included gas, electricity, telephones, telegraph, water services, pipelines, and warehouses used in connection with rail and ship transportation.

As authorized, the legislature passed unanimously the Public Utilities Act, which the governor signed into law on December 23, 1911. Accordingly, the number of commissioners was increased from three to five and they were to be appointed by the governor as opposed to being elected as previously was the case. All public utilities in the state fell within the jurisdiction of the commission, except for those incorporated exclusively in cities or towns.

Johnson's stress on efficiency and economy, hallmarks of progressivism nationwide, is evident in the establishment of the Board of Control in 1911. The legislature created the board to monitor the state's finances. The agency conducted annual audits of the accounts of the state's hospitals, prisons, bureaus, and commissions, as well as other institutions. By 1913, 16 state officers had been investigated, fired, and required to repay the monies they embezzled. The cost of funding the board amounted to $42,000 a year. As of January 1, 1913, according to the chair of the board, the state registered net savings of $750,000. The complaints of critics about the cost of regulation rang hollow in the face of these figures.

As an earlier defender of labor unions, Johnson's governorship addressed workers' concerns. In response to pressure from labor unions and public officials, in 1911 the legislature passed and the governor signed a workers' compensation law to protect the interests of employees injured on the job. The measure provided for voluntary compensation, paid by employers. No such payments would be made, however, if employers could show that workers' negligence had played a role in their injuries. Seeing these provisions as inadequate in terms of safeguarding workers, the California Department of Insurance board of commissioners refused to enforce the law. Instead, the commissioners turned to a New Zealand workers' compensation law for guidance. As a result the state legislature created a state insurance monopoly, as New Zealand had earlier. The monopoly took the form of a mutual insurance company, that is, an entity owned by citizen policyholders, who, unlike investors in commercial enterprises, had no incentive to pursue profitmaking. This discouraged private sector competitors from entering and controlling the workers' compensation market, keeping job-related accident insurance affordable for employers and workers. In 1913 a new California workers' compensation statute went into effect, making employer participation in a broadened state insurance program compulsory, except in agriculture. In accounting for the new and more effective measure, commission chairman A.J. Pillsbury declared "We borrowed the idea from New Zealand."

In the area of labor relations, reformer and journalist William E. Smythe of San Diego encountered limits as to how progressive the state would be. In 1901–2 he promoted compulsory arbitration of labor disputes. To him, a recent strike in San Francisco constituted "a blot on the history of California." "Thousands of men were idle for weeks. . . . Assaults were committed and blood was shed." The fact that the Pacific dominion of New Zealand had successfully implemented compulsory arbitration of disputes between workers and employers had caused Smythe to underestimate the culture of property ownership and a relatively weak regulatory state that prevailed on the American side of the ocean. In the face of employer opposition, his efforts came to nothing. In the early 1900s, California, at least, was not ready for the arbitration reform championed by some progressives.

Labor market reforms, nevertheless, came on other fronts. At the turn of the century in California, children of poor families worked in fields, factories, and canneries, often enduring exploitative conditions and earning wages that were a fraction of those paid to adults. In 1913 California progressives, led by Katherine Philips Edson, pushed for and secured a minimum wage law for women and children, and the establishment of the Industrial

Welfare Commission, which, among its other duties, investigated the wages, hours, and working conditions of children. The information gathered helped lead to the passage of another minimum wage law for children and others three years later. Working conditions for women further improved in 1913 when Berkeley socialist Elvina Beals and her female colleagues secured an amendment to the existing eight-hour-day law, extending its provisions to women employed in public lodging houses, apartment buildings, hospitals, and other places exempted from the original statute.

Democratizing Politics, Subsidizing Education

Governor Johnson and his fellow progressives repeatedly declared their intent to transfer political decision-making from the parties and economic interests directly to "the people." This was the antithesis of what many conservatives believed, namely, that the American system of government was representative rather than democratic; the common people, accordingly, were unfit to handle affairs of state. Progressives, on the other hand, adhered to a Jeffersonian faith in the goodness of human beings that when nurtured by public education would lead to the building of a just and good society. They believed that democratizing politics and subsidizing education were curatives for what ailed a state in need of reform.

Making good on the Lincoln–Roosevelt League's platform of instituting the initiative, referendum, recall, and direct primaries, as noted, Johnson fought for and won the legislature's approval of constitutional amendments incorporating these devices. In a special election held on October 10, 1911, voters ratified the amendments, rendering California a national leader, along with Oregon, in democratizing electoral politics at the state level. Thereafter, an initiative could be placed on the ballot when 8 percent of the voters participating in a preceding gubernatorial election signed a petition supporting a proposed measure. A referendum qualified for the ballot with 5 percent. Initiatives and referendums have had unintended consequences, in that powerful corporations and special interests (the progressives' adversaries) have since made effective use of these instruments. The Proposition 13 initiative, for example, passed by voters in 1978 purportedly to reduce the property taxes of elderly homeowners, was pushed by commercial real-estate interests and has resulted in long-term impacts on public education and many other state services. For recalls, variable percentages were required depending on whether the official was elected by a political subdivision of California or voters statewide. The legislature in 1911 amended the Direct Primary Law of 1909, enabling voters to indicate their choice for U.S. Senator.

Displeased with political parties, while desirous of Republican support, conflicted progressives took a momentous step in securing ratification of a cross-filing amendment in 1913. Thereafter candidates could vie for nomination in the primaries of other parties as well as their own without indicating any affiliation. This measure, operative until repealed in 1959, weakened California's political organizations. At times, uninformed voters fell prey to the deceptions of candidates whose agendas remained masked by the non-partisan label. Cross-filing's most immediate effect was that it enabled former Republicans who had joined the new Progressive Party to file for the nominations of both parties in 1912.

Democratizing politics, per these progressive reforms, required a robust exercise of citizenship, which, in turn, necessitated a quality, state-subsidized education system to foster an informed electorate. Such a system was infused with the ideals of social philosopher John Dewey and others, which focused on educating the whole child, deemphasizing rote memorization, and creating an informal learning environment that allowed for a measure of experimentation. Aspects of this approach appeared at several levels of public education.

The kindergarten movement illustrates the application of progressivism to early childhood education. Started in Germany, the movement spread into California cities and elsewhere throughout the United States before and after 1900. Premised on the perfectibility of humans and the establishment of an environment conducive to that goal, Californian Sarah Cooper became the spokesperson for kindergartens on the Pacific Coast. Eventually, she became known as a theorist, organizer, and fundraiser of the movement nationwide and abroad. Such a pre-school experience was the best hope, Cooper held, of ameliorating the suffering and ignorance of poor children. Kindergartens, progressives believed, would put disadvantaged pre-schoolers on the road to becoming empowered, responsible citizens.

Simultaneously, junior (now called community) colleges appeared in California and throughout the nation. Progressives established these tax-supported institutions to train teachers, prepare students for university study, and provide vocational education. Founded in 1913, Fullerton College in Orange County is the oldest continuously operating two-year public college in the state.

UCLA, established in 1919 as the Southern Branch of the University of California, exemplifies the progressives' seriousness about making higher education available to the state's citizenry. Many of the engineers, lawyers, journalists, scientists, and other experts needed to ensure high-quality professional services and efficiency in public policy – key progressive aims – and southern California's continued economic growth would be produced there.

Women's Suffrage and Public Morals

The nation's and California's Progressive Era coincided with an ongoing movement for women's voting rights that had gained momentum in the 1890s. Women wanted the vote not only to be men's civil equals, but also to raise the standards of public morality. Throughout the nineteenth and early twentieth centuries both sexes agreed that women constituted society's "beacons of virtue." Accordingly, the Women's Christian Temperance Union (WCTU), a group committed to realizing total abstinence from alcohol consumption in the United States, established its California chapter in 1879 to combat the scourge of male alcoholism. In the 1880s leaders in that organization had started chapters within the Pacific Basin in Hawai'i, New Zealand, Australia, Japan, Korea, and China. Throughout this maritime region, as in California, WCTU members pushed for voting rights. Lacking sufficient public support for abstinence in California, WCTU members embarked on a suffrage campaign, hoping that a female electorate eventually would help win the battle against alcohol consumption in the state through the passage of a prohibition law.

The convergence of progressivism and the women's suffrage campaign just after the turn of the century boosted the prospects of both efforts, as the two became mutually supportive. If reform-minded women could obtain the ballot, so they reasoned, they could more effectively elevate public morality. As voters, and presumably elected and appointed officials, they would protect their communities from the vices of male alcoholism, race track gambling, and prostitution.

Led by the WCTU and other upper-middle-class mostly white women's groups, suffragettes organized the California Woman's Congress in 1894. The purpose of the organization was to unify women in the demand for voting rights as a prerequisite to exercising full citizenship rights. The following year the state legislature approved a constitutional amendment providing for suffrage; it could not become law, however, until ratified by male voters in the 1896 election. Meanwhile, wealthy suffragettes crossed class lines, garnering support from working and socialist women. The leaders excluded non-whites, however, particularly African Americans and Mexican Americans. These leaders, assuredly, were not immune to the prevailing white racism of the times, but equally important to them was the fact that the struggle for women's rights was sufficiently difficult without further complicating and encumbering their efforts by simultaneously championing racial equality. Spokespersons, like the famed Susan B. Anthony who came to the Bay Area to help lead the cause, emphasized that America needed white women to bring order out of the chaos and human misery plaguing factory cities across the land. Voters, nevertheless, refused to ratify the suffrage amendment.

Members of chapters of the California Federation of Women's Clubs, headed by Clara Burdette in 1900, quickly took up the reform cause, stressing women's role in working for civic "improvement" and downplaying suffrage. In 1903 they tasked themselves with restoring El Camino Real (the historic King's Highway) of California's mission period; in this way they were acting in the public sphere while evoking the state's romantic past and stirring civic pride. Moreover, clubwomen volunteered their services in public schools, and – joined by professional men – led a rapidly growing City Beautiful movement by planting trees and building parks and playgrounds in the state's urban centers. The success of the movement in cities such as San Francisco even inspired City Beautiful advocates across the Pacific in Australia and New Zealand to spruce up their municipalities. Soon additional women's groups formed in the Golden State, for example the California Club in San Francisco and the Civic League of Los Angeles, to help in beautifying cities and enhancing social services. The leadership and membership in both organizations included only the white social elite.

To demonstrate their non-radical, mainstream thinking, clubwomen showcased their patriotism and support for American empire-building in Pacific waters. For example, in 1903 Katherine Hittell, a California Club officer, told the San Francisco Merchants' Association that world power was shifting to the Pacific Basin and that the City of St. Francis would become the commercial hub of the new American overseas empire. Accordingly, municipal bonds should be approved to give San Francisco the infrastructure and look of an imperial maritime trade center. Show the "world that we have confidence in the destiny of our queen city [of the Pacific Coast]," she urged.

Clubwomen backed their speeches with actions that demonstrated their qualifications for full citizenship rights, including voting. In the aftermath of the 1906 San Francisco earthquake, they formed a Women's Sanitation Committee. The committee volunteered its services to wage a "war on rats" as part of a government effort to battle the city's post-earthquake outbreak of bubonic plague. When some of the city's businesspersons tried to end the graft prosecutions, the 2,000-member women's auxiliary of the male Citizens' League of Justice called for a boycott of those merchants urging an end to the trials.

At the 1908 state Republican convention suffragettes paraded into the gathering and demanded endorsement of women's right to vote. They based their case on women's entitlement to full citizenship rights. When the male attendees politely rejected the demand of the "ladies" and thanked them for attending, the suffragettes booed and hissed. "We don't want your thanks – we want justice," they replied. Led by William F. Herrin, the Southern Pacific machine controlled the convention and would not budge on any significant reforms.

With backing from the Lincoln–Roosevelt Leaguers, the herculean efforts of Caroline Maria Severance, Katherine Philips Edson, and others brought results. By a small margin of 2 percent, and despite Hiram Johnson's noncommittal stance on the issue, California's male voters ratified a women's suffrage amendment in 1911.

Armed with the vote, female progressives carried forward their crusade against liquor consumption. Local prohibition laws closed bars in about half of the state by 1913. Statewide

Figure 9.2 Cartoon, "The Suffragette," *San Francisco Call*, August 29, 1908. The Roman goddess of wisdom, Minerva, representing California women, is drawn in shackles that render her powerless in the face of male party bosses like William F. Herrin who do not want to be bothered by women seeking the ballot. Courtesy of California Digital Newspaper Collection, Center for Bibliographic Studies and Research, University of California, Riverside, <http://cdnc.ucr.edu>.

prohibition came to California only when the federal government oversaw the ratification of the Eighteenth Amendment to the U.S. Constitution in 1919 and Congress passed the Volstead Act later that year to implement the amendment.

Race track gambling and prostitution, often connected to saloons, greatly concerned California progressives. A 1911 law forbade betting on horse races. Slot machines were disallowed by another measure. Female reformers, in particular, fought prostitution because they felt it degraded members of their sex. In 1913 the state legislature passed a Red Light Abatement Act, which criminalized pimping and allowed police to padlock brothels. Despite these steps, the targeted social vices persisted, especially in San Francisco and other large cities.

Water: Cities in a State of Thirst

As much of the foregoing suggests, progressivism, nationwide, was an urban-based movement attuned to meeting the most basic needs – such as water – of city dwellers. The interests of rural, farming communities were often an afterthought in the dynamics of progressive politics, while at times private individuals exploited public water projects for financial gain. As California's two largest municipalities, San Francisco and Los Angeles, grew in population, provision had to be made for supplying their citizens with an adequate amount of water. The public projects undertaken to do so were sweeping in scope and enmeshed in controversy.

At the beginning of the twentieth century, San Francisco was by far the state's and the Pacific Coast's leading city, boasting a population of 342,782 in 1900. With limited nearby water resources and an increasing demand for electricity, the city's progressive officials eyed Yosemite National Park's Tuolumne River. If that river's flow could be impounded in a reservoir to be situated at Hetch Hetchy Valley, as urged by the city's engineer, San Francisco's water and power needs could be met far into the future. To that end, Mayor James D. Phelan applied, unsuccessfully, to the U.S. secretary of the interior for authorization to transform the Hetch Hetchy Valley into a gargantuan water storage and electricity-generating facility.

For more than a decade a fierce political battle ensued among progressive conservationists – a battle between those valuing nature primarily for spiritual and aesthetic reasons, and those valuing nature as consumers, for sustainable and efficient use of its resources. With few exceptions, Sierra Club conservationists, ably led by John Muir (see Chapter 7), fit best into the spiritual and aesthetic group. Phelan and those supporting a Hetch Hetchy reservoir, on the other hand, aligned more with the utilitarian cohort, for which the water and power needs of city residents trumped all else.

To appreciate the intensity of the opposition to Phelan and the Hetch Hetchy project, it is essential to understand Muir's thinking. His environmental philosophy informed virtually every aspect of his adult life, accounting for his determination to prevent Hetch Hetchy from becoming a reservoir. Muir gravitated toward a naturalistic belief in the goodness, humanness, and sacred beauty of wilderness. "The whole of wilderness seems to be alive and familiar, full of humanity," he wrote. "The very stones seem talkative, sympathetic, brotherly." Filling the Hetch Hetchy Valley with water would be equivalent to drowning the valley's "brotherly" stones and vegetation, or, put another way, to flooding nature's cathedral.

From 1901 to 1913, Muir and his supporters succeeded in stopping the transformation of Hetch Hetchy into a reservoir. However, with the beginning of President Woodrow Wilson's first administration in the latter year, a new secretary of the interior – Franklin K. Lane from California – gave permission to proceed with the hydroelectric project. After holding hearings, Congress followed suit with passage of the Raker Act in 1913, which was then signed into law by Wilson. Named after California Representative John E. Raker, the measure granted the City of San Francisco the right to build a reservoir in the Hetch Hetchy Valley, provided that the water and electricity made available by the project would not be sold to any private individual or corporation. Utilitarian conservationists insisted on the sales prohibition. They were intent on preventing Pacific Gas and Electric (PG&E), a private utilities corporation, from selling water and power derived from a federally owned source for profit. Passage of the Raker Act left Muir worn out and disheartened. He died in 1914.

In the years that followed, the City of San Francisco could not get sufficient votes to pass the bond measures that would have enabled the project to remain entirely publicly owned. PG&E then purchased electricity from the city and resold it at a profit to San Franciscans, a violation of the spirit if not the letter of the Raker Act. In 1934 the aqueduct was completed and the city's inhabitants experienced their first taste of Hetch Hetchy water.

Los Angeles, with a population of 102,479 in 1900 that would double over the next five years, similarly found a water source in the Sierra Nevada – the Owens River, located on the eastern side of the range. The controversy over building an aqueduct that would divert water from that river and convey it 233 miles southward to Los Angeles was even bitterer than that engulfing the Hetch Hetchy project.

In 1904, Fred Eaton, an engineer and former Los Angeles mayor, reported to municipal officials that in Owens Valley he had found a major source of water that could supply the city's needs into the foreseeable future. William Mulholland, the city engineer and former protégé of Eaton, supported the idea strongly.

Eaton expected to enrich himself by transferring to Los Angeles land and water rights he had been buying in Long Valley, located at the upper end of the Owens River watershed. There a reservoir could be built, which would make his property even more valuable to Los Angeles and, consequently, more profitable for himself. For his scheme to work, however, a U.S. Reclamation Service plan to irrigate Owens Valley farms had to be derailed and Los Angeles had to finance the building of an aqueduct.

Both of these obstacles were met and overcome. Joseph B. Lippincott, the Reclamation Service's supervising engineer, decided that the valley's water should go to Los Angeles rather than to the federal agency's planned irrigation project for the area. The fact that Lippincott and Eaton had been close friends who proceeded to work together on Los Angeles' acquisition of land and water rights for an aqueduct suggests that Eaton may have influenced the Reclamation Service's willingness to give up the irrigation plan. In any case such influence, if it existed, was not decisive as President Roosevelt favored Los Angeles' going forward with the aqueduct system. The second obstacle – funding the waterworks – was addressed in 1907 by Los Angeles' passage of a nearly $25 million bond issue to cover construction costs.

Figure 9.3   The opening of the Owens Valley–Los Angeles Aqueduct, November 5, 1913. About 30,000 onlookers attended the aqueduct's opening ceremony. Courtesy of the Los Angeles Department of Water and Power. © Los Angeles Department of Water and Power.

Meanwhile, a syndicate of Los Angeles investors led by Harrison Gray Otis and Henry Huntington, among others, confidentially informed of the Owens Valley aqueduct plans, began acquiring options to 16,000 acres of San Fernando Valley land thought to be the site of a reservoir serving Angelinos and nearby farmers. The syndicate paid $35 an acre and later sold the parcels for millions when aqueduct water reached their holdings. Construction of the Los Angeles Aqueduct began in 1908 and was completed on November 5, 1913.

Meanwhile, the anger of Owens Valley farmers mounted in the 1920s as dry weather parched their fields and the river flow that had in earlier times relieved drought went almost entirely to Los Angeles. Growers in the water-starved region dynamited sections of the aqueduct in 1924. When Eaton's envisioned Long Valley dam began operating in 1941, several years after his death, the descendants of the Owens Valley growers were still disgruntled. Signs in public restrooms read: "Don't flush the toilet. Los Angeles needs the water."

The Owens Valley's residents could fume as long as they wanted. Their protests made little difference to those living in the metropolitan Southland. With a profitable and reliable supply of water, the business elite and progressives were well on their way to building their "Great Los Angeles," the Pacific Coast's new super city.

Pacific Profile: George Freeth, Southern California Surfer Extraordinaire

George Douglas Freeth, Jr. (1883–1919) was born on Oahu in the Hawaiian Islands. Historian Arthur Verge, an authority on the figure, credits the part-Polynesian Freeth with introducing surfing in southern California and establishing professional lifeguard services along the region's shoreline. Moreover, his celebrated aquatic feats as a Pacific surfer, diver, and swimmer boosted the Southland's coastal real-estate development and helped establish the beach culture from Santa Monica to San Diego. In short, he exemplified the ever-growing ties between California and Hawai'i from the gold rush era to the present.

Freeth descended from a prominent family in Hawai'i. Drawn to the ocean from an early age, young George, who taught acclaimed California author Jack London to surf at Waikiki, became known as the preeminent board rider in the islands. Having revived surfing in Hawai'i, which New England missionaries in the islands had once banned for its "immodesty and idleness," Freeth's departure for California in 1907 made front-page news in Honolulu's leading paper, the Pacific Commercial Advertiser. The headlines (July 3, 1907) declared that he would introduce "Hawaiian Surfriding to People in California." Armed with a letter of introduction from the Hawai'i Promotion Committee, which worked to increase tourism from the mainland to the Polynesian archipelago, Freeth shipped to California, where his surfing exploits at Venice beach quickly gained recognition in the local press.

Southern California real-estate tycoons Abbot Kinney and Henry E. Huntington relied on Freeth's surfing exhibitions to publicize their respective Venice and Redondo beachfront developments. Huntington hired Freeth to perform as a celebrity wave rider and organize lifeguard services at Redondo. The advanced ocean rescue techniques Freeth taught reflected the Progressive Era's emphasis on professionalizing public services. "Innovation" and "efficiency" were his watchwords.

On the afternoon of December 16, 1908, Freeth's lifesaving skills and courage were put to a major test. A Pacific squall had whipped up gale-force winds and towering waves off Venice, where several boats carrying a total of 11 Japanese fishermen were in danger of crashing on the rocky breakwater. Diving off the Venice pier into the chilly, stormy sea he single-handedly saved seven of the fishermen at the risk of losing his own life to hypothermia. The remaining four were rescued by the Venice Lifesaving Corpsmen, who had been trained by Freeth. The entire two-and-a-half-hour ordeal had been watched by thousands of beach spectators. Afterward the rescued fishermen awarded Freeth a gold watch, gave him a financial donation, and changed the name of their fishing village near today's Pacific Palisades from Maikura to Port Freeth. In 1911 a newspaper reporter found that the villagers were performing nightly Shinto rituals in honor of the Hawaiian hero who had saved them. On the recommendation of Abbot Kinney, whose son participated with Venice's rescue crewmen, and written testimonials from eyewitnesses to the drama of that December afternoon, Freeth was awarded in 1910 the nation's highest civilian commendation, the Congressional Gold Medal.

His last years were spent in San Diego, where he coached rowing, taught ocean swimming, and, as along Los Angeles County's shoreline, organized professional lifeguard services. The influenza pandemic of 1918–19 took the life of this aquatic marvel, whose exploits anticipated the increasing importance of southern California's beach culture and ties to Hawai'i.

San Francisco, Transpacific Racial Tensions, and Angel Island

Denouncing the Asian presence in the Golden State was nearly an unwritten requirement for white candidates seeking elective office in Progressive Era California. Republicans, Democrats, Populists, and socialists alike agreed that immigrants from the Far East posed problems to the entire West Coast. The Bay Area having America's largest cluster of trans-pacific immigrants, San Francisco became the flashpoint of racial tensions in California, particularly with respect to relations between whites and incoming Japanese aliens. Under-scoring the Golden State's connection to the Asian Pacific Rim, these tensions led to a diplomatic crisis between Japan and the United States. As the immigrants' Pacific gateway to the United States, Angel Island, in San Francisco Bay, served as the clearing house for those who would be admitted into America, or deported.

Most of the 55,000 Japanese immigrants entering the United States from 1900 to 1908 settled in California, with some 1,781 residing in San Francisco in 1900. Most of those living in the outlying areas and in the Southland worked as farm hands. Having been pivotal in the nation's recent anti-Chinese movement, the city and its press objected to more "Orientals" arriving on its shores in the 1890s. These objections grew more strident in the immediate aftermath of Japan's stunning 1904–5 military defeat of Russia. The victory of a non-white nation (Japan) over a white one (Russia) magnified the fears of San Francis-cans and a growing number of Americans that Japan was fast becoming a serious threat to the Pacific interests of the United States. Those interests included expanding maritime trade with China while protecting America's recently acquired Pacific stepping stones to that trade in Hawai'i and the Philippines, and defending the West Coast in case of attack.

Fearing the "silent invasion" of Japanese immigrants, in 1905, 67 organizations – mainly labor unions – founded the national Asiatic Exclusion League (AEL), headquartered in San Francisco. Labor groups had been similarly involved in anti-Chinese agitation in the 1870s (see Chapter 6). The AEL's California branch alone boasted 100,000 members. Its primary goal was to prevent Japanese people from working in agriculture and industry, as well as to stop the influx of such immigrants into the United States. Its methods included distrib-uting propaganda, lobbying for anti-Japanese legislation, holding rallies, and conducting boycotts.

On October 11, 1906, amid the earthquake's smoldering ruins, rising levels of anti-Japanese violence, and sensational graft trials, the San Francisco Board of Education responded to pressure from the AEL and ordered Japanese students to attend an Oriental Public School in Chinatown. The board statement read in part: "children should not be placed in any position where their youthful impressions may be affected by association with pupils of the Mongolian race." Sacramento Assemblyman Grove Johnson put into more explicit language his concern for the safety of innocent white schoolgirls who might be seated next to older Japanese boys "with their evil oriental thoughts."

An international crisis quickly developed. The Japanese press denounced the board's policy as insulting and ungrateful in view of a $250,000 donation from Japan to aid San Francisco's recovery from the recent earthquake and fire. Japan's government lodged a protest in Washington, D.C., declaring that the action of the San Francisco board violated a treaty guaranteeing Japanese children equal educational opportunities in the United States. Acutely aware of Japan's predominant position in Asian Pacific waters and the difficulty of defending America's territory in the Philippines, President Theodore Roosevelt ridiculed the board's policy as a "wicked absurdity."

To resolve the issue, in early 1907 Roosevelt arranged for San Francisco Mayor Eugene Schmitz and the board members to meet with him in the nation's capital. There a deal was struck that afterward was incorporated into the informal Gentlemen's Agreement of 1907–8 between the United States and Japan. According to that agreement, only overage students and those unable to speak English might be sent to separate San Francisco schools. This stipulation would apply to all foreign-born students and not exclusively to those from Japan. In return for this concession, Japan promised not to permit workers, skilled or unskilled, to immigrate to the United States.

In the immediate aftermath of the Gentlemen's Agreement, San Francisco and other major California ports played highly publicized roles in America's follow-up show of naval strength to Japan. Convinced that relations with Japan would remain stable and peaceful only if that nation feared the United States, Roosevelt ordered the entire American battleship armada, known as "The Great White Fleet," on a round-the-world "goodwill cruise" that included a stop at Yokohama, a leading port city near Tokyo. En route to Japan from Hampton Roads, Virginia, the fleet was welcomed by crowds at San Diego, San Pedro, and especially San Francisco where half a million enthralled spectators cheered the warships as they steamed through the Golden Gate.

Despite the Gentlemen's Agreement and naval show of strength, Japanese immigration to the United States mainly via San Francisco resulted in a further 120,000 new arrivals by 1924. This increase was due largely to so-called "picture brides" shipping to California, swelling the population of alien Japanese in the state. Such brides were so called because having seen only photographs of their prospective husbands of Japanese descent residing in America, the young women participated in marriage ceremonies in Japan. Now wed, the female spouses boarded San Francisco-bound vessels. On arrival, the new wives joined their waiting husbands.

Many of the picture brides labored with their farmer husbands in the fields of the Central Valley. Initially, these families (*issei* or first generation) farmed as laborers; before long, through their knowledge of growing and their herculean work ethic, some acquired acreage of their own. By 1910 they owned some 17,000 acres and leased more than 80,000. They introduced rice farming in the state and, like Chinese farmers decades earlier, grew potatoes commercially. Soon white growers complained about competition from the state's immigrant Japanese farmers, particularly those owning their own land and prospering.

Ingrained anti-Asian racism and fear of competition in farming led to the passage, with support from Hiram Johnson and all political parties, of the state's Alien Land Act of 1913. By its terms "aliens ineligible to citizenship" could not buy California land or lease it for more than three years. Because a federal law of 1790 specified that naturalized citizens must be white, Japanese residents in California were ostensibly prohibited from owning their own farmland or leasing acreage for more than three years. However, the intended targets of the law found legal loopholes. For example, Japanese immigrants bought land in the name of their American-born (*nisei*, or second generation) children, who were U.S. citizens,

Figure 9.4   Japanese "picture brides." The original caption appearing in the *San Francisco Examiner*, March 9, 1919, read in part: "Here are a number of 'picture brides' from the land of cherry blossoms, photographed on the deck of a ship just pulling into San Francisco harbor. They are destined to be the wives of Japanese residents of California." Courtesy of California State Parks, 2012. Image 231-18-9.

or they partnered with whites in co-ownership arrangements. To combat the perceived subterfuge, in 1920 the Native Sons of the Golden West and the American Legion, two groups that identified closely with California's pioneering and the nation's military traditions respectively, succeeded in securing tighter alien land-owning restrictions.

Land-seeking and other Japanese newcomers to America usually passed through San Francisco's Angel Island Immigration Station. Situated just inside the Bay, the station served as the United States Pacific gateway, much as Ellis Island in New York City had been functioning as America's Atlantic gateway with at least one critically important difference – Angel Island was established largely for the purpose of *excluding* Asians, particularly the Chinese. Built in 1910, largely to enforce the policy of Chinese exclusion, the station processed immigrants from about 80 nations throughout the Pacific Basin and beyond.

Unlike Chinese arrivals, Japanese immigrants detained at Angel Island between 1910 and 1924 were seldom deported. Those sent back to Japan were usually rejected because of diseases diagnosed by examining physicians at Angel Island. Hookworm, an intestinal malady sometimes afflicting Japanese picture brides, led to quarantine and treatment at the station, followed by admission into the United States on receiving medical clearance. Still, detention on Angel Island was unpleasant; quarters were cramped and unclean, privacy was lacking, and the station was described as a prison by some detainees.

African Americans, Hispanics and Filipinos, Sikhs, and Indians

As the struggles of Asians in early twentieth-century California might suggest, in most instances white progressives made little effort to cross the color line and help nonwhite ethnic minorities. Native Americans – a major casualty of American migration to California since the gold rush – were the one exception to this trend and did receive some support from government officials and reformers. To secure any measure of social justice, African Americans, Hispanics and Filipinos, and Sikhs often had to mobilize their own ethnic communities rather than depend on help coming from outside their respective groups.

Despite the racial exclusivity of most white reformers, some African Americans embraced the cause of progressivism. However, constituting only about 2 percent of California's population on the eve of World War I, blacks, who experienced discrimination in housing and employment, had little effect on the state's major battles in the Progressive Era. Conversely, says historian Douglas Flamming, the era had a powerful effect on them by empowering African American leaders to organize their constituents to fight racial injustices.

An instance of this occurred when California chapters of the National Association for the Advancement of Colored People and the Urban League protested showings of David W. Griffith's film *The Birth of a Nation* in 1915. Overall, these protests were ineffectual: calls for censoring the film's degrading depictions of negroes went largely unheeded; boycotts in Los Angeles and New York failed to stop showings; and the film went on to become one of Hollywood's highest-grossing movies before World War II. Popular nationwide, the film was made entirely in California and depicted a chivalrous Ku Klux Klan struggling to restore order and decency in the Union-occupied American South in the post-Civil War period.

African Americans also organized political campaigns for statewide and local offices. While contending with black voter apathy, in 1918 African American progressives succeeded in electing the first black assemblyman in California, Frederick M. Roberts, who won in Los Angeles' 74th District.

An important Pacific dimension to black self-help efforts is seen in the move of clusters of African Americans from Los Angeles to Baja California in the 1910s and 1920s, an episode that is also illustrative of the extensive history of Greater California's influence in Baja. At the invitation of the Mexican government, these former Angelinos established a colony they called Little Liberia, situated between Tijuana and the port of Ensenada. In search of fairer treatment and more opportunities they established farms on thousands of acres, cultivating citrus, wheat, vegetables, alfalfa, and potatoes.

Similarly, Hispanics, particularly Mexican Americans and Spanish-speaking Filipinos, were marginalized by white progressives, who seemed to pay little attention to the increasing numbers of these groups. The near decade-long revolution that erupted in Mexico in 1910 resulted in tens of thousands of its people crossing the border into California and parts of the Southwest. With few exceptions, these new arrivals from south of the border tended to be poor, in need of jobs, and politically unorganized. They assuredly impacted the state by supplying menial labor and carving out *barrios* (ethnic neighborhoods) in San Diego, Los Angeles, and other cities, and *colonias* (ethnic settlements) in farming areas. Still, some of these arrivals became merchants, thereby augmenting a small but growing Hispanic middle class. For example, in the Belvedere neighborhood, a barrio of Los Angeles, Mexican American businessman Zeferino Ramírez became a successful mortician and organized his compatriots to promote public education and civic improvements. Like Mexican Americans, Filipinos constituted an important labor source for the state's canneries and farms, and were tolerated when not ignored by white progressives. In 1920 nearly half (2,674) of the West Coast's Filipinos lived in California, where most supported themselves as farm hands and domestic workers. California's Filipino workers were slower to unionize than their Japanese and Mexican counterparts. Largely without union membership and lacking progressive advocates on their behalf, the state's Filipino laborers remained low-paid for decades. Some, however, found other ways to support themselves, such as enlisting in the military, or opening small businesses. Filipino American Felix Budhi, for example, arrived in San Diego in 1908, and joined the U.S. Navy for financial reasons. A very few of his fellow Filipinos, according to him, "owned small restaurants combined with pool and gambling tables."

Sikhs from the Punjab area of northern India constituted a largely non-union agricultural labor force in early twentieth-century California. Coming to the Golden State via British Columbia, Sikhs, working in the Central and Imperial valleys, undercut unionized Japanese and white field laborers. Consequently, on the evening of January 28, 1908, white farm hands attacked Sikh orchard pruners in Live Oak, a town located 10 miles north of Marysville. They beat the Sikhs and stole $2,500 from them before driving their victims out of town. When the turban-wearing Asian Indians tried to prosecute two of their attackers the townspeople testified that the white defendants had not been at the camp. Despite such flagrant mistreatment, Sikhs were not content to remain hired farm workers. They pooled their money, leased acreage, and prospered from their orchards and other agricultural holdings.

With the rare exception of attention-grabbing newspaper headlines when a dramatic event involving an Indian occurred, Native Americans were the least visible minority in Progressive Era California. The gripping story of Ishi, the last known survivor of the Yani tribe who turned up in the northern California town of Oroville in 1911, has been recounted (see Chapter 1). An even more dramatic if less publicized incident of the times involving a California Indian occurred in the southern part of the state. Willie Boy, a young Paiute-Chemehuevi Indian wrongly accused of murdering another Chemehuevi man and his daughter in 1909, according to historians James A. Sandos and Larry E. Burgess, was the object of a sensationalized desert manhunt for a "wild" Indian thought to be a homicidal killer.

Such anomalous occurrences aside, some California progressives advocated for Indian rights. One reason for this advocacy was that by the early 1900s most Californians no longer saw the small population of 17,000 Indians in the state as a threat; the influx of Asians, especially Japanese farmers and other laborers, came to preoccupy many Anglos fearful of "the yellow peril." Whites who defended Indian rights could by then do so safely, unlike in the gold rush era half a century earlier. Southland reformer and booster Charles F. Lummis, working with reform-minded Stanford University President David Starr Jordan and others, succeeded in obtaining federal aid for the Cupeño tribe that had been forced to move from land near Warner's Hot Springs in San Diego County. In northern California Frederick G. Collette, a Methodist minister, organized the Indian Board of Cooperation in 1913. The board, whose members were white, worked to improve educational opportunities for Indian children and to extend citizenship rights to most indigenous peoples in the state.

While indigenous peoples depended on white advocates, some Indians actively defended their own rights. Annie Jarvis, for example, furnishes a striking example of Indian self-help. She was a head Dreamer, that is, a spiritual leader of the dream dance, among her Kashaya Pomo tribespeople. The dream dance conjured up apocalyptic visions at times associated with a joyous restoration of Indian ways before the coming of whites. Women, like Jarvis, usually led these dances. For three decades, beginning in 1912, in addition to her spiritual functions, she campaigned successfully for a prohibition on marriage with non-Indians, the outlawing of gambling and drinking, and an end to government officials sending Native American children to boarding schools.

Maritime Trade and the Panama Pacific Exposition

America's acquisition of a Pacific empire around 1900 put the nation's West Coast ports increasingly in the international spotlight. This was particularly true of California's maritime centers of San Francisco and Los Angeles, with its new harbor at San Pedro. The Panama Pacific Exposition of 1915 heralded San Francisco's rebuilding after the 1906 earthquake and California's arrival as a major global player in transoceanic commerce.

Based partially on the state's growing maritime economy in the latter half of the nineteenth century (see Chapter 7), business leaders had been predicting a rosy future for California and its seagoing commerce. The president of the California State Board of Trade, N.P. Chapman, envisioned a twentieth-century Golden State whose economic growth would be more dependent on its Pacific connections than on its ties to the nation's interior regions. In an article titled "Greater California and the Trade of the Orient," appearing in the *Overland Monthly* magazine in September 1899, he described a state bursting with economic energy beyond its borders and shoreline. Its trade relations would extend in all directions but most prominently toward the Asian Pacific Rim.

Evincing a progressive's concern for urban infrastructure development by supplying water and electrification for cities and for conserving California's timber and other resources for efficient use – that is, harvesting and extracting in a sustainable manner – Chapman urged state policymakers to concentrate on supplying China's teeming population with the state's products, especially foodstuffs, timber, and manufactures. Readers were urged to support California's China trade, otherwise that commerce would fall to the West Coast "cities of Portland, Seattle, and Tacoma" where "an aspiring and energetic people . . . will not yield us supremacy without a struggle." Greater California's northern rivals, he concluded, "are active and aggressive and do not intend that San Francisco shall be the great mart for Pacific Ocean trade on this Coast."

Chapman's vision for California's Pacific maritime commerce became a reality in the Progressive Era and into the early1920s. During that period San Francisco and Los Angeles were among the world's 13 leading seaports in terms of the aggregate value of trade respectively clearing their harbors. While the seagoing commerce of rival ports in Oregon and Washington grew, the Golden State retained its dominance of coastal and transpacific exchange.

San Francisco's Panama Pacific Exposition of 1915 celebrated this trade dominance and portrayed it as an engine of California's economic growth. The completion and opening of the Panama Canal that year was the occasion for holding the international fair. A model of the canal fascinated viewers. Pacific Basin-themed exhibits predominated. Replicas of a Mexican pueblo, a Samoan village, and Chinese and Japanese settlements were featured. China was portrayed as a country ripe for American investment and trade.

Everything about the fair was on a grand scale. Thirty-one nations and many states provided exhibits. The extravaganza ran for nine months and was attended by an estimated 19 million people.

Beyond the glitz and commercialism of the fair, the occasion was notable for the 948 "congresses" devoted to subjects as diverse as engineering, insurance, and the role of the Pacific in world history. Prominent scholars met at a Historical Congress to assess the opening of the Panama Canal against a backdrop of past and present occurrences. Speakers made various remarks linking California and the United States to the Pacific world. One commented that America "became a Pacific Coast power by the annexation of California." Another presenter celebrated the recent "enormous" growth in North Pacific commerce. Goods from "Japan, China, the [East] Indies], and the Philippines" were shipped across the Pacific to "San Francisco, [the] Hawaiian Islands and through the Panama Canal." A third speaker observed presciently that in world affairs: "The seat of [American] empire begins to shift from the Atlantic to the Pacific." As the future would show, California's trade and coastal military installations would become increasingly important components of a United States Pacific shift.

The Twilight of Progressivism

After the heyday of California progressivism from 1910 to 1913, the movement nationwide entered a gradual decline that lasted into the 1920s. Naturally, America's entry into World War I in 1917 forced the entire nation to focus less on reform and more on shoring up the home front and prevailing militarily overseas. Other factors, even more specific to California politics, also led to the waning of progressivism.

Between 1914, when World War I erupted in Europe, and America's entry into the conflict three years later, politicians and publicists in the United States debated whether the nation should intervene militarily. Neutrality, President Woodrow Wilson's declared policy, was proving hard to maintain.

In San Francisco, as elsewhere throughout the nation, some business leaders advocated going to war against Germany and its Triple Alliance partners. They appealed to patriotism to build public support for entering hostilities. In 1916, while the city was experiencing labor strife, a self-appointed Law and Order Committee and prominent businesspeople planned a parade for July 22, to demonstrate preparedness for war. Union members, socialists, pacifists, and some progressives boycotted the parade. Amid the flag-waving procession a bomb exploded at the intersection of Market and Steuart Streets. Nine people died and 40 were injured.

Suspects were arrested and trials held. Warren K. Billings, who had earlier been imprisoned for illegally transporting a suitcase filled with dynamite, was convicted and sentenced to life in prison. Next, Thomas J. Mooney, a radical trade union socialist and mentor of the younger Billings, was convicted and handed a death sentence. While the two were in prison, Mooney awaiting execution, their defenders nationwide demonstrated for release of the men. President Woodrow Wilson set up a Mediation Commission to investigate Mooney's supposed guilt; the commission found no evidence to support the conviction. Thereafter, Governor William D. Stephens commuted Mooney's sentence to life in prison in 1918, despite evidence that witnesses for the prosecution had committed perjury and that they had been encouraged to do so by District Attorney Charles M. Fickert. In 1939 Governor Culbert Olson pardoned both Mooney and Billings.

While the Mooney and Billings cases kept the issue of loyalty alive on the home front, more than 130,000 Californians served in the military. About 4,000 of them died in combat or from other war-related causes, such as disease or accidents.

In the aftermath of World War I, public suspicions about enemy saboteurs escalated into a coast-to-coast campaign to arrest and prosecute those thought to have been unpatriotic. In 1919 the California legislature enacted a criminal syndicalism law. By its terms, any person "advocating . . . unlawful acts of force and violence" aimed at changing ownership of industries or transforming the political system was liable to prosecution. Hundreds of Californians underwent trials for allegedly violating this law.

The most publicized of these trials was that of philanthropist, socialist, and suffragette Charlotte Anita Whitney. An outspoken opponent of American entry into World War I, with other Socialist Party members she helped form the more radical Communist Labor Party. In November 1919 she was arrested for violation of the criminal syndicalism law. Her trial and conviction the following year resulted in a prison sentence of one to 14 years. While she was free on bail for seven years, her attorney, John Francis Neylan, appealed the case until it landed in the U.S. Supreme Court in 1927. That tribunal upheld her earlier conviction and the constitutionality of California's criminal syndicalism law. However, Governor Clement C. Young pardoned the by then 60-year-old woman, who, rather than being a real "criminal," had devoted her life, in his view, to helping the less fortunate.

In addition to being eclipsed by the nation's war-related preoccupations, California progressivism suffered from squabbling between factions of reformers within the state's Republican Party. Strife between progressive factions erupted when Francis J. Heney ran for the U.S. Senate in 1914. Governor Johnson, just reelected to a second term, viewed Heney as a future rival and withheld endorsement. Heney lost the election and Johnson won an enemy.

In the elections of 1916, California progressives enjoyed a fleeting moment of victory that ended with a widening cleavage in their ranks. Regarding the presidential race that year, the state's Republican conservatives, led by William H. Crocker, son of the Big Four's Charles Crocker, organized a speaking tour for their party's candidate, Charles Evans Hughes. Thinking that Johnson's influence had evaporated, Crocker made no effort to court the progressive governor's help. Feeling snubbed, an embittered Johnson, who was running for the U.S. Senate that year, put little effort into campaigning for Hughes in the Golden State. When the votes were tallied, Hughes lost in California by fewer than 4,000 votes. Had he carried the state he would have been elected president. Johnson, on the other hand, won a resounding victory in his Senate bid, beating his opponent by nearly 300,000 votes. In the wake of the 1916 elections, the split between Johnson and the California conservatives widened and the state Republican Party lay in ruins. The victory for progressives, however, would not be enjoyed for long.

The glow of the progressive victory in the 1916 elections faded fast due largely to Johnson's mishandling of the matter of his successor following the untimely death of California's lieutenant governor in February of that year. Were Johnson to win his U.S. Senate race, which he did, the lieutenant governor would accede to the governorship. Reluctant to fill the vacant office with William D. Stephens, a former president of the Los Angeles Chamber of Commerce, Johnson delayed stepping down as governor even after winning his Senate seat. Johnson groundlessly feared that Stephens would not support progressive policies, and on one occasion referred to him as a "mere swine with his head in a trough." Consequently, for two weeks in the March 1917 transition period Johnson held the offices of governor and Senator simultaneously. Stephens, with strong support from southern California progressives, became the next governor despite Johnson's denunciations and delaying tactics. The political fallout from this and other instances of infighting among reformers left the state's progressive movement in tatters. A new, post-reform era in California began to unfold.

SUMMARY

Progressive Era California bore the markings of a Pacific-oriented state. The Southern Pacific Railroad's domination of California's economy and politics fueled the reform movement. However, the socialist thinking of some prominent leaders, such as Dr. John Randolph Haynes and Elvina Beals, coupled with the social democratic policies of the South Pacific dominion of New Zealand, guided the state's urban-based reformers. Republican Governor Hiram Johnson embodied many of the ideals of the movement and oversaw the passage of numerous laws that broke the hold of the Southern Pacific on the state's economy while cleaning up and democratizing politics. Without taking a stand on women's suffrage, he signed the legislation that gave females the right to vote. Urban and farm sector growth were assured by the undertaking of major water projects.

California's Progressive Era Pacific orientation is seen sharply in international affairs, immigration, and maritime trade. San Francisco was the flashpoint of a major dispute between Japan and the United States over immigration, while the federal government established Angel Island in the Bay Area to serve as the Pacific Coast screening station for Asians and others seeking entry into the United States. San Francisco and Los Angeles dominated West Coast trade, and the City of St. Francis's hosting of the 1915 Panama Pacific Exposition highlighted California's lead in transpacific shipping. America's entry into World War I and a host of other factors related to feuds within the state's Republican Party led to the steady decline of California progressivism in the 1920s.

REVIEW QUESTIONS

- What were the long-range and immediate causes of California's progressive movement?
- In what ways was California's progressive movement Pacific-oriented?
- In what ways did the state's progressive movement reflect the geographical reach of a Greater California?
- What do you regard as the five most important reforms of the California progressives and why?
- What factors led to the decline of California progressivism in the 1920s?

FURTHER READINGS

Mansel G. Blackford, *The Politics of Business in California, 1890–1920* (Columbus, OH: Ohio State University Press, 1977). A clearer, more comprehensive treatment of the subject matter would be hard to find.

Jacqueline R. Braitman, "A California Stateswoman: The Public Career of Katherine Philips Edson," *California History*, 65 (June 1986), 82–95. Edson's work with the state Bureau of Labor Statistics and her advocacy of the 1913 minimum wage law for women and children are highlighted in this authoritative article.

Gray Brechin, *Imperial San Francisco: Urban Power, Earthly Ruin* (Berkeley: University of California Press, 1999). This work analyzes San Francisco's turn-of-the-century imperial stature and self-image from the perspectives of art, architecture, urban design, and environmental studies.

Peter Browning, ed., *John Muir in His Own Words: A Book of Quotations* (Lafayette, CA: Great West Books, 1988). The editor offers a treasure trove of Muir's statements drawn from his autobiographical works, travel narratives, and reflections on the natural world.

Thomas R. Clark, "Labor and Progressivism," *California History*, 66 (September 1987), 196–207. Studying labor voting patterns, the author found that workers voted in accordance with their perceived economic interests rather than for progressive candidates and measures as such.

William Deverell and Tom Sitton, eds., *California Progressivism Revisited* (Berkeley: University of California Press, 1994). This is an indispensable anthology presenting the recent findings of historians regarding early twentieth-century reform in the Golden State.

Ellen Dubois, "Woman Suffrage: The View from the Pacific," *Pacific Historical Review*, 69 (November 2000), special issue. The entire issue contains articles placing women's suffrage in a transpacific, comparative perspective.

Gayle Gullett, *Becoming Citizens: The Emergence and Development of the California Women's Movement* (Urbana, IL: University of Illinois Press, 2000). The author reveals how California women crafted their own gendered image of citizenship at the same time that they assumed a larger, more active role in the public sphere.

Abraham Hoffman, *Vision or Villainy: Origins of the Owens Valley–Los Angeles Water Controversy* (College Station, TX: Texas A & M University Press, 2001). This is a well-researched, reliable account of a highly controversial California water project.

Lynn M. Hudson, "This Is Our Fair and Our State: African Americans and the Panama–Pacific International Exposition," *California History*, 87 (2010), 26–45. The fair's negative stereotypes of African Americans are presented largely through the reporting of Delilah L. Beasley, a leading black journalist of the Progressive Era who visited the exposition.

William L. Kahrl, *Water and Power: The Conflict over Los Angeles' Water Supply in the Owens Valley* (Berkeley: University of California Press, 1982). The history, politics, and economics of this dramatic episode in California history are covered in this detailed study.

Michael Kazin, *Barons of Labor: The San Francisco Building Trades and Union Power in the Progressive Era* (Urbana, IL: University of Illinois Press, 1989). Politics and economics are deftly woven into this history of the labor movement in one of America's foremost unionized cities.

James T. Kloppenberg, *Uncertain Victory: Social Democracy and Progressivism in European and American Thought, 1870–1920* (New York: Oxford University Press, 1986). The international roots and dimensions of early twentieth-century reform in the Western world are presented in this illuminating volume.

Lon Kurashige, "Immigration, Race, and the Progressives," in William Deverell and David Igler, eds., *A Companion to California History* (Malden, MA: Wiley-Blackwell, 2008). Editor Chester Rowell's changing discourse about race is offered as a cautionary tale about the dangers of classifying influential progressives as "racist," based on a selective reading of their statements.

Erika Lee and Judy Yung, *Angel Island: Immigrant Gateway to America* (New York: Oxford University Press, 2010). The authors trace not only the Asian experiences at the Angel Island Immigration Station but also present the struggles of newcomers from some 80 countries who were processed at America's Pacific gateway.

Richard Coke Lower, *A Bloc of One: The Political Career of Hiram W. Johnson* (Stanford, CA: Stanford University Press, 1993). This is a detailed, reliable, and mostly sympathetic study of Johnson's career as a reform politician.

Spencer C. Olin, Jr., *California's Prodigal Sons: Hiram Johnson and the Progressives, 1911–1917* (Berkeley: University of California Press, 1968). Though written decades ago, the author's rigorous analysis and balanced conclusions about Johnson and his supporters remain largely intact.

Thomas G. Paterson, "California Progressives and Foreign Policy," *California Historical Society Quarterly*, 47 (December 1968), 329–42. This is one of the few studies in print on a much-neglected topic in the literature on California progressivism.

Eric F. Petersen, "The Struggle for the Australian Ballot in California," *California Historical Quarterly*, 51 (Fall 1972), 227–43. The author places this important late nineteenth-century California reform in a transpacific context.

Jackson K. Putnam, "The Persistence of Progressivism in the 1920s: The Case of California," *Pacific Historical Review*, 35 (November 1966), 395–411. Contrary to most studies, this article traces the progressive impulse well into the 1920s.

James J. Rawls, *Indians of California: The Changing Image* (Norman, OK: University of Oklahoma Press, 1984). A leading California historian provides one of the most accessible, coherent, and anthropologically informed overviews of the state's indigenous peoples in print.

Tom Sitton, *John Randolph Haynes: California Progressive* (Stanford, CA: Stanford University Press, 1992). The achievements and legacy of a prominent Los Angeles physician, Christian socialist, and progressive are treated in this nuanced and well-researched biography.

Arthur Verge, "George Freeth: King of the Surfers and California's Forgotten Hero," *California History*, 80 (Summer 2001), 83–105. This is a very sympathetic portrait of a Hawaiian who introduced surfing and professional lifeguarding on southern California's beaches.

10

Good Times and Bad in a Pacific Rim Super State

For California, as for the rest of the nation, the 1920s marked a period of prosperity, and the 1930s, by contrast, a time of depression. Despite the seemingly sharp break between the two decades in California history, some remarkable continuities existed throughout the interwar years. Motion pictures and other forms of mass entertainment continued to shape national perceptions of life in the Golden State. Most importantly business associations and governing officials, working separately and in concert, transformed the physical environment by building aqueducts, dams, oil rigs, highways, airports, bridges, and port facilities. Agribusiness and oil companies thrived. Notably, too, shipping, naval, and other maritime enterprises raised California's already formidable profile as a Pacific Rim super state while the automotive and aviation industries grew apace from the 1920s to the Thirties. Politically, also, a fair amount of continuity existed through good times and bad: progressivism continued to retreat and most often Republicans dominated statewide politics. Throughout these decades California had its religious and social messiahs while it continued to register impressive cultural achievements, particularly in the arts and architecture.

Pacific Eldorado: A History of Greater California, First Edition. Thomas J. Osborne.
© 2013 Thomas J. Osborne. Published 2013 by Blackwell Publishing Ltd.

Timeline

1918	Evangelist Aimee Semple McPherson settles in Los Angeles, shortly afterward founding the International Church of the Foursquare Gospel
1920	DiGiorgio Fruit Company, a Central Valley agribusiness giant, is incorporated
1921	Signal Hill, in Long Beach, is covered with oil rigs, becoming the world's richest reserve in terms of barrels pumped per acre
1922	The Swing–Johnson Act, passed by Congress, authorizes the building of a high dam in Boulder Canyon on the Arizona–Nevada border and an All-American Canal to transport water to irrigate California's Imperial Valley
	T. Claude Ryan establishes the first daily scheduled passenger flight route in the United States – the air corridor between San Diego and Los Angeles
1923	Hollywood director Cecil B. DeMille releases his first blockbuster movie, *The Ten Commandments*
1924	Los Angeles' Nishi Hongwanji congregation erects the largest Buddhist temple in North America
1924–30	Los Angeles oil mogul Edward L. Doheny is implicated but not convicted in a national bribing scandal involving the lease of U.S. naval petroleum reserves in Elk Hills, California
1925	Three-fourths of all ships using the Panama Canal either enter or depart from the Port of Los Angeles
1928	Australian Charles Kingsford-Smith and his three-man crew are the first to pilot a plane, the *Southern Cross*, across the Pacific from California to Australia, and then to circumnavigate the globe by air, returning to the Bay Area
1931	Cannery workers' strike in Santa Clara Valley, led by Luisa Moreno and others
1932	Los Angeles hosts the international Summer Olympics
1933	The state passes the California Central Valley Project Act authorizing construction of dams, canals, and power transmission lines to provide farmers with water and workers with jobs
1934	West Coast dock strike originates in San Francisco, led by Harry Bridges of the International Longshoremen's Association; the ILA wins the right to control the hiring hall
	Socialist turned Democrat Upton Sinclair runs for governorship on an "End Poverty in California" platform; conservative Republican Frank Merriam wins the governor's race
	Long Beach physician Francis E. Townsend promotes a plan for the government to give every retired citizen over 60 years of age $200 a month, paid for by a tax, providing the recipient spends the stipend within 30 days; Townsend Clubs attract 1.5 million members nationwide
1935	The Boulder (renamed Hoover in 1947) Dam becomes operational
1936	San Francisco/Oakland Bay Bridge opens
1937	The Golden Gate Bridge, reputedly the world's most photographed span, is completed, linking San Francisco to Sausalito
1939	The Golden Gate International Exposition is held in San Francisco
	John Steinbeck's novel *The Grapes of Wrath* is published and wins a Pulitzer Prize; William Saroyan's play *The Time of Your Life* wins a Pulitzer Prize, but the author rejects the award and prize money

Mass Entertainment: Hollywood Movies, Pacific Fun Zones, and the Olympics

Hollywood movies and ocean front amusement zones enthralled paying customers during the interwar decades. A more fleeting but no less thrilling spectacle, the 1932 Olympics brought worldwide attention to Los Angeles. To varying degrees, all of these types of attractions heralded the arrival of ongoing mass entertainment in the Golden State.

Though beginning on the East Coast in the early 1900s, America's film industry moved to California to escape the monopoly that Thomas Edison's Motion Picture Patents Company wielded and to take advantage of the state's weather and locations. Nationwide, the industry had become synonymous with Hollywood by the interwar years. In the early 1920s some 250,000 film company employees worked in Los Angeles in what had become a billion-dollar business. Director David W. Griffith's blockbuster movie, *The Birth of a Nation* (see Chapter 9) unfortunately helped revive and spread the white supremacist Ku Klux Klan throughout the nation in the 1920s. Thomas Dixon's novel *The Klansmen* provided the inspiration and much of the material for the movie, which, for its technical aspects alone set a high standard. By the time sound movies or talkies appeared in 1927, *Birth of a Nation* had grossed $18 million; a hundred million people had seen it by 1930. Filmed in southern California, this early blockbuster resulted in Hollywood surpassing New York to become the cinema capital of America, a status that this district in Los Angeles has retained. Despite its glaring endorsement of white racism in the post-Civil War South, historian Kevin Starr rightly notes that today *The Birth of a Nation* is regarded as "among the two or three finest films ever made."

In the 1920s the American middle class became increasingly enamored of Hollywood movies. The growing public interest was facilitated by the "star" system and the construction of posh theaters. To increase revenues, Hollywood studios selected actors and actresses deemed likely to have mass appeal, and then carefully honed and promoted public images of these "stars," sometimes by changing their names and invariably by publicizing them in the media, especially in movie magazines. Canadian Gladys Smith, for example, was renamed Mary Pickford; she became known as "America's Sweetheart" while earning $500,000 a year by 1915. Charlie Chaplin raised film comedy to an art form and in so doing became an international star, earning $10,000 a week in the World War I era. Douglas Fairbanks, Jr., Joan Crawford, and Greta Garbo were other box-office draws in the early years of cinema. Grauman's Chinese Theater in Hollywood, built in 1927, affords a striking example of the luxurious movie houses of the time.

Off to a promising start, the Hollywood film industry was rocked by early scandals involving the off-screen conduct of some of its matinee idols. One of the most sensational of these involved comedian and actor Roscoe "Fatty" Arbuckle (so called because he weighed nearly 300 pounds) and a young starlet, Virginia Rappe. The two had attended a drunken party held by a group of Hollywood celebrities in early September 1921 in a San Francisco hotel. Accounts of what happened conflict, but one witness testified that she saw a naked, bleeding, inebriated Rappe, who had been sexually ravaged by Arbuckle. Several days after the bash, Rappe died. Arbuckle was arrested, charged with manslaughter, and went through three trials before gaining acquittal. News of this scandal and others, usually involving alcohol and/or sexual promiscuity, led to a call from some civic leaders for stricter standards of conduct for the Hollywood set and censorship of movies. To head off possible federal censorship, the newly formed, industry-run Motion Picture Producers and Directors Association appointed a movie czar, Will H. Hays, to see to it that immorality in film scenes led to punishment of the transgressing characters on the silver screen. Self-regulation and an effort to enhance the industry's respectability took other forms as well. A leading director of the period, Cecil B. DeMille of Paramount Pictures, made movies that brimmed with Judeo-Christian content, such as *The Ten Commandments* (1923) and *The King of Kings* (1927). According to film historian Carlos Clarens, DeMille insisted that "during production, the actors portraying Christ and the apostles refrain from drinking, gambling, cussing, night-clubbing and even having intercourse with their wives." Despite Hays's oversight and DeMille's rules, scenes of sex and violence still found their way into Hollywood films.

Even during the Depression era, with people's discretionary spending reduced, Hollywood prospered, largely because Americans sought escape. Momentarily, at least, the antics of the Marx Brothers in such movies as *Duck Soup* (1933) and the swashbuckling exploits of Errol Flynn in *Captain Blood* (1935), co-starring the talented Olivia de Havilland, provided relief from the pangs of distress. Much of the footage for these two movies was shot on location in Pasadena and Laguna Beach, respectively. Escapism was also served when filmmakers chose far-off islands in exotic places, like the vast reaches of the Pacific world, to situate human dramas that could momentarily relieve people's fears about being able to care for their families. Pacific-themed movies of the time included *Treasure Island* (1934) and *Mutiny on the Bounty* (1935). *Treasure Island* was filmed mainly in California, including the Channel Islands and Laguna Beach (which stood in for tropical Pacific isles), and Hawai'i. It featured major Hollywood stars Wallace Beery, Jackie Cooper, and Lionel Barrymore. *Mutiny on the Bounty* was shot in California, including the Channel Islands, and French Polynesia and starred Charles Laughton and Clark Gable. It won the 1936 Academy Awards Oscar for the Best Picture.

Film-producing companies and directors were indispensable to Hollywood's meteoric rise in the 1920s and 1930s. The major companies included Loew's (and its Metro-Goldwyn-Mayer subsidiary), Warner Brothers, Paramount, Radio-Keith-Orpheum, and Twentieth Century Fox. Behind these leaders were Columbia, Universal, and United Artists. Included among the successful directors of the time were some women, particularly Elinor Glyn and Dorothy Arzner.

Besides going to movies, Californians and tourists alike spent time and money at the state's Pacific fun zones. Singly or in combination, these beach venues featured boardwalks, piers, roller coasters, and dance halls. San Francisco's Playland included several roller coasters, a Fun House with a mirror maze and 200-foot indoor slide, a Ferris wheel, and nearly a hundred concessionaires. Santa Cruz's Boardwalk comprised a ballroom, plunge, pier, and, after its 1924 opening, the Giant Dipper roller coaster that for 15 cents would hurtle screaming riders up and down its winding course at 55 miles per hour. The coaster appeared in several Hollywood films. In the Southland, Venice Beach advertised itself as "The Coney Island of the Pacific." Like its New York City counterpart, Venice featured numerous attractions. In 1921 the descendants of Abbot Kinney, the developer of Venice, reportedly invested $3 million in building a new pier extending 1,200 feet in length and 525 feet in width. The so-called Venice Amusement Pier featured three roller coasters, a fun house, dance hall, and other rides. On a much smaller scale, nearby Santa Monica added a carousel and ballroom to its Pacific fun zone in the 1920s.

Besides fun zones, the City of Angels treated the world to a premier athletic spectacle during the 1930s. In the summer of 1932, 37 countries sent 1,300 athletes to compete in the Games of the X Olympiad in Los Angeles. The city's Memorial Coliseum was expanded to 105,000 seats for the international competition. A hundred thousand spectators attended the opening ceremonies. Hollywood stars, including Charlie Chaplin and Marlene Dietrich, promoted ticket sales through entertainment. Babe Didrikson, arguably America's best female athlete, won gold medals in the javelin and hurdles. Despite the hard times economically, the Olympics was a success.

Extending California's Water Infrastructure

Movies, Pacific fun zones, and other public attractions drew numerous people to California, many of whom stayed, swelling the populations of cities. Naturally, the most immediate need of newcomers was water. Without large quantities of available water California's metropolitan centers could not provide for their growing populations, the agricultural sector could not prosper, and the oil-refining industry could not have developed as it did, given the fact that some 77,000 gallons of water were needed to refine 100 barrels of petroleum. Simply put, California's urban and economic growth in the 1920s and 1930s was water-dependent, which necessitated the further development of infrastructure to direct flows to cities, fields, and industrial plants.

The Hetch Hetchy and Owens Valley aqueducts, which, respectively, supplied San Francisco and Los Angeles with water (see Chapter 9), were components of what became, in the interwar decades, the most extensive system of waterworks in the United States if not the world. To these components were added O'Shaughnessy Dam, Boulder Canyon (later renamed Hoover) Dam and its accompanying All-American Canal, the Colorado River Aqueduct, and the Central Valley Project.

While the Hetch Hetchy Aqueduct was under construction, San Francisco engineer Michael S. O'Shaughnessy oversaw the building of a huge dam that would impound the waters of the Tuolumne River. Work on the O'Shaughnessy (also known as the Hetch Hetchy) Dam began in 1919. When the mammoth structure's first phase was completed in 1923, it had attained a height of 227 feet. The hydroelectric power generated by the project supplied more than 80 percent of San Francisco's needs by the mid-1930s.

The Boulder Canyon Project was necessitated by the phenomenal growth of Los Angeles and southern California, whose water needs soon outstripped flows from Owens Valley and the Imperial Canal farther south. With a population of 576,673 in 1920, Los Angeles surpassed San Francisco and has since remained the state's largest city. Ten years later Los Angeles' population had nearly tripled, to 1,470,516. Much more water was needed for both household and commercial use, as, in addition to the water-dependent petroleum refineries, tire manufacturing had come to the city. The Good Year Tire and Rubber Company, for example, required 8 million gallons of water a day to operate its Los Angeles plant. Because of these developments, city engineer William Mulholland urged building an aqueduct from the Colorado River to the City of Angels.

The scale, cost, and benefits of this undertaking were of such magnitude that the federal government oversaw the project that took some 20 years to complete. After considerable negotiation, seven states located in the Colorado River watershed – Wyoming, Colorado, Utah, New Mexico, Nevada, Arizona, and California – signed an agreement in November 1922 ensuring that the first four of these states would receive half of the river flow. Meanwhile, earlier that same year two California congressmen, Representative Phil Swing and Senator Hiram Johnson, cosponsored the Swing–Johnson bill providing for construction of a high dam to be built in Boulder Canyon for the purposes of generating hydroelectric power and preventing flooding. The bill also authorized construction of an All-American Canal (so called because the waterway would supersede the earlier Imperial or Alamo Canal, much of which lay in Mexico) that would be located entirely on U.S. soil just above the Mexican border. Alarmed by demands from the Mexican government for half of the flow through the canal on its territory, California farmers had pressed for an All-American canal to be located entirely on U.S. soil. This new canal would facilitate irrigation of Imperial Valley farmland, turning a desert into a garden.

Concerted opposition from many Republicans and private corporations hindered passage of the measure. Conservative *Los Angeles Times* editor Harry Chandler charged that the bill was socialistic and, hence, a threat to American capitalism. His ownership of 862,000 acres of Baja land near the defunct Imperial Canal exemplifies the Pacific Rim reach of Greater California business interests in the early decades of the 1900s. This huge land holding may have given Chandler even more cause to oppose the All-American Canal, whose adjacent real estate on the U.S. side of the border would increase in value relative to his Mexican holdings located near the old Imperial Canal. Nevertheless, the election of moderate Republican Herbert Hoover, a Stanford-educated engineer and supporter of the project, to the presidency in 1928 provided the momentum needed to pass the dam and canal bill that same year. Outgoing President Calvin Coolidge signed the measure, renamed the Boulder Canyon Project Act, into law on December 21.

Both the dam and the canal quickened urbanization and agricultural development in southern California. In 1935 Boulder Dam, then the world's largest, was completed and christened by President Franklin D. Roosevelt. A year later the Southland began receiving hydroelectric power, mostly publicly owned, generated by the project. In 1947 Congress renamed the water-impounding colossus Hoover Dam (as it has since been called), after the former U.S. president who supported its building. Work on the All-American Canal began in 1934 and the channel was in use by 1940. Today more than half a million acres of land are irrigated by the waters flowing through the waterway, the world's largest irrigation canal.

Meanwhile, in 1931 voters in the Metropolitan Water District of Southern California approved a $220 million bond issue to construct a 242-mile aqueduct from what would become Arizona's dam-made Lake Havasu, filled by the Colorado River, to southern California's Pacific Coast. Los Angeles Basin residents and factories began receiving the pipeline's flow in 1941.

These extraordinary water projects reflect the energies and reach of a Greater California. Hoover Dam, situated on the Nevada–Arizona border, was largely the handiwork of California politicians, engineers, water and power organizations, and construction companies. "It was . . . for all practical purposes, a California enterprise in conjunction with the federal government," noted historian Kevin Starr. Arizona's Lake Havasu is the source of the Colorado River Aqueduct that supplies much of the Southland's water. In these two instances, the Golden State did not hesitate to cross borders – or to figuratively extend its borders – to meet its water needs.

As in the Southland, large farms in the Central Valley, California's agricultural heartland, required additional water resources in the 1930s. Because additional land was being cultivated, more water was needed. While the number of farms increased in the 1920s and 1930s, so too did the acreage of the largest growers. For example, by 1935, 70 percent of Sacramento Valley and San Joaquin Valley farmland belonged to agribusiness (large-scale, corporate farming that includes the production, processing, and distribution of crops as well as equipment use) interests holding 1,000 acres or more. Such extensive agricultural development generated a great thirst in this interior region of the Golden State.

Efforts by Progressives in the 1920s to quench that thirst by advancing government-sponsored irrigation projects in the Central Valley were blocked by Pacific Gas and Electric Company, a powerful opponent of publicly owned utilities ventures. Some major growers opposing a statutory 160-acre per person limit on land irrigated by Bureau of Reclamation projects allied themselves with PG&E. However, with 20 percent of Californians on depression-era relief, many politicians and their constituents looked increasingly to government at all levels to create public works programs so that the able-bodied unemployed could earn paychecks.

In response to the needs of farmers and jobless workers, the state legislature overcame PG&E opposition and passed the California Central Valley Project Act in 1933. A statewide $170 million bond measure won voter approval later that same year, but revenues were insufficient to start work until the federal government released emergency relief funds two years later. At that point the Bureau of Reclamation assumed responsibility for the project, on which work was begun in 1937.

When completed in the 1950s, the extensive network of agricultural plumbing included dams, canals, and power transmission lines. Shasta Dam, 602 feet high, impounded flows from the Sacramento, McCloud, and Pitt rivers into Shasta Lake. Other principal components of the CVP included the Keswick, Folsom, and Friant dams, and the Contra Costa, Delta–Mendota, Madera, and Friant–Kern canals. Though owned by PG&E, the transmission lines were made available to the state by an agreement with the federal government. As a result, hydroelectric power generated by the Shasta and Keswick dams could be transmitted to pump water through the Delta–Mendota and Contra Costa canals.

Agribusiness and Banking

Within the state, farming, or agribusiness, produced more wealth than many other sectors of the economy. This was especially the case as government-funded irrigation projects

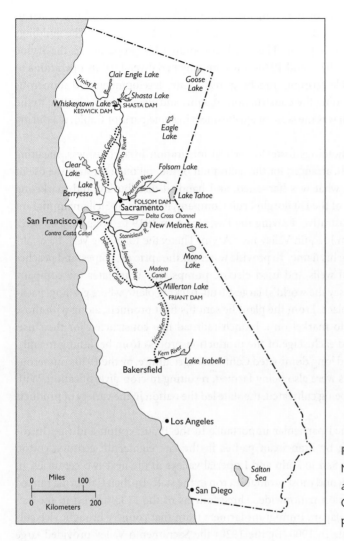

Figure 10.1   The Central Valley Project. Based on Norris Hundley, Jr., *The Great Thirst: Californians and Water: A History* (Berkeley: University of California Press, c.2001), p. 256. Reproduced with permission of University of California Press.

proliferated from the northern to the southern interior regions of the state. California's agricultural productivity was the highest in the world during the interwar years. The state's canning industry, a spinoff of crop-raising, flourished in these decades and, similarly, led the world. Banks in the state were instrumental in supplying capital to corporate farmers and funds for agricultural research.

This period witnessed a furthering of the ongoing shift from family farming to agribusiness or "factories in the fields." Many corporate giants – such as Miller and Lux, Standard Oil, and the Irvine Company – owed their growth and success to their capacity to buy huge tracts of land and their use of the latest equipment, machinery, and fertilizers to maximize yields of grain, fruits, nuts, and other crops. The Irvine Company affords an example. In

1894 James Irvine II, founder of the company, inherited from his father a huge ranch in Orange County, assembled from three adjoining Mexican land grants. The holdings exceeded 100,000 acres at one point. The son incorporated his properties as the Irvine Company that year. By the 1920s and 1930s, the company had diversified its operations to include citrus and vegetable farming, ranching, real-estate development, and numerous hydrological projects, including the construction of dams and even a water pipeline to the City of Laguna Beach. Such was the scale of agribusiness in some parts of California during the interwar years.

Consolidation of land holdings fostered vertical integration in agribusiness, meaning owners purchased croplands, arranged for the cultivation of the soil often through the use of tenant farmers, processed what was harvested, and handled distribution and marketing of their products. The case of the DiGiorgio Fruit Company, founded by Sicilian immigrant Giuseppe DiGiorgio, is illustrative. Leaving the East Coast, in 1919 he bought 5,845 acres of land in the southern San Joaquin Valley near Arvin. There, the following year, he established the company bearing his name. To provide water for the apricots, grapes, and peaches he grew, DiGiorgio drilled wells and used electric pumps. Ten years later the company operated America's (some say the world's) largest fruit-packing plant, where grading, packaging, and shipping took place. From the plant he sent his fruit products, along with those of other nearby growers, to market on a branch railroad line constructed for their use. DiGiorgio, then, controlled each stage of the production process from beginning to end.

While citrus growing had long dominated California agriculture, by the 1920s numerous vegetables and other plants were also being farmed, resulting in crop diversification. With nearly 200 different crops being cultivated, the state led the nation in the variety of products coming from the soil.

Two such products gained particular importance in the 1930s: cotton and rice. Introduced into Alta California by Franciscan padres in the late eighteenth century, cotton cultivation spread into the San Joaquin and Imperial valleys in the next two centuries. In the early 1930s it was the second most profitable crop in the state. By then California ranked eleventh in cotton production nationwide. Three-fourths of the 1933 harvest in the San Joaquin Valley was sold to Japan. Immigrant farmers from that country brought rice cultivation to the Golden State in 1900. By the 1920s the Sacramento Valley provided large quantities of that staple, rendering California the third-ranking rice-producing state in the nation. The yield per acre was the highest in America. In 1937 the state produced 10 million bushels of the grain. By then the Rice Growers Association of California, a farmer-owned cooperative aimed at ensuring quality and increasing sales, had opened Pacific Rim export markets that would become increasingly lucrative.

Livestock and poultry raising comprised another segment of California agriculture. Dairying was sufficiently robust, due in part to cooperatives, to meet the state's domestic needs for milk, butter, and cheese. During the 1930s only Wisconsin and its few surrounding states surpassed California as producers of these foods. In the beef and pork markets, California lagged well behind Texas and Iowa respectively. Chicken and turkey ranching spread into the semi-arid parts of the state.

The agribusiness sector of California's economy in the interwar years grew because of bank loans. Corporate farmers relied on bank credit to cover the enormous outlays of cash needed for land, equipment, fertilizer, and insurance. Credit was available because banks in the state had in the early decades of the twentieth century grown their assets by building branch offices and extending large mortgage loans to land developers and other business interests. Amadeo P. Giannini founded the Bank of Italy in San Francisco in 1904 and spent the next few decades expanding his interests in New York and Italy, and developing branch banks within the state. By 1927 his bank owned one of every 11 mortgages in California's major farming areas. In 1930 he established and endowed the Giannini Foundation of Agricultural Economics at UC Berkeley (later joined by UC Davis and UC Riverside), which promoted and supported agricultural research and rural development in California. That same year, Giannini consolidated his holdings into the newly chartered Bank of America, which by 1940 had emerged as the world's largest private banking institution, demonstrating the growing financial clout of Greater California. A similar process of consolidation through bank mergers occurred in Los Angeles. There in 1929, entrepreneur Joseph Sartori absorbed the Farmers and Merchants Bank into his new Pacific Security Bank. Eventually, this financial institution would become the sixth largest bank in the United States and an investor in numerous non-banking ventures internationally.

The 1920s Oil Boom

While agribusiness and banking prospered, California's petroleum industry registered spectacular growth. A second oil boom, the first having occurred in the 1890s (see Chapter 7), began in Huntington Beach and swept parts of the state in the 1920s. On November 13, 1920 Standard Oil began pumping operations in this Orange County seaside community with a well yielding 2,000 barrels a day. Within a few years Huntington Beach lots overlooking the Pacific were dotted with a forest of derricks. By June of the following year Signal Hill in Long Beach was similarly covered with oil rigs, only these belonged to Shell Oil Company and they tapped into the world's richest reserves in terms of barrels per acre. Meanwhile, a third southern California oil bonanza occurred on land leased by George Franklin Getty on Telegraph Hill, Santa Fe Springs. By 1923 Telegraph Hill wells pumped 70 million barrels a year.

So productive were these and additional drilling operations, for example in the San Joaquin Valley, that the oil industry far surpassed all others in profitability, including agriculture and its related canning business, in the state in the 1920s. More than $2.5 billion-worth of this "black gold" was extracted from California's oil fields during this prosperous decade.

Along with quick riches sometimes come major scandals. Such was the case involving Los Angeles oil mogul Edward L. Doheny, who was implicated in a scandal that made national headlines from 1924 to 1930. Doheny had arranged with his friend Albert B. Fall, secretary of the interior, to lease federal oil lands in Elk Hills, located in Kern County. Oil reserves at that site were to be used in the event that the United States should find itself at war in the Pacific. Doheny was to build and fill oil storage tanks on the West Coast and at Honolulu, Hawai'i. In 1924 the public learned that while Doheny had negotiated the lease with Fall, the oilman had transferred $100,000 to the secretary of the interior. Was this a bribe, or a loan?

A federal investigation led to prosecutions. In October 1929, Fall was convicted of receiving the $100,000 as a bribe and went to prison. In a separate trial later that year, however, Doheny, who had insisted that the transferred money was an interest-free loan to a dear friend, was acquitted of bribery. The different outcomes hinged on criminal intent: Fall, as a federal cabinet official, was seen by a jury as having received tainted money while administering public lands; Doheny, on the other hand, was able to show a long-time practice of generously aiding friends and charities. While Doheny was acquitted in a courtroom in 1930, the scent of scandal followed him to his grave. As the result of a separate civil suit, the federal government cancelled the oil leases on the ground that they had been obtained by bribery.

By the time this scandal fizzled at the end of the 1920s, California's oil boom had come and gone. The petroleum industry would remain important, but other business endeavors, some with longer histories in the Golden State, would prove more vital to the economy.

Maritime Enterprises

Pacific maritime pursuits were the linchpin for the state's economy in the interwar years as earlier. Only New York handled a larger volume of foreign commerce than California. The Golden State's agricultural and petroleum sectors were dependent on seaborne transport, which accounted for the growth of ocean-trafficking ports in the Bay Area, Sacramento and Stockton in the Delta region, and Los Angeles. Commercial saltwater fishing and canning augmented the state's burgeoning maritime economy.

The Bay Area waterfronts were the busiest on the West Coast. Though its dominance was lessening, San Francisco maintained its status as the western shoreline's leading port in the 1920s and 1930s. In terms of merchant marine tonnage it ranked second to New York. The War Department and the U.S. Shipping Board affirmed in 1933: "San Francisco Bay is the best harbor on the Pacific coast and one of the finest in the world." Three-fourths of San Francisco's exports consisted of petroleum, fruits and vegetables, and grains. Farm products reached the City by the Bay via the interior river/Pacific ports of Sacramento and Stockton. Most of Hawai'i's sugar and substantial quantities of its coffee and other tropical products arrived in San Francisco by sea. Eighty steamship lines, including Pacific cruise ship giants Robert Dollar Company and Matson Navigation Company, made that city a regular port of call. Still, nearby Oakland, whose seaborne commerce increased by 25 percent from 1932 to 1933, was catching up fast. For all the above reasons, in 1929 the state legislature chose the Bay Area for locating and establishing the California Maritime Academy, the only college of its kind on the Pacific Coast. Two years later the school, whose mission was to train officers for the merchant marine and other professionals in the maritime industries, occupied a 50-acre site in the Bay Area city now called Tiburon.

Los Angeles–San Pedro harbor, a man-made port, was home to the fastest-growing maritime trade facility on America's Pacific shoreline while San Diego became the West

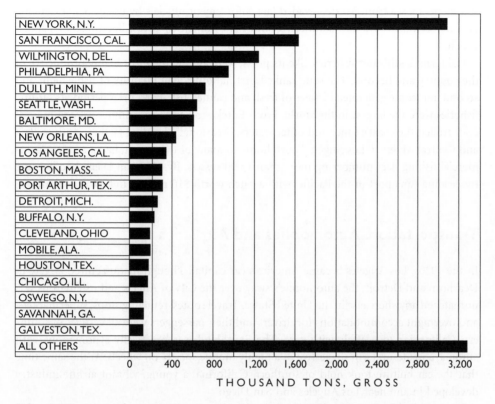

Figure 10.2   Bar graph comparing tonnage at America's principal ports. From Eliot G. Mears, *Maritime Trade of Western United States* (New York: Stanford University Press, 1935), p. 180. Used with permission of Stanford University Press.

Coast's leading naval base. By 1925 three-fourths of the ships using the Panama Canal were either bound for or departing Los Angeles. Huge quantities of California oil were shipped from Los Angeles through the canal, en route to Atlantic ports and world markets. Five years later the Port of Los Angeles and the adjacent Port of Long Beach handled more than a billion dollars'-worth of cargoes. Along with San Diego and Pearl Harbor (Honolulu), Los Angeles and Long Beach became anchorages for the U.S. Navy's Pacific Fleet, which brought federal monies to the Golden State. By the end of the 1920s San Diego, calling itself the "Gibraltar of the Pacific," claimed to have the largest naval base on the West Coast and the second largest in the nation. The navy had become vital to that city's economy, accounting for 30 percent of San Diego's payroll in 1930.

Especially in this era of Prohibition (1919–33), illicit Pacific Coast smuggling must be factored into overall maritime commerce. In 1926 the *Los Angeles Times* reported that contraband alcohol from Canada, often carried to San Pedro in lumber schooners, comprised a major industry in the Southland. As many as 7,000 cases of bootlegged scotch whiskey arrived in a single voyage. Over the course of a single year some $10 million of this beverage arrived by ship at or near the Port of Los Angeles. Similarly, illegal alcohol shipments by sea from Mexico evaded law enforcement officials by use of Santa Catalina Island's secluded bays and southern California's numerous coves, like those of Laguna Beach.

California's saltwater fisheries, like its ports, were among the most highly productive in the country and beyond. The state ranked first nationwide in quantity of fish caught and second in income generated by sales of fresh and canned fish. For a brief period, its sardine fisheries were the largest in the world. From Eureka to San Diego, numerous commercial craft trolled the coast's inner and outer waters, occasionally heading farther south to Baja and Central America. Los Angeles' port, home to many of these craft, had a resident commercial fishing fleet numbering more than 1,000 vessels. By 1939 San Diego had become the leading tuna port of the Pacific, with a catch worth $10 million in that year alone.

Transportation: Automobiles and Airplanes

In the 1920s, Los Angeles became America's car capital. Though manufactured largely in Dearborn and Detroit, the automobile's sway over the City of Angels and its environs was unmatched anywhere else in the United States. Travel routes, refueling stops, supermarkets, and overnight accommodations for drivers and their passengers were all vestiges of southern California's love affair with cars. The Southland was practically synonymous with autopia, a made-up term suggestive of a highly mobile society on wheels. At the same time that the car culture took hold of southern California, a young, vibrant airline industry developed in and near Los Angeles and San Diego.

Motor vehicle ownership was widespread in Los Angeles County in the decade after World War I. In 1927, for example, there were 560,136 automobiles in the county, which meant one car for every 3.2 people or about twice the national average. Writing in the *New Republic* magazine that same year, journalist Bruce Bliven observed with little exaggeration: "Any Angeleno without his automobile is marooned, like a cowboy without his horse." While women throughout the state, as throughout the nation, were not nearly as likely as men to own cars, females in ever-increasing numbers learned to drive, largely to enjoy the mobility it afforded. Realizing that females influenced male car purchases, automobile manufacturers paid attention to what women wanted in style, color, comfort, and price. The average price of a new car in 1930, according to one authority, was $640; by the end of the decade that figure had increased to $700. Naturally, more expensive automobiles were available in the 1930s, such as the pricey Auburn 1935 851 Boattail Speedster, which sold for $2,250. Motorists paid about 10 cents a gallon for gasoline in 1930.

With sound factual backing, historian Kevin Starr has remarked: "For the first time in urban history a city [Los Angeles] was building itself around the automobile." That was largely true for the county as well. From 1917 to 1927, Los Angeles County invested $24 million in building 1,300 miles of paved roads. The following year the county appropriated an additional $5.2 million for road construction. Some 450 filling stations sold gasoline to motorists. The spread of the city westward toward the Pacific via a 16-mile extension of Wilshire Boulevard was facilitated by the automobile. Bullocks Wilshire department store, with its rear area parking lot, was situated along a segment of this major thoroughfare known as the "Miracle Mile," perhaps the world's first business district designed to accommodate the automobile. American supermarkets first appeared along Los Angeles' roadways, affording motorists the tantalizing option of one-stop grocery buying. Respite for weary drivers was provided by a new type of lodging, the motor inn or motel. Similarly, the automobile and the new access routes it entailed went hand in hand with the subdivision and development of real-estate tracts in Los Angeles' mushrooming suburbs in the 1920s. Assured of convenient automotive transportation to and from the metropolis, by the middle of the decade suburbanites turned increasingly away from using the excellent Pacific Electric rail system and toward driving their own cars.

The Automobile Club of Southern California, founded in 1900 and headquartered in Los Angeles, promoted a car-centered lifestyle by advocating for road construction and touring by motor vehicles. The Auto Club posted numerous traffic signs throughout the Southland before the State of California took over that responsibility in the 1950s. Its magazine *Touring Topics* (later renamed *Westways*) provided thoughtful articles on travel destinations and routes, while promoting the pleasures of driving. In 1927 the non-profit organization had enrolled 124,000 motorists as recipients of its services.

California's car craze was less evident in the Bay Area. Most likely the vastness of the bay and the geographical compactness of San Francisco, compared to Los Angeles, slowed the spread of a car-oriented society until bridges traversing the huge inlet were built in the 1930s. Still, the area had its northern counterpart to the Auto Club – the California State Automobile Association, headquartered in San Francisco.

Less formidable than the automotive industry, aviation constituted a new and growing sector of California's interwar transportation economy. While aircraft manufacturing started in the East in the early 1900s, within several decades Los Angeles emerged as the nation's aviation capital. The Southland's clear skies and open spaces attracted the pioneers in the fledgling industry. In the 1910s two of the earliest aviators – Glenn Curtiss and Glenn Martin – were building their own planes. Meanwhile, in Santa Barbara the brothers Allen and Malcolm Loughead joined with John K. Northrop in assembling aircraft. After World War I they transferred their Lockheed (derived from Loughead) Aircraft Company to Hollywood-Burbank.

Throughout the 1920s the state's aircraft industry outgrew its infancy. With an initial investment of $600, aeronautical engineer Donald Douglas began designing airplanes in a small space inside a Los Angeles barber shop. Unable to secure a bank loan, Douglas was advanced $15,000 by a group of investors led by *Los Angeles Times* publisher Harry Chandler. With the money Douglas set up a successful factory in Santa Monica. In 1922 another aviation pioneer, T. Claude Ryan, established the first daily scheduled passenger flight route in the United States: the air corridor between San Diego and Los Angeles. The most famous aircraft of the decade, the *Spirit of St. Louis*, which Charles A. Lindbergh piloted into aviation history by making the first transatlantic flight in 1927, was built on the Pacific Coast in Ryan's San Diego factory. The first crossing of the Pacific by airplane occurred the following year (see Pacific Profile below).

The mid-1930s witnessed the beginning of commercial transpacific flights to and from California. On November 22, 1935, amid great fanfare and media attention, Pan American Airlines' *China Clipper* launched its first transpacific flight, covering a distance of 8,000 miles. The large Martin M-130 seaplane departed from Alameda, in the Bay Area, and island-hopped to Oahu, Midway Island, Wake Island, Guam, and the Philippines before arriving in Canton, China, with a cargo of mail. A year later Pan American inaugurated passenger flights over the same route. In the new era of transpacific air travel, California was the indisputable national leader.

Pacific Profile: Charles Kingsford-Smith's Transpacific Flight

Though not nearly as well known in the United States as Charles Lindbergh, Australian flying ace Charles Kingsford-Smith (1897–1935) and his three crewmen (only one of whom could fly a plane but was unlicensed) accomplished a feat as daring and arguably even more remarkable than Lindbergh's. Before this success, Kingsford-Smith had won medals for valor as a fighter pilot in the Australian Flying Corps in World War I. His 1928 flight in the *Southern Cross* made aviation history by being the first to cross the Pacific, from California to Australia, and, after a brief stop in Sydney to then circumnavigate the globe, returning to the Bay Area.

The epic flight, financed by California businessman and former sea captain G. Allan Hancock, was divided into three transpacific segments: Oakland to Honolulu, Hawai'i; Honolulu to Suva, Fiji; Suva to Brisbane, Australia. The longest, stormiest stretch was the more than 3,000-mile segment from Hawai'i to Fiji. Shortly after landing in Brisbane, the four men visited Sydney, where they were hailed as aviation heroes by 300,000 cheering people.

On completion of the Pacific-crossing portion of the round-the-world flight, President Calvin Coolidge wired Kingsford-Smith saying: "Hearty congratulations to you and your companions on successful flight Oakland to Australia. Your brilliant and courageous pioneering has advanced the cause of aviation and strengthened bonds between your commonwealth and our country." Hancock also wired Kingsford-Smith, telling the Australian pilot that the money advanced to finance the flight need not be repaid.

Overlooked in U.S. and California history textbooks, Kingsford-Smith's Pacific crossing opened this vast track of ocean to commercial air travel in the late 1930s. The Golden State has been an integral hub in this air traffic from the start. For his role in pioneering transpacific flight and other aeronautical achievements, the highly decorated pilot was knighted, with the title "Sir" added to his name. His last flight occurred in November 1935. Taking off in England en route to his Australian homeland, he and his copilot failed to arrive in Singapore, one of their planned stopovers, and were never heard from again. Two years later, fishermen found part of their plane's wreckage on the shores of an island off the coast of present-day Myanmar.

Conservatism Restored

The growth of the Golden State's economy in the 1920s went hand in hand with nationwide prosperity, and a pro-business, conservative swing of the political pendulum away from reform. California's politics remained largely a Republican affair, only it was the right wing of the party rather than its progressive element that wielded the power. Gone was the influence of Hiram Johnson, who by then was serving his state in the U.S. Senate. In addition to the changing mood of America and splits in the Republican Party, there were certain demographic and structural factors specific to California that account for the rightward shift.

Evidence of a conservative renaissance in the 1920s is seen in the almost complete failure of Democrats to gain elective office. They failed to win a single executive-level statewide office and won only a few lower-echelon partisan contests.

Johnson's successor, Governor William D. Stephens, held office from 1917 to 1923. He was a transitional figure embodying a combination of progressive and conservative leanings. On the one hand he was a Republican prohibitionist who spoke out against labor unions while supporting the Criminal Syndicalism Act in 1919. On the other hand, he had been a member of the Progressive Party in its earlier heyday and as governor secured an increase in the state budget and a 35 percent corporate tax hike to finance it.

Stephens was followed in office by a solidly conservative Republican governor, Friend W. Richardson of Berkeley. Richardson denounced his predecessor's tax and spending policies, making deep cuts in the budgets for education and welfare. When the state legislature passed spending bills, he usually vetoed them.

Richardson's unwavering conservatism caused a liberal backlash, led by the Progressive Voters League and resulting in the candidacy of Berkeley Republican Clement C. Young in the gubernatorial election of 1926. A former teacher turned businessperson, Young entered politics, serving as assembly speaker and lieutenant governor before campaigning for the state's highest office. His progressive platform called for governmental efficiency, highway-building, development of hydroelectric power and water delivery systems, and conservation. Richardson campaigned on a platform calling for government austerity. Young barely won nomination over the incumbent, Richardson, but went on to win the general election decisively.

Imbued with progressive intentions, Young was able to undo some of Richardson's most reactionary policies. Government aid to the needy and physically handicapped was provided. America's first state-sponsored old-age pension law was passed. Conservation and public parks were supported. These achievements made progressives happy, but they strongly opposed the Young administration's roll-back of regulations allowing the proliferation of branches of the California-based Bank of Italy. Such proliferation triggered progressives' fears of a banking monopoly in the making; in California and throughout the nation these reformers battled trusts in order to extend economic opportunity to entrepreneurs and prevent corporate domination of politics.

Young lost his bid for reelection in 1930 due to the split in the prohibitionist vote between him and another "dry" candidate in the Republican primary. The split resulted in the party's nomination going to James ("Sunny Jim") Rolph, Jr., a "wet," as anti-prohibitionists were called. A conservative Republican, Rolph went on to win the governorship in the November general election.

Aside from such splits within Republican ranks, there were both demographic and structural factors specific to California that helped ensure a pro-business, conservative cast to the state's politics in the 1920s. Midwestern newcomers to southern California, whose population led the state after 1920, were markedly traditional in religious and political matters. What drew them to the Southland? A leading journalist of the time, Bruce Bliven, noted that many of these newcomers were retirees who had farmed the prairies most of their lives. "[G]narled and weather-worn, exhausted by the long struggle against [Midwestern] cyclones, blizzards, drought, locusts and low prices," they sold their farms and came to southern California where the climate was so wonderful that "no one ever dies." The growing numbers of these and others coming into the Golden State gave new emphasis to the issue of political representation in Sacramento.

Structurally, in the face of southern Californians' growing discontent over their region's underrepresentation in the state legislature, voters considered two opposing initiatives, framed as constitutional amendments on the 1926 ballot. Both measures dealt with the apportionment of seats in the Sacramento legislature. One initiative, designated "the federal plan," called for the apportionment of the assembly on the basis of population and of the senate on the basis of counties. Accordingly, no county could have more than one senator and no senator could represent more than three counties. The other initiative, officially known as the All Parties proposal, provided for the apportionment of seats in both houses of the legislature on the basis of population. Supported by powerful growers and San Francisco business interests, the federal plan won adoption. Consequently, southern California continued to be underrepresented in the state legislature for another four decades and conservatives consolidated their hold on state politics.

Religious Awakenings and Developments

By the 1920s California already had a reputation for exoticism in spiritual matters. For example, in the late 1800s Mennonite pacifists settled on farms in the Central Valley, and in the southern reaches of the state mainstream Christians and Jews were joined by Mormons, Adventists, and Spiritualists (who believed in communication with the dead). As the 1920s unfolded and led into the hard times of the 1930s, the state's reputation grew as a nesting ground for spiritual groups beyond the pale of the traditional Judeo-Christian denominations.

Aimee Semple McPherson was the state's most charismatic and impactful evangelist of the times. "Sister Aimee," as she was called, migrated from the East Coast, settling in Los Angeles in 1918. There she built the 5,000-seat Angeles Temple, headquarters of the International Church of the Foursquare Gospel that she founded. At the temple she preached dramatic, radio-aired sermons and tended the sick and infirm. Her son Rolf McPherson later recalled: "Often Mother would . . . go down and pray for someone on a stretcher. They would get up off the stretcher and the stretcher would be carried off empty."

In 1926 scandal rocked the new church. McPherson had disappeared after swimming near Venice Beach on May 18, only to resurface a month later in Mexico, claiming she had been kidnapped. Researchers have gathered considerable evidence to show that she had spent part of her time in "captivity" in a honeymoon cottage in Carmel, accompanied by her church's radio station engineer, Kenneth Ormiston, a married man. Her charisma helped her weather the incident. Despite suffering a nervous breakdown in 1930, and eloping with a choir member and divorcing him several years later, she held herself and her church together well enough to provide meals for thousands of unemployed Angelinos during the depression-ridden 1930s. At the time of her death in 1944, reportedly from an accidental overdose of barbiturates, the Church of the Foursquare

Gospel counted 410 churches in North America, 29,000 members worldwide, and assets totaling $2,800,000.

Minister Robert P. Shuler, a rival and adversary of McPherson, increased his Trinity Methodist Church's membership from 900 in 1920 to 42,000 10 years later. He, too, used radio to reach listening audiences. His messages scorned Jews, Catholics, movies, evolution, and dancing. A defender of the Ku Klux Klan, he stressed the importance of preserving the Anglo-Saxon purity of Los Angeles, "the one city in the nation in which the white, American, Christian idealism predominates."

A different spiritual message – one of inclusiveness – appealed to some Angelinos who became followers of Paramahansa Yogananda. Born in India, he arrived in Los Angeles in 1925. There he established his temple and the international headquarters of the Self-Realization Fellowship, which blended Hindu and Christian teachings with yoga philosophy. Spiritual enlightenment, he preached, came through a process of self-realization of the divine that could be reached by practicing physical exercises, breath control, and meditation. Monks and nuns were expected to adhere to non-violence, chastity, obedience, and a simple lifestyle. Lush SRF meditation centers were located on prime real estate mostly along or near the coast in Pacific Palisades, Hollywood, Encinitas, and San Diego. With more than 600 such facilities in 62 countries today, this California-based religious movement has stood as an early link between the religions of the East and those of the West.

A stronger East–West, transpacific religious tie was exemplified in the continued growth of Buddhism in California. The port cities of San Francisco and Los Angeles, with their sizable populations of Chinese and Japanese, nurtured their respective Buddhist heritages in California, which reached back into the latter half of the nineteenth century. In 1924, for example, Los Angeles' Nishi Hongwanji congregation erected the largest Buddhist temple in North America.

Freedom-Minded and Other Women

During the interwar years, women, like men, splintered along ethnic and class lines in their gender roles. A number of white, middle-class women were more freedom-minded than religion-focused in California, as in some other parts of the nation. They sought a wider range of gender options and roles than their predecessors had enjoyed. Non-white women, generally having less education and fewer economic resources at hand, confined themselves to more traditionally prescribed family roles until the depression of the 1930s hit. With husbands often out of work, many sought paid labor while keeping their families intact. Single women of the working class and all ethnicities may have had to scramble the most to find jobs with which to support themselves.

Increasingly, white middle-class women entered the professions and philanthropies. Julia Morgan, a UC Berkeley engineering graduate and preeminent Bay Area architect, designed numerous educational institutions, conference centers, Young Women's Christian Association buildings, churches, and private residences (some of which are discussed later in this chapter). Physician Adelaide Brown was a leader in the movement to advance preventive medicine and birth control in the state. In the 1920s she traveled throughout the Far East, surveying the health of women and children. Women excelled in law and business, as well as in the arts, including photography. Californians comprised nearly 30 percent of America's female airplane pilots. Estelle Doheny was a major figure in philanthropy and art collecting. In the mid-1920s Ellen Browning Scripps endowed one of the Claremont Colleges for women named in her honor. Gaining elective political office, however, remained elusive. Florence Prag Kahn was California's only female representative in Congress. A graduate of UC Berkeley, she was instrumental in the establishment of Alameda Naval Base in the Bay Area and advocated for the extension of American citizenship to the China-born wives of Chinese American men.

Both as voters and job holders, women formed an array of business and professional organizations in California, all of which aimed at promoting opportunities for whites of their gender and class. As of May 1922, 21 women's business and professional associations existed in the state, with a total of 1,964 members. A sampling of these groups includes: the Los Angeles Business Women's Civic Club; the San Diego Business and Professional Women's Club; the Woman's Lawyers' Club of Los Angeles; the Faculty Club of the University of California, Southern Division (UCLA); the Business Woman's Forum, Oakland; and the Secretarial Association of Los Angeles. These organizations and others like them assured their members of a growing presence and influence in the business world.

Besides enjoying improved occupational and professional mobility, middle-class white women adopted some aspects of male behavior: they smoked, drove cars, and drank alcohol. Influenced by the relaxed sexual mores of the era, they wore dresses with lowered necklines and raised hemlines, and used birth control. Within marriage, these women enjoyed a measure of equality and independence largely unknown to their mothers' generation.

Both white and non-white married, working-class women were increasingly forced beyond their traditional maternal and homemaking roles and into the wage-labor market as the depression of the 1930s cost more of their husbands their jobs. Historian Judy Yung, in her book *Unbound Feet: A Social History of Chinese Women in San Francisco* (1995), recounts the plight of Wong Shee Chan, Yung's "Grandaunt," who lived in San Francisco's Chinatown where she raised her six children during the depression. "Those were the worst years for us," recalled Grandaunt. "Life was very hard. I just went from day to day. . . . A quarter was enough for dinner. With that I bought two pieces of fish to steam, three bunches of vegetables (two to stir-fry and the third to put in the soup), and some pork for the soup." After her formerly laid-off husband found work as a seaman, Yung's Grandaunt cared for their children while studying for and gaining a hairdresser's license. She kept the children in a beauty parlor with her while she worked from 7 a.m. to 11 p.m. seven days a week. In this manner, Wong Shee Chan kept her family together while her husband was at sea.

Working-class single women, including widows and divorced mothers, of all ethnicities, struggled mightily during the 1930s to support themselves and sometimes dependent relatives as well. Faced with few job prospects, some of them urged removing married females from the workforce. A mother from Redondo Beach, California, complained about employing wedded women: "It keeps our Boys and Girls from getting work and they are the ones that need it."

The Great Depression: Strikes and Panaceas

Like the rest of the nation, California was hit hard by the Great Depression that followed the stock market crash of 1929 and lasted until American entry into World War II in 1941. Across the country many factories closed, and joblessness plagued both cities and farmlands. In 1932–3 unemployment soared to about 25 percent of the workforce as some 13 to 17 million laborers nationwide were without jobs. Those who were employed often suffered wage cuts. The United States, like much of the rest of the world, found itself in the throes of the worst economic collapse in its history. Amid the fallout from this collapse, union members fought back against pay reductions, often by going on strike, that is, stopping all work until their various demands were met. In California labor strife was particularly acute in the fields and on the docks. State officials were hard-pressed to maintain order and offer some semblance of economic relief. A prominent socialist ran for governor of California, and bizarre remedies for economic relief found their way into politics.

Labor conditions throughout the state were bad in the 1930s; they were at their worst in the fields, where union organizing made the fewest inroads. Desperate Okies and Arkies, so called because they migrated out of the soil-impoverished states of Oklahoma and Arkansas in the hope of finding work, arrived in the Central Valley farmlands in jalopies. These seasonal laborers were joined by Mexicans and Filipinos in the Imperial Valley, who comprised the remainder of the state's farm labor force.

Wage cuts amid deplorable working conditions led to a number of strikes in California's fields and canneries in the 1930s. A strike led by lettuce pickers in the Imperial Valley in 1930 was the first of many such stoppages. Five thousand field hands joined the strike, which, like a magnet, drew in communist organizers who persuaded the aggrieved workers to join the Cannery and Agricultural Workers Industrial Union (CAWIU). Meanwhile, cannery workers in the state, nearly three-fourths of whom were women, grew restive about their 16-hour workdays for a wage of 15 cents an hour. Such conditions led to a 1931 cannery workers' strike in the Santa Clara Valley. Latinas, like Luisa Moreno, held key leadership positions in the United Cannery, Agricultural, Packing, and Allied Workers of America union representing the laborers. Some of the strikes led by Moreno and others in the early 1930s brought positive results. For example, by August of 1933 agricultural wages had risen from 16 to 25 cents an hour.

Fearing that unionization was spreading, major growers and their business allies formed the Associated Farmers in 1934. Horrified at the specter of Bolshevism (the anti-capitalist doctrines of the radical socialists who won the Russian Revolution) in the state, the Associated Farmers helped fund the prosecution of CAWIU leaders suspected of being Communist Party members. Seventeen members of this union were tried for violation of the 1919 Criminal Syndicalism Act (see Chapter 9) in 1935; eight were convicted.

Beyond the fields and canneries, unions met with greater success along California's waterfronts. Successful dock strikes in San Francisco and San Pedro in 1923 served as preludes to the much more extensive longshoremen's strike of 1934, which erupted in the City by the Bay and spread along the entire Pacific coastline. San Francisco's Embarcadero, a strip of land abutting the city's port that includes a roadway and wharves, was ground zero for the drama that unfolded.

In response to a weekly wage of about $10 and employer demands for faster work, Pacific Coast leaders of the International Longshoremen's Association (ILA), a powerful maritime union whose West Coast office was located in San Francisco, met in that city in February 1934. They authorized a coast-wide strike if the ILA and shippers could not come to a satisfactory agreement on wage rates and hours. As negotiations dragged into March, the ILA added more demands. The union insisted on a dollar-an-hour wage rate, overtime pay at $1.50 an hour, a six-hour workday and 30-hour work week, union-run hiring halls, a prohibition on employers using the facilities of one Pacific port to undermine a strike at another, and a demand that the employers bargain for all of the West Coast ports simultaneously.

The shipping companies and their allies in the maritime industries rejected the union's demands as radical, charging that ILA organizer Harry Bridges was a communist. Bridges, an avowedly militant trade unionist who emigrated from Australia to California, denied the charge and his accusers never proved it.

On May 9, 1934, West Coast longshoremen went on strike. Other maritime unions and the teamsters soon joined. By mid-May 34,700 dockworkers and others from Tacoma, Washington, in the north to San Diego in the south brought Pacific Coast shipping to a halt. San Francisco shippers retaliated by bringing in three squads of UC Berkeley football players to break the strike. Though the teamsters refused to haul cargoes to and from vessels, a so-called Belt Line railroad, owned by the State of California, remained in operation to perform that service. Longshoremen emulated the nonviolent followers of Mohandas Gandhi in India by sitting on the tracks and roadbed. The strike cost San Francisco port businesses an estimated $1 million a day; to stanch this hemorrhaging of money, company executives enlisted support from the city's police department, whose intervention would prove calamitous.

Matters came to a violent head on July 5, "Bloody Thursday." Police armed with extra-heavy riot sticks and teargas canisters defended the strikebreakers. Union workers overturned and burned trucks, strewing their cargoes onto the streets. Shots were fired, killing two strikers as scores of their fellow workers were beaten by police. Governor Frank Mirriam sent 1,700 National Guardsmen with fixed bayonets and machine guns to the Embarcadero. Labor officials responded to this show of armed force by declaring a general strike on July 16, that is, a union stoppage of business throughout the city.

Four days later the ILA ended the general strike and by late July, after 83 days of turmoil and bloodshed, the shippers agreed to unconditional federal arbitration. On October 12 the arbitration board gave unions almost total control over hiring halls at the docks, a key demand of the ILA.

In addition to validating some of the ILA demands and spurring a growth in its membership, the 1934 San Francisco dock strike underscored how significant the city's Pacific maritime economy was. When shipping was shut down, the West Coast's leading mercantile city was shut down. In the wake of the longshoremen's strike, the October 14, 1935, edition of the *San Francisco Examiner* contained a special section titled "Century of Commerce," which traced the central role of seagoing trade in the city's and the state's history during the preceding 100 years. "It is only because of the unsurpassed maritime service San Francisco has enjoyed for so many years," stated the article, "that California is able to compete in the markets of the world with her manufactured goods and her vast agricultural products. Fruits, cotton, hay and grain grown in the great inland valleys all find their way to wide flung markets of the world by way of The Embarcadero [the city's ship-loading waterfront]." This statement bears testimony to the dependence of California's agricultural sector on the state's Pacific trade.

While the state's maritime economy struggled yet remained afloat, the nationwide depression caused sufficient suffering to prompt California voters to support Franklin D. Roosevelt for president in 1932, and to put non-Marxian socialism on the ballot in the election of 1934. To the unease of Washington, D.C., New Dealers seeking to reform rather than replace capitalism, former Socialist Party member Upton Sinclair reregistered as a Democrat, securing his party's nomination for the governorship that year. In order to promote his campaign, he wrote an idealistic novel, *I, Governor of California, and How I Ended Poverty: A True Story of the Future* (1933). The acronym designating Sinclair's campaign, EPIC, derives from the book title. In effect, it was an imagined, socialistic recounting of how during the years from 1933 to 1938 good times returned to the Golden State. For example, Sinclair pretended that farm lands and factories were publicly owned and operated as agricultural and industrial cooperatives.

The Republicans nominated conservative Frank Merriam, the incumbent governor. Louis B. Mayer, the movie mogul who ran Metro-Goldwyn-Mayer, worked with other business leaders to portray Sinclair as an atheist, free love advocate, and communist whose policy prescriptions would draw trainloads of hobos to California. In the absence of support from President Roosevelt, the Republican strategy succeeded in discrediting Sinclair by showing him as outside of the mainstream of American society. Sinclair's candidacy was also hurt by his opposition to the plan of Long Beach physician Francis E. Townsend calling for an old-age retirement program. Accordingly, a business transaction tax would fund monthly payments of $200 to every retired citizen over 60 years of age, with the requirement that recipients spend the money within the month. Townsend clubs attracted 1.5 million members nationwide, showing the reach of a Greater California in the public policy arena, and pushed President Roosevelt toward sponsoring the Social Security Act of 1935. Merriam's support of the Townsend Plan probably helped win his reelection.

Governor Merriam's conservatism proved highly pragmatic and somewhat supportive of Roosevelt's New Deal. He antagonized a number of his most reactionary supporters by securing the adoption of a state income tax, and increasing imposts on banks and other corporations. By repealing the sales tax on food and providing a modicum of aid to the elderly, he showed some affinity for the spirit of the New Deal. The substance of the New Deal, however, resided in federal programs implemented in the state. For example, the Works Project Administration and Civilian Conservation Corps built numerous schools and other public buildings as well as parks in the Golden State.

Despite the practical New Deal programs brought to the state, California continued to flirt with more exotic responses to the depression. One such response, the Los Angeles-based Technocracy movement of the early 1930s, envisioned the evolution of a cooperative utopia ushered in by technology and the application of science to public policy. Capitalism's benefits would thereby be more rationally and equitably distributed. The pension panacea that arose and enlivened California's 1938 election serves as another example of an unconventional approach to the economic downturn. Informally called "Ham and Eggs" by a promoter, the scheme qualified as a ballot initiative titled Thirty Dollars Every Thursday. Its advocates proposed that the state pay $30 every Thursday to unemployed Californians over 50. The "Ham and Eggs" initiative went down in defeat on election day, along with incumbent Republican gubernatorial candidate Merriam, who had opposed the measure.

Democrat Culbert L. Olson, whose campaign took no clear stance on "Ham and Eggs," won the governorship in 1938. Though more identified with New Deal policies than his predecessor Merriam, Olson was hampered by Republican control of the state Senate and by a bare, fractious Democratic majority in the assembly. Still, the new governor pardoned Tom Mooney (see Chapter 9) and oversaw modest reform of the state's penal and mental health-care systems.

Cultural Expression of a High Order

In the interwar years, California assuredly experienced its share of combative politics and economic poverty; yet culturally it was a Pacific Eldorado whose achievements could scarcely be matched by any other state. This was particularly true of the Golden State's literary output, photographic works, and architectural marvels.

The state's literary masters included John Steinbeck, William Saroyan, and Robinson Jeffers. Steinbeck was raised by upper-middle-class parents in Salinas and attended but did not graduate from Stanford University. His fictional works were set mostly in the farmlands and coastal areas of Central California. Critical notoriety and commercial success awaited publication of his novel *Tortilla Flat* (1935), which narrated the drunken and romantic escapades of a group of poor, mixedblood Spanish, Mexican, Indian, and Caucasian male idlers in Monterey whose complexions were "like that of a well-browned meerschaum pipe." The following year Steinbeck published *In Dubious Battle*, which dramatized the plight of migratory farm workers who, led by communists, went on strike for more humane working conditions. Steinbeck's road trips throughout the San Joaquin Valley beginning in 1936 resulted in his journalistic writings and epic novel on the travails of the Okies and Arkies in depression-era California, *The Grapes of Wrath* (1939). The book won a Pulitzer Prize. Steinbeck was fascinated by marine life and wrote his next book, a work of nonfiction titled *The Sea of Cortez* (1941), about his Pacific expedition to Baja's Gulf of California with his biologist friend Edward F. Ricketts. In this marine specimen-gathering voyage from Monterey into Baja's gulf waters, Steinbeck probed deeply into what this Pacific excursion revealed to him about the natural world and humankind's place in it: "The disappearance of plankton, although the components are microscopic, would probably in a short time eliminate every living thing in the sea and change the whole of man's life.... One [species of marine life] merges into another ... until what we know as life meets and enters what we think of as non-life; barnacle and rock, rock and earth ... And the units nestle into the whole and are inseparable from it.... [O]ne thing is all things – plankton, a shimmering phosphorescence on the sea and the spinning planets and an expanding universe, all bound together by the elastic string of time." The public quarreled far less with these reflections than with the author's political views. Denounced more than praised in Salinas because of his left-wing politics and unflattering depictions of big growers, Steinbeck received the Nobel Prize in Literature in 1962.

William Saroyan's talent was almost entirely self-developed. Raised in poverty in Fresno, he did not graduate from high school, nor attend college. For much of his hardscrabble career he lived and wrote in San Francisco, where he turned out the book that launched his success, *The Daring Young Man on the Flying Trapeze* (1934). In addition to other critically acclaimed novels and short stories, he wrote plays, including the Pulitzer Prize-winning *The Time of Your Life* (1939). The drama portrayed the lives of hapless, good-hearted men who frequented a dockside San Francisco tavern. Characteristically, Saroyan rejected the Pulitzer award and prize money, insisting that art remain free of the taint of money and authority.

Robinson Jeffers was and remains California's greatest poet. Ensconced in Tor House, the stone family citadel he built with his own hands on a Carmel bluff overlooking Pacific rollers, Jeffers etched into verse nature's sculpting of the Big Sur coast, and similarly, fate's often turbulent shaping of human lives. "Great poetry," he wrote, "appeals to the most primitive instincts. . . . It is a beautiful work of nature." In poems such as *Tamar* (1924) and *Roan Stallion* (1925), Jeffers showed the power of untamed human capacities for incest and murder – morality and civilization notwithstanding.

Just as Jeffers's poems captured the grandeur of the Big Sur coast, the photographs of Edward Weston, Ansel Adams, and Dorothea Lange similarly captured the grandeur of the Central California shoreline, Yosemite Valley, and the human spirit respectively. Weston and Adams lived in Carmel, hungrily photographing its Pacific seascape. However, it was Adams's stunning black and white depictions of Yosemite Valley that would ensure his fame. Lange's iconic photograph titled *Migrant Mother* spoke volumes about the hardships endured by the Okies and Arkies entering California in the 1930s.

Architecturally, the Golden State abounded with noteworthy structures and brilliant designers. Some 700 buildings nationwide, including those on the campuses of UC Berkeley and Mills College in Oakland, were the handiwork of Julia Morgan. Hearst Castle, overlooking the Pacific in San Simeon, was one of her masterpieces of design. In the Bay Area the landscape was graced by the M.H. de Young Memorial Museum, the West Coast's leading art gallery, and by the California Palace of the Legion of Honor museum, as well as by the world's most photographed structure of its kind – the Golden Gate Bridge linking San Francisco to Sausalito, completed in 1937 as a public works project. In southern California, the soon to become famous bungalow style of homebuilding was introduced by the Pasadena brothers Charles and Henry Greene. Scripps College in Claremont, founded in 1926, is known throughout the country for the understated elegance of its Spanish Revival architecture and aesthetic landscaping. By contrast, the Watts Towers in Los Angeles, sculpted during the years 1921–55 by Simon Rodia from Pacific sea shells, Chinese pottery shards, broken glass, bathroom tiles, and other cast-off material, symbolized the energies and refuse of a city on the move.

Architect William Alexander Levy (later known simply as William Alexander) designed Hangover House, so called because it was perched on a hillside overlooking Aliso Canyon

Figure 10.3 *Migrant Mother*, photographed by Dorothea Lange. This image captures the poverty and uncertainty experienced by so many Dust Bowl migrants who relocated to California's Central Valley during the Great Depression of the 1930s. Courtesy of Library of Congress, LC-USF34- 009058-C.

in Laguna Beach. Affording a dramatic view of the Pacific, this flat-roofed, modern-style glass, steel, and concrete residence was completed in 1938. Though Alexander, who worked briefly with Frank Lloyd Wright, was not preeminent in his field, architectural historian Ted Wells has attested to the national importance of the three-bedroom, multi-storied, structure that anticipated by nearly 20 years a home design that would later become very popular in California. The owner, Richard Halliburton, was a celebrity adventurer and lecturer, known for having swum the length of the Panama Canal, climbed the Matterhorn, flown around the world in an open cockpit biplane, and with the aid of a ghost writer regaled readers with numerous travel books recounting his journeys. His last adventure, sailing a Chinese junk from Hong Kong to San Francisco, ended in his death in a Pacific storm in 1939.

The physical structure that best represents California during the interwar decades was the 80-foot statue of the mythical goddess Pacifica, erected on Treasure Island, the site of the 1939 Golden Gate International Exposition. Created by artist Ralph Stackpole, the semi-Buddhist mother goddess figure represented the ambitions of San Francisco, indeed of all California, to become the commercial hub of the entire Pacific Basin. An approaching war from across that ocean would temporarily thwart that dream.

Figure 10.4 Statue of the Court of Pacifica at the Golden Gate International Exposition on Treasure Island, 1939. San Francisco History Center, San Francisco Public Library.

SUMMARY

During the 1920s and 1930s Greater California emerged as the super state of the Pacific Rim. Its world-class infrastructure and economy were unmatched by any other state and few, if any, nations in that ocean region. Oil derricks, aqueducts and water irrigation systems, dams, croplands, highways, bridges, shopping centers and motels geared to the emergent car culture, movie houses, and Pacific fun zones transformed the landscape. They afforded physical evidence of an extraordinarily diversified economy that included movie-making, agribusiness, and petroleum, maritime, automotive, aircraft, and banking enterprises. As ever, California's economy was hitched largely to Pacific Basin markets and trade routes. Charles Kingsford-Smith's epic transpacific flight dramatically symbolized this.

As California returned to political conservatism in the 1920s, new religious forces made themselves felt mainly along the coast from San Francisco down to San Diego. The

International Church of the Foursquare Gospel, the Self-Realization Fellowship, and Buddhist temples attracted followers. Meanwhile, women, having earlier obtained voting rights, succeeded in gaining a larger measure of equality with men in both society and the professions. Middle-class white females enjoyed a far greater measure of this equality, and accompanying rights and opportunities, than did women of color and those in the working class.

The Great Depression of the 1930s hit California hard. The state's voters supported Democrat Franklin D. Roosevelt's election to the presidency in 1932. Labor strikes in the fields and ports, culminating in a 1934 San Francisco-centered shutdown of the nation's West Coast docks, rocked the state, showing how critical Pacific shipping was to California's economy. That same year a socialist ran for the governorship, and throughout the decade an assortment of panaceas was offered by citizens to help the elderly and unemployed. Though poverty was widespread, cultural production in the state was of a high order, as evidenced in literature and the other arts. The building of the world-renowned Golden Gate Bridge and the erecting of the statue of Pacifica in San Francisco Bay testified to an irrepressible optimism among Californians – an optimism that as usual looked westward to the Pacific for brighter days.

REVIEW QUESTIONS

- What evidence is given in the chapter in support of the claim that California became a super state in the 1920s and 1930s?
- Describe the state's major aqueduct-irrigation-hydroelectric generation projects of the 1920s and 1930s. What was their significance?
- What factors led to the development of California's car culture?
- In what ways was California a Pacific Eldorado during the Great Depression of the 1930s?
- What was the significance of the 1934 West Coast dock strike, spearheaded in San Francisco?

FURTHER READINGS

Jeremiah B.C. Axelrod, *Inventing Autopia: Dreams and Visions of the Modern Metropolis in Jazz Age Los Angeles* (Berkeley: University of California Press, 2009). Los Angeles' sprawl in the 1920s was envisioned and planned more than previously thought, according to this critically acclaimed study.

Giles Brown, *Ships that Sail No More: Marine Transportation from San Diego to Puget Sound, 1910–1940* (Lexington, KY: University Press of Kentucky, 1966). This well-researched book is one of the few comprehensive histories of West Coast shipping during its halcyon years.

California History, 87/2 (2010). The entire issue, replete with telling photographs, is devoted to the work and influence of California poet Robinson Jeffers.

Philip L. Fradkin, *A River No More: The Colorado River and the West* (New York: Alfred A. Knopf, 1996). As the title suggests, the author traces the diminishing supply of Colorado River water available to western states in recent times of drought, hoping that clearer hindsight will result in better foresight in the shaping of public policy regarding the river.

Camille Guerin-Gonzales, *Mexican Workers and American Dreams: Immigration, Repatriation, and California Farm*

Labor, 1900–1939 (New Brunswick, NJ: Rutgers University Press, 1994). The forced repatriation in the 1930s of half a million Mexican workers and some Mexican Americans and its impact on their national and cultural identity is explored in this work.

Michael Hiltzik, *Colossus: Hoover Dam and the Making of the American Century* (New York: Free Press, 2010). The author treats the immensity, benefits, and human costs – in terms of labor exploitation, lax safety practices, and deaths – of this epic construction project.

Robert V. Hine, *California's Utopian Colonies* (San Marino, CA: Huntington Library, 1953). This classic study of religious experimentalism and exoticism in nineteenth-century California provides a prologue for somewhat similar developments in the 1920s and 1930s.

Roger W. Lotchin, *Fortress California, 1910–1961: From Warfare to Welfare* (New York: Oxford University Press, 1992). According to the writer, a partnership beginning in the 1920s between cities and the military led to the establishment of bases and airfields in California.

Carey McWilliams, *Factories in the Field: The Story of Migratory Farm Labor in California* (Berkeley: University of California Press, 2000). The encounter between corporate farming and migratory labor in the fields of depression-ridden California is traced in this classic exposé and brief on behalf of agricultural workers, first published in 1939.

Bruce Nelson, *Workers on the Waterfront: Seamen, Longshoremen, and Unionism in the 1930s* (Urbana, IL: University of Illinois Press, 1990). Labor conditions, unionism, and radicalism are at the heart of this account on Pacific Coast maritime workers during a tumultuous decade.

John Niven, *The American President Lines and Its Forebears, 1848–1984* (Newark, DE: University of Delaware Press, 1987). The history of America's maritime trade with Asia, going back to the gold rush era, is related through the dealings of shipping magnate Robert Dollar and his successors.

Stephanie S. Pincetl, *Transforming California: A Political History of Land Use in California* (Baltimore: Johns Hopkins University Press, 2003). In addition to chronicling California land use policy since 1850, this book calls for an invigorated understanding of citizenship to combat environmental degradation and create public spaces more nurturing than shopping malls.

Charles F. Queenan, *The Port of Los Angeles: From Wilderness to World Port* (Los Angeles: Government and Community Relations Division, Los Angeles Harbor Department, 1983). Within this sweeping history of the Port of Los Angeles, an entire chapter is devoted largely to the dredging, expansion, and commerce of the harbor from 1921 to 1945.

Walter A. Radius, *United States Shipping in Transpacific Trade, 1922–1938* (New York: Stanford University Press, 1944). One of the few studies in its field, this book is an invaluable source of statistics and commentary on America's Pacific commerce in the interwar years.

Robert Chao Romero, *The Chinese in Mexico, 1882–1940* (Tucson, AZ: University of Arizona Press, 2010). California's role in a Chinese transnational commercial network, operating from Mexico, is detailed in this provocative volume.

Vicki Ruiz, *Cannery Women, Cannery Lives: Mexican Women, Unionization, and the California Food Processing Industry, 1930–1950* (Albuquerque, NM: University of New Mexico Press, 1987). Mexicana and Mexican American women are at the center of this study of the struggles and successes of the United Cannery, Agricultural, Packing, and Allied Workers of America Union during the Great Depression in California.

George J. Sanchez, *Becoming Mexican American: Ethnicity, Culture, and Identity in Chicano Los Angeles, 1900–1945* (New York: Oxford University Press, 1993). Just as American history cannot be understood apart from its immigrant roots, this book shows how a segment of Los Angeles history in the twentieth century is best seen as an amalgam of negotiated identities and allegiances among border-crossing Mexicans.

Harvey Schwartz, ed., *Solidarity Stories: An Oral History of the ILWU* (Seattle, WA: University of Washington Press, 2009). The history of the International Longshore and Warehouse Union, an outgrowth of the 1934 San Francisco and West Coast dock strikes, is told sympathetically through first-hand recollections.

David F. Selvin, *A Terrible Anger: The 1934 Waterfront and General Strikes in San Francisco* (Detroit: Wayne State University Press, 1996). The San Francisco dock strike at the center of a tie up of West Coast trade is viewed through the eyes of a witness who happens to be a labor historian.

Tom Sitton and William Deverell, eds., *Metropolis in the Making: Los Angeles in the 1920s* (Berkeley: University of California Press, 2001). This collection of essays reveals the dynamism of America's first decentralized city while showcasing the promise of urban studies scholarship.

Kevin Starr, *Endangered Dreams: The Great Depression in California* (New York: Oxford University Press, 1996). The strikes, fears of communism, and social messiahs of depression-era California are featured in this engaging work.

Kevin Starr, *Golden Gate: The Life and Times of America's Greatest Bridge* (New York: Bloomsbury Press, 2010). The construction and meaning of America's gateway to the Pacific are treated in this work by a master historian.

Kevin Starr, *Material Dreams: Southern California through the 1920s* (New York: Oxford University Press, 1990). This volume offers both a panoramic overview and a detailed account of southern California's dramatic rise in the early twentieth century.

John Steinbeck, *Harvest Gypsies: On the Road to the Grapes of Wrath* (Berkeley: Heyday Books, 1988). This compilation of seven newspaper articles written by the prominent California novelist served as the basis of Steinbeck's fictional masterpiece, *The Grapes of Wrath*.

Richard A. Walker, *The Conquest of Bread: 150 Years of Agribusiness in California* (New York: The New Press, 2004). One of the signal contributions of this study is that it connects California's agricultural dominance in the United States with the use of numerous Mexican farm laborers from the state's Pacific Rim neighbor to the south.

Judy Yung, *Unbound Feet: A Social History of Chinese Women in San Francisco* (Berkeley: University of California Press, 1995). Drawing heavily from interviews, the author provides testimonies of women who lived in America's largest Chinese enclave from the turn of the century to World War II.

11

America's Pacific Bulwark: World War II and Its Aftermath

Because of its Pacific preeminence and connections, California's role in World War II was largely unmatched by any other state. The 40-year clash between the state and its Japanese population, beginning in 1900, set the stage for the Pearl Harbor attack of December 7, 1941, that thrust America into the war. That attack led to the mass removal of California's residents of Japanese ancestry to barbed wire encampments. Meanwhile, the state's military installations, shipyards, and airplane factories were instrumental in waging war in the Pacific, while UC Berkeley's leadership in the atomic bomb project ensured a decisive and controversial end to the global conflict.

In the war's aftermath, California emerged as more thoroughly industrialized, more heavily populated, and an even more dominant force in Pacific commerce and security affairs as well as aerospace enterprises than in the depression era. While the Pacific Coast states of Oregon and Washington likewise experienced wartime growth, in most regards they were greatly eclipsed by California. The Golden State's phenomenal military infrastructure, necessitated by war, gave rise to a long-lasting, economic boom beginning in the late 1940s and undergirded by agriculture. During the war years and afterward, Greater California's influence in the Far West, the nation, the Pacific Basin, and globally became greater still.

Pacific Eldorado: A History of Greater California, First Edition. Thomas J. Osborne.
© 2013 Thomas J. Osborne. Published 2013 by Blackwell Publishing Ltd.

Timeline

1941   Japan launches a surprise attack on U.S. naval vessels and military installations at Pearl Harbor and elsewhere on Oahu in the Hawaiian Islands, resulting in America's declaration of war on Japan and entry into World War II

1942   Aviation replaces filmmaking as southern California's leading industry

A Japanese submarine shells the coast just north of Santa Barbara

The Congressionally authorized bracero labor program begins, legalizing California's use of Mexican farm workers

1942–5   Long Beach serves as the major anchorage for the U.S. Navy's Pacific Fleet

UC Berkeley physicist J. Robert Oppenheimer heads the scientists working on the top-secret Manhattan Project to build an atomic bomb

1942–6   Americans of Japanese descent, three-fourths of whom live in California, are sent to concentration camps

1943   Zoot Suit riots in Los Angeles involve off-duty U.S. sailors beating adolescent Mexican American males

1944   Physicist Theodore von Karman co-founds the Jet Propulsion Laboratory at Caltech in Pasadena

An explosion at the Port Chicago Naval Magazine results in the deaths of 320 servicemen, two-thirds of whom are blacks in a segregated unit

1945   The United Nations Charter, founding the international organization, is drafted in San Francisco

1946   By defeating Jerry Voorhis in a Congressional election in southern California, Richard Nixon gains national prominence as a leader of the anti-communist crusade

1947   In *Mendez v. Westminster*, judges in the federal Ninth Circuit Court of Appeals hold that the California constitution prohibits the segregation of Mexican-origin children into separate schools

RAND Corporation, a leading public policy think tank, opens in Santa Monica

1948   California becomes America's leading farm state in terms of value of agricultural output

1949   The regents of the University of California adopt a loyalty oath requiring personnel to swear that they are not communists and "do not support any party or organization that believes in, advocates, or teaches the overthrow of the United States Government . . ."

1950   The state legislature passes the Levering Act requiring all state employees, including professors, to take a loyalty oath or risk being fired; in 1967 the state supreme court ruled this oath unconstitutional, largely on First Amendment grounds

Los Angeles surpasses San Francisco in maritime cargo shipping, due to containerization

1951   The San Francisco Peace Treaty is signed, formally ending World War II between the United States and its allies and Japan

The U.S. Naval Postgraduate School moves from Annapolis, Maryland, to Monterey, California, signaling the Department of Defense's increasing focus on the strategic importance of California and the Pacific Basin

The 117-mile-long Delta–Mendota Canal is in operation, transporting water southeasterly from Tracy in the San Joaquin Valley to Mendota, 30 miles west of Fresno, completing the Central Valley Project

1952	In *Tolman v. Underhill*, the state supreme court strikes down the UC regents' loyalty oath as unconstitutional
	Richard M. Nixon and Dwight D. Eisenhower are elected as vice president and president respectively
1953	President Eisenhower appoints California Governor Earl Warren as chief justice of the U.S. Supreme Court, inaugurating a major shift of that tribunal toward support for civil rights and racial justice
	California surpasses New York, becoming America's leading state in terms of military appropriations

Military Installations: Forts, Naval Bases, and Airfields

California's forts, naval bases, and airfields in operation in the 1930s were expanded and supplemented by more such facilities during the war years. The state's pre-war military installations included San Francisco's Presidio, Fort Ord, Mare Island's U.S. Naval Shipyard, San Diego's naval base, and March airfield. As a result of America's entry into World War II, California became a garrison state serving as one of the nation's two major training and staging areas for military operations, Texas being the other.

Modest in its beginnings, California's war-related infrastructure grew dramatically after Pearl Harbor. From 16 military bases in 1941, the number grew to 41 by 1945, more than those in the five states combined that were ranked just beneath California.

After the Pearl Harbor attack, the San Francisco Bay area served as the command center for America's West Coast. The city's Presidio was headquarters for the Army's Western Defense Command, under Lieutenant General John L. DeWitt. DeWitt's 4th Army was also headquartered at the Presidio. Situated in San Francisco Bay, Mare Island served as the nation's largest naval ship repair facility. Warships of all kinds ringed the island; damaged naval vessels from the Pearl Harbor assault, like the U.S.S. *Shaw*, were refitted there and put back into battle. Camp Stoneman, abutting the Carquinez Strait that empties into San Francisco Bay, provided the major training center and staging area for the more than 1 million soldiers who afterward voyaged through the Golden Gate en route to the Pacific theater of military operations. The Western Sea Frontier, the U.S. Navy command responsible for protecting the West Coast from Alaska down to and including Mexico, was headquartered on Treasure Island lying between Oakland and San Francisco. Moreover, the man-made island served as a command center for the Coast Guard. Northern California's Navy Pre-Flight School, one of four such centers nationwide, was located on the campus of St. Mary's College in the East Bay community of Moraga. Crissy Field and Hamilton Field, both of which were located on the Bay's perimeter, accommodated Army Air Force warplanes as did nearby Travis Air Force Base. Numerous smaller war-related facilities – forts, depots, and piers – dotted the area.

Approximately 80 miles south of the Bay Area, Monterey County's Fort Ord served as home to the Army's 7th Infantry Division, under the command of Brigadier General Joseph Stilwell. Fort Ord doubled in size from 15,000 acres in World War I to 30,000 acres in World War II. Utilizing the beaches of Monterey Bay, it became a major training area for the amphibious warfare that characterized much of the Pacific fighting between 1942 and 1945.

Southern California, too, was garrisoned. With Pearl Harbor in ruins, Long Beach furnished the major anchorage for the U.S. Navy's Pacific Fleet from 1942 to 1945. San Diego, as well, provided an important harbor for that fleet's warships, a training area for amphibious landings along the Coronado Strand, and the West Coast's center for naval aviation. The Marine Corps established an air base at El Toro in Orange County, and purportedly the world's largest military installation, occupying 123,000 acres, at Camp Pendleton in San Diego County. In 1944 nearly 87,000 Marines and other military personnel were stationed at Camp Pendleton. Also in the Southland, the Army Air Force used the San Bernardino Air Field and Depot (much later renamed Norton Air Force Base), as well as March Field in Riverside County, and operated its West Coast Training Center in nearby Santa Ana, which taught pre-flight maneuvers to some 20,000 cadets. Those completing the program then went on to pilot, bombardier, or navigator instruction at the Victorville Army Flying School or at the Army Air Force's Advanced Flying School at Sacramento's Mather Field.

California's forts, naval bases, and airfields tell only part of the story of the state's role in fighting World War II. Fueled by Pentagon expenditures and driven by wartime production demands, the civilian sector of the state's economy became equally consequential in transforming California from a peacetime, consumer-based society into a preeminent defense juggernaut.

The Wages of War: Shipyards, Aircraft Plants, and Universities

Although the term "military-industrial complex" was not coined until President Eisenhower used it in 1961, the web of connections between the Pentagon, military contractors, and universities was woven during World War II. California in the 1940s – with its military installations, shipyards and aircraft plants, and universities – played a leading role in shaping America's emergent military-industrial complex. Huge outlays of federal dollars sustained the three linked components of the complex. Of the $360 billion the federal government spent in the continental United States from 1940 to 1946 to prosecute the war and provide for defense, $35 billion went to California, which made sense given the state's geographical proximity to the Pacific theater of fighting, its ports, and the need to transport artillery and troops across the vast ocean lying at its doorstep. No other state west of the Mississippi received nearly as much federal money; only Michigan and New York received more. These expenditures provided employment opportunities, with good wages, that drew millions of job-seekers into the state, triggering a second gold rush.

In World War II the Bay Area, with its more than 30 shipyards and $5 billion in federal expenditures, boasted the largest shipbuilding complex in world history. The bayside towns of Richmond and Sausalito were home to the major yards producing Liberty ships – large military cargo vessels carrying weapons, munitions, tanks, jeeps, and other war matériel to battlefronts – as well as to 50 escort aircraft carriers, tankers, and other vessels.

From his corporate office in Oakland, industrialist Henry J. Kaiser, a key builder of the Boulder/Hoover Dam and founder of the Golden State's first steel plant in Fontana, oversaw the production of Liberty ships – and their larger variant, Victory ships – in Richmond

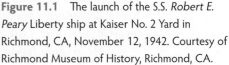

Figure 11.1   The launch of the S.S. *Robert E. Peary* Liberty ship at Kaiser No. 2 Yard in Richmond, CA, November 12, 1942. Courtesy of Richmond Museum of History, Richmond, CA.

California, Oregon, and Washington. More than 100,000 incoming workers and their families swelled the population of the once quiet bayside town that housed four interconnected shipbuilding yards. Using assembly-line and pre-fabrication techniques, Kaiser's Richmond shipyard set a record by building the S.S. *Robert E. Peary* in 4 days, 15 hours, and 26 minutes from the time the keel (the lengthwise bottom plate structure of the vessel) was laid. "Richmond yards . . . have produced more ships than any other yards in the country," concluded Vice Admiral H.L. Vickery in 1945 after surveying shipbuilding nationwide for President Roosevelt. The fact that Kaiser built 30 percent of America's wartime shipping, most of which was assembled in the Bay Area, speaks to the impact of the publicly financed private sector of Greater California. Progressive in his thinking, Kaiser provided workers with high wages, medical care for which Kaiser Permanente hospitals would become renowned, and exemption from military service since their labors were considered critical to the war effort.

In 1945–7, the war having been won, congresspersons critical of the New Deal and the billions of federal dollars that had gone into shipbuilding, charged that Kaiser had been a "war profiteer." Henry Kaiser responded sarcastically: "I recall quite vividly that it was important at one time to win the war [and] that ships were necessary to win the war."

Meanwhile, on the northern shore of the Bay other industrial magnates, including the Bechtel brothers (Kenneth and Stephen), built Liberty ships in the upscale Marin County town of Sausalito. Marinship, the name of their new company and assembly yard, employed 19,000 workers in 1942, and delivered 93 vessels including Liberty ships and tankers. A Master Agreement provided for a closed shop (union workers only), and an hourly wage of $1.20 for journeymen laborers, that is, those having gone through an apprenticeship and considered competent in their trade or craft. As at Richmond, the daily work cycle included three eight-hour shifts. Twelve to 15 percent of the workers lived in Marin City, an on-site public housing project that included its own post office, library, nursery and elementary schools, grocery stores, laundry and dry-cleaning establishments, a cafeteria, and a gymnasium. Rental housing ranged from dormitory rooms for $5.50 a week, to one-room apartments for $29 a month and six-room detached houses costing $43.50 a month. Rents included utilities and health care. Despite worker absenteeism and juvenile delinquency, the on-site living arrangement succeeded. Surveying "hundreds of war housing projects" nationwide in 1943, Massachusetts Congressman George Bates proclaimed Marin City "the best administered and best organized war housing project that I have seen." The relatively high pay and congenial working conditions attracted job-seekers from throughout the United States.

While shipbuilding and commercial transoceanic voyaging had a long and impressive record in California, the state's aircraft industry by contrast remained in its early stages of development until the late 1930s, when southern California surpassed New York as the leading builder of planes. As with shipbuilding, the Pearl Harbor attack led to a cascade of federal dollars being poured into the making of warplanes, which, in turn, catapulted California aviation even further into national prominence.

In 1942 aviation replaced filmmaking as the leading industry in southern California. The region's nearly year-round clear, safe weather conditions proved ideal for manufacturing and test-flying aircraft. President Roosevelt's call for 60,000 planes that year and 125,000 the following year doubtlessly spurred production, especially when accompanied by federal outlays for construction. The major airframe assembly plants, some virtually the size of cities, were located in Los Angeles and San Diego counties. In 1943 they employed 280,300 workers. Douglas, Lockheed, North American, and Northrop operated largely out of Los Angeles; Convair and Ryan were headquartered in San Diego. Lockheed, the most socially progressive of these companies, offered its workers food service, counseling, medical provision that included dental and optometry care, banking, and more. In 1944 the company was Los Angeles County's largest employer, with a workforce numbering 90,000.

Aviation spawned a major component of the nation's emerging military-industrial complex – government- and corporate-subsidized university research facilities. By the late 1930s the California Institute of Technology (Caltech) in Pasadena had become America's leading center for aeronautical engineering. Physicist Theodore von Karman, a foremost expert on rocketry at Caltech, interfaced with Army Air Corps Major General Henry (Hap) Arnold and other top military brass. In 1944 von Karman co-founded the school's Jet Propulsion Laboratory and chaired the Pentagon's Scientific Advisory Board, which explored space weapons technology in the coming decades.

Though other American universities contributed greatly to the war effort, the University of California played the most determinative role in World War II because of its leadership of the top-secret, federally subsidized Manhattan Project (1942–5) that developed the atomic bomb that ended the war. Two of the most gifted physicists in the world, Nobel Laureate Ernest O. Lawrence and J. Robert Oppenheimer, were UC Berkeley faculty members. In 1930 Lawrence invented the cyclotron, a device that whirled nuclear particles in a chamber at speeds sufficient to smash atoms. Later he built a Calutron, a device based on the cyclotron, while working in the Manhattan Project. By enabling the making of weapons-grade uranium, the Calutron paved the way for the creation of the atom bomb. Lawrence's colleague, Oppenheimer, recruited and managed brilliantly the team of scientists from other prominent universities throughout the nation who gathered in Los Alamos, New Mexico, to build such a weapon before Germany, Japan, and the Soviet Union did. America's dropping of two atomic bombs – one on Hiroshima and another on Nagasaki, Japan, in August 1945 – quickly ended the conflict while ushering in the nuclear age.

Finally, Scripps Institution of Oceanography, founded in 1903 and later attached to UC San Diego, also comprised the state's World War II-generated military-industrial complex.

Figure 11.2 J. Robert Oppenheimer. Oppenheimer graduated with the highest academic honors at Harvard, focusing on the sciences and Asian religions. He earned his doctorate in theoretical physics from the University of Göttingen in Germany, afterward teaching at Caltech and UC Berkeley. His leadership on the Manhattan Project later unsettled him. "I feel we have blood on our hands," he told President Harry S. Truman in the aftermath of America's use of atom bombs on Japan. Courtesy of the Los Alamos National Laboratory, New Mexico.

During the war the federal government extended $12 million in grants to Scripps for research into submarine acoustics.

The war demonstrated that California's universities were in the forefront of scientific research. By the late 1940s, Stanford took its place in the state's formidable military-industrial complex, as a major center for Pentagon-financed Cold War projects.

Opportunities and Prejudice: Women and Minorities

While the War Department segregated black servicemen into their own fighting units in World War II, with separate African American blood banks for those who were injured, on the home front workers of various ethnic backgrounds at times experienced a considerable degree of integration, especially in factories and shipyards. Wartime needs created unprecedented employment opportunities for women as so many able-bodied men were taken out of the workforce and sent overseas by the military. Shipyards needed more laborers than ever before, which also meant job openings for blacks and other nonwhites who entered the state in droves seeking work. Not all war industries, however, were open to ethnic minorities. As beneficial as the new economic opportunities were for previously marginalized groups, the stresses of war at times exacerbated white racism, causing ugly confrontations.

Jobs for women, mainly whites, on the home front were plentiful, particularly in the shipyards and aircraft factories. Women accounted for 23.3 percent of the total workforce at Marinship. Their presence angered some male employees, who felt that men were being displaced. Female employee Vianne Cochran reported in 1942 that one man "coughed and spat a big gob on my cheek." As she leaped at her tormenter, a security guard restrained her. Cochran then took her grievance to management with the result that the offending man was fired. Given the labor shortage, Marinship valued its female employees and took their concerns seriously. By late 1943 the company had more than 4,000 female employees; co-owner Kenneth Bechtel called them "first rate workers." In addition to serving as cafeteria and clerical personnel, many held positions in the skilled trades, such as welding. While women received pay equal to men in various job categories, females were less likely to be promoted than their male counterparts. Most likely, latent male sexism in the workplace was responsible for this. Still, under workplace conditions that had improved since World War I but were far less than ideal, women contributed mightily on the home front. As one Marinship executive put it: "America's wartime achievements in shipbuilding could not have been realized without women workers."

Across San Francisco Bay in Richmond, women comprised more than 27 percent of Kaiser shipyard's workforce. Most of them were married, and those who were parents took advantage of Kaiser's childcare facilities. About 40 percent of Kaiser's welders were female. The Rosie the Riveter Memorial, situated in Richmond, honors the women workers who contributed greatly to the wartime shipbuilding effort. Unions were less appreciative of female riveters, welders, and other workers who performed jobs customarily done by men. Because most shipyard unions affiliated with the American Federation of Labor were conservative in their social policies, many of the most powerful unions would not admit women into their ranks.

Women fared as well, if not better, in southern California's aircraft plants, where they were paid 60 cents an hour when the state's minimum wage was 40 cents an hour. In 1943 women constituted 42.4 percent of aviation's workforce in the region. Moreover, in comparison to males, females received comparable pay for comparable work. Generally smaller than men, women were able to weld and perform other tasks in tight places, making them particularly valuable employees in the aircraft industry. With increasing numbers of women working with men, aircraft plants became more sexualized. North American Aviation provided bands, dances, and date-counseling services. Lockheed contended with the problem of employees using its bomb shelters for lovemaking.

Like Anglo women, numerous non-Anglos of both sexes found jobs and encountered varying degrees of discrimination in wartime California. Circumstances mostly brightened for Chinese Americans. Many blacks secured work in the shipyards. Particularly embittering for African Americans was the prejudice directed at them while serving in the military. As Mexican nationals labored in the fields and on railroads, adolescent Mexican American males in East Los Angeles were targeted by U.S. servicemen on leave for bullying and beatings.

With China being an ally of the United States in World War II, Congress repealed the Chinese Exclusion Act in 1943. Consequently, employment opportunities outside of Chinatown opened for California's population of Chinese ancestry. Many took jobs in the Bay Area shipyards. One defense worker at Mare Island, Maggie Gee, took flying lessons in Nevada and afterward piloted military supply transports throughout the country for the Army Air Corps.

Prospects of employment in the war industries spurred a mass migration of blacks out of the rural South and into the urban North and West. The black population in the Bay Area alone jumped from fewer than 20,000 in 1940 to more than 60,000 by 1945. Seventy percent of the workers in this group were employed in shipbuilding. At Marinship blacks and whites worked peacefully together, though blacks were not allowed membership in the "lily white" Brotherhood of Boilermakers union.

Half of the West Coast-bound black migrants settled in Los Angeles. The city's African American population stood at 55,114 in 1940 and had more than doubled by 1944, reaching 118,888. Most working-age newcomers took jobs in the shipyards, with some 5,000 blacks employed by Calship. As in the Bay Area, major unions, such as the Boilermakers, denied them membership due to race but encouraged them to join "auxiliary locals," which gave them no voting rights in union affairs and smaller insurance benefits than white workers. Affiliated with all-white major unions, auxiliary locals were clearly second-class organizations whose members paid dues and yet their treasuries were controlled by the officers of the major unions. African American Fred Jones, among others, objected to this subordinate status, noting: "We have been forced into a Jim Crow outfit [meaning inferior auxiliary locals]." When Jones initially applied for shipyard work and admittance in the union he listed himself as "Hindu." Full union membership followed. Afterward, on telling labor officials that he was a "Negro," they switched his membership to auxiliary status.

In aviation, unlike shipbuilding, employment opportunities for African Americans did not materialize in the war years due to race-based discrimination. Most aircraft plants refused to hire blacks and made no secret of it. A spokesperson for the firm

Consolidated-Vultee wrote to the Los Angeles Council of the Negro Congress in August 1940: "I regret to say that it is not the policy of this company to employ people other than that of the Caucasian race." The following year the president of North American Aviation said: "Regardless of their training as aircraft workers we will not employ Negroes in the North American plant. It is against company policy."

An explosion of munitions in 1944 at the Port Chicago Naval Magazine, a weapons storage and transfer depot on the south shore of Suisun Bay north of San Francisco, laid bare racial tensions between blacks and whites in the military. The handling of ammunition was back-breaking, life-threatening work, and the navy assigned it almost exclusively to enlisted African American men. On the evening of July 17 a horrific explosion occurred at the depot, killing 320 servicemen, two-thirds of whom were blacks serving in a segregated unit. Another 233 of them were injured to varying degrees. On being told to return to their weapons-handling duties afterward, 50 members of the surviving unit refused to do so, citing the unsafe conditions. All were tried and convicted of mutiny, and sentenced to prison. Later, the navy admitted that "there can be no doubt that racial prejudice was responsible for the posting of African Americans" to the site of the disaster. Not until January of 1946, after the National Association for the Advancement of Colored People (NAACP) intervened, were 47 of the Port Chicago sailors released from prison and reassigned to ship duty. Two others were still in the hospital, and a third was detained for bad conduct while incarcerated.

While servicemen of Mexican descent were not segregated in the armed forces, where their valor was recognized, their adolescent civilian counterparts in Los Angeles found themselves increasingly at odds with law enforcement officers. Also, the press associated the young Latino males with delinquency. The Sleepy Lagoon murder trial, the round-up and arrest of Latino youths, followed by the Zoot Suit riots, exemplified the strains that war placed on Anglo-Hispanic racial relations on the home front.

On August 1, 1942, Jose Diaz had attended a party at a house near an East Los Angeles quarry called Sleepy Lagoon, often used by Hispanic youth for swimming. The next day he was found unconscious on a road near the house. He was taken to a nearby hospital, where he died. No direct evidence of murder was produced, nor were there any known witnesses to the mishap. A police investigation determined that the night before the body was found the alleged 38th Street Mexican American gang had crashed the party attended by Diaz and fighting had ensued. Later that month authorities indicted 23 members of that group, most of whom had jobs and were hard workers, for murder. In a courtroom presided over by a notoriously anti-Mexican judge, an all-white jury convicted 17 of the defendants of crimes ranging from assault to first-degree murder. Sheriff Department Lieutenant Ed Duran Ayres testified before the grand jury that Mexican Americans were given to blood lust and violence, traits inbred in them from their Aztec ancestors. He urged the imprisonment of all suspected Latino gangsters in the city, not just 38th Street gang members. Though the Second District Court of Appeals overturned the convictions on October 4, 1944, media depictions of Latino males remained negative.

Local Mexican American leaders challenged these negative depictions. Josefina Fierro de Bright, activist and president of El Congreso del Pueblo de Habla Española, with help from the city's largest Spanish-language newspaper *La Opinión*, worked to mobilize and defend

Los Angeles' Hispanic community. Their struggle would not end anytime soon. Though Mexican Americans distinguished themselves in combat overseas, in the wake of the Sleepy Lagoon murder trial the police, courts, and Hearst newspapers depicted young Angelinos of Mexican descent in East Los Angeles and elsewhere in the city as subversive and criminal. This was wartime, and public fears were easily heightened to hysteria by the media and officials.

Mass arrests of juvenile Latinos further strained racial relations in the City of Angels. The police in Los Angeles County kept a close watch on the pro-Axis Unión Nacional Sinarquista, a group with a colony in Baja California and some 400 members in southern California, a reminder of the continuous interchanges between the two Californias. When, on August 10, 1942, police in the county rounded up and arrested more than 600 Mexican American male youths on flimsy charges, the Sinarquistas warned that Californians of Hispanic heritage might soon be imprisoned in concentration camps. To many Anglos, Angelinos of Mexican descent were linked with the America-bashing Sinarquistas, and therefore were disloyal. Besides, these young men were not in the military, which made them vulnerable to the charge of being unpatriotic draft dodgers.

The Anglo racism stirred by the publicized Sleepy Lagoon incident and evidenced in the mass arrests of Latino youths that same year spilled over into press accounts of the Zoot Suit riots the following year, 1943. *Pachucos*, as the defiant adolescent Mexican American males living in barrios were called, resented off-duty American servicemen making advances to young Latinas in the dance halls and bars of Los Angeles. Sexual competition for females heightened tensions at the same time that the long hair and stylized dress of the *pachucos* seemed a rebuke of the plainer, clean-cut military look. *Pachuco* attire included long coats with well-padded shoulders and wide lapels, pleated pants, raised shoes, a watch or keys attached to a long chain, and a wide-brimmed hat. So conspicuously and self-consciously clad, zoot suiters were easy targets for police and servicemen.

Beginning on June 3, 1943, white sailors, soldiers, and civilians began a six-day hunt through parts of Los Angeles looking for zoot suiters to harass. When they found them, fighting ensued. The outnumbered, hapless *pachucos* were often beaten, stripped of their clothes, and shorn of their hair. Fortunately, no one was killed and only one serious injury resulted from the rioting. These assaults ended only when the navy cancelled leave into the city. Whatever the explanation for these attacks, they left a residue of racial ill will in Los Angeles that lasted long after World War II ended, and gave birth to a growing consciousness of what came to be known by the 1960s as Chicano cultural identity.

The prejudice and mistreatment that some Anglos directed at African Americans and Mexican Americans were bad. Yet these were not the only minority ethnic groups who suffered at the hands of the Caucasian majority in wartime California.

Japanese Imprisonment

California was pivotal to the federal government's program from 1942 to 1946 of removing and imprisoning people mainly of Japanese descent living along and beyond America's Pacific Rim from Alaska southward to Peru. War hysteria, racism, and political expedience in California led to the policy, say historians Donald T. and Nadine I. Hata, which affected tens of thousands of Japanese in California alone. "Military necessity," however, was the federal government's explanation for imprisoning people of Japanese ancestry in World War II.

War hysteria on the coast spread when on February 23, 1942, a Japanese submarine, 8 miles off the shore just north of Santa Barbara, fired shells at oil storage tanks. The salvo failed but put residents along the coast on edge. A *Los Angeles Times* headline read: "SUB-MARINE SHELLS SOUTHLAND OIL FIELD." During the next two weeks that same submarine sank several American cargo vessels along the California coast. Two days later military units in and near Los Angeles went on alert, and nighttime blackouts were ordered. Though these incidents occurred several days *after* Roosevelt's directive calling for Japanese removal from the Pacific Coast, they kept the public fear level high, sustaining widespread support for the imprisonment policy.

Anti-Japanese racism, rife in California since the beginning of the twentieth century, became even more virulent after the Pearl Harbor attack. In the immediate aftermath of that assault, General DeWitt declared: "The Japanese race is an enemy race and while many second and third generation Japanese born on American soil, possessed of United States citizenship, have become 'Americanized,' the racial strains are undiluted." Regardless of Americanization, he said, "a Jap is a Jap." DeWitt's view was expressed by many others, including media spokespersons and government officials pushing for incarceration. The anti-Japanese racism that helped lead to the removal policy is evident in the fact that German Americans and Italian Americans did not experience mass imprisonment during the war.

Political expediency, too, played a role in Japanese incarceration. Various social organizations and economic interests with lobbying clout urged removal. Among others, such groups included the American Legion, the Native Sons and Daughters of the Golden West, the American Growers Protective Association, the State Federation of Labor, and the Los Angeles Chamber of Commerce. Politicians, including Governor Culbert Olson, Attorney General Earl Warren, Los Angeles Mayor Fletcher Bowron, and many in California's congressional delegation had a great deal of public support in urging incarceration. According to DeWitt, the pressure for the removal policy came from "the best people of California."

The official rationale for removal was "military necessity," that is, fear of sabotage, or "fifth column" subversion on the home front. Accordingly, on February 19, 1942, President Roosevelt signed Executive Order 9066, which effectively authorized the removal and relocation of those of Japanese descent. While the Golden State did not house all of the war prisoners from the Pacific Coastal region, three-fourths of America's population of Japanese descent lived in California and most of them were imprisoned there. Others, including 3,000 Peruvians and other Latin Americans of Japanese ancestry, were removed to "Relocation Centers" in at least nine other states. Alaskan Indians, considered to be of Asian stock and in need of protection from Japanese forces that had recently seized some of the Aleutian Islands, were forcefully removed from their homeland in the northwestern parts of the then territory to its southwestern shores. Still, the command center for the incarceration program on the United States Pacific Coast was located in San Francisco where Lieutenant General John L. DeWitt carried out the removal policy that he had helped shape.

In 1942 some 93,000 Japanese Americans, designated by some scholars as Nikkei, lived in California, where virtually all were imprisoned at two camps: Manzanar in Owens Valley, and Tule Lake, just below the Oregon border. Most of these were *nisei*, meaning they had been born in the United States and, consequently, were American citizens. Their Japan-born parents, the *issei*, were categorized by the federal authorities as enemy aliens. Such legal distinctions made no difference in the matter of identifying those to be incarcerated. Overall, two-thirds of the Nikkei sent to American concentration camps were United States citizens.

Few Californians publicly opposed removal. Those who did acted courageously. Liberal journalist and historian Carey McWilliams denounced removal in his book *Prejudice: Japanese Americans, Symbol of Racial Intolerance* (1944). Chester H. Rowell, the prominent one-time editor of the *San Francisco Chronicle*, similarly was nearly a lone voice in his profession when he repudiated the policy. Quakers, too, publicly opposed Nikkei removal. Too few in numbers and influence to guide policymaking, all of these dissenters became witnesses to a race-based incarceration they could not stop.

While Germany's World War II concentration camps, where deaths in the millions occurred, were far worse than those in the United States, still conditions were horrid in America's "relocation" or "internment" camps, as they were oftentimes euphemistically called. President Roosevelt and other high-ranking officials used the term "concentration camps" when referring to the incarceration sites for Japanese aliens and U.S. citizens alike. En route to these barbed wire encampments still under construction, Nikkei were herded into assembly centers, which served as temporary quarters. Race tracks, fairgrounds, and other enclosed public venues served the purpose. Prisoners took up housekeeping, for example, in foul-smelling, insanitary stables at Santa Anita race track in Arcadia. From such places the War Relocation Authority moved prisoners to more permanent barracks, hastily built, mainly in desolate areas.

Understanding what conditions were like in these camps, with guard towers manned by machine-gun-bearing guards, does not require much imagination. Incarcerees have provided vivid accounts of what they experienced. Said one: "We lined up together for everything – cheek to cheek, tit to tit, and butt to butt. In order to build partitions to separate families, or kids from married couples, we first hung blankets or pieces of cloth. But it was so cold, we needed the blankets. Later, us kids slipped into the restricted lumber area and stole wood. But even then everyone could hear everything – from whispered lovemaking, to farts and family arguments . . . day after day, week after week. . . ." In addition to overcrowding, cold weather, and lack of privacy, inmates contended with poor food, frequent diarrhea, dust storms, and violence at the hands of guards and other prisoners. The psychological trauma, compounded by the embarrassing and humiliating living circumstances, is incalculable.

The most troublesome Nikkei prisoners, that is, those thought to be "disloyal" based on allegations of informants or answers incarcerees provided on a questionnaire to the effect that they were unwilling to swear unqualified allegiance to the United States and/or were unwilling to serve in the U.S. Armed Forces, were transferred to the concentration camp at Tule Lake. Approximately 18,000 prisoners were housed there. A thousand army military police plus tanks guarded the facility. At times the guards resorted to violence in their

Figure 11.3   A Manzanar evacuee resting on his cot after moving his belongings to this bare barracks room. Photo: Clem Albens. Courtesy of Bancroft Library, UC Berkeley.

treatment of "troublemakers." An FBI report, dated August 2, 1945, noted that three Nikkei prisoners "suspected of dissident behavior . . . [were] detained, savagely beaten, tortured and thrown into the stockade. One . . . suffered permanent mental impairment, one committed suicide, and the third, disillusioned with American justice, renounced [his U.S. citizenship] and repatriated to Japan."

Despite the harsh treatment the federal government meted out to Nikkei, including their losses of an estimated $400 million in property, which they sold for what they could get within days of their being rounded up and relocated by the authorities, some of the incarcerees volunteered for duty in the U.S. Armed Services. They formed the racially segregated 100th Infantry Battalion and the 442nd Regimental Combat Team, which fought in the European theater of conflict. These Japanese American units suffered 9,486 casualties, including 650 killed in action, and were awarded one Congressional Medal of Honor, 560 Silver Stars, 9,486 Purple Hearts, and seven Presidential Distinguished Unit Citations. For their numerical size, these were the most battle-decorated American units in World War II.

While Nikkei soldiers were fighting in Europe, their counterparts on the home front brought suit against the U.S. government, challenging the constitutionality of the removal policy. In one of several such cases, Fred Korematsu, a Californian, refused to be evacuated. His attorneys raised the issue of whether American citizens, because of their Japanese ancestry, could be imprisoned in what were "actually concentration camps." In 1944 the U.S. Supreme Court decided against Korematsu, contending that "the gravest imminent danger to the public safety" and the doubtful loyalty of persons of Japanese descent justified Executive Order 9066. In short, the removal policy was constitutional.

Though the Supreme Court deemed incarceration constitutional, was the policy a military necessity? In the hindsight of history, the answer is "no." The Japanese had no plans to invade the Pacific Coast, nor did DeWitt or other top military personnel claim otherwise. Even more telling, a U.S. Office of Naval Intelligence report in 1942 affirmed that Japanese Americans did not present a threat to American military security, and that there was no evidence of their alleged disloyalty. Before the Korematsu and other decisions, the U.S. Solicitor General at that time, Charles Fahy, deliberately withheld the report from the Supreme Court justices, which constituted an alarming dereliction of duty at the very least. Moreover, after the Battle of Midway in early June, 1942, Japan no longer had enough aircraft carriers to wage war anywhere in the central or eastern Pacific. Yet inmates were moved from the assembly centers to the camps after that battle. Shortly after the war ended, Californians came to see that a grave injustice had been committed against its Nikkei population. In 1988 the U.S. government formally apologized for its wartime removal and imprisonment policy.

Pacific Profile: Jeanne Wakatsuki Houston, Manzanar Inmate and Writer

Born in Inglewood, California, Jeanne Toyo Wakatsuki's life (1934–) seems much like those of others of Japanese descent who were forced into wartime captivity in Manzanar, among more than 10,000 other incarcerees. A major difference between her and her fellow prisoners, however, was that she worked through feelings of pain and humiliation enough to co-write a book, *Farewell to Manzanar: A True Story of Japanese-American Experience during and after the World War II Internment* (1973).

The youngest of 10 children whose father had been a commercial fisherman near Santa Monica, along with her family she was imprisoned at the age of 7 in 1942. Years after her family's release in 1945, she went on to graduate from San Jose State University, followed by study at the Sorbonne, University of Paris. Nearly 30

years transpired from the time of her imprisonment before she co-authored her unsentimental account, *Farewell to Manzanar*, at age 37. The time lag between her Manzanar experience and her reportage of it speaks to the deep psychological trauma, accompanied by felt shame, which she and others struggled with long after their farewells to the high desert prison camp. The time lag reveals something else as well: she had taken to heart a San Jose State journalism professor's advice that that field, which she wanted to enter, was essentially closed to aspiring Asian female writers. For years to come, she put her goal of becoming a journalist aside.

Even had she begun a journalism career on graduating, a delayed reaction to the travails of imprisonment served as a major block to telling her family's story. As she later explained to a *Los Angeles Times* contributor,

(Continued)

her experiences made her feel "sullied, like when you are a rape victim. . . . You feel you must have *done* something. You feel you are part of the act." Perhaps this is why, as she acknowledged, members of her family could only talk about their Manzanar years superficially, if at all.

This changed dramatically when her nephew, a student at UC Berkeley taking a sociology class, asked her in 1971 not about camp routines – the lousy food, "the Manzanar runs," communal showers, dust storms, and recreational activities – but rather how she *felt* "about being locked up like that." In an interview, she reflected: "He asked me a question no one had ever asked before, a question I had never dared to ask myself. Feel? How did I feel? For the first time I dropped the protective cover of humor and nonchalance. I allowed myself to 'feel.' I began to cry. I couldn't stop crying." Unable to regain her composure, they rescheduled their discussion.

Her nephew had opened a floodgate. She tried to write about it to satisfy the curiosity of her other many young nieces and nephews but made little progress. It fell to her husband, writer James Houston, to help steer her through the flood of emotions, memories, and pain

that gushed through that new opening into the once guarded part of her life.

"I'm having trouble writing this memoir," she told her husband. "What memoir is this?" he asked, not having been told of her project. For that matter, she had not yet confided even to him her rage and the psychological toll that imprisonment had taken on her life. "What seems to be the problem?" he asked. Embarrassed, she explained, "I can't stop crying whenever I try to write about Manzanar. I think I'm going crazy."

"Let's talk about it," he said, thus beginning their collaboration on *Farewell to Manzanar*. Published in 1973, she recalled that "my life changed" with the project. "I reclaimed pride in my heritage. I rediscovered my ability to write." The book has sold more than a million copies, and has been the subject of an award-winning television film. Public school libraries throughout California and other states have incorporated both the film and book into their curricula on history and civil rights. Jeanne Wakatsuki Houston has continued to write both works of fiction and non-fiction, and to speak to audiences across the country about civil rights in wartime and Asian American women's issues.

The Postwar Military-Industrial Complex and International Relations

Not only did federal military spending catapult the West Coast out of the depression, it also primed the region's economy for continued post-World War II growth. Most of that growth took place in California, whose military-industrial complex quickly grew into the most extensive nationwide. Meanwhile, San Francisco played a key postwar role in international relations, including Pacific security.

California's role as America's Pacific fortress became even more imposing after hostilities ended in 1945. In addition to the state's wartime military bases, many of which remained in operation after Japan's surrender, the Department of Defense took a major step in 1951 by relocating its Naval Postgraduate School (NPS) from Annapolis, Maryland, to a site overlooking the Pacific in Monterey, California. NPS, founded in 1909, has been a premier institution of higher learning for educating naval officers and defense specialists in military science and strategic planning. The move to California's shores speaks to the importance that the Department of Defense attached to the Pacific state's role in global security affairs.

In addition to Department of Defense facilities, war-related industries constituted a major component of the state's evolving military-industrial complex. Shipbuilding and aviation were of particular importance to California's postwar economic development.

Shipbuilding and repairing in postwar California took place mainly in the Bay Area, Long Beach, and San Diego, and had both naval and civilian sectors. Members of Congress whose districts included these port cities saw to it that federal appropriations subsidized naval shipbuilding and maintenance operations in these urban maritime centers. The United States Merchant Marine, with its own service academy in the Bay Area, was an auxiliary of the navy, and thus received federal military funding. The rationale for these naval-related disbursements was invariably the same and invariably succeeded: national security. Just beneath the surface, however, loomed the always significant matter of jobs. The Long Beach naval shipyard, which had closed after the war ended, reopened in 1951, thereby cutting the state's unemployment rate by half.

Civilian shipbuilders also sought and benefited from federal defense outlays. In 1949 the federal government assigned to Bay Area shipyards five of the 35 shipbuilding contracts awarded nationwide. These contracts gave a needed boost to the state's postwar maritime economy and translated into jobs for Bay Area workers.

While the shipbuilding and repairing industry struggled to remain alive in the late 1940s and early 1950s, aircraft-related enterprises prospered more than ever before. The Cold War was on, the U.S. Air Force emerged as a separate branch of the armed services in 1947, and California had the nuclear weapons laboratory, the aircraft companies and their ancillary manufacturers, and the university research programs to put the state in the forefront of the new aerospace industries. These enterprises included the designing of jet aircraft for commercial and military uses as well as the building of missiles and other space weapons.

In the first postwar decade and a half, Douglas, Lockheed, and North American were joined by Rocketdyne, Aerospace Corporation, and Litton Industries as major defense contractors. These companies were based in southern California. Numerous smaller spinoff businesses, for example, Aerocraft Heat Treating, founded in Paramount in 1947 by gifted entrepreneur William Dickson to provide metallurgical services related to aircraft manufacture and maintenance, dotted the Southland.

By 1960, 25 percent of America's defense expenditures and 42 percent of Pentagon research contracts went to firms and universities in the Golden State. The cluster of California's universities engaged in military research was unmatched in any other state, and included UC Berkeley, Caltech, and Stanford. Berkeley, under contract with the federal Atomic Energy Commission, ran the Los Alamos Scientific Laboratory in New Mexico, the Livermore Laboratory in the Bay Area, and the radiation laboratory on its own campus. Caltech's Jet Propulsion Laboratory developed guided missiles. Stanford, partnering with General Electric Company and Lockheed, began receiving Defense Department contracts for electronic research in the 1950s, drawing the Silicon Valley into the state's military-industrial complex. Like these leading universities, RAND Corporation (an acronym signifying scientific research and development) produced knowledge on which public policy could be based. It was initially part of Douglas but established itself as an independent "think tank" in Santa Monica in 1947. Much but by no means all of RAND's contract work has been related to military security.

The jobs created by the military-industrial complex, particularly in aircraft plants and shipyards, continued to draw blue-collar and white-collar workers into California after 1945. High-tech engineers and scientists also followed the job market to the Golden State, whose population increased dramatically in the aftermath of World War II.

Beyond the scale of its huge military-industrial economy, California's role in postwar international relations was equaled by few, if any, other states. The Golden State's role was underscored in the writing of the United Nations Charter, and the negotiation of two treaties regarding Allied–Japanese relations and military security in the western Pacific region.

After several earlier efforts had met with little success, the Western world's centuries-old dream of creating a concert of peace-seeking nations to end the scourge of major war made headway in San Francisco. For two months beginning on April 25, 1945, delegates from approximately 50 countries assembled in that city for a high-level conference that wrote the charter founding the United Nations. Accordingly, the gathered powers established a Trusteeship Council to handle the disposition of islands once ruled by Japan; permanent members of the powerful Security Council (the United States, the Soviet Union, Britain, France, and China) were installed, each with the right of veto; a General Assembly giving voice to the smaller nations was set up; and the International Court of Justice was born. U.S. President Harry S. Truman arrived at the conference and gave his approval of its work. Inspired by their city's role in giving birth to the United Nations, in 1947 San Franciscans founded the West Coast's largest foreign policy organization, the northern California chapter of the prestigious World Affairs Council that brings together international leaders, academicians, and business luminaries to weigh and discuss the leading foreign policy issues of the time.

Japan, meanwhile, remained occupied by the U.S. military, which oversaw the pacification of that nation from 1945 until 1951, when, again in San Francisco, a major international conference was held. The purpose of the meeting was twofold: first, to negotiate a peace treaty between 46 World War II allied nations, led by the United States, and their former enemy; and second, to ensure peaceful relations in the Asian Pacific region, meaning the countries in the western Pacific near or bordering the Asian continent. The San Francisco Peace Treaty, as it is often called, returned sovereignty to Japan while committing that country and the signatory powers to the peaceful resolution of disputes, allowing for the negotiation of agreements providing for U.S. bases on Japanese islands in the Pacific, and renouncing any Allied rights to reparations from Japan. The pact went into effect in 1952. While the peace treaty was being negotiated, top American and Japanese officials also signed the Japan–U.S. Security Treaty, pledging the United States to defend Japan in return for the right to establish bases on its territory. Taken together, MIT historian John Dower terms these two agreements "The San Francisco System," which has shaped U.S.–Japan relations and Pacific security ever since. All of this happened in the City by the Bay in a California whose international stature in the mid-twentieth century, especially in the Pacific Basin, was becoming greater by the day.

Population Growth, Housing, and Discrimination

California's population, which had grown considerably during World War II, continued to swell afterward. In 1945 the state's residents numbered 9.3 million; five years later that figure had increased to just below 10.6 million people. Returning servicemen, including those who had lived in other states before the war, comprised a large segment of the growth.

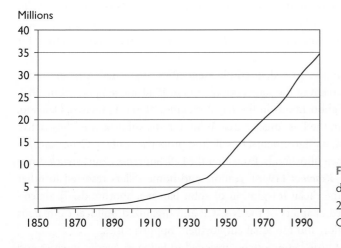

Figure 11.4   California's population has increased dramatically over time. Source: *Cal Facts* (December 2000), p. 13. Legislative Analyst's Office, State of California.

While accurate counts are lacking, a good many gay men and lesbians were among the returning veterans who settled in San Francisco and Los Angeles, where they found greater acceptance than elsewhere. Los Angeles in 1945 became the fourth largest U.S. city, and home to 1.9 million people blanketing 451 square miles. In 1962 Greater California eclipsed New York, becoming the most populous state in the nation.

Such a dramatic population increase put severe strains on the state's infrastructure. Governor Earl Warren observed in August 1948: "The stampede has visited us with unprecedented civic problems, partly because we did not expect to digest so much population in so short a time, and partly because even if we had been forewarned we could have done but little to prepare for the shock during the stringent war years. So we have an appalling housing shortage, our schools are packed to suffocation, and our highways are inadequate and dangerous. We are short of water and short of power, and our sanitation and transportation systems are overtaxed. Our hospitals and our corrective institutions are bursting at the seams." This lament, probably unintentionally, laid out California's infrastructure-building agenda for the next two decades.

To alleviate the need for homes, the late 1940s saw the beginning of California's tract housing boom. Tract houses usually were built on small, subdivided lots, adjacent to one another; developers simultaneously constructed multiple homes, using a small number of floor plans and prefabricated materials – all of which kept building costs and purchase prices down. Agricultural lands were encroached on, and new suburbs appeared up and down the state but mostly in the Southland. Lakewood, located 10 miles southeast of Los Angeles, arose in 1950 out of a former beet field and within three years boasted a population of 70,000 inhabitants living in affordable, detached, single-family tract homes. The construction industry profited enormously. As armed services veterans, a large number of Lakewood's residents enjoyed federal GI Bill home financing and worked at the nearby Douglas plant. The so-called Lakewood Plan of retaining budgetary power in local matters while contracting with Los Angeles County for road repair, sewer services, and fire protection was adopted in new communities throughout many parts of the country. To the north, parts of the suburban Bay Area also registered a tract housing boom, especially in Santa Clara Valley communities like San Jose, where orchards were cleared for home-building.

While the state's white suburbs thrived, its ethnic inner cities languished. African Americans, who constituted 1.8 percent of the state's population in 1940 and 4.3 percent in 1950, lived largely in all-black neighborhoods in the Bay Area cities of San Francisco, Oakland, and Berkeley, and in Watts in the Los Angeles area. Whites in the suburbs used "restrictive covenants," that is, homeowners' agreements, to sell their properties only to Caucasians, to control home sales in their neighborhoods. Even after the U.S. Supreme Court struck down such contracts in *Shelley v. Kraemer* (1948), realtors and home sellers resorted to other informal ploys to prevent the racial integration of suburban neighborhoods. To defend their interests, blacks formed chapters of the NAACP and organized political campaigns against housing discrimination and for equal employment opportunities.

Mexican Americans fared little better, often consigned to living in *barrios* in cities and some suburbs. Like blacks, Latinos fought discrimination against them by working through organizations like LULAC, the League of United Latin American Citizens. In one particularly notable instance of combating segregation in public schools, Orange County residents Gonzalo and Felicitas Mendez brought a class action suit against the Westminster and several other Orange County school districts, charging discrimination against the couple's young children who in 1943 were denied admission to the 17th Street School in Westminster. Officials said that the children were dark-skinned and could not speak English. The parents were told to enroll their children in a Mexican school 10 blocks away from the white school.

The Mendez parents refused, took their case to court, and won, first in the Los Angeles Federal District Court, and then in the federal judiciary's 9th Circuit Court of Appeals. In *Mendez v. Westminster* (1947), the judges held that the California constitution prohibited segregation of Mexican-origin children into separate schools. National (Mexican) origin, not race, was the issue in this case. Still it set a precedent in seemingly being the first case leading to the eventual overturning of *Plessy v. Ferguson* (1896), in which the U.S. Supreme Court upheld the "separate but equal" doctrine in public facilities. According to that doctrine, separate public facilities were legal or constitutional as long as the facilities in question were equal. In *Plessy v. Ferguson* the constitutionality of racially segregated train cars was at issue. Some of the arguments used by the plaintiffs' attorneys in *Mendez v. Westminster* were used by plaintiff attorney Thurgood Marshall in the U.S. Supreme Court's landmark decision in *Brown vs. the Board of Education* (1954), which struck down the "separate but equal" doctrine once and for all. Thereafter, white schools throughout the nation could no longer bar students of other ethnic backgrounds.

Meanwhile in 1949 Mexican American Edward Roybal won election to the Los Angeles city council, the first person of his ethnicity to do so since the late 1800s. With help from community organizer Fred Ross and the politically charged Community Service Organization of East Los Angeles, Roybal had campaigned on ending discrimination in housing, employment, and education. With his victory, Hispanics began to sense their political clout when they mobilized voters.

Green Gold: Agribusiness and Labor

In World War II's aftermath, California's rapidly growing military and civilian populations had to be fed, necessitating a further increase of cropland productivity. In the postwar era and through the 1950s commercial agriculture continued to be the leading sector in the state's burgeoning economy. Throughout that time, crops accounted for 61 percent of the state's agricultural output, and livestock 39 percent. Cheap, plentiful water, an inexpensive labor force, and further mechanization of farming lowered production costs, ensuring affordable prices for California farm products in a national market. By 1950 an "agricultural-industrial complex" had formed, taking modernization of farming to a new level. The lucrative fruits (and their derivatives such as wine), nuts, vegetables, and other plants from the state constituted, in effect, "green gold."

Water for irrigation was the key to California's farming economy. In 1951 the 117-mile-long Delta–Mendota Canal was in operation, transporting water southeasterly from Tracy in the San Joaquin Valley to Mendota, 30 miles west of Fresno, completing the Central Valley Project. Growers in that agricultural hinterland thereafter had a reliable supply of water for field irrigation. By 1960, in part due to irrigation, the Central Valley's farm products were valued at $3 billion, nearly 9 percent of the total value of U.S. farm income. Similarly, growers in the southern desert valleys could count on ample quantities of Colorado River water to make their arid lands bloom into gardens.

Ample water, however, came at an environmental cost. Agribusiness, enticed by record profits and an expanding national market for California fruit, wine, wheat, cotton, and vegetables, tapped into aquifers (pools of underground water) to increase cultivated acreage. When aquifers were thereby drained, the ground above often sank, creating depressions 30 or more feet in depth. Subsided land tended to be dry, leaving a soil that became dusty and windswept.

A low-paid, dependable labor force was scarcely less important than water. Such farm workers were recruited from Mexico, underscoring the economic interdependencies between California and its Pacific Rim neighbor to the south. In 1942 the U.S. Department of Agriculture oversaw a program authorized by a Congressional Act and treaty that brought Mexican farm workers called *braceros* (the term means "strong-armed ones") to harvest California crops. The federal government thereby assured agribusiness a captive labor force whose contracts with growers prohibited strikes. In 1957 growers had 192,438 *braceros* working in California's fields. Two years later the AFL-CIO (American Federation of Labor-Congress of Industrial Organizations) launched a campaign to stop the flow of these foreign workers into the United States on the grounds that they lowered wages and working conditions for American field hands. The program ended in 1964. As important as *bracero* labor was, it constituted only 30 percent of the entire migrant workforce from Mexico that harvested California's crops.

Mechanization of farming further facilitated agribusiness. Diesel engines came into use on tractors and other equipment. Aircraft seeded, fertilized, and dusted crops with various chemical compounds aimed at preventing plant diseases and curbing insect blights. By mid-century an "agricultural-industrial complex" had emerged. The state supplied water

Figure 11.5   Dorothea Lange, *First Braceros*,
c.1942. © The Dorothea Lange Collection, Oakland
Museum of California, City of Oakland. Gift of Paul
S. Taylor.

from the Central Valley Project and scientists from UC Davis, California's preeminent
agricultural institution of higher education; manufacturers produced chemical fungicides,
herbicides, and pesticides developed by UC Davis scientists; and large growers, assured of
water and chemicals, expanded their acreage. The result was a network of ties between
researchers, manufacturers, and agribusiness that made California the nation's leading state
beginning in 1948 in terms of the value of its agricultural output. Los Angeles County
alone, according to University of California agronomist Rachel Surls, surpassed Iowa and
all other Midwestern states in the value of crop production in the early 1950s.

Governor Earl Warren: Progressive Republican

The return of prosperity in wartime California, occasioned in part by agricultural growth,
made it easy for Republican Earl Warren to defeat Democratic incumbent Culbert L. Olson
in the gubernatorial campaign of 1942. With the depression ended, Warren's tax cuts resonated with business interests. A state economy booming with federal wartime spending
allowed him to save public money that in the late 1940s could be invested in highway
construction and higher education. These later expenditures made him popular and able
to withstand criticism of his essentially progressive policies from his party's right wing.

Born in Los Angeles in 1891, Warren grew up in Bakersfield and graduated from UC
Berkeley and its law school before gaining notoriety as a public prosecutor. He had served
as attorney general before winning the governorship, and went on to establish a record by

occupying that office for 10 years and 8 months, having been elected in 1942, 1946, and 1950. Warren's electoral successes and rise to national prominence by mid-century were due in part to his and the state's non-partisanship orientation.

Non-partisanship favored Republicans. Though Democrats outnumbered Republicans in California from 1942 to 1958, the former usually elected Republicans to the higher state offices. This peculiar pattern developed for mainly two reasons: first, cross-filing allowed candidates' names to appear on the primary ballots of the opposing party with no affiliation indicated; and second, incumbents' names appeared at the top of those ballots. Generally, Republicans were better educated and informed about party affiliation and their candidates played down their party membership. Democratic voters gravitated toward choosing the name at the top of the primary ballot, which was usually that of a Republican. Those candidates winning the primaries of both parties, as Warren did in 1950, won elections.

Republicans were also helped greatly by the wealth of business interests in their party and editorial assistance from the state's most influential newspapers, including the *Los Angeles Times*, the *San Francisco Chronicle*, and the *Oakland Tribune*. As businesses themselves, these powerful newspapers liked the Republicans' emphasis on low taxes and minimal regulation. All of these factors benefited Warren, despite his drift toward progressivism, which antagonized the Republican right but appealed to Democrats and unions.

The first indications of Warren's center-left leanings came in 1945. As western European countries were repairing and strengthening their welfare states, Warren alarmed California conservatives by urging passage of a compulsory health insurance law, a measure that had been unsuccessfully promoted by a few progressives in 1916. Opposition from the California Medical Association, insurance companies, and political conservatives blocked action on Warren's proposal, distancing him from right-leaning Republicans. In 1947 oil and trucking lobbies fought unsuccessfully Warren's bid to increase the gasoline tax to finance the system of highways and freeways that he saw as necessary for the state's postwar economic growth.

Warren's staunch support for the University of California and his environmentalism endeared him to many liberals. He served on the UC Board of Regents, and all six of his children graduated from the university's various campuses. Earl Warren College, founded in 1974 on the campus of UC San Diego, was named in his honor, as was a legal institute at UC Berkeley's law school. Though the term environmentalist had not yet come into use, Warren was an outdoorsman who loved to hike, hunt, and fish in the wilds of the state. He worked with UC Berkeley Professor Emanuel Fritz to expand the state's Forestry Service and replenish timberland, while promoting wildlife preservation and the licensing of fishing and hunting.

Though Warren was an unsuccessful contender for the Republican nomination for the White House in 1952, he remained a national figure in that party. The following year President Eisenhower appointed the then California governor as chief justice of the U.S. Supreme Court. Meanwhile, the nation and California were caught up in the Cold War and combating Soviet influence abroad and at home. California politics became polarized, even frenzied, in the late 1940s and early 1950s as Richard M. Nixon first gained statewide and then national attention in the fight against communism.

Richard Nixon and the Anti-Communist Crusade

Even before Japan's surrender in 1945, the Soviet–American wartime alliance began to unravel under mounting strain. The United States was displeased about Soviet expansion into eastern Europe and the Soviet Union felt uneasy about the United States' development of an atomic bomb. Even as World War II was ending, the Cold War was beginning.

The political climate nationally and in the state was ripe for ambitious politicians to challenge office-holding Democrats on the issues of national security and loyalty. In the Golden State, heated disputes regarding communism arose in Hollywood's film industry and on several campuses of the University of California.

Orange County, a stronghold of Republican conservatism, was home to Richard Milhous Nixon, a rising young politician who knew just how to turn Cold War issues to his electoral advantage. Born in Yorba Linda to Quaker parents who owned a small store, Nixon entered Whittier College on a scholarship. On graduating, he went on to earn a law degree at Duke University. Following a World War II stint in the U.S. Navy, serving as a lieutenant commander in the South Pacific, he returned home and entered politics.

Some Orange County millionaires saw in Nixon the drive and other qualities they desired in a Congressperson. Consequently, they backed his candidacy as the Republican challenger to unseat Democratic Representative Jerry Voorhis in the 1946 election. The liberal, scholarly, genteel Voorhis never knew what hit him as the bare-knuckle political tactics employed by the Nixon campaign carried the day. For example, Nixon claimed that Voorhis's voting record in Congress was "Socialistic and Communistic." Just days before the election, voters received anonymous phone calls: "Did you know that Jerry Voorhis is a Communist?" Afterward, Nixon acknowledged: "Of course I knew that Jerry Voorhis wasn't a Communist, but I had to win . . . Nice guys . . . don't win many elections." Nixon used similar smear tactics, for which he became known, in his successful 1950 campaign for the U.S. Senate, defeating Democratic nominee Helen Gahagan Douglas. A liberal Democrat, Douglas was mischaracterized as "the Pink Lady" whose voting record in Congress allegedly reflected her communist sympathies.

Nixon's rising profile in the Republican Party landed him a place on the party's victorious ticket in the 1952 election, in which he ran as Dwight D. Eisenhower's vice-presidential running mate. The California Senator's political prospects suddenly brightened.

Meanwhile, the House Un-American Activities Committee (HUAC), founded in 1938 to investigate subversives nationwide, turned its attention on the Hollywood film industry, which was suspected of employing communists. In 1947 HUAC worked from a list of 250 actors, writers, and directors it suspected of having communist ties; they were all eventually fired. During the next five years, film moguls Jack Warner, Louis B. Mayer, and Walt Disney were joined by the president of the Screen Writers Guild, Ronald Reagan, in helping HUAC investigators ferret out "Reds." Some cinema stars, including Humphrey Bogart, Lauren Bacall, Judy Garland, and Katherine Hepburn, endangered their careers by publicly denouncing the "Red Scare" and its ruination of careers.

At the same time that film people were placed in the crosshairs of HUAC, Jack B. Tenney of Los Angeles served as chair of a joint California legislature Fact-Finding Committee on

Un-American Activities. In response to the committee's charges of communist activity and affiliations among University of California faculty, the university's regents adopted a loyalty oath in early 1949.

The regents' oath required university personnel to swear that they were not communists and "did not support any party or organization that believes in, advocates, or teaches the overthrow of the United States Government . . ." In August 1950, 32 professors who refused to sign the oath were terminated for insubordination. Many distinguished scholars who had no communist ties refused to take the oath on the grounds that it violated academic freedom and the California constitution. UC Berkeley psychology professor Edward C. Tolman led the non-signers in suing the regents, represented by the board's secretary and treasurer, Robert M. Underhill. A state supreme court decision in *Tolman v. Underhill* (1952) declared the oath invalid since only the legislature possessed the power to impose it. Consequently, the professors were offered reinstatement.

Meanwhile, three happenings in Pacific Rim nations in the mid-twentieth century intensified the loyalty oath debate in postwar California politics: the Soviet Union's detonation of an atomic bomb (August 29, 1949), the communists' takeover of China (October 1949), and the outbreak of the Korean War (June 25, 1950). Amid these Cold War developments, in 1950 the California legislature passed the Levering Act, requiring *all* state employees, including university faculty, to take an even more stringent loyalty oath or risk losing their jobs. The Levering oath, too, met with resistance from some faculty members. In 1967 the state's supreme court ruled that this oath was unconstitutional largely on grounds that it violated First Amendment rights and that membership in an organization did not, in itself, prove disloyalty.

The Red Scare of the mid-twentieth century evoked a liberal backlash that slowly gained momentum in the 1950s. An era known for free expression, reform, and major government-sponsored infrastructure upgrades was at hand.

SUMMARY

War in the Pacific followed by Cold War, particularly in the Asia-Pacific region, shaped developments in the Golden State in the 1940s and early 1950s. The Japanese attack on Pearl Harbor resulted in California becoming the West Coast's command center and staging area for U.S. military operations in the Pacific theater of World War II. Overnight the state's shipyards, aircraft plants, and public universities – particularly UC Berkeley – merged into a military-industrial complex that would influence national policy and ensure robust economic growth in California for the next half-century. Women and minorities enjoyed defense industry employment opportunities unimagined before America's entry into the war. Racial discrimination, assuredly, did not disappear, as demonstrated in the Zoot Suit riots, the imprisonment of civilian Japanese Americans on the basis of their ethnicity (later seared into the consciousness of readers worldwide by Jeanne Wakatsuki Houston's memoir *Farewell to Manzanar*), and the explosion at the Port Chicago Naval Magazine. San Francisco captured international attention as the founding city of the United Nations and later venue for the treaty-making ending America's war with Japan.

In the aftermath of World War II, many discharged service people settled in California at the same time that job-seekers from throughout America streamed into the state where opportunities invariably bumped up against racial prejudice against non-whites. Feeding and housing newcomers led to booms in agriculture and construction. *Braceros* from California's Pacific seaboard neighbor, Mexico, worked the fields for a pittance under conditions that few whites could, or would, endure. Mexican Americans fought discrimination against their children in the state's public schools as blacks opposed restrictive covenants aimed at keeping them from living in white neighborhoods.

Developments along the Pacific Rim – the Soviet Union's detonation of an atomic bomb, China's fall to the communists, and the Korean War – shaped politics. Tapping into and at times stoking voters' fears of communism, Republicans usually triumphed at election time. Governor and then U.S. Supreme Court Chief Justice Earl Warren was the face of progressive-minded Republicanism in Cold War California while Congressman and later vice president Richard Nixon was the face of militant Republican anti-communism.

REVIEW QUESTIONS

- What accounts for California's commanding home front role in the Pacific theater of World War II?
- What were the major components of California's military-industrial complex in World War II, and what role did that cluster of institutions play in the state's economy in the immediate aftermath of the conflict?
- What factors were responsible for the imprisonment of American citizens of Japanese ancestry in California during World War II?
- What were the major instances of racial discrimination against non-whites in California during the 1940s?
- In what ways did international developments along the Pacific Rim, for example, the communists' takeover of China, in the late 1940s and early 1950s shape California politics?

FURTHER READINGS

Bruce Cumings, *Dominion from Sea to Sea: Pacific Ascendancy and American Power* (New Haven, CT: Yale University Press, 2009). This book is a leader among recent studies giving the Pacific its due significance in shaping the history of the United States, the Far West, and California.

Roger Daniels, *Concentration Camps USA: Japanese Americans and World War II* (New York: Holt, Rinehart & Winston, 1972). This classic account provides a cautionary tale about the injustices that racist-minded majorities in a democracy can inflict on ethnic minorities.

Edward J. P. Davis, *The United States Navy and U.S. Marine Corps at San Diego* (San Diego, CA: Pioneer Press, 1955). The author provides one of the few detailed studies of San Diego's Navy-Marine Corps history during World War II.

Iris Engstrand, *San Diego: California's Cornerstone* (San Diego, CA: Sunbelt Publications, 2005). A leading historian of Pacific maritime affairs provides sound coverage of San Diego during World War II and its immediate aftermath.

Mark S. Foster, *Henry J. Kaiser: Builder in the Modern American West* (Austin, TX: University of Texas Press,

1989). For a reliable, balanced, thoroughly researched account of this entrepreneurial California capitalist who worked closely with government, this book is unmatched.

David G. Gutiérrez, *Walls and Mirrors: Mexican Americans, Mexican Immigrants, and the Politics of Ethnicity* (Berkeley: University of California Press, 1995). The author shows that government and regional businesses have actively recruited workers from Mexico, and that immigrants from that country have maintained their cultural identity by living in Spanish-speaking American enclaves.

Donald T. Hata and Nadine I. Hata, *Japanese Americans and World War II: Mass Removal, Imprisonment, and Redress* (Wheeling, IL: Harlan Davidson, 2011). This invaluable small book gives an overview of the removal policy and redress movement, and updates readers on the appropriate terminology and recent scholarship on the subject.

Marilyn S. Johnson, *The Second Gold Rush: Oakland and the East Bay in World War II* (Berkeley: University of California Press, 1993). The author contends that the changes that World War II brought to the Bay Area, particularly through its shipbuilding industry, were as great as those occasioned by the gold rush era.

Roger W. Lotchin, *The Bad City in the Good War: San Francisco, Los Angeles, Oakland, and San Diego* (Bloomington, IN: Indiana University Press, 2003). While cities are often stereotyped as centers of crime and graft, this work shows that the state's urban areas were indispensable in weapons production and provided major military installations in World War II, the so-called "good war."

Roger W. Lotchin, *Fortress California, 1910–1961: From Warfare to Welfare* (New York: Oxford University Press, 1992). This work traces the close ties between California's cities, particularly those on the coast, and the emergent military-industrial complex that became such an important component of the state's economy.

Abraham F. Lowenthal, *Global California: Rising to the Cosmopolitan Challenge* (Stanford, CA: Stanford University Press, 2009). Though not essentially a work of history, the book places the opportunities and challenges facing California today within a context of the state's ever-increasing global presence.

Carey McWilliams, *Prejudice: Japanese-Americans, Symbol of Racial Intolerance* (Boston: Little, Brown, 1945). This volume, written by a journalist-historian who publicly denounced the removal policy at the time of its implementation, examines the historical roots of the racial prejudice directed at Japanese Americans in World War II.

Gerald D. Nash, *World War II and the West: Reshaping the Economy* (Lincoln, NE: University of Nebraska Press, 1990). The author argues that large-scale federal investment in the American West during the war years reshaped the region's economy, resulting in the Pacific Coast states – particularly California – becoming the cultural pacesetters for the nation.

Walter Nugent, *Into the West: The Story of Its People* (New York: Vintage Books, 2001). Moving beyond Anglocentric and politically focused histories of the West, the author narrates the region's rich multicultural past, giving due attention to urbanization as well.

John B. Rae, *Climb to Greatness: The American Aircraft Industry, 1920–1960* (Cambridge, MA: MIT Press, 1968). Though not a recent publication, this critically acclaimed volume is still the starting point for the serious study of twentieth-century aviation in the United States.

Kevin Starr, *Embattled Dreams: California in War and Peace, 1940–1950* (New York: Oxford University Press, 2002). This comprehensive account treats the social, economic, and political history of California in the 1940s with a novelist's sensibility for narrative, poignancy, and detail.

John Tateishi, *And Justice for All: An Oral History of the Japanese American Detention Camps* (New York: Random House, 1984). Based on interviews with men and women of Japanese descent who were incarcerated, as well as with incarcerees who enlisted in the famed 442nd Regimental Combat Team, this is a work of testimony given by those who experienced wartime imprisonment due largely to race.

Arthur C. Verge, *Paradise Transformed: Los Angeles during the Second World War* (Dubuque, IA: Kendall/Hunt Publishing, 1993). Contemporary concerns about defending Los Angeles from attack, race relations, rapid economic growth, and more are treated expertly in this study of wartime Los Angeles.

Richard A. Walker, *The Conquest of Bread: 150 Years of Agribusiness in California* (New York: The New Press, 2004). This highly regarded volume analyzes the environmental, labor, capital, biochemical, and technological components that together have turned the state into the world's most productive agricultural region.

Charles Wollenberg, *Marinship at War: Shipbuilding and Social Change in Wartime Sausalito* (Berkeley: Western Heritage Press, 1990). This brief book is particularly strong in its treatment of class, gender relations, and race at a major wartime shipbuilding facility in the San Francisco Bay Area.

12

Liberalism at High Tide

California's post-World War II boom coincided with a center-left political era during which state government became increasingly activist in ways favored more by liberals than by conservatives. Huge federal and state government outlays provided for jobs, flood control, water distribution, highways, new schools, and a world-class public higher education system. The incoming tide of political liberalism peaked during the governorship of Edmund G. "Pat" Brown in the late 1950s and early 1960s.

Growth was the mantra of the times. California became the nation's most populous state, boasting the world's most productive farmland. Because of these and related developments, Governor Brown noted that "the balance of the most powerful nation of the world will shift from the Atlantic to the Pacific. . . . The implications are vast." To him and many others, the Golden State would be the epicenter of this Pacific shift that would showcase the economic, political, and cultural prominence of a rising California.

However, the tide on which prosperity and public spending washed over the state also brought with it crowding and continued hardship for many people of color. A major race riot erupted in Los Angeles. With increasing numbers of students, public institutions of higher learning became more bureaucratic and seemingly unresponsive to students' demands for racial equality and a voice in educational policy matters. Nationwide UC Berkeley was viewed as ground zero for the playing out of the heady idealism and mounting tensions that characterized California during its liberal heyday. The conservative opposition that arose is treated in Chapter 13.

Pacific Eldorado: A History of Greater California, First Edition. Thomas J. Osborne.
© 2013 Thomas J. Osborne. Published 2013 by Blackwell Publishing Ltd.

Timeline

1955   The Hollywood movie *Rebel Without a Cause* catapults James Dean and Natalie Wood into stardom

The Disneyland amusement park opens in Anaheim

Allen Ginsberg reads his controversial poem "Howl" at San Francisco's famed Six Gallery arts venue

1958   The New York Giants and Brooklyn Dodgers professional baseball teams relocate to San Francisco and Los Angeles, respectively

Congress passes a law abolishing 41 California Indian reservations

1959   The Unruh Civil Rights Act passes in the state legislature, prohibiting businesses from discriminating on the basis of race, gender, sexual orientation, religion, and medical condition, and providing for redress in the courts when evidence of bias exists

The state legislature passes the Water Resources Development Bond (Burns–Porter) Act authorizing putting before California voters a $1.75 billion bond issue incorporated in Proposition 1

Cross-filing is abolished in California elections

1960   The Minneapolis Lakers professional basketball team relocates to Los Angeles

California hosts the Winter Olympics at Squaw Valley near Lake Tahoe

A Master Plan for Higher Education in California, 1960–1975, creating a world-class system of public higher education, is put into effect

Voters approve the Burns–Porter bond issue, marking the beginning of the epic State Water Project

25 percent of America's defense expenditures and 42 percent of Pentagon research contracts go to firms and universities in the Golden State

1962   Esalen Institute is founded at Big Sur

Cesar Chávez, along with Dolores Huerta, Gilbert Padilla, and others, found the National Farm Workers Association (NFWA)

The electorates in San Francisco, Alameda, and Contra Costa counties pass a measure establishing the Bay Area Rapid Transit District (BART), which becomes operational ten years later

California eclipses New York, becoming the most populous state in America

1963   The state legislature passes the Rumford Fair Housing Act, prohibiting discrimination based on race in the sale and rental of real estate

1964   The American Council on Education ranks UC Berkeley the "best balanced distinguished university," public or private, in the United States

The Free Speech Movement is launched at UC Berkeley and spreads across the nation

Voters pass Proposition 14, repealing the Rumford Fair Housing Act

The Los Angeles Music Center, a major performing arts venue, opens and is dedicated

The *bracero* program ends

1965   The Watts riots result in 34 deaths and 1,000 injuries reported, while some 4,000 people are arrested; property damage amounts to $40 million

The Delano Grape Strike is launched

Congress passes the Immigration and Nationality Act that abolishes national origins as a basis for entry for foreigners relocating in the United States, resulting in a large influx of Asians

1966   Largely Hispanic field workers march 300 miles from Delano to Sacramento drawing national attention to their call for boycotts of grapes and wine until their demands for collective bargaining and other rights are recognized

Huey P. Newton and Bobby G. Seale organize the Black Panther Party for Self-Defense in 1966 in Oakland

1967   75,000 young people drawn from throughout the nation celebrate the "Summer of Love" in San Francisco

America's first large-scale popular music gathering of the 1960s, the Monterey International Pop Festival, is held

The nation's first Trader Joe's market opens in Pasadena

1968   San Francisco State College appoints linguist S.I. Hayakawa as president; he gains national attention by confronting student protesters and eventually quashing a major student strike on campus

1969   UC Berkeley students and others attempt to seize a block of university property for use as a "People's Park"

Indians from California and other states occupy Alcatraz Island in San Francisco Bay

1970   UC Santa Barbara students living in Isla Vista riot and torch a branch of the Bank of America in the college enclave

Prosperity, Suburbanization, and Consumerism

California in the 1950s and 1960s was quintessentially Pacific Eldorado, a coastal land whose citizens enjoyed the good life, which was found in the mushrooming suburbs, especially but not only in the Southland. Job opportunities in the aircraft and other industries ensured a high level of consumer spending.

Agriculture led the state's economy, and California's farmers led the nation in crop productivity. In 1970 farm products exceeded $4 billion in value. In addition to the usual fruits, nuts, vegetables, and animal products covered in earlier chapters, winemaking gained international attention, thanks in part to vinicultural researchers at UC Davis, whose graduates included some of Europe's leading vintners. The state's more than 250 wineries began producing varietals, that is, wines made from particular grapes and named for those grapes, for example, Chardonnays and Cabernet Sauvignons. In a prestigious blind wine-tasting competition in Paris in 1976 Napa Valley Chardonnay and Cabernet Sauvignon wines bested for the first time what were reputed to be their elite competitors in France.

The industrial sector of the state's economy hummed. Oil wells pumped 350 million barrels annually. Los Angeles was second only to Detroit in tire manufacturing and automobile assembly. Aircraft and aerospace enterprises accounted for an even larger share of California's jobs and prosperity. America's wars across the Pacific, first in Korea (1950–3) and then in Vietnam (1964–75), boosted the state's economy as 25 percent of all Pentagon spending, amounting to $50 billion between 1952 and 1962, came to California. This was twice what any other state received. In 1953 California surpassed New York, becoming the nation's leading recipient of military appropriations. By 1963 40 percent of the Pentagon's research and development budget of $8.5 billion went to California.

Naturally, defense spending at such a high level produced numerous jobs, especially for engineers and scientific researchers. Mare Island Naval Shipyard in San Francisco Bay built nuclear-powered Polaris submarines. Santa Clara County, where Lockheed's Aircraft Missile System division was located, flourished economically. Aerojet-General, the nation's leading producer of rocket engines, was headquartered in Azusa and employed 33,500 workers from California to the East Coast, many living in the Southland. Convair Astronautics employed 25,000 workers at its San Diego plant. The Aerospace Corporation, Hughes, Lockheed, North American, Northrop, and Douglas – all headquartered in southern California – provided most of the 400,000 well-paying jobs that went to both blue- and white-collar defense workers in the 1950s. In short, one out of every 15 California workers owed their employment to federal military spending, which buoyed the Golden State's growing economy through consumer purchases and the payment of taxes.

The civilian-based commercial airlines industry also expanded during this time. Statewide air travel doubled in volume during the 1960s as the flight corridor between the Pacific Coast cities of Los Angeles and San Francisco became the most heavily trafficked in the world.

Maritime enterprises such as transpacific trade, shipbuilding, passenger voyaging, fishing, and surfing constituted a major sector of the state's economy in the 1950s and 1960s. Transpacific trade was given a significant boost by the advent of containerization that would lead to California's domination of American seagoing commerce in the near future. "Containerization" refers to the use of portable, tamper-proof compartments to store and transport goods on ships. At docks containers were lifted by large cranes from vessels for transfer onto trucks or trains, as well as hoisted by cranes from wharves onto awaiting ships. Containerization saved time and money: whereas before this innovation a crew of 16 to 18 longshoremen could handle 8–10 tons per hour, this change enabled a five-man crew to handle 450 tons per hour! The turnaround time for a ship was thereby reduced from 10 days to 36 hours. Oakland, like Los Angeles in 1950, surpassed San Francisco in cargo shipping by adopting containerization, which the City by the Bay had refused to do. Matson Navigation Company introduced containerized shipping to the West Coast at Los Angeles in 1958. Oil was exported in huge quantities by seagoing tankers, while gargantuan shipments of lumber entered the port. By the late 1950s the bulk of the port's trade was with Japan, whose economy would soon be second in the world only to that of the United States. The Pacific shift of America's economy heralded by Governor Brown was well under way. Accordingly, Japanese automobiles began arriving at the port; among other items, Los Angeles sent consumer electronic goods to Japan. In the early 1960s, Todd Ship-

Figure 12.1   Cranes like that pictured in this photograph taken at Los Angeles Harbor were instrumental in ushering in the containerization of maritime trade. Courtesy of the Los Angeles Harbor Department.

yards won three contracts totaling $84 million to build five container vessels and guided missile frigates for the navy. Ocean fishing (particularly for tuna, a $30-million-a-year business in San Diego in 1950); transpacific passenger voyaging via Matson liners to Hawai'i, the South Seas, and Asia; recreational sailing; and surfing added greatly to California's bustling economy. Of these Pacific-related enterprises, surfing in the 1960s began its ascent into a multi-billion-dollar industry by the century's end.

The prosperity of the times, much of which was generated by Pacific-related enterprises, was reflected in the movement of Californians to the suburbs. Most of the state's 10,586,223 residents in 1950 lived in densely populated cities and towns. For the remainder of the century, however, both newcomers and others – especially middle-class whites – moved to the suburbs, which sprang up on the peripheries of such coastal urban centers as San Francisco, Los Angeles, and San Diego, as well as in Orange County, in the form of housing tracts, or subdivisions. California financiers like Howard Ahmanson, who headed America's largest thrift (a business that holds money deposits and offers credit to individuals) – Home Savings and Loan – extended attractive loans to middle-class families to purchase tract homes. Often schools, shopping centers, and parks to serve the new communities were still under construction as houses were being built. In many instances, especially in Orange County, citrus orchards had been cleared to provide the land for new construction. Drawn by the prospect of escaping what many regarded as Los Angeles' urban blight – crowding, choking traffic, crime, and air pollution – rapidly suburbanizing Orange County's population soared from 220,000 in 1950 to 700,000 a decade later. In short, urban congestion led to suburban sprawl, especially along or near the coastal sections of southern California from Santa Barbara to San Diego.

The new suburbanites had the incomes to consume discretionary goods and services. They bought cars, new furniture, television sets, household appliances and gadgets, sporting goods equipment, and power tools. In suburban San Fernando Valley, where $2.6 billion in wages was paid in 1959, 45 percent of the families owned two automobiles, and Anthony Brothers swimming pools graced the backyards of thousands of middle-class residents. With growing numbers of women entering the workforce, fast-food outlets, like McDonald's (founded in San Bernardino in 1940 and franchised nationwide in the mid-1950s), spread throughout the state. Selling precooked, 15-cent hamburgers to busy commuters on their way home from work in city offices, warehouses, and factories fit neatly into the emergent suburban California lifestyle. As throughout much the rest of America, consumption became an ever more important generator of profits in the state's burgeoning economy.

Entertainment Media, Sports, and Amusement Parks

Consumers of entertainment media and sports opted for television over Hollywood movies. New York challenged Los Angeles for status as America's media capital. As a result, the moviemaking business suffered while commercial television followed an upward trajectory of viewership. When not spending their leisure hours in front of a screen, Californians – and tourists from throughout the nation and the world – could visit the state's amusement parks.

Though cinema's golden era had passed, only one major Hollywood studio, Radio-Keith-Orpheum, closed in the 1950s. With important exceptions like *Dr. Strangelove or: How I Learned to Stop Worrying and Love the Bomb* (1964) and *Who's Afraid of Virginia Wolf?* (1966), studios favored movies about disaffected youth. Seemingly, the more the American Dream of home ownership and living a middle-class lifestyle of consumerism amid relative suburban security became accessible, the more movie audiences were drawn to films about individualistic, rebellious youth. Fascination with motorcycle gang violence, played out against the backdrop of a small and quiet town in middle-class America, brought people into theaters to see a surly Marlon Brando in *The Wild One* (1953). Thereafter, adolescent males in increasing numbers bought black leather jackets and rode motorcycles. *Rebel Without a Cause* (1955) captured the as yet unfocused anger of youth, catapulting James Dean and Natalie Wood into stardom. *West Side Story* (1961), again, played to a younger audience, with the added attraction of Technicolor. The movie featured Natalie Wood, Rita Moreno, and other notables. Budgeted for an estimated $6 million, it grossed $43,656,822 at the box office and won ten Academy Awards. By the late 1960s some filmmakers dared to put America's entire suburban-based, consumption- and business-driven value system on cinematic trial. *The Graduate* (1967) depicted youthful disillusionment with corporate culture and the perceived phoniness of upper-middle-class suburbanites obsessed with keeping up appearances of propriety beneath which lurked unsatisfying marriages, and secret addictions to alcohol and illicit sex. Dustin Hoffman, Anne Bancroft, and Katherine Ross starred in this box office bonanza that featured scenes of the stunning Big Sur coastline. The Mike Nichols-directed film won four Academy Awards and earned $104,397,102 in profits.

Commercial television transitioned from 1950s programming that kept viewers within their comfort zone to 1960s and 1970s shows that at times dealt with serious social issues in the news, often satirically. Fifties sitcoms, like *I Love Lucy* (aired 1951–7) and *The Adventures of Ozzie & Harriet* (aired 1952–66), projected middle-class, intact, two-parent, white families whose predicaments sparked laughter but rarely treated a chronic social issue. Two sitcoms of the late 1960s and early 1970s, on the other hand, were among the first to take on social issues: *All in the Family* (aired 1971–9) and *MASH* (aired 1972–83). Issues of war, race, class, sexual behavior, and gender became fodder in each episode of *All in the Family*, an Emmy Award-winning program. Ostensibly, the setting for *MASH*, directed by Robert Altman, was the Korean War being waged on the other side of the Pacific but little audience imagination was required to see that the sometimes humorous inanities portrayed in fighting that war applied to the ongoing Vietnam conflict, covered extensively and wrenchingly on nightly television news.

Through television, professional and collegiate sporting events entered California homes. The Los Angeles Rams professional football team had many of its games televised, as did the Los Angeles Dodgers professional baseball team, newly relocated from Brooklyn in 1958. In 1961 the professional Los Angeles Angels (later moving to Anaheim), now a Major League expansion team, played their first game. In 1960 the Lakers professional basketball team relocated to Los Angeles from Minneapolis. San Francisco became the new home of the former New York Giants professional baseball team in 1958. In professional football San Francisco featured the cerebrally endowed 49ers, many of whose players had graduated from UC Berkeley, Stanford, and the University of Santa Clara. During the 1960s the San Diego Chargers had a home field and won four division professional football championships. In 1969 San Diego retained the name of the Padres for its major league professional baseball team. The college football scene was enlivened by the "Big Game" between cross-Bay rivals Cal and Stanford, and the annual gridiron contest in Los Angeles between UCLA and USC. Of all the West Coast teams playing in the coveted Rose Bowl game, televised nationwide, USC holds the record for number of appearances and wins. In college basketball, UCLA, coached by the legendary John Wooden, became America's dominant team, winning an unprecedented 10 national championships between 1964 and 1975.

California's Squaw Valley Winter Olympics in 1960 was the first to be televised nationwide, and to be held in the western United States. The largest competition of its kind, 34 nations had entrants, and nearly half a million spectators watched the sports spectacle involving 1,000 premier athletes from all over the globe.

For all of California's achievements on fields, courts, and slopes, arguably no sport defined it more readily for Americans than surfing. With the possible exception of Hawai'i, no other state could match the surfing cachet of California, though Hawai'i's and Mexico's beaches, and later Australia's, were part of a Pacific surfing circuit centered on the Golden

State's coast. From Santa Cruz in the north to San Diego in the south, California had the beaches, the waves, the weather, the bronzed wave riders, the competitions, the music, the films, the boards, and the attire that branded it the Mecca of surfing – and its offspring, wind surfing – worldwide.

Films, magazines, and music did much to popularize California surfing. The Hollywood teen romance movie *Gidget* (1959), according to cultural historian Kirse Granat May, "provided international exposure to the state's surfing scene for the first time." Filmmaker John Severson, meanwhile, pioneered a new genre of movies that were short on romance and long on the thrills of the sport, including *Surf Safari*, *Surf Fever*, *Big Wednesday*, and *Pacific Vibrations*. In 1960 Severson founded *Surfer* magazine, which circulated far beyond the state. Another filmmaker, Greg MacGillivray of Laguna Beach, co-created the iconic surf film, *Five Summer Stories* (1972). Surf films featured the music of Dick Dale and the Del-Tones, the Beach Boys, Jan and Dean, and other vocal/instrumental groups.

Middle-class Californians during this period had discretionary income to spend at the Southland's booming amusement parks. Disneyland in Anaheim, a creation of Walt Disney, opened amid much fanfare in 1955. Much like the image of the Golden State itself, it was America's Magic Kingdom, affording visitors a romantic, sanitized version of America's past in Frontierland, an idealized portrayal of Main Street, USA, and a glimpse into the wonders of the Space Age in Tomorrowland. Nearby Knott's Berry Farm in Buena Park, founded by Walter and Cordelia Knott in 1920, upgraded its 160-acre site to compete with Disneyland. At Knott's children could pan for gold in an artificial stream, drink sarsaparilla (a root beer-like soft beverage) in a faux saloon, tour Constitution Hall, and go home with souvenirs to remind them of how the West had been won by intrepid, self-sufficient American pioneers. For an ocean-minded clientele, Marineland opened in 1954 in Palos Verdes, providing ticketholders sitting in outdoor bleachers with dolphin, whale, and seal performances in huge tanks situated atop a headland looking out on the Pacific. It became the prototype for similar aquatic parks nationwide. To see terrestrial creatures, the San Diego Zoo offered visitors the world's largest wild animal collection.

The San Francisco Renaissance and the Arts

California's prosperity facilitated an energized art scene. Bay Area Bohemians loosely joined by Big Sur writers gave birth to a literary revival, the San Francisco Renaissance, which anticipated a countercultural movement soon to sweep much of America. In Los Angeles, on the other hand, non-Bohemian, socially elite arts patrons busily invested their resources in creating cultural venues commensurate with the city's wealth, size, and aspirations to become a world super city.

The Bay Area headquarters of the poetry renaissance was San Francisco's City Lights Bookstore, co-founded by poet, painter, and publisher, Lawrence Ferlinghetti. A galaxy of the leading Beats, so called because their work supposedly embodied the beatitudes of Jesus as well as a sense of being beaten down, gathered there to read each other's output. City Lights literati included Kenneth Rexroth, Allen Ginsberg, Gary Snyder, William Everson, Jack Kerouac, Alan Watts, and other notables.

In addition to poetry, some of the Beats also wrote prose that oftentimes evinced Pacific images. In his acclaimed novel titled *On the Road* (1959), which narrates his car trip across America to California through fictional characters, Kerouac rhapsodized about catching his first glimpse of the City by the Bay and the vast ocean outside its Golden Gate: "It seemed like a matter of minutes when we began rolling in the foothills before Oakland and suddenly reached a height and saw stretched out ahead of us the fabulous white city of San Francisco on her eleven mystic hills with the blue Pacific and its advancing wall of potato-patch fog beyond, and smoke and goldenness in the late afternoon of time."

The poems and prose emanating from the San Francisco Renaissance often satirized corporate America's consumerism, nationalism, and militarism. Ginsberg's poem "Howl," addressed to his close friend, Carl Solomon, aimed its controlled fury at these targets. The bard gave his poem its first public reading in 1955 at San Francisco's famed Six Gallery arts venue. Some authorities hold that by then Ginsberg had accepted his own homosexuality. Certain passages contained explicit homoerotic imagery that led to a major court battle involving the charge that Ginsberg's book, *Howl and Other Poems*, which appeared the following year, was obscene. Ferlinghetti, whose City Lights Bookstore had published the work, successfully waged the fight against the obscenity charge. His attorney was able to demonstrate that the book was written without lewd intent and had "redeeming social importance." The legal victory, according to the *Los Angeles Times Book Review*, "set a landmark precedent enabling the publication of books by, among others, [William S.] Burroughs, Henry Miller and Vladimir Nabokov."

Asian religions, particularly Buddhism, informed the works of many of the Bay Area and Big Sur writers. A Buddhist and Taoist reverence for nature infused many of their writings. Some – Gary Snyder, Alan Watts, Kenneth Rexroth, and Allen Ginsberg – studied in Asia. Others, like Everson and Kerouac, imbibed Asian religions from their San Francisco associations and readings.

Prominent novelist Henry Miller lived and wrote in Big Sur, a picturesque village situated above towering cliffs overlooking the Pacific and located about 120 miles south of San Francisco. His novel *Tropic of Cancer* (1934), a semi-autobiographical work focusing on his life in Paris in the 1920s and 1930s, was banned in the United States until 1961 for its explicit sexuality. Nevertheless, it won critical acclaim, with renowned British poet T.S. Eliot calling it a "magnificent piece of work."

Ken Kesey was another major Beat-influenced Bay Area author. After studying writing at Stanford, he worked in a Menlo Park hospital. His novel *One Flew Over the Cuckoo's Nest* (1962) depicts the struggles of institutionalized people to gain a modicum of agency in a society that punished nonconformity. With a group known as the Merry Pranksters, Kesey toured America in a kaleidoscopically painted bus in the 1960s.

UC Berkeley-educated author Joan Didion did not fit the bohemian mode. She published her first novel in 1963, *Run River*, which dissected the troubles of a California rancher's daughter going insane. Before moving to New York City, Didion lived in Los Angeles for 20 years, during which she gathered material for her collection of essays on California in the 1960s, *Slouching Towards Bethlehem* (1968). Though Didion saw a glowing side to California, bright warm days "when Catalina floats on the Pacific horizon and the air smells of orange blossoms," on balance she presented a state in decline. The "center . . . was not holding," meaning that California's children "grew up cut loose from the web of cousins and great-aunts and family doctors and lifelong neighbors who had traditionally . . . enforced society's values." To her the state's youth were not so much in rebellion against traditional values as ignorant of those values in the first place.

While San Francisco boasted one of the nation's best opera companies, complemented by art venues such as the de Young Museum, the Palace of the Legion of Honor, and the Museum of Modern Art, Los Angeles patrons decided to enter their city into the ranks of those known internationally for art. Dorothy Buffum Chandler, wife of the publisher of the *Los Angeles Times*, headed a fundraising drive resulting in the building of the Music Center, dedicated in 1964. The Hollywood Bowl provided summer concertgoers an outdoor amphitheater where they could hear the world-renowned Los Angeles Philharmonic Orchestra under the direction of Zubin Mehta. Oil magnate J. Paul Getty's Malibu mansion served as an art museum, exhibiting ancient sculptures and other works he had collected in Italy. After completion of his seaside villa, these works went on display to the public beginning in 1974.

San Diego, too, tended to its arts sites. By 1965 the San Diego Civic Theater had been built, providing a concert hall for the city's symphony. A year later, the city's Museum of Art expanded by adding a west wing, doubling exhibit space for its modern European collection of paintings.

Like the state's big-city art centers, smaller ones also were located mainly along the coast, which provided ideal settings for *plein air* (outdoor-painted) seascapes. Mendocino, Carmel, and Laguna Beach continued to draw painters, bolstering those cities' national reputations as art colonies and travel destinations.

Architecturally, three styles prevailed: modernism, Tiki, and ranch. Austrian-born Richard Neutra, who settled and worked in Los Angeles, was known worldwide as an innovator in modernist designs. He employed machine patterns in the design of homes and commercial buildings. Sea Ranch, a modernist resort area on the Sonoma coast, was planned by architect Al Boeke, who conceived of building clusters of unpainted wooden houses and a lodge that fit with the natural environment. There, landscape architect Lawrence Halperin let the Pacific Coast inspire his design, which fused public and private space into a seamless outdoor setting. Internationally renowned Hideo Sasaki, whose modernist landscape designs can be seen at Los Altos Hills' Foothill College and San Francisco's Embarcadero, similarly insisted that the environment must guide his projects. Bay Area architect Joseph Eichler designed modern, steel-and-glass-encased, atrium-centered, single-family residences. Thousands were built, selling in 1957 for between $18,000 and $25,000. Throughout the Bay Area, Asian motifs were particularly evident in interior décor, furniture, and landscaping. Garrett Eckbo, a leading state architect, exalted the Japanese Zen garden as the aesthetic ideal for use of outdoor space.

Tiki (represented as a Polynesian warrior) architecture was most popular in the Bay Area but could also be found in the Southland. Many San Francisco shipping magnates, such as Roger Lapham, president of the American-Hawaiian Steamship Company and former city mayor, had traveled extensively throughout Polynesia and were enamored of the island lifestyle, which they incorporated into their homes. This often meant having rattan furniture, tropical plants, and artwork reflecting Pacific island cultures. These prominent residents and others held backyard luaus, or Hawaiian feasts, lit by Tiki torches. Businesses also adopted Hawaiian motifs. Trader Vic's restaurant, for example, popularized Aloha shirts and other attire, and many hotels featured Tiki bars, where exotic rum drinks were served. The national chain of Trader Joe's markets, beginning with the first in Pasadena in 1967, has utilized the South Seas theme in interior décor and branding products from then to now, according to founder Joe Coulombe.

Ranch-type residences evoked California's connections to the American Southwest. Such houses, whose low, sprawling, horizontal lines were accented, bespoke California's Spanish-Mexican past when rancheros dotted the hillsides. Like other aspects of California life, ranch-style architecture, inspired mainly by the designs of Cliff May, had spread to many parts of America by the mid-1960s.

Politics: Goodwin Knight, Pat Brown, and Reforming Government Operations

Governors Goodwin J. Knight and Edmund G. "Pat" Brown, the first a moderate-to-liberal Republican and the second a liberal Democrat, were progressive-minded. "Pat" was a nickname traced to an impassioned Patrick Henry-like speech Brown delivered as a youth. Both politicians saw government as an instrument for ensuring social justice and advancing the well-being of the public through an impartial justice system, regulatory oversight, and infrastructure projects. During Brown's administrations reforms were implemented regarding government operations.

Goodwin Knight, who had once campaigned for Hiram Johnson and worked his way through Stanford, practiced law before entering politics as a self-made millionaire. His work experience as a hard-rock miner made him sympathetic to organized labor, which, in turn, supported him. As lieutenant governor under Earl Warren, Knight assumed the governorship in 1953 when Warren became chief justice of the U.S. Supreme Court. The following year, Knight was elected governor in his own right.

As governor, Knight continued Warren's progressive policies. The new governor repelled conservative attempts to pass "right to work" legislation that would have hobbled unions by undermining the solidarity needed in workplaces for effective collective bargaining. Knight supported a Feather River dam, raised benefits for the unemployed and seniors, increased the state's education budget, addressed Los Angeles' smog problem, tightened regulations on alcohol and boxing, appointed the first female regent of the University of California, and oversaw the transfer of Hearst Castle in San Simeon to the State of California.

Despite these achievements, Knight's reelection bid in 1958 was hurt by a rift within the state's Republican Party between himself and challenger William F. Knowland. Knowland was the candidate put forward by conservative, anti-union southern California Republicans, aircraft and oil companies, and *Los Angeles Times* publisher Norman Chandler. Stung by this development, Knight withdrew from the governor's race and ran for the U.S. Senate, leaving the Republican gubernatorial nomination to Knowland.

With Republicans split by the Knight–Knowland feud, the way was clear for a Democrat to win the governorship. That Democrat was the affable former attorney general Pat Brown, who garnered support from the state's 1.5 million union members who detested Knowland. With a slowing Californian economy, candidate Brown said that Knowland offered only "a bigger dose of trickle-down economics," referring to the Republican Party's faith in the free market as the remedy for economic ills coupled with an aversion to income redistribution through taxes. According to this theory, only by the rich getting richer would prosperity trickle down to the rest of society in the form of more jobs and higher wages. Brown, on the other hand, had a New Dealer's faith in an activist state that redistributed wealth in order to make "life a little more comfortable for the average human being."

Brown won in a Democratic landslide, capturing 60 percent of the vote, while his party won all of the top state offices, as well as majorities in both houses of the state legislature. Moreover, Democrats won a 16 to 14 majority in California's House of Representatives delegation, and a seat in the U.S. Senate that went to Clair Engel, who defeated Knight. The 1958 election would prove a major turning point in the state's history.

The Golden State's new governor did not attend college but graduated from an evening law school, and was a lifelong Catholic who openly opposed the death penalty. In 1960 his delaying of the execution of Caryl Chessman, a convicted rapist, brought public scorn. Brown embraced the liberal view that in church–state relations the Constitution must protect everyone "even atheists and agnostics." Never an ideologue nor shrill anti-communist Cold Warrior, the new governor was a pragmatic politician. He counted on the support of his wife, Bernice, who had little love for politics, and his three children, one of whom would occupy the statehouse later. Buoyed by a sunny countenance, a belief in California's greatness, and his family, Brown's governorship ushered in liberalism's high tide.

To make politics more transparent and responsive to the masses of voters, Assemblyman Jesse M. Unruh, chair of the Ways and Means Committee and later assembly speaker, oversaw reforming government operations. In 1959 cross-filing was abolished so that voters would know candidates' party affiliations. Additionally, hitherto underrepresented urban voters received more equitable treatment through reapportionment. In 1964 the U.S. Supreme Court ruled in *Reynolds v. Sims* that legislative voting districts in states must have approximately equal numbers of voters. Before this ruling, hugely populated Los Angeles County with some 6 million residents had the same number of votes in the state senate as the Alpine-Mono-Inyo District with slightly more than 14,000 inhabitants. As a result of reapportionment control of the state senate passed to southern California, which had enjoyed assembly majorities since the 1930s.

Heartened by his first term, Brown ran for reelection in 1962 against Richard Nixon, who had lost his bid for the presidency two years earlier to John F. Kennedy. Nixon charged that Brown was "soft on communism," a strategy that had worked well for the red-baiting Orange County Republican in years past. Still, Nixon lacked Brown's command of California issues and had made some enemies among his fellow Republicans who found his methods unsavory. Brown won a second term, and an angry Nixon made newspaper headlines, saying that journalists would not have him "to kick around any more." The victor was now positioned to continue building the progressive mega-state of his dreams.

Enhancing the Super State: Water, Transit, and Universities

If the comparative word "greater" applied to the state in earlier times, it made even more sense during the Pat Brown era, when so many things about California were greater than before and greater compared to other states: population size, the extent of the state's water infrastructure and freeway systems, the scale and quality of public higher education, the scope of the student and farm labor protest movements, and more. In terms of population growth, as noted, California became the largest state in the Union in 1962, surpassing New York. Americans poured into what seemed a Pacific Eldorado, replete with jobs and the promise of a good life, at the rate of 1,000 a day in the first half of the 1960s, edging the population up near the 20 million mark. Los Angeles County became the nation's most populous, while Orange and San Diego counties grew apace. To continue its growth, the super state was in need of enhancements: the Southland needed water; suburbanites needed transit to their workplaces; and the burgeoning economy needed an educated workforce.

Enhancing the mega-state would be costly. Unapologetically, Brown raised income, inheritance, and corporate taxes as well as those on tobacco products. Imposts for the poor were lowered. Altogether, the increases netted the state an additional $256 million a year. "I have nothing but contempt for those who say that no new taxes are necessary," Brown confided in his diary.

En route to making California even greater, one of the governor's proudest achievements was the State Water Project. The project envisioned the building of the Oroville Dam, the tallest in the United States, on the Feather River to provide flood control and water to San Joaquin Valley corporate landholders. From the Sacramento–San Joaquin Delta the so-called California Aqueduct would be built to meet the future water needs of an expanding Southland population. A Peripheral Canal, skirting the delta in order to feed only non-saline water into the aqueduct, was included in the plan.

Even with the unprecedented strength of Democrats in Sacramento, Brown had to fight for the project. Opposition arose from San Francisco, nearly always resistant to measures supplying northern California water to the parched Southland. The California Labor Federation decried the cheap water that would go to corporate land owners, since the federal stipulation that only farms of 160 acres or less could receive water flows was not contained in the measure. Even the Metropolitan Water District of Southern California opposed the project initially, fearing the district's claim to Colorado River water might be weakened in an ongoing Supreme Court trial brought by Arizona.

Brown met and beat the opposition. The 1959 passage of the Water Resources Development Bond (Burns–Porter) Act authorized putting before California voters a $1.75 billion bond issue incorporated in Proposition 1. Throughout America's states and cities, expensive public works projects, such as that encompassed in the Burns–Porter Act, have often been financed by the sale of bonds to investors who are contractually entitled to a rate of interest on the money loaned to a given state or municipal government. State or city taxpayers will eventually pay off such bonds; in the meantime a given project will go forward and usually be completed long before the bond is retired. Historian Kevin Starr rightly holds that the Burns–Porter bill called for "the most ambitious water storage and distribution system in the history of the human race." Brown deployed the full range of his lobbying skills to secure passage of the measure in June, after which he signed the landmark legislation. In November 1960 California voters went to the polls and by a thin margin of 174,000 votes out of 5.8 million cast approved the water bonds, which financed the early stage of the State Water Project. Except for the Peripheral Canal, the major components of the project have been completed, including the Oroville Dam, 32 reservoirs, 17 pumping stations, and 662 miles of canals and pipelines.

In addition to more water, the super state needed more highways and modern metropolitan rail transit. With a population of 15 million people in 1959, California led the nation in the number of cars, with 7 million registered automobiles and as many drivers. In the southern reaches of the state where the car was king the Sacramento government built America's first freeway, the Arroyo Seco Parkway, in 1940. Freeways were so called because, unlike expressways on the East Coast, they were toll-free. In 1959 Brown signed the Freeway and Expressway Act calling for $10.5 billion of construction during the next 20 years. State spending, at ever higher levels, kept the highway-building trend going well into Brown's governorship. When he took office the state's gas tax stood at 6 cents per gallon; in 1963 it went up another cent, by which time California was spending more than $633.5 million a year on highways. These funds were supplemented by federal dollars resulting from Congress's passage of the Federal-Aid Highway Act of 1956, which aimed to link the nation by building 41,000 miles of freeways/expressways by 1972. In the 1960s and 1970s, these federal funds built the San Diego, Golden State, Santa Monica, San Bernardino, Foothill, and San Gabriel River freeways.

The geographically compact Bay Area was not nearly as supportive of freeway construction as was the sprawling Southland. San Franciscans defeated plans to build seven freeways linking the Embarcadero waterfront to the Golden Gate Bridge, then passing through scenic and historic Golden Gate Park and crisscrossing the city. Instead, San Franciscans opted for electric-powered, fast, light rail transit. Thus in 1962, by which time Los Angeles had dismantled its excellent Pacific Electric "Red Car" rail network, voters in San Francisco, Alameda, and Contra Costa counties passed a measure establishing the Bay Area Rapid Transit District (BART). Since 1972 the BART system has been providing commuters with a low-cost, convenient, automated, computerized rail service.

Public higher education was a third major policy area of concern for Brown as he set about building an even greater California. His challenge was twofold: to supply highly educated professionals needed to sustain economic growth; and to find a solution to the ongoing disputes between the state colleges and universities regarding the awarding of doctorates and the funding of discipline-oriented research. By the late 1950s the number of state colleges had grown to 15 and their enrollments had, overall, tripled in that decade. The leaders of these institutions, founded to graduate teachers, wanted to award doctorates and receive research funding, just like the UCs. To end the competition between the two systems of higher education, maintain and enhance the quality of the UCs, and ensure public access to post-secondary education, Brown supported what came to be called *A Master Plan for Higher Education in California, 1960–1975*. The plan was put into operation when the Donohoe Act, named after Assemblywoman Dorothy M. Donohoe who chaired the committee that wrote it, was passed by the state legislature and signed by Governor Brown on April 26, 1960.

The historic master plan established a three-tiered, tuition-free, system of public higher education. Students graduating in the top one-eighth (12.5 percent) of their high-school class would be eligible for UC admission. The UCs could award bachelor's, master's, and doctoral degrees. Those graduating in the top one-third (33.3 percent) would be directed to the state colleges, renamed "universities" or CSUs in 1971. These institutions could award bachelor's and master's degrees. All other students, high-school graduates or not, could attend two-year junior (later called community) colleges, where they could earn associate of arts degrees before transferring to the UCs or state colleges, or pursue career/vocational training.

California's master plan quickly drew national and worldwide praise. *Time* magazine ran a feature story on it and posted University of California President Clark Kerr, who had spearheaded negotiations on that plan, on its cover. While a profound thinker and respected labor economist, President Kerr was also known for his wit, as when he earlier served as UC Berkeley's chancellor he quipped that many saw his primary responsibilities as "providing parking for the faculty, sex for the students, and athletics for the alumni." The blueprint for public higher education, however, is what put him on the *Time* cover and would shape his legacy. Meeting in Paris, the European Organization for Economic Cooperation Development declared that the master plan "represents the most advanced effort to construct a system of mass higher education . . . while maintaining a quality of research and education . . . unsurpassed anywhere . . . in the world." By the late 1960s, 23 other states had put into operation similar master plans.

Meanwhile, UC Berkeley's academic reputation continued to soar, as did that of UCLA, which had joined the top tier of national universities. By the 1950s Berkeley had the largest number of Nobel Laureates on its faculty of any American university. Speaking at Berkeley in 1962, President John F. Kennedy, a Harvard graduate, stated: "When I observe the men who surround me in Washington, I am forced to confront an uncomfortable truth – the New Frontier may well owe more to Berkeley than to Harvard." In 1964 the American Council on Education rated Berkeley the "best balanced distinguished university," public or private, in the United States. Writing in the early 1970s, Harvard economist John Kenneth Galbraith noted that nearly one-third of the professors of economics at his venerable university had been recruited "from the University of California at Berkeley."

Governor Brown remained a strong advocate of California's master plan for higher education. During his governorship, state spending on the UCs more than doubled, and more than tripled for the state colleges. Three new university campuses and four new state colleges were established, while funding was increased for community colleges and the K-12 system. By almost any measure, during the Pat Brown era Greater California had spawned America's, and arguably the world's, greatest system of public higher education.

Students in Dissent, Campuses in Revolt

Governor Brown was unable to bask for long in the glories of his super state, with its super system of higher education. In the 1960s a national civil rights movement and growing U.S. military involvement in Vietnam engaged the attention of collegians, resulting in escalating turmoil on campuses within and outside the state.

While youth at the University of Michigan were launching the Students for a Democratic Society in 1960, Berkeley and San Francisco State College students in April of that year protested their exclusion from a hearing of the House Un-American Activities Committee held in San Francisco's city hall. When students refused to leave the premises, police used fire hoses and clubs to disperse them. These happenings in different regions of America signaled that the "silent generation" of 1950s students, who had pursued higher education for jobs and material gain, was being succeeded by a new wave of more affluent, idealistic, and politically active collegians.

By the 1960s, according to Kerr, "Berkeley . . . had a historical ambiance of a liberal-radical flavor that attracted sympathetic students and faculty." Also, some outspoken conservative students were part of the campus mix. All of these groups insisted on their right to advocate on university property for political causes.

Amid these developments, Berkeley's Free Speech Movement arose in the fall of 1964. Mario Savio, valedictorian of his New York City high-school class, and a coterie of fellow students had returned to campus after having volunteered in the South during Freedom Summer. They had been registering blacks to vote. In doing so, these students developed organizing skills and the courage to stand up to Ku Klux Klan and police violence. Trained, toughened, and impassioned, in September they organized "sit-ins" at Bay Area businesses thought to discriminate on the basis of race in hiring, paying, and promoting employees. A "sit-in" was a nonviolent form of protest, such as occupying seats or public buildings and refusing to move until arrested, if then.

That same month university officials declared that a sidewalk at the south end of campus that students had been using to circulate political leaflets was off limits for such activity due to the institution's policy of remaining free from "political or sectarian influence in the appointment of regents and the administration of its affairs." The fact that the university prohibited student politicking based on a policy aimed at ensuring the political neutrality of the institution itself made no sense according to Berkeley's own attorneys. In other words, while the administration was required to perform its duties in a politically neutral fashion, from a legal standpoint the students did not forfeit their right to freedom of speech by enrolling at the university. Backed by the U.S. Supreme Court's decision in *Edwards v. South Carolina* (1963) upholding students' rights to on-campus political speech that did not "constitute a clear and present danger," Savio and others, including the Young Republicans, continued their forbidden leafleting and speechmaking. To leftist students the ban on campus political activity proved that the university aimed at "turning out corporate drones" rather than encouraging the critical thinking and social responsibility essential to "participatory democracy."

October 1, 1964, marked a milestone in the development of the Free Speech Movement (FSM). A few minutes before noon, Jack Weinberg, a Berkeley mathematics graduate student, set up a makeshift podium in front of the Sproul Hall administration building in preparation for a rally. Several deans and a lone police officer arrested Weinberg when he refused to dismantle the structure. Meanwhile, students gathered in the plaza, causing the police officer to go for help. When more police arrived, Weinberg, trained in the South to go limp (meaning he would not resist arrest but would have to be carried to be moved), refused to get into the squad car. By the time police placed him in the car, hundreds of peaceful students had surrounded the vehicle and someone had let the air out of at least one tire. The immobilized car then became a rostrum. Student speakers removed their shoes and sequentially addressed the awaiting throng from the roof of the police car. Professors, too, spoke. Savio negotiated a truce with the administration and after 32 hours Weinberg was allowed to leave the car. Governor Brown was relieved but annoyed by the students' "total disrespect for the law."

By this point an FSM coalition had formed at Berkeley and Savio was its titular spokesperson. In one of his most celebrated orations, delivered before a throng of listeners on campus in early December, he declared: "There is a time when the operation of the machine becomes so odious, makes you so sick at heart, that you can't take part, can't even tacitly take part; and you've got to put your bodies upon the gears and upon the wheels, upon the levers, upon all the apparatus, and you've got to make it stop." Jo Freeman, Jackie Goldberg, Bettina Aptheker, and others also took leadership roles in slowing if not stopping the apparatus or operation of the university. In its struggle, the FSM prevailed. The faculty senate, by a large margin, voted to support the students' demands. At the end of 1964 the administration repealed the ban on campus political activity. Berkeley, by then, was seen as the cockpit of student protests that from the shores of the Pacific began sweeping the nation, and within a few years would erupt at elite universities in Paris, Prague, Rome, Berlin, Warsaw, Tokyo, and Mexico City.

Figure 12.2 Berkeley students marching through Sather Gate en route to the UC Board of Regents' meeting, November 20, 1964. Mario Savio, wearing a coat and tie, is in the front line, second from the right of the banner. Photo: Don Kechely. Courtesy of Bancroft Library, UC Berkeley.

As American involvement in Vietnam deepened, student opposition to the war mounted at Berkeley, San Francisco State, and other institutions throughout California and the nation. At Stanford, David Harris, who had participated in the 1964 campaign to register black voters in Mississippi, returned to campus where as student body president two years later he led a movement to empower students, advance civil rights, and oppose the Vietnam War. In 1968, as campus protests throughout America became more destructive of property, Stanford's ROTC building was destroyed by arson. The following year, UCLA, which ABC correspondent John Davenport described as a model of stability, became newsworthy when black philosophy professor Angela Davis, an avowed communist, was fired by the UC Board of Regents. If students and faculty at UCLA remained relatively quiet, the academic environment at other prominent Southland schools was quieter still, for example at the Claremont Colleges and USC. On the other hand, in mid-May 1969 students and non-students at UC Berkeley tried to seize a block of university-owned land for use as a "People's Park." They tore down fences and burned signs posted around the property. National Guardsmen called to the scene sprayed the thousands of protesters with shotgun pellets while police fired teargas into the rampaging crowd. In 1970 violence erupted near UC Santa Barbara when students rioted in the off-campus housing neighborhood of Isla Vista and torched the city's Bank of America. One student was killed in the mayhem. According to UC Berkeley Professor Todd Gitlin, a student movement that had ushered in years of hope in the early 1960s was ending in days of rage.

Pacific Profile: S.I. Hayakawa, San Francisco State College President

Samuel Ichiye Hayakawa (1906–92) was an eminent semanticist, college professor and president, and U.S. Senator. Of Japanese ancestry, he was born and raised in Vancouver, Canada, after which he immigrated to the United States, where he earned his Ph.D. from the University of Wisconsin at Madison. Receiving American citizenship in 1954, he was regarded as an authority in his field, particularly on how dictators such as Hitler, Stalin, and Mussolini had used words and symbols in the 1930s as tools of totalitarian propaganda. His textbook *Language in Action* (1941) was used by colleges and universities throughout the United States.

San Francisco State College hired Hayakawa in 1955. He seemed sympathetic to Berkeley's FSM initially and favored a broadening of the curriculum at San Francisco State. However, as campus turmoil spread and students became increasingly destructive of property and disruptive of classroom instruction, Hayakawa's views changed. He became convinced that students in the late 1960s at Berkeley and elsewhere had become

too radicalized and that administrators needed to assert their authority.

In November 1968 Hayakawa was appointed president of San Francisco State. By then student protests had gone global as rioters and dissenters challenged authorities at the universities of Paris, Mexico, Peking (now Beijing, China), and elsewhere, including a two-month strike at San Francisco State at the very moment that Hayakawa assumed the presidency.

His response to the strike on his campus was dramatic and decisive. "We have a standing obligation to the 17,500 or more students – white, black, yellow, red and brown – who are not on strike and have every right to expect continuation of their education," he declared. Next he called for 600 San Francisco police officers to come onto campus to maintain order. On December 2, with a megaphone in hand, he mounted a protester's truck and ripped out the wires to an amplifying system. He then stepped down and waded through the angry crowd of students, returning to his office. A photograph of the incident appeared in newspapers across the country. From then on, if not before, Hayakawa became a polarizing figure in America: conservatives praised him; liberals denounced him. In March 1969 the campus strike ended, with the college making some concessions, such as establishing a black studies department.

National politics beckoned. In August 1973, Hayakawa resigned his presidency and changed his party affiliation from Democrat to Republican. The leadership he had shown on campus and the media attention that followed made him attractive to Republican strategists. Accordingly, at 70 years of age he ran for the U.S. Senate in 1976 against Democratic incumbent John Tunney and won.

"Sleepin' Sam," as he was called because he dozed off in committee meetings, opposed busing to integrate schools, and fought affirmative action to diversify student bodies. He had been a courageous and influential educator but was ineffective in the Senate. Hayakawa did not run for a second term and died in 1992, having brought distinction to Asian Pacific Californians.

Minorities and Women

During the 1950s and 1960s California's minority groups and women became increasingly assertive of their rights. These groups made headway during Pat Brown's governorship. His journey to appreciation of ethnic diversity and gender justice had been a long one. Growing up and as a young man he reflected the prejudices of his times. He recalled as a boy throwing bricks at Chinese laundry wagons. As a prosecutor he ridiculed San Francisco's gays and lesbians, and until becoming governor had given little "thought about women with respect to equal rights." As times changed, so did his views on rights for minorities and women.

African Americans, who continued moving into California in the 1950s, were the most vocal minority. Those who left the American South, where segregationist Jim Crow laws restricted black people's seating on city buses and use of public facilities, encountered a somewhat different set of challenges in California. Once resettled in the Golden State, a land supposedly brimming with opportunities, blacks found that they needed to insist on equal rights in jobs, housing, and education. In the Bay Area city of Richmond in 1950, for example, 29 percent of non-white workers were unemployed while only 13 percent of white workers were jobless. In southern California, where most of the state's incoming blacks settled, conditions were worse. Jobs were hard to get, in that factories had moved out of Los Angeles to the suburbs. Black city dwellers, numbering some 500,000 by 1960, did not have rapid transit systems to get them to and from work. For more than a decade after its opening in 1955, Disneyland in Orange County refused to hire blacks in "people contact" positions, except for the one African American who played Aunt Jemima for visitors reliving "the days of the Old South." Racially restrictive housing covenants (though declared unenforceable in a 1948 Supreme Court decision) slowed blacks' moving into white neighborhoods, while banks refused to lend to African Americans attempting to buy houses in such areas.

African Americans and their white supporters fought back, but ingrained racism gave little ground. In 1959 the Sacramento legislature passed the Unruh Civil Rights Act, named for the assembly speaker. The measure prohibited businesses from discriminating on the basis of race, sex, sexual orientation, religion, and medical condition and disability; it provided for the collection of damages through the courts in instances where unfair treatment could be proven. With help from white liberals, many of them Jewish, African Americans Gilbert Lindsay, Tom Bradley, and Billy Mills won Los Angeles city council seats in the early 1960s. Incensed by restrictive covenants in housing, Governor Brown insisted: "No man should be deprived of the right of acquiring a home of his own because of the color of his skin." In 1963 the state legislature passed the Rumford Fair Housing Act, advocated by black Berkeley Assemblyman Byron Rumford, barring racial discrimination in the sale and rental of real estate. Passage of Proposition 14 the following year repealed the Rumford Act, to the frustration of blacks. Amid these gains and setbacks, discrimination persisted in housing and the job market, fueling black anger.

Racial tension exploded into deadly riots in Watts, a crowded black neighborhood in southeast Los Angeles, during the summer of 1965. The uprising was touched off by a police arrest of a young black man for drunken driving. At the arrest scene a rumor spread that two African American women had been mistreated by police. Six days of rioting, burning, and looting followed, capturing coast-to-coast television coverage. Brown sent his aide, William Becker, to Watts to find out what residents wanted. Becker summed up their complaints in one sentence: "We want the kind of life the white man has." In the wake of the violence, finally quelled by National Guard forces, 34 deaths and 1,000 injuries were reported, while some 4,000 people were arrested. Property damage amounted to $40 million.

After the Watts riots, as before, progress toward racial equality remained halting. In 1966 the state supreme court declared Proposition 14 unconstitutional, a decision validated by the U.S. Supreme Court a year later. Still, neighborhoods and schools reflected de facto segregation. In 1970, nearly two decades after the U.S. Supreme Court struck down "separate but equal" in *Brown v. Board of Education* (1954), 90 percent of the black students in the Los Angeles Unified School District attended all-black public schools.

Angry and dismissive of Martin Luther King's nonviolent approach to securing social justice, two black radicals in Oakland – Huey P. Newton and Bobby G. Seale – organized the Black Panther Party for Self-Defense in 1966. Armed with guns and law books, they followed police cars, making sure African Americans who were pulled over did not become victims of racialized mistreatment. Influenced by the teachings of Karl Marx, Vladimir Lenin, Mao Tse-tung, and especially Malcolm X, they adopted a platform calling for "black power," community self-help, and militant self-protection from police and other government agents. In the late 1960s, Panthers were involved in a number of Bay Area shootouts with police resulting in deaths on both sides. By then the Panther organization was at the peak of its strength, claiming thousands of members in 40 states and known throughout the world. Eldridge Cleaver, the Panther's minister of information, ran for president on the Peace and Freedom Party ticket in 1968. An even more radical, left-wing group, the Symbionese Liberation Army (SLA), saw itself as being in the vanguard of the black power movement. It was particularly active in the Bay Area from 1973 to 1975, during which time its members murdered Oakland superintendent of schools Marcus Foster, abducted wealthy heiress Patricia Hearst, robbed banks, and engaged in numerous shootouts with police. A fierce gun battle with the authorities in Los Angeles in 1975 resulted in the deaths of many of its leaders and the demise of the SLA.

Inspired by African Americans and the charismatic labor organizer Cesar Chávez, Mexican Americans, California's largest ethnic minority in the latter half of the twentieth century, championed "brown power" in the fields and cities of the state. In 1962 Chávez, along with Dolores Huerta, Gilbert Padilla, and others, founded the National Farm Workers Association (NFWA). Led by Chávez, the union stressed nonviolent resistance, such as marches, boycotts, and strikes, as the path to securing higher wages and better working conditions. Once the *bracero* program ended in 1964, the new union had the benefit of greatly reduced competition from a low-paid foreign labor force.

The Delano Grape Strike, launched on September 8, 1965, by Filipino members of the Agricultural Workers' Organizing Committee (AWOC), an AFL-CIO affiliate, drew in Chávez and the NFWA. The work stoppage put a national spotlight on the grim labor conditions endured by California field workers, whose contracts did not allow for collective bargaining, payment of the legally sanctioned minimum wage, social security benefits, or unemployment insurance. Carrying banners bearing images of the Virgin of Guadalupe and Mexican flags, in spring 1966 workers and their supporters marched 300 miles from Delano to Sacramento. These Mexican symbols bore testimony to the labor connection between California and its Pacific Rim neighbor republic to the south. Media coverage of the pilgrimage spoke to the consciences of Americans, many of whom supported the workers' demands by boycotting California wines and table grapes. During the next five years the major California winemakers signed union contracts with the by then combined NFWA and AWOC, renamed the United Farm Workers Organizing Committee. In 1966 the powerful DiGiorgio Fruit Company, which had claimed repeatedly that its workers did not want to be unionized, finally allowed its field hands to vote on union membership. Its laborers voted overwhelmingly in favor of unionizing. Chávez paid tribute to the sacrifices and rewards represented by these victories: "Ninety five percent of the strikers lost their homes and cars. But I think that in losing those worldly possessions they found themselves, and they found that only . . . through serving mankind, and . . . the poor, and those . . . struggling for justice, only in that way could they really find themselves."

In the cities, where 85 percent of California's 75,000 Spanish-surnamed people lived in the mid-1960s, a more rhetorically militant form of Mexican American pride characterized the Chicano/a movement. Tracing their roots southward along the Pacific Rim to Mexico's Aztec civilization, the youth who started and dominated this movement accentuated differences between themselves – "La Raza," literally the race that supposedly still carried Aztec bloodlines – and Anglos.

Daunting problems confronted urban Mexican Americans and their Chicano/a leaders. They had twice as many families living below the official federal poverty line as families in any other ethnic group. Twice as many Latino/a students dropped out of high school as Anglos. Worse still, voter turnout for Mexican Americans was extremely low. Many Chicanos/as viewed the Vietnam War as a major problem for them in the late 1960s, pointing out that Mexican Americans were grossly overrepresented among the war dead.

Asian Americans, whose numbers increased dramatically after passage of the 1965 Immigration and Nationality (Hart–Cellar) Act, fared better than any ethnic minority group during these times. This law was pivotal. By removing immigrants' "national origins" as the basis of entry into the United States, it resulted in Asia replacing the western hemisphere

Figure 12.3   Farm labor organizer Dolores Huerta speaking to workers at end of the 300-mile march from Delano to Sacramento. Photo: John Kouns (b. 1929). Courtesy of the Phillip & Sala Burton Center for Human Rights; image provided by Farmworker Movement Documentation Project R2011.1301.003.

as the major source of most of America's newcomers. Located on the Pacific Rim, California received a disproportionate share of Asian immigrants. Those of Chinese and Japanese descent did particularly well. They lived on average seven years longer than native whites; these two groups also outranked native whites and all other ethnic minorities in education level and earnings, and had lower levels of juvenile delinquency. Thus, to a good many whites Asians seemed the model minority, provoking relatively little Anglo racist prejudice even after the early 1970s when Southeast Asian refugees, mainly Vietnamese, began arriving in California. During that decade some 80,000 fled Vietnam after the communist takeover in 1975, and came to the Golden State; most of these had been supporters of the defeated South Vietnam government and anticipated being tortured and forced into "reeducation" (brainwashing) centers if they did not escape their homeland. They resettled in California, especially Orange County, because they were accustomed to a warm climate and preferred living near other Vietnamese, who had established themselves in and around the City of Westminster.

No ethnic group in California has suffered longer and with more devastating consequences than Indians, who remained the state's most impoverished minority. Throughout much of the twentieth century, their unemployment rate more than tripled that of whites.

Numbering 75,000 in 1965, they approved a settlement of their land claims in the state for a little more than $29 million for 64 million acres of land. After paying lawyers, this amounted to about 45 cents an acre, or $600 per eligible recipient.

Meanwhile, in the 1950s the federal government implemented its new policy of "termination," which ended its custodial responsibility for holding Indian lands in trust. Thereafter, those lands were to be sold. In 1958 Congress passed a measure abolishing 41 California reservations. Native Americans were to move into America's cities. Relocation was followed by the federal Bureau of Indian Affairs' withdrawal of all health services for California's Indians, who were thereafter expected to fend for themselves like all other citizens in vying for local, county, and state assistance.

California's Indians in the 1960s found ways to publicly express their group identity and assert what they regarded as their long-ignored rights. Invoking "Red Power" and joined by tribespeople from other parts of the nation, they occupied Alcatraz Island, situated in San Francisco Bay, from 1969 to 1971. Since then, American Indian Studies centers and departments have been established on university campuses, San Francisco State University's being among the first in 1969.

Gays and lesbians, too, struggled for equal rights and better treatment in the 1960s. By then same-sex bars had been spreading into cities across America since the 1940s. In 1964 *Life* magazine described San Francisco as America's "gay capital," touching off a nationwide gay/lesbian migration to the City by the Bay. Homosexuals in San Francisco's Castro District and Los Angeles County's West Hollywood area were particularly public about their lifestyles and active in what came to be called the "gay liberation" movement that began in the late 1960s.

Finally, California's women evidenced a higher degree of political activism in the 1950s and 1960s than at any time since the Progressive Era. The salient point about this activism is that it was divided between liberal and conservative causes.

Comprising nearly one-third of California's workforce in 1950 while earning 40 percent less than their male counterparts, women with center-left political leanings grew increasingly concerned about hiring opportunities, equal pay for equal work, maternity leave, and chances for promotion. Accordingly, a reluctant Governor Pat Brown appointed a state Commission on the Status of Women in 1964. The commission's report, submitted in 1967 to Brown's successor, Ronald Reagan, went far beyond workplace matters to include findings on childcare, abortion, and divorce while offering proposals for legislation. Reagan was considerably less supportive of feminist causes than Brown, and, therefore, little came of the recommendations.

Taking advantage of a greater social acceptance of female involvement in the public sphere, largely suburban white women joined Republican-dominated women's clubs, where they worked for conservative causes, including guidance of public school policies. These women became an important component of a rising conservatism in the state in the late 1960s.

Coastal Counterculture in the 1960s

Rooted in the San Francisco poetry renaissance and largely youth-oriented, a California-based counter cultural movement decidedly at odds with mainstream American values emerged in the 1960s. It was a Pacific-influenced and situated phenomenon found primarily along the coastline from the Bay Area southward to Laguna Beach.

Counterculture values stressed an earthy lifestyle and disdain for material wealth; nonviolence; "free love," meaning an acceptance of non-exclusive sexual relationships; an embrace of Asian and Native American metaphysics; and an openness to experimentation with consciousness-altering drugs. Youthful adherents of this ethos were called "hippies," a word derived from "hipster," a 1950s term for a bohemian. Hippies held that people over 30 years of age who held jobs, paid mortgages, and supported families were part of corporate America's "Establishment," thought to be the cause of society's wars, racism, and poverty.

In the northern reaches of the state, San Francisco's 1967 "Summer of Love" captured much of the counterculture's idealism, whimsy, and downside. Centered in the Haight-Ashbury neighborhood, it was attended by some 75,000 young people from throughout the nation and memorialized in Scott McKenzie's song, "San Francisco." There, hippies, or "flower children" as they were also called because of blossoms worn in their hair, listened to the music of the Grateful Dead and other groups, while eating communally, dancing, and taking drugs. "Make love not war" was emblazoned on placards and t-shirts. Allen Ginsberg chanted Hindu mantras before leading processions to the ocean to watch a Pacific sunset. Before summer's end, youthful exuberance gave way to drug abuse, malnutrition, violent crime, and a public health menace.

In June 1967, at another coastal California site, the nation's first large-scale popular music event of the 1960s was held: the Monterey International Pop Festival. The three-day concert included performers Simon and Garfunkel, the Animals, Ravi Shankar, The Byrds, Jefferson Airplane, Janis Joplin, Jimi Hendrix, and other musical artists. A Buddha statue placed at the site provided a sense of Asian-Pacific spirituality. On the third day of the festival the crowd swelled to 60,000. Marijuana and stronger hallucinogens were pervasive, including a new type of LSD (lysergic acid diethylamide), called Monterey Purple, that made its debut.

Farther south in Big Sur an older, wealthier, and more contemplative clientele frequented the hot springs and classes at the Esalen Institute. Perched on a Big Sur cliff overlooking the Pacific, Esalen, founded by two Stanford graduates in 1962, offered classes in meditation and Asian spiritual and psychological development.

In southern California, Topanga Canyon and Laguna Beach became major hippie haunts. Rustic Topanga Canyon was home to rock musicians who played at Los Angeles clubs. Neil Young, The Doors, and The Eagles were onetime canyon residents. Laguna Beach, an artsy Orange County enclave known for its seascape, attracted former Harvard psychologist Dr. Timothy Leary and author Ken Kesey, both of whom lived there in the late 1960s. The so-called Brotherhood of Eternal Love, which coalesced around LSD guru Leary, trafficked in psychedelic drugs and surfed Laguna's scenic beaches. The group's drug and surfing ties extended to Mexico, Hawai'i, and Afghanistan.

By then California's liberalism had seen its better days. An era that had defined anew the promise and perils of America's Pacific Eldorado had run its course. Having lost his 1966 bid for a third term as governor, Pat Brown put it aptly: "We fought hard but the tide was just going out."

Figure 12.4 The "Summer of Love:" hippies in Haight Ashbury, San Francisco, 1967.

SUMMARY

As wars in Korea and then Vietnam shifted America's attention increasingly toward the Pacific Rim, politically and figuratively California was awash in a rising tide of liberalism from the early 1950s to the late 1960s. The Golden State became even more of a Pacific Eldorado during these years of remarkable economic growth and prosperity. Agriculture, oil, the aerospace and commercial airlines industries, Hollywood movie-making and television, tourism, and especially defense appropriations and Pacific maritime trade and other ocean-related enterprises powered what was becoming the nation's leading economy. In 1962 California surpassed New York as America's most populous state. Tract homes went up in the Bay Area and Southland suburbs, whose growing numbers of residents pursued ever more consumerist lifestyles that included spending time and money at Disneyland and other theme parks, sporting events, and, famously, beach recreations.

Greater California's materialism went unquestioned except for a maverick group of writers whose poetry and prose launched the San Francisco Renaissance in the 1950s.

Lawrence Ferlinghetti's City Lights Bookstore served as the nerve center of this movement. The Asian Pacific-influenced works of Allen Ginsberg, Jack Kerouac, Gary Snyder, and others paved the way for a wholesale repudiation of mainstream American values that came in the 1960s.

Political progressivism, or liberalism, marked the governorships of Goodwin Knight and even more of Edmund G. "Pat" Brown. These two state leaders put in place a world-class infrastructure of water distribution, transportation, and educational systems. Brown's pragmatic liberalism drew fire from conservatives who opposed his governmental activism and principled stand against the death penalty, and did not go far enough for UC Berkeley's Free Speech Movement organizers. San Francisco State College's President S.I. Hayakawa's quelling of a student strike on his campus catapulted him into national prominence and a seat in the U.S. Senate. Meanwhile, outside of college campuses women and ethnic minorities struggled for fair and equal rights in employment, housing, and the administration of justice. A major race riot in the Watts neighborhood of Los Angeles in 1965 reverberated across the country, unmasking the horrid conditions under which a predominantly black population lived. Meanwhile Mexican Americans became a force in local and state politics and a 1965 immigration law removed barriers to Asians entering California and other parts of the nation.

Political liberalism was accompanied by cultural liberalism – oftentimes called the countercultural movement – during the 1960s. The countercultural movement rejected the "Establishment's" business-world values, and urged a mix of non-materialism, Asian religions, "free love," and experimentation with drugs. This alternative lifestyle was associated largely with California's Pacific Coast. Youth from all over the nation gathered in San Francisco, Monterey, Big Sur, Topanga Canyon, and Laguna Beach to celebrate a decade of sun, surf, sex, rock music, and drugs. By the end of the storied era their rollicking, like the liberal reforms and super state enhancements of governors Knight and Brown, began to ebb into memory.

REVIEW QUESTIONS

- What were the major achievements of the governorships of Goodwin Knight and Edmund G. "Pat" Brown?
- What were the major sectors of California's diversified economy in the 1950s and 1960s and how did each contribute to the prosperity of the times?
- How did California's Pacific connections influence developments in the Golden State from the early 1950s to the late 1960s?
- Being sure to include the experiences of people of color, what were the promises and perils of California life in the 1960s?
- How were the San Francisco Renaissance of the 1950s and the countercultural episode of the 1960s connected? Were these two separate movements or simply different stages of one long social phenomenon the energies of which were directed against the corporate "Establishment"?

FURTHER READINGS

Jonathan Bell, *California Crucible: The Forging of Modern American Liberalism* (Philadelphia: University of Pennsylvania Press, 2012). The social democracy that characterized American public policies from the late 1940s to the mid-1970s, this book shows, was rooted in and driven by California's liberal movement that crested in the governorship of Edmund G. "Pat" Brown.

Edmund G. Brown et al., *California: The Dynamic State* (Santa Barbara: McNally & Loftin, 1966). Governor Pat Brown laid out his ambitious plans for California's growth in this volume.

John and LaRee Caughey, eds., *Los Angeles: Biography of a City* (Berkeley: University of California Press, 1976). This anthology covers Los Angeles' history from the time of Indian *rancherías* (villages) to the rise of the late twentieth-century megalopolis.

Robert Cohen, *Freedom's Orator: Mario Savio and the Radical Legacy of the 1960s* (New York: Oxford University Press, 2009). The rise of the Free Speech Movement and its peerless student orator is chronicled with understanding and in detail in this thoroughly researched biography.

Robert Cohen and Reginald E. Zelnik, eds., *The Free Speech Movement: Reflections on Berkeley in the 1960s* (Berkeley: University of California Press, 2002). This anthology provides a comprehensive analysis of the Free Speech Movement from the perspectives of students, faculty, and administrators at UC Berkeley in the 1960s.

Michael Davidson, *The San Francisco Renaissance: Poetics and Community at Mid-Century* (New York: Cambridge University Press, 1989). An understanding of the urban, romantic, proletarian poetry movement in 1950s San Francisco, which this book offers, is indispensable to fathoming California in the 1960s.

Mike Davis, *City of Quartz: Excavating the Future in Los Angeles* (New York: Vintage Books, 1990). The author exposes the wide gap between the utopian dreams of Los Angeles' promoters and the tawdry underside of greed, exploitation, and violence that characterize the history of a city that augurs America's future.

John A. Douglass, *The California Idea and American Higher Education: 1850 to the 1960 Master Plan* (Stanford, CA: Stanford University Press, 2001). The intellectual origins and development of the Master Plan for Higher Education in California are traced with sympathetic care in this seminal study.

Iris Engstrand, *San Diego: California's Cornerstone* (San Diego, CA: Sunbelt Publications, 2005). This is a highly readable and reliable account of a major California city from its Native American past to its importance as a modern high-technology metropolitan center situated on the Pacific Rim.

Marcia A. Eymann and Charles Wollenberg, eds., *What's Going On? California and the Vietnam Era* (Berkeley: University of California Press, 2004). This illustrated history offers visually arresting photographs and incisive commentary on the California home front during the turbulent Vietnam War years.

Jo Freeman, *At Berkeley in the Sixties: The Education of an Activist* (Bloomington, IN: Indiana University Press, 2004). The author tells how she became a liberal political activist on entering UC Berkeley at age 16, how she dealt with her fears of being arrested for the first time, and her dissatisfaction with the subordinate role of female students in the Free Speech Movement.

Louis Heath, ed., *The Black Panther Leaders Speak: Huey P. Newton, Bobby Seale, Eldridge Cleaver and Company Speak Out through the Black Panther Party's Official Newspaper* (Metuchen, NJ: Scarecrow Press, 1976). This is a valuable source for understanding the ideas, goals, and activities of the radical, urban-based "black power" movement.

Norris Hundley, Jr., *The Great Thirst: Californians and Water, a History* (Berkeley: University of California Press, 2001). A more comprehensive, balanced, and detailed account of California's twentieth-century water projects would be hard to imagine.

Troy Johnson and Donald Fixico, *The American Indian Occupation of Alcatraz Island: Red Power and Self-Determination* (Lincoln, NE: University of Nebraska Press, 2008). Drawing on extensive interviews and government documents, the authors narrate the goals and living conditions of the Indians who seized the island for 19 months beginning in 1969.

Clark Kerr, *The Gold and the Blue: A Personal Memoir of the University of California, 1949–1967*, 2 vols. (Berkeley: University of California Press, 2001). The president of the University of California tellingly explains the crossfire he was caught in between students, professors, regents, and the governor during the Free Speech Movement.

Rob Kling, Spencer Olin, and Mark Poster, eds., *Postsuburban California: The Transformation of Orange County since World War II* (Berkeley: University of California Press, 1991). Orange County's phenomenal post-World War II transformation from a rural appendage of Los Angeles into a high-technology export business center is traced in this groundbreaking anthology.

James Andrew LaSpina, *California in a Time of Excellence: School Reform at the Crossroads of the American Dream* (Albany, NY: State University of New York, 2009). The author analyzes the politics involved in framing the 1960s Master Plan for Higher Education and instituting K-12 reforms in the following decades.

Kirse Granat May, *Golden State, Golden Youth: The California Image in Popular Culture, 1955–1966* (Chapel Hill, NC: University of North Carolina Press, 2002). This slim volume chronicles the rise of California's youth culture and its portrayal in the media.

Carlos Muñoz, *Youth, Identity, Power: Chicano Movement* (New York: Verso, 1989). Written by a leader in the Chicano movement, the author traces the movement's origins back to the 1930s and situates its blossoming and decline within the broader civil rights crusade of the 1960s.

Charles F. Queenan, *The Port of Los Angeles: From Wilderness to World Port* (Los Angeles: Government and Community Relations Division, Los Angeles Harbor Department, 1983). The rise of maritime Los Angeles to international stature on the Pacific Rim is chronicled in this illustrated account.

Ethan Rarick, *California Rising: The Life and Times of Pat Brown* (Berkeley: University of California Press, 2005). This is a well-balanced yet sympathetic political biography of one of California's most determinative governors in the twentieth century.

Theodore Rosak, *The Making of a Counterculture: Reflections on the Technocratic Society and Its Youthful Opposition* (Berkeley: University of California Press, 1995). In this foundational study, the author shows how youthful opposition to the corporate world and its technologies helped produce the 1960s counterculture.

Nicholas Schou, *Orange Sunshine: The Brotherhood of Eternal Love and Its Quest to Spread Peace, Love, and Acid to the World* (New York: St. Martins Griffin, 2010). A journalist sheds new light on a countercultural group of surfers, hippies, and drug users/dealers whose operations ranged from Laguna Beach to Mexico, Hawai'i, and Afghanistan.

Kevin Starr, *Golden Dreams: California in an Age of Abundance, 1950–1963* (New York: Oxford University Press, 2009). The ties between economic abundance and cultural growth in the postwar era are detailed in this account of modern California's purported golden age.

13

"Gold Coast" Conservatism and the Politics of Limits

During liberalism's high tide in the 1960s, a small but growing opposition to progressive politics coalesced around Hollywood actor-turned-politician Ronald Reagan, who lived in affluent Pacific Palisades "Where the Mountains Meet the Sea." He did not so much lead the conservative backlash that influenced California politics into the early twenty-first century as symbolize it and speak for it. The conservatism that he embodied had a singular quality about it: it was most formidable along southern California's so-called "Gold Coast," a stretch of Pacific shoreline stretching from Santa Barbara to San Diego and inhabited by many wealthy, powerful business leaders with close ties to government officials in Sacramento and Washington, D.C. Newport Beach, located in notably Republican Orange County, was and remains its vital center. During the presidency of Richard M. Nixon, however, seaside San Clemente, where the Republican head of state spent much time at his Western White House, Casa Pacifica, momentarily vied for that distinction. From the "Gold Coast," elite conservative Republicans would by the late 1960s dominate state politics, and thereby exert increasing influence throughout the nation.

Political conservatives believed that the past should have a strong hold on the present and future. Change, especially rapid change promoted by government, was viewed with skepticism. Similarly, they revered the free market economy, resisting tax increases and governmental interference with and regulation of business. They publicly avowed traditional Christian beliefs and values. In foreign policy matters, they tended to be hawkish. "Gold Coast" conservatives embraced these characteristics but did so in a mainstream style, largely devoid of the conspiratorial views and apocryphal evangelical pronouncements of many right-wing conservatives elsewhere, especially those living in rural America. In the words of Harvard historian Lisa McGirr, the Orange County conservative Republicans were "suburban warriors" – respectable, well organized, combative, and politically consequential.

Powered largely by "Gold Coast" Republicans, California's rightward shift in the 1960s can be attributed to such major factors as Cold War fears about communism, public anger about student protests at UC Berkeley and other UC campuses, taxpayers' frustration about the mounting costs of the liberal agenda, rising levels of urban crime and violence, and dissatisfaction with long-serving, center-left, secular-leaning politicians in the state capital. These factors gave rise to a conservatism that would structurally impede the financing of the public sector, shorten the tenure of liberal Democratic legislators in Sacramento, and usher in a politics of limits that embraced minimal government regulation of the economy and a rollback of programs aimed ostensibly at promoting environmentalism, social welfare, and racial justice.

Pacific Eldorado: A History of Greater California, First Edition. Thomas J. Osborne.
© 2013 Thomas J. Osborne. Published 2013 by Blackwell Publishing Ltd.

Timeline

1961   San Marino Republican and John Birch Society leader John H. Rousselot wins election to the 25th Congressional District

1962   The Lincoln Club, a power center of "Gold Coast" conservatism, is founded and headquartered in Newport Beach

1967   The California Air Resources Board is established to set air-quality standards and enforce laws

California establishes the State Water Resources Control Board, responsible for setting water-quality standards

1968   Southern California Edison operates the state's first nuclear power plant at San Onofre, along the coast just south of San Clemente

1969   A major oil spill off Santa Barbara's coast blackens beaches, kills thousands of seabirds, and causes millions of dollars in damage

California, Nevada, and the federal government establish the Tahoe Regional Planning Agency to manage growth and protect the ecology of the lake

1970   The California Environmental Quality Act is passed, requiring the preparation of environmental impact reports for major construction projects having the potential of affecting the natural environment

1971–2   Governor Ronald Reagan increases salary withholding, sales, bank, and corporation taxes

1973   Tom Bradley is elected as Los Angeles' first black mayor

1975   The state legislature passes the Agricultural Labor Relations Act, providing safeguards for the United Farm Workers Union

1976   The landmark California Coastal Act passes and is signed into law, empowering the Coastal Commission to "protect, conserve, restore, and enhance [the] . . . resources of the California coast and ocean"

1977   Governor Jerry Brown appoints Rose Elizabeth Bird as chief justice of the California supreme court; she is the first woman to serve on that tribunal

1978   Voters pass Proposition 13, which limits taxes on both residential and commercial properties to 1 percent of the assessed value, and restricts tax increases for both types of properties to 2 percent per year, based on 1975 valuations; any new taxes would require a two-thirds vote in the state legislature

In the U.S. Supreme Court decision, *Regents of the University of California v. Bakke*, white plaintiff Allan Bakke sues and wins admission to UC Davis's medical school in a case that strikes down racial quotas for admission

Former San Francisco Supervisor Daniel White shoots and kills Mayor George Moscone and Supervisor Harvey Milk; White's attorney employs the "Twinkie Defense"

1990   California passes a law mandating that automobile manufacturers produce and make available non-polluting vehicles by 1998

Voters pass Proposition 140, amending the constitution to set term limits for lawmakers.

1992	The Rodney King riots erupt in Los Angeles, resulting in the deaths of more than 50 people and property damage of $1 billion
	Diane Feinstein is elected to the U.S. Senate, joining Barbara Boxer, and marking the first time in American history that a state has been represented by two female Senators at the same time
1993	California registers America's highest rate of residential and commercial real-estate foreclosures
1994	The Northridge earthquake kills 60 people and injures more than 7,000; approximately $20 billion in damage results; the temblor is felt in Greater California's surrounding areas of Nevada, Utah, and Baja
	Voters pass Proposition 187 denying non-emergency medical treatment, public schooling, and other specified social services to undocumented immigrants
	Voters pass Proposition 184, the "Three Strikes" initiative, providing that those convicted of a third felony will receive a mandatory prison sentence of 25 years to life
	Orange County government is derailed by the nation's largest municipal bankruptcy
1995	In a criminal trial a predominantly black jury acquits O.J. Simpson of killing his wife Nichole Brown Simpson and Ronald L. Goldman
1996	Governor Wilson signs a bill removing the cap on consumers' electricity rates
	Voters pass Proposition 209, prohibiting state and local government agencies from using race, gender, color, or national background in the awarding of contracts, hiring, or admission of students
	Twentieth Century Fox establishes Baja Studios, located on the Pacific Coast just south of Rosarito Beach; much of *Titanic* was filmed there
1997	In a civil trial the families of murder victims Nichole Brown Simpson and Ronald L. Goldman win a $33.5 million verdict against O.J. Simpson
	30 dated levees in the Sacramento–San Joaquin Delta break, resulting in nine deaths and $2 billion in property damage
	Fueled by Pacific-centered enterprises and the "dot com gold rush," the state's trillion-dollar economy ranks with that of leading nations
	The Getty Center art museum opens near UCLA
1998	The Internet search company Google is co-founded in 1998 by two Stanford graduate students, Larry Page and Sergey Brin
early 2000s	California's nation-sized economy ranks 6th in the world; 40 percent of America's waterborne imports pass through the linked Pacific ports of Los Angeles–Long Beach
2001	California experiences "rolling blackouts" due to Texas-based Enron's gaming of the state's energy market
2002	Los Angeles' Cathedral of Our Lady of the Angels is completed
2003	Los Angeles' Walt Disney Concert Hall opens
2004	California's export trade with Pacific Rim countries is valued at $110 billion

From Ultra-Right-Wingers to Mainstream Suburban Warriors

"Gold Coast" conservatism underwent a shift in the 1960s from marginal credibility to mainstream respectability. The John Birch Society exemplified the marginality in the early stages of conservatism's rise. Founded in 1958 by a wealthy, retired Boston candy manufacturer, Robert W. Welch, Jr., the society to this day has been an ultra-right-wing advocacy organization. It was named after a Baptist medical missionary in China who was assassinated by communists in August 1945. Welch and his followers held that the graduated income tax, social security, fluoridation of public drinking water, and civil rights legislation were all due to a gigantic communist conspiracy to undermine the United States. Moreover, they alleged that the United Nations was a communist organization in the process of creating a world government, and therefore the United States must withdraw from it. Welch is remembered for having called Republican President Dwight D. Eisenhower, supreme commander of Allied forces in World War II, a "conscious, dedicated agent of the communist conspiracy." Birchers furthermore claimed that Republican U.S. Supreme Court Chief Justice Earl Warren was a communist agent. Though William F. Buckley, Jr., arguably conservatism's leading spokesperson, dismissed Welch and the Birchers in the early 1960s as "idiotic" and "paranoid," the society established a strong presence in the southern California Republican enclaves of San Marino and Orange County.

In San Marino, Republican John H. Rousselot won election to the 25th Congressional District in 1961 as a member of the John Birch Society. Several years later he served as regional director of the society from his San Marino office, heading Bircher operations in the Far West. Beginning in 1970 he won half a dozen terms in the House of Representatives.

Orange County was equally friendly to the John Birch Society, where, according to McGirr, it had some 5,000 members in 1965. Society organizers in the county, known nationwide as a bastion of conservatism, promoted Republican candidates for public office. For example, Bircher and Santa Ana College philosophy and political science professor John Schmitz gained election to the state senate in 1964, serving two terms before winning a seat in the House of Representatives' 35th Congressional District in 1970. In 1972 he ran for the presidency on the American Independent Party ticket as the conservative alternative to Richard Nixon, who prided himself on opening relations with the communist government of mainland China. "I have no objection to President Nixon going to China," Schmitz quipped, "I just object to his coming back." Schmitz received 1.1 million votes in that campaign. "I lost the presidency by a mere 44 million votes," he afterward reportedly joked. He believed citizens should be free to carry loaded guns in their cars, that state universities should be sold to private corporations to curb student rebellions, and that sex education in public schools should be banned. The Watts riots of 1965, he held, were "a Communist operation." Though trounced in the presidential election, his polling of more than a million votes is a barometer of the number of Americans who supported the far right. In the early 1980s, by which time he had stepped up his verbal attacks on women's rights advocates and publicly supported General Augusto Pinochet's right-wing military dictatorship in Chile, the John Birch Society expelled him for "extremism."

While a force within southern Californian Republican circles in the 1960s, the John Birch Society thereafter declined substantially in numbers and influence. Near the end of that decade some Birchers grew impatient with the society's unsupported conspiracy theories and tired of being labeled in the media as fringe-type people. The society did not appeal to Republican moderates, nor to conservative/libertarian-leaning independent thinkers, nor to entrepreneurs and middle-of-the road voters generally. Many such Republicans living along the "Gold Coast" formed the nucleus of a broader constituency that would one day rule national politics.

While Eric Hoffer did not fit the profile of Gold Coast conservatives, who led affluent lifestyles in southern California, nevertheless from the 1950s into the 1980s he was a consequential and popular figure among political moderates and right-leaning people nationwide. Of German descent, Hoffer had no schooling, lived simply (for a brief period he was a hobo), and after arriving in California from his home state of New York, picked crops in the Central Valley before becoming a San Francisco longshoreman. During much of this time, Hoffer read numerous books checked out from public libraries, becoming a self-educated citizen philosopher. In many of the more than 10 books he wrote, beginning with *The True Believer* (1951), Hoffer warned about zealots and the mass movements they often led. "The fanatic is not really a stickler to principle. He embraces a cause not primarily because of its justness or holiness but because of his desperate need for something to hold onto." Abrupt societal change, the goal of such movements, could be catastrophic for humans; measured change over time was best. He viewed the student radicalism of the 1960s as the result of privileged youth, who, not having had to enter the paid labor force, had not found the meaning in their lives that comes with growing up and earning a living. Affluence kept college-age young people in a state of perpetual adolescence. Eschewing the label of "intellectual," he preferred to be called a "longshoreman." UC Berkeley saw him as an important thinker and hired him as an adjunct instructor. President Eisenhower read and expressed admiration for some of Hoffer's books, and President Lyndon B. Johnson invited the dock worker and writer to the White House for conversation.

Meanwhile, in conservatism's southern California heartland, the Lincoln Club, founded in 1962 and headquartered in Newport Beach, provided much of the leadership for a powerful right-wing cohort of voters. The non-profit business organization aimed to shrink the scope and size of government, reduce taxes, and expand economic freedom. It took its name from Abraham Lincoln, whom it quotes as having said: "In all that people can individually do as well for themselves, the government ought not do for them." Herein was the "Gold Coast" evocation of the politics of limits. Club members included such corporate and political elites as Dr. Arnold O. Beckman, the founder of Beckman Instruments; Walter Knott, the founder of Knott's Berry Farm; Si Fluor of the Fluor Corporation; soon-to-become president Richard Nixon; and movie star John Wayne.

At the non-elite, grassroots level of local politics Orange County's widening base of conservatives formed advocacy groups that battled "obscenity" in speech and print, opposed sex education in the public schools, and campaigned against abortion. Looking back, one conservative parent in Orange County, for example, recalled: "It was so bad . . . all the rock groups, their music . . . the movies, television. Everything was changing, the whole system of values that we treasured in this country. . . . You know that Mario Savio thing from

Berkeley, 'If it feels good, do it.'" That this was a wholly mistaken characterization of Mario Savio, who was highly disciplined, cerebral, and critical of "hippieness" and drug use, did not matter. No moral issue so galvanized the broader constituency as abortion. On this issue some Democrats linked with Republicans and many evangelical Protestants joined with Catholics, particularly in Orange County, to support a pro-life (meaning anti-abortion) movement. One former Democrat, Beverly Cielnicky, reregistered as a Republican and joined the Central Baptist Church in Huntington Beach, which she viewed as "very, very pro-life." To such converts to Republican conservatism must be added a large share of the hundreds of thousands of people buying homes in Orange County in the 1960s and 1970s. Many of these upper-middle-class, mainly white professional suburban denizens worked in the defense-aerospace sector, which virtually assured their support for high military expenditures to thwart the spread of communism. Hughes Aircraft, TRW, Ford Aerospace, Nortronics, Autonetics, and other military contractors provided well-paying jobs to this phalanx of high-tech "suburban warriors."

Ably led by the Lincoln Club, this broader, more mainstream, vanguard of "Gold Coast" voters stood in need of political candidates who could garner mass appeal. They were in luck.

Ronald Reagan: The "Cowboy" Governor

Amid these conservative Republican stirrings, the glow of the Pat Brown era of achievements (see Chapter 12) faded fast. The Free Speech Movement at UC Berkeley later became militant as America stepped up the drafting of college-age males being sent to fight in Vietnam; a six-day race riot incinerated much of Watts in 1965 (see Chapter 12); California growers became increasingly resistant to the demands of unionized farm workers; and Governor Pat Brown's ambitious reforms had left little money in the state treasury. White taxpayers in the state had grown angry with the Democrats who had been in charge in Washington, D.C., and Sacramento during the first half of the 1960s. Into these roiling political waters stepped Ronald W. Reagan, who, like a frontier sheriff, promised to restore "law and order" for the working and middle classes who felt their voices went unheard in Sacramento. The Lincoln Club and other wealthy southern California Republicans, situated mainly along the "Gold Coast," promoted his candidacy.

Such was the backdrop for the state's 1966 gubernatorial election. Brown came to symbolize a politics that went beyond the limits, a government and society reeling out of control. After defeating former San Francisco Mayor George Christopher for the party's nomination, Reagan became the Republican candidate for governor, campaigning to restore "common sense" and economy to government. Reagan pledged to clean up the "mess at Berkeley," repeal the Rumford Fair Housing Act, reduce welfare, and safeguard California's cities whose "streets are jungle paths after dark, with more crimes of violence than New York, Pennsylvania and Massachusetts combined." Regarding his opposition to the Rumford measure, Reagan insisted that he was motivated by reverence for private property, not racial bigotry. On November 8 he won the governorship by a margin of close to 1 million votes. Most other statewide offices also went to Republicans while the Democrats' majorities in the Sacramento legislature were reduced.

While combative, the new governor was also likable. Reagan had been born in Illinois in 1911 and graduated from Eureka College, where he excelled in drama and athletics. Throughout much of his life, he exhibited the optimism, Midwestern folksiness, and communication skills that marked his political style. While his style remained unchanging, his politics had shifted significantly from New Deal liberalism to post-World War II conservatism as he grew alarmed about communism in the Hollywood studios. Having starred in several westerns early in his movie career, he was fond of dressing in cowboy boots and other equestrian attire. At his ranch overlooking the Pacific in the Santa Ynez Mountains north of Santa Barbara, Reagan indulged his cowboy persona more fully.

Governor Reagan's inaugural address, delivered on January 5, 1967, went to the core of his public philosophy: "We are going to squeeze and cut and trim until we reduce the cost of government." Unlike his more urbane immediate predecessors – Earl Warren, Goodwin Knight, and Pat Brown – Reagan did not see a positive role for government in making California a better place for all. He suspected that many state services "were just goodies dreamed up for our supposed betterment." Consequently, budget cuts were in store for colleges, mental health care, and welfare.

Figure 13.1 Governor Ronald Reagan riding at his ranch. Courtesy of the Ronald Reagan Library, Simi Valley, CA.

Reagan thought cutting state funding for colleges would serve two purposes. First, it would trim government spending, and second, it "would help get rid of undesirables," that is, those "there to agitate and not to study." He also saw to it in 1970 that UC students for the first time would pay tuition, technically described as an "education fee." While higher education budgets were reduced and tuition imposed, Reagan helped secure the Board of Regents' firing of the president of the UC system, Clark Kerr. Academics nationwide viewed Kerr's removal as an anti-intellectual attack on America's preeminent public university system. A *New York Times* editorial, titled "Twilight of a Great University," predicted that the budget cuts and firing of Kerr would result in top professors leaving the system, which in turn would decline in quality and prestige. Some 2,500 student marchers assembled at the state capital. They came from the UC's nine campuses, demanding a restoration of ample budgets and a rescinding of the tuition policy. Reagan refused. His policies toward the three-tiered higher education system remained unchanged throughout his two terms in office and had large public support.

Regarding mental health, California had one of the nation's most progressive programs until Reagan took office. That program had institutionalized the seriously incapacitated while providing outpatient care in communities for those who were more functional. The new governor closed hospitals, reduced the number of public mental health workers by 2,500, and shut down numerous outpatient facilities.

To Reagan, downsizing California's "monster" welfare programs was essential to restoring a politics of limits. He believed that welfare pushed the costs of government "out of control" and made people lazy and dependent even though only 1 percent of male recipients were physically fit to work. About three-fourths of those on federal and/or state aid were blind, aged, or disabled, and the rest were children being raised by single mothers. Undeniably, welfare spending had increased significantly as Reagan entered the governor's mansion. Federal welfare payments, in the form of Aid to Families with Dependent Children (AFDC), went to more than twice as many Californians in 1967 (769,000) as in 1963 (375,000). By 1970, when Reagan defeated Democrat Jesse Unruh by half a million votes, the state's AFDC recipients numbered 1,566,000, or nearly one out of every 13 Californians. The state had supplemented payments to these recipients in additional programs, such as Medi-Cal, which provided health care to low-income families with children, pregnant women, the elderly, and the disabled. As governor, Reagan secured stiffer prerequisites for AFDC recipients and a work requirement for able-bodied people on the welfare rolls; however the courts blocked his attempt to reduce Medi-Cal expenses.

Many of his campaign pledges went unfulfilled. Reagan was unable to deliver on his promise to reduce the cost of government. In fact, state budgets doubled during his governorship, climbing from $5 billion in 1967–8 to more than $10 billion in 1974–5. The operations of the Department of Health Care Services furnish one example of rising government expenditures. When Reagan entered the governorship that "department" was really little more than an office with four or five employees. Three years later, in 1970, that office had ballooned into a full-fledged department with about 1,000 employees. By then the state was wrestling with the new question of how much preventive medical care Californians could expect to receive. To keep the government financially solvent, Reagan raised taxes by introducing a salary withholding policy in 1971 and upping sales, bank, and corporation levies the following year. Reagan backed off of his earlier campaign pledge to repeal the Rumford Fair Housing Act, citing the measure's "symbolism" to black communities. With the Watts riots (see below) freshly in mind, both Republicans and Democrats in Sacramento were mindful of what could happen if racial tensions went ignored. Though often criticized for being a right-wing ideologue, the Republican governor was highly pragmatic. Regarding his retreat on the Rumford matter, biographer Lou Cannon simply noted: "Reagan was a conservative beyond a doubt. He was also a practical and resourceful politician."

Despite the fact that his policies in some important instances were at odds with his conservative rhetoric, voters liked Reagan. The charismatic politician's eventful two terms contributed to his rising profile in national politics. Though losing to Richard Nixon in a bid to gain the Republican presidential nomination in 1968, Reagan's stature and popularity continued to grow. He presented a formidable, if unsuccessful, challenge to incumbent Republican President Gerald Ford's nomination in 1976. Four years later his party and the nation would be ready for a Reagan presidency.

Governor Jerry Brown: The Zen of Politics and Frugality

Narrowly defeating Republican gubernatorial nominee Houston Flournoy in 1974, Edmund G. ("Jerry") Brown, Jr., son of former Governor Pat Brown, ushered in a more progressive variant of the politics of limits. If Ronald Reagan evoked the materialistic, cowboy image, Jerry Brown's persona by contrast was that of a self-denying, Zen philosopher who rather than living in the governor's mansion resided in a rented room, with his bedding on the floor. Instead of being chauffeured in a Cadillac like his immediate predecessor, he chose a Plymouth sedan. Unlike the folksy, parochial, detail-averse Reagan, Brown was an aloof cosmopolitan – having graduated from UC Berkeley in classics and from Yale Law School – known for his impressive command of policy matters. A former Jesuit novitiate, the new governor was a bachelor and public intellectual, who had served on the Los Angeles Community College District board of trustees, and then as California's secretary of state.

A pragmatic political liberal and independent thinker, Brown understood that the times called for reducing public spending and maximizing the use of limited resources. Wide-ranging in his reading, he thought highly of British economist E.F. Schumacher's book *Small is Beautiful: Economics as if People Mattered* (1973). The volume was a minor classic, persuasively making the case for reducing consumption of goods, buying locally produced foods and other products, and for economies serving residential communities rather than profit-focused corporations. Fortunately for Brown, as he went about implementing his approach of enlightened austerity, Democrats enjoyed majorities in both houses of the state legislature and in California's congressional delegation. They also held most of the higher administrative offices in Sacramento. In short, the governor could count on considerable support for his policies from the apparatus of government.

Policy-wise, Brown's first term was more progressive than his second. The Agricultural Labor Relations Act of 1975 provided safeguards for the United Farm Workers Union. To ensure enforcement, Brown appointed Rose Elizabeth Bird to the Agricultural Labor

Figure 13.2   Edmund G. ("Jerry") Brown, at his 1961 UC Berkeley graduation, being congratulated by his father, Governor Edmund G. ("Pat") Brown. San Francisco History Center, San Francisco Public Library.

Relations Board. In 1977 he installed her as chief justice of the state supreme court, making Bird the first woman to serve on that tribunal. He appointed more women, African Americans, Latinos, and Asian Americans to high state office than any other governor in California history. Business leaders balked when Brown placed conservationists on the Air Resources Board and the Energy Commission. To maintain wilderness areas and provide young unemployed workers with jobs, Brown established the California Conservation Corps. Though implemented without tax increases, the governor's policies did not solve the stubborn problem of unemployment in California, driven as it was by a nationwide recession.

Brown's attempt to gain the Democratic presidential nomination in 1976 failed, as he won primaries in only a few states. He tried again in 1980 but President Jimmy Carter's incumbent status posed an insurmountable barrier.

Meanwhile, Brown had won reelection to the governorship in 1978, handily defeating state Attorney General Evelle Younger by more than a million votes. In response to conservative critics, Brown appointed pro-business people to a number of commissions and departments. To increase California's share of the burgeoning Pacific Rim economy, Brown traveled to Japan, Canada, and Mexico. Envisioning an economic windfall from satellite technologies, he urged a major role for aerospace and electronics companies in planning for space colonization, for which Chicago journalist Mike Royko dubbed Brown "Governor Moonbeam." Royko later apologized publicly for so caricaturing Brown. Regarding the criminal justice system, Brown approved bills meting out harsher penalties for those convicted of violent crimes. Like his father, however, he opposed capital punishment while reluctantly agreeing to follow the law regarding its imposition. The governor's 1977 veto of a bill reinstating the death penalty was trumped a year later by voters' passage of an initiative reestablishing it. State funding for public higher education, including community colleges, more than doubled during his governorship.

During Brown's second term California's public sector was hit by a taxpayers' revolt, of far-reaching consequences. In 1978 Howard Jarvis and Paul Gann founded the United Organization of Taxpayers to place an initiative on the ballot – Proposition 13 – aimed at preventing property tax increases. The measure limited taxes on both residential and commercial properties to 1 percent of the assessed value, and restricted tax increases for both types of properties to 2 percent per year, using 1975 valuations as the baseline for assessments. Reassessments could occur only in the cases of improvements or sale, and any new taxes would require a two-thirds vote in the state legislature rather than the then required simple majority. The proposed constitutional amendment easily qualified for the ballot. Brown and many other officeholders opposed the measure when it was introduced, warning that it would benefit those possessing apartments and other businesses more than homeowners, undercut government services, force layoffs of state workers, and result in severely underfunding public education at all levels. Later developments, after Brown left the governorship, proved the validity of many of these warnings, especially after per-pupil spending in the K-12 system declined dramatically and the state's physical infrastructure began to deteriorate. With a well-publicized $3.5 billion surplus in the state treasury, accumulated by Brown's austerity, voters felt that funds were more than adequate to pay for state services, such as public education, maintaining highways and bridges, staffing parks, and carrying out numerous other functions. After Proposition 13 passed overwhelmingly in 1978 and became law, the governor found favor with it, acknowledging that it was compatible with his "era of limits" thinking. The two-thirds super-majority required to increase state taxes would remain a contentious political issue for decades afterward.

In addition to the taxpayers' revolt, Brown's second term was dogged by a controversy regarding the use of chemical pesticides to combat an infestation of Mediterranean fruit flies that threatened commercial crops in the Santa Clara Valley. Initially, the governor sided with residents fearful of the health effects of aerial spraying and supported ground spraying as an alternative and the use of sterile fruit flies to block reproduction. At this point, President Ronald Reagan imposed a quarantine on all California produce, thereby forcing Brown to resume aerial spraying. The fruit fly controversy damaged the governor's standing with both the public and business interests in California.

Another battle shaping up during Brown's second term was waged over affirmative action, that is, the policy of government agencies giving preferential consideration, often through quotas, to underrepresented minorities in admission to public universities, hiring, and letting contracts. Allan Bakke, a white student, was twice rejected when applying to UC Davis's medical school though each time minority candidates with grade point averages and test scores below his were admitted. This was due to the university's policy of reserving 16 percent of its seats for incoming students for underrepresented minority applicants. Seeing this as reverse racial discrimination, Bakke sued and won at the state level and in the U.S. Supreme Court decision, *Regents of the University of California v. Bakke* (1978), resulting in his admission. While not prohibiting the university's use of race as a factor in admissions, racial quotas were outlawed. Brown kept a low profile in the controversial Bakke matter, which some voters saw as an indication that leadership in the governor's office was lacking.

Crime and Racial Tensions

By the 1980s an escalating crime rate and mounting racial tensions were tarnishing the quality of life and image of California. The assassination of two top San Francisco officials by a vengeful office-seeker drew national headlines. As levels of inner city crowding and poverty rose, well-armed street gangs organized along ethnic lines, some with strong Pacific Basin ties, posed an increasing problem to law-abiding citizens and police. Tensions between South Central Los Angeles' black population and white law enforcement officers erupted in a massive riot when policemen, who had been videotaped beating a motorist, were found not guilty of using excessive force. International attention was riveted on Los Angeles by a double murder in upscale Brentwood that implicated a former USC Heisman Trophy winner and television celebrity. Such happenings strengthened the conservatives' case for getting tough on crime and criminals.

In broad daylight on November 27, 1978, former San Francisco Supervisor Daniel White entered City Hall and shot and killed Mayor George Moscone and Supervisor Harvey Milk. White was a "law and order" advocate, strongly supported by conservatives, who had been angered by the mayor's refusal to rescind his (White's) earlier resignation and Milk's cham-

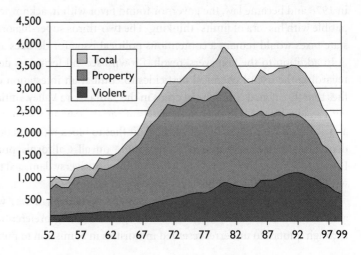

Figure 13.3   California's crime rate, 1952–99. The crime rate peaked in 1980, declined for several years, increased slightly in the late 1980s, and dropped significantly each year from 1991. Source: *Cal Facts* (Sacramento, CA: Legislative Analyst's Office, 2000), p. 75.

pioning of gay and lesbian rights. He readily admitted to the killings. White's attorney offered the "Twinkie Defense," claiming that his client had committed the killings while in a condition of "diminished capacity" caused by sugary substances that skewed his judgment. Swayed by this argument, the jury convicted White of voluntary manslaughter rather than murder. This outraged the city's homosexuals, who saw Milk – one of America's first openly gay municipal officials – as a martyr to their cause.

Meanwhile, Los Angeles remained a simmering cauldron of racial ferment in the wake of the 1965 Watts riots. Rising expectations among middle-class blacks in Los Angeles and statewide provide a backdrop to their unrest. In the 1970s and 1980s, African Americans Maxine Waters, Mervyn Dymally, and Yvonne Braithwaite Burke – all Angelinos – won seats in the House of Representatives, as did Ronald Dellums of Berkeley, who joined Augustus Hawkins who had been representing his Los Angeles district since the 1960s. Wilson Riles in 1970 had become the first African American to be elected superintendent of public instruction. Blacks also had swelled their ranks in the state legislature, where San Francisco's Willie Brown presided as assembly speaker in the 1980s, afterward becoming that city's first African American mayor. The election of Tom Bradley as the first black mayor of the City of Angels in 1973 doubtlessly helped keep conflicts from escalating out of control. With these successes in mind, South Central Los Angeles residents were torn between trusting the police for protection while fearing law enforcement officers' reputed brutality.

Such was the situation on the eve of the April 30–May 5, 1992, Los Angeles riots, one of the worst eruptions of racial discord in American history. On March 3 of the previous year Rodney King, a black man, had been arrested after a high-speed chase and beaten severely by baton-wielding Los Angeles policemen. The pummeling of a prostrate King had been recorded on camera with repeated showings on national television network news. Four police officers were brought to trial in 1992 and acquitted the following year of the charge of using excessive force by a San Fernando Valley jury consisting of 10 whites, one Latino, and a Filipino American. The verdict sparked five days of what came to be called the Rodney King riots, an uprising far worse than its Watts counterpart of 1965. More than 50 people were killed and property damage reached an estimated $1 billion. In the wake of the 1992 riots the widely reported words of Rodney King remain etched in many minds: "People, I just want to say . . . can we all get along? Can we get along?"

Racial relations in Los Angeles were again strained in 1994 with the headline-grabbing murders of Nicole Brown Simpson and Ronald L. Goldman. Ms. Simpson had been the attractive Caucasian wife of African American football star and television sports commentator Orenthal James (known as O.J.) Simpson, and Goldman, a waiter at a nearby restaurant. On June 12, Ms. Simpson and Goldman had been stabbed and slashed to death outside her Brentwood residence. A trial monitored worldwide ended in October 1995 when a predominantly African American jury acquitted the defendant, Mr. Simpson, of both killings. Many African Americans believed that the verdict had been just; a number of whites were convinced that the defendant had literally gotten away with murder. In a civil trial ending in 1997 the victims' families won damages from Mr. Simpson amounting to $33.5 million. The racial aspects of the killings and the criminal trial became fodder for public discourse for years afterward.

Gang violence constituted another major category of ethnic-related crime in late twentieth-century California. In police terminology, gangs are groups of three or more persons joining together to engage in criminal activity. Tom Hayden, author of *Street Wars: Gangs and the Future of Violence* (2004), has concluded that about 25,000 people, mainly gang members themselves, have died in Los Angeles' street wars since the 1970s.

Many of the state's street gangs drew members from immigrant families with roots in Pacific Basin countries and dependencies. These included Mexico, El Salvador, American Samoa, Vietnam, and Cambodia. La Eme (Spanish for the letter "M"), a Mexican American gang, was founded in California prisons in 1956. Known as the Mexican mafia, La Eme aimed at protecting fellow Hispanic prisoners from other inmates, especially the white supremacist Aryan Brotherhood, but soon engaged in extortion, drug trafficking, and contract killings. From Folsom and San Quentin prisons, La Eme members directed drug dealing in the Southland, Baja California, and on Mexico's mainland. Mara Salvatrucha (known as MS), translated as "Salvadoran neighborhood," grew out of El Salvador's civil war in the 1980s, which led to an exodus of Salvadorans to California. Discriminated against in Los Angeles, these impoverished immigrants formed MS, one of the most violent gangs on the entire West Coast. It has since spread to San Francisco, Reno, New York City, Long Island, and Texas – all the while retaining drug ties to El Salvador and competing with La Eme for control of that country's narcotics market. After suffering the ravages of the Vietnam War, some of the younger immigrants from that nation and Cambodia formed Asian gangs to protect themselves in central Orange County, where Santa Ana's Mexican American gangs dominated. Meanwhile, on the East side of Long Beach the Sons of Samoa (SOS) formed in 1980. Its members banded together for protection against black and Mexican American gangs. Soon SOS spread throughout parts of the Southland, San Jose, Hawai'i, and Utah. To all of these gangs must be added the African American rivals – the Crips and the Bloods. Both were formed in Los Angeles in the mid- to late 1960s. They dealt mainly in cocaine trafficking. By 1991 investigative reports held that Crips or Bloods had spread to 32 states and more than 100 cities nationwide. All of these gangs remain active in California and beyond. Thus gang activity, like so many other aspects of the state, reflected the geographical reach of Greater California.

Business and Labor

Despite a public sector whose vitality had been compromised by Proposition 13, California on the whole outpaced the rest of the nation and many countries in economic growth, job-creation, and per capita income from 1980 to 2000. This was true despite a severe recession in the first half of the 1990s. By the early 2000s, California's trillion-dollar gross product, that is, the value of the goods and services it produced yearly, placed the state 6th among the world's nations. In 2001 Los Angeles County's $352 billion economy ranked 16th in the world, ahead of Russia's.

This spectacular economic growth can be attributed to many factors. The diversification of California's economy was a major strength: its agricultural production continued to lead the nation, earning $14 billion in 1986; manufacturing thrived, especially as Japanese firms established assembly plants in the state; banking remained robust in San Francisco and Los Angeles; construction, particularly commercial, showed no abatement; tourism garnered $75 billion annually by 2000; and California dominated the world's film and television markets. To these engines of economic growth must be added two others of even greater consequence: the state's further integration into the bustling Pacific Rim economy, and the spectacular high-technology enterprises in Silicon Valley and elsewhere along or near California's coastline.

The state's turbo-charged business activity from the 1980s to the early twenty-first century had much more to do with California's connections to the Pacific world than with its ties to America's interior and Atlantic regions. While much of Europe in the 1980s was emerging from the stresses and military spending of the Cold War, the nations of East Asia had been industrializing. Its international security assumed largely by the United States, Japan parlayed its people's vaunted work ethic and corporate culture into making it the richest country in Pacific Asia. South Korea, Taiwan, and Hong Kong, similarly, grew their economies, while China stood on the cusp of becoming the trade and banking giant of Pacific Asia. All of these powers outpaced Europe's leading nations in generating wealth. This was the transpacific business environment of which California – America's most Asian state in terms of population – was a part. This huge oceanic region, the new hub of the global economy, remains the most dynamic commercial zone in the world.

Maritime commerce has been at the heart of California's involvement in the $3 trillion Pacific Rim trading economy. "By 1980 two-thirds of California's exports went to Asian destinations," noted historian Bruce Cumings, "and American trade with Asia eclipsed that with Europe." The state's business transactions with Pacific Rim countries in 1985 amounted to $65 billion and most of America's commerce with those nations passed through California's ports. In 2004 California's exports to those countries were valued at $110 billion. "Our future is with the Pacific Basin," remarked the head of the California Office of International Trade. "We're right in the middle of it. If the Basin prospers, we prosper." Since 1999 Mexico has become America's leading trading partner, due largely to the United States entry into the North American Free Trade Agreement that established a continent-wide tariff-free zone. In the early 2000s, 40 percent of the United States waterborne imports came through the linked Pacific ports of Los Angeles–Long Beach, the nation's largest, busiest harbor complex. Oakland held strong in fourth place. Seventy percent of America's Asian trade flows through these ports. The state has been helped in tracking these statistics and providing information to businesses by its institutions of higher education. For example, the University of San Francisco's Center for the Pacific Rim and UC San Diego's Graduate School of International Relations and Pacific Studies have supplied focused information required by Pacific Basin investors and traders. Pomona College's Pacific Basin Institute brings together the region's business leaders, academicians, and government officials.

Regarding labor, waterfront employment as dockworkers and even clerkships went almost entirely to males until a 1983 U.S District Court decision required that the International Longshore and Warehouse Union "adopt the long range goal of employing women as marine clerks . . . at the Port [of Los Angeles] in sufficient numbers to eliminate the continuing effects of any possible past discrimination." To implement his decision, the

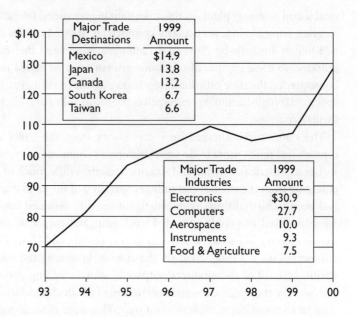

Major Trade Destinations	1999 Amount
Mexico	$14.9
Japan	13.8
Canada	13.2
South Korea	6.7
Taiwan	6.6

Major Trade Industries	1999 Amount
Electronics	$30.9
Computers	27.7
Aerospace	10.0
Instruments	9.3
Food & Agriculture	7.5

Figure 13.4   California's major export markets and the nature of the goods sold are shown in this graph. Source: *Cal Facts* (Sacramento, CA: Legislative Analyst's Office, 2000), p. 6.

presiding judge set hiring quotas for women. As gender bias in hiring declined, the Port of Los Angeles provided 203,000 jobs in a nearby five-county area in fiscal year 1991–2. Port pilots, who navigate container ships and oil tankers through the harbor, were among the highest-paid employees, receiving $150,000 to $300,000 a year in the early 2000s.

Equally important in fueling California's extraordinary economic growth beginning in the 1980s was the bonanza of technological innovation issuing from Silicon Valley. Far removed from the more traditional business culture associated with America's Atlantic seaboard, casually clad young computer geniuses on the Pacific Coast blazed their own trails across the frontier of information technologies. A good share of these prodigies was affiliated with Stanford University, situated in the heart of Silicon Valley. Located slightly south of San Francisco Bay, the valley has been the epicenter for the computer-related high-technology industries that have shaped the way business and communications have functioned worldwide. In the early 1990s a subset of the 900,000 Asian Pacific Islanders living in the Bay Area included tens of thousands of Taiwanese engineers and other computer specialists who owned homes in Taiwan and Silicon Valley. They commuted by plane back and forth across the Pacific, and the décor of their homes in both places reflected what authority Shenglin Chang calls "transcultural lifestyles," meaning the residences and even identities of the Pacific-crossers were a mix of Taiwanese and Californian culture. Highly educated Asian-born women continue to comprise a good number of these ambitious transpacific professionals.

Numerous firms sprouted in Silicon Valley's fertile intellectual environment. Steven Jobs, a college dropout and student of Buddhism, and Stephen Wozniak, a UC Berkeley engineering graduate, co-founded Apple Computers. Robert Noyce, co-inventor of the silicon microchip, led Fairchild Semiconductor and then Intel. Internet search companies such as

Yahoo, Excite, Lycos, Infoseek, and Netscape sprang up, the handiwork of young computer entrepreneurs. The giant-to-be of them all, Google, was co-founded in 1998 by two Stanford graduate students, Larry Page and Sergey Brin. Tens of billions of dollars in profits attested to the success of these firms, which created hundreds of Silicon Valley millionaires in the 1980s and 1990s.

UC Berkeley's dean of the School of Information, AnnaLee Saxenian, calls the engineering-related professionals who founded and managed these enterprises the "new Argonauts." Like the gold-seekers of 1849, they have been drawn to California's universities and unsurpassed high-technology sector. "They are the best and brightest from places like India and China. . . . They have been marinated in Silicon Valley and learn how the start-up culture works here." She says they either return to their Asian or Asian Pacific countries of origin and start their own companies, or remain active in the economies of their homeland and California. Intel's CEO Paul Otellini, while an American, fits the "new Argonaut" profile in every other way. With an MBA from UC Berkeley, he oversaw the 1996 expansion of his microprocessing corporation into China, where he employed 3,500 workers, and later into Vietnam.

High earnings and career opportunities in Silicon Valley, however, did not go as readily to women as men. Carly Fiorina's 1999 rise to president and CEO of Hewlett-Packard, the oldest and most revered Silicon Valley firm, came only after many other talented women, like her, had demonstrated that running a complex business was not solely within the province of males. Historian Glenna Matthews notes: "In 1970, women held 4 percent of professional jobs in the Valley and 0.5 percent of the managerial ones; in 1980, the figures were 17 percent and 14 percent, respectively." By the 1990s a number of women had risen to the upper echelons of management in valley corporations.

Inspired by the Silicon Valley phenomenon, the Southland witnessed a proliferation of computer, electronics, and related businesses. Kingston Technologies, founded by Chinese immigrants to Los Angeles, showed sales approaching $1 billion in 1994. Its workforce numbered 300 employees. That same year some 1,200 Chinese-owned computer firms were operating in southern California. By 1997 Orange County's Irvine Spectrum High Technology Park was home to offices of Western Digital, AT&T, Mazda Motors, Toshiba, and other firms.

In the late twentieth century California emerged as the world's biotechnology leader. The new enterprise, located mainly along or near the Pacific Coast, served as a drive-wheel of the state's nation-sized economy. By 2000 nearly 40 percent of America's research and manufacturing in biotechnology was done in California, where the industry's yearly earnings ranged between $6 and $10 billion. The Bay Area, the Los Angeles Basin, Orange County, and San Diego drew on close university connections to develop pharmaceuticals and related medical technologies that would advance health care. UC San Francisco set the pace by building a 43-acre biomedical research complex. In the Southland, Amgen, Inc., the world's largest biotech company, operated out of Thousand Oaks, offering genetically engineered treatments for cancer, kidney disease, and osteoporosis while financially underwriting biotechnology research in some of the state's universities. In 2000 Amgen's sales reached $3 billion. UC San Diego, working with the nearby Salk Institute, became a leader in biotech research, as did UC Irvine's Paul Mirage School of Business, which has served as an incubator of numerous entrepreneurial biomedical enterprises. In 1997 Claremont's Keck Institute of Applied Life Sciences was founded to provide graduate education for those pursuing biotechnology careers. UCLA, UC Santa Barbara, Caltech, and USC, similarly, engaged in research and teaching related to biotechnology.

Those employed in the biotechnology field exemplified what Claremont Graduate University management authority Peter F. Drucker called "knowledge workers." They comprised the vanguard of highly educated employees of the new information-based economy that was eclipsing the traditional heavy manufacturing one. By late 1997 about 210,000 such professionals were employed in California's booming biotechnology businesses. Their average salaries amounted to $50,000 a year. By then California had clearly become a Pacific Eldorado for scientists, entrepreneurs, venture capitalists, and others in the high-technology workforce.

Pacific Profile: Jerry Yang, Co-founder and CEO, Yahoo! Inc.

"New Argonaut" Jerry Yang (1968–) was born in Taipei, Taiwan. His career trajectory in Silicon Valley's computer industry dazzled onlookers before trailing off a bit. In 2009 *Forbes* magazine listed his wealth at $1.25 billion, ranking him 317th among the 400 richest Americans. His story embodies the California Dream of a Pacific-crosser of modest means, prodigious talent, and soaring ambition making a fortune and carving a niche in history.

Yang's family emigrated from Taiwan to San Jose, California, in 1978, when Jerry was 10 years old. His father having died, Yang's family consisted of his mother, his younger brother, and himself. Though his mother taught English, Yang claims that the only word in that language that he and his brother knew upon arriving in the United States was "shoe." "We got made fun of a lot at first. I didn't even know who the faces were on the paper money," he remembered. "But when we had a math quiz in school I'd always blow everyone else away. And by our third year, my brother and I had gone from remedial English to advanced-placement English." Yang graduated as valedictorian of his Piedmont High School class, where he had served as student body president. He was accepted at UC Berkeley, Stanford, and Caltech, and chose Stanford because it was closer to home and didn't require him to pick a major in his first year of studies. There, he earned bachelor's and master's degrees in engineering while making financial ends meet by working part-time in the university library.

That useful employment taught him about how information was catalogued and organized using the Dewey Decimal System.

Yang was enrolled in a Ph.D. program in engineering at Stanford when he and fellow graduate student, David Filo, decided to start their own Internet search company in 1994–5. Taking an extended leave of absence, they launched Yahoo! Inc. "We started to make money almost from day one. . . . Our audience metrics never slowed down," Yang recalled in 2005. By then Yahoo! was America's leading search engine, and capitalized at nearly $48 billion. Filo ran the technical side of operations; Yang, as CEO, managed nearly everything else until several members of the board of directors complained about revenues not growing fast enough, which led to him stepping down and serving as a director himself. He remains the public face of Yahoo, while charting its course in "voice recognition" and other commercially viable innovations.

Yang married a Stanford engineering student of Japanese descent, Akiko Yamazaki. In addition to contributing millions of dollars to their alma mater, the two have been financial patrons of San Francisco's Asian Art Museum, UC Berkeley's East Asian Library, and the San Francisco Ballet.

Jerry Yang's story remains unfinished. As a computer entrepreneur and philanthropist, his already noteworthy Pacific profile is still in the making.

Protecting the Environment and Supplying Energy

California's economic growth surge of the 1960s and afterward came at the price of environmental degradation. At the same time, the state, with its growing population and power needs, was hit by several energy crises beginning in the 1970s.

A new set of environmental challenges faced Californians in the last decades of the twentieth century. A major oil leak on January 28, 1969, from a well just off the Santa Barbara coast, blackened the city's picturesque Pacific beaches, killed thousands of seabirds and marine mammals, and caused millions of dollars in property damage. In the early 1980s some of Silicon Valley's high-tech companies were found to have leaking underground storage tanks filled with toxic chemicals that presented a health hazard to the public's water supply. Agribusiness was using 120 million pounds of pesticides yearly, causing birth defects and illnesses among farm workers' families, and endangering wildlife. Chemical and other plants were producing nearly 26 million truckloads of contaminants annually by 1985. In the 1990s Governor Peter ("Pete") Wilson authorized the relaxation of environmental laws, such as the California Endangered Species Act, to create jobs and help businesses. The state's Pacific coastline, bays, and adjacent wetlands were becoming polluted largely by urban runoff and industrial emissions, while increasing development restricted public access to beaches. In 1997, 30 dated levees in the Sacramento–San Joaquin Delta broke, resulting in nine deaths and $2 billion in property damage. To all of this must be added the toxic cleanups necessitated by the closure of military bases in the state, such as the El Toro Marine Corps Air Station in Orange County that shut down in 1999. The federal government's discovery of residues of the chemical degreaser TCE, Trichloroethylene, a cancer-causing substance, heightened public fears about the extent to which people living near the base were at risk.

Santa Barbara's oil catastrophe rallied local residents, especially after Union Oil Company President Fred Hartley trivialized his firm's colossal spill, publicly insisting it had not been a "disaster" and had merely resulted "in the loss of a few birds." Angry Santa Barbarans and many others demanded no more offshore drilling; meanwhile, citizens throughout the state organized to safeguard the coast and prevent unchecked development from despoiling the natural environment. San Francisco, home to a hundred environmental organizations including the powerful Sierra Club, led the way. From there, environmentalism, also known as the ecology movement to distinguish it from the early twentieth-century conservation effort to make more efficient use of natural resources, gained momentum as a force in politics nationwide.

The Santa Barbara oil spill triggered the state legislature's passage of the California Environmental Quality Act (CEQA) in 1970. Passed over resistance from pro-growth business and labor groups, the law required the preparation of environmental impact reports for major construction projects undertaken by private parties and government agencies that had the potential of affecting the natural environment. State officials could disallow such projects on environmental grounds. The CEQA process stopped the Peripheral Canal and many other large-scale projects.

Building on a 1960 state law, the first in the nation, to reduce automobile emissions causing smog, environmentalists secured the passage of numerous measures that addressed multiple concerns. The California Air Resources Board was established in 1967 to set standards and enforce laws. In the 1970s the state's clean air regulations imposed fines on car manufacturers whose vehicles violated legal standards. Enforcement was sporadic under governors Reagan and George Deukmejian who, in the 1970s and 1980s respectively, viewed regulations as an unwarranted interference with the free market. In 1990 California passed a law mandating that automobile manufacturers produce and make available non-polluting vehicles by 1998. At the federal level the Environmental Protection Agency helped by enforcing national emission and air-quality standards that had met with resistance from some states, and some counties – such as Los Angeles, America's car capital.

To safeguard drinking water and resolve other water-related issues, California established the State Water Resources Control Board in 1967. The board sets water-quality standards and was instrumental in blocking the proposed Peripheral Canal that would have diverted fresh water flows around the Sacramento–San Joaquin Delta. Those flows have a cleansing effect on Delta waters and help keep the saline content in check. The charge of the board was daunting and despite its success in the Delta region, much else remained to be done. For example, a 1979 Congressional study identified 177 toxic dumps in California that leaked contaminants into water systems. Seven years later voters passed an initiative making it illegal to discharge known carcinogens into public watercourses and holding government officials criminally liable if they neglected to stop such dumping. In the 1980s Governor Deukmejian's administration took a long time listing the toxics to be regulated, which slowed implementation of the initiative measure. Corporate dischargers were doubtlessly alarmed when in 1996 investigatory work by a law office file clerk led to a court verdict awarding $333 million to 600 residents of Hinckley, California, whose health had suffered due to Pacific Gas and Electric's leakage of hexavalent chromium, a carcinogen, into the city's water supply. The file clerk's name was Erin Brockovich and a movie by that name, released in 2000, told her story.

California is known the world over for the grandeur of its 1,264-mile Pacific coastline. Steady population growth and the built environment, with their accompanying landform alterations, urban runoff, and habitat destruction, however, have exacted a toll on the Golden State's shoreline. To meet these challenges, attorney Peter M. Douglas co-drafted and citizens passed Proposition 20 in 1972, establishing a temporary Coastal Commission. The commission was to be an independent, quasi-judicial state agency tasked with regulating land and water use within the coastal zone. This zone embraces an offshore three-mile-wide band of ocean, and inland a swath of terrain varying from several hundred feet in urban areas to 5 miles in rural regions. To make the commission perma-nent, the state legislature passed and Governor Jerry Brown signed the California Coastal Act of 1976, co-authored by Douglas. The Coastal Commission's charge is to: "Protect, conserve, restore, and enhance environmental and human-based resources of the Califor-nia coast and ocean for environmentally sustainable and prudent use by current and future generations." Public access to coastal beaches and waters falls within the purview of the commission.

As the passage and enforcement of this Act suggest, no region in the state since the mid-1970s has occasioned more public and private concern than the ribbon of coveted coastline under the charge of the Coastal Commission. At the center of that concern was Douglas, who from 1985 until his retirement in 2011 served as the commission's high-profile executive director. To environmentalists he was a champion of coastal preservation and public access; to developers and their Sacramento-based ally – the Pacific Legal Foundation – Douglas was often portrayed as an overzealous government regulator and enemy of private property.

Governor Deukmejian vowed to abolish the commission in order to promote business. While he did not succeed, he did cut the agency's budget by 19 percent and reduced its staff of experts by one-quarter.

Lake Tahoe, much like California's coast, needed protection from development-driven silting, urban runoff, and sewage contamination. Since the deep, sapphire-colored lake straddles the Nevada–California border, both states had jurisdiction over its use. In 1969 the two states and the federal government established the Tahoe Regional Planning Agency (TRPA) to manage growth and protect the ecology of the lake. Concerted action required agreement by the delegates from both states. California's members' favored environmental protections while Nevada's insisted on economic development. The standoff undermined TRPA's effectiveness.

Environmentalists made more headway in their efforts to save Mono Lake, located 13 miles east of Yosemite National Park, which was being drained by a thirsty, growing population of Angelinos. The lake has served as a stopover along the Pacific Flyway, an aerial corridor taken yearly by millions of migratory birds from Asia and the Americas. A lawsuit against the City of Los Angeles, initiated in 1979 by the Audubon Society and Friends of the Earth, resulted in a victory for environmentalists. The decision handed down by the state supreme court in 1983 held that the common law principle of "public trust" (meaning tidal areas and submerged lands belong to the people en masse, not private parties) allowed for the alteration and even revocation of deeded water rights. In addition to this precedent-setting case, the struggle to save Mono Lake marked the first time, in 1994, that the state's Water Resources Control Board rescinded water rights on environmental grounds. Los Angeles thereby lost access to most of the water it had previously received from the Mono Basin, making possible the replenishment of the lake's water.

Less well known, but ecologically consequential nevertheless, has been the work of the Bolsa Chica Land Trust founded in 1992 to preserve one of the last marine wetlands in southern California. A dozen or so visionaries, led by biologist Flossie Horgan among others, built an organization that successfully staved off a coastal development project that would have situated more than 4,884 homes in wetlands and surrounding upland mesas located in Huntington Beach.

To forestall the Pacific Lumber Company's plans to harvest old-growth redwoods in Humboldt County, in December 1997 Earth First activist Julia Butterfly Hill climbed a thousand-year-old giant tree named Luna, and lived atop its huge branches for two years. The media publicity she aroused saved the tree and raised public awareness nationwide about the potential harm unchecked economic growth posed to the state's forests.

Environmental issues, as the Santa Barbara oil spill along the coast underscored, are at times closely tied to energy matters. During the last four decades of the twentieth century Californians and their officials in Sacramento grappled with the difficult challenge of supplying the state with safe, affordable energy.

Against the backdrop of the 1973 Arab oil embargo, Governor Jerry Brown created the Office of Appropriate Technology to investigate and advance where advisable alternative energies, including solar, wind, geothermal, and nuclear power. The office also stressed conservation of resources and recycling. The California Energy Commission, established in 1975, set efficiency standards for new houses and businesses. Wall insulation, double-paned windows, and low-intensity lighting were promoted, leading to energy savings.

Alternative energy gained traction. In 1986 construction began on the world's largest solar thermal electricity facility, located in the Mojave Desert. Soon afterward rooftop solar panels that converted sunlight into electricity made their appearance. Pacific winds that once filled the sails of Spanish galleons plying California's coast were now harnessed by the world's largest concentration of windmills, sited on hills around Livermore. Wind-generated electricity was soon produced in the Tehachapi Mountains near Bakersfield and at San Gorgonio Pass in Riverside County.

Nuclear power proved more controversial. Southern California Edison's nuclear facility at San Onofre, located along the Pacific shoreline in San Diego County and in operation since 1968, was the first power station of its kind in California. By 1980 the plant generated 4 percent of Edison's power. In 1969 Pacific Gas and Electric began construction of a nuclear facility farther north along the Pacific Coast at Diablo Canyon, near San Luis Obispo. The problem of safely disposing of nuclear waste from these plants led to mounting public opposition to this form of energy. In 1976 the state legislature ordered the California Energy Commission to stop giving clearances for the building of more nuclear power plants until the federal government solved the problem of radioactive waste disposal. Since then the nuclear power industry has not built another facility in the state.

As a result of the foregoing developments, California remained oil-dependent. An expanding population's reliance on fossil fuels for transportation and other needs paved the way for an impending and calamitous energy crisis.

The untimely convergence of the deregulation of California's energy providers, the state's ever-increasing power needs, and out-of-state corporate greed struck with full force in early 2001. As a result of pressure from Pacific Gas and Electric, San Diego Gas and Electric, and Southern California Edison, Governor Wilson, on September 23, 1996, signed a bill removing the cap on consumers' electricity rates, assuming that competition would increase supply and lower charges. Instead, as public demand for energy increased, supplies fell short, especially when expected natural gas resources did not materialize. Meanwhile, wholesale energy prices rose dramatically, tripling many consumers' electricity bills. Among 30 out-of-state providers, Texas-based Enron Corporation manipulated the state's energy market, a later investigation revealed, as California began experiencing "rolling blackouts" in January 2001. Homes and businesses suffered electricity outages. Enron took plants off line at will for "maintenance," adding artificial power shortages to the existing ones. Taped phone conversations captured Enron executives laughing about "Grandma Millie" and other luckless Californians held in the grip of their corporation's control over the previously regulated energy market. Kenneth Lay, Enron's chief executive officer, was eventually convicted of criminal fraud and conspiracy. The crisis passed in 2002 as new supplies came online.

Governor George Deukmejian's Right Turn

Jerry Brown's successor as governor was George Deukmejian. Positioning himself as "tough on crime," Deukmejian, a transplanted New Yorker and "Gold Coast" Republican conservative who lived near the shore in Long Beach, served California successively in the assembly, the senate, and as attorney general. In 1982 he defeated Los Angeles Mayor and Democratic candidate Tom Bradley in a close-fought gubernatorial campaign, and did so in a rematch four years later. In their first face-off, 6 percent of polled voters admitted that race (Bradley being African American) decided their support for Deukmejian.

When Deukmejian took office in January 1983 California's treasury was nearly bare. Proposition 13 had cut property tax revenues in half. Government spending coupled with inflation consumed most of what was left. The state unemployment rate stood at 11.2 percent and the treasury surplus of the late 1970s had shifted to a $1.5 billion deficit. Faced with a Democratic-controlled legislature, he changed the criminal justice system, vetoed numerous spending bills, and reduced funding for some government offices. As much as his immediate predecessor, the new governor was a practitioner of the politics of limits with one important exception: Deukmejian spent a lot of money on penal institutions.

To fight crime, Deukmejian promoted the building of prisons, whose purpose was punishment of inmates, not rehabilitation. Strongly supporting capital punishment, he increased prison capacity 250 percent, upped the budget of the Department of Corrections 310 percent, and tripled the number of incarcerates. Before leaving office, Deukmejian had through his judicial appointments secured a three-fourths majority of the judges in the state court system; these appointees had been screened to ensure that their views reflected those of the governor.

Despite his huge increase in the prison budget, the governor kept his campaign promise to not levy new taxes and to hold government expenditures in check. For example, he saw to it that community colleges imposed a $50 student fee, which led to an enrollment drop of 20 percent between 1980 and 1985. State funding for the UCs and CSUs fared better. Like Jerry Brown before him, Deukmejian presided over the state's deteriorating infrastructure of highways, bridges, and K-12 schools. Moreover, he cut social and environmental program budgets. In the process, workers' and consumers' rights suffered erosion, in keeping with the governor's pro-business, limited government outlook.

Deukmejian liked conservative Orange County's preference for toll roads rather than state-funded freeways. One naysayer, a *Los Angeles Times* (July 27, 1987) reader wrote: "The proposal to build a toll road in Orange County is, again, reflective of the mentality which would lower services to the poor and allow the rich to purchase personal services for themselves. When I grew up, this country had a viable middle class, and there was a good deal of opportunity for children of the poor. Public education was strong. Public highways and parks were well supported. Ayn Rand had projected a different kind of world based upon personal self-interest. The 'toll-road' concept fits that philosophy." Ayn Rand, prominent author of *The Fountainhead* (1943) and other works, favored laissez-faire capitalism and unfettered individualism. Some conservatives and many libertarians have been drawn to her views. The founding of the Ayn Rand Institute, committed to spreading her philosophy, in beachfront Marina del Rey in 1985 and its relocation to Irvine in 1992 exemplifies "Gold Coast" conservatism's momentum during Deukmejian's governorship.

Deukmejian's minimalist approach to government may have been accepted by the public in large part due to the upturn in the nation's economy during the mid-1980s. Once again, California was a major recipient of federal military spending, which increased dramatically when Ronald Reagan entered the White House. By the late 1980s, both the nation and California slipped back into recession and remained there as Deukmejian left office in 1991.

Voter Resentment, Term Limits, and Wedge Politics

Voter resentment was particularly acute during the recession-ridden late 1980s and early 1990s. Californians were disgusted with the hold of special interests and their lobbyists on Sacramento lawmakers. Also, especially on the political right, the belief that immigrants were the cause of the state's economic woes was palpable. Finally, middle- and working-class whites were angered by what they perceived as reverse discrimination in the policy of affirmative action, which gave weight to racial and gender factors in hiring, awarding government contracts, and university admissions, in order to mitigate the consequences of past injustices.

In response to disgruntlement about special interests dominating California's legislature, voters passed Proposition 140 in November 1990, which amended the constitution to set term limits for lawmakers. The rationale behind the proposition was that the state needed to replace professional politicians with citizen-legislators who, after serving limited terms, would return to their regular jobs. This way, supposedly, they would not remain on a political treadmill of endless fundraising and limitless reelection cycles. Accordingly, Proposition 140 limited assemblypersons to three two-year terms, and senators to two four-year terms.

Percentage of the population that is foreign born, 1870–2009

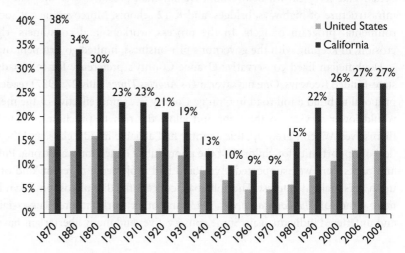

Figure 13.5 Percentage of the California population that is foreign-born, 1870–2009. Note the dramatic increase in immigration to California from 1980 to 2000. Source: Hans Johnson, "Just the Facts: Immigrants in California," Public Policy Institute of California, April 2011.

Growing public agitation about non-Anglo immigration, mainly originating from the state's Pacific Rim neighbor countries to the south – such as Mexico, Guatemala, and El Salvador – led to voter passage of Proposition 187 in 1994. Republicans and Independents supported the proposition by large majorities; Democrats, including President Bill Clinton and U.S. Senators Diane Feinstein and Barbara Boxer, opposed it in large numbers and led the campaign against its passage. This measure denied non-emergency medical treatment, public schooling, and other specified social services to undocumented immigrants. Politicians whose constituencies were comprised of substantial numbers of older white suburban voters got on the Proposition 187 bandwagon, which galvanized their support groups. Consequently, the measure served as a wedge issue, delineating a class-ethnic divide with important political payoffs and costs, especially for Republicans. Though most of Proposition 187 was invalidated by federal courts, it had several lasting effects. It increased ill will between certain whites, mainly Republicans, and many Latinos, whose interests were defended by the Catholic Church, labor unions, and prominent Democratic spokespersons. Second, it activated newly arrived Spanish-speaking Californians to become citizens and vote.

Affirmative action constituted another political wedge issue, again separating voters along class-ethnic fault lines. As competition for business contracts intensified in recession-plagued California in the early 1990s and numerous students vied for admission to the UCs and CSUs, angry whites, joined by a few leaders of minority ethnic backgrounds, promoted Proposition 209. The controversial initiative forbade state and local government agencies from using criteria of race, gender, color, or national background in awarding contracts, hiring workers, or in the admission of students. Voters passed the measure in November 1996. Pete Wilson, a rising Republican leader, was a beneficiary of the campaign for Proposition 209 and of the escalating level of voter resentment in California politics.

Governor Pete Wilson and a Roller-Coaster Economy

In 1990 California voters elected former assemblyman, San Diego Mayor, and U.S. Senator Pete Wilson as governor. Before entering politics, Wilson had graduated from Yale University and UC Berkeley's School of Law, and served in the U.S. Marine Corps. His defeated Democratic opponent in the 1990 gubernatorial contest, San Francisco Mayor Dianne Feinstein, went on to win a U.S. Senate seat in 1992, joining fellow California Democrat Barbara Boxer, who had also just won election to that chamber. This marked the first time in U.S. history that a state had been represented by two female Senators at the same time. Public attention, however, was focused on the economy. Few, if any, of the state's chief executives have experienced a more dramatic downturn and upturn in California's economy than Wilson did during his two terms in office.

As a moderately conservative "Gold Coast" resident, Wilson understood California's connection to the Pacific world. The new governor's Inaugural Address, delivered on January 7, 1991, showed appreciation of the state's pivotal position on the Pacific Rim: "For the better part of two centuries, Californians have followed the sun westward, [to] the broad Pacific. And then they joined with Californians from the ancient lands and cultures

U.S. and California Unemployment Rates

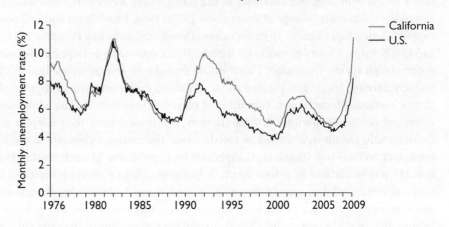

Figure 13.6 U.S. and California unemployment rates, 1976–2009. Source: "Just the Facts: California's Rising Unemployment," Public Policy Institute of California, March 2009.

of Asia and Mexico, and created new frontiers – intellectual, scientific and cultural." Before those new frontiers dazzled the world in the latter half of the 1990s, Wilson had to contend with a slumping economy as Cold War military spending evaporated.

Signs of severe recession were manifold. A $12.6 billion state deficit confronted Wilson's administration. Approximately 75,000 California workers in defense plants lost their jobs in the single year from July 1990 to July 1991. Some businesses moved out of state, costing California the corporate taxes they once paid. Between 1990 and 1993 about 820,000 Californians were out of work; in the latter year the state had the nation's highest unemployment rate, at 9.4 percent. By April 1993 California registered America's highest rate of residential and commercial foreclosures.

The shaky economy shook even more on January 14, 1994, when a devastating earthquake, centered in San Fernando Valley's city of Northridge, threatened homes, toppled some buildings, and ignited fires. Sixty people were killed and more than 7,000 were injured by the temblor that was felt in Greater California's surrounding areas of Nevada, Utah, and Baja. Approximately $20 billion in damage resulted. This was a reminder that California was geologically situated on the Pacific Ring of Fire (see Chapter 1) and that every so often, as in the Loma Prieta quake near Santa Cruz five years earlier that caused 63 deaths, the state's preparations for such calamities are tested.

A little-known aspect of the Northridge disaster is that the people of Nagoya, Japan (also located on the Ring of Fire), sent relief across the Pacific to the victims of the Northridge quake. The relief was an outgrowth of the Sister City relationship formed in 1959 between Los Angeles and Nagoya to promote peace, cultural exchange, and business under the auspices of Sister Cities International, an organization headquartered in Washington, D.C. The goodwill aid from Nagoya in 1994 was soon reciprocated. In early 1995 the city of Kobe, located not far from Nagoya, was hit by a severe earthquake. Both aid and letters of support came from Angelinos. One of the letters, characteristic of others, read in part: "I am Mexican-American and grew up on Juanita Street . . . among a lot of Japanese people. They all spoke Spanish to me, as that was my first language. Just the kindness of these people was very important in my life. . . . I'm an artist and was a guest of the city of Nagoya when one of my sculptures was given by the city of Los Angeles as a celebration of the 25th year of sister cities. . . . I just love the Japanese people. Please accept this small donation for the Kobe Relief fund. . . . I wish it was within my means to contribute more. [signed] Dolores de Larios, Los Angeles." Since the occurrences of these major temblors Los Angeles and Nagoya have carried on a mutually supportive transpacific exchange regarding emergency preparedness.

As troubling as these times were, Northridge recovered while a new California economy was in the making. It was computer-based but also included entertainment, foods, financial services, banking, insurance, pharmaceuticals, and mega-retail enterprises. Intel Corporation, the world's largest semiconductor manufacturer, posted a net worth of $24 billion in 1992, signaling a coming boom. Besides, historian Kevin Starr notes: "Aerospace brainpower was not about to migrate from Southern California." The blue-collar assembly jobs had been lost but the "research, development, design, and engineering of aircraft would remain solidly centered in the Southland." In 1993 Hewlett-Packard's sales soared to $21.4 billion. Orange County government eventually rebounded from the nation's largest municipal bankruptcy, declared in 1994 and resulting from the county's sale of bonds from a risky investment pool. The state's trillion-dollar economy in 1997 ranked with that of leading nations. In short, Wilson had successfully steered California's economy into the so-called "dot com gold rush" of the years 1995–2000.

Meanwhile, the center-right governor moved with deliberation and speed in other public policy areas. He both raised taxes and slashed most state expenditures. In the K-12 schools, Wilson reduced class size, froze teachers' salaries, fought "social promotion" of students who did not qualify for grade advancement, and advocated for statewide student performance standards. Also, he reduced welfare benefits and cut workers' compensation expenditures by 30 percent. His popular "tough on crime" stance resulted in the 1994 passage of Proposition 184, the "Three Strikes" initiative. Accordingly, those convicted of a third felony would receive a mandatory prison sentence of 25 years to life.

In the 1994 gubernatorial election, State Treasurer Kathleen Brown, sister of former Governor Jerry Brown and daughter of former Governor Pat Brown, was the Democratic candidate. She blamed the incumbent governor for the state's ailing economy. Wilson, on the other hand, used Ms. Brown's known opposition to the death penalty to characterize her as weak on crime. This worked and along with Brown's missteps assured his easy reelection to a second term, which on balance proved less eventful than his first.

Proposition 184 has had major impacts on criminal justice, politics, and the state's budgetary woes. Unwittingly, it resulted in California having the nation's largest prison population (160,000 inmates in 2000), the cost of which contributed to the serious economic downturn that lay just ahead. "The Three Strikes law . . . produced 5,000 life sentences by September 1999. Half of these defendants were non-violent offenders; one is now in jail for 25 years because he stole a pizza," declared Jewelle Taylor Gibbs, professor emerita of social welfare at UC Berkeley. The California Correctional Peace Officer's Association, a major beneficiary of Proposition 184 spending, has been a key contributor to the political campaigns of candidates running on "law and order" platforms. Moreover, claims Gibbs, "There is a relationship . . . between prisons and lack of educational resources in the state."

Architecture and Fine Arts, Sports, and Entertainment

While the economy fluctuated dramatically from the 1960s to the early 2000s, the state's profile in architecture and fine arts, sports, and entertainment trended upward. California became increasingly prominent in each of these areas.

Regarding public architecture and the fine arts, California boasted a number of modernist structures receiving international acclaim. In 1997 the Getty Center art museum opened, atop a hill near UCLA. Internationally known architect Richard Meier designed sweeping walls of Roman travertine stone. Inside, visitors enjoyed spectacular exhibitions, featuring paintings, photography, clothing, and more. Los Angeles' Cathedral of Our Lady of the Angels, completed in 2002, was designed by world-renowned architect José Rafael Moneo and constitutes a study in sun lighting that serves as a visual metaphor of the believer's pilgrimage toward salvation. The futuristic Walt Disney Concert Hall is situated near the cathedral. Designed by famed architect Frank Gehry and opening in 2003, it is the home of the Los Angeles Philharmonic, and its acoustics match the grandeur of the steel-curved exterior, making it one of the world's finest concert halls. San Francisco featured mostly older though equally respected performance venues, such as its downtown Performing Arts Center. The new home of the M.H. de Young Museum was an exception to this. Designed by the San Francisco firm of Fong & Chan Architects, its modernist copper exterior and sylvan setting in Golden Gate Park render it a singular arts site. Beginning in 1986 structural components of the privately built Orange County Performing Arts Center made their appearance, the family of Renée and Henry Segerstrom having donated the land and much of the seed money to start construction of the huge arts complex.

San Francisco and Los Angeles vied with each other and with Seattle for recognition as the fine-arts capital of the Pacific Rim. Asian and Mexican-themed artwork became pervasive. Mesami Teraoka's 1990 watercolor *Geisha and AIDS Nightmare* and Isamu Noguchi's outdoor sculptures captured the infusion of Japanese aesthetic sensibilities into California art. Similarly, Charles "Chaz" Bojórquez, a former graffiti artist, portrayed street life in the barrios of East Los Angeles in his serigraph (color-print silk screen) *Los Avenues*.

Sports-wise, the state continued its ascendancy regionally, nationally, and internationally. In professional football the San Francisco 49ers won five Super Bowl Championships between 1981 and 1994. The Oakland/Los Angeles Raiders won three such crowns, in 1977, 1981, and 1984. California's professional baseball teams – the San Francisco Giants, Oakland Athletics, Anaheim Angels, and San Diego Padres – won a combined total of seven World Series championships between 1972 and 2002. In professional basketball the Los Angeles Lakers won nine National Basketball Association championships. The San Diego/Los Angeles Clippers struggled in the shadow of the Lakers during those years. In ice hockey, the San Jose Sharks (named after the Pacific Ocean predator fish) began their first season of competition in 1991. To the south, the Los Angeles Kings played their first season in 1967–8 and made it to the Stanley Cup Finals in 1993. The Anaheim Ducks, in Orange County, played their first season in 1993 and won the Stanley Cup in 2007. The Los Angeles Galaxy professional soccer team won the Western Conference five times between 1996 and 2002, setting an enviable standard for the state's other soccer franchises. In professional

Figure 13.7   Walt Disney Concert Hall in Los Angeles. Photo: Palette7 / Shutterstock.com.

surfing, Kelly Slater – a resident of Florida, California, and Hawai'i – has won 10 world titles since 1992; Rochelle Ballard of Montebello, California, was ranked fourth among women surfers in the world in 1988 and 1990. Southern California sisters Serena and Venus Williams have ranked among the top female tennis players in the world since the late 1990s, and Eldrick Tont ("Tiger") Woods similarly dominated professional golf into the early 2000s. Since 2006, Amgen, the pharmaceutical giant, has been sponsoring the Amgen Tour of California, which the *Los Angeles Times* has called "North America's most prominent cycling race." The scenic, nearly 800-mile Tour of California has drawn top professional bicycle racers worldwide and has been watched by television viewers in several hundred countries and territories.

In college sports UCLA and USC did well in basketball and football, respectively, while UC Berkeley and Stanford excelled in other sports such as men's and women's rowing and cross-country, respectively. In the years 1977–1998, USC won seven national baseball championships. Los Angeles' stature as an international amateur sports center was enhanced by its hosting of the 1984 Summer Olympics. President Reagan opened the games.

Many of these sporting events and much else were covered by the media headquartered in America's entertainment capital: Los Angeles. The movie and recording industry seemed recession-proof, with the blockbuster 1997 film *Titanic* grossing $1.8 billion by 2003. Much of the Oscar-winning best movie was filmed along the Pacific Coast of Baja California and in Long Beach. Hollywood's fondness for filming below the border, where production costs are minimal, is evidenced in Twentieth Century Fox's establishment in 1996 of Baja Studios, located just south of Rosarito Beach. *Pearl Harbor* (2001) and *Master and Commander* (2003) were both shot at that 35-acre facility and along its adjoining Pacific coastline. Households were beginning to purchase integrated media systems combining radio, television, Internet, motion picture, music, and other services. Still, for those who wished, Universal Studios, Disneyland, Knott's Berry Farm, Sea World, malls, parks, stadiums, campgrounds, and the storied California beaches awaited them. Thus, the "Gold Coast" was not just about conservative politics at the state and national levels; it was also about play.

SUMMARY

For three decades beginning in the 1960s California's affluent "Gold Coast" Republicans spearheaded a national conservative comeback launched from their corporate boardrooms and residences situated along the pricey shoreline from Santa Barbara southward to San Diego. Newport Beach, in Orange County, was and remains the nerve center of conservative politics in the Western United States, if not the entire nation. The Lincoln Club, headquartered there, helped catapult Richard Nixon and Ronald Reagan into the national political arena. Denouncing UC Berkeley protesters, Reagan mobilized voter support for a politics of limits, that is, the conservative agenda of downsizing state government and cutting its social services budget. Governor Edmund G. (Jerry) Brown, Jr., a Democrat, was the antithesis of Reagan. Brown supported migrant farm workers' rights, brought more women into government, doubled funding for public education, and approved environmental safeguards, while restraining state spending and championing his own variant of a politics of limits. Though opposed to Proposition 13 before its 1978 passage, he adapted to the measure that was to have major impacts on state budgets for decades afterward.

A high urban crime rate gave credence to the conservatives' call for "law and order." Mounting gang violence and inner-city racial tensions, connected to an increased flow of Pacific Rim immigration, formed a backdrop to the 1992 Los Angeles riots and the O.J. Simpson murder trials held several years later.

Increasingly, California was America's Pacific Eldorado in terms of economic growth, which despite serious recessions emerged as the world's sixth-largest economy in the early 2000s. The Golden State's prosperity was due largely to its diverse sectors, especially Pacific maritime-related enterprises and high technology. By 1980 America's trade with Asia eclipsed that with Europe, and California was a major player in the $3 trillion Pacific Rim economy. Silicon Valley became the world's leader in the development and marketing of computers and software products. Yahoo CEO Jerry Yang helped keep California on the cutting edge of the information-processing industry.

Economic growth resulted in environmental problems. Struggling against corporate-backed conservative lawmakers, liberal-leaning environmentalists secured some measure of environmental protection. The computer industry and agribusiness produced chemical waste that endangered public health. Urbanization and tourism polluted San Francisco Bay and Lake Tahoe respectively. A gigantic oil spill off the coast of Santa Barbara in 1969 sparked an environmental movement leading to the passage of the landmark California Environmental Quality Act in 1970 and the establishment of the statewide Coastal Commission shortly afterward. Pacific Gas and Electric's contamination of public drinking water led to a huge courtroom verdict in favor of cancer victims in the desert community of Hinckley and the making of the Hollywood film *Erin Brockovich*. Governor Pete Wilson's removal of the cap on consumers' energy rates resulted in Texas-based Enron and other providers gaming California's energy market in ways that eventuated in criminal prosecution of that corporation's top executives.

The period from the late 1960s to the early 2000s was not just about "Gold Coast" conservatism and a politics of limits. Leisure-time pursuits and play mattered as well. Cultural and entertainment venues from the Bay Area southward into Baja provided Californians with art treasures, dance, theater, opera, professional and collegiate sports, movies and television, theme parks, and stretches of beaches known worldwide.

REVIEW QUESTIONS

- How would you define "Gold Coast" conservatism? What specific examples can you give of how "Gold Coast" conservatism shaped a politics of limits?
- What impacts did Pacific Rim immigration have on California during the last three decades of the twentieth century?
- What profound shift had taken place in America's foreign trade by 1980? What was significant about this shift for California's economy?
- What major environmental problems confronted California from the 1960s through the early 2000s? What steps did environmentalists and the state government take to address these problems?
- What examples can you give of California having become a national/international venue for the arts, entertainment media, and sports from the 1960s through the early 2000s?

FURTHER READINGS

Mark Baldassare, *A California State of Mind: The Conflicted Voter in a Changing World* (Berkeley: University of California Press, 2002). A public opinion analyst explains how the unstable economy in the 1990s shaped Californians' concerns, policy views, and distrust of government.

Jerry Brown, *Dialogues* (Berkeley: Berkeley Hills Books, 1998). Brown interviews some of America's leading religious thinkers, scientists, and artists in a book that demonstrates the author's analytical brilliance and quest to integrate ideas with actions in the public sphere.

Lou Cannon, *Governor Reagan: His Rise to Power* (New York: Public Affairs, 2003). The author provides a temperate yet sympathetic view of Ronald Reagan's governorship.

Shenglin Chang, *The Global Silicon Valley Home: Lives and Landscapes within the Taiwanese American Trans-Pacific Culture* (Stanford, CA: Stanford University Press, 2006). The author examines how some Taiwanese Americans with homes in California and across the Pacific in Taiwan have adapted their identities and landscapes accordingly.

Bruce Cumings, *Dominion from Sea to Sea: Pacific Ascendancy and American Power* (New Haven, CT: Yale University Press, 2009). The author situates California in the vanguard of America's nearly continuous Pacific shift, detailing trade matters in the late twentieth century.

Serge Dedina, *Wild Sea: Eco-Wars and Surf Stories from the Coast of the Californias* (Tucson: University of Arizona Press, 2011). The author narrates the shared ecological concerns and joint activist efforts linking surfers and environmentalists in Baja and southern California.

Peter Drucker, *Post-Capitalist Society* (New York: HarperCollins, 1993). A foremost management authority contends that in the computer age capital, land, and labor are no longer the major resources; instead, knowledge workers will shape the economies of competing nations.

James Flanigan, *Smile Southern California, You're the Center of the Universe* (Stanford, CA: Stanford University Press, 2009). This is a very readable treatise on southern California's outsized role in the Pacific Rim economy in the late 1990s and early 2000s.

Alex L. Fradkin and Philip L. Fradkin, *The Left Coast: California on the Edge* (Berkeley: University of California Press, 2011). The product of a father–son team, this visually sumptuous work pays tribute to the history, character, ecology, and beauty of the California coast.

Tom Hayden, *Street Wars: Gangs and the Future of Violence* (New York: The New Press, 2004). The author attributes much of the responsibility for the formation of California-connected Pacific Rim gangs to America's neglect of urban poverty at home and the arming of warring factions in Central America.

Erik J. Heikkila and Rafael Pizarro, eds., *Southern California and the World* (Westport, CT: Praeger, 2002). This is a highly theoretical anthology that analyzes California's roles as a center of international communication and economic flows, a microcosm of the world's cultural diversity, and an exporter of its own values and aspirations to other countries.

Rob Kling, Spencer Olin, and Mark Poster, eds., *Postsuburban California: The Transformation of Orange County since World War II* (Berkeley: University of California Press, 1991). This anthology traces Orange County's shift from a collection of cities and suburbs to a new kind of social formation replete with distinct and sepa-rable centers that include residential neighborhoods, malls, and industrial parks.

Joel Kotkin and Paul Grabowicz, *California, Inc.* (New York: Rawson, Wade, 1982). The authors treat California's prosperity in the 1960s and 1970s as an outgrowth of its growing trade with Pacific Rim countries.

Abraham F. Lowenthal, *Global California: Rising to the Cosmopolitan Challenge* (Stanford, CA: Stanford University Press, 2009). Californians must develop a global mindset, contends this work, in order to address pressing international challenges that include climate change, environmental pollution, and trade competition.

Gerald C. Lubenow, ed., *Governing California: Politics, Government, and Public Policy in the Golden State* (Berkeley: Regents of the University of California, 2006). This brief anthology provides an overview of how California government operates, offering insightful thumbnail sketches of governors from Ronald Reagan to Arnold Schwarzenegger.

Lisa McGirr, *Suburban Warriors: The Origins of the New American Right* (Princeton, N.J.: Princeton University Press, 2002). The building of a powerful, respectable grassroots conservative movement in 1960s Orange County is detailed in this book on how the Republican Party recovered from Barry Goldwater's defeat in his bid for the presidency.

Glenna Matthews, *Silicon Valley, Women, and the California Dream: Gender, Class, and Opportunity in the Twentieth Century* (Stanford, CA: Stanford University Press, 2002). This penetrating study views the transition of Silicon Valley from a farming area to a high-technology Mecca from the perspectives of the women whose lives were bound up with that transformation.

Thomas J. Osborne, "Pacific Eldorado: Rethinking Greater California's Past," *California History*, 87/1 (2009), 26–45. Reframing California history within a Pacific Basin context, this article anticipates the present textbook.

Robert Pack, *Jerry Brown: The Philosopher-Prince* (New York: Stein and Day, 1978). Brown is treated as a young political outlier, whose unconventional thinking and governance have been as unique as the state he has led.

Peter Schrag, *Paradise Lost: California's Experience, America's Future* (New York: The Free Press, 1998). A liberal-minded columnist chronicles California's descent in terms of governance following passage of Proposition 13.

Peter Schrag, *California: America's High-Stakes Experiment* (Berkeley: University of California Press, 2008). Disinvestment in California's infrastructure, attributed to Proposition 13 and similar initiative-driven measures, is treated as a warning to both the state and nation in the twenty-first century.

Michael A. Shires, *Patterns in California Government Revenues since Proposition 13* (San Francisco: Public Policy Institute of California, 1999). This empirical study shows that all units of local government in the state have experienced a significant drop in their "self-controlled revenue" between 1978 and 1995 due to Proposition 13.

Michael A. Shires et al., *Has Proposition 13 Delivered? The Changing Tax Burden in California* (San Francisco: Public Policy Institute of California, 1998). The authors conclude that, controlling for inflation, by 1998 per capita state revenues declined by 16 percent since 1978, when Proposition 13 went into effect.

Kevin Starr, *Coast of Dreams: California on the Edge, 1990–2003* (New York: Oxford University Press, 2004). Packed with illustrative detail, this book narrates the effects of California's roller-coaster economy on society and culture.

14

The Ongoing Pacific Shift

California was born of a cataclysmic, Pacific-driven shift of tectonic plates (see Chapter 1). Ever since that geologic event eons ago no other factor has had the explanatory force of that ocean basin in shaping historical developments in what much later became the Golden State. As has been shown, the Pacific figured prominently in the earliest human seaborne migration to California's landmass, in the European encounter and colonization of that landmass during the age of sail, in the province's maritime fur and hide-and-tallow trades, in its once world-dominant whaling industry and later commercial fishing enterprises, in the shipboard transport of gold and gold-seekers, in the conception and construction of the first transcontinental railroad as a Golden State pathway to Asian markets, in the export of California's agricultural staples and oil, in the state's tourism and recreation, in the global reach of its high-tech businesses, in its containerized transoceanic commerce, in the rise of its "Gold Coast" conservatism, in its strategic role in America's overseas wars and defense posture since 1898, and more.

By the late twentieth century the Pacific world had replaced the Atlantic community as the epicenter of the global economy. Some analysts project that half of the world's economic growth in the early twenty-first century will occur in East Asia. This Pacific ascendancy has been under way for more than a century. That said, how does California's most recent past – especially regarding immigration, politics, economics, the environment, and international security – fit into the unfolding drama of the world's historic Pacific shift?

Pacific Eldorado: A History of Greater California, First Edition. Thomas J. Osborne.
© 2013 Thomas J. Osborne. Published 2013 by Blackwell Publishing Ltd.

Timeline

1990 Dr. Chang-Lin Tien is appointed chancellor of UC Berkeley, becoming the first Chinese American to head a major American research university

1998 Voters pass Proposition 227, an initiative measure outlawing bilingual education and requiring English-only instruction except in stipulated cases

2000 Latinos/as constitute 16 percent of California's electorate

2001 The *Stanford Report* (September 5, 2001) newsletter finds: "California's universities and research institutions claim more Nobel laureates than any state or country in the world"

2002 The state legislature passes the Clean Cars Law requiring that all new cars sold in California have to cut greenhouse gas emissions by 30 percent by 2016

2003 In a statewide election, Governor Gray Davis is recalled and Arnold Schwarzenegger is chosen as Davis's replacement

Governor Schwarzenegger signs an executive order repealing restoration of the full vehicle license fee and later borrows money from an education fund to operate the government; the repeal costs the state more than $4 billion in revenue

2005 Antonio Villaraigosa is installed as the first Latino mayor of Los Angeles in 133 years

Los Angeles–Long Beach port trade with Pacific Rim nations amounts to $300 billion

California has more military installations and personnel than any other state in the nation

Disneyland in Hong Kong, China, opens to the public

2007 The state establishes the Water Quality Monitoring Council to check water quality and report its findings to the public via a website

2008 According to a *Time* magazine cover story, "California's wipeout [recession-ridden] economy attracted more venture capital than the rest of the nation combined"

In San Marino, the Huntington Library's long-awaited and highly publicized Chinese Garden of Flowing Fragrance opens to the public

Proposition 8 narrowly passes, amending the state constitution to declare that "only marriage between a man and a woman is valid or recognized in California"

2009 Los Angeles financier Donald Tang founds CSIP Group, a China-focused cross-border financial services firm, headquartered in Los Angeles

The U.S. Department of Commerce ranks California's nation-sized $1.8 trillion economy as the eighth largest in the world, just behind Italy and ahead of Brazil and Spain

(Continued)

2010　Members of UC Irvine's Muslim Student Union are charged with disrupting a speech by the Israeli ambassador to the United States, Michael Oren; afterward, the university suspends the MSU for one year, followed by a probationary year, and disciplines the students involved in the disturbance

According to the U.S. Census Bureau, California's population is 37.3 million people (most of whom live near or along the Pacific Coast); Hispanics comprise 37.6 percent of the state's population; Asians account for 13 percent and are designated as California's fastest-growing ethnic group

The California State Lands Commission issues a report saying that most of the state's 40 ports and shipping hubs are not prepared for the expected 16-inch rise in sea levels by 2050

California's budget deficit reaches $25.4 billion, and its unemployment rate is 12.4 percent (the national rate is 10 percent)

Voters pass Proposition 25, which ends the previously required two-thirds legislative majority to pass budgets; hereafter, a simple majority will suffice

2011　Assembly Bill 131 (known as the California Dream Act) passes, enabling high-achieving undocumented students in higher education to apply for and receive scholarships drawn from non-state funds and, beginning January 1, 2013, for financial aid partially derived from state funds

The multi-billion-dollar restaurant chain, Panda Restaurant Group, Inc., is headquartered in Rosemead and operates at more than 2,000 locations nationwide, employing more than 17,000 workers

In *Brown v. Plata* the U.S. Supreme Court holds that California's prison conditions are so appalling as to be in violation of the Constitution's Eighth Amendment, outlawing "cruel and unusual punishment"

Los Angeles Mayor Antonio Villaraigosa leads a city trade delegation to Asian countries resulting in transpacific business partnerships and Hyundai Merchant Marine agreeing to build a new terminal at the Port of Los Angeles

San Pedro Bay shipping complex surges back from the recession, handling 20.3 percent more cargo in 2011 than the year before

With a market valuation of $350 billion, Apple becomes the world's leader in computer products

President Barack Obama, Secretary of State Hillary Clinton, and Secretary of Defense Leon Panetta announce that America's foreign and strategic policy is undergoing a major Pacific "shift" since that ocean basin is now the center of the global economy

Nationwide, California ranks low – 43rd in 2011 – in spending per pupil

2012　Trucks entering and leaving the Los Angeles–Long Beach port complex must adhere to Federal Clean Truck Emissions Standards or be banned from the harbor.

Chinese Americans Edwin Lee and Jean Quan are serving as mayors respectively of San Francisco and Oakland; Quan is the first Asian American woman to head a major city in the United States

Headquartered in Cupertino, California, Apple Incorporated, with a market valuation of $500 billion, becomes the most valuable corporation in the world, surpassing Exxon Mobil

Hawthorne, California-based SpaceX completes the world's first private industry-sponsored space mission, docking at the orbiting International Space Station 250 miles above northwest Australia

Immigration, Diversity, and the Politics of Multiculturalism

Throughout recorded history, the bulk of California's population – 37.3 million, according to the U.S. Census Bureau's 2010 count – has been concentrated in coastal areas. The immigrants occupying these areas have come overwhelmingly from Pacific-bordering nations in Asia and Latin America, creating America's most ethnically and culturally diverse state. Such diversity, in turn, has played a major role in shaping California's politics and will continue doing so into the early decades of the twenty-first century, during which minorities – immigrants and residents alike – will continue to constitute the state's majority.

According to the 2010 Census, Latinos comprise 37.6 percent of California's population. Demographers say non-Latino whites, who constituted 40.1 percent of the population, will be surpassed by a new majority of Hispanics by 2025. For various cultural and economic reasons, Latinas have a high fertility rate compared to all other women. For example, outreach workers often cite machismo and social and religious pressures to account for the relatively high birth rate among Latinas. Only 20 percent of the growth of the Hispanic population since 1980 has been due to immigration; to these considerations must be added an estimated 2.8 million unauthorized Mexican immigrants in California in 2009. Still, Hispanics, particularly Mexicans, constituted the largest group of newcomers to the state, approximately three-quarters of whom hailed from Pacific Rim countries.

Southern California has been home for most of the state's Hispanic residents and recent arrivals. Those gaining legal entry usually cross at a border station, such as San Diego or Calexico; a growing number of unauthorized Hispanic immigrants are entering the state by sea at night in shallow-hulled boats, which use secluded anchorages in Catalina's coves and at beaches along San Diego, Orange, and Los Angeles counties to deposit passengers and oftentimes cargoes of illicit drugs as well.

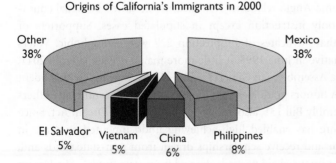

Origins of California's Immigrants in 2000

Other 38%

Mexico 38%

El Salvador 5%   Vietnam 5%   China 6%   Philippines 8%

Figure 14.1 Chart of the origins of California immigrants in 2000. Department of Finance, State of California. Ten countries (Mexico, the Philippines, China, Vietnam, El Salvador, India, Nicaragua, Taiwan, Korea, and Guatemala) contributed 75 percent of the state's immigrants in 2000. Source: State of California, Department of Finance, *They Came to California: Legal Immigration in 2000* (Sacramento, CA, March 2003).

California's expanding Latino/a population has raised its economic profile throughout the state in the early 2000s. Enrique Hernandez, Jr., hailed from a struggling immigrant family, graduated from Harvard and that university's law school, and then headed a security firm employing 30,000 workers and earning $2 billion annually in revenue. Similarly, Daniel D. Villanueva, a former place kicker for the Dallas Cowboys and Los Angeles Rams, became a founder of one of the first Spanish-language television stations in the Southland, KMEX, Channel 34, which made him a multi-millionaire. In the early 2000s he co-founded Bastion Capital, which invested in Spanish-language radio stations. On a more modest scale of enterprise, there are some 650,000 Hispanic-owned small to medium-sized businesses in the state – 25,000 of these garner more than $1 million a year in revenues. Latinos/as wield more than $200 billion in buying power in southern California alone, a portion of which goes to the state in the payment of sales taxes. The $6 billion they send annually, in the form of remittances, to family members south of the border speaks to the familial and economic reach of Greater California. However, for all of the successes of Hispanics, and their contributions to the state economy, they remain among the lowest-paid workers.

With an increasing population and economic clout, Hispanics have steadily gained political power since the 1990s. In the latter half of that decade 1 million California Latinos/as registered to vote. Helped by Spanish-language newspapers, like *La Opinión*, they have become more politicized. By 2000 Hispanics constituted 16 percent of the state's electorate. They have maintained Miguel A. Pulido in office as mayor of the City of Santa Ana since 1994, elected Representative Loretta Sanchez to the 47th Congressional District in 1996 and her sister, Representative Linda Sanchez, to the 39th Congressional District in 2003, placed Cruz Bustamente in the office of lieutenant governor in 1998, elected Rocky Delgadillo as Los Angeles' city attorney in 2001, and installed Antonio Villaraigosa in the office of mayor of that city in 2005. Villaraigosa thus became the first Latino mayor of the City of Angels in 133 years. On the national stage, Californian Hilda L. Solis has served as secretary of labor in Washington, D.C., since 2009.

As Hispanics' political clout grew, tensions mounted between them and Anglos over multicultural issues in politics. In the late 1990s, public debate over Proposition 227 became a flashpoint in Hispanic-Anglo relations. That measure outlawed bilingual education and required English-only instruction except in stipulated cases. Supporters of bilingual teaching charged that advocates of Proposition 227 were xenophobic. Voters passed the controversial initiative in June 1998. A little more than a decade later, in 2011, Mexican American California Assemblyman Gilbert Cedillo of Los Angeles – with student leadership from recent UCLA honors graduates Tam Tran, Cinthya Felix, and many others – secured the passage of Assembly Bill 131, also known as the California Dream Act. Since January 1, 2012, that measure has enabled high-achieving undocumented students in higher education to apply for and receive scholarships drawn from non-state funds and, beginning January 1, 2013, for financial aid partially derived from state funds. "The Dream Act benefits us all by giving top students a chance to improve their lives and the lives of all of us," said Governor Jerry Brown on signing the measure. Since the 1980s, Hispanic-Anglo tensions have also played out at polling stations. Claiming Democratic voter fraud, in a 1988 statewide election Republicans posted uniformed security guards at Hispanic polling sites in parts of Orange County. The Orange County registrar of voters investigated and found no evidence of fraud. On the other hand, charging voter intimidation, five Latino plaintiffs received $400,000 from the Republican Party in settlement of a lawsuit over the heated matter. Poll-watching remains a volatile issue in the early 2000s. As these developments indicate, Hispanics have become a major force in California politics.

While Hispanics comprise a large and growing segment of California's population, the U.S. Census Bureau has designated "Asian and Pacific Islanders" as the fastest-increasing ethnic group in the state. According to the 2010 federal census, Asians comprised 13 percent of California's population, with Chinese and Filipinos posting the largest numbers. The Golden State had America's largest population of Native Hawaiians and other Pacific Islanders, followed by Hawai'i, and Washington. Orange County's Little Saigon neighborhood has the largest concentration of Vietnamese outside their homeland.

Asians have been especially successful in business. Founded in 1971, the California-Asia Business Council (Cal-Asia) has become increasingly active in promoting commercial ties

(a)

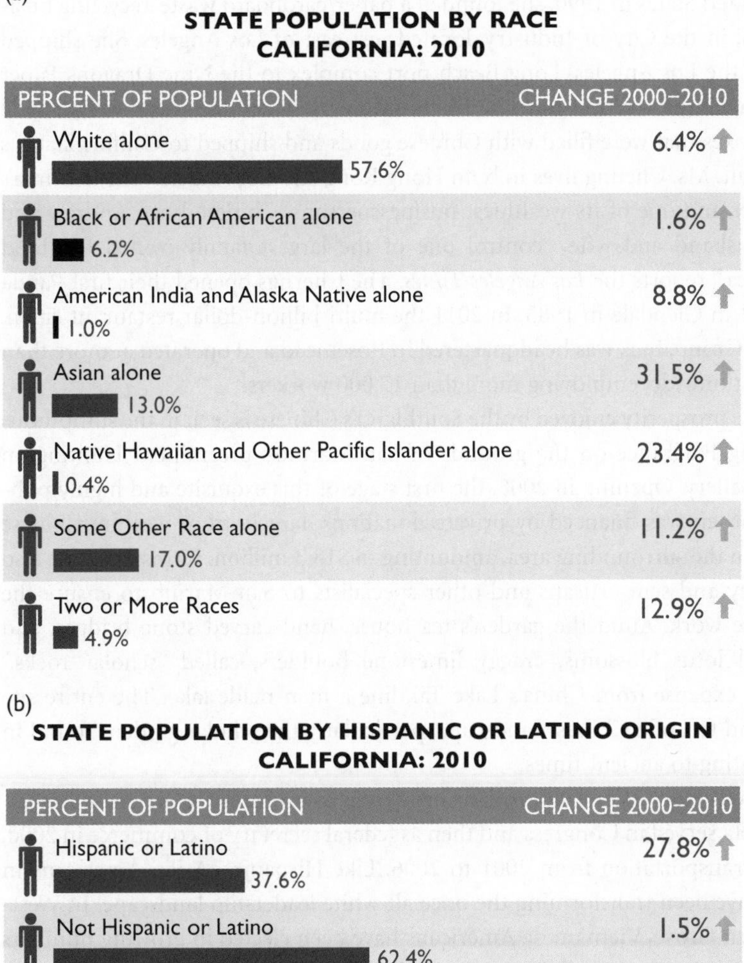

STATE POPULATION BY RACE
CALIFORNIA: 2010

PERCENT OF POPULATION	CHANGE 2000–2010
White alone 57.6%	6.4% ↑
Black or African American alone 6.2%	1.6% ↑
American India and Alaska Native alone 1.0%	8.8% ↑
Asian alone 13.0%	31.5% ↑
Native Hawaiian and Other Pacific Islander alone 0.4%	23.4% ↑
Some Other Race alone 17.0%	11.2% ↑
Two or More Races 4.9%	12.9% ↑

(b)

STATE POPULATION BY HISPANIC OR LATINO ORIGIN
CALIFORNIA: 2010

PERCENT OF POPULATION	CHANGE 2000–2010
Hispanic or Latino 37.6%	27.8% ↑
Not Hispanic or Latino 62.4%	1.5% ↑

Figure 14.2   (a) State population by race, California, 2010; (b) State population by Hispanic or Latino/a origins, California, 2010. Source: United States Census Bureau, Washington, D.C.

between the state and the nations of Pacific Asia and India. Cal-Asia, for example, partnered with the USC Marshall School of Business in organizing the 2011 Asia Pacific Business Outlook Conference in Los Angeles, which featured 60 sessions plus private consultations focused on strengthening California's commercial connections with 14 Asian economies.

A number of Asian American businesspersons are promoting these connections. Donald Tang is among them. Born in Shanghai and educated in California, Tang founded in 2009 CSIP Group, a China-focused cross-border financial services firm, headquartered in Los Angeles. Tang envisions Los Angeles becoming the hub of the global economy: "We have a shot at attracting headquarters of international business operations from Japan, Korea, Singapore, India, and China." Similarly, Dominic Ng, originally from Hong Kong, augmented the Chinese presence in Southland commercial banking. He became chairman of the East West Bancorp, Inc., which by 2007 had grown its assets to $11.6 billion, while employing 1,200 workers at 72 California branches and one office in Hong Kong. "We are now the largest Chinese bank in the United States," Ng claimed. Yan Cheung exemplifies the talents and energies of a female Asian American entrepreneur in California and China. Coming to the United States in 1990, she founded a paper/cardboard waste-recycling business, Chung Nam, in the City of Industry, located just east of Los Angeles. She shipped paper waste from the Los Angeles–Long Beach port complex to the Nine Dragons Paper Mill in Dongguan, China – a mill that she built and owns. There the waste was remade into corrugated boxes that were filled with Chinese goods and shipped to California, thus completing a circuit. Ms. Cheung lives in both Hong Kong and Los Angeles; she is China's largest papermaker and one of its wealthiest businesspersons. Chinese-born Andrew and Peggy Cherng, husband and wife, "control one of the largest family-owned fast-food empires in America," reports the *Los Angeles Times*. The Cherngs opened their first Panda Express restaurant in Glendale in 1983. In 2011 the multi-billion-dollar restaurant chain, Panda Restaurant Group, Inc., was headquartered in Rosemead and operated at more than 2,000 locations nationwide, employing more than 17,000 workers.

A measure of the prosperity enjoyed by the Southland's Chinese is seen in the sumptuous Garden of Flowing Fragrance on the grounds of San Marino's preeminent Huntington Library and Art Gallery. Opening in 2008, the first stage of this exquisite and highly publicized classical garden was financed by private donations, largely from wealthy Chinese Americans living in the surrounding area, amounting to $18.3 million. Firms in China also contributed money and sent artisans and other specialists to San Marino to ensure the authenticity of the work. Amid the garden's tea house, hand-carved stone bridges, and plum, peach, and lotus blossoms, craggy limestone boulders, called "scholar rocks," imported at great expense from China's Lake Tai, line a man-made lake. The entire site evokes the look and feel of a Chinese landscape, particularly the scholar gardens found in Suzhou, China, dating to ancient times.

In the public sector, too, Asian Californians have risen to prominence. Japanese American Norman Mineta served in Congress and then as federal secretary of commerce in 2000, and secretary of transportation from 2001 to 2006. Like Hispanics, Asian Americans in Orange County have been transforming the once all-white leadership landscape. In Westminster and Garden Grove, Vietnamese Americans have been elected in growing numbers to school boards and city councils. In Irvine in 2008, Sukhee Kang became the first Korean

American to be elected mayor of a major city; he was reelected in 2010. Chinese American Gilbert Wong served in 2011 as mayor of Cupertino, home of Apple computers and a rapidly growing population of Chinese. In 2012 Chinese Americans Edwin Lee and Jean Quan were serving as mayors respectively of San Francisco and Oakland. Quan is the first Asian American woman to head a major city in the United States. Chinese American March Fong Eu rose through the political ranks to become California secretary of state from 1974 to 1994. Her son, Matthew Fong, held the post of state treasurer from 1995 to 1998. Dr. Chang-Lin Tien served as chancellor of UC Berkeley from 1990 to 1997, becoming the first Chinese American to head a preeminent American research university. Wilma Chan, an assemblywoman from Oakland, served as leader of that chamber from 2002 to 2004. In 2006 Dr. Leland Yee, of Chinese descent, became the first Asian American to be elected to the state senate; he was reelected in 2010. Since 2009 UC Berkeley physicist and Nobel laureate Dr. Steven Chu, a Chinese American, has served as U.S. secretary of energy.

Unlike Hispanic and Asian Californians, blacks have not experienced dramatic population growth, and relative to these other groups African Americans' political and economic influence may have stagnated since the turmoil of the Los Angeles riots and O.J. Simpson trials of the 1990s (see Chapter 13). According to the 2000 U.S. Census, California had 2.2 million blacks, about 6.5 percent of the state's population; in 2010 these numbers changed to 2.3 million and 6 percent, respectively. By the early 2000s African Americans were migrating from their traditional population centers in Los Angeles, San Francisco, Oakland, Compton, and Inglewood to more suburban and often remote inland cities such as Antioch and Stockton in the northern part of the state, and to Palmdale, Moreno Valley, Lancaster, and Fontana in southern California. Lower residential real-estate prices in these inland areas prompted much of this migration. The problem of violent crime in large metropolitan areas also doubtlessly contributed to the move. U.S. Census Bureau statistics indicate that in 2007 blacks owned 4 percent of California's businesses. UC Irvine Chancellor Dr. Michael V. Drake, appointed in 2005, exemplifies the high level of leadership attained by some African Americans in recent years.

California's population in the early 2000s of more than 1 million Muslims, largely of Middle Eastern descent, has succeeded in business while anecdotal evidence suggests their children have performed well in schools. The September 11, 2001, terrorist assaults on the United States resulted in reprisal shootings, beatings, and arson attacks directed at Arab Americans and Muslim Americans in many parts of the United States, including the California cities of San Francisco, San Jose, and Los Angeles. Simmering hostilities between some Muslims and Jewish students erupted at UC Irvine on February 8, 2010, when members of the campus Muslim Student Union (MSU) were charged with disrupting a speech by the Israeli ambassador to the United States, Michael Oren. Afterward, the university suspended the MSU for one year, followed by a probationary year, and disciplined the students involved in the disturbance.

Even with significant coverage of their casino operations, California's Native Americans are the least visible in the media of the above groups. According to U.S. Census Bureau figures, as of July 1, 2008, the state had America's largest population of Indians, numbering 738,978. By almost any standard, they are not faring well compared to other ethnic minorities. Poverty is widespread among them. Their high-school dropout rate in 2000 was 14.2

percent, nearly twice that of whites. Riverside's Sherman Indian High School, founded in 1892, exemplifies some of the problems. Amid an enrollment decline from 640 students in 2006–7 to 452 in 2010–11, the school laid off 35 teachers, dorm staffers, and other personnel for budgetary reasons in 2009. Student disciplinary problems and homesickness, reportedly, are major causes of declining enrollments. Beyond the educational challenges, alcoholism and other health problems confront California's Indians.

To provide jobs and save their cultures, some tribes began operating gambling casinos in the 1980s. With the legality of such operations in question and faced with opposition from a few governors, some tribes pushed for and achieved passage of Proposition 1A in 2000, legalizing their gaming ventures. Billions of dollars in profits have since poured in, resulting in some tribes, mainly in southern California, reaping financial windfalls that have helped preserve their cultures and sense of self-determination. Recipient tribes have used this money to build museums showcasing their respective heritages, support their elders, and educate tribal youth. Still, gaming proceeds have offered no panacea; most California Indians have received no benefit from these revenues. This is because only Indian groupings acknowledged as tribes by the U.S. government were eligible to run gaming enterprises on reservations, and most self-identified California Indians do not belong to such tribes. Gaining federal acknowledgment involves a long, complex process with no assurance of success. Indian affairs attorney Stephen V. Quesenberry noted in 2008 that in California "over forty tribes have submitted petitions for federal acknowledgment" and "only one . . . was acknowledged." Meanwhile, gaming profits have given some California tribes new-found political clout in electoral politics as Democratic and Republican candidates, as well as interest groups, vie for Indian financial support.

Pacific Profile: Novelist Isabel Allende

Born in Peru to Chilean parents, Isabel Allende Llona (1942–) is a world-acclaimed novelist and playwright living in the Bay Area. She identifies herself as a Chilean American, though a strong affinity for California informs many of her works. Going back to the gold rush era, the ties between Chile and California are laid out in her fictional stories about seagoing Chileans migrating across the Pacific from Valparaíso to San Francisco. These stories are grounded in a solid grasp of history.

Her parents divorced when she was a child, and she and her mother moved to Santiago, Chile, where young Allende lived with her grandparents and graduated from a private high school at age 16. A house filled with books, coupled with her grandmother's stories, kindled her interest in writing. In 1962 she married her first husband, Miguel Frías, an engineer.

Allende then entered the working world, taking a secretarial job with the United Nations Food and Agriculture Organization in Santiago. A few years later she turned to reporting news, editing, and conducting television interviews. She describes her interview with famed Chilean poet and Nobel Laureate Pablo Neruda as follows: "I went to visit him and it was a very pleasant lunch until he said that I was a lousy journalist – the worst in the country, and that I . . . lied all the time, I couldn't be objective. If I didn't have a story, I made it up. Why didn't I switch to literature, where all those defects are virtues? So that's what I've done." In doing so, she became a beloved author worldwide.

Many of her novels are centered in Chile and/or California, for example, *House of the Spirits* (1982), *The Infinite Plan* (1991), *Daughter of Fortune* (1999), *Portrait in Sepia* (2001), and *Zorro* (2005). Her non-fiction memoir of the life and death of her daughter Paula (the title of the work) tells of a mother's love for her beautiful 28-year-old dying daughter, who, suffering from a rare blood disease, porphyria, fell into a coma. Allende transported Paula to northern California, where the comatose young woman spent her last days in an old house overlooking the Pacific, tended by a mother who was with her to the end.

Before and after Paula's 1992 death, politics figured into many of Allende's books. The liberal, anti-authoritarian bent in some of her works may derive from the fact that she was a niece of Chile's socialist president, Salvador Allende, who was overthrown in a U.S.-supported 1973 coup led by General Augusto Pinochet. Writer Allende saw firsthand the cruelties, imprisonments, and "disappearances" of her fellow Chileans under Pinochet's dictatorship. The suffering of the people, especially women, at the hands of the rich and powerful grated on her. In honor of her daughter Paula, who had worked with the poor in Venezuela, in 1996 the celebrated author established the Isabel Allende Foundation, which donates money from her book sales to select nonprofits in the San Francisco Bay Area and Chile that work to provide women and girls with reproductive rights, health care, education, and protection from violence.

Leaving Chile, in 1988 Allende remarried in California and settled into a home in Marin, becoming an American citizen in 1993. Her experiences and impressions of the multicultural Bay Area and the Golden State as a whole, from the perspective of a Latina newcomer, are telling: "The entire world passes through San Francisco. . . . The city is filled with foreigners; I am not an exception. In the streets you hear a thousand tongues, temples are raised for all denominations, and the scent of food from the most remote points of the world fills the air. . . . No one watches me or judges me, they leave me in peace. The negative side of that is that if I drop dead in the street, no one will notice . . . but . . . that is a cheap price to pay for liberty. The price I would pay in Chile would be high indeed, because there diversity is not as yet appreciated. In California the only thing that isn't tolerated is intolerance."

Governor Gray Davis: An Able Moderate under Fire

As has been shown, the demographic developments just surveyed impacted public affairs in many ways during the late 1990s and early 2000s. Meanwhile, a Democratic triumph was in the making.

Californians have perennially searched for leaders who embody the Golden State dream of limitless opportunity, voice their hopes, and steer the state through cycles of boom and bust. This is a tall order, especially for governors who, though able and experienced, may lack charisma and are not visionaries. In a time of crisis, especially, those in the governor's office must not only be skilled but also be perceived as effective and in charge. Such was the context in which Joseph ("Gray") Davis, a talented political moderate, came under fire.

The gubernatorial election of 1998 resulted in a Democratic Party landslide, ushered in on the seismic voting power of Hispanics, labor groups, and women. More than 70 percent of the Latino/a vote went to Davis and other Democrats. Labor unions, including the California Teachers' Association, spent in excess of $33 million to support him and others. Women, who especially valued reproductive rights and social services, lent their energies and dollars to Democratic candidates. Winning 58 percent of the votes compared to Republican Dan Lungren's 38.4 percent, Davis became the state's new governor. Democrat Barbara Boxer was reelected to the U.S. Senate and the majority of those elected to the House of Representatives were her fellow party members. Also, the lieutenant governor, attorney general, auditor, and treasurer were Democrats.

Davis entered office well qualified but wanting in terms of public appeal. Graduating with honors from Stanford and Columbia Law School, he received a Bronze Star for service in the Vietnam War and held several state offices before being inaugurated as the state's chief executive in 1999. Eschewing political liberalism and conservatism, the only "ism" that this self-described moderate might embrace would have been pragmatism. Davis's middle-of-the-road approach to governance contributed to his lackluster persona that eventually took its toll.

Governor Davis, nonetheless, registered a number of impressive achievements. With help from Democratic legislators he oversaw the enactment of more stringent gun control laws, strengthened health care, fought global warming, extended gay rights, safeguarded depositors' privacy information from sale by banks to marketers, and raised educational standards. He won passage of a ban on semiautomatic weapons and restrictions on the manufacture and sale of the infamous handguns known as "Saturday night specials," so called because they could be purchased easily and cheaply on any given Saturday night, when criminal activity was thought to be at a weekly peak. Under him state health insurance coverage was expanded to include an additional 1 million children. To advance the frontiers of medicine, he was the first governor in the nation to authorize stem cell research. Davis signed reputedly the first law in the nation to curb global warming by reducing greenhouse gasses and promoting alternative fuels. Education, he said, was "the first, second, and third priority" of his governorship. Accordingly, more rigorous curricular standards were established and student scores on standardized tests improved while he increased state spending on education. This was an enviable record that helped Davis win reelection against wealthy Republican businessman William Simon in November 2002.

Then came the power outages crippling state government by draining its resources (see Chapter 13), thereby setting the stage for a campaign to recall Davis. The governor took a characteristically moderate approach to stanch the hemorrhaging of money from the state treasury to buy electricity: he cut government spending and restored the full vehicle license fee. Fee restoration was projected to raise $4 billion that would help balance the budget. The cost to individual vehicle owners amounted to approximately $150 annually. Public discontent mounted, fanned by Davis's Republican opponents, turning the license fee issue into a blazing symbol of unwarranted taxation by an extravagant government. A vocal segment of Californians was inflamed when Davis signed a measure allowing illegal immigrants to receive drivers' licenses. Representative Darrell Issa, a Republican from Vista in San Diego County seeking the governorship, spent $1.7 million of his own money to finance a recall campaign that he acknowledged as "fundamentally a conservative Republican mainstream movement." Davis's achievements lapsed into insignificance. August polls showed that more than 50 percent of those sampled favored recall.

The "Governator:" Arnold Schwarzenegger

The state's budgetary crisis doomed Davis but provided an opportunity for aspiring office-seekers. According to state law a recall election could be held when signatures had been gathered from 12 percent of the number of voters participating in the preceding gubernatorial balloting. On July 23, 2003, the secretary of state announced that the requisite number of signatures had been acquired and that the state's first recall election would go forward. On October 7 California voters cast ballots on two matters, the first asking whether Gray Davis should be recalled, and the second offering a slate of candidates from which to choose a replacement.

One hundred and thirty-five hopefuls ran but Issa was not among them. He had tearfully withdrawn his name shortly after Arnold Schwarzenegger entered the contest. The Austrian-born former world champion bodybuilder and Hollywood action-movie star put $10 million of his own money into campaigning. In television ads, Schwarzenegger denounced his rivals for taking money from "special interests," such as Indian gaming casinos. "Special interests are going to go crazy because they know I'm going to kick some serious butt." Posteriors may have figured into his campaign in another way as well: more than a dozen women publicly claimed that during Schwarzenegger's bodybuilding and movie careers he had groped them. At first Schwarzenegger acknowledged and apologized for "behaving badly" around women in his earlier days; later he emphatically denied the allegations as "absolutely untrue." With his telegenic then-wife, Maria Shriver, at his side and attesting to his good qualities as a husband and father, Schwarzenegger won handily. About 55 percent of the vote, which included more than 30 percent of the Hispanic electorate as well as many Democrats and Independents, called for Davis's removal. Schwarzenegger became the "Governator," a media reference to him playing on the title of his movie *The Terminator* and coupling the film's portrayal of an action-hero with his new position as Golden State governor.

In his Inaugural Address, Governor Schwarzenegger, ever the builder of high expectations, declared: "This election was not about replacing one man. It was not about replacing one party. It was about changing the entire political climate of this state." Lacking experience in governmental leadership, such an aim was implausible. Near the close of his speech he echoed the vision of several former American presidents and other luminaries throughout history when he said, "I see California as the golden dream by the sea." This idea, evocative of California being a Pacific Eldorado of beauty and bounty, resonated with the press.

An avowed fiscal conservative and social moderate, the newly installed chief executive set about dealing with the issues facing a distressed state. Overall, the media-magnetic governor lost as many policy battles as he won, tacking pragmatically to the political right and left to satisfy his conservative base and yet ensure broader support as needed. Budgetary problems plagued his governorship: to liberals revenues were insufficient; to conservatives spending was excessive. Trying to satisfy both groups, which were becoming increasingly polarized nationwide, proved impossible. His good initial working relationship with the Democratic-controlled legislature grew harder to maintain, especially after he began referring to his opponents as "girlie men." Starting with an impressive 65 percent approval rating in 2003, two years later the figure dropped to 34 percent, as even support from his base eroded.

Shortly after his inaugural speech the new governor moved into action. He signed an executive order repealing the restoration of the full vehicle license fee and later borrowed money from an education fund to operate the government. While the governor's anti-tax supporters cheered, the repeal cost the state $4 billion in revenue that could have gone toward deficit reduction. Unwilling to raise taxes, Schwarzenegger acquired funds to run the government by negotiating an agreement with educators to borrow for a short and specified time $2 billion otherwise dedicated to the schools and community colleges. As he had promised in the recall campaign, the new governor achieved repeal of the law permitting undocumented residents to obtain drivers' licenses.

To get the state's finances in order, Schwarzenegger proposed a $15 billion deficit-bond measure along with a balanced budget initiative. Both measures passed easily. He secured approval of a law aimed at reining in workers' compensation payouts. His attempt to privatize public employee retirement systems stirred such a storm of protest from civil service workers that he abandoned the effort. Similarly, a plan he supported to change the way teachers were compensated, from length of service and educational level to merit pay based vaguely on what students had learned in the classroom, failed. He had not been clear about how student learning would be measured. According to the *San Francisco Chronicle* "the governor was short on details." After antagonizing teachers with this idea, the governor sought to impede a law Davis had signed stipulating a minimum nurse-to-patient ratio in hospitals. When nurses protested, Schwarzenegger denounced the health-care givers as "special interests," threatening to "kick their butt."

As his poll numbers declined even among Republicans, the governor moved to the political right. Assailing illegal immigration seemed a sure way to rally supporters. "Close the borders in California and all across Mexico and in the United States," Schwarzenegger urged publicly in April 2005. Hispanic voters grew increasingly uneasy about the governor some of them had helped elect.

Unable to get political mileage from what some said was his mishandling of the illegal immigration issue, Schwarzenegger campaigned hard to secure passage of several initiatives which, if passed in a special November 2005 election, might rescue his public standing. For example, one would have allowed him the discretion to make budget cuts. Others would have extended the time required for teachers to gain permanent job status, and undercut the power of unions, many of which contributed to the Democratic Party.

When none of these measures passed, the governor appointed a new chief of staff, a paintball-playing, cigar-smoking Democratic woman, Susan Kennedy. To whatever extent Schwarzenegger was able to rekindle public support, she was a major reason for it. His tough public talk became more tempered; he promised to increase per-pupil spending; and he voiced concern about human-generated climate change, going so far as endorsing California's Global Warming Solutions Act (AB 32), drafted by Democrat Fabian Núñez. The press proclaimed that a "New Arnold" had emerged.

In 2006 the "New Arnold" ran for reelection against Democratic nominee Phil Angelides, former state treasurer. In contrast to the incumbent, Angelides was politically experienced, Harvard-trained, and highly knowledgeable about public policy. Much of the challenger's thunder, however, was stolen when Schwarzenegger campaigned on a plan to invest more than $200 billion in the state's aging infrastructure of ports, highways, levees, schools, bridges, and prisons. The money would be raised through bond sales. As with Davis earlier, even in hard times Angelides' proven competency could not trump Schwarzenegger's celebrity power, especially when combined with his new, more progressive style. Even though Democrats outnumbered Republicans by 8 percentage points (42.5 to 34.3 percent, respectively) in voter registration, Schwarzenegger easily won reelection, his bipartisan appeal having been restored. Otherwise, the election resulted in a Democratic near-sweep in California, with Diane Feinstein being reelected to the U.S. Senate. Of six executive branch offices, only one went to a Republican.

The reelected governor tacked more to the political center during his second term, antagonizing his conservative base. He became more vocal about the importance of AB 32, the Global Warming Solutions Act, as a means of combating climate change. The measure passed and received the governor's signature in 2006. Accordingly, California would reduce the fossil fuel emissions causing global warming to 1990 levels by the year 2020. His fellow Republicans, many of whom warned that this measure would hurt business, were angered. Any support of President George W. Bush's policies became more muted. The governor's vetoing of the 2006 California Dream Act, which would have enabled undocumented college students to apply for institutional aid and Cal Grants, doubtlessly played well with what was left of his Republican base, but disappointed many others. When voters passed Proposition 1A in 2008, authorizing the building of a 220 miles-per-hour high-speed rail system connecting San Diego to San Francisco, Schwarzenegger traveled to China looking for investors. Work was to begin in 2012. Many budget-conscious conservatives opposed the then $9 billion project. The governor's public support for same sex-marriages marked another clear departure from his conservative political base. In a bitterly fought battle in 2008, Proposition 8 narrowly passed, amending the state constitution to declare that "only marriage between a man and a woman is valid or recognized in California." Afterward, Schwarzenegger told backers of gay marriage that "they should never give up." Opponents of Proposition 8 have since brought suit in the courts, which will determine the constitutionality of the controversial measure. Schwarzenegger's commutation of the sentence meted out to former Democratic Assembly Speaker Fabian Núñez's son, who had pled guilty to voluntary manslaughter in the killing of a 22-year-old victim, caused an outcry. This was especially the case as the exiting governor, when accused of cronyism, responded: "Well, hello! I mean, of course you help a friend." Conservative hardliners, especially with respect to crime, were not pleased. It's still too early to offer any more than a preliminary assessment of Schwarzenegger's governorship. In 2011 veteran California commentator Dan Walters noted that when Schwarzenegger's second term ended, he left office with a budget deficit "just as bad, and perhaps even worse, than the one he inherited from predecessor Gray Davis. And regardless of what else he may have accomplished, that will leave an indelible stain on his gubernatorial record." As for "changing the entire political climate of this state," as he said he aimed to do when entering office, that would have required major constitutional changes that have yet to be made.

Infrastructure Matters: Schools, Transportation, Health Care, and Prisons

A hugely expanding California population has exerted pressure on the half-century-old infrastructure dating to the governorships of Earl Warren, Goodwin Knight, and Pat

Brown. The results have been manifold: aging school and other public buildings, crowded and deteriorating highways, increased health-care needs, and teeming prisons. This is not to say that infrastructure matters have been ignored since that earlier time. Rather they have not received the funding necessary to keep pace with growing demands for quality public education, efficient transit, accessible and affordable medical services, and more incarceration facilities.

The proud possessor of one of the nation's model K-12 systems of public education in the 1950s and 1960s, the state's schools have plummeted in quality in more recent decades. In mid-August 2011, the *Los Angeles Times* reported that according to just-released Department of Education findings California students, grades 2 to 11, made "moderate gains in English and math on standardized test scores." Overall, 54 percent scored at the "proficient" level in English and 50 percent scored proficient or better in math. The newspaper reported a "sharp achievement gap separating Asian and white students from Latino and black students." These results indicate some improvement, but show that much remains to be done. Educators give many reasons for the overall decline in quality of public education. Importantly, the state ranks low – 43rd in 2011 – in spending per pupil. Since Proposition 13 (see Chapter 13), funding has become increasingly problematic. Proposition 98, enacted in 1988, aimed at investing about 40 percent of the state's budget in public education. However, dwindling available revenues and other factors have undercut public school financing under that measure. Then, too, Governor Schwarzenegger failed to restore the $2 billion he borrowed from the measure's fund. In addition to being underfunded, the state's schools must teach students from vastly different cultures and language traditions, which greatly complicates the tasks of education. The large number of high-school graduates underprepared in terms of job market skills hurts the state's businesses and economy.

Statewide, public higher education has fared better than the K-12 system, especially in terms of reputation. Though the state's share of the costs for educating college/university students has steadily declined during recent decades, the UCs have continued to be highly rated. In the 2011 *Times Higher Education Supplement* (London) ranking of universities, public and private, for teaching and research, UC Berkeley placed fourth worldwide. Among American universities, only Harvard and MIT bested Berkeley. UCLA and UC San Diego ranked 12th and 30th respectively. UC Berkeley Chancellor Robert Birgeneau reported that in 2004 the state provided 35 percent of his university's funding and in 2011 just 12 percent. For the first time in the history of the UCs, students in 2011 paid a greater portion of the cost of their education than did the state. UC officials say the present funding level renders the operation of the system unsustainable. The 23 CSUs and 112 community colleges (the nation's largest system of higher education) have, likewise, suffered from deep budget cuts. In fact, recent reductions in public funding have become so draconian that commentators are increasingly asking whether California's vaunted Master Plan for Higher Education of 1960 (see Chapter 12) is still viable.

To address the state's deteriorating transportation system of highways and bridges, voters passed in November 2006 a measure to raise $19.9 billion through the sale of general obligation bonds, that is, fundraising instruments requiring no collateral assets of the issuer. Gas taxes, federal funds, and private investments were part of the total financial

Figure 14.3   UC Berkeley and the Bay as seen from the hill above the campus. Photo: Ginger T. Osborne.

package. This measure was part of Governor Schwarzenegger's ambitious 10-year Strategic Growth Plan to upgrade California's infrastructure. The monies allocated to transportation, $107 billion, were to be used to relieve traffic congestion, particularly in the Bay Area, including Silicon Valley, and the Los Angeles Basin, as well as to promote highway safety and reduce pollution. Meanwhile, light rail transit made headway in the traffic-congested Los Angeles Basin. In addition to operating interurban Metro Blue Lines, Red Lines, and Green Lines, inner-city Los Angeles was connected by rail links to outlying areas in Ventura, Orange, San Bernardino, and Riverside counties.

Health care constitutes another key segment of the state's infrastructure. At the same time that California has been a world leader in medical technologies and treatments, in the early 2000s it ranks near the bottom of states making health care available to low-income families. State law requires that hospital emergency rooms admit anyone in an emergency condition, yet rising costs for treatment in these expensive urgent-care facilities have been resulting in some closures. While Medi-Cal offers health coverage for low-income people, still 8.4 million Californians had no medical insurance in 2010 according to the UCLA Center for Health Policy Research. Schwarzenegger vetoed legislation aimed at providing health insurance for children. Though Phil Angelides campaigned for the governorship in 2006 on a platform calling for a government-operated system of universal health care, that possibility was dashed by his defeat. Despite tight resources, California has been a national leader in funding research and treatment for AIDS (acquired immunodeficiency syndrome) sufferers.

Like schools, roads, and hospitals, prisons are a major component of the state's infrastructure. California has America's largest prisoner population. No state-run facilities are more crowded than its 33 prisons, housing some 140,000 inmates. These institutions were built to hold 80,000 individuals. With reference to the cockroaches, rodents, standing water, broken plumbing, and filth found in her own and other penal institutions, Jeanne Woodford, former San Quentin warden for 27 years, declared recently: "These prisons are falling apart." In late May 2011 she told a *Los Angeles Times* columnist that California incarcerates "many more prisoners than is necessary for the safety of the public." That same month in *Brown v. Plata* the U.S. Supreme Court, in a 5:4 decision, concluded that California's prison conditions were so appalling as to be in violation of the Constitution's Eighth Amendment, outlawing "cruel and unusual punishment." Accordingly, the court ordered the state to reduce its prison population by about 30,000 during the next two years. Serious budget constraints are likely to play a major role in how the Golden State manages prison and other criminal justice-related issues in the near future.

The High-Stakes Gubernatorial Election of 2010

California's gubernatorial election of 2010 was one of many other off-year elections held nationwide. Candidates running for governor in California faced daunting challenges, most of which derived from the state's dire financial situation, symbolized by the $25.4 billion budget deficit. Providing for public safety, funding education, keeping state parks open, attracting business and investment, and other key governmental functions as well were all tied to the financial condition of California in a time of recession. Unemployment ran at 12.4 percent, well above the national rate of 10 percent. Naturally, this kept the housing market, plagued by mortgage foreclosures, depressed. The flagging economy was the campaign's central issue. The field of candidates running to replace Schwarzenegger eventually narrowed to two: Margaret Cushing ("Meg") Whitman and Edmund Gerald ("Jerry") Brown, Jr. Their rivalry made for a high-stakes election in at least two ways: record amounts of money were spent, and to many it seemed that the state's near future rode on the outcome.

The two leading gubernatorial candidates presented a contrast to voters. Republican Whitman, a New Yorker by birth and upbringing, graduated from Princeton and earned an MBA at Harvard Business School. After having held a number of high-level corporate positions, eBay, an online auction site headquartered in San Jose, California, hired her as CEO in 1998. Moving to California, Whitman took what she described as a "no-name Internet company" with fewer than two dozen employees and remade it into the online marketing giant and Fortune 500 Company it has since become. In the process she became a billionaire. Democrat Jerry Brown, age 71, was a California native and a leading public intellectual who at one time hosted a Bay Area radio program, *We the People*, with a national listening audience; he interviewed scientists, religious thinkers, poets, educational reformers, and others working for societal change. Though coming from a prominent political family, he did not possess great wealth. Brown had spent decades in public office, including two terms as a former Golden State governor (see Chapter 13) and, among other positions, had served a stint as mayor of Oakland.

A Field Poll taken in October 2009 showed Brown well ahead of Whitman by a margin of 50 percent to 29 percent, but by mid-2010 the frontrunner's lead had dwindled. Whitman pumped an estimated $160 million of her own money into the governor's race, mainly for television ads. One such ad portrayed Brown as an opportunist who publicly denounced Proposition 13 until it passed in 1978, immediately after which he described himself as a "born-again tax cutter." Without the funding resources to run counterattack ads, Brown repeatedly challenged Whitman to televised debates, to little avail. Her ads and scripted speeches to select audiences worked; a Field Poll in September 2010 showed them tied at 41 percent each. Consequently, she agreed to a maximum of three debates.

In these televised encounters, Whitman attacked President Barack Obama's health-care plan as too costly, pledged to shrink the size of government, complained the capital gains tax was a jobs-killer, promised to lower taxes and rein in regulations, and tried to explain why she supported Arizona's harsh anti-immigration law while holding that that law was inappropriate for California. She praised Proposition 13 for limiting property taxes. Brown supported President Obama's health-care plan as "a framework to bring in children and to bring in people who have no other way of getting their health insurance." He said eliminating the capital gains tax would be great for billionaires but not for the citizenry at large, and minimized talking about Proposition 13. Brown charged Whitman with being too hard on immigrants in her support of the Arizona law, and, unlike her, pledged to support the California Dream Act in order to give undocumented students educational opportunities.

As important as all of these issues were in the campaign, none ignited as much media attention and controversy as the revelation that Whitman had hired and later fired her undocumented housekeeper. The longer prime time coverage dragged on, the lower her poll numbers dropped.

On November 2, 2010, voters elected Jerry Brown to his second tenure as governor by the substantial margin of 53.8 percent to Whitman's 40.9 percent. The contest for California's governorship was the costliest race of its kind in American history. That election also resulted in passage of Proposition 25, which ended the previously required two-thirds legislative majority to pass budgets; thereafter, a simple majority would suffice. In other results, Democratic U.S. Senator Barbara Boxer was reelected, and all of the highest state administrative offices went to Democrats. In nearly all other states the 2010 elections resulted in Republican victories. California's Democratic sweep did not mean that that party could govern as it wished. Brown's ability to lead in Sacramento would be limited significantly by the challenge of gaining the constitutionally required two-thirds super majority needed to raise taxes.

An Economic and Political Colossus

California's problems, as highlighted in the 2010 election, are real; just as real, however, is the fact that the Golden State remains America's economic and political colossus. California is America's wealthiest state in terms of its "gross product", that is, the sum value of all the goods and services the state produces. In 2009 the U.S. Department of Commerce ranked California's nation-sized $1.8 trillion economy as the eighth largest in the world, just behind Italy and ahead of Brazil and Spain. Agriculture, entertainment/media, high technology, cargo shipping by sea and air, and sports-fitness and beachwear enterprises attest to the state's economic predominance regionally, nationally, and in some instances globally. Politically, no state comes close to matching the 55 electoral votes California wields in presidential elections. Moreover, in the early 2000s a number of the state's leaders have held or hold key positions in Washington, DC.

Few, if any, other states exercise so much reach beyond their borders. An article in the venerable journal *Foreign Affairs* (Spring 1993) referred to California variously as a virtual "nation," in need of its own foreign policy, and minimally as "a distinct region within the United States." The construct of "Greater California" clearly conforms to this expansive view of the Golden State's distant and immediate past.

In 2010 California continued leading the nation in agriculture, as it had for more than half a century, both in terms of receipts, which totaled a record $37.5 billion, and in the abundance of its more than 400 commodities. The state's fruits, nuts, and wines, especially, are world-renowned. As the nation's largest producer of fruits and nuts, California's earnings from these crops grew to $13.3 billion in 2010. According to the Wine Institute, a San

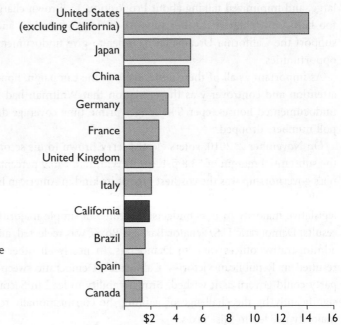

Figure 14.4   The world's top 10 economies. The next-largest state economy – Texas – is about 60 percent the size of California's. Source: *Cal Facts* (Sacramento, CA: Legislative Analyst's Office, 2011). The figures are in trillions of dollars.

Francisco trade group, during the first 10 months of 2011 California was on course to set a record in wine exports, which at that time totaled $1.14 billion. That represented a 23 percent increase over that same period in 2010. Most exported California wines still go to European countries, but the Chinese market is rapidly expanding due to that nation's astounding economic growth and demand for consumer goods. In the first 10 months of 2011 the state's wine sales to China increased 35 percent over such sales during that same period in 2010. In the latter year Hong Kong, California's third-largest wine export market, spent $116 million on the beverage.

The Golden State, particularly the Los Angeles region, remains the world capital of the entertainment/media industry, which includes movies, television, video games, the making of training videos for the Department of Defense, theme parks, and more. Digital and related technologies are transforming the industry. This is evident in filmmaking and is likely to become increasingly the case in the distribution of content over the Internet. Meanwhile, 3D movie formats are being combined with IMAX projection on to towering 80-foot screens, thrilling audiences worldwide while turning big profits. For example, the June 2011 release of *Transformers 3: Dark of the Moon*, a science fiction action blockbuster, had grossed $348,540,006 by late August. Two-thirds of Hollywood's movie revenues come from sales overseas, particularly along the Pacific Rim. Studio officials are especially interested in expanding sales to Latin America and Asia. The Global Entertainment and Media Outlook 2010–14 report by PricewaterhouseCoopers, one of the world's largest professional services and accountancy firms, anticipates a 12 percent annual increase in movie sales to China, the fastest-growing market in Asia.

Hollywood's Pacific Basin influence and connections go far beyond film sales to include production partnerships, on-site shooting, and foreign actors who have either moved to the Los Angeles area or have a highly visible presence there. The Chinese martial arts thriller *Crouching Tiger, Hidden Dragon* (2000) was a co-production of Hollywood's Columbia Pictures, and other companies in China, Taiwan, and Hong Kong. It won four Academy Awards. Regarding on-site shooting, *Avatar* (2009), the highest-grossing movie in Hollywood history ($2.8 billion) and winner of three Academy Awards, was filmed in Los Angeles and New Zealand, and distributed worldwide by Twentieth Century Fox, a Los Angeles-based production company owned by Australian media mogul Rupert Murdoch. Canadian-born director James Cameron, who lives in seaside Malibu and was educated at California State University at Fullerton, sent the cast to Hawai'i's rainforests before production in order for the actors to gain a feel for the tropical setting in *Avatar*, which explores the conflict between American invaders and the native population of another planet. Thus the movie, like many others, underscores Hollywood's extensive Pacific Basin connections. Those ties are also seen among some of the leading actors in the industry. For example, New Zealand and Australia together have provided Hollywood with some of its major box-office draws: Nicole Kidman, Russell Crowe, Naomi Watts, Mel Gibson, Cate Blanchett, the late Heath Ledger, and Geoffrey Rush.

Theme parks, likewise, contribute to California's entertainment economy. For example, the Walt Disney Company, headquartered in Burbank, in Los Angeles County, is the world's largest entertainment conglomerate, reportedly earning more than $40 billion in 2011. In addition to Anaheim's Disneyland (see Chapter 12) and other such theme parks in

North America and Europe, the corporate giant – either singly or in foreign business part-nerships – has established Disneyland parks across the Pacific in Tokyo, Japan, in 1983 and in Hong Kong, China, in 2005, and is currently building another in nearby Shanghai.

Regarding California's high-technology enterprises, Apple, with a market valuation of $500 billion and rising in early 2012, has ascended to the rank of the world's leader in computer products, and recently surpassed Exxon Mobil to become the most valuable company on the planet. Market valuation constitutes the total combined worth of all of a corporation's shares of stock. The company's sales to China alone in 2011 amounted to $13 billion, up from $3 billion the preceding year. Apple's co-founder the late Steve Jobs has been surrounded in Bay Area high-tech circles by numerous entrepreneurial geniuses like himself. Mark Zuckerberg, CEO and co-founder of Facebook, an internet social networking service, dropped out of Harvard and with his girlfriend Priscilla Chan relocated in Palo Alto, where his firm has thrived. Zuckerberg was *Time* magazine's Person of the Year in 2010, when Facebook had more than 400 million users worldwide. Forbes, a premier news service and publisher of financial information, estimated his wealth a year later at $17.5 billion, making the 1984-born whiz one of the youngest billionaires in the world. A Hol-lywood movie, *The Social Network*, dramatizing Zuckerberg's story as Facebook's titular leader, was released in 2010 and won three Academy Awards. In early 2012 Facebook claimed to have more than 800 million users per month and industry analysts estimated its then impending IPO (Initial Public Offering, that is, the worth of the company when it sells stocks publicly) to be between $50 and $100 billion. A number of glitches attended the corporation's IPO on May 18, and shares that opened at $38 dropped steadily in value to $25.52 during the next weeks causing jitters among investors. Still, Facebook's Asian Pacific market has been booming: as of March 31, 2012, Zuckerberg's social networking corporation reported that it had 195,034,380 Facebook users in that region, which is but a fraction of the potential users in that highly populated part of the world. Drew Houston is another of the Bay Area's young entrepreneurial computer savants. Scoring a perfect 1600 on his SATs, he attended MIT before coming to California and settling into a modest San Francisco apartment, from where his rise began. The 28-year-old co-founder and president of Dropbox, an online file-sharing and storage company with 50 million users, built his San Francisco-based business into a $4 billion enterprise by 2012. Houston rejected Steve Jobs's offer three years earlier to buy Dropbox, a clear sign that the young CEO has big plans for his company.

California's national lead in high-technology industries has recently been broadened to include space exploration and missions. In late May 2012 the world learned of the success of the first private sector-sponsored space mission: the docking of SpaceX's Dragon capsule at the orbiting International Space Station 250 miles above northwest Australia. SpaceX is the shortened name for Space Exploration Technologies Corp, headquartered in Haw-thorne, California and led by 40-year-old billionaire Elon Musk who founded the company and serves as its chief executive. A dream and hard work on the part of Musk and his 1,800 employees made this happen. Addressing the significance of this accomplishment, National Aeronautics and Space Administration spokesperson Charles Bolden stated: "Now that a U.S. company has proven its ability to resupply the space station, it opens a new frontier for commercial opportunities in space – and new job creation opportunities right here in the U.S." The Pacific splash-down of the capsule 560 miles west of the coast of Baja California symbolizes SpaceX's recent landing of a $1.6 billion NASA contract to haul U.S. government cargo to the orbiting space outpost.

A *Time* magazine cover story (November 2, 2009), titled "Why California Is Still the Nation's Future," recognized the Golden State's unmatched innovation in advanced technology. While acknowledging the state's serious budget problems, the author inserted an arresting and seldom-mentioned piece of information: "In 2008, California's wipeout economy attracted more venture capital than the rest of the nation combined." The article then pointed out that the state's next gold rush is already in the making: clean technology. For example, SunPower, a world leader in solar energy technologies for homes and commercial properties, is headquartered in San Jose, California. From modest beginnings in the 1970s it employed more than 5,000 workers in 2009. Other pioneering California firms in the solar business include BrightSource, eSolar, and Nanosolar. "The San Francisco utility Pacific Gas & Electric, which recently bolted the U.S. Chamber of Commerce over climate policy, has 40 percent of the nation's solar roofs in its territory," the article continued. In biotechnology San Diego is home to more than 500 research-intensive companies that have established that city as "the world capital of algae-to-fuel experiments."

While the *Time* magazine article had good reason to be cheery about the prospects for California's solar power industry, the road forward has been rocky. Solyndra, a former solar panel producer headquartered in the Bay Area City of Fremont, stunned alternative energy enthusiasts when after receiving a $535 million loan guarantee from the U.S. Department of Energy in 2009 the corporation suspended operations and declared bankruptcy in 2011. Still, the buzz surrounding two major commercial solar energy conferences in the state – the Solar POWER-GEN & Renewable Energy World Conference & Expo in Long Beach in February 2012 and the other sponsored by IntertechPira in San Diego in April of that year – suggests that California will maintain its lead in the solar power industry. Moreover, China's production of solar panels has had the effect of lowering prices for utilizing this energy source, which, in turn, promotes competition, stirring further California business activity in this enterprise.

At the same time that the Golden State has been advancing in various high-technology sectors, its maritime commerce has continued to grow impressively. International trade, particularly with Pacific Rim nations, is a pillar of California's economy in the early 2000s. The ports in the Bay Area, including those in the Delta region, San Pedro Bay, and San Diego, are all involved to varying degrees in this burgeoning maritime commerce. Consequently, the Los Angeles–Long Beach port complex has maintained its number one ranking in the United States in terms of both volume and value of cargoes handled. Jock O'Connell, international trade adviser to Beacon Economics of San Rafael, California, affirms: "As long as China remains the principal source of U.S. imports, then the Los Angeles and Long Beach ports should thrive." Oakland, similarly, has retained its number four ranking among the nation's ports.

California's China trade, mainly in Silicon Valley high-technology exports, is centered in the Bay Area, which also sends an array of agricultural goods to other parts of Asia. Forty percent of the Central Valley's agricultural exports go to East Asia, 22 percent to Canada, and the remainder to Europe and Russia. Most often, these products are transported by

Leading California Export Markets
(In $ U.S. Billions)

Partner	2008	2009	2010	2011
World Total	144.806	120.080	143.269	159.354
Mexico	20.472	17.473	21.002	26.037
Canada	17.850	14.314	16.149	17.194
China	10.981	9.744	12.468	14.196
Japan	13.061	10.901	12.181	13.096
South Korea	7.746	5.912	8.046	8.403
Hong Kong	5.688	5.799	6.760	7.683
Taiwan	5.149	4.119	6.523	6.253
Germany	5.758	4.441	5.127	5.313
Netherlands	4.348	3.565	4.139	4.618
United Kingdom	5.537	3.916	4.193	4.154
Singapore	4.084	3.221	4.026	4.132
India	2.329	2.178	3.295	3.796

Figure 14.5 Chart of leading California export markets, 2008–11. Exports from California accounted for 11 percent of total U.S. exports in 2011. California's top trading partners are Mexico, Canada, China, Japan, and South Korea. California trade and exports translate into high-paying jobs for over 1 million Californians. Source: U.S. Department of Commerce.

sea. For example, the inland Delta sea/river ports of Sacramento and Stockton, connected by waterways to San Francisco Bay, regularly ship nearly half of the state's rice harvest to Japan, Taiwan, and Korea.

Foreign trade is the leading element in southern California's mammoth economy, says James Flanigan, author of *Smile Southern California, You're the Center of the Universe* (2009). According to UC San Diego political scientist Steven Erie, the twin ports of Los Angeles–Long Beach have become America's "Gateway for the Pacific Rim," evidenced by the increase of that maritime trade from $200 billion in 1999 to $300 billion in 2005, and its projected growth to $661 billion by 2020. The Los Angeles County Economic Development Corporation estimates that in the 2010s the ports will need to operate 24/7 to handle the growing transpacific commerce. A 20-mile-long Alameda Corridor from San Pedro Bay to downtown Los Angeles, completed in April 2002 at a cost of $2.4 billion, enables the whisking of container cargoes to and from the twin ports by rail. A 2007 report found that that trade corridor was responsible for creating 3.3 million jobs nationwide, a measure of Greater California's impact on America's economy. Within California, the *Los Angeles Times* noted in September 2011 that the two San Pedro Bay ports "are the primary reason more than half of the state's 1.1 million logistics jobs are in Southern California." In December Los Angeles Mayor Villaraigosa headed a trade mission to Asia, comprised of former federal officials, current city administrators, and Southland business executives. Among other yields, including new and lucrative business partnerships between Asian and Los Angeles firms, the group returned with South Korean shipping conglomerate Hyundai Merchant Marine agreeing to build a new terminal at the Port of Los Angeles. The *Los Angeles Times* reported on December 30 that the San Pedro Bay shipping complex had surged back from the recession, handling 20.3 percent more cargo in 2011 than the year before. Southward, trade at the Port of San Diego was dwarfed by its counterpart at Los Angeles–Long Beach. In 2010, for example, San Diego's imports amounted to slightly more than $4.5 billion and exports totaled almost $88 million.

Several challenges to California's dominance of Pacific maritime trade lie on the horizon. One of these is Mexico's building of a $4 billion port at the village of Punta Colonet, 150 miles below Tijuana along the Baja coast. Scheduled for completion in 2014, Asian shippers may find it cheaper and easier to use that facility, where loose environmental standards and lower labor costs serve as inducements to doing business. Similarly Canada's Prince Rupert port is upgrading its cargo-handling and railroad-transporting capacity in hopes of becoming a major Asian gateway to goods destined for the United States. Additionally, and perhaps most importantly, the widening and deepening of the Panama Canal (scheduled for completion in 2014) could divert as much as 25 percent of Asia's transpacific shipping away from the linked ports of Los Angeles–Long Beach. To meet all of these challenges, Los Angeles port officials and their business and labor allies are continuing their efforts to expedite the transfer of goods by upgrading terminals and shortening transit times along the above-mentioned Alameda Corridor. Mayor Villaraigosa announced in early 2012 that $1.5 billion in capital improvements would be invested in the port during the next five years. Regardless of how well California meets these challenges, for which it is preparing, they underscore the extent to which the Golden State's future, like so much of its past, is connected to the Pacific maritime world.

On a much smaller scale, trade cargoes leave California for foreign and domestic destinations by air. In 2006 Los Angeles International Airport ranked as the world's fifth-busiest passenger and eleventh-busiest cargo airport. LA/Ontario International Airport, located approximately 38 miles east of downtown Los Angeles, is a major hub for United Parcel Service packages bound for Pacific Rim destinations. "Four of the six direct weekly flights UPS sends to China originate at Ontario," says USC international relations expert Abraham F. Lowenthal.

Sports-wise, in addition to the numerous revenue-generating activities mentioned previously (see Chapters 12 and 13), San Francisco is anticipating windfall profits from its hosting of what many regard as the world's premier sailing competition: the 34th America's Cup race in 2013, which will take place on California's Pacific coastline. As the defending world champion, the San Francisco Yacht Club's BMW Oracle Racing Team will compete against top international challengers on the waters of San Francisco Bay. According to the city's website: "The economic impact of San Francisco hosting the 34th America's Cup is significant, and includes an estimated 8,800 jobs, distributed widely across occupations from food and beverage to hospitality, transportation, and the construction trades, and nearly $1.4 billion in economic impacts to San Francisco and the Bay Area region." In addition to these expected material benefits, California's already formidable stature in maritime history should be enhanced even further by the hosting of this premier event in the City by the Bay.

Closely related to sports, the state's fitness gym industry reflects southern California's image as a Pacific playground of sun, sand, and surf, enjoyed by people with well-toned bodies. LA Fitness, a corporate purveyor of this image, is headquartered in Irvine. In 2010 LA Fitness generated nearly $1 billion in revenue. The following year it purchased Chicago-based Bally health clubs, formerly America's largest gym chain. With more than 500 clubs throughout the country, including the East Coast, LA Fitness is the nation's leader in its field and an embodiment of the economic and cultural reach of Greater California.

As in its economic clout, in national politics, too, the Golden State continues to wield outsized power. Besides the state's unrivaled numerical dominance in Congress and the Electoral College, in recent times a number of Californians have held and continue to hold prominent positions in the Federal Government. Representative Nancy Pelosi served as Speaker of the House from 2007 to 2011, the first woman to hold that high office. Since that time she has been serving as the House Democratic (or Minority) Leader. Leon E. Panetta served as director of the Central Intelligence Agency from 2009 to 2011, after which President Obama appointed him secretary of defense. As noted, since 2009 Steven Chu has been serving as secretary of energy in the Obama Administration, and since that year Hilda L. Solis has occupied the secretary of labor cabinet post. From 2009 to 2010 UC Berkeley economics Professor Christina Romer chaired the president's Council of Economic Advisors.

Figure 14.6   Hilda Solis, U.S. secretary of labor. Her high-school counselor told her mother that the girl should forget about college and become a secretary. Courtesy of U.S. Department of Labor.

Major Environmental and Energy Challenges

Like most large states with populations to match their expanse, California in the early 2000s faces multiple environmental and energy challenges. Some of the major environmental concerns include the provision of healthful drinking water, safeguarding air quality, combating global climate change, and attending to the threatened marine ecosystem. Equally daunting is the task of supplying affordable clean energy to a state whose population is slated to reach nearly 50 million by 2025.

To better provide safe drinking water, amid the contaminants from fertilizers and other industrial-based chemical agents seeping into waterways and aquifers (see Chapter 13), the state government established the Water Quality Monitoring Council in 2007. The council works with the California Environmental Protection Agency and other designated state offices to monitor, assess, and report to the public – via a website – its water-quality findings. In the non-governmental civic sector, the Natural Resources Defense Council, a citizens' advocacy group led by scientists and lawyers, reported in 2002 that overall the quality of drinking water in Fresno, Los Angeles, San Diego, and San Francisco was "mediocre yet acceptable."

Air quality continues to vex the state's largest cities, particularly those in Los Angeles, Orange, Riverside, and San Bernardino counties. The U.S. Environmental Protection Agency estimates that 25 percent of Los Angeles County's air pollution originates in China and is carried across the ocean by transpacific air flows. The remaining bulk of unhealthful air in the Southland comes from nearby sources: diesel emissions from ships and trucks, refineries, manufacturing plants, and especially automobile emissions that raise ozone levels when interacting with nitrogen oxides and sunlight. The resulting smog is connected to respiratory ailments among Angelinos. In Los Angeles, according to the American Lung Association's 2011 State of the Air Report, an estimated 1 million adults and 300,000 children had asthma, "outranking 23 other congested cities." In response to a public outcry about diesel emissions at the Los Angeles–Long Beach port complex, harbor officials adopted federal clean truck emission standards. Accordingly, beginning January 1, 2012, all trucks not meeting these standards are banned from the port. Some trucks hauling cargoes to and from that port are now using clean liquefied natural gas. Port authorities expect to see an 80 percent reduction in harmful truck emissions. "The trucks here at the port now meet the strictest clean air and safety standards of any major port in the world," said Los Angeles Mayor Villaraigosa in mid-January.

Climate warming, according to the California Academy of Sciences and the National Academy of Sciences, will continue taking its toll on the state's water-dependent and climate-sensitive agricultural economy, and has other major impacts as well. For example, among other authorities, including the National Research Council, Dr. Peter Roopnarine, Curator of Geology and Paleontology at the California Academy of Sciences in San Francisco, attributes sea-rise to global warming. One result of this would be the imperiling of the low-lying airports in San Francisco and Oakland. Moreover, in 2010 the California State Lands Commission issued a report saying that most of the state's 40 ports and shipping hubs were not prepared for the expected 16-inch rise by 2050 in sea levels that would prove damaging to ground-level facilities and toxic storage sites at the San Pedro Bay harbor complex while slowing the handling of cargoes. Geraldine Knatz, executive director of the Port of Los Angeles, was quoted in the *Los Angeles Times* (December 10, 2009) as warning: "We need to start planning for these things now, so that we're not caught having to do a lot of remedial repair work 15 years to 20 years in the future." In response to this and other scientific reports, many of the state's coastal cities are preparing for an anticipated sea rise. Newport Beach, a conservative enclave in Orange County that recently had a city council member professing disbelief in global warming, commissioned a study in 2008 that warned of impending sea-rise damage to the city's high-end real estate. That city is reportedly taking steps to make sure that existing sea walls are sufficiently high. Global warming has U.S. Geological Survey scientists and others concerned about how the state's majestic redwood groves will hold up under climate change. Because passenger vehicles and light duty trucks produce nearly a third of the emissions that cause climate change, the state legislature passed the Clean Cars Law in 2002 requiring that all new automobiles sold in California had to cut greenhouse gas vapors by 30 percent by 2016. This was the first statute of its kind in the nation; more than a dozen other states have since passed similar laws.

California's marine ecology and resources, which are vitally important to the state's citizenry, are closely linked to climate change and a number of other factors as well. Since oceans absorb most of the greenhouse gases generated on land, California's coastal waters register the impacts of the resulting warming. According to the California Academy of Sciences, 70 percent of the world's reefs may disappear by 2020 due to global warming, which causes acidification of the corals and ocean pollution. As elsewhere, California's reefs furnish nutrient-rich marine life habitats unless they are ravaged by acidification and the chemical and bacterial contaminants resulting from urban runoff emptying into the Pacific. Mercury, a toxic element in urban runoff, continues to be found in large fish, such as tuna, caught along the state's coast. Runoff, especially in storm water, often includes plastics as well. In 2009 researchers at Scripps Institution of Oceanography at UC San Diego found that 9.2 percent of the fish caught in the middle depths of the northern Pacific Ocean are ingesting plastic, at the rate of 24,000 tons of the substance each year. Scientists caught a sample of these fish in the so-called Pacific Garbage Patch, a slow-moving gyre of debris roughly the size of Texas located 1,000 miles off California's coast. Overfishing, in addition to these other perils, compounds the problem of rescuing California's Pacific waters before the ecological damage becomes irreversible.

Government agencies, universities, citizen groups, and some business leaders are working to nurse the state's marine environment back to health. Since 1985 Santa Monica's Heal the Bay citizen's organization has succeeded in gaining enforcement of the 1972 federal Clean Water Act in order to upgrade the treatment of effluent at the Hyperion Sewage Wastewater Treatment Plant. In the early 2000s surfers in the vicinity of the Bay have reported fewer infections, and marine habitats near the Hyperion outfall have become healthier. The California Coastal Commission (see Chapter 13), the Department of Fish and Game, commercial and recreational anglers, and civic-sector ocean advocate groups have worked together since passage of the Marine Life Protection Act in 1999 to map and establish Marine Protected Areas (MPAs) in California's coastal waters. An MPA is an ocean area where human activity, such as fishing, is more restricted than in surrounding waters. The Act was passed to protect the state's marine life and ecosystems and replenish diminishing fish stocks, all through the use of scientific management practices. In Laguna Beach the Bluebelt Coalition, a civic-sector advocate group, worked successfully to secure the city council's approval of MPA safeguards for the municipality's entire coastline. After lobbying the state's Department of Fish and Game for MPA recognition, the coalition and city council had to settle for a slightly smaller stretch of coastline protection, which nevertheless marked a major step toward replenishing depleted fish stocks.

To better inform the public on these and related ocean matters, the Newkirk Center for Science and Society at the University of California, Irvine held a major conference on "Enhancing the Future of the California Coast," in early March 2011. In addition to presentations by marine biologists and leaders of citizens' groups, Greg MacGillivray, president of MacGillivray Freeman Films in Laguna Beach, spoke about the urgency of rescuing the Earth's ocean environment. He informed attendees about a "One World One Ocean" nonprofit, global initiative that he and his family had recently launched with their money and that of other donors. The goals of the initiative are, first and foremost, to educate people about the declining health of the oceans, and second, to inspire action on three goals: to extend marine protected areas or sanctuaries to 10 percent of the area covered by the world's oceans by 2020; to change the way people eat sea-life so that consumption habits foster sustainable fishing practices; and to encourage people to reduce their usage of single-use disposable plastic. The MacGillivrays plan to make four to six 3D IMAX films, an eight-part television series, a 3D theatrical documentary, and a robust social media platform to show viewers the beauty and importance of the oceans and to inspire public support for their marine recovery campaign.

Energy challenges in the early 2000s will continue to drive research in new technologies for harnessing the power of the sun, wind, and sea algae, as already mentioned. Additionally, some entrepreneurs, like Mark Holmes and David New who partner in heading Green Wave Energy Corporation of Newport Beach, are looking into utilizing the power of Pacific breakers. The March 11, 2011, meltdown at Japan's Fukushima–Daiichi nuclear plant raised public fears in California and around the world about the safety of this energy source. In addition to the search for power sources other than those based on fossil fuels and atoms, utility companies are employing technologies to help ratepayers conserve on energy use. For example, in 2011 San Diego Gas and Electric (SDG and E) installed smart meters, which relay energy-usage figures to customers via the Internet, in homes and businesses throughout the region it serves. A pilot study that SDG and E ran earlier showed that when ratepayers could privately and conveniently track their energy usage during times of high demand, electricity use and bills declined 14 percent.

The Pacific, the U.S Military, and California

U.S. Secretary of State Hillary Clinton said in November 2011: "As we end the war in Iraq and begin bringing troops back from Afghanistan, we are making an important pivot. The world's strategic and economic center of gravity is shifting east, and we are focusing more on the Asia-Pacific region." Secretary of Defense Leon Panetta, a Californian, amplified this view as reported by an Australian radio public affairs program in January 2012, which quoted him as saying: "The U.S. military will increase its institutional wake and focus on enhanced presence, power projection and deterrence in Asia Pacific. This region is growing in importance to the future of the United States in terms of our economy and our national security." A base in Darwin, Australia, will be used as a staging area for U.S. Marines. California will figure prominently in America's historic Pacific "pivot." Because of North Korea's and especially China's arms buildups, the Pentagon is taking a keen interest in the state's international security role.

China's military buildup during the last two decades has focused on strengthening its sea power. A paper published in the Naval Post Graduate School (NPS) journal *Strategic Insights* (January 2003) notes a major change in Chinese military policy beginning in the 1990s. Since then "the PLA [People's Liberation Army] has transformed its military focus from a 'continental' defense to a 'peripheral' defense of the coastal and maritime regions of China."

That nation's nuclear submarines, and launching of its first aircraft carrier in mid-2011, exemplify China's augmented naval presence in Asian Pacific waters. With China and the United States being the strongest powers in that region, and given America's security commitments there, the Pentagon wishes to reduce tensions and manage relations between the two governments. Accordingly, since 2005 Monterey's NPS, a leading center of research and teaching related to Pacific affairs, has been facilitating talks between mid-level Chinese and American military strategists on prevention of an arms race and control of nuclear forces.

Thus, the U.S. Navy tracks changes in Chinese military policy and adapts its operations accordingly. The U.S. Pacific Fleet, the world's largest naval juggernaut, is charged with defending America's interests in that ocean basin. Though headquartered at Pearl Harbor, Hawai'i, San Diego is the principal homeport of the Pacific Fleet, and its base accommodates one-sixth of all of America's warships. Camp Pendleton, the West Coast's largest Marine Corps amphibious training center, is located nearby. Other naval installations dot California's coast up to Monterey's NPS, plus a few air stations inland.

The best measure of the U.S. government's concern about maintaining the Golden State's military readiness to respond to developments in the Asian Pacific is federal spending. Despite the ending of the Cold War in the late twentieth century, and the resulting base closures in the state, in 2005 California still had more military installations and personnel than any other state in the nation, according to Department of Defense figures. The state's 424 military facilities support nearly 200,000 service people and civilians. Pentagon spending in California in the early 2000s amounts to about $40 billion annually. Clearly, as in all of America's major conflicts since the Spanish–American War of 1898, California remains the nation's West Coast bastion.

Still the Pacific Eldorado

Prophecies of California's imminent downfall, much like the state's economic cycles of booms and busts, come and go. Amid a recession in 1993 such alarms were sounded by pundits and policymakers alike. Then came the dot-com revolution that dazzled and led the world. In January 2010, as a huge budget deficit, insufficient revenues, and a gridlocked state legislature further reduced government expenditures for education, state parks, and other services, *Newsweek* magazine published an article titled "California: America's First Failed State." This perception of a state on its last legs, however questionable, has made its way into the national media.

The *Newsweek* article gave no indication of how the Golden State compared to other states struggling to make ends meet in a down national economy. Put differently, the state's epitaph may have been written prematurely, for despite the bad news, no other state matches California as an innovator and producer of wealth. This is why Nicolas Berggruen, a billionaire entrepreneur who travels the world calling no place home, in 2011 donated $20 million to the Think Long Committee for California that is working to break through the state's political gridlock, thereby leading it and the nation out of the doldrums. "California, even with the troubles that it has today," he said recently, "has this window into our future. . . . And frankly California will have an influence on the world." No other state has a public university system that comes close to matching the University of California's promise of "access and excellence." The *Stanford Report* (September 5, 2001) newsletter stated matter-of-factly: "California's universities and research institutions claim more Nobel laureates than any state or country in the world." As noted, even in the nationwide recession beginning in 2008 California attracted more venture capital than all of the other states combined. The Golden State's rare balance of economic resources, including ports, farmlands, high technology, entertainment/media, tourism, and the recreational economy is unequaled in America. If the world's largest ocean basin continues to be the epicenter of global economics, and if the Golden State's past offers any indication of its future, Greater California can be expected to remain the Pacific Eldorado.

SUMMARY

No state has been more integral to America's ongoing Pacific shift than California. Surveying such areas as immigration, politics, the economy, the environment, and international security shows this to be the case.

In 2000 the majority of immigrants entering the Golden State came from Pacific Rim countries. Mostly Asians and Hispanics, these newcomers have made California the most populous and ethnically diverse state in the Union, while contributing immensely to its economy, culture, and politics. They have started myriad businesses, both hired and provided their own labor, and have paid taxes, all of which have added to the state's economic health. Coming to the Bay Area from Chile, writer Isabel Allende applauds California's cultural pluralism, especially its rich variety of languages and foods. Newcomers have shaped politics increasingly through voting and office-holding. Wedge issues like bilingual education and financial aid to undocumented college students galvanized Pacific Rim immigrants into a political force that helped lead to the 2011 passage of Assembly Bill 131. Also known as the California Dream Act, this measure made some funding available to undocumented collegians.

In addition to addressing Pacific Rim immigration, the state's political leaders grappled with the fallout from the recall of Governor Gray Davis and his replacement by Arnold Schwarzenegger in 2003. As a result of the new governor's repeal of a measure to restore the full vehicle license fee and his unwillingness to raise other taxes, California's infrastructure of schools, transportation systems, health care, and prisons continued its downward slide from past decades. While Schwarzenegger's second term was ending in 2010, the most expensive governor's race in American history began. With but a fraction of Republican candidate Meg Whitman's financial resources, Democrat Jerry Brown won the campaign convincingly. Moreover, all of the highest administrative offices went to his fellow Democrats. In winning, Brown took over a state with a $25.4 billion deficit and 12.4 percent unemployment rate. Since his election, Brown has struggled to keep the government running in the face of meeting Proposition 13's requirement of gaining a two-thirds legislative majority to raise taxes.

Though the state's infrastructure stood at great risk due to structural impediments to its upgrading, California's economy and political clout in the early 2000s rendered the state a colossus. A diversified economy powered especially by Pacific Rim trade and an unmatched high-tech sector have secured the state's eighth-place ranking among the world's wealthiest nations. At the same time that pundits speculated about California's economic demise during the onset of a severe nationwide recession in 2008, the Golden State attracted more investment capital than all of America's other states combined.

California's nation-sized economy has spawned some major environmental challenges. Even with its compromised public sector, the state has established governmental agencies to monitor and protect air, drinking water, and its magnificent coastline from industrialization and urbanization. Particularly noteworthy is Assembly Bill 32, enacted into law in 2006, putting California in the lead nationwide in combating climate warming.

As the federal government shifts its focus to the Asia Pacific region, the epicenter of the global economy and sphere of influence of a naval-building China, California remains the nation's foremost recipient of Pentagon spending, and San Diego serves as the principal home port of America's Pacific Fleet. If the world's largest ocean basin continues to be ground zero in the international struggle for wealth and power, and if the Golden State's history is prologue to its future, Greater California is likely to remain the Pacific Eldorado.

REVIEW QUESTIONS

- What is the meaning of the chapter's title: "The Ongoing Pacific Shift"? What evidence is offered of such a shift in U.S. foreign policy, and how does California fit into this context?
- In what ways do the life, works, and activities of writer Isabel Allende represent transpacific ties between Chile and California? Do you agree with her statement: "In California the only thing that isn't tolerated is intolerance." Why, or why not?
- What evidence is offered for the deterioration of California's infrastructure of schools, transportation systems, health care, and prisons?

- In what ways may it be said that California remains a Pacific Eldorado, an economic and political colossus, in the early twenty-first century?
- What are the major environmental challenges confronting the state in the early 2000s, and what is being done by government and citizens to address these problems?

FURTHER READINGS

Isabel Allende, *My Invented Country: A Nostalgic Journey through Chile* (New York: HarperCollins, 2003). The author shares memories of living in her homeland, and in doing so occasionally but tellingly comments on life in California.

Mark Baldassare, *A California State of Mind: The Conflicted Voter in a Changing World* (Berkeley: University of California Press, 2002). Voters' distrust of California's government to handle the challenges of racial, ethnic, and regional diversity is the salient message of this book.

Mark Baldassare, *California in the New Millennium: The Changing Social and Political Landscape* (Berkeley: University of California Press, 2000). The importance of voter participation in California's decision-making process is stressed in this study.

Margaret Caldwell et al., *Pacific Ocean Synthesis: Scientific Literature Review of Coastal and Ocean Threats, Impacts, and Solutions* (Monterey, CA: Center for Ocean Solutions, Stanford University, 2009). Written in language accessible to laypersons, policymakers, and scientists, this work provides a distillation of the latest research on the challenges, particularly that of global warming, to the Pacific's various ecological regions.

Bruce Cumings, *Dominion from Sea to Sea: Pacific Ascendancy and American Power* (New Haven, CT: Yale University Press, 2009). This book is singular and path-breaking in its rebalancing of American history so as to give adequate scope to the Pacific world.

Steven P. Erie, *Globalizing L.A.: Trade, Infrastructure, and Regional Development* (Stanford, CA: Stanford University Press, 2004). The author skillfully blends history and policy analysis to explain Los Angeles' rise as a global city.

James Flanigan, *Smile Southern California, You're the Center of the Universe* (Stanford, CA: Stanford University Press, 2009). Through biographical sketches, coupled with quantitative data, the author makes a case for southern California being an economic model for the United States and the world.

Alex L. Fradkin and Philip L. Fradkin, *The Left Coast: California on the Edge* (Berkeley: University of California Press, 2011). The authors, father and son, provide engaging narrative and evocative photographs to convey the history of California's littoral from the Spanish period to the early 2000s, with a strong focus on the environmental impacts of human settlement.

Gary Griggs, Kiki Patsch, and Lauret Savoy, eds., *Living with the Changing California Coast* (Berkeley: University of California Press, 2005). In a little more than 500 pages, this densely factual volume offers comprehensive and up-to-date coverage of the natural history of every stretch of California's coast.

Michael Grunwald, "Why California Is Still America's Future (And That's a Good Thing Too)," *Time*, 174/17 (November 2, 2009), 26–32, 34. This article makes a strong case for recession-ridden California being the most innovative and economically dynamic state in the nation.

Erik J. Heikkila and Rafael Pizarro, eds., *Southern California and the World* (Westport, CT: Praeger, 2002). Aimed at academics, this compact volume probes the roles of filmmaking, religion, and immigration in creating southern California's hybrid, globalized society.

Gus Koehler, *California Trade Policy* (Sacramento, CA: California Research Bureau, 1999). This monograph provides a compendium of trade information appearing in few other single sources.

Abraham F. Lowenthal, *Global California: Rising to the Cosmopolitan Challenge* (Stanford, CA: Stanford University Press, 2009). This is an essential work that contains surprisingly little on the challenges to California's Pacific-related economy and maritime ecosystem.

Abraham F. Lowenthal and Katrina Burgess, eds., *The California–Mexico Connection* (Stanford, CA: Stanford University Press, 1993). An anthology of stimulating essays, this volume probes the ever-increasing ties between California and the nation on its southern border.

R. Jeffrey Lustig, ed., *Remaking California: Reclaiming the Public Good* (Berkeley: Heyday Books, 2010). While analyzing the litany of problems facing California today, the contributing writers pay special attention to the state's constitutional crisis that impedes so many of the solutions offered in this volume.

Paul McDonald and Janet Wasko, eds., *The Contemporary Hollywood Film Industry* (Malden, MA: Blackwell Publishing, 2008). This collection of writings is especially strong on the international aspects of Hollywood filmmaking and marketing, with particular attention given to Asia.

Joe Matthews and Mark Paul, *California Crackup: How Reform Broke the Golden State and How We Can Fix It* (Berkeley: University of California Press, 2010). This book analyzes the historical development of the state's major political and economic problems in the early 2000s and prescribes thoughtful, practical remedies.

Peter Schrag, *California: America's High-Stakes Experiment* (Berkeley: University of California Press, 2008). The author offers an incisive analysis of the state's current problems while at the same time glimpsing the possibilities of recapturing the hope that California once afforded its people and the nation.

Kevin Starr, *California: A History* (New York: Random House, 2005). This is essentially a one-volume abridgement of the author's preeminent series of books on California's social and cultural history.

Kevin Starr, *Coast of Dreams: California on the Edge, 1990–2003* (New York: Oxford University Press, 2004). Written with the author's well-known eye for colorful, revelatory detail, this volume narrates the human impacts of California's economic troubles and boom during this eventful time-span.

Roger Waldinger and Mehdi Bozorgmehr, eds., *Ethnic Los Angeles* (New York: Russell Sage Foundation, 1996). This is a sociologically based history of Los Angeles' ethnic groups and their communities that focuses largely on the second half of the twentieth century.

Kent Wong, Janna Shadduck-Hernandez, Victor Narro, Abel Valenzuela, and Fabiola Inzunza, eds., *Undocumented and Unafraid: Tam Tran, Cinthya Felix, and the Immigrant Youth Movement* (Los Angeles: UCLA Center for Labor Research and Education, 2012). This important work highlights the role of student leaders in advocating for undocumented collegians.

Michael Zielenziger, "Chinafornia," *California* (UC Berkeley alumni magazine), 117/1 (January/February 2006), 30–8. The cultural and economic impacts of Chinese immigration to California, and especially the Bay Area, in the early 2000s are traced in this article.

Appendix: Governors of California, 1768–2012

The Spanish Period in Alta California (1767–1821)

Gaspar de Portolá, 1768[?]–1770
Pedro Fages, 1770–1774
Fernando Rivera y Moncada, 1774–1777
Felipe de Neve, 1777–1782
Pedro Fages, 1782–1791
José Antonio Roméu, 1791–1792
José Joaquín de Arrillaga, 1792–1794
Diego de Borica, 1794–1800
Pedro de Alberni, 1800
José Joaquín de Arrillaga, 1800–1814
José Argüello, 1814–1815
Pablo Vicente de Solá, 1815–1822 (ending in the Mexican period)

The Mexican Period in Alta California (1821–1846)

[Pablo Vicente Solá, 1815–1822]
Luis Argüello, 1822–1825
José María de Echeandía, 1825–1830
Manuel Victoria, 1830–1831
Pío Pico, 20 days, between January and February 1832
José María Echeandía, 1832–1833

Pacific Eldorado: A History of Greater California, First Edition. Thomas J. Osborne.
© 2013 Thomas J. Osborne. Published 2013 by Blackwell Publishing Ltd.

Agustín Vicente Zamorano (in the north only), 1832–1833
José Figueroa, 1833–1835
José Castro (acting governor), 1835–1836
Nicolás Gutíerrez, acting governor for four months, between January and May 1836
Mariano Chico, acting governor for three months, between May and August 1836
Nicolás Gutíerrez, acting governor for three months, between August and November 1836
José Castro, between November and December 1836
Juan Bautista Alvarado, December 1836–1842
Manuel Micheltoreña, 1842–1845
Pío Pico, 1845–1846
José María Flores, 1846–1847
Andrés Pico, January 11–13, 1847

American Military Governors (1846–1849)

Commodore John D. Sloat, July 7 – July 29, 1846
Commodore Robert F. Stockton, July 29, 1846 – January 19, 1847
Colonel John C. Frémont, January 19 – March 1, 1847
General Stephen W. Kearny, March 1 – May 31, 1847
Colonel Richard B. Mason, acting governor, May 31, 1847 – February 28, 1849
General Persifor F. Smith, February 28 – April 12, 1849
General Bennett Riley, April 12 – December 20, 1849

The American Period (1849–2012) and Party Affiliation

Peter H. Burnett, 1849–1851, Democrat
John McDougal, 1851–1852, Democrat
John Bigler, 1852–1856, Democrat
J. Neely Johnson, 1856–1858, Know-Nothing
John B. Weller, 1858–1860, Democrat
Milton S. Latham, January 1860, Democrat
John G. Downey, January 1860–1862, Democrat
Leland Stanford, 1862–1863, Republican
Frederick F. Low, 1863–1867, Union
Henry H. Haight, 1867–1871, Democrat
Newton Booth, 1871–February 1875, Republican
Romualdo Pacheco, between February and December 1875, Republican
William Irwin, December 1875–1880, Democrat
George C. Perkins, 1880–1883, Republican
George Stoneman, 1883–1887, Democrat
Washington Bartlett, between January and September 1887, Democrat
Robert W. Waterman, September 1887–1891, Democrat

Henry H. Markham, 1891–1895, Republican
James H. Budd, 1895–1899, Democrat
Henry T. Gage, 1899–1903, Republican
George C. Pardee, 1903–1907, Republican
James N. Gillett, 1907–1911, Republican
Hiram W. Johnson, 1911–1917, Progressive/Republican
William D. Stephens, 1917–1923, Republican
Friend W. Richardson, 1923–1927, Republican
Clement C. Young, 1927–1931, Republican
James Rolph, Jr., 1931–1934, Republican
Frank F. Merriam, 1934–1939, Republican
Culbert L. Olson, 1939–1943, Democrat
Earl F. Warren, 1943–1953, Republican
Goodwin J. Knight, 1953–1959, Republican
Edmund G. "Pat" Brown, 1959–1967, Democrat
Ronald W. Reagan, 1967–1975, Republican
Edmund G. "Jerry" Brown, Jr., 1975–1983, Democrat
George Deukmejian, 1983–1991, Republican
Peter "Pete" Wilson, 1991–1999, Republican
Joseph Graham "Gray" Davis, 1999–2003, Democrat
Arnold Schwarzenegger, 2003–2011, Republican
Edmund G. "Jerry" Brown, Jr., 2011– , Democrat

Index